STRATEGY SYNTHESIS

RESOLVING STRATEGY PARADOXES TO CREATE COMPETITIVE ADVANTAGE

TEXT AND READINGS

BOB DE WIT Maastricht School of Management, The Netherlands

RON MEYER Rotterdam School of Management, Erasmus University, The Netherlands

Australia · Canada · Mexico · Singapore · Spain · United Kingdom · United States

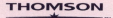

Strategy Synthesis: Resolving Strategy Paradoxes to Create Competitive Advantage (Text and Readings)

Copyright © 2005 Thomson Learning

The Thomson logo is a registered trademark used herein under licence.

For more information, contact Thomson Learning, High Holborn House, 50–51 Bedford Row, London, WC1R 4LR or visit us on the World Wide Web at: http://www.thomsonlearning.co.uk

British Library Cataloguing-in-Publication Data
A catalogue record for this book is available from the British Library

South-Western ISBN
0-324-28272-9

ternational Thomson Business Press

Text design by Design Deluxe, Bath
Typeset by J&L Composition, Filey, North Yorkshire
Printed in Italy by G. Canale & C. S.p.A.

BRIEF CONTENTS

To our children,
Liza de Wit and
Suzanne, Thomas and Simone Meyer,
our ultimate works of synthesis

CONTENTS

LIST OF EXHIBITS

ACKNOWLEDGEMENTS

*It could be said of me that in this book I have only made up
a bunch of other men's flowers, providing of my own
only the string that ties them together.*
Montaigne (1533–1592); French moralist and essayist

As Montaigne, we have created a book that is a 'bouquet of other people's flowers' – we have brought together many of the leading ideas, concepts, frameworks and theories in the field of strategic management and have arranged them in a way that each complements the 'beauty' and 'fragrance' of the others. While we are proud of the job we have done in selecting the most attractive flowers and arranging them into a lush bouquet, we are aware that we are much indebted to the hundreds of authors whose contribution to the topic of strategy we have used to compose this book.

Even when it comes to the string tying the flowers together, we have received considerable support, which should not go unmentioned. During the six years since the publication of the first edition, many colleagues and readers from around the world have provided valuable feedback, leading to considerable changes in the book. We have also benefited from the comments and suggestions received from our students and executive program participants, as we have had the opportunity to present our ideas at universities and companies in dozens of countries around the world. To all of these people, we would like to express our gratitude – and we would like to encourage all to keep on contributing towards the next edition.

Just before the publication of the first edition, we decided to apply some strategic thinking to our own activities and to challenge the traditional model of the vertically integrated business school. The result was the founding of two related organizations: *Strategy Academy*, which does research and teaching, and functions as a specialized supplier to various business schools, corporate universities and company training departments; and *Strategy Works*, a strategy consulting and process facilitation firm. Since then our clients and employees have been a rich source of inspiration, ideas and feedback, while providing a constant 'reality check' for our evolving concepts and frameworks. We greatly appreciate their openness to our ideas and their trust in our ability to bring into practice what we preach.

We started the process of creating this new edition in the autumn of 2002, by organizing a Strategic Management Society mini-conference in Rotterdam entitled 'Plurality, Perspectives and Paradoxes in Strategy' at which a number of topics were explored that are central to our approach to strategy. We would like to thank the participants of this conference, and in particular Charles Hampden-Turner, Anne Huff, Barry Johnson, Marianne Lewis, John McGee, Jane McKenzie, Andrew Pettigrew, Rob van Tulder and Richard Whittington for their inputs and inspiration.

Following the conference, we were able to find a number of colleagues willing to participate in reviewing chapter rewrites and in supplying material for short cases. We greatly appreciate the contribution of the following team:

Ard Pieter de Man

Peer Ederer

Wolter Lemstra

Marc Padberg

Martin Rademakers

Winfried Ruigrok

Rob van Tulder

Leonard Zijlstra

We would also like to highlight the essential role of our research assistants, Renske Bartels, Henk van de Berg, Casper van der Veen and Geert van Deth, who spent months doing anything and everything needed to ensure that the second edition would be completed on time. And in the background, of course, always our office manager, Karin Feteris, making sure the place didn't fall apart in the meantime.

Finally, we also want to thank the team at Thomson Learning and Southwestern for working so hard with us at creating a truly global book. While many books are written for a national audience and then exported to other countries, Thomson/Southwestern has shared our ambition to create a book suited to readers all around the world. In particular we would like to thank our former editor, Anna Faherty, who pleasantly, but unrelentingly, hounded us to start on the second edition, and our current co-editors, Geraldine Lyons in London and John Szilagyi in Mason, Ohio, who have successfully taken up the challenge of coordinating this book project across so many national borders. And last, but not least, we would like to thank the man who got us started as 'flower arrangers' so many years ago, our first editor, David Godden, who has now retired to a life of growing real flowers in New Zealand.

PREFACE

Not only is there an art in knowing a
thing, but also a certain art in teaching it.
Cicero (106–43 BC); Roman orator and statesman

What is a good strategy for teaching and learning about the topic of strategy? Judging by the similarity of the strategic management textbooks currently available, there seems to be a general consensus among business professors on the best approach to this task. It is not an exaggeration to say that strategic management education is dominated by a strong *industry recipe* (Spender, 1989). Almost all textbooks share the following characteristics:

- *Few differing perspectives*. Only a limited number of perspectives and theories are presented, often as accepted knowledge, from which prescriptions can easily be derived.

- *Step-by-step structure*. A step-by-step strategic planning approach is used as the books' basic structure, to decompose strategy-making into a number of simple sequential activities.

- *No primary material*. The key academic articles and books on strategy are reworked into the textbook authors' own words to create consistent and easily digestible pieces of text.

- *Domestic orientation*. Despite fancy subtitles referring to globalization, the choice of perspectives, theories, examples and cases are heavily biased towards the textbook authors' own domestic context.

It is interesting to speculate on the causes of this isomorphism in the 'strategic management education' industry. Institutionalists would probably point to the need for legitimacy, which leads textbook authors to conform to widely accepted practices and to avoid major innovations (e.g. Abrahamson, 1996; Powell and DiMaggio, 1991). Social psychologists would likely suggest that over the years shared cognitive structures have developed within the strategic management community, which makes the prevailing educational paradigm difficult to challenge (e.g. Smircich and Stubbart, 1985; Walsh, 1995). Theorists taking a new institutional economics perspective would probably interpret the uniformity of strategic management textbooks as a form of lock-in, caused by the large investments already made by publishers and business professors based on a shared educational 'standard' (e.g. Arthur, 1996; David, 1994). Whatever the reason, it is striking that the character of strategic management textbooks has not significantly changed since the founding of the field.

But what would strategy education look like if educational orthodoxy were actively challenged and the industry rules broken? How might strategy be taught if the current constraints were thrown aside and the teaching process was boldly reinvented? In short, what would happen if some strategic thinking were applied to the teaching of strategy?

During the last 15 years, we have continuously asked ourselves these questions. Our conclusion is that all four of the above features of current strategic management textbooks greatly inhibit the development of independent strategic thinkers and therefore urgently need to be changed. It is for this reason that we decided to create a book ourselves, with the following characteristics:

■ *Multiple strategy perspectives*. A broad range of differing, and often conflicting, perspectives and theories are presented, reflecting the richness of current debate among academics and practitioners in the field of strategic management.

■ *Issue-based structure*. An issue-based book structure is used, with each chapter focusing on a key strategic issue, which is discussed from a variety of angles, leaving readers to draw their own conclusions.

■ *Original readings*. A large number of original articles and book chapters are included, to offer readers a first hand account of the ideas and theories of influential strategy thinkers.

■ *International orientation*. A strong international orientation is at the core of this book, as reflected in the choice of topics, theories, readings, examples and cases.

In the following paragraphs the rationale behind the choice for these characteristics will be explained. Following this discussion, the structure of the book and the ways in which it can be employed will be further clarified.

USING MULTIPLE STRATEGY PERSPECTIVES

*Education, n. **That which discloses to the wise and disguises
from the foolish their lack of understanding.***
The Devil's Dictionary, Ambrose Bierce (1842–1914); American columnist

What should students learn in a strategic management or business policy course? It seems an obvious question to start with, especially for professors who teach about objective setting. Yet, in practice, the large majority of strategic management textbooks do not make their teaching objectives explicit. These books implicitly assume that the type of teaching objectives and teaching methods needed for a strategic management course do not radically differ from any other subject – basically, strategy can be taught in the same way as accounting or baking cookies. Their approach is based on the following teaching objectives:

■ *Knowledge*. To get the student to clearly understand and memorize all of the major 'ingredients'.

■ *Skills*. To develop the student's ability to follow the detailed 'recipes'.

■ *Attitude*. To instill a disciplined frame of mind, whereby the student automatically attempts to approach all issues by following established procedures.

This is an important way of teaching – it is how all of us were taught to read and write, do arithmetic and drive a car. This type of teaching can be referred to as *instructional*, because students are told what to know and do. The instructor is the authority who has all of the necessary knowledge and skills, and it is his/her role to transfer these to the students. Thus the educational emphasis is on communicating know-how and ensuring that students are able to repeat what they have heard. Students are not encouraged to question the knowledge they receive – on the contrary, it is the intention of instructional teaching to get students to absorb an accepted body of knowledge and to follow established recipes. The student should *accept*, *absorb* and *apply*.

However, while instructing students on a subject and programming their behavior might be useful in such areas as mathematics, cooking and karate, we believe it is not a very good way of teaching strategy. In our opinion, a strategic management professor should have a different set of teaching objectives:

- *Knowledge.* To encourage the understanding of the many, often conflicting, schools of thought and to facilitate the gaining of insight into the assumptions, possibilities and limitations of each set of theories.

- *Skills.* To develop the student's ability to define strategic issues, to critically reflect on existing theories, to creatively combine or develop conceptual models where necessary and to flexibly employ theories where useful.

- *Attitude.* To instill a critical, analytical, flexible and creative mind-set, which challenges organizational, industry and national paradigms and problem-solving recipes.

In other words, strategy professors should want to achieve the opposite of instructors – not to instill recipes, but rather to encourage students to dissect and challenge recipes. Strategic thinking is in its very essence questioning, challenging, unconventional and innovative. These aspects of strategic thinking cannot be transferred through instruction. A critical, analytical, flexible and creative state of mind must be developed by practicing these very qualities. Hence, a learning situation must encourage students to be critical, must challenge them to be analytical, must force them to be mentally flexible and must demand creativity and unconventional thinking. Students cannot be instructed to be strategists, but must learn the art of strategy by thinking and acting themselves – they must *discuss*, *deliberate* and *do*. The role of the professor is to create the circumstances for this learning. We therefore refer to this type of teaching as *facilitative*.

This teaching philosophy has led to a radical departure from traditional textbooks that focus on knowledge transfer and application skills, and that have often been written from the perspective of just one paradigm. In this book the fundamental differences of opinion within strategic management are not ignored or smoothed over. On the contrary, it is the mission of this book to expose students to the many, often conflicting, perspectives in the field of strategy. It is our experience that the challenge of comparing and reconciling rivaling strategy perspectives sharpens the mind of the 'apprentice' strategists. Throwing students into the midst of the central strategy debates, while simultaneously demanding that they apply their thinking to practical strategic problems, is the most likely way to enhance the qualities of creativity, flexibility, independence and analytical depth that students will need to become true strategic thinkers.

FOCUSING ON STRATEGY ISSUES

Some people are so good at learning the tricks of the trade
that they never get to learn the trade.
Sam Levenson (1911–1980); American teacher and comedian

While it is the objective of this book to increase students' strategic thinking abilities by exposing them to a wide range of theories and perspectives, it is not the intention to confuse and disorient. Yet in a subject area like strategic management, in which there is a broad spectrum of different views, there is a realistic threat that students might go deaf listening to the cacophony of different opinions. The variety of ideas can easily become overwhelming and difficult to integrate.

For this reason, the many theories, models, approaches and perspectives have been clustered around ten central strategy issues, each of which is discussed in a separate chapter. These ten strategy issues represent the key questions with which strategists must deal in practice. Only the theorists whose ideas have a direct bearing on the issue at hand are discussed in each chapter.

The advantage of this issue-based book structure is that it is *decision-oriented* – each chapter is about a key type of strategic decision that needs to be made. Students are challenged to look at a strategic issue holistically, taking various aspects and perspectives into account, and to arrive at a proposed course of action. This type of decision-focus closely reflects what strategizing managers need to do in practice. Step-by-step books are much more *tool-oriented*, teaching students how to go through each phase of a strategic planning process and how to use each analysis framework – useful, especially for junior analysts, but unlikely to stimulate real strategic thinking and to provide insight into difficult strategic choices.

Within each chapter, the conflicting perspectives on how the strategic issue should be approached are contrasted with one another by staging a virtual 'debate'. Two opposite perspectives are presented to kick off the debate and highlight areas of disagreement, after which the students (and their professors) are invited to further debate the issue and decide on the value and limitations of each point of view. While the chapter text offers a general introduction to the nature of the strategic issue and gives an overview of the hotly debated questions, no attempt is made to present the 'right answer' or provide a 'grand unifying theory' – students must make up their own minds based on the arguments placed before them.

The advantage of this debate-based chapter structure is that it encourages the students' engagement and that it provokes critical thinking. As students need to determine the strengths and weaknesses of each strategy perspective, they also become more adept at combining different 'lenses' to gain a fuller understanding of a problem, while becoming more skilled at balancing and mixing prescriptions to find innovative solutions to these problems. Some students will feel ill at ease not being presented with the 'right approach' or the 'best practice', as they are used to getting in many other books, but this is all the more reason to avoid providing these – as strategizing managers the security of one truth won't get them far, so it is preferable to learn to deal with (and benefit from) a variety of opinions as soon as possible.

USING ORIGINAL READINGS

Education is not filling a bucket but lighting a fire.
William Butler Yeats (1865–1939); Irish poet and dramatist

There are no better and livelier debates than when rivals put forward their own ideas as forcefully as they can. For this reason, we have chosen to strengthen the strategy debates by letting influential theorists state their own case. In Section VI, 20 readings have been included, which is two for each of the main chapters. Each duo has been selected as representative of the two poles in each debate. These works, by influential theorists from each camp, offer the reader a first-hand account of the key ideas, concepts and theories that are central to these two perspectives on strategy. They are our 'discussants', making the strategy debates more tangible and allowing the reader to judge the arguments of the two opposite positions without our 'interpretive filter'.

These two readings per chapter have been selected with a number of criteria in mind. As a starting point, we were looking for the articles or books that are widely judged to be classics in the field of strategy. However, to ensure a good debate, we occasionally looked beyond established classics to find a challenging minority point of view. Finally, discussants are only as good as their ability to communicate to the non-initiated, and therefore we have sometimes excluded certain classics as too technical.

To keep the size of the book within acceptable limits, most readings have had to be reduced in length, while extensive footnotes and references have had to be dropped. At all times this editing has been guided by the principle that the author's key ideas and arguments must be preserved intact. To compensate for the loss of references in each article, a combined list of the most important references has been added at the end of this book.

TAKING AN INTERNATIONAL PERSPECTIVE

He who knows only his side of the case,
knows little of that.
John Stuart Mill (1806–1873); English philosopher

While almost all strategic management textbooks have been mainly produced for their author's domestic market and are later exported overseas, this book has been explicitly developed with an international audience in mind. For students, the international orientation of this book has a number of distinct advantages:

■ *Cross-cultural differences.* Although there has been relatively little cross-cultural research in the field of strategy, results so far indicate that there are significant differences in strategy styles between companies from different countries. This calls into question the habit among strategy researchers to present universal theories, without indicating the cultural assumptions on which their ideas have been based. It is not unlikely that strategy theories have a strong cultural bias and therefore cannot be simply transferred from one national setting to another. Much of the debate going on between strategy theorists might actually be based on such divergent cultural assumptions. As this book does not take one position, strategists are encouraged to ask themselves the question whether some theories and perspectives are more appropriate in some countries than in others.

■ *International context.* Besides the issue of potentially needing to adapt one's strategy-making style to the specific country one is in, many companies have the additional complexity of operating in a variety of countries at the same time. In this international arena they are confronted with a distinct set of issues, ranging from global integration and coordination, to localization and transnationalization. This set of issues presented by the international context is debated in depth in Chapter 10.

■ *International cases and illustrations.* To explore how the various strategy perspectives can be applied to different national contexts, it is imperative to have cases and illustrations from a wide variety of countries, spread around the world. In this book the 31 cases and illustrations cover more than 20 countries and most have an international orientation. It must be noted, however, that we have had a bias towards well-known firms from developed economies, as these examples are more recognizable to most audiences around the world.

IMPROVEMENTS TO THE SECOND EDITION

Change is not made without inconvenience,
even from worse to better.
Samuel Johnson (1709–1784); English lexicographer

While high fashion designers launch their new collections on an annual basis, we have taken the automotive industry as our inspiration, bringing out a new 'model' every four to six years. This long 'cycle time' has allowed us to thoroughly test new ideas and to distinguish which of the developments in the field of strategic management are important innovations and which are short-lived fashions. It has also given us the opportunity to do a major 'overhaul', instead of a more superficial 'make over'.

The result is a second edition that contains a number of significant improvements when compared to the previous version. While the basic approach and structure have remained largely the same, major revisions have been implemented. These alterations are partially due to new advances in the field of strategic management, but also reflect the continual learning that has taken place as these ideas have been tested in practice via consulting and teaching. The main improvements over the previous edition are the following:

■ *New structure within chapters.* All chapters have been thoroughly restructured to enhance readability. In the previous edition, each chapter started with a central debate, highlighting points of disagreement between strategists. This left some readers confused, as they had difficulty understanding the key issues being debated. Therefore, in the new edition, each chapter begins with a review of the key strategy issues, explaining important strategy concepts and frameworks, after which the central debate is introduced. This revised order should greatly improve the reader's ability to critically evaluate the arguments raised in each debate.

- *New readings section*. While in the previous edition the readings were dispersed throughout the book, in this edition they have been clustered into one section at the end of the book. The advantage of this set-up is that the text and the readings are much more distinct and that both can be more easily used as stand-alone materials where necessary. At the same time, all readings have been clearly numbered according to the chapter to which they correspond, to ensure ease of use.

- *New topics*. Besides a new structure, all chapters have also been significantly expanded to give a more comprehensive coverage of the main topics in the area of strategic management. A number of new topics have been added, including strategic renewal, business models, alliance capabilities, business ecosystems, disruptive technologies and co-evolution, while others have been given much more space, such as sources of competitive advantage, market segmentation, value chain analysis, corporate integration mechanisms, multi-business synergy, post-acquisition integration, strategic alliances, industry development, strategic leadership, corporate governance and strategy implementation.

- *New illustration boxes*. A new feature is the addition of two extensive illustrations per chapter (20 in total). For each strategy perspective described in the book, an exhibit has been included, describing a well-known company that employs this strategy perspective. These examples make it much easier to see how a particular strategy perspective leads to concrete organizational behavior in practice. As with all of the examples and cases in the book, these illustrations have been taken from a broad range of industries and countries, to emphasize that the concepts being discussed are widely applicable.

- *New short cases*. In addition to the two illustrations per chapter, this edition again includes 11 short cases that provide a good example of the debate at hand. The short cases are an interesting challenge to readers, to see how complex strategy issues can be solved in a variety of different ways, depending on the strategy perspective employed. These cases are also an excellent alternative to traditional long cases and have proven to be particularly valuable in executive programs and in-company courses, where managers can read and discuss them on the spot. All of these short cases are new or revised.

- *New web site materials*. For professors and students using this book as their strategy textbook, new supplementary materials have been developed and posted on our web site (www.strategy-academy.org or www.thomsonlearning.com). This material includes a multiple choice test bank for professors, practice questions for students, PowerPoint slides, links to the case companies and course outlines.

- *New alternative editions*. A new feature is that this book is available in three different 'weight categories'. The 'heavyweight' version is entitled *Strategy – Process, Content, Context: An International Perspective* and includes four readings per chapter and 22 long cases. The edition in front of you is the intermediate, 'welterweight' version, in which the core text is supplemented by 20 readings, one for each of the 20 perspectives presented in this book. There is also an even more slimmed down version available, without any readings. This 'featherweight' edition, entitled *Strategy Synthesis: Concise Version*, is particularly suited to short courses and executive education programs.

We are aware that these changes might bring some inconvenience, even though in Samuel Johnson's words they are 'from worse to better'. As every strategist knows, 'software updates' come with switching costs that require users to invest time and energy to acquaint themselves with the new version. However, we trust that previous 'users' will find the 2.0 version of our book well worth the additional investment.

CONTACT US

A stand can be made against invasion by an army; no stand can be made against invasion by an idea.
Victor Hugo (1802–1885); French poet, novelist and playwright

Books are old-fashioned, but based on a proven technology that is still the most appropriate under most circumstances. One drawback, however, is that a book is unidirectional, allowing us to send a message to you, but not capable of transmitting your comments, questions and suggestions back to us. This is unfortunate, as we are keen on communicating with our audience and enjoy hearing what works and doesn't work 'in the field'.

Therefore, we would like to encourage managers, students and professors to establish contact with us. You can do this by visiting our web site (www.strategy-academy. org or www.thomsonlearning.com) to check out the extra features we have for you and to leave your comments and suggestions. But you can also contact us directly by email at b.dewit@strategy-academy.org or r.meyer@strategy-academy.org.

STRATEGY

INTRODUCTION

Men like the opinions to which they have become accustomed from youth; this prevents them from finding the truth, for they cling to the opinions of habit.
Moses Maimonides (1135–1204);
Egyptian physician and philosopher

Where there is much desire to learn, there of necessity will be much arguing, much writing, many opinions; for opinion in good men is but knowledge in the making.
John Milton (1608–1674); English poet

THE NATURE OF STRATEGY

In a book entitled *Strategy*, it seems reasonable to expect Chapter 1 to begin with a clear definition of strategy that would be employed with consistency in all subsequent chapters. An early and precise definition would help to avoid conflicting interpretations of what should be considered strategy and, by extension, what should be understood by the term 'strategic management'. However, any such sharp definition of strategy here would actually be misleading. It would suggest that there is widespread agreement among practitioners, researchers and theorists as to what strategy is. The impression would be given that the fundamental concepts in the area of strategy are generally accepted and hardly questioned. Yet, even a quick glance through current strategy literature indicates otherwise. There are strongly differing opinions on most of the key issues and the disagreements run so deep that even a common definition of the term strategy is illusive.

This is bad news for those who prefer simplicity and certainty. It means that the topic of strategy cannot be explained as a set of straightforward definitions and rules to be memorized and applied. The strongly conflicting views mean that strategy cannot be summarized into broadly agreed on definitions, rules, matrices and flow diagrams that one must simply absorb and learn to use. If the fundamental differences of opinion are not swept aside, the consequence is that a book on strategy cannot be like an instruction manual that takes you through the steps of how something should be done. On the contrary, a strategy book should acknowledge the disagreements and encourage thinking about the value of each of the different points of view. That is the intention of this book.

The philosophy embraced here is that an understanding of the topic of strategy can only be gained by grappling with the diversity of insights presented by so many prominent thinkers and by coming to terms with the fact that there is no simple answer to the question of what strategy is. Readers who prefer the certainty of reading only one opinion, as opposed to the intellectual stimulation of being confronted with a wide variety, should read no further – there are plenty of alternatives available. Those who wish to proceed should lay aside their 'opinions of habit', and open their minds to the many other opinions presented, for in these pages there is 'knowledge in the making'.

IDENTIFYING THE STRATEGY ISSUES

If the only tool you have is a hammer, you treat everything like a nail.
Abraham Maslow (1908–1970); American psychologist

The approach taken in this book is in line with the moral of Maslow's remark. To avoid hammering strategy issues with only one theory, a variety of ways of viewing strategic questions will be presented. But there are two different ways of presenting a broad spectrum of theoretical lenses. This point can be made clear by extending Maslow's hammer-and-nail analogy. To become a good carpenter, who wisely uses a variety of tools depending on what is being crafted, an apprentice carpenter will need to learn about these different instruments. One way is for the apprentice to study the characteristics and functioning of all tools individually, and only then to apply each where appropriate. However, another possibility is for the apprentice to first learn about what must be crafted, getting a feel for the materials and the problems that must be solved, and only then to turn to the study of the necessary tools. The first approach to learning can be called 'tools-driven' – understanding each tool comes first, while combining them to solve real problems comes later. The second approach to learning can be termed 'problem-driven' – understanding problems comes first, while searching for the appropriate tools is based on the type of problem.

Both options can also be used for the apprentice strategist. In a tools-driven approach to learning about strategy, all major theories would first be understood separately, to be compared or combined later when using them in practice. A logical structure for a book aiming at this mode of learning would be to allot one chapter to each of the major theories or schools of thought. The advantage of such a theory-based book structure would be that each chapter would focus on giving the reader a clear and cohesive overview of one major theory within the field of strategy. For readers with an interest in grasping the essence of each theory individually, this would probably be the ideal book format. However, the principal disadvantage of a theory-by-theory summary of the field of strategy would be that the reader would not have a clear picture of how the various theories relate to one another. The apprentice strategist would be left with important questions such as: 'Where do the theories agree and where do they differ? Which strategy phenomena does each theory claim to explain and which phenomena are left unaccounted for? Can various theories be successfully combined or are they based on mutually exclusive assumptions? And which strategy is right, or at least most appropriate under particular circumstances? Not knowing the answers to these questions, how could the apprentice strategist try to apply these new theoretical tools to practice?

This book is based on the assumption that the reader wants to be able to actively solve strategic problems. Understanding the broad spectrum of theories is not an end in itself, but a means for more effective strategizing. Therefore, the problem-driven approach to learning about strategy has been adopted. In this approach, key strategy issues are first identified and then each is looked at from the perspective of the most appropriate theories. This has resulted in an issue-based book structure, in which each chapter deals with a particular set of strategy issues. In each chapter, only the theories that shed some light on the issues under discussion are brought forward and compared to one another. Of course, some theories are relevant to more than one set of issues and therefore appear in various chapters.

In total, ten sets of strategy issues have been identified that together largely cover the entire field of strategic management. These ten will be the subjects of the remaining ten chapters of this book. How the various strategy issues have been divided into these ten sets will be explained in the following paragraphs.

Strategy dimensions: Process, content and context

The most fundamental distinction made in this book is between strategy process, strategy content and strategy context (see Figure 1.1). These are the three dimensions of strategy that can be recognized in every real-life strategic problem situation. They can be generally defined as follows:

- Strategy process. The manner in which strategies come about is referred to as the strategy process. Stated in terms of a number of questions, strategy process is concerned with the *how*, *who* and *when* of strategy: how is, and should, strategy be made, analyzed, dreamt-up, formulated, implemented, changed and controlled; who is involved; and when do the necessary activities take place?

- Strategy content. The product of a strategy process is referred to as the strategy content. Stated in terms of a question, strategy content is concerned with the *what* of strategy: what is, and should be, the strategy for the company and each of its constituent units?

- Strategy context. The set of circumstances under which both the strategy process and the strategy content are determined is referred to as the strategy context. Stated in terms of a question, strategy context is concerned with the *where* of strategy: where (that is in which firm and which environment) are the strategy process and strategy content embedded.

FIGURE 1.1   Dimensions of strategy and the organizational purpose

It cannot be emphasized enough that strategy process, content and context are not different parts of strategy, but are distinguishable dimensions. Just as it is silly to speak of the length, width and height parts of a box, one cannot speak of the three parts of strategy either. Each strategic problem situation is by its nature three dimensional, possessing process, content and context characteristics, and only the understanding of all three dimensions will give the strategist real depth of comprehension. In particular, it must be acknowledged that the three dimensions interact (Pettigrew and Whipp, 1991; Ketchen, Thomas and McDaniel, 1996). For instance, the manner in which the strategy process is organized will have a significant impact on the resulting strategy content, while likewise, the content of the current strategy will strongly influence the way in which the strategy process will be conducted in future. If these linkages are ignored, the strategist will have a flat view instead of a three-dimensional view of strategy. A useful analytical distinction for temporarily unraveling a strategic problem situation will have turned into permanent means for fragmenting reality.

However, it is possible to concentrate on one of the strategy dimensions if the other two are kept in mind. In fact, to have a focused discussion it is even necessary to look at one dimension at a time. The alternative is a debate in which all topics on all three dimensions would be discussed simultaneously: such a cacophony of opinions would be lively, but most likely less than fruitful. Therefore, the process–content–context distinction will cautiously be used as the main structuring principle of this book, splitting the text into three major sections.

A fourth section has been added to these three, although strictly speaking it is not about strategy. In the above list, the questions of how, who, when, what and where were mentioned, but not yet the question of *why* – why do organizations exist and why do their strategies move them in a certain direction? This is the issue of organizational purpose – the impetus to strategy activities. Making strategy is not an end in itself, but a means for reaching particular objectives. Organizations exist to fulfill a purpose and strategies are employed to ensure that the organizational purpose is realized. Given the importance of this topic to the understanding of strategy, purpose has been given an equal position next to process, content and context as a separate section of this book.

This four-fold structure fits closely with the situation within the academic field of strategic management. To a large extent, strategy literature is divided along these lines. Most strategy research, by its very nature, is more atomistic than holistic, focusing on just a few variables at once. Consequently, most writings on strategy, including most of the theories discussed in this book, tend to favor just one, or at most two, strategy dimensions, which is usually complex enough given the need to remain comprehensible. In particular, the divide between strategy process and strategy content has been quite pronounced, to the extent of worrying some scholars about whether the connections between the two are being sufficiently recognized (Pettigrew, 1992). Although sharing this concern, use of the process–content–context–purpose distinction here reflects the reality of the current state of debate within the field of strategic management.

Strategy process: Thinking, forming and changing

Section II of this book will deal with the strategy process. Traditionally, most textbooks have portrayed the strategy process as a basically linear progression through a number of distinct steps. Usually a split is made between the strategy analysis stage, the strategy formulation stage and the strategy implementation stage. In the analysis stage, strategists identify the opportunities and threats in the environment, as well as the strengths and weaknesses of the organization. Next, in the formulation stage, strategists determine which strategic options are available to them, evaluate each and choose one. Finally, in the implementation stage, the selected strategic option is translated into a number of concrete activities, which are then carried out. It is commonly presumed that this process is not only linear, but also largely rational – strategists identify, determine, evaluate, choose, translate and carry out based on rigorous logic and extensive knowledge of all important factors. Furthermore, the assumption is frequently made that the strategy process is comprehensive – strategy is made for the entire organization and everything can be radically changed all at once.

All of these beliefs have been challenged. For instance, many authors have criticized the strong emphasis on rationality in these traditional views of the strategy process. Some writers have even argued that the true nature of strategic thinking is more intuitive and creative than rational. In their opinion, strategizing is about perceiving strengths and weaknesses, envisioning opportunities and threats and creating the future, for which imagination and judgment are more important than analysis and logic. This constitutes quite a fundamental disagreement about the cognitive processes of the strategizing manager. These issues surrounding the nature of strategic thinking will be discussed in Chapter 2.

The division of the strategy process into a number of sequential phases has also drawn heavy criticism from authors who believe that in reality no such identifiable stages exist. They dismiss the linear analysis–formulation–implementation distinction as an unwarranted simplification, arguing that the strategy process is messier, with analysis, formulation and implementation activities going on all the time, thoroughly intertwined with one another. In their view, organizations do not first make strategic plans and then execute them as intended. Rather, strategies are usually formed incrementally, as organizations think and act in small iterative steps, letting strategies emerge as they go along. This represents quite a difference of opinion on how strategies are formed within organizations. These issues surrounding the nature of strategy formation will be discussed in Chapter 3.

The third major assumption of the traditional view, comprehensiveness, has also been challenged. Many authors have pointed out that it is unrealistic to suppose that a company can be boldly redesigned. They argue that it is terribly difficult to orchestrate an overarching strategy for the entire organization that is a significant departure from the current course of action. It is virtually impossible to get various aspects of an organization all lined up to go through a change at the same time, certainly if a radical change is intended. In practice, different aspects of an organization will be under different pressures, on different timetables and have different abilities to change, leading to a differentiated approach to change. Moreover, the rate and direction of change will be seriously limited by the cultural, political and cognitive inheritance of the firm. Hence, it is argued, strategic change is usually more gradual and fragmented than radical and coordinated. The issues surrounding this difference of opinion on the nature of strategic change will be discussed in Chapter 4.

These three chapter topics – strategic thinking, strategy formation and strategic change – do not constitute entirely separate subjects. Let it be clear that they are not phases, stages or elements of the strategy process that can be understood in isolation. Strategic thinking, strategy formation and strategic change are different aspects of the strategy process, which are strongly linked and partially overlapping (see Figure 1.2). They have been selected because they are sets of issues on which there is significant debate within the field of strategy. As will become clear, having a particular opinion on one of these aspects will have a consequence for views held on all other aspects as well.

FIGURE 1.2   Aspects of the strategy process

Strategy content: Business, corporate and network levels

Section III of this book will deal with the strategy content. Strategies come in all shapes and sizes, and almost all strategy writers, researchers and practitioners agree that each strategy is essentially unique. There is widespread disagreement, however, about the principles to which strategies should adhere. The debates are numerous, but there are three fundamental sets of issues around which most conflicts generally center. These three topics can be clarified by distinguishing the level of strategy at which each is most relevant.

Strategies can be made for different groups of people and/or activities within an organization. The lowest level of aggregation is one person or task, while the highest level of aggregation encompasses all people and/or activities within an organization. The most common distinction between levels of aggregation made in the strategic management literature is between the functional, business and corporate levels (see Figure 1.3). Strategy issues at the *functional level* refer to questions regarding specific functional aspects of a company (operations strategy, marketing strategy, financial strategy, etc.). Strategy at the *business level* requires the integration of functional level strategies for a distinct set of products and/or services intended for a specific group of customers. Often companies only operate in one such business, so that this is the highest level of aggregation within the firm. However, there are also many companies that are in two or more businesses. In such companies, a multi-business or *corporate level* strategy is required, which aligns the various business level strategies.

A logical extension of the functional–business–corporate distinction is to explicitly recognize the level of aggregation higher than the individual organization. Firms often cluster together into groups of two or more collaborating organizations. This level is referred to as the multi-company or *network level*. Most multi-company groups consist of only a few parties, as is the case in strategic alliances, joint ventures and value-adding partnerships. However, networks can also have dozens, even hundreds, of participants. In some circumstances, the corporation as a whole might be a member of a group, while in other situations only a part of the firm joins forces with other organizations. In all cases, when a strategy is developed for a group of firms, this is called a network level strategy.

In line with the generally accepted boundaries of the strategic management field, this book will focus on the business, corporate and network levels of strategy, although this

FIGURE 1.3 Levels of strategy

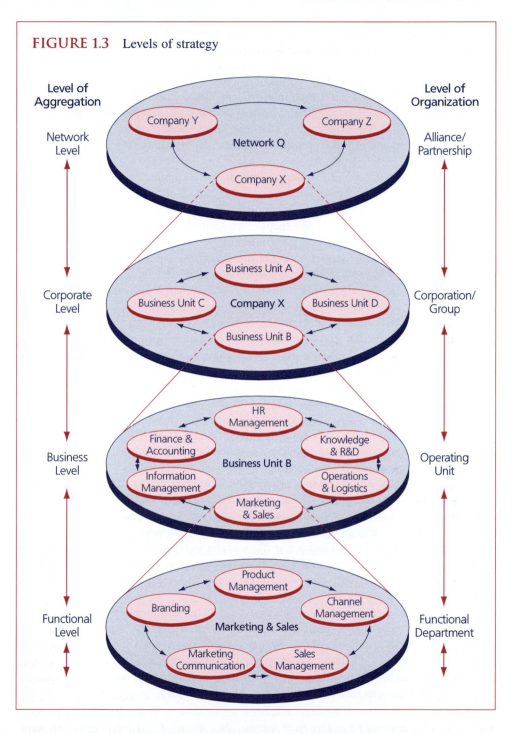

will often demand consideration of strategy issues at the functional level as well. In Section II, on the strategy process, this level distinction will not be emphasized yet, but in Section III, on the strategy content, the different strategy issues encountered at the different levels of strategy will be explored. And at each level of strategy, the focus will be on the fundamental differences of opinion that divide strategy theorists.

Chapter 5 will deal with strategy issues at the business level. Here the fundamental debate is whether firms are, and should be, primarily market-driven or resource-driven. Some authors argue that firms should be strongly externally oriented, engaged in a game of positioning vis-à-vis customers, competitors, suppliers and other parties in the environment, and should adapt the firm to the demands of the game. In other words, companies should think 'outside-in'. Yet, other authors strongly disagree, stressing the need for companies to exploit and expand their strengths. They recommend a more 'inside-out' view, whereby companies search for environments and positions that best fit with their resource base.

Chapter 6 is concerned with strategy issues at the corporate level. The fundamental debate in this chapter is whether corporations are, and should be, run as federations of autonomous business units or as highly integrated organizations. Some authors argue that corporate strategists should view themselves as investors, with financial stakes in a portfolio of business units. As a shrewd investor, the corporate center should buy up cheap companies, divest underperforming business units, and put money into its business units with the highest profit potential, independent of what industry they are in. Each business unit should be judged on its merits and given a large measure of autonomy, to be optimally responsive to the specific conditions in its industry. However, other authors are at odds with this view, pointing to the enormous potential for synergy that is left untapped. They argue that corporations should be tightly knit groupings of closely related business units that share resources and align their strategies with one another. The ensuing synergies, it is forecast, will provide an important source of competitive advantage.

Chapter 7 focuses on the strategy issues at the network level. The fundamental debate in this chapter revolves around the question whether firms should develop long-term collaborative relationships with other firms or should remain essentially independent. Some authors believe that competition between organizations is sometimes more destructive than beneficial, and argue that building up durable partnerships with other organizations can often be mutually advantageous. Participation in joint ventures, alliances and broader networks requires a higher level of inter-organizational trust and interdependence, but can pay off handsomely. It is therefore recommended to selectively engage in joint – that is, multi-company – strategy development. Other authors, however, are thoroughly skeptical about the virtues of interdependence. They prefer independence, pointing to the dangers of opportunistic partners and creeping dependence on the other. Therefore, it is recommended to avoid multi-company level strategy development and only to use alliances as a temporary measure.

Again, it must be emphasized that the analytical distinction employed here should not be interpreted as an absolute means for isolating issues. In reality, these three levels of strategy do not exist as tidy categories, but are strongly interrelated and partially overlapping. As a consequence, the three sets of strategy issues identified above are also linked to one another. In Section III it will become clear that taking a stand in one debate will affect the position that one can take in others.

Strategy context: Industry, organizational and international

Section IV in this book is devoted to the strategy context. Strategy researchers, writers and practitioners largely agree that every strategy context is unique. Moreover, they are almost unanimous that it is usually wise for managers to strive for a fit between the strategy process, strategy content and the specific circumstances prevalent in the strategy context.

However, disagreement arises as soon as the discussion turns to the details of the alignments. Does the context determine what the strategizing manager must do, or can the manager actually shape the context? Some people argue or assume that the strategy context has a dynamic all its own, which strategists can hardly influence, and therefore that the strategy context sets strict confines on the freedom to maneuver. The context is not malleable and hence the motto for the strategist is 'adapt or die'. Others believe that strategists should not be driven by the context, but have a large measure of freedom to set their own course of action. Frequently it is argued that strategizing managers can, and should, create their own circumstances, instead of being enslaved by the circumstances they find. In short, the strategy context can be determined, instead of letting it determine.

In Section IV, the difference of opinion on the power of the context to determine strategy surfaces when discussing the various aspects of the strategy context. The section has been split into three chapters, each focusing on a different aspect of the strategy context. Two distinctions have been used to arrive at the division into three chapters (see Figure 1.4). The first dichotomy employed is that between the organization and its industry environment. The *industry context* will be the subject of Chapter 8. In this chapter, the strategic issues revolve around the question whether the industry circumstances set the rules to which companies must comply, or whether companies have the freedom to choose their own strategy and even change the industry conditions. The *organizational context* will be dealt with in Chapter 9. Here, the key strategic issues have to do with the question of whether the organizational circumstances largely determine the strategy process and strategy content followed, or whether the strategist has a significant amount of control over the course of action adopted.

The second dichotomy employed is that between the domestic and the international strategy context. The domestic context does not raise any additional strategic issues, but the *international context* clearly does. Strategists must deal with the question of whether adaptation to the diversity of the international context is strictly required or whether companies have considerable freedom to choose their strategy process and content irrespective of the international context. The difference of opinion between writers on the international

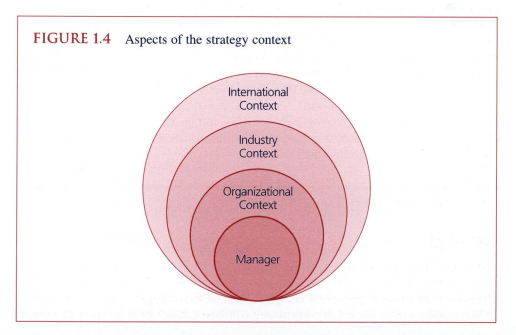

FIGURE 1.4   Aspects of the strategy context

context actually goes one step further. Some authors predict that the diversity of the international context will decline over time and that companies can encourage this process. If global convergence takes place, it is argued, adaptation to the international context will become a non-issue. Other authors, however, disagree that international diversity is declining and therefore argue that the international context will remain an issue that strategists must attempt to deal with. This debate on the future of the international context is conducted in Chapter 10.

Organizational purpose

Oddly enough, most authors write about strategy without any reference to the organizational purpose being pursued. It is generally assumed that all organizations exist for the same basic reasons, and that this purpose is self-evident. However, in reality, there is extensive disagreement about what the current purposes of organizations are, and especially about what their purpose should be. Some people argue that it is the business of business to make money. In their view, firms are owned by shareholders and therefore should pursue shareholders' interests. And it is the primary interest of shareholders to see the value of their stocks increase. On the other hand, others believe that companies exist to serve the interests of multiple stakeholders. In their opinion, having a financial stake in a firm should not give shareholders a dominant position vis-à-vis other groups that also have an interest in what the organization does. Other stakeholders usually include employees, customers, suppliers and bankers, but could also include the local community, the broader industry and even the natural environment.

This is a very fundamental debate, with broader societal implications than any of the other strategy issues. Given the important role played by business organizations in modern times, the purposes they attempt to fulfill will have a significant impact on the functioning of society. It is not surprising, therefore, to see that organizational purpose is also discussed by people other than strategy theorists and practitioners. The role of firms and the interests they should pursue are widely debated by members of political parties, environmental conservation groups, unions, the media, political action groups and the general public.

Arguably, in a book on strategy, organizational purpose should be discussed before moving on to the subject of strategy itself – as Figure 1.1 visualizes, organizational purpose is the impetus for strategy activities. In principle this is true, but the 'issue of existence' is not an easy topic with which to start a book – it would be quite a hefty appetizer with which to begin a strategy meal. Therefore, to avoid intellectual indigestion, the topic of purpose will be saved for dessert. The last text part of the book, Section V, will be devoted to the issues surrounding purpose. This section comprises only one chapter, Chapter 11 entitled 'Organizational purpose', as the discussion will be staged broadly, asking what drives organizations forward.

STRUCTURING THE STRATEGY DEBATES

For every complex problem there is a simple solution that is wrong.
George Bernard Shaw (1856–1950); Irish playwright and critic

Every real-life strategic problem is complex. Most of the strategic issues outlined earlier in this chapter will be present in every strategic problem, making the prospect of a simple solution an illusion. Yet, even if each set of strategy issues is looked at independently, it seems that strategy theorists cannot agree on the right way to approach them. On each of the topics, there is widespread disagreement, indicating that no simple solution can be expected here either.

Why is it that theorists cannot agree on how to solve strategic problems? Might it be that some theorists are right, while others are just plain wrong? In that case, it would be wise for problem-solvers to select the valid theory and discard the false ones. While this might be true in some cases, it seems unlikely that false theories would stay around long enough to keep a lively debate going. Eventually, the right (i.e. unfalsified) theory would prevail and disagreements would disappear. Yet, this does not seem to be happening in the field of strategic management.

Could it be that each theorist only emphasizes one aspect of an issue – only takes one cut of a multi-faceted reality? In that case, it would be wise for problem-solvers to combine the various theories that each look at the problem from a different angle. However, if this were true, one would expect the different theories to be largely complementary. Each theory would simply be a piece in the bigger puzzle of strategic management. Yet, this does not explain why there is so much disagreement, and even contradiction, within the field of strategy.

It could also be that strategy theorists start from divergent assumptions about the nature of each strategy issue and therefore logically arrive at a different perspective on how to solve strategic problems. In that case, it would be wise for problem-solvers to combine the various theories, in order to look at the problem from a number of different angles.

All three possibilities for explaining the existing theoretical disagreements should be kept open. However, entertaining the thought that divergent positions are rooted in fundamentally different assumptions about strategy issues is by far the most fruitful to the strategist confronted with complex problems. It is too simple to hope that one can deal with the contradictory opinions within the field of strategy by discovering which strategy theories are right and which are wrong. But it is also not particularly practical to accept all divergent theories as valid depictions of different aspects of reality – if two theories suggest a different approach to the same problem, the strategist will have to sort out this contradiction. Therefore, in this book the emphasis will be on surfacing the basic assumptions underlying the major theoretical perspectives on strategy, and to debate whether, or under which circumstances, these assumptions are appropriate.

Assumptions about strategy tensions

At the heart of every set of strategic issues, a fundamental tension between apparent opposites can be identified. For instance, in Chapter 7 on network level strategy, the issues revolve around the fundamental tension between competition and cooperation. In Chapter 8 on the industry context, the fundamental tension between the opposites of compliance and choice lies at the center of the subject (see Figure 1.5). Each pair of opposites creates a tension, as they seem to be inconsistent, or even incompatible, with one another; it seems as if both elements cannot be fully true at the same time. If firms are competing, they are not cooperating. If firms must comply with the industry context, they have no choice. Yet, although these opposites confront strategizing managers with conflicting pressures, somehow they must be dealt with simultaneously. Strategists are caught in a bind, trying to cope with contradictory forces at the same time.

The challenge of strategic management is to wrestle with these tricky strategy tensions. All strategy theories make assumptions, explicitly or implicitly, about the nature of these

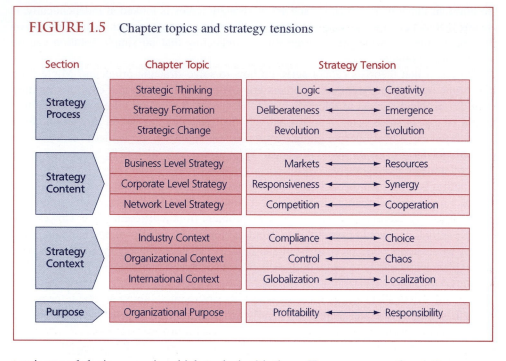

FIGURE 1.5   Chapter topics and strategy tensions

tensions and devise ways in which to deal with them. However, every theorist's assumptions differ, giving rise to a wide variety of positions. In fact, many of the major disagreements within the field of strategic management are rooted in the different assumptions made about coping with these strategy tensions. For this reason, the theoretical debate in each chapter will be centered around the different perspectives on dealing with a particular strategy tension.

Identifying strategy perspectives

The strategy issues in each chapter can be viewed from many perspectives. On each topic there are many different theories and hundreds of books and articles. While very interesting, a comparison or debate between all of these would probably be very chaotic, unfocused and incomprehensible. Therefore, in each chapter the debate has been condensed into its most powerful form – two diametrically opposed perspectives are confronted with one another. These two poles of each debate are not always the most widely held perspectives on the particular set of strategy issues, but they do expose the major points of contention within the topic area.

In every chapter, the two strategy perspectives selected for the debate each emphasize one side of a strategy tension over the other (see Figure 1.6). For instance, in Chapter 7 the discrete organization perspective stresses competition over cooperation, while the embedded organization perspective does the opposite. In Chapter 8, the industry dynamics perspective accentuates compliance over choice, while the industry leadership perspective does the opposite. In other words, the two perspectives represent the two extreme ways of dealing with a strategy tension, emphasizing one side or emphasizing the other.

In the first part of each chapter, the core strategic issue and the underlying strategy tension will be explained. Then, the two strategy perspectives will be introduced as the

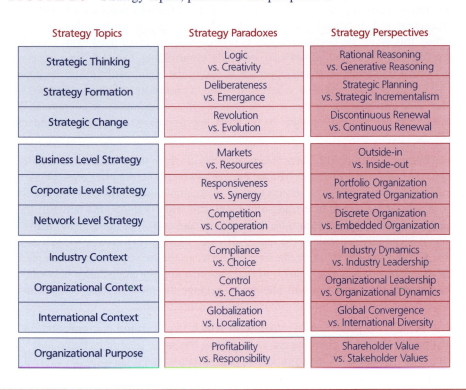

FIGURE 1.6   Strategy topics, paradoxes and perspectives

Strategy Topics	Strategy Paradoxes	Strategy Perspectives
Strategic Thinking	Logic vs. Creativity	Rational Reasoning vs. Generative Reasoning
Strategy Formation	Deliberateness vs. Emergence	Strategic Planning vs. Strategic Incrementalism
Strategic Change	Revolution vs. Evolution	Discontinuous Renewal vs. Continuous Renewal
Business Level Strategy	Markets vs. Resources	Outside-in vs. Inside-out
Corporate Level Strategy	Responsiveness vs. Synergy	Portfolio Organization vs. Integrated Organization
Network Level Strategy	Competition vs. Cooperation	Discrete Organization vs. Embedded Organization
Industry Context	Compliance vs. Choice	Industry Dynamics vs. Industry Leadership
Organizational Context	Control vs. Chaos	Organizational Leadership vs. Organizational Dynamics
International Context	Globalization vs. Localization	Global Convergence vs. International Diversity
Organizational Purpose	Profitability vs. Responsibility	Shareholder Value vs. Stakeholder Values

contestants in a virtual strategy debate and they will be given the opportunity to state their case. Each chapter will be wrapped up by giving an overview of the main differences between the two positions. What will not be done – and cannot be done – is to give readers the outcome of the debate. This readers will have to decide for themselves.

Viewing strategy tensions as strategy paradoxes

So, what should readers be getting out of each debate? With both strategy perspectives emphasizing the importance of one side of a strategy tension over the other, how should readers deal with these opposites? Of course, after hearing the arguments, it is up to readers to judge for themselves how the strategy tensions should be handled. However, there are four general ways of approaching them:

- As a puzzle. A puzzle is a challenging problem with an optimal solution. Think of a crossword puzzle as an example. Puzzles can be quite complex and extremely difficult to analyze, but there is a best way of solving them. Some of the most devious puzzles are those with seemingly contradictory premises. Strategy tensions can also be viewed as puzzles. While the pair of opposites seems to be incompatible with one another, this is only because the puzzle is not well understood yet. In reality, there is one best way of relieving the tension, but the strategist must unravel the problem first. Some writers seem to suggest that there are optimal ways of dealing with strategy tensions under all circumstances, but others argue that the optimal solution is situation dependent.

- ■ **As a dilemma.** A dilemma is a vexing problem with two possible solutions, neither of which is logically the best. Think of the famous prisoner's dilemma as an example. Dilemmas confront problem-solvers with difficult either-or choices, each with its own advantages and disadvantages, but neither clearly superior to the other. The uneasy feeling this gives the decision-maker is reflected in the often-used expression 'horns of a dilemma' – neither choice is particularly comfortable. Strategy tensions can also be viewed as dilemmas. If this approach is taken, the incompatibility of the opposites is accepted, and the strategist is forced to make a choice in favour of either one or the other. For instance, the strategist must choose either to compete or cooperate. Which of the two the strategist judges to be most appropriate will usually depend on the specific circumstances.

- ■ **As a trade-off.** A trade-off is a problem situation in which there are many possible solutions, each striking a different balance between two conflicting pressures. Think of the trade-off between work and leisure time as an example – more of one will necessarily mean less of the other. In a trade-off, many different combinations between the two opposites can be found, each with its own pros and cons, but none of the many solutions is inherently superior to the others. Strategy tensions can also be viewed as trade-offs. If this approach is taken, the conflict between the two opposites is accepted, and the strategist will constantly strive to find the most appropriate balance between them. For instance, the strategist will attempt to balance the pressures for competition and cooperation, depending on the circumstances encountered.

- ■ **As a paradox.** A paradox is a situation in which two seeming contradictory, or even mutually exclusive, factors appear to be true at the same time (e.g. Poole and Van de Ven, 1989; Quinn and Cameron, 1988). A problem that is a paradox has no real solution, as there is no way to logically integrate the two opposites into an internally consistent understanding of the problem. As opposed to the either-or nature of the dilemma, the paradox can be characterized as a 'both-and' problem – one factor is true and a contradictory factor is simultaneously true (e.g. Collins and Porras, 1994; Lewis, 2000). Hence, a paradox presents the problem-solver with the difficult task of wrestling with the problem, without ever arriving at a definitive solution. At best, the problem-solver can find a workable reconciliation to temporarily cope with the unsolvable paradox. Strategy tensions can also be viewed as paradoxes. If this approach is taken, the conflict between the two opposites is accepted, but the strategist will strive to accommodate both factors at the same time. The strategist will search for new ways of reconciling the opposites as best as possible. To take the same example as above, the strategist faced with the tension between competition and cooperation will attempt to do both as much as possible at the same time, with the intention of reaping the 'best of both worlds'.

Most people are used to solving puzzles, resolving dilemmas and making trade-offs. These ways of understanding and solving problems are common in daily life. They are based on the assumption that, by analysis, one or a number of logical solutions can be identified. It might require a sharp mind and considerable effort, but the answers can be found.

However, most people are not used to, or inclined to, think of a problem as a paradox. A paradox has no answer or set of answers – it can only be coped with as best as possible. Faced with a paradox, one can try to find novel ways of combining opposites, but one will know that none of these creative reconciliations will ever be *the* answer. Paradoxes will always remain surrounded by uncertainty and disagreements on how best to cope.

So, should strategy tensions be seen as puzzles, dilemmas, trade-offs or paradoxes (see Figure 1.7)? Arguments can be made for all, but viewing strategy tensions as strategy

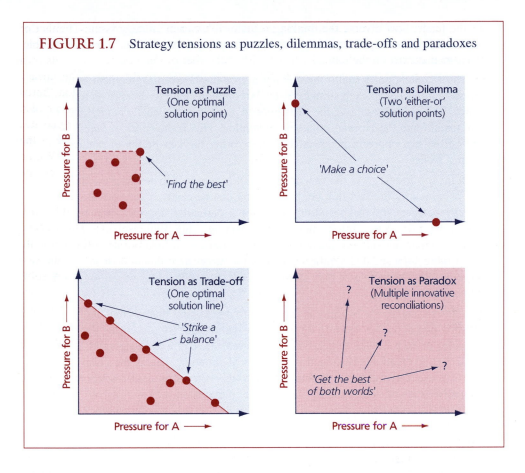

FIGURE 1.7 Strategy tensions as puzzles, dilemmas, trade-offs and paradoxes

paradoxes is the ultimate intellectual challenge. Looking at the tensions as paradoxes will help readers to avoid 'jumping to solutions' and will encourage the use of creativity to find ways of benefiting from both sides of a tension at the same time. Hence, throughout this book, the strategy tensions will be presented as strategy paradoxes, and readers will be invited to view them as such.

Taking a dialectical approach

As stated earlier, the debate in each chapter has been condensed into its most powerful form – two diametrically opposed perspectives are confronted with one another, each emphasizing one pole of the paradox. These two opposite positions are in fact the thesis and the antithesis of the debate, challenging the reader to search for an appropriate synthesis somewhere between the two extremes. This form of debate is called 'dialectical inquiry' – by using two opposite points of view, the problem-solver attempts to arrive at a better understanding of the issue and a 'higher level resolution' that integrates elements of both the thesis and the antithesis. This approach has a number of advantages:

- Range of ideas. By presenting the two opposite poles in each debate, readers can quickly acquire an understanding of the full range of ideas on the strategy issue. While these two extreme positions do not represent the most widely held views, they do clarify for the reader how diverse the thinking actually is on each strategy issue. This is the *book-end function* of presenting the two opposite perspectives – they 'frame' the full set of views that exist on the topic.

- Points of contention. Usually there is not across-the-board disagreement between the various approaches to each strategy issue, but opinions tend to diverge on a number of critical points. By presenting the two opposite poles in each debate, readers can rapidly gain insight into these major points of contention. This is the *contrast function* of presenting the two opposite perspectives – they bring the key points of contention into sharper focus.

- Stimulus for bridging. As the two opposite poles in each debate are presented, readers will be struck by the fact that neither position can be easily dismissed. Both extreme strategy perspectives make a strong case for a particular approach and readers will experience difficulty in simply choosing one over the other. With each extreme position offering certain advantages, readers will feel challenged to incorporate aspects of both into a more sophisticated synthesis. This is the *integrative function* of presenting the two opposite perspectives – they stimulate readers to seek a way of getting the best of both worlds.

- Stimulus for creativity. Nothing is more creativity evoking than a challenging paradox whereby two opposites seem to be true at the same time. By presenting the two opposite poles of each debate, which both make a realistic claim to being valid, readers are challenged to creatively resolve this paradoxical situation. This is the *generative function* of presenting the two opposite perspectives – they stimulate readers to generate innovative ways of 'transcending' the strategic paradox.

Each debate starts with the most traditional pole as the thesis, which is then contrasted with the less-established opposite pole as the antithesis. As for the synthesis, that is up to each strategist to find (see Figure 1.8).

Using the cases

One of the best ways of exploring synthesis possibilities is to examine practical examples and see whether an innovative solution can be found 'beyond the trade-off line'. Therefore, at the end of each debate, a short case will be introduced describing the strategy paradox

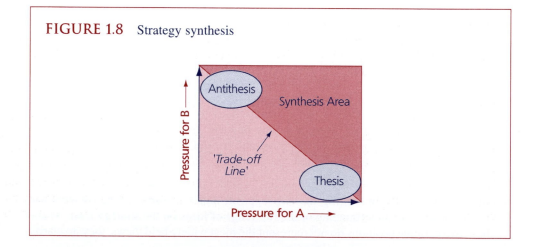

FIGURE 1.8   Strategy synthesis

facing a particular international company. Each case has been selected because the paradox debated in the chapter 'in theory' is so clearly frustrating these firms 'in practice'. When going through these cases, readers should challenge themselves to view the core strategic problem from both strategy perspectives and see if they can find a way of resolving the strategy paradox as best as possible.

Besides these 'open-ended' cases, each chapter also contains two company illustrations. These two short exhibits give examples of companies whose approach to strategy comes very close to the strategy perspectives discussed in the chapter. These illustrations should make the theoretical arguments of each side much more tangible. As with the cases, the companies that have been selected as illustrations come from a wide range of countries and industries.

In this chapter, while there is no single strategy paradox being debated, in the following pages a short case will be presented. Reading this case on Disney should not only be stimulating and fun, but should make clear that in reality strategists usually face all ten strategy paradoxes simultaneously – not what you would normally call a 'Mickey Mouse problem'.

EXHIBIT 1.1 SHORT CASE

DISNEY: ANY MAGIC LEFT IN THE MOUSE HOUSE?

It is little known that the world's most famous mouse, who goes by such names as Topolino in Italy, Musse Pigg in Sweden and Mi Lao Shu in China, actually used to be a bunny. The main character in Walt Disney's first cartoon was a creature named Oswald the Lucky Rabbit, but after Disney was cheated out of his copyrights, he modified the ears and renamed him Mickey Mouse. What is more widely known is that Walt, and his brother Roy, subsequently captured the attention of audiences around the world with Mickey as *Steamboat Willie* (1928), in the first cartoon with synchronized sound. After some modest successes with such new characters as Goofy and Donald Duck, the business of Disney Brothers Studios really started to accelerate when they moved into full-length animated films, releasing blockbusters such as *Snow White and the Seven Dwarfs* (1937), *Pinocchio* (1940) and *Bambi* (1942). Soon Disney discovered the lucrative merchandising business, licensing the use of Disney characters for such things as clothing, pencils and soda-cans. On the basis of this success, Disney branched out into TV programs, film music and live-action movie productions. In 1955, Walt's dream of creating a 'Magical Kingdom' was realized when Disneyland was opened in Anaheim, California. After Walt's death in 1966, Roy carried on to build Disney World in Orlando, Florida, which was completed just before he passed away in 1971.

While the empire the brothers left behind carried on to entertain billions of children and adults the world over, the creative pipeline dried up completely. After the release of Walt's last project, *Jungle Book*, in 1967, the Disney studios spent the 1970s looking for ways to emulate the founder's magic, but without result. By 1983, only 4% of US movie-goers went to a Disney picture, and the 15-year drought of hit movies was being severely felt in the sales of Disney merchandise and licensing income. In the same year, the Disney Channel was launched in the United States, but did not get off to a flying start. Making things worse, the hordes that initially swamped the theme parks were getting bored with Disney's dingy image and visitor numbers began to shrink, while at the same time Disney was incurring heavy costs to finish the Epcot Center at Disney World. To stem the tide, a new management team was hired in 1984, consisting of a brash young executive from Paramount Studios, Michael Eisner, who became CEO, and a level-headed operational man from Warner Brothers, Frank Wells, who became COO.

At Paramount, Eisner had produced hit movies such as *Raiders of the Lost Ark* and *Grease*, as well as the successful television shows *Happy Days* and *Cheers*. He was known as passionate, creative and hands-on, with a fanatical attention to detail, to the extent of getting involved in reading scripts and selecting costumes. Wells, on the other hand, was known for his operational planning and people skills. Together they quickly set out to rejuvenate Disney, beginning with the business they knew best – movies. In the live-action movie business, they redirected Disney towards lower budget films, using promising scripts from less-established writers and actors who seemed at the end of their careers. Through a new subsidiary, Touchstone Pictures, Disney also entered the attractive market for films for the teen and young adult audience. With hits such as *Good Morning Vietnam* and *Down and Out in Beverly Hills,* Disney reached a 19% US box office share by 1988, causing Eisner to comment that 'nearly overnight, Disney went from nerdy outcast to leader of the popular crowd'. Later Disney was responsible for successes such as *Pretty Woman* (1990) and *Pulp Fiction* (1994) – the latter made by Miramax, an avant-garde movie studio Disney had acquired a year before.

The animation part of the business was also revitalized, with major investments made in new animation technology and new people – in particular a new creative producer, Jeffrey Katzenberg. Eventually, this resulted in a series of very successful films: *The Little Mermaid* (1989), *Beauty and the Beast* (1991), *Aladdin* (1992) and *The Lion King* (1994). To keep the new movies in the limelight, alliances were formed with McDonald's and Coca-Cola involving promotional tie-ins. And to get spin-off merchandise flowing in greater volumes, Eisner moved beyond mere licensing, building up a global chain of Disney stores. Helped by a little luck, Disney also profited from the new home video trend that was sweeping the world. Not only could Disney release its new movies twice – first in the theatres and then on video – it could also re-release a steady stream of classic pictures for home audiences.

In the theme park business, the major innovation spearheaded by Eisner and Wells was to make Disneyland and Disney World more appealing to adults. In 1989 the Disney-MGM Studios theme park was opened near Disney World, as well as the Pleasure Island nightlife complex. Based on the success of Tokyo Disneyland, which was opened in 1983, Disney also built a theme park outside of Paris, called Euro Disney, which opened in 1992. It turned out that while the Japanese visitors appreciated an almost replica of Disney World in Tokyo, European tastes were very different, requiring a long period of adaptation to the local market conditions and causing Euro Disney (later renamed Disneyland Paris) to suffer significant losses over a number of years.

Then, in 1994, Frank Wells was killed in a helicopter crash, Eisner had bypass heart surgery, and a period of boardroom infighting commenced, leading to the high profile departure of the studio head, Katzenberg (who later received US$250 million in compensation and teamed up with Steven Spielberg and David Geffen to found a new independent film company, DreamWorks SKG). Other executives also left, pointing to Eisner's overbearing presence. 'People get tired of being second guessed and beaten down,' a former studio executive remarked. 'When people came out of Michael's office wounded, Frank was the emergency room,' another Disney insider reported to *Fortune*, but with Wells gone, no one was there to repair damaged egos and sooth hurt feelings. However, Eisner viewed the situation differently: 'I've never had a problem with anybody who was truly talented ... This autonomy crap? That means you're off working alone. If you want autonomy, be a poet.'

During this period, Eisner made his biggest move yet, acquiring Capital Cities/ABC for US$19.6 billion. This deal included the ABC Television Network (distributing to 224 affiliated stations), the ABC Radio Networks (with 3400 radio outlets) and an 80% share of ESPN, a sport-oriented network, which includes various cable channels and radio stations. Ironically, Eisner had previously worked for ABC as daytime programmer, and felt that he had a lot to add to ABC: 'I would love, every morning, to go over and spend two hours at ABC. Even though my children tell me that I am in the wrong generation and I don't get it anymore, I am totally convinced that I could sit with our guys and make ABC No. 1 in two years.' To help him manage during this period, Eisner hired Michael Ovitz as second man, but this ended in divorce within 16 months, and a US$100 million severance package.

Soon after this episode, Disney's artistic and financial performance began to deteriorate. Between 1984 and 1997, operating income grew more than 20% per year, reaching US$4.5 billion, but between 1998 and 2003 the company got nowhere near this level. Eisner's major headache was ABC, which was the top-rated network at the time of the acquisition, but quickly fell to third place in the ratings. The network had a short-lived success in 2000 with one blockbuster show, *Who Wants to be a Millionaire?*, but once this fad had ebbed away, ABC sunk back into last place. In an attempt to turn around fortunes, Eisner fired the head of ABC Entertainment, Stu Bloomberg, in 2002, and installed Susan Lyne. She immediately indicated that she was reconsidering Disney's vertical integration strategy, whereby Disney subsidiary, Touchstone Television, provides the majority of programs for ABC. This strategy is beneficial when shows turn out to be hits, because Touchstone can then supply reruns and related materials to other parts of the Disney family. The downside of wanting to do everything itself is that Disney runs all risks alone and that ABC cannot tap into multiple talent pools.

At the same time, Disney's animation track record has been wobbly since Katzenberg left – movies such as *Pocahontas* (1995) and *Tarzan* (1999) did not do too badly, although soaring costs made them only mildly profitable. Other features, such as *Atlantis* (2001) and *Treasure Island* (2002) were box office fiascos. Disney's real animation successes have come from the organization's deal with Pixar, an independent studio specializing in computer-generated animations, run by former Apple CEO, Steve Jobs. Such co-productions as *Toy Story* (1995), *Monsters Inc.* (2000) and *Lilo and Stitch* (2002) have been hits in the cinemas and on DVD. Yet, this makes Disney all the more dependent on Pixar, raising the question whether Disney should develop these capabilities in-house instead of sticking to current animation competences.

In the area of live-action films, Disney's approach changed dramatically after Joe Roth took over in 1994. Instead of Katzenberg's policy of setting a 'financial box' within which the creatives had to operate, Roth moved to bigger budgets, big names and big special effects – and just a few too many big disasters. Illustrative were *Pearl Harbor* (2001) and *Gangs of New York* (2002), both with immense production budgets, yet unable to live up to their promise. The result has been a high market share for Disney films, but profitability hovering just above zero, so Roth too has exited the company. Add to this that Disney seriously over-built the number of Disney Stores, necessitating the closing of about a quarter of the 550 US outlets, while in the mature theme park business, tight consumer spending and a general fear of traveling have plagued operations. The head of this division, Paul Pressler, also left the company in 2002, further thinning the ranks of long-term senior managers.

All these developments have led analysts to raise some big question marks. For instance, in *The Economist* the question was asked whether Eisner had upset the balance between the suits and the ponytails – the logic-oriented managers and the creative types – placing too much emphasis on rationalistic management systems. Moreover, it was wondered whether Eisner had gone overboard in his micro-management of all aspects of the business, trying to influence everything from the program schedule of ABC to the furniture at the new Animal Kingdom Lodge, not allowing for enough individual autonomy. Another question was whether Eisner had just basically run out of good ideas to challenge the rules of the game in the entertainment industry and had become too settled. Could it also be that striving for synergy within Disney had led to insufficient responsiveness to the specific characteristics of each separate business?

Eisner's response to these questions has been characteristically upbeat: 'Maybe I'm crazy, but I don't consider this a crisis,' Eisner told *Fortune*. 'We're being buried a little prematurely here . . . I spend my life being Odysseus. I tie myself to the mast, and don't listen to the Sirens. The Sirens in my business are agents, investment bankers, the media, people saying that your testosterone level is gone because you haven't made an acquisition in the last ten minutes.' He points out that major turnaround initiatives have been introduced, chopping thousands of jobs. And Disney is well positioned to gain from the accelerating sales of DVDs and the commercial downloading of songs, games and characters into a wide variety of new gadgets, such as personal digital assistants and cell phones. In Anaheim, Downtown Disney and Disney's California Adventure were opened in 2001, while overseas the new Tokyo Disney Sea Park was opened in 2000, Disneyland Paris is being expanded and a new park is set to open in Hong Kong in 2006.

As Eisner says: 'We've solidified our company . . . when the economy turns, and when the fear of flying goes away, when we get a couple of hits on ABC – and because of how lean we've made the company – I believe it becomes a gusher. I want to be here to take advantage of all the work we've done and all the crap we took . . . we'll be the premier growth company in the business.' But then again, the clock might strike 12 and the magic might be over.

Sources: Disney *Annual Report 2002*; *The Economist*, September 28 2002 and January 16 2003; *Fortune*, December 23 2001; *Harvard Business Review*, January–February 2000; *Business Week*, June 24 2002; http://disney.go.com.

FURTHER READING

Woe be to him who reads but one book.
George Herbert (1593–1632); English poet

At the end of each chapter, a number of follow-up books and articles will be suggested for readers who wish to delve deeper into a particular topic and avoid the dangers of reading only one book. These lists of recommended readings will be selective, instead of exhaustive, to assist readers in finding a few key works that can provide a stimulating introduction to the subject and a good starting point for further exploration.

As a follow up to this chapter, readers interested in tensions and paradoxes have a number of stimulating sources to examine. A recent article by Marianne Lewis in the *Academy of Management Review*, entitled 'Exploring Paradox: Toward a More Comprehensive Guide', is very good, as is the classic on this topic, 'Using Paradox to Build Management and Organization Theories', by Marshall Scott Poole and Andrew Van de Ven. Also stimulating is an older book by Robert Quinn, *Beyond Rational Management*. A very valuable hands-on approach to dealing with paradoxes is provided by Barry Johnson in his book *Polarity Management*. Another highly recommended work is *Building Cross-Cultural Competence: How to Create Wealth from Conflicting Values* by Charles Hampden-Turner and Fons Trompenaars, which looks at cross-cultural management paradoxes.

An older book by Charles Hampden-Turner, *Charting the Corporate Mind: From Dilemma to Strategy*, is also thought-provoking in its account of how dialectics can be employed as a problem-solving approach. In the same way, Richard Mason and Ian Mitroff's book *Challenging Strategic Planning Assumptions* makes for very good reading.

STRATEGY PROCESS

Follow the course opposite to custom and you will almost always do well.

Jean Jacques Rousseau (1712–1778); French philosopher

Given the variety of perspectives on strategy, finding a precise definition with which all people agree is probably impossible. Therefore, in this book we will proceed with a very broad conception of strategy as 'a course of action for achieving an organization's purpose'. In this section, it is the intention to gain a better insight into how such a course of action comes about – how is, and should, strategy be made, analyzed, dreamt-up, formulated, implemented, changed and controlled; who is involved; and when do the necessary activities take place?

The process by which strategy comes about can be dissected in many ways. Here, the strategy process has been unraveled into three partially overlapping issues, each of which requires managers to make choices, and each of which is (therefore) controversial (see Figure II.1):

- **Strategic thinking**. This issue focuses on the *strategist*. The question is how managers should organize their thinking to achieve a successful strategic reasoning process.

- **Strategy formation**. This issue focuses on the *strategy*. The question is how managers should organize their strategizing activities to achieve a successful strategy formation process.

- **Strategic change**. This issue focuses on the *organization*. The question is how managers should organize changes to achieve a successful strategic renewal process.

The most important term to remember throughout this section is *process*. In each chapter the discussion is not about one-off activities or outcomes – a strategic thought, a formed strategy or a strategic change – but about the ongoing processes of thinking, forming and changing. These processes need to be organized, structured, stimulated, nurtured and/or facilitated over a prolonged period of time and the question concerns which approach will be successful in the long term, as well as in the short term.

FIGURE II.1   The strategy process chapters

STRATEGIC THINKING

Rational, adj. Devoid of all delusions save those of observation, experience and reflection.

The Devil's Dictionary, Ambrose Bierce (1842–1914); American columnist

INTRODUCTION

What goes on in the mind of the strategist? A fascinating question that is easy to ask, but difficult to answer. Yet, it is a question that is important in two ways – generally and personally. Generally, knowing what goes on in the minds of managers during strategy processes is essential for understanding their choices and behaviors. Opening up the 'black box' of the strategist's mind to see how decisions are made can help to anticipate or influence this thinking. Grasping how managers shape their strategic views and select their preferred actions can be used to develop more effective strategy processes. It is due to this importance of strategic thinking that a separate chapter in this book is devoted to the subject. Yet, for each reader personally, the topic of strategic thinking is also of key importance, as it automatically raises the questions 'what is going on in *my* mind?' and 'how strategic is *my* thinking?'. Exploring the subject of strategic thinking triggers each person to explore their own thought processes and critically reflect on their own strategy preferences. Ideally, wondering about the mind of the strategist should inspire readers to constantly question their own assumptions, thoughts, beliefs and ideas, and to sharpen their strategic thinking, as they move through the following chapters. For this reason, it seems only appropriate to start the book with this topic.

So, what goes on in the mind of the strategist? Well, a lot, but if reduced to its bare essentials it can be said that strategists are engaged in the process of dealing with *strategic problems*. Not problems in the negative sense of troublesome conditions that need to be avoided, but in the neutral sense of challenging situations that need to be resolved – a strategic problem is a set of circumstances requiring a reconsideration of the current course of action, either to profit from observed opportunities or to respond to perceived threats. To deal with these strategic problems, managers must not simply think, but they must go through a *strategic reasoning process*, searching for ways to define and resolve the challenges at hand. Managers must structure their individual thinking steps into a reasoning process that will result in effective strategic behavior. The question is how managers actually go about defining strategic problems (how do they identify and diagnose what is going on?) and how they go about solving strategic problems (how do they generate, evaluate and decide on potential answers?). It is this issue of strategic reasoning, as a string of strategic thinking activities directed at defining and resolving strategic problems, that will be examined in further detail below.

THE ISSUE OF STRATEGIC REASONING

The mind of the strategist is a complex and fascinating apparatus that never fails to astonish and dazzle on the one hand, and disappoint and frustrate on the other. We are often surprised by the power of the human mind, but equally often stunned by its limitations. For the discussion here it is not necessary to unravel all of the mysteries surrounding the functioning of the human brain, but a short overview of the capabilities and limitations of the human mind will help us to understand the issue of strategic reasoning.

The human ability to know is referred to as 'cognition'. As strategists want to know about the strategic problems facing their organizations, they need to engage in *cognitive activities*. These cognitive activities (or strategic thinking activities) need to be structured into a strategic reasoning process. Hence, the first step towards a better understanding of what goes on in the mind of the strategist is to examine the various cognitive activities making up a strategic reasoning process. The four main cognitive activities will be discussed in the first sub-section below. To be able to perform these cognitive activities, people need to command certain mental faculties. While very sophisticated, the human brain is still physically strictly limited in what it can do. These limitations to people's *cognitive abilities* will be reviewed in the second sub-section. To deal with its inherent physical shortcomings, the human brain copes by building simplified models of the world, referred to as *cognitive maps*. The functioning of cognitive maps will be addressed in the third sub-section.

In Figure 2.1 the relationship between these three topics is visualized, using the metaphor of a computer. The cognitive abilities of our brains can be seen as a hardware level question – what are the physical limits on our mental faculties? The cognitive maps used by our brains can be seen as an operating system level question – what type of platform/language is 'running' on our brain? The cognitive activities carried out by our brains can be seen as an application level question – what type of program is strategic reasoning?

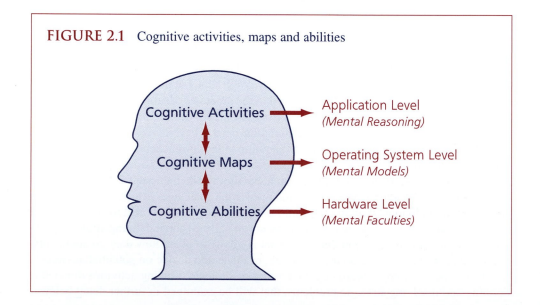

FIGURE 2.1 Cognitive activities, maps and abilities

Cognitive activities

The strategic reasoning process consists of a number of strategic thinking elements or cognitive activities – mental tasks intended to increase the strategist's knowing. A general distinction can be made between cognitive activities directed towards *defining* a strategic problem, and cognitive activities directed at *solving* a strategic problem. Each of these two major categories can be further split in two (see Figure 2.2), leading to the following general elements of a strategic reasoning process:

- Identifying. Before strategists can move to benefit from opportunities or to counter threats, they must be aware of these challenges and acknowledge their importance. This part of the reasoning process is variably referred to as identifying, recognizing or sense-making.

- Diagnosing. To come to grips with a problem, strategists must try to understand the structure of the problem and its underlying causes. This part of the reasoning process is variably referred to as diagnosing, analyzing or reflecting.

- Conceiving. To deal with a strategic problem, strategists must come up with a potential solution. If more than one solution is available, strategists must select the most promising one. This part of the reasoning process is variably referred to as conceiving, formulating or imagining.

- Realizing. A strategic problem is only really solved once concrete actions are undertaken that achieve results. Strategists must therefore carry out problem-solving activities and evaluate whether the consequences are positive. This part of the reasoning process is variably referred to as realizing, implementing or acting.

A structured approach to these four cognitive activities is to carry them out in the above order, starting with problem identification and then moving through diagnosis to conceiving solutions and finally realizing them (i.e. clockwise movement in Figure 2.2). In this

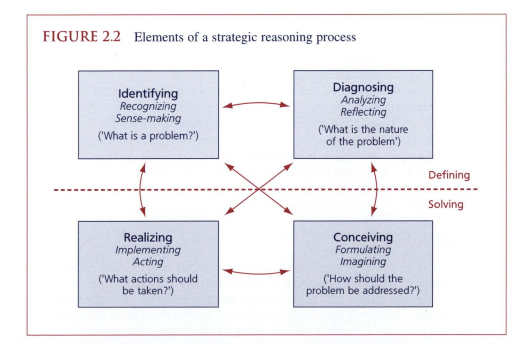

FIGURE 2.2   Elements of a strategic reasoning process

approach the first step, identifying strategic problems, would require extensive external and internal scanning, thorough sifting of incoming information and the selection of priority issues. In the next reasoning step, the strategic problems recognized would have to be diagnosed by gathering more detailed data, and by further analyzing and refining this information. Once the problem had been properly defined, a strategy could be formulated by evaluating the available options and deciding which solution would be best. In the final phase, realization, the strategist would need to ensure execution of the proposed solution by consciously planning and controlling implementation activities. In this case, the four elements of the strategic reasoning process could actually be labeled recognizing, analyzing, formulating and implementing.

However, strategists do not always reason in this step-by-step fashion. Their thinking is often less orderly, with identifying, diagnosing, conceiving and realizing intermingled with one another – even going on at the same time. Nor are the cognitive activities as straightforward as portrayed above. The identification of strategic problems is often not about objective observation, but rather subjective interpretation – by looking at the world from a particular angle, strategists see and value particular strengths, weaknesses, opportunities and threats. Such sense-making activities (Weick, 1979; Gioia and Chittipeddi, 1991) lead to attention being paid to some issues, while others do not make the strategic agenda (Dutton, 1988; Ocasio, 1997). Likewise, diagnosing strategic problems is not always a structured analytical process. Gaining a deeper understanding of strategic problems may involve explicit analysis, but also intuitive reflecting – by employing unconscious reasoning rules strategists often quickly form a general picture of how key aspects of a strategic problem are interrelated.

Conceiving strategic solutions can be equally 'messy' and subjective. Often, strategic options are not chosen from an available repertoire of potential solutions, but they are invented. In other words, new options are often not selected, discovered or figured out, but are envisioned – strategists imagine how things could be done. Such idea generation can involve reasoning by analogy or metaphor, brainstorming or pure fantasizing. New potential solutions may come to the strategist in a flash (eureka!) or emerge over time, but usually require a period of incubation beforehand and a period of nurturing afterwards. Furthermore, strategists often find it impossible to objectively prove which new idea would be the best solution. Therefore, the process of deciding on the solution to be pursued may involve more judgment than calculation.

Finally, it must be emphasized that action does not always come last, in the form of solution implementation. Often, strategists do not wait for a problem to be precisely defined and for a solution to be fully conceived before starting to act. On the contrary, strategists often feel they must first act – they must have experience with a problem and know that the current strategy will not be able to overcome the problem. To find a suitable solution it is often also necessary to test certain assumptions in practice and to experiment. Hence, acting regularly precedes, or goes hand in hand with, all other cognitive activities.

Cognitive abilities

People are not omniscient – they do not have infinite knowledge. To some extent this is due to the nature of reality – many future events are inherently unpredictable, due to factors that are uncertain or unknowable. Yet, humans are also burdened with rather imperfect cognitive abilities. The human brain is severely limited in what it can know (Simon, 1957). The limitation to human's cognitive abilities is largely due to three factors:

■ Limited information sensing ability. Humanity's first 'handicap' is a limited informa-tion-sensing ability. While the senses – touch, smell, taste, hearing and seeing – are bombarded with stimuli, much of reality remains unobservable to humans. This is par-tially due to the physical inability to be everywhere, all the time, noticing everything. However, people's limited ability to register the structure of reality is also due to the inherent superficiality of the senses and the complexity of reality. The human senses cannot directly identify the way the world works and the underlying causal relation-ships. Only the physical consequences of the complex interactions between elements in reality can be picked up by a person's sensory system. Therefore, the mental represen-tations of the world that individuals build up in their minds are necessarily based on circumstantial evidence.

■ Limited information processing capacity. Unfortunately, a second drawback is that humans do not have unlimited data processing abilities. Thinking through problems with many variables, complex relationships and huge amounts of data is a task that peo-ple find extremely difficult to perform. Approaching every activity in this way would totally overload a person's brain. For this reason, humans hardly ever think through a problem with full use of all available data, but necessarily make extensive use of men-tal shortcuts, referred to as 'cognitive heuristics' (Janis, 1989). Cognitive heuristics are mental 'rules of thumb' that simplify a problem, so that it can be more quickly under-stood and solved. Cognitive heuristics focus a person's attention on a number of key variables that are believed to be most important, and present a number of simple deci-sion rules to rapidly resolve an issue. The set of possible solutions to be considered is also limited in advance.

■ Limited information storage capacity. Another human cognitive shortcoming is poor memory. People have only a limited capacity for storing information. Remembering all individuals, events, dates, places and circumstances is beyond the ability of the human brain. Therefore, people must store information very selectively and organize this infor-mation in a way that it can be easily retrieved when necessary. Here again, cognitive heuristics are at play – 'rules of thumb' make the memorization process manageable in the face of severe capacity limitations. Such heuristics help to simplify complex clus-ters of data into manageable chunks and help to categorize, label and store this information so that it can be recalled at a later time.

To deal with these severe physical limitations, the brain has come up with more than only simple cognitive heuristics. The human mind has come to work with more holistic cognitive maps.

Cognitive maps

Knowledge that people have is stored in their minds in the form of 'cognitive maps' (e.g. McCaskey, 1982; Weick and Bourgnon, 1986), also referred to as 'cognitive schemata' (e.g. Anderson, 1983; Schwenk, 1988), 'mental models' (e.g. Day and Lord, 1992; Knight et al., 1999), 'knowledge structures' (e.g. Lyles and Schwenk, 1992; Walsh, 1995) and 'construed reality' (Finkelstein and Hambrick, 1996). These cognitive maps are represen-tations in a person's mind of how the world works. A cognitive map of a certain situation reflects a person's beliefs about the importance of the issues and about the cause and effect relationships between them.

Cognitive maps are formed over time through education, experience and interaction with others. Based on the inputs of their senses, people will infer causal relationships between phenomena, making guesses about unobservable factors and resolving inconsistencies between the bits of information received. In turn, people's cognitive maps steer their senses; while cognitive maps are built on past sensory data, they will consequently direct which new information will be sought and perceived. A person's cognitive map will focus attention on particular phenomena, while blocking out other data as noise, and will quickly make clear how a situation should be perceived. In this way, a cognitive map provides an interpretive filter or perceptual screen, aiding the senses in selecting and understanding external stimuli (Starbuck and Milliken, 1988). Furthermore, cognitive maps help to direct behavior, by providing an existing repertoire of 'problem-solving' responses (also referred to as 'scripts' or 'recipes') from which an appropriate action can be derived.

In building their cognitive maps, people acquire a lot of their knowledge by means of direct experience. They learn to communicate, play an instrument, drive a vehicle and solve problems by doing. This knowledge is added to people's cognitive maps without being explicitly articulated. In other words, knowledge gained through experiential learning is usually not codified into formal rules, principles, models or theories, but remains tacit (Polanyi, 1966; Nonaka, 1991). People formulate implicit models and draw conclusions, but do so largely unconsciously. In this way, cognitive maps evolve without people themselves being entirely aware of their own cognitive map. Hence, when people use their 'intuition', this is not a mystical or irrational way of reasoning, but thinking guided by the tacit knowledge they have acquired in the past (Behling and Eckel, 1991). Intuitive thinking is the opposite of analytical thinking – informal and holistic (Von Winterfeldt and Edwards, 1986). Informal means that the thinking is largely unconscious and based on assumptions, variables and causal relationships not explicitly identifiable by those doing the thinking. Holistic means that the thinker does not aim at unraveling phenomena into their constituent parts, but rather maintains a more integrated view of reality.

Yet, people's cognitive maps are not developed independently, but rather in interaction with one another. People tend to construct a shared understanding of the world by interacting with each other within a group over an extended period of time. By exchanging interpretations of what they see, it is said that they *enact* a shared reality (Daft and Weick, 1984; Smircich and Stubbart, 1985). The resulting shared cognitive map is variably referred to as the group's dominant logic (Prahalad and Bettis, 1986), common paradigm (Kuhn, 1970) or belief system (Noorderhaven, 1995). Such a shared worldview can exist within small social units, such as a firm or a family, but also within larger units, such as an industry or a nation.

As individuals can belong to different groups, they can be influenced by different belief systems simultaneously. As members of a national culture, their cognitive maps will to a certain extent be influenced by the beliefs dominant within the nation. As employees of a company, their cognitive maps will be affected by the beliefs common within the firm and the industry as well. In the same manner, people can be impacted by the professional community to which they belong, their religious affiliation, their political party and any other groups in which they interact with others (Hambrick et al., 1993; Sutcliffe and Huber, 1998). Due to the mutually inclusive nature of group membership, an individual's cognitive map will be a complex combination of elements taken from different group-level dominant logics. While these paradigms on which an individual draws can be complementary, or overlapping yet consistent, it is quite possible that inconsistencies arise (Schein, 1985; Trice and Beyer, 1993).

As shared beliefs develop over time through interaction and are passed on through socialization, they remain largely tacit. The shared cognitive map of a group is literally 'common sense' – sense shared by a common group of people. However, where members of different groups come into conflict with one another, or where an individual needs to deal with the inconsistencies brought on by multiple group memberships, beliefs can become more artic- ulated. Different behaviors, based on different cognitive maps, will often lead to the identi- fication and codification of beliefs, either to protect them or to engage in debate with people with other views. As paradigms become more articulated, they also become more mobile, making it possible to transfer ideas to people without direct interaction.

The downside of cognitive maps is that they exhibit a high level of rigidity. People are generally not inclined to change their minds. Once people's cognitive maps have formed, and they have a grip on reality, they become resistant to signals that challenge their con- ceptions. As McCaskey (1982) remarks, the mind 'strives mightily to bring order, sim- plicity, consistency, and stability to the world it encounters', and is therefore reluctant to welcome the ambiguity presented by contradicting data. People tend to significantly over- estimate the value of information that confirms their cognitive map, underestimate dis- confirming information, and they actively seek out evidence that supports their current beliefs (Schwenk, 1984). Once an interpretive filter is in place, seeing is not believing, but believing is seeing. People might have the impression that they are constantly learning, but they are largely learning within the bounds of a paradigm. When an individual's map is supported by similar beliefs shared within a firm, industry or country, the ability to ques- tion key aspects of a paradigm will usually be rather limited. Not only does the individual have no 'intellectual sounding board' for teasing out new ideas, but deviation from the dominant logic might also have adverse social and political ramifications within the group (e.g. DiMaggio and Powell, 1983; Aldrich and Fiol, 1994). Not for nothing the old proverb is: 'old ideas never change; they eventually die out' (Kuhn, 1970).

For strategists, cognitive rigidity is particularly worrying. Strategists should be at the forefront of market developments, identifying changing circumstances and new opportu- nities before their competitors. Strategic thinking is by its very nature focused on under- standing and shaping the future, and therefore strategists must have the ability to challenge current beliefs and change their own mind. They must be able to come up with innovative, but feasible, new strategies that will fit with the unfolding reality. This places extraordi- nary cognitive demands on strategists – they must be able to overcome the limitations of their own cognitive maps and develop a new understanding.

THE PARADOX OF LOGIC AND CREATIVITY

Information's pretty thin stuff, unless mixed with experience.
Clarence Day (1874–1935); American essayist

Many management theorists have noted that the opposites of intuition and analysis create a tension for managers (e.g. Langley, 1989, 1995; Pondy, 1983). While some researchers make a strong case for more formal analysis (e.g. Isenberg, 1984; Schoemaker and Russo, 1993), there is a broad understanding that managers need to employ both intuitive and ana- lytical thinking, even if they are each other's opposites.

The extensive use of intuitive judgment among managers is understood by most as nec- essary and beneficial. A manager's intuition is built up through years of experience and contains a vast quantity of tacit knowledge that can only superficially be tapped by formal analysis. Intuition can also give a 'richer' assessment, by blending in all types of qualita- tive information. Moreover, intuitive thinking is often better at capturing the big picture than analytical thinking. And very practically, intuition is needed to cut corners: without the widespread use of cognitive heuristics, management would grind to a halt, overloaded by the sheer complexity of the analyses that would need to be carried out. Such a situation of rationality gone rampant is referred to as 'paralysis by analysis' (Lenz and Lyles, 1985; Langley, 1995).

However, it is equally clear to most that human intuition is often unreliable. Cognitive heuristics are 'quick and dirty' – efficient, but imprecise. They help people to intuitively jump to conclusions without thorough analysis, which increases speed, but also increases the risk of drawing faulty conclusions. The main danger of cognitive heuristics is that they are inherently biased, as they focus attention on only a few variables and interpret them in a particular way, even when this is not appropriate (e.g. Tversky and Kahneman, 1986; Bazerman, 1990). For this reason, many academics urge practitioners to bolster their intuitive judgments with more explicit rational analysis. Especially in the case of strategic decisions, more time and energy should be made available to avoid falling prey to common cognitive biases. Otherwise the ultimate result might be a 'corporate gravestone' with the epitaph *'extinct by instinct'* (Langley, 1995).

While the tension between intuition and analysis is important, it does not go to the heart of the strategic reasoning issue. For strategists the more fundamental question is how they can escape getting stuck with an outdated cognitive map. How can they avoid the danger of building up a flawed picture of their industry, their markets and themselves? As strategists must be acutely aware of the unfolding opportunities and threats in the environment, and the evolving strengths and weaknesses of the organization, they must be able to constantly re-evaluate their views.

On the one hand, this requires rigorous *logical thinking*. All the key assumptions on which a strategist's cognitive map have been based need to be reviewed and tested against developments in the firm and its environment. On the other hand, strategists must have the ability to engage in *creative thinking*. To be able to see new opportunities and strengths, strategists must be able to think beyond current models of reality. Both demands on strategists will now be reviewed in more detail.

The demand for logical thinking

It is clear that if managers only base their strategic decisions on heavily biased cognitive maps, unconsciously built up through past experience, this will lead to very poor results. Managers need to have the ability to critically reflect on the assumptions they hold, to check whether they are based on actual fact, or on organizational folklore and industry recipes. They must be capable of making their tacit beliefs more explicit, so that the validity of these mental models can be evaluated and they can be further refined. In short, to be successful strategists, managers need to escape the confines of their own cognitive maps – and those of other stakeholders engaged in the strategy process.

Assessing the validity of a cognitive map requires strong logical thinking. Logical thinking is a disciplined and rigorous way of thinking, on the basis of formal rules. When employing logic, each step in an argumentation follows from the previous, based on valid principles. In other words, a logical thinker will only draw a conclusion if it is arrived at by a sound succession of arguments.

Logical thinking can be applied to all four cognitive activities outlined in Figure 2.2. When identifying and diagnosing a strategic problem, logical thinking can help to avoid the emotional interpretations that so often color people's understanding of environmental opportunities and threats, and organizational strengths and weaknesses. Logical thinking can also expose a person's bullish or bearish bias and can be instrumental in discarding old 'theories' of how the firm and its environment function. By analyzing the empirical facts and rigorously testing the hypotheses on which the firm's shared cognitive map has been built, the strategist can prevent building a false model of reality.

When conceiving and realizing a strategic solution, logical thinking can help to avoid the danger of following outdated habits and routines. Routines are programed courses of action that originally were deliberately conceived, but have been subsequently internalized and are used automatically (March and Simon, 1993). Habits are programed courses of action that have developed unconsciously. By explicitly formulating strategic options and subjecting them to formal evaluation, the strategist can break away from such established behavior and develop new approaches to gaining and retaining competitive advantage. Moreover, logical thinking can aid in making a distinction between fantasy and feasibility. Sound logic can serve to weed out strategic options that are flights of fancy, by analyzing the factors that will determine success or failure.

The demand for creative thinking

Creative thinking is the opposite of logical thinking. As described above, when employing logic, a thinker bases each step in a train of thought on the previous steps, following formal rules of valid thinking. De Bono (1970) refers to this pattern of thought as 'vertical thinking'. However, when creativity is used, the thinker does not take a valid step, but takes a leap of imagination, without being able to support the validity of the mental jump. In creative thinking a person abandons the rules governing sound argumentation and draws a conclusion that is not justified based on the previous arguments. In this way the thinker generates a new understanding, but without objective proof that the new idea 'makes sense'. De Bono refers to this pattern of thought as 'lateral thinking'.

In essence, creative thinking takes liberty in following thinking rules. One idea might lead to another idea, without formal logic interfering. One variable might be linked by the thinker to another, without a sound explanation of why a correlation is assumed. Creativity in effect creates a new understanding, with little attention paid to supporting evidence. Often logic is used afterwards to justify an idea that was actually generated by creative means.

When identifying and diagnosing strategic problems, creative thinking is often needed. Old cognitive maps usually have a very compelling logic, locking people into old patterns of thinking. These old cognitive maps are usually tried and tested, and have become immune to external signals that they are no longer fitting. Thinking within the boundaries of a shared cognitive map is generally accepted and people tend to proceed rationally – that is, they try to avoid logical inconsistencies. Challenging a cognitive map's fundamental assumptions, however, cannot be done in a way that is logically consistent with the map itself. Contradicting a paradigm is illogical from the point of view of those who accept the paradigm. Therefore, changing a rigid and subjective cognitive map, rooted in a shared paradigm, requires strategists to imagine new ways of understanding the world that do not logically follow from past beliefs. Strategic thinkers need to be willing and able to break with orthodoxy and make leaps of imagination, that are not logically justified, but needed to generate novel ways of looking at old problems.

The same is true when conceiving and realizing strategic solutions. New strategies often do not follow from the facts, but need to be invented – they are not analyzed into existence, but need to be generated, if they are to be innovative and distinctive. Creative solutions do not follow from the dominant logic, but are the unexpected answers that emerge when the grip of the dominant logic is loosened.

Unfortunately, the conclusion must be that logical thinking and creative thinking are not only opposites, but that they are partially incompatible as well. They are based on methods that are at odds with one another. Strategizing managers would probably love to be fully logical and fully creative at the same time, but both require such a different mindset and range of cognitive skills that in practice it is very difficult to achieve both simultaneously. The demand for logic and creativity is not only contradictory for each individual, but also within teams, departments and the overall firm: while strategizing groups would like to be fully capable of logical and creative thinking, finding ways of incorporating both forms of strategic thinking into a workable strategy process is extremely challenging. Commonly, conflicting styles lead to conflicting people, and therefore a blend between the two is not that simple. It is for this reason that we speak of the 'paradox of logic and creativity' – the two demands on managers seem to be contradictory, yet both are required at the same time.

EXHIBIT 2.1 SHORT CASE

SMIT: SALVAGING STRATEGY?

When in 2001 Russian president Vladimir Putin promised his nation to raise the sunken nuclear submarine *Kursk* and to give its crew an honorable land burial, few believed that it would be possible to salvage such a dangerous wreck, at such a depth, in the cold and stormy arctic waters before the onset of winter. The company that was able to pull off this amazing feat was Smit, the world's leading provider of maritime services, working together with the heavy transport company, Mammoet. Besides its headline-grabbing salvage business, Smit is involved in a broad range of 'ship-based' services, such as harbor towage (getting an ocean-faring boat into and out of dock), heavy lift and transport (getting big objects like oil rigs and bridge parts to the right destination) and offshore terminal support (operational services and getting supplies to offshore oil platforms). With its base in the world's largest harbor, Rotterdam, and regional headquarters in Singapore, Cape Town and Houston, Smit operates on a worldwide basis, employing approximately 2900 people. In 2002 the company's revenues totaled €319 million, earning an operating result of €13 million.

The company, founded in 1842 by Fop Smit, has a history filled with many remarkable achievements, inspired by the company's long-time slogan 'any job, any sea'. For example, in 1896, Smit was the first company in the world to tow a ship dock overseas, from Rotterdam to Angola, even though there were no suitable ocean-going tugboats available. The company has also been involved in many complex salvage operations: for instance, it recently raised the Japanese training vessel, Ehime Maru, which had sunk in deep water near Hawaii after colliding with a US submarine. Typical for all these operations has been the company's 'can do' attitude and the improvisation skills of its crews. More than 100 years ago a senior Smit manager was famously quoted as saying 'experience or not, we'll do it and we'll go there!', and this attitude has remained central to the Smit culture ever since.

This entrepreneurial 'get up and go' has been the major factor driving the growth of Smit throughout most of the 20th century, leading the company to enter many new foreign markets and new lines of business. From 1921 to 1980, the company was run by two members of the Smit family, first Murk Lels and then Piet Kleyn van Willigen, both with a strong entrepreneurial streak, yet with little interest in doing extensive strategic analyses. Their decision to enter a new country or to offer a new service was largely dependent on two criteria: it needed to be maritime and it needed to be lucrative. In their view, a business was potentially lucrative if it promised significant sales opportunities – with little regard to the question whether a market was structurally attractive or not. This mode of thinking brought the company into many new areas. For instance, in the 1960s Smit was asked to start towing oil rigs and terminal platforms for the emerging off-shore oil industry, which triggered the company's jump into terminal provisioning services, sea-going firefighting and terminal maintenance, requiring various specialized ships to be built. In the 1970s, Smit saw growing opportunities to tow ultra-heavy objects across the ocean (e.g. icebergs from Antarctica to the Persian Gulf) and therefore had three giant tugboats built. Within the company the joke circulated that a new business was actually only interesting if new ships were necessary – growth was driven by 'new toys for the boys'.

When in 1980 the last family member of the board of directors decided to retire, it was determined that an emotionally detached outsider should take the helm and restructure the extensive portfolio of businesses that Lels and Kleyn van Willigen had built up. From 1980 to 1988, Koos Groenendijk, a former shipping company manager, worked at trimming the corporate portfolio, while from 1988 to 1998 Fred Busker, a former Royal Dutch Shell manager, attempted to achieve more focus. 'We threw sentiments overboard and took a rational look at things', said Mr Busker, leading to the closing down and selling off of many unprofitable business units. But while 'sinking leaky businesses' went relatively well, the difficulty faced by Groenendijk and Busker was that they did not have the intimate industry knowledge to find new growth opportunities. Both missed the experienced-based intuition and sense of

entrepreneurial risk-taking that their predecessors had long been able to tap. Moreover, while there were still many 'can-do' people in the organization, few had the capability to develop a good business case to justify the huge investments needed to launch a new type of service. After some failed attempts to try something new, both CEOs retreated to optimizing the existing businesses within the current rules of the game.

Yet, at the same time, other companies were nibbling at Smit's core businesses. In the Rotterdam harbor a new towing competitor emerged, without the high costs of an overengineered and overstaffed fleet. In heavy transport and lifting the company was being challenged by low cost 'Mom and Pop' outfits on the one hand, and new entrants from the shipping and construction industries on the other. All of this had an increasingly negative impact on the company's growth and profitability.

In 1997 the Smit family decided to float 100% of the company's shares on the Amsterdam Stock Exchange, after which a new CEO was installed, Nico Buis, a highly regarded former navy officer and director of the Dutch intelligence and security service. Although Buis was very well connected in the maritime sector and did an excellent job representing the company to the outside world, he too did not know how to revive the slipping business fortunes. In 2000, despite the buoyant global economy, Smit was forced to issue its first profit warning, while also being reprimanded by the stock exchange for providing the warning too late. The company was doubly punished by shareholders, who felt that the company did not have a clear strategic direction, while also not having its financial reporting systems adequately organized.

Anticipating the retirement of Buis in 2002, a search was started in 2000 to find a successor with the capability to reinvigorate the company and set a clear strategic course for the Smit fleet of companies. Within the organization many competent managers were identified, but it was felt that they excelled at operational management, not strategic leadership: most talented managers had worked hard at developing their ability to solve challenging client problems, not at building new businesses and strengthening the competitive advantage of existing ones. Within the company, improvisation skills and 'technical inventiveness' were qualities in abundance, but strategizing skills and 'business innovativeness' were insufficiently developed. For this reason, once more an outsider was sought, resulting in the hiring of Ben Vree in November 2000.

Vree was headhunted from Van Ommeren / Vopak, a large international company in the tank storage business (e.g. storing oil and chemicals in tanks in harbors). With his background in business-to-business marketing in the oil and maritime industries, Vree was seen as someone who could bring marketing and strategic thinking into the operationally minded Smit company. Vree was also a charismatic leader, with a forceful presence, yet a listening ear and a warm personality, making him the right person, it was felt, to lead the needed change process within the company.

Vree was given a year and a half, until June 2002, to get to know the business and to prepare himself for taking over as CEO. His very first task was to lead the strategy review process that Buis had started in response to the profit warning. What Vree found was a technically competent company, with an excellent reputation, strategically adrift and under competitive pressure from all sides. He also saw that the lack of central direction, coupled with entrepreneurial drive, had led foreign subsidiaries to 'do their own thing', with little regard to synergy with the rest of the company. Even more worrying was the impending brain drain – many of the key operational people storing the tacit knowledge on which Smit depended for its competitive advantage would be retiring within a few years. And at the root of all of these problems Vree found that the strategic thinking capability at Smit was woefully inadequate, which had led to the dominance of operational thinking.

Vree and Buis quickly took measures to redirect the company and improve the operating results. The sprawling portfolio of localized business units was reorganized into four global divisions: Harbor Towage, Terminals, Salvage and Transport & Heavy Lift. In these new divisions the autonomy of the foreign subsidiaries was strongly restrained, to start building consistent business strategies for Smit's international customers (e.g. shipping companies, oil firms and international ship insurers). Various non-performing businesses were sold or closed. Much emphasis was also placed on fortifying the company's current position and increasing profitability, to fend off the threat of operating losses.

But a month after taking over the helm in June 2002, Vree was forced to issue the second profit warning in the company's history. In particular, the results in the economically volatile Transport & Heavy Lift division had deteriorated quickly. For Vree it was clear that Smit could not downsize itself out of this difficult strategic position. Besides the necessary cost cutting and restructuring that he had already initiated, the company needed to find its way back to growth. New opportunities had to be identified and diagnosed, and new strategies conceived and realized. But how to get Smit to do this successfully was the question on Vree's mind. How could he improve the strategic thinking capability of his organization to achieve the necessary strategic reorientation? For Vree there was no doubt that getting his crew to set the right course was much more preferable than letting others salvage his business once it had run aground.

Sources: www.smit-international.com; company interviews.

PERSPECTIVES ON STRATEGIC THINKING

Irrationally held truths may be more harmful than reasoned errors.
T.H. Huxley (1825–1895); English biologist

While the need for both logical and creative thinking is clear, this does place strategists in a rather awkward position of needing to bring two partially contradictory forms of thinking together in one strategic reasoning process. Logical thinking helps to make the strategic reasoning process more *rational* – rigorous, comprehensive and consistent, instead of haphazard, fragmentary and ad hoc. Creative thinking, on the other hand, helps to make the strategic reasoning process more *generative* – producing more unorthodox insights, imaginative ideas and innovative solutions, instead of having a bland, conformist and conservative output. In finding a balance between these opposite forms of thinking, the main question is whether the strategic reasoning process should actually be a predominantly rational affair, or a much more generative process. Is strategizing largely a rational activity, requiring logical thinking to be the dominant modus operandi, with occasional bits of creativity needed here and there to generate new ideas? Or is strategizing largely a generative activity, requiring creative thinking to be the standard operating procedure, with occasional bits of logical analysis needed here and there to weed out unfeasible ideas?

The answer to this question should be found in the strategic management literature. Yet, upon closer inspection, the opinions outlined in both the academic and popular literature show that views vary widely among researchers and managers alike. A wide spectrum of differing perspectives can be recognized, each giving their own angle on how strategic thinking should use logic and creativity – sometimes explicitly mentioning the need for both, but more commonly making implicit assumptions about the role of logic and creativity in strategy processes.

As was outlined in Chapter 1, it is not the intention here to summarize all of the 'schools of thought' on the topic of strategic thinking. Instead, only the two most opposite points of view will be presented in this section. These two poles in the debate are not necessarily the most popular points of view and at times they might seem somewhat extreme, arguing in terms of 'black-and-white' instead of shades of gray. Yet, as the two pure 'archetypes' they do form the ultimate pair for a good debate – a clear-cut thesis and antithesis in a process of dialectical inquiry.

At the one end of the spectrum, there are those who argue that strategic reasoning should be a predominantly rational process, requiring logic to be the main form of thinking in use. This point of view is referred to as the 'rational reasoning perspective'. At the other pole, there are those who argue that the essence of strategic reasoning is the ability to break through orthodox beliefs and generate new insights and behaviors, requiring the extensive use of creativity. This point of view will be referred to as the 'generative reasoning perspective'.

The rational reasoning perspective

Strategists employing the rational reasoning perspective argue that strategic reasoning is predominantly a 'logical activity' (Andrews, 1987). To deal with strategic problems the strategist must first consciously and thoroughly analyze the problem situation. Data must be gathered on all developments external to the organization, and this data must be processed to pinpoint the opportunities and threats in the organization's environment. Furthermore, the organization itself must be appraised, to uncover its strengths and weaknesses and to establish which resources are available. Once the problem has been defined, a number of alternative strategies can be identified by matching external opportunities to internal strengths. Then, the strategic options must be extensively screened, by evaluating them on a number of criteria, such as internal consistency, external consonance, competitive advantage, organizational feasibility, potential return and risks. The best strategy can be selected by comparing the scores of all options and determining the level of risk the strategist is willing to take. The chosen strategy can subsequently be implemented.

This type of intellectual effort requires well-developed analytical skills. Strategists must be able to rigorously, consistently and objectively comb through huge amounts of data, interpreting and combining findings to arrive at a rich picture of the current problem situation. Possible solutions require critical appraisal and all possible contingencies must be logically thought through. Advocates of the rational reasoning perspective argue that such reasoning strongly resembles the problem-solving approach of chess grand masters (Simon, 1987). They also thoroughly assess their competitive position, sift through a variety of options and calculate which course of action brings the best chances of success. Therefore, the reasoning processes of chess grand masters can be used as an analogy for what goes on in the mind of the strategist.

While depicted here as a purely step-by-step process of recognition, analysis, formulation and implementation, proponents of the rational reasoning perspective note that in reality strategists often have to backtrack and redo some of these steps, as new information becomes available or chosen strategies do not work out. Strategists attempt to be as comprehensive, consistent and rigorous as possible in their analyses and calculations, but of course they cannot know everything and their conclusions are not always perfect: even with the most advanced forecasting techniques, not all developments can be foreseen; even with state of the art market research, some trends can be missed; even with cutting edge test marketing, scenario analyses, competitive simulations and net present value calculations, some selected strategies can turn out to be failures. Strategists are not all knowing, and do make mistakes – their rationality is limited by incomplete information and imperfect cognitive abilities. Yet, strategists try to be as rational as possible. Simon (1957) refers to this as 'bounded rationality' – 'people act intentionally rational, but only limitedly so'. This coincides with Ambrose Bierce's famous sarcastic definition of logic as 'the art of thinking and reasoning in strict accordance with the limitations and incapacities of the human misunderstanding'.

The (boundedly) rational strategist must sometimes improvise to make up for a lack of information, but will try to do this as logically as possible. Inferences and speculation will always be based on the facts as known. By articulating assumptions and explicitly stating the facts and arguments on which conclusions have been based, problem definitions and solutions can be debated within the firm to confirm that they have been arrived at using sound reasoning. This strongly resembles the scientific method, in that hypotheses are formulated and tested as a means for obtaining new knowledge. Only by this consistent alignment of mental models with empirical reality can the strategist avoid the danger of becoming stuck with an outdated cognitive map.

The alternative to this rational approach, it is often pointed out, is to be irrational and illogical, which surely cannot be a desirable alternative for the strategist. Non-rational reasoning comes in a variety of forms. For instance, people's thinking can be guided by their emotions. Feelings such as love, hate, guilt, regret, pride, anxiety, frustration and embarrassment can all cloud the strategist's understanding of a problem situation and the possible solutions. Adherents of the rational reasoning perspective do not dispute the importance of emotions – the purpose of an organization is often based on 'personal values, aspirations and ideals', while the motivation to implement strategies is also rooted in human emotions. However, the actual determination of the optimal strategy is a 'rational undertaking' par excellence (Andrews, 1987: 32).

Neither is intuitive thinking an appealing alternative for strategists. Of course, intuition can often be useful: decision rules based on extensive experience (cognitive heuristics) are often correct (even if they have been arrived at unconsciously) and they save time and effort. For example, Simon argues that even chess grand masters make many decisions intuitively, based on tacit rules of thumb, formulated through years of experience. Yet, intuitive judgments must be viewed with great suspicion, as they are difficult to verify and infamously unreliable (e.g. Hogarth, 1980; Schwenk, 1984). Where possible, intuitive thinking should be made explicit – the strategist's cognitive map should be captured on paper (e.g. Anthony et al., 1993; Eden, 1989), so that the reasoning of the strategist can be checked for logical inconsistencies.

Creative thinking is equally suspicious. Of course, creativity techniques can be beneficial for triggering some unexpected ideas. Whether it is by means of brainstorming, six thinking caps or action art, creative thinking can spark some unconventional thoughts. Even a rational scientist like Newton has remarked that 'no great discovery was ever made without a bold guess'. But this is usually where the usefulness of creativity ends, and to which it should be limited. In creative thinking anything goes and that can lead to anything between odd and ludicrous. To be able to sift the sane from the zany, logic is needed. To make sense of the multitude of new ideas the logical thinker must analyze and evaluate them. A more serious drawback is that in practice many 'creative ideas' are just someone's unsupported beliefs, dressed up to sound fashionable. 'Creative thinking' is often just an excuse for intellectual laziness.

In conclusion, advocates of the rational reasoning perspective argue that emotions, intuition and creativity have a small place in the strategic reasoning process, but that logical thinking should be the dominant ingredient. It could be said that the rational reasoning process of the strategist strongly resembles that of the scientist. The scientific methods of research, analysis, theorizing and falsification are all directly applicable to the process of strategic reasoning – so much so, that the scientific method can be used as the benchmark for strategy development processes. Consequently, the best preparation for effective strategic reasoning would be to be trained in the scientific tradition.

EXHIBIT 2.2 THE RATIONAL REASONING PERSPECTIVE

BERKSHIRE HATHAWAY: CONTROL YOUR EXCITEMENT

At the peak of the 'new economy', few people were derided as much as Warren Buffett, chairman of the insurance and investment conglomerate Berkshire Hathaway. Buffett – admiringly nicknamed the 'Sage of Omaha' – had gained a phenomenal reputation as an investor during the 1980s and 1990s, but to most it was clear that he had not grasped the opportunities presented by the internet. The grand old man might have been the guru of the old economy, but he simply did not understand the new rules of the information economy. He was considered a pitiful example of a once brilliant mind that had not been able to make the leap beyond conventional beliefs and comprehend the 'new paradigm'. The investment strategy of Berkshire Hathaway was deemed hopelessly outdated. At the peak of the dot.com boom, in September 1999, when almost all funds were rushing into new economy shares, the investment portfolio of Berkshire consisted of companies like Coca-Cola, Walt Disney, Gillette and *The Washington Post*. The shares of Berkshire traded at their lowest level in years.

The person least perturbed by this new, dubious status was Buffett himself. In his 1999 annual 'Letter to the Berkshire Hathaway Shareholders', he displayed an untouched faith in the fundamentals that had created an empire worth US$51 billion: 'If we have a strength, it is in recognizing when we are operating well within our circle of competence and when we are approaching the perimeter. . . . we just stick with what we understand. If we stray, we will have done so inadvertently, not because we got restless and substituted hope for rationality'. He refused to invest in internet stocks, which he considered 'chain letters', in which early participants get rich at the expense of later ones.

When valuing companies, Buffett's approach was based on a solid analysis of company fundamentals, 'to separate investment from speculation'. In his view, ultimately, share prices reflect a company's fundamentals and therefore nothing can substitute for a thorough diagnosis of these fundamentals. Another part of Buffett's approach was focus, concentrating the bulk of the investments in a limited number of stocks, and sticking to this. Furthermore, he avoided investing in ill-understood businesses and in fast-changing industries, 'in which the long-term winners are hard to identify'. Conscientious and consistent application of these principles had led to an exceptional track record – between 1965 and 1998 Berkshire shares outperformed the S&P 500 in all but three years. The compounded annual return over this period of Berkshire was 24.7%, against 10.5% for the S&P 500.

By 2001 the dot.com boom was history and Buffett was proven right – again. From the moment the stock market started to plunge, Berkshire shares were on the rise. Buffett had resisted the irrational emotions by emphasizing the need for rational reasoning, even when the conclusions were not fashionable. Nothing was more characteristic of this attitude than his 2000 'Letter to the Berkshire Shareholders', in which he wrote: 'We have embraced the 21st century by entering such cutting-edge industries as brick, carpet, insulation and paint. Try to control your excitement.'

Sources: www.berkshirehathaway.com; www.economist.com; *The Economist,* March 15 2001.

The generative reasoning perspective

Strategists taking a generative reasoning perspective are strongly at odds with the unassailable position given to logic in the rational reasoning perspective. They agree that logic is important, but stress that it is often more a hindrance than a help. The heavy emphasis placed on rationality can actually frustrate the main objective of strategic reasoning – to generate novel insights, new ways of defining problems and innovative solutions. Analysis can be a useful tool, but as the aim of strategic reasoning is to tear up outdated cognitive maps and to reinvent the future, creative thinking should be the driving force, and logical thinking a supporting means. For this reason, proponents of the generative reasoning perspective argue that strategists should avoid the false certainty projected by rational approaches to strategic reasoning, but should nurture creativity as their primary cognitive asset.

In the generative reasoning perspective, emphasis is placed on the 'wicked' nature of strategic problems (Rittel, 1972; Mason and Mitroff, 1981). It is argued that strategic problems cannot be easily and objectively defined, but that they are open to interpretation from a limitless variety of angles. The same is true for the possible solutions – there is no fixed set of problem solutions from which the strategist must select the best one. Defining and solving strategic problems, it is believed, is fundamentally a creative activity. As such, strategic reasoning has very little in common with the thought processes of the aforementioned chess grand master, as was presumed by the rationalists. Playing chess is a 'tame' problem. The problem definition is clear and all options are known. In the average game of chess, consisting of 40 moves, 10 120 possibilities have to be considered (Simon, 1972). This makes it a difficult game for humans to play, because of their limited computational capacities. Chess grand masters are better at making these calculations than other people and are particularly good at computational short cuts – recognizing which things to figure out and which not. However, even the best chess grand masters have been beaten at the game by highly logical computers with a superior number crunching capability. For the poor chess grand master, the rules of the game are fixed and there is little room for redefining the problem or introducing innovative approaches.

Engaging in business strategy is an entirely different matter. Strategic problems are wicked. Problem definitions are highly subjective and there are no fixed sets of solutions. It is therefore impossible to 'identify' the problem and 'calculate' an optimal solution. Opportunities and threats do not exist, waiting for the analyst to discover them. A strategist understands that a situation can be 'viewed' as an opportunity and 'believes' that certain factors can be threatening if not approached properly. Neither can strengths and weaknesses be objectively determined – a strategist can employ a company characteristic as a strength, but can also turn a unique company quality into a weakness by a lack of vision. Hence, doing a SWOT analysis (strengths, weaknesses, opportunities and threats) actually has little to do with logical analysis, but in reality is nothing less than a creative interpretation of a problem situation. Likewise, it is a fallacy to believe that strategic options follow more or less logically from the characteristics of the firm and its environment. Strategic options are not 'deduced from the facts' or selected from a 2×2 matrix, but are dreamt up. Strategists must be able to use their imaginations to generate previously unknown solutions. If more than one strategic option emerges from the mind of the strategist, these cannot be simply scored and ranked to choose the optimal one. Some analyses can be done, but ultimately the strategist will have to intuitively judge which vision for the future has the best chance of being created in reality.

Hence, a generative reasoning process is more than just brainstorming or having a wild idea every once in a while. In a generative reasoning process all strategic thinking activities are oriented towards creating, instead of calculating – 'inventing' instead of 'finding' (Liedtka, 2000). This type of creative thinking is very hard work, as strategists must leave the intellectual safety of generally accepted concepts to explore new ideas, guided by little else than their intuition. They must be willing to operate without the security of a dominant logic; experimenting, testing, arguing, challenging, doubting and living amongst the rubble of demolished certainties, without having new certainties to give them shelter. To proponents of the generative reasoning perspective, it is essential for strategists to have a slightly contrarian (Hurst, Rush and White, 1989), revolutionary predisposition (Hamel, 1996). Strategists must enjoy the challenge of thinking 'out of the box', even when this disrupts the status quo and is not much appreciated by those with their two feet (stuck) on the ground. As Picasso once remarked, 'every act of creation is first of all an act of destruction' – strategists must enjoy the task of eroding old paradigms and confronting the defenders of those beliefs. And if some analyses can be done to support this effort, then they can serve a valuable purpose in the overall strategy process.

In conclusion, advocates of the generative reasoning perspective argue that the essence of strategic reasoning is the ability to creatively challenge 'the tyranny of the given' (Kao, 1996) and to generate new and unique ways of understanding and doing things. As such, strategic reasoning closely resembles the frame-breaking behavior common in the arts. In fields such as painting, music, motion pictures, dancing and architecture, artists are propelled by the drive to challenge convention and to seek out innovative approaches. Many of their methods, such as brainstorming, experimentation, openness to intuition, and the use of metaphors, contradictions and paradoxes, are directly applicable to developing strategy. Consequently, the best preparation for strategic reasoning might actually be to be trained in the artistic tradition of iconoclastic creativity and mental flexibility.

EXHIBIT 2.3 THE GENERATIVE REASONING PERSPECTIVE

3M: KISSING FROGS

When Bill Hewlett of Hewlett Packard was asked which company he most admired for its innovative capability, his response was immediate: '3M! . . . You don't know what they're going to come up with next. The beauty of it is that they probably don't know what they're going to come up with either!' For almost 100 years, 3M (Minnesota Mining and Manufacturing) has been known for its ability to come up with surprising new products and frame-breaking approaches to business. The US$16 billion company continually reinvents itself – as a rule, 30% of the company revenues come from products that are less than four years old. Examples of successful 3M product innovations are the sticky Post-it Notes, Thinsulate thermal insulation material and Scotch cellophane tape. Many of these innovative products created new markets, while others have fundamentally changed the rules of the game in existing markets. While the company started as a mining and abrasive manufacturing firm, today 3M has leading positions in areas such as office products, display and graphics materials, electronics and telecommunications, healthcare, safety, security and protection services, and transportation.

With such a track record in new product development, one might expect 3M to have an enormous R&D department, which is half true – the entire firm is one big R&D organization. Instead of limiting creative thinking to a few people in white coats, 3M's approach has been to get everyone in the organization involved in innovation. Technical employees can spend up to 15% of their time 'bootlegging' – freely working on their individual pet ideas that they hope will one day become useful innovations for the company. They have access to additional financial and material resources to support them in this. An inter-disciplinary venture team then tries to push the idea further or sends it back to the drawing board. These innovations can be product ideas, but process innovations are equally welcome. And innovation is not limited to the techies – employees in marketing, sales and administrative functions are also stimulated to come up with innovative practices.

An inherent part of the 3M culture is the belief that developing winning ideas is a process requiring enormous perseverance: 'You have to kiss a lot of frogs to find the prince,' according to a 3M researcher. Critical in finding the new prince is encouraging the organization to take risks and not to be afraid of making mistakes. Within 3M, the corporate hero is the one who has continued against all odds to create a successful innovation from something everyone thought frivolous. The top management wants no boundaries to its people's imagination and allows them to have a 'healthy disrespect for the rules' – it's better to ask forgiveness than ask permission. Very often, a venture team rejection motivates developers to work even harder on an idea. As one 3M manager remarked: 'It takes six to seven years to kill an idea in 3M.'

3M acknowledges the inspirational value of stories about innovations and the story of Post-it Notes is a classic example. In 1968, a 3M scientist trying to improve acrylate adhesives for tapes discovered an adhesive that did not permanently stick. After fruitless efforts to sell the idea internally, a new company recruit in 1973 was directly convinced of the potential and developed products as tiles and tapes for bulletin boards. The ultimate niche application was found later in the 1970s when Art Fry, a new-product development researcher, while singing in church suddenly realized that the adhesive would be the solution to the scrap paper bookmarks that kept falling out of his church choir hymn book. In the company many remained skeptical, pointing to processing difficulties and extreme waste production, to which Fry responded: 'Really, that is great news! If it were easy, then anyone could do it. If it really is as tough as you say, then 3M is the company that can do it.' Market analysis also did not reveal any customer demand for the product, so Fry suggested giving away sales samples to create demand.

Typical for the lateral thinking used by 3M is taking a technology from one business area and using it somewhere else. This is how the medical division started – automotive masking tape was adapted to the needs of surgeons to have a better way of attaching surgical drapes. Over the last ten years 3M has worked on improving the efficiency and speed of the new product development process. This has led to tension with the slack and mind-set required to come up with out-of-the box ideas. Conscious of this, the company has worked hard to structure the right conditions for spontaneity and creativity, and remains committed to nurturing a generative culture. And for good reason, as pointed out by one 3M researcher: 'Remember, one prince can pay for a lot of frogs.'

Sources: www.3M.com; Insead, case nr. 802–002–1; *The Economist*, February 18 1999.

TOWARDS A SYNTHESIS

When you have eliminated the impossible, whatever remains, however improbable, must be the truth.

'Sherlock Holmes', Arthur Conan Doyle (1859–1930); English novelist

Imagination is more important than knowledge.

Albert Einstein (1879–1955); German-American physicist

So, how should managers engage in strategic reasoning processes and how should they encourage fruitful strategic reasoning within their organizations? Should managers view strategic reasoning primarily as a rational and deductive activity or as a more imaginative

and generative process? Should strategists train themselves to follow procedural rationality – rigorously analyzing problems using scientific methods and calculating the optimal
course of action? Or should strategists practice to 'boldly go where no one has gone
before' – redefining problems and inventing new courses of action?

In Table 2.1 the main arguments of the two opposite poles in this debate have been summarized. It would make the life of managers much simpler if the outcome of this debate
would be that one side was obviously right and the other side was blatantly wrong.
However, there is little consensus to be found on the topic of strategic thinking, neither
among strategy theorists, nor among strategizing managers. Therefore, readers will have
to make up their own minds on the best way to approach strategic reasoning, based on the
arguments presented.

As you as reader make up your own mind, you are reminded of the challenge outlined
in Chapter 1, to consider that both sides in the debate might be simultaneously right, but
each only to a certain extent. Both perspectives might be shedding light on valuable
aspects of strategic thinking, but not giving the entire picture. Each might be overempha-
sizing one side of the paradox, while not sufficiently recognizing the importance of the
other side of the coin. If this is the case, the challenge for managers would be to take these
two opposite poles – the *thesis* and the *antithesis* – and to find a *synthesis*, combining the
'best of both worlds' in a way that suits each manager's specific circumstances. Ideally,
such a blend of the two perspectives would not only combine the strengths of both sides,
but would also avoid as many of their weaknesses as possible.

Yet, finding a synthesis once is only part of the challenge that readers should be willing to embrace. If there is not one definitive solution to the paradox of logic and creativity that is the optimal answer always and everywhere, being able to develop a synthesis
once is not good enough. If different organizational and market conditions require a different blend of the two perspectives, managers will need to update the balance they have
struck between the conflicting demands as circumstances change. And even where the circumstances are not shifting, managers might still be able to use experimentation and experience to come up with new and improved ways of getting the best of both worlds. Hence,
each synthesis is merely a workable resolution of the paradox at a particular moment. The

TABLE 2.1   Rational reasoning versus generative reasoning perspective

	Rational reasoning perspective	*Generative reasoning perspective*
Emphasis on	Logic over creativity	Creativity over logic
Dominant cognitive style	Analytical	Intuitive
Thinking follows	Formal, fixed rules	Informal, variable rules
Nature of thinking	Deductive and computational	Inductive and imaginative
Direction of thinking	Vertical	Lateral
Problem defining seen as	Recognizing and analyzing activities	Reflecting and sense-making activities
Problem solving seen as	Formulation and implementation activities	Imagining and doing activities
Value placed on	Consistency and rigor	Unorthodoxy and innovativeness
Assumption about reality	Objective, (partially) knowable	Subjective, (partially) creatable
Thinking hindered by	Incomplete information	Adherence to current cognitive map
Decisions based on	Calculation	Judgment
Metaphor	Strategy as science	Strategy as art

real challenge for managers is not to find a synthesis once, but to manage the paradox on an ongoing basis, continuously developing new syntheses along the way.

For this reason, the outcome of the debate in this chapter must be left open-ended. It is up to managers to determine their own perspective. However, it can be concluded that managers would be wise to practice their ability at seeing the issue of strategic thinking from both perspectives and to improve their skill at actively balancing the paradox of logic and creativity on a continual basis.

FURTHER READING

Those who judge by their feelings do not understand reasoning, for they wish to get an insight into a matter at a glance, and are not accustomed to look for principles. Contrarily, others, who are accustomed to argue from principles, do not understand the things of the heart, seeking for principles and not being able to see at a glance.

Blaise Pascal (1623–1662); French scientist and philosopher

Anyone interested in the topic of strategic thinking will sooner or later run into the work of Herbert Simon. His concept of bounded rationality was originally explored in the book *Models of Man*, which is still interesting reading, but *Organizations*, written together with James March, is a more comprehensive and up-to-date source with which to start. Also, a good introduction to (bounded) rationality is given by Niels Noorderhaven, in his book *Strategic Decision Making*, which additionally covers the topics of emotions, intuition and cognition in relationship to the strategy process. Another excellent book exploring the role of emotions in economic decision-making behavior and engaging in a debate with rational choice theorists is *Alchemies of the Mind: Rationality and the Emotions*, by Jon Elster.

For a more in-depth discussion on the interplay between cognition and strategic decision-making, a stimulating book is R. Hogarth's *Judgement and Choice: The Psychology of Decision*. Also an excellent book is *The Essence of Strategic Decision Making*, by Charles Schwenk, in particular with regard to the discussion of cognitive biases. A good research article summarizing the role of cognition in (strategic) management is James Walsh's (1995) 'Managerial and Organizational Cognition: Notes From a Trip Down Memory Lane'. On the topic of the social construction of reality, Karl Weick's *The Social Psychology of Organizing* is still the classic that should be read. A shorter article on the same topic is 'Strategic Management in an Enacted World' by Linda Smircich and Charles Stubbart (1985).

A good example of the rational reasoning perspective is in the work of Kenneth Andrews, one of the 'godfathers' of the field of strategic management. His book *The Concept of Corporate Strategy* takes a strongly rational reasoning position, as does his well-known textbook *Business Policy* (Christensen, Andrews, Bower, Hamermesh and Porter, 1987). A good example of the generative reasoning perspective can be found in the well-known book, *The Mind of the Strategist*, by Kenichi Ohmae.

Readers interested in the link between creativity and strategic thinking might want to start with *Creative Management*, an excellent reader edited by John Henry, which contains many classic articles on creativity from a variety of different disciplines. A second step would be to read Gareth Morgan's imaginative book, *Imaginization: The Art of Creative*

Management, or John Kao's *Jamming: The Art and Discipline of Business Creativity*, both of which make challenging proposals for improving an organization's creative thinking. Also stimulating is the book *Strategic Innovation*, by Charles Baden-Fuller and Martyn Pitt, which contains a large number of cases on companies exhibiting creative thinking. For a practical guide to creative thinking Stephen Reid's recent book, *How to Think: Building Your Mental Muscle*, is quite useful.

STRATEGY FORMATION

To plan, v. To bother about the best method of accomplishing an accidental result.

The Devil's Dictionary, Ambrose Bierce (1842–1914); American columnist

INTRODUCTION

There are many definitions of strategy and many ideas of how strategies should be made. In the introduction to Section II of this book on 'Strategy process', our definition of strategy was kept basic to encompass the large majority of these different views – 'strategy is a course of action for achieving an organization's purpose'. Taking this definition as a starting point, a major distinction can be observed between people who see strategy as an *intended* course of action and those who regard strategy as a *realized* course of action. Mintzberg and Waters (1985) have remarked that these two views of strategy are not contradictory, but complementary. Intended strategy is what individuals or organizations formulate prior to action (a *pattern of decisions*), while realized strategy refers to the strategic behavior exhibited in practice (a *pattern of actions*). Of course, not all behavior is necessarily strategic – if the actions do not follow a pattern directed at achieving the organization's purpose, it does not qualify as strategy.

The process by which an intended strategy is created is called 'strategy formulation'. Normally strategy formulation is followed by strategy implementation. However, intentions sometimes end up not being put into practice – plans can be changed or canceled along the way. The process by which a realized strategy is formed is called 'strategy formation'. What is realized might be based on an intended strategy, but it can also be the result of unplanned actions as time goes by. In other words, the process of strategy formation encompasses both formulation and action. Strategy formation is the entire process leading to strategic behavior in practice.

For managers with the responsibility for getting results, it would be too limited to only look at the process of strategy formulation and to worry about implementation later. Managers must ask themselves how the entire process of strategy formation should be managed to get their organizations to act strategically. Who should be involved, which activities need to be undertaken and to what extent can strategy be formulated in advance? In short, for managers finding a way to realize a strategic pattern of actions is the key issue.

THE ISSUE OF REALIZED STRATEGY

Getting an organization to exhibit strategic behavior is what all strategists aim to achieve. Preparing detailed analyses, drawing up plans, making extensive slide presentations and holding long meetings might all be necessary means to achieve this end, but ultimately it is the organization's actions directed at the market-place that count. The key issue facing managers is, therefore, how this strategic behavior can be attained. How can a successful course of action be realized in practice?

To answer these questions, it is first necessary to gain a deeper understanding of the 'who' and 'what' of strategy formation – 'what type of strategy formation activities need to be carried out?' and 'what type of strategy formation roles need to be filled by whom?'. Both questions will be examined in the following sections.

Strategy formation activities

In Chapter 2 it was argued that the process of strategic reasoning could be divided into four general categories of activities – identifying, diagnosing, conceiving and realizing. These strategic problem-solving activities, taking place in the mind of the strategist, are in essence the same as those encountered in organizations at large. Organizations also need to 'solve strategic problems' and achieve a successful pattern of actions. The difference is that the organizational context – involving many more people, with different experiences, perspectives, personalities, interests and values – leads to different requirements for structuring the process. Getting people within an organization to exhibit strategic behavior necessitates the exchange of information and ideas, decision-making procedures, communication channels, the allocation of resources and the coordination of actions.

When translated to an organizational environment, the four general elements of the strategic reasoning process can be further divided into the eight basic building blocks of the strategy formation process, as illustrated in Figure 3.1.

Strategic issue identification activities.   If a strategy is seen as an answer to a perceived 'problem' or 'issue', managers must have some idea of what the problem is. 'Identifying' refers to all activities contributing to a better understanding of what should be viewed as problematic – what constitutes an important opportunity or threat that must be attended to if the organization's purpose is to be met. The key activities here are:

■ Mission setting. What the organization sees as an issue will in part depend on its mission – the enduring set of fundamental principles outlining what purpose the organization wishes to serve, in what domain and under which conditions. A company's mission, encompassing its core values, beliefs, business definition and purpose, forms the basis of the organization's identity and sets the basic conditions under which the organization wishes to function. Where a company has a clearly developed mission, shared by all key players in the organization, this will strongly color its filtering of strategic issues. The mission does not necessarily have to be formally captured in a mission statement, but can be informally internalized as a part of the company culture. The topic of mission is discussed at more length in Chapter 11.

■ Agenda setting. Besides the organizational mission as screening mechanism, many other factors can contribute to the focusing of organizational attention on specific strategic

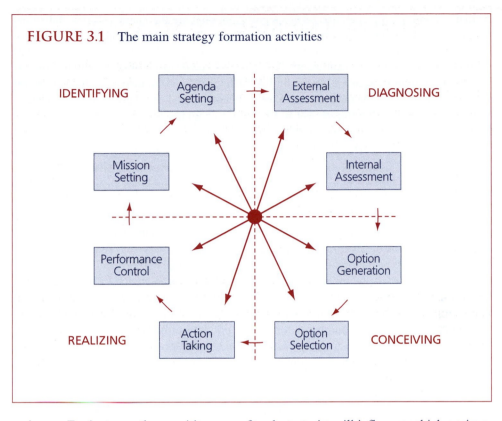

FIGURE 3.1   The main strategy formation activities

issues. For instance, the cognitive map of each strategist will influence which environmental and organizational developments are identified as issues. Furthermore, group culture will have an impact on which issues are discussible, which are off-limits to open debate, and under what conditions discussions should take place. Getting people to sit up and take notice will also depend on each actor's communication and political skills, as well as their sources of power, both formal and informal. Together these attention-focusing factors determine which issues are picked up on the 'organizational radar screen', discussed and looked into further. It is said that these issues make it on to the 'organizational agenda', while all other potential problems receive less or no attention. Many of these organizational factors are discussed more extensively in Chapters 4 and 9.

Strategic issue diagnosis activities.   To come to grips with a 'problem' or 'issue', managers must try to comprehend its structure and its underlying causes. Especially since most strategic issues are not simple and straightforward, but complex and messy, it is very important to gain a deeper understanding of 'what is going on' – which 'variables' are there and how are they interrelated? This part of the strategy formation processes can be divided into the following activities:

- External assessment. The activity of investigating the structure and dynamics of the environment surrounding the organization is commonly referred to as an external assessment or analysis. Typically such a diagnosis of the outside world includes both a scan of the direct (market) environment and the broader (contextual) environment. In both cases the analyst wants to move beyond observed behavior, to understand 'what makes the system tick'. What is the underlying structure of the industry and the market that is conditioning each party's behavior? And what are the characteristics and strategies of each important actor, including customers, competitors, suppliers, distributors, unions, governments and financiers? Furthermore, only understanding the current state of affairs is generally insufficient; it is also necessary to analyze in which direction external circumstances are developing. Which trends can be discerned, which factors seem to be driving the industry and market dynamics, and can these be used to forecast or estimate future developments? In Chapters 5, 7 and 8, these questions surrounding external assessment are discussed in more detail.

■ Internal assessment. The activity of investigating the capabilities and functioning of the organization is commonly referred to as an internal assessment or analysis. Typically such a diagnosis of the inner workings of the organization includes an assessment of the *business system* with which the firm creates value and the *organizational system* that has been developed to facilitate the business system. When dissecting the business system, attention is directed at understanding the resources and chain of value-adding activities that enable the firm to offer a set of products and services. To gain insight into the functioning of the organizational system, it is necessary to determine the structure of the organization, the processes used to control and coordinate the various people and units, and the organizational culture. In all these analyses a mere snapshot of the firm is generally insufficient – the direction in which the organization is developing must also be examined, including a consideration of the main change drivers and change inhibitors. Furthermore, for strategy making it is important to compare how the organization scores on all aforementioned factors compared to rival firms. In Chapters 4 and 5 these topics are investigated in more depth.

Strategy conception activities.   To deal with a strategic 'problem' or 'issue', managers must come up with a potential solution. A course of action must be found that will allow the organization to relate itself to the environment in such a way that it will be able to achieve its purpose. 'Conceiving' refers to all activities that contribute to determining which course of action should be pursued. In this part of the strategy formation process, the following categories of activities can be discerned:

■ Option generation. Creating potential strategies is what option generation is about. Sometimes managers will immediately jump at one specific course of action, limiting their strategic option generation activities to only one prime candidate. However, many managers will be inclined to explore a number of different avenues for approaching a specific strategic issue, thereby generating multiple strategic options. Each option can range in detail from a general outline of actions to be taken, up to a full-blown strategic plan, specifying goals, actions, tasks, responsibilities, resource allocation, milestones and performance measures. Which questions each strategic option should address is the main focus of discussion in the strategy content section of this book.

■ Option selection. The potential 'solutions' formulated by managers must be evaluated to decide whether they should be acted upon. It must be weighed whether the strategic option generated will actually lead to the results required and then it must be concluded whether to act accordingly. Especially where two or more strategic options have come forward, managers need to judge which one of them is most attractive to act on. This screening of strategic options is done on the basis of evaluation criteria, for instance perceived risk, anticipated benefits, the organization's capacity to execute, expected competitor reactions and follow-up possibilities. Sometimes a number of the evaluation criteria used are formally articulated, but generally the evaluation will at least be partially based on the experience and judgment of the decision-makers involved. Together, these activities of assessing strategic options and arriving at a selected course of action are also referred to as 'strategic decision-making'.

Strategy realization activities.   A strategic 'problem' or 'issue' can only be resolved if concrete actions are undertaken that achieve results. Managers must make adjustments to their business or organizational system, or initiate actions in the market – they must not only think, talk and decide, but also do, to have a tangible impact. 'Realizing' refers to all these practical actions performed by the organization. If there is a clear pattern to these actions, it can be said that there is a realized strategy. In this part of the strategy formation process, the following activities can be distinguished:

- Action taking. A potential problem solution must be carried out – intended actions must be implemented to become realized actions. This performing of tangible actions encompasses all aspects of a firm's functioning. All hands-on activities, more commonly referred to as 'work', fall into this category – everything from setting up and operating the business system to getting the organizational system to function on a day-to-day basis.
- Performance control. Managers must also measure whether the actions being taken in the organization are in line with the option selected and whether the results are in line with what was anticipated. This reflection on the actions being undertaken can be informal, and even unconscious, but it can be formally structured into a performance monitoring and measuring system as well. Such performance measurement can be employed to assess how well certain people and organizational units are doing vis-à-vis set objectives. Incentives can be linked to achieving targets, and corrective steps can be taken to ensure conformance to an intended course of action. However, deviation from the intended strategy can also be a signal to re-evaluate the original solution or even to re-evaluate the problem definition itself. An important issue when engaging in performance control is the determination of which performance indicators will be used – micro-measuring all aspects of the organization's functioning is generally much too unwieldy and time-consuming. Some managers prefer a few simple measures, sometimes quantitative (e.g. financial indicators), sometimes qualitative (e.g. are clients satisfied?), while others prefer more extensive and varied measures, such as a balanced scorecard (Kaplan and Norton, 2001; Simons, 1995).

Note that these strategy formation activities have not been labeled 'steps' or 'phases'. While these eight activities have been presented in an order that seems to suggest a logical sequence of steps, it remains to be seen in which order they should be carried out in practice. In Figure 3.1 the outer arrows represent the logical clockwise sequence, similar to the rational reasoning process discussed in Chapter 2. The inner arrows represent the possibility to jump back and forth between the strategy formation activities, similar to the irregular pattern exhibited in the generative reasoning process in Chapter 2.

Strategy formation roles

In all strategy formation processes the activities discussed above need to be carried out. However, there can be significant differences in who carries out which activities. Roles in the strategy formation process can vary as tasks and responsibilities are divided in alternative ways. The main variations are due to a different division of labor along the following dimensions:

- **Top vs. middle vs. bottom roles.** Strategy formation activities are rarely the exclusive domain of the CEO. Only in the most extreme cases will a CEO run a 'one-man show', carrying out all activities except realization. Usually some activities will be divided among members of the top management team, while other activities will be pushed further down to divisional managers, business unit managers, and department managers (e.g. Bourgeois and Brodwin, 1983; Floyd and Wooldridge, 2000). Some activities might be delegated or carried out together with people even further down the hierarchy, including employees on the work floor. For activities such as external and internal assessment and option generation it is more common to see participation by people lower in the organization, while top management generally retains the responsibility for selecting, or at least deciding on, which strategic option to follow. The recurrent theme in this question of the vertical division of activities is how far down activities can and should be pushed – how much *empowerment* of middle and lower levels is beneficial for the organization?

- **Line vs. staff roles.** By definition line managers are responsible for realization of strategic options pertaining to the primary process of the organization. Because they are responsible for achieving results, they are often also given the responsibility to participate in conceiving the strategies they will have to realize. Potentially, line managers can carry out all strategy formation activities without staff support. However, many organizations do have staff members involved in the strategy formation process. Important staff input can come from all existing departments, while some organizations institute special strategy departments to take care of strategy formation activities. The responsibilities of such strategy departments can vary from general process facilitation, to process ownership to full responsibility for strategy formulation.

- **Internal vs. external roles.** Strategy formation activities are generally seen as an important part of every manager's portfolio of tasks. Yet, not all activities need to be carried out by members of the organization, but can be 'outsourced' to outsiders (e.g. Robinson, 1982). It is not uncommon for firms to hire external agencies to perform diagnosis activities or to facilitate the strategy formation process in general. Some organizations have external consultants engaged in all aspects of the process, even to the extent that the outside agency has the final responsibility for drawing up the strategic options.

In organizing the strategy formation process, a key question is how formalized the assignment of activities to the various potential process participants should be. The advantage of formalization is that it structures and disciplines the strategy formation process (e.g. Chakravarthy and Lorange, 1991; Hax and Maljuf, 1984). Especially in large organizations, where many people are involved, it can be valuable to keep the process tightly organized. Formalization can be achieved by the establishment of a strategic planning system. In such a system, strategy formation steps can be scheduled, tasks can be specified, responsibilities can be assigned, decision-making authority can be clarified, budgets can be allocated and evaluation mechanisms can be put in place. Generally, having unambiguous responsibilities, clearer accountability and stricter review of performance will lead to a better functioning organization. The added benefit of formalization is that it gives top management more control over the organization, as all major changes must be part of approved plans and the implementation of plans is checked.

Yet, there is a potential danger in using formal planning systems as a means to make strategy. Formalization strongly emphasizes those aspects that can be neatly organized such as meetings, writing reports, giving presentations, making decisions, allocating resources and reviewing progress, while having difficulty with essential strategy-making activities that are difficult to capture in procedures. Important aspects such as creating new insights, learning, innovation, building political support and entrepreneurship can be sidelined or crushed if rote bureaucratic mechanisms are used to produce strategy. Moreover, planning bureaucracies, once established, can come to live a life of their own, creating rules, regulations, procedures, checks, paperwork, schedules, deadlines and double-checks, making the system inflexible, unresponsive, ineffective and demotivating (e.g. Marx, 1991; Mintzberg, 1994a).

THE PARADOX OF DELIBERATENESS AND EMERGENCE

The ability to foretell what is going to happen tomorrow, next week, next month and next year. And to have the ability afterwards to explain why it didn't happen.
Winston Churchill (1874–1965); British prime minister and writer

Strategy has to do with the future. And the future is unknown. This makes strategy a fascinating, yet frustrating, topic. Fascinating because the future can still be shaped and strategy can be used to achieve this aim. Frustrating because the future is unpredictable, undermining the best of intentions, thus demanding flexibility and adaptability. To managers, the idea of creating the future is highly appealing, yet the prospect of sailing for *terra incognita* without a compass is unsettling at best.

This duality of wanting to intentionally design the future, while needing to gradually explore, learn and adapt to an unfolding reality, is the tension central to the topic of strategy formation. It is the conflicting need to figure things out in advance, versus the need to find things out along the way. On the one hand, managers would like to forecast the future and to orchestrate plans to prepare for it. Yet, on the other hand, managers understand that experimentation, learning and flexibility are needed to deal with the fundamental unpredictability of future events.

In their influential article, 'Of Strategies: Deliberate and Emergent', Mintzberg and Waters (1985) were one of the first to explicitly focus on this tension. They argued that a distinction should be made between deliberate and emergent strategy (see Figure 3.2). Where realized strategies were fully intended, one can speak of 'deliberate strategy'. However, realized strategies can also come about 'despite, or in the absence of, intentions', which Mintzberg and Waters labeled 'emergent strategy'. In their view, few strategies were purely deliberate or emergent, but usually a mix between the two.

Hence, in realizing strategic behavior managers need to blend the conflicting demands for deliberate strategizing and strategy emergence. In the following paragraphs both sides of this paradox of deliberateness and emergence will be examined further.

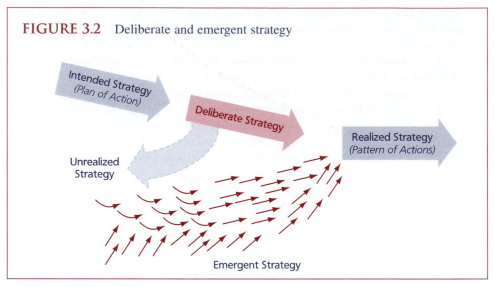

FIGURE 3.2   Deliberate and emergent strategy

Intended Strategy
(Plan of Action)

Deliberate Strategy

Realized Strategy
(Pattern of Actions)

Unrealized
Strategy

Emergent Strategy

Source: Mintzberg and Waters, 1985; reprinted with permission from *Strategic Management Journal*, © 1985 John Wiley and Sons Ltd.

The demand for deliberate strategizing

Deliberateness refers to the quality of acting intentionally. When people act deliberately, they 'think' before they 'do'. They make a plan and then implement the plan. A plan is an intended course of action, stipulating which measures a person or organization proposes to take. In common usage, plans are assumed to be articulated (made explicit) and documented (written down), although strictly speaking this is not necessary to qualify as a plan.

As an intended course of action, a plan is a means towards an end. A plan details which actions will be undertaken to reach a particular objective. In practice, however, plans can exist without explicit objectives. In such cases, the objectives are implicitly wrapped up in the plan – the plan incorporates both ends and means.

All organizations need to plan. At the operational level, most firms will have some degree of production planning, resource planning, manpower planning and financial planning, to name just a few. When it comes to strategic behavior, there are also a number of prominent advantages that strongly pressure organizations to engage in deliberate strategizing:

■ Direction. Plans give organizations a sense of direction. Without objectives and plans, organizations would be adrift. If organizations did not decide where they wanted to go, any direction and any activity would be fine. People in organizations would not know what they were working towards and therefore would not be able to judge what constitutes effective behavior (e.g. Ansoff, 1965; Chakravarthy and Lorange, 1991).

■ Commitment. Plans enable early commitment to a course of action. By setting objectives and drawing up a plan to accomplish these, organizations can invest resources, train people, build up production capacity and take a clear position within their environment. Plans allow organizations to mobilize themselves and to dare to take actions that are difficult to reverse and have a long payback period (e.g. Ghemawat, 1991; Marx, 1991).

- Coordination. Plans have the benefit of coordinating all strategic initiatives within an organization into a single cohesive pattern. An organization-wide master plan can ensure that differences of opinion are ironed out and one consistent course of action is followed throughout the entire organization, avoiding overlapping, conflicting and contradictory behavior (e.g. Ackoff, 1980; Andrews, 1987).

- Optimization. Plans also facilitate optimal resource allocation. Drawing up a plan disciplines strategizing managers to explicitly consider all available information and consciously evaluate all available options. This allows managers to choose the optimal course of action before committing resources. Moreover, documented plans permit corporate level managers to compare the courses of action proposed by their various business units and to allocate scarce resources to the most promising initiatives (e.g. Ansoff and McDonnell, 1990; Bower, 1970).

- Programming. Last, but not least, plans are a means for programming all organizational activities in advance. Having detailed plans allows organizations to be run with the clockwork precision, reliability and efficiency of a machine. Activities that might otherwise be plagued by poor organization, inconsistencies, redundant routines, random behavior, helter-skelter fire fighting and chaos, can be programmed and controlled if plans are drawn up (e.g. Grinyer et al., 1986; Steiner, 1979).

Given these major advantages, it can come as no surprise that organizations feel the pressure to engage in deliberate strategizing. Deliberateness is a quality that the strategy formation process cannot do without.

The demand for strategy emergence

Emergence is the process of becoming apparent. A strategy emerges when it comes into being along the way. Where there are no plans, or people divert from their plans but their behavior is still strategic, it can be said that the strategy is emergent – gradually shaped during an iterative process of 'thinking' and 'doing'.

Emergent strategy differs from ad hoc behavior in that a coherent pattern of action does evolve. While managers may have no prior intentions, they can explore, learn and piece together a consistent set of behaviors over time. Such an approach of letting strategy emerge has a number of major advantages that organizations also need to consider:

- Opportunism. As the future is unknown and therefore unpredictable, organizations must retain enough mental freedom to grab unforeseen opportunities as they emerge. Organizations must keep an open mind to sense where positive and negative circumstances are unfolding, so that they can respond rapidly to these new conditions – proactively riding the wave of opportunity, using the momentum in the environment and/or the organization to their advantage. This ability to 'play the field' is an important factor in effective strategy formation (e.g. Quinn, 2002; Stacey, 2001).

- Flexibility. Not only must managers keep an open mind, they must keep their options open as well, by not unnecessarily committing themselves to irreversible actions and investments. Letting strategy emerge means not prematurely locking the organization in to a preset course of action, but keeping alternatives open for as long as practically possible. And where commitments must to be made, managers need to select 'robust' options, which permit a lot of leeway to shift along with unfolding events. This pressure to remain flexible is also an important demand on strategizing managers (e.g. Beinhocker, 1999; Evans, 1991).

- **Learning**. Often, the best way to find out what works is to give it a try – to act before you know. Letting strategy emerge is based on the same principle, that to learn what will be successful in the market must be discovered by experimentation, pilot projects, trial runs and gradual steps. Through the feedback obtained by hands-on 'doing', a rich insight can grow into what really works. As Thomas Alva Edison is well known for remarking, invention is 5% inspiration and 95% perspiration, and this is probably equally true for 'inventing the corporate future'. Learning is hard work, but it is an essential part of strategy formation (e.g. Pascale, 1984; Mintzberg, 1994b).

- **Entrepreneurship**. Building on the previous point, often the best way to find out what works is to let various people give it a try – to tap into the entrepreneurial spirits within the organization. Different people in the organization will have different strategic ideas and many of them will feel passionately about proving that their idea 'can fly'. By providing individuals, teams and/or entire units with a measure of autonomy to pursue innovative initiatives, firms can use the energy of 'intrapreneurs' within the organization, instead of forcing them to conform or start on their own (e.g. Amabile, 1998; Pinchot, 1985). As true incubators, firms can facilitate various divergent projects simultaneously, increasing commitment or closing them down as their potential unfolds (e.g. Burgelman, 1983, 1991; Lyon, Lumpkin and Dess, 2000).

- **Support**. A major shift in strategy generally requires a major shift in the political and cultural landscape of an organization – careers will be affected, vested departmental interests will be impacted and cultural values and beliefs will be challenged. Rarely can such shifts be imposed top-down by decree. Getting things done in organizations includes building coalitions, blocking rivals, convincing wavering parties, confronting opposing ideas and letting things 'sink in', all with the intention of gradually building enough support to move forward. Yet, finding out where enough support can be mustered to move forward, and where side steps or even reversals are needed, is an ongoing process and cannot be predicted in advance. Hence, strategizing managers must understand the internal political and cultural dynamics of their organizations and pragmatically shape strategy depending on what is feasible, not on what is ideal (e.g. Allison, 1971; Quinn, 1980a).

Each of these points seems to be the opposite counterpart of the advantages of deliberate strategizing – while deliberateness creates commitment, emergence allows for flexibility; while deliberateness gives direction, emergence allows for opportunism; while deliberateness facilitates fixed programming, emergence allows for ongoing learning. This places managers in a paradoxical position. While both deliberate strategizing and strategy emergence seem to have advantageous characteristics, they are each other's opposites and are to a certain extent contradictory – a firm cannot be fully committed to detailed and co-ordinated long-term plans, while simultaneously adapting itself flexibly and opportunistically to unfolding circumstances, ongoing learning and unpredictable political and cultural processes. With two conflicting demands placed on the strategy formation process at the same time, managers need to choose one at the expense of the other, trying to strike the best possible balance between deliberateness and emergence.

EXHIBIT 3.1 SHORT CASE

AIRBUS: PLANNING BEYOND PLANES?

When aviation pioneers Orville and Wilbur Wright flew their first aircraft more than a century ago, they probably never imagined that some successors of their Flyer would carry a price tag of over US$200 million per aircraft and require R&D investments in excess of US$10 billion per model. Yet, this is the current reality facing the two remaining makers of large passenger aircraft in the world – Boeing in Seattle, USA, and Airbus, headquartered in Toulouse, France. Other large manufacturers such as McDonnell Douglas and Lockheed have had to bow out of this high stakes game, as they were not capable of realizing the economies of scale in production and R&D needed to survive in this industry. Only the long-time market leader Boeing and the upstart challenger Airbus have had an attractive enough range of aircraft models to achieve the volume needed to survive the shakeout.

While Boeing is a straightforward company, with a traditional structure, Airbus is a somewhat odd firm, with an odd history. Back in 1969, a consortium of French and German firms was formed with the intention of jointly developing an aircraft that could compete with the American giants. This consortium was later expanded to include Spanish and British companies as well. The consortium was often derided as a mere job-creation program and a less-than-subtle vehicle for funneling state aid into a 'strategic industry'. The consortium also had many teething problems, as it needed to develop cross-border decision-making processes involving many parties, many interested local and national governments and without strong central leadership. Yet, despite the internal difficulties and the external criticisms, Airbus was able to create the successful A300B passenger jet. Within

ten years of its inception, Airbus captured a strong foothold in the market for large passenger jets, having 256 orders from 32 customers. This encouraged the consortium partners to turn their loose alliance into a more structured federation and to conceive a long-term vision to develop a complete family of large aircraft, ranging from 100-seat to 400-seat passenger jets. Underpinning this vision was the assumption that a broad choice of aircraft types would enable airlines to switch more easily to Airbus.

So by the early 1980s Airbus was looking for a second type to add to its line up. Given the economic downturn and increased fuel prices at that time, airlines indicated that they were interested in a new type of aircraft with the ability to carry the same number of passengers over the same distance as the well-established Boeing 727–200, while burning just half as much fuel. Airbus's answer was the A320, which was launched in 1984. In 1987 the product range was further extended with two larger aircraft, the four-engine A340 and twin-engine A330. In 1993, in the midst of the worst financial crisis suffered by the airline industry until then, Airbus launched a relatively small passenger jet, the A319. This move ensured that adequate numbers of this type of plane were available to meet a recovery of demand that, according to Airbus planners, would occur in 1996. They were right – from 1995 onwards, US air carriers started to replace part of their fleets, as 25% of their planes were over 20 years old. Moreover, new anti-noise regulations came into effect in many markets, which favored the relatively quiet Airbus jets.

Despite a strongly expanded market share, the Airbus consortium members were still not convinced that they would be able to compete with Boeing in the long run, especially as Boeing had been able to entice

McDonnell Douglas, into a merger in 1996, even though Airbus had been courting McDonnell Douglas for years. Three worries were foremost in the minds of the Airbus executives. First, the consortium structure was proving to be a severe burden on strategic decision-making. Every decision required the consent of all participating companies and negotiations on 'who would get what' could be long and bitter. There was a growing feeling that if the 'parents' had so many 'children' together, it was about time they got around to marrying. Secondly, after deregulation of the airline industry, the boom and bust cycles in the aircraft industry had become more severe. In the past, the state-owned flag carriers could plan their fleet expansion and renewal without much concern for the swings in demand among air passengers. The privatized carriers and new commercial airlines, however, were much more vulnerable to swings in demand, leading them to order aircraft in good times and to cancel orders *en masse* as soon as the market declined. The Airbus companies felt that something would need to be done to make Airbus less vulnerable to such cyclicality, especially since Boeing had a lot of stable military business in its portfolio to offset swings in the commercial aircraft business. Thirdly, it worried Airbus that Boeing still had a monopoly at the top end of the market with its 747 jumbo jet. The resulting revenues gave Boeing the advantage of having higher investment power than Airbus. Therefore, it was felt that the only way to keep up with Boeing would be to attack it directly in the heart of its empire.

Finding an answer to these worries took the Airbus partners several years, but in 2000 major steps were taken to address all three. It was announced that from January 1 2001 the consortium would be transformed into a single corporate entity. Furthermore, to ensure that the company would have a balanced portfolio of businesses, Airbus was made part of a larger, newly established company, the European Aeronautic Defense and Space Corporation (EADS), which brings together a broad range of companies with airborne activities (i.e. commercial and defense airplanes and helicopters, missiles, satellites and rocket launchers). Moreover, it was announced that Airbus would start to develop a 555-seat double-decker mega jet, the A380, to overtake the Boeing 747 at the high end of the market.

With a long history of complex and prolonged negotiations between partner organizations, no one was surprised that the CEO of the unified Airbus, Noël Forgeard, made centralization of strategic decision-making one of his top priorities. He wanted to make use of the momentum to create an effective and efficient strategy formation process that fits well with the challenges faced by the company. It was clear to him that strong strategic planning would be required, given the inevitability of deciding on new aircraft types far in advance. With R&D investments for a new aircraft type surpassing US$10 billion and years of development time, strategists did not have the luxury of test marketing a few different product types and keeping the best one – they had to get it right first time. The payback period of the average aircraft is in excess of ten years and aircraft designs can last up to 50 years, placing a premium on forecasting which product will fit the needs for many years to come. For instance, the Boeing 747 jumbo jet has been in production for more than 30 years and is still being sold, which has netted Boeing more than US$20 billion in profits. On the other hand, getting it wrong can mean billions down the drain and years of delay in developing an alternative.

Yet, planning in the aircraft industry has never been more difficult. It used to be easier to calculate when airlines would need to replace old planes and to project market growth. But the old airlines have been in turmoil since deregulation – new competitors are entering and the traditional business model of a 'hub-and-spoke' airline network is being challenged by low cost 'point-to-point' carriers. This difficulty in forecasting industry developments has led to sharp contrasts between the future expectations of Boeing and Airbus. In deciding to pursue the 555-seat A380, Airbus based itself on the projection that air traffic would grow by 5% per year and that crowded airport hubs, with limited starting and landing capacity, would need bigger aircraft. Its forecasts showed that over the next 20 years there would be an attractive US$300 billion market for 1400 mega carriers that could carry up to 600 passengers. Boeing, on the contrary, believed that air travel was going to fragment, and most growth would not come from routes connecting crowded hub airports, but from long-haul point-to-point services such as Singapore–Los Angeles. Therefore, smaller and faster planes would have a bright future, and Boeing decided to unfold plans to develop a new aircraft, the Sonic Cruiser, which would be smaller than the 747, but would travel at 95% of the speed of sound.

Since then, the market for aircraft has proven to be even more unpredictable than anticipated. The post-internet bubble economic downturn, followed by the events of September 11 2001, the Second Gulf War and the SARS scare of 2003 have sent the airline industry into a tailspin. Airlines have delayed or canceled orders, sending prices plunging down to earth and leading to huge overcapacity at Airbus and Boeing. With the future unclear and little market enthusiasm for its Sonic Cruiser, Boeing has quietly shelved its grand plans and instead has come up with relatively low-cost plans for a super-stretched version of the 747 jumbo jet. Airbus, however, has already committed itself to multi-billion investments for its

A380 program and can hardly reduce its engineering resources as the project is in full swing.

To Forgeard the challenge of making strategy in an unpredictable environment is not restricted to the big 'aircraft type' decisions taken every eight to ten years. More and more, Airbus wants to make its money on options added to an aircraft and the services surrounding the aircraft, instead of only on the basic product itself. Forgeard is thinking of services such as fleet planning, maintenance, financing and refurbishing, plus extra options such as in-flight internet. Yet, the difficulty is that his organization is used to making long-term product strategies, based on market forecasts and a strong measure of technology-push. It is not used to identifying potential service needs and developing innovative offerings to fulfill them. A different approach to strategy formation might be required.

Hence, the question facing Forgeard and Airbus is how they should go about shaping their strategy in future. Is it a matter of making even better forecasts or are there other ways of dealing with the unpredictability and unknowability of industry developments? And can Airbus use the same approach to strategy formation for the task of developing new options and services as it has used to develop new aircraft? The answer is vital, since Forgeard has pledged that Airbus will become bigger than Boeing before 2007 – which means adding a few billion to its current sales of US$17 billion, while not crash landing in the meantime.

Sources: *Airfinance Journal*, September 2002; *Aviation Week*, July 2 2000; *Aviation Week and Space Technology*, December 24 2001; *Business Week*, January 21 2002; *Financial Times*, September 8 2000; *Fortune*, August 2 1999 and March 5 2001; *Industry Week*, June 11 2001.

PERSPECTIVES ON STRATEGY FORMATION

It is impossible for a man to learn what he thinks he already knows.
Epictetus (c. 60–120); Roman philosopher

In Hollywood, most directors do not start shooting a movie until the script and storyboard are entirely completed – the script details each actor's words, expression and gestures, while the storyboard graphically depicts how each scene will look in terms of camera angles, lighting, backgrounds and stage props. Together they form a master plan, representing the initial intentions of the director. However, it frequently happens that a director has a new insight, and changes are made to the script or storyboard 'on the fly'. Yet, on the whole, most 'realized movies' are fairly close to directors' initial intentions.

For some directors this is madness. They might have a movie idea, but in their mind's eye they cannot yet picture it in its final form. Some elements might have already crystallized in their thoughts, but other parts of the film can only be worked out once the cameras are rolling and the actors start playing their roles. In this way, directors can let movies emerge without having a detailed script or storyboard in advance to guide them. It can be said that such movies are shaped by gradually blending together a number of small intentional steps over a long period of time, instead of taking one big step of making a master plan and implementing it. This approach of taking many small steps is called 'incrementalism'.

The question is how this works for managers making strategy. Is it best to deliberately draw up a storyboard for the film and trust that the 'actors' are flexible enough to adapt to minor changes in the script as time goes by? Or is the idea of a master plan misplaced, and are the best results achieved by developing a strategy incrementally, emergently responding to opportunities and threats as they unfold along the way? In short, how should strategizing managers strike a balance between deliberateness and emergence?

Unfortunately, the strategic management literature does not offer a clear-cut answer to this question. In both the academic journals and the practitioner-oriented literature, a wide spectrum of views can be observed on how managers should engage in strategy formation. While some writers suggest that there might be different styles in balancing deliberateness and emergence (e.g. Chaffee, 1985; Hart, 1992), most seem intent on offering 'the best way' to approach the issue of strategy formation – which often differs significantly from 'the best way' advised by others.

To come to grips with this variety of views, here the two diametrically opposed pole positions will be identified and discussed. On the basis of these two 'points of departure' the debate on how to deal with the paradox of deliberateness and emergence can be further explored. At one pole we find those managers and theorists who strongly emphasize deliberateness over emergence. They argue that organizations should strive to make strategy in a highly deliberate manner, by first explicitly formulating comprehensive plans, and only then implementing them. In accordance with common usage, this point of view will be referred to as the 'strategic planning perspective'. At the other pole are those who strongly emphasize emergence over deliberateness, arguing that in reality most new strategies emerge over time and that organizations should facilitate this messy, fragmented, piecemeal strategy formation process. This point of view will be referred to as the 'strategic incrementalism perspective'.

The strategic planning perspective

 Advocates of the strategic planning perspective argue that strategies should be deliberately planned and executed. In their view, anything that emerges unplanned is not really strategy. A successful pattern of action that was not intended cannot be called strategy, but should be seen for what it is – brilliant improvisation or just plain luck (Andrews, 1987). However, managers cannot afford to count on their good fortune or skill at muddling through. They must put time and effort into consciously formulating an explicit plan, making use of all available information and weighing all of the strategic alternatives. Tough decisions need to be made and priorities need to be set, before action is taken. 'Think before you act' is the strategic planning perspective's motto. But once a strategic plan has been adopted, action should be swift, efficient and controlled. Implementation must be secured by detailing the activities to be undertaken, assigning responsibilities to managers and holding them accountable for achieving results (e.g. Ansoff and McDonnell, 1990; Chakravarthy and Lorange, 1991).

Hence, in the strategic planning perspective, strategies are intentionally designed, much as an engineer designs a bridge. Building a bridge requires a long formulation phase, including extensive analysis of the situation, the drawing up of a number of rough designs, evaluation of these alternatives, choice of a preferred design, and further detailing in the form of a blueprint. Only after the design phase has been completed do the construction companies take over and build according to plan. Characteristic of such a planning approach to producing bridges and strategies is that the entire process can be disassembled into a number of distinct steps that need to be carried out in a sequential and orderly way. Only by going through these steps in a conscious and structured manner will the best results be obtained (e.g. Armstrong, 1982; Powell, 1992).

For advocates of the strategic planning perspective, the whole purpose of strategizing is to give organizations direction, instead of letting them drift. Organizations cannot act rationally without intentions – if you do not know where you are going, any behavior is fine, which soon degenerates into 'muddling through' (e.g. Ansoff, 1991; Steiner, 1979). By first setting a goal and then choosing a strategy to get there, organizations can get 'organized'. Managers can select actions that are efficient and effective within the context of the strategy. A structure can be chosen, tasks can be assigned, responsibilities can be divided, budgets can be allotted and targets can be set. Not unimportantly, a control system can be created to measure results in comparison to the plan, so that corrective action can be taken.

Another advantage of the planning approach to strategy formation is that it allows for the *formalization* and *differentiation* of strategy tasks. Because of its highly structured and sequential nature, strategic planning lends itself well to formalization. The steps of the strategic planning approach can be captured in planning systems (e.g. Kukalis, 1991; Lorange and Vancil, 1977), and procedures can be developed to further enhance and organize the strategy formation process. In such strategic planning systems, not all elements of strategy formation need to be carried out by one and the same person, but can be divided among a number of people. The most important division of labor is often between those formulating the plans and those implementing them. In many large companies the managers proposing the plans are also the ones implementing them, but deciding on the plans is passed up to a higher level. Often other tasks are spun off as well, or shared with others, such as diagnosis (strategy department or external consultants), implementation (staff departments) and evaluation (corporate planner and controller). Such task differentiation and specialization, it is argued, can lead to a better use of management talent, much as the division of labor has improved the field of production. At the same, having a formalized system allows for sufficient coordination and mutual adjustment, to ensure that all specialized elements are integrated back into a consistent organization-wide strategy (e.g. Grinyer et al., 1986; Jelinek, 1979).

Last, but not least, an advantage of strategic planning is that it encourages long-term thinking and commitment. 'Muddling through' is short-term oriented, dealing with issues of strategic importance as they come up or as a crisis develops. Strategic planning, on the other hand, directs attention to the future. Managers making strategic plans have to take a more long-term view and are stimulated to prepare for, or even create, the future (Ackoff, 1980). Instead of just focusing on small steps, planning challenges managers to define a desirable future and to work towards it. Instead of wavering and opportunism, strategic planning commits the organization to a course of action and allows for investments to be made at the present that may only pay off in the long run (e.g. Ansoff, 1991; Miller and Cardinal, 1994).

One of the difficulties of strategic planning, advocates of this perspective will readily admit, is that plans will always be based on assumptions about how future events will unfold. Plans require forecasts. And as the Danish physicist Niels Bohr once joked, 'prediction is very difficult, especially about the future'. Even enthusiastic planners acknowledge that forecasts will be inaccurate. As Makridakis, the most prolific writer on the topic of forecasting, writes (1990: 66), 'the future can be predicted only by extrapolating from the past, yet it is fairly certain that the future will be different from the past'. Consequently, it is clear that rigid long-range plans based on such unreliable forecasts would amount to nothing less than Russian roulette. Most proponents of the strategic planning perspective therefore caution for overly deterministic plans. Some argue in favor of 'contingency planning', whereby a number of alternative plans are held in reserve in case key variables in the environment suddenly change. These contingency plans are commonly based on different future 'scenarios' (Van der Heyden, 1996; Wilson, 2000). Others argue that organizations should stage regular reviews, and realign strategic plans to match the altered circumstances. This is usually accomplished by going through the planning cycle every year, and adapting strategic plans to fit with the new forecasts.

The strategic planning perspective shares many of the assumptions underlying the rational reasoning perspective discussed in Chapter 2. Both perspectives value systematic, orderly, consistent, logical reasoning and assume that humans are capable of forming a fairly good understanding of reality. And both are based on a calculative and optimizing view of strategy-making. It is, therefore, not surprising that many managers who are rationally inclined also exhibit a distinct preference for the strategic planning perspective.

EXHIBIT 3.2 THE STRATEGIC PLANNING PERSPECTIVE

SAMSUNG ELECTRONICS: SHOOTING FOR THE STARS

At the end of the 1960s, Byung-Chull Lee was chairman of the Samsung Group, one of the major South Korean *chaebol* – a con-glomerate manufacturing a wide array of products, ranging from clothing to ships. Samsung had worked hard to overcome the devastation of the Korean War (1951–1954), but Lee had even more ambitious plans. He wanted to move beyond traditional low value-added industries, into a more attractive industrial sector – electronics. So, in 1969 he launched Samsung Electronics, initially oriented towards the manufacturing of 'white goods' (home appliances), such as refrigerators, stoves and vacuum cleaners. The founding of Samsung Electronics fitted perfectly in the South Korean government's 'Eight-Year Development Plan for Electronics Industries', which provided the firm with significant government support in R&D, the establishment of new plants and access to cheap loans.

Once Samsung Electronics had established a position in white goods by the start of the 1980s, Lee went to Japan to personally investigate where further growth opportunities could be found. Here he observed how the developments in semiconductors were speedily opening up enormous opportunities for new high-tech products. He became convinced that Samsung should not move cautiously in this area, following Sony and Matsushita, but should try to boldly grab a leadership role for itself – becoming an innovative industry shaper instead of remaining a reactive copycat. But for this to be successful, Samsung could not allow its strategy to slowly emerge, but rather would need to set extremely ambitious long-term goals and commit the organization to a disciplined roadmap to go from being a 'nobody' to becoming 'number one'.

Based on Lee's vision, a business project team for semiconductors was secretly formed in 1982. The team ran a study to find out what the most attractive semiconductor product would be, which resulted in forecasts and strategic options for a range of different electronic components. In 1983, after thorough evaluations, Samsung decided to enter the DRAM (dynamic random access memory) chip industry. A long-term strategic plan was drawn up which would take the company from acquiring relatively simple technologies, to modifying imported technology, to designing new products through reverse engineering, to eventually develop-

ing advanced products. Finally, Samsung would become a 'black-belt master' in product and process innovation. To further refine this broad, long-term strategic plan, Samsung hired a group of US-educated South Korean engineers and sent them with a team of managers to the United States to work on the DRAM business project. Their assignment was to write a more detailed business plan and to recruit more engineers. Once the 'blueprint' was finished and approved by Lee, Samsung started DRAM assembly activities for the US-based Micron Technologies.

Over the next ten years, Samsung followed its strategy largely as planned and by the early 1990s had become the industry leader in DRAMs. Its approach of setting extremely ambitious goals and then developing detailed plans to be implemented with a relentless discipline, also paid off in the subsequent years. During 1997 and 1998 the industry was hit by a dramatic dip in demand and prices for memory chips. But while some competitors became nervous about short-term profitability and 'adapted' themselves to the unfolding circumstances, slashing capital spending and production capacity, Samsung remained committed to its long-term plans and continued to invest and strengthen its memory chip production operations. When the bust cycle turned into boom again, Samsung was one of the few companies with sufficient DRAM manufacturing capacity to reap the benefit.

Since then, Samsung Electronics has gone from strength to strength, building on its DRAM know-how. By 2003, it had become world market leader in TFT-LCD screens, computer monitors, VCRs and microwave ovens, and number two in many more areas. The company employs approximately 55 000 people and generates more than US$23 billion in revenues, accounting for about 18% of South Korea's exports. In 1999 the company was spun off from the Samsung conglomerate, with new ambitious plans, targeting yet other chip-based product categories as areas where it wanted to become number one or two, such as cellular telephones and notebook computers. So far, its strategic planning approach has made huge steps in this direction. Samsung has clearly lived up to its name, meaning 'three stars' in Korean, and written with the characters that translate as 'large, strong and lasting forever'.

Sources: www.samsung.com; *Far Eastern Economic Review,* September 14 2002; Yu, 1999; Haour and Cho, 2000.

The strategic incrementalism perspective

 To advocates of the strategic incrementalism perspective, the planners' faith in deliberateness is misplaced and counter-productive. In reality, incrementalists argue, new strategies largely emerge over time, as managers proactively piece together a viable course of action or reactively adapt to unfolding circumstances. The strategy formation process is not about rigidly *setting* the course of action in advance, but about flexibly *shaping* the course of action by gradually blending together initiatives into a coherent pattern of actions. Making strategy involves sense-making, reflecting, learning, envisioning, experimenting and changing the organization, which cannot be neatly organized and programmed. Strategy formation is messy, fragmented, and piecemeal – much more like the unstructured and unpredictable processes of exploration and invention than like the orderly processes of design and production (e.g. Mintzberg, 1990; Quinn, 1978).

Yet proponents of the strategic planning perspective prefer to press strategy formation into an orderly, mechanistic straightjacket. Strategies must be intentionally designed and executed. According to strategic incrementalists, this excessive emphasis on deliberateness is due to planners' obsession with rationality and control (e.g. Wildavsky, 1979; Mintzberg, 1993). Planners are often compulsive in their desire for order, predictability and efficiency. It is the intention of strategic planning to predict, analyze, optimize and program – to deliberately fine-tune and control the organization's future behavior. For them, 'to manage' is 'to control' and therefore only deliberate patterns of action constitute good strategic management.

Incrementalists do not question the value of planning and control as a means for managing some organizational processes, but point out that strategy formation is not one of them. In general, planning and control are valuable for routine activities that need to be efficiently organized (e.g. production or finance). But planning is less suitable for non-routine activities – that is, for doing new things. Planning is not appropriate for innovation (e.g. Hamel, 1996; Kanter, 2002). Just as R&D departments cannot plan the invention of new products, managers cannot plan the development of new strategies. Innovation, whether in products or strategies, is not a process that can be neatly structured and controlled. Novel insights and creative ideas cannot be generated on demand, but surface at unexpected moments, often in unexpected places. Nor are new ideas born full-grown, ready to be evaluated and implemented. In reality, innovation requires brooding, tinkering, experimentation, testing and patience, as new ideas grow and take shape. Throughout the innovation process it remains unclear which ideas might evolve into blockbuster strategies and which will turn out to be miserable disappointments. No one can objectively determine ahead of time which strategic initiatives will 'fly' and which will 'crash'. Therefore, managers engaged in the formation of new strategies must move incrementally, letting novel ideas crystallize over time, and increasing commitment as ideas gradually prove their viability in practice. This demands that managers behave not as planners, but as 'inventors' – searching, experimenting, learning, doubting, and avoiding premature closure and lock-in to one course of action (e.g. Stacey, 1993a; Beinhocker, 1999).

Recognizing that strategy formation is essentially an innovation process has more consequences. Innovation is inherently subversive, rebeling against the status quo and challenging those who are emotionally, intellectually or politically wedded to the current state of affairs. Creating new strategies involves confronting people's cognitive maps, questioning the organizational culture, threatening individuals' current interests and disrupting the distribution of power within the organization (e.g. Hamel, 1996; Johnson, 1988). None of these processes can be conducted in an orderly fashion, let alone be incorporated into a planning system. Changing people's cognitive maps requires complex processes of unlearning and learning. Cultural and political changes are also difficult processes to program. Even for the most powerful CEO, managing cognitive, cultural and political changes is not a matter of deliberate control, but of incremental shaping. Less powerful managers will have an even weaker grip on the unfolding cognitive, cultural and political reality in their organization, and therefore will be even less able to plan. In short, managers who understand that strategy formation is essentially a disruptive process of organizational change will move incrementally, gradually molding the organization into a satisfactory form. This demands that managers behave not as commanders, but as 'organizational developers' – questioning assumptions, challenging ideas, getting points on the strategic agenda, encouraging learning, championing new initiatives, supporting change and building political support.

Incrementalists point out that planning is particularly inappropriate when dealing with wicked problems. While solving tame problems can often be planned and controlled, strategizing managers rarely have the luxury of using generic solutions to fix clearly recognizable strategic problems. Strategic problems are inherently wicked – they are essentially unique, highly complex, linked to other problems, can be defined and interpreted in many ways, have no correct answer, nor a delimited set of possible solutions. The planning approach of recognizing the problem, fully analyzing the situation, formulating a comprehensive plan and then implementing the solution, is sure to choke on a wicked problem. A number of weaknesses of planning show up when confronted with a wicked problem:

- Problems cannot be simply recognized and analyzed, but can be interpreted and defined in many ways, depending on how the manager looks at it. Therefore, half the work of the strategizing manager is *making sense* out of complex problems. Or, as Rittel and Webber (1973) put it, the definition of a wicked problem is the problem! Managers must search for new ways for understanding old problems and must be aware of how others are reinterpreting what they see (e.g. Liedtka, 2000; Smircich and Stubbart, 1985). This inhibits strategic planning and encourages strategic incrementalism.

- A full analysis of a wicked problem is impossible. Due to a wicked problem's complexity and links to other problems, a full analysis would take, literally, forever. And there would always be more ways of interpreting the problem, requiring more analysis. Strategic planning based on the complete understanding of a problem in advance therefore necessarily leads to paralysis by analysis (e.g. Langley, 1995; Lenz and Lyles, 1985). In reality, however, managers move proactively despite their incomplete understanding of a wicked problem, learning as they go along. By acting and thinking at the same time, strategizing managers can focus their analyses on what seems to be important and realistic in practice, gradually shaping their understanding along the way.

■ Developing a comprehensive plan to tackle a wicked problem is asking for trouble. Wicked problems are very complex, consisting of many sub-problems. Formulating a master plan to solve all sub-problems in one blow would require a very high level of planning sophistication and an organization with the ability to implement plans in a highly coordinated manner – much like the circus performers who can keep ten plates twirling at the ends of poles at the same time. Such organizations are rare at best, and the risk of a grand strategy failing is huge – once one plate falls, the rest usually come crashing down. This is also known as Knagg's law: the more complex a plan, the larger the chance of failure. Incrementalists therefore argue that it is wiser to tackle sub-problems individually, and gradually blend these solutions into a cohesive pattern of action.

■ Planners who believe that formulation and implementation can be separated underestimate the extent to which wicked problems are interactive. As soon as an organization starts to implement a plan, its actions will induce counteractions. Customers will react, competitors will change behavior, suppliers will take a different stance, regulatory agencies might come into action, unions will respond, the stock markets will take notice and company employees will draw conclusions. Hence, action by the organization will change the nature of the problem. And since the many counterparties are intelligent players, capable of acting strategically, their responses will not be entirely predictable. Planners will not be able to forecast and incorporate other parties' reactions into the plans. Therefore, plans will be outdated as soon as implementation starts. For this reason, incrementalists argue that action must always be swiftly followed by redefinition of the problem and reconsideration of the course of action being pursued. Over time, this iterative process of action–reaction–reconsideration will lead to the emergence of a pattern of action, which is the best possible result given the interactive nature of wicked problems.

■ This last point, on the unpredictability of external and internal reactions to a plan, leads up to a weakness of strategic planning that is possibly its most obvious one – strategy has to do with the future and the future is inherently *unknown*. Developments cannot be clearly forecast, future opportunities and threats cannot be predicted, nor can future strengths and weaknesses be accurately foreseen. In such unknown terrain, it is foolhardy to commit oneself to a preset course of action unless absolutely necessary. It makes much more sense in new and unpredictable circumstances to remain flexible and adaptive, postponing fixed commitments for as long as possible. An unknown future requires not the mentality of a train conductor, but of an explorer – curious, probing, venturesome and entrepreneurial, yet moving cautiously, step-by-step, ready to shift course when needed.

To proponents of the strategic incrementalism perspective, it is a caricature to call such behavior ad hoc or muddling through. Rather, it is behavior that acknowledges the fact that strategy formation is a process of innovation and organizational development in the face of wicked problems in an unknown future. Under these circumstances, strategies must be allowed to emerge and 'strategic planning' must be seen for what it is – a contradiction in terms.

EXHIBIT 3.3 THE STRATEGIC INCREMENTALISM PERSPECTIVE

YOSHINOYA: ONE STORE AT A TIME

Yoshinoya's first east coast outlet opened on Times Square in 2002. Yoshinoya is Japan's answer to McDonald's – fast food Japanese-style. With its 845 outlets across Japan and 171 outlets overseas, mainly in the United States, Yoshinoya may not be as big as McDonald's yet, but its growth is phenomenal and its profitability enough to make Ronald McDonald jealous. In 2001 the company recorded a ¥16.7 billion pre-tax profit. And Yoshinoya still has enormous ambitions. Shuji Abe, president of Yoshinoya, has indicated that he believes that it should be possible to grow to 1200 outlets in Japan and 1000 restaurants abroad by 2006. But, Abe emphasizes, this growth must be realized 'one store at a time' and not on the basis of some pre-set strategic plan.

Yoshinoya was founded in Tokyo in 1899 and became the first fast-food chain in Japan in the 1960s, serving only *gyudon* – a bowl of rice topped with thin-sliced braised beef. The company's slogan has been 'fast, delicious and cheap', and its positioning has been one of stressing the importance of the customer, personal service and quality. But instead of standardizing the fast-food formula and then rolling it out across Japan, Yoshinoya's philosophy has been to avoid a 'cookie-cutter' approach and a rigid expansion blueprint. In Abe's view, such a 'copy-paste' program of expansion would be dangerous, and would make insufficient use of the company's ability to learn, improve and adapt along the way. In the Japanese food service industry, with its many local characteristics and unfolding rules of the game, much still remains to be discovered en route. Hence, Yoshinoya considers ongoing experimentation and innovation crucial, making extensive use of pilot projects, which are flexibly and rapidly exploited whenever they prove viable. The company has also established a corporate university, Yoshinoya College, partially to secure high operational standards via training, but as a platform for bottom-up innovation and continuous improvement as well. The company slogan of 'one store at a time' is a reflection of Yoshinoya's dedication to grow organically and in a sure-footed manner, building on its emerging insights into where the fast-food business is headed and can be shaped.

Yoshinoya's approach of strategic incrementalism has also worked well for its expansion abroad. Again, Yoshinoya sees internationalization as an ongoing learning process, requiring a pioneering mentality, instead of that of a conqueror, imposing itself on its environment. Yoshinoya gained its first foothold in the US market in Los Angeles in 1979 and gradually expanded towards 96 outlets in California. Along the way, Yoshinoya gradually reshaped its formula to fit the US market circumstances better. For instance, it deviated from the franchise method used in Japan, finding out that fully owned restaurants worked better. Management systems were changed and the company found out what type of local items to add to its menu. Given its success in California, in 2002 Yoshinoya decided that it was time to look for opportunities in the rest of the United States, starting along the east coast.

What Yoshinoya will look like in the coming years might not be entirely certain, but the company has at least determined one clear long-term intention: 'We are reshaping the fast-food experience.' It might be time for the competition to consider a McRice-Bowl as a response.

Sources: *Nation's Restaurant News*, November 8 2002; *The Nikkei Weekly*, November 13 2000; *Financial Times*, December 21 1992; www.yoshinoyausa.com; www.yoshinoya.com/eng.

TOWARDS A SYNTHESIS

Those who triumph compute at their headquarters a great number of factors prior to a challenge. Little computation brings defeat. How much more so with no computation at all!

Sun Tzu (5th century BC);
Chinese military strategist

It is a mistake to look too far ahead. Only one link of the chain of destiny can be handled at a time.

Winston Churchill (1874–1965);
British prime minister and writer

So, how should strategies be formed in practice? Should managers strive to formulate and implement strategic plans, supported by a formalized planning and control system? Or should managers move incrementally, behaving as inventors, organizational developers and explorers? As no consensus has yet developed within the field of strategic management on how to balance deliberateness and emergence, it is up to each individual to assess the arguments put forward in the ongoing debate and to form their own opinion.

In Table 3.1 the main arguments of the two opposite poles in this debate have been summarized. From this overview it is quite clear that the thesis and antithesis are 'worlds apart'. The challenge for managers is now to see whether they can create a synthesis combining the 'best of both worlds'. Can the advantages of strategic planning be 'fused' with those of strategic incrementalism? As with fusion in other areas of life – such as in cooking, music and physics – bringing together the two sides into a new whole often requires ingenuity and large amounts of energy, but when it works the results can be enormously rewarding.

TABLE 3.1 Strategic planning versus strategic incrementalism perspective

	Strategic planning perspective	Strategic incrementalism perspective
Emphasis on	Deliberateness over emergence	Emergence over deliberateness
Nature of strategy	Intentionally designed	Gradually shaped
Nature of formation	Figuring out	Finding out
View of future	Forecast and anticipate	Partially unknown and unpredictable
Posture towards the future	Make commitments, prepare	Postpone commitments, remain flexible
Formation process	Formally structured and comprehensive	Unstructured and fragmented
Formation process steps	First think, then act	Thinking and acting intertwined
Decision-making	Hierarchical	Dispersed
Decision-making focus	Optimal resource allocation and coordination	Experimentation and parallel initiatives
Implementation focused on	Programming (organizational efficiency)	Learning (organizational development)
Strategic change	Implemented top-down	Requires broad cultural and cognitive shifts

FURTHER READING

What we anticipate seldom occurs; what we least expect generally happens.
Benjamin Disraeli (1804–1881); British prime minister and novelist

For readers interested in an overview of the strategy formation literature, the best place to start is with *Strategy Safari: A Guided Tour Through the Wilds of Strategic Management*, by Henry Mintzberg, B. Ahlstrand and Joseph Lampel. Two other interesting overviews are 'How Strategies Develop in Organizations', by Andy Bailey and Gerry Johnson, and 'An Integrative Framework for Strategy-Making Processes', by Stuart Hart.

There are many books that give a detailed rendition of how strategic planning should be conducted within organizations. Igor Ansoff's and E. McDonnell's well-known textbook, *Implanting Strategic Management*, is an excellent, yet taxing, description of strategy-making from a planning perspective, while George Steiner's *Strategic Planning: What Every Manager Must Know* is a more down to earth prescription. Between these two extremes is a whole range of widely sold planning-oriented textbooks, such as Arthur Thompson and A.J. Strickland's *Strategic Management: Concepts and Cases*, and Thomas Wheelen and David Hunger's *Strategic Management and Business Policy*. For further reading on formal planning systems, Balaji Chakravarthy and Peter Lorange's book *Managing the Strategy Process: A Framework for a Multibusiness Firm* is a good place to start. On the link between planning and forecasting, the book *Forecasting, Planning and Strategy for the 21st Century*, by Spiro Makridakis, provides a useful introduction. A good book on scenarios is by Kees van der Heyden, entitled *Scenarios: The Art of Strategic Conversation*.

The most articulate critic of planning is probably Henry Mintzberg, whose book *The Rise and Fall of Strategic Planning* makes for thought-provoking reading. David Hurst's article 'Why Strategic Management is Bankrupt' also provides many interesting arguments against strategic planning. For a more extensive description of the strategic incrementalism perspective, James Brian Quinn's book *Strategies for Change* is still a good starting point. The fascinating book *Competing on the Edge: Strategy as Structured Chaos*, by Shona Brown and Kathleen Eisenhardt, also incorporates incrementalist approaches, as does Ralph Stacey's excellent textbook *Strategic Management and Organizational Dynamics*. Also highly recommended are Ikujiro Nonaka's article 'Toward Middle-Up-Down Management: Accelerating Information Creation' and Robert Burgelman's article 'Corporate Entrepreneurship and Strategic Management: Insights from a Process Study'.

For a better understanding of the political processes involved in strategy formation the reader might want to turn to Andrew Pettigrew's article 'Strategy Formulation as a Political Process', or to Jeffrey Pfeffer's book *Power in Organizations*. Graham Allison's classic book *The Essence of Decision: Explaining the Cuban Missile Crisis* is also highly recommended. The cultural processes are vividly described in Gerry Johnson's *Strategic Change and the Management Process*, and more popularly in Rosabeth Moss Kanter's *The Change Masters*. Further articles and books that explore the link between strategy formation and strategic change are presented at the end of Chapter 4.

STRATEGIC CHANGE

There is nothing more difficult to take in hand, more perilous to conduct, or more uncertain in its success, than to take the lead in the introduction of a new order of things. Because the innovator has for enemies all those who have done well under the old conditions, and lukewarm defenders in those who may do well under the new.

Niccolo Machiavelli (1469–1527); Florentine statesman and political philosopher

INTRODUCTION

In a world of new technologies, transforming economies, shifting demographics, reforming governments, fluctuating consumer preferences and dynamic competition, it is not a question of whether firms *should* change, but of where, how and in what direction they *must* change. For 'living' organizations, change is a given. Firms must constantly be aligned with their environments, either by reacting to external events, or by proactively shaping the businesses in which they operate.

While change is pervasive, not all change in firms is strategic in nature. Much of the change witnessed is actually the ongoing operational kind. To remain efficient and effective, firms constantly make 'fine-tuning' alterations, whereby existing procedures are upgraded, activities are improved and people are reassigned. Such operational changes are directed at increasing the performance of the firm within the confines of the existing system – within the current basic set-up used to align the firm with the environment. Strategic changes, on the contrary, are directed at creating a new type of alignment – a new fit between the basic set-up of the firm and the characteristics of the environment. Strategic changes have an impact on the way the firm does business (its 'business system') and on the way the organization has been configured (its 'organizational system'). In short, while operational changes are necessary to maintain the business and organizational systems, strategic changes are directed at renewing them.

For managers the challenge is to implement strategic changes on time, to keep the firm in step with the shifting opportunities and threats in the environment. Some parts of the firm's business system and organizational system can be preserved, while others need to be transformed for the firm to stay up-to-date and competitive. This process of constantly enacting strategic changes to remain in harmony with external conditions is called 'strategic renewal'. This chapter examines the issue of the series of strategic change steps required in order to bring about a process of ongoing strategic renewal.

THE ISSUE OF STRATEGIC RENEWAL

There are many actions that constitute a strategic change – a reorganization, a diversification move, a shift in core technology, a business process redesign and a product portfolio reshuffle, to name a few. Each one of these changes is fascinating in itself. Yet, here the discussion will be broader than just a single strategic change, looking instead at the process of how a series of strategic changes can be used to keep the firm in sync with its surroundings (see Figure 4.1). How can 'a path of strategic changes' be followed to constantly renew the firm and avoid a situation whereby the firm 'drifts' too far away from the demands of the environment (Johnson, 1988).

To come to a deeper understanding of the issue of strategic renewal, the first step that must be taken is to examine what is actually being renewed during a process of strategic renewal. The areas of strategic renewal will be explored in the next section. After this initial analysis of 'what' is being changed, a distinction will be made between the magnitude and the pace of change. The magnitude of change refers to the size of the steps being undertaken, whereby the question is whether managers should move in bold and dramatic strides, or in moderate and undramatic ones. The pace of change refers to the relative speed at which the steps are being taken, whereby the question is whether managers should move quickly in a short period of time, or more gradually over a longer time span.

Areas of strategic renewal

Firms are complex systems, consisting of many different elements, each of which can be changed. Therefore, to gain more insight into the various areas of potential change, firms need to be analytically disassembled into a number of component parts. The most fundamental distinction that can be made within a firm, is between the business system and the organizational system:

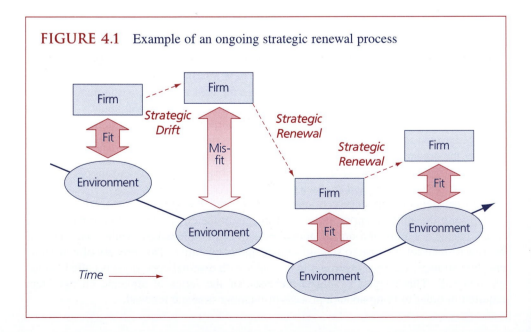

FIGURE 4.1   Example of an ongoing strategic renewal process

- **Business system.** The term business system refers to the way a firm conducts its business. A simple definition would be 'how a firm makes money'. A more formal definition of business system is 'the specific configuration of resources, value-adding activities and product/service offerings directed at creating value for customers'. Each firm has its own specific system for taking certain resources as inputs (e.g. materials and know-how), adding value to them in some type of manner (e.g. production and branding) and then selling a particular package of products and/or services as output. As such, a firm's business system (or 'value creation system') is particular to the type of business that the firm is in – an airplane manufacturer conducts its business differently to an airline.

- **Organizational system.** The term organizational system refers to the way a firm gets its people to work together to carry out the business. A simple definition would be 'how a firm is organized'. A more formal definition of the organizational system would be 'how the individuals populating a firm have been configured, and relate to one another, with the intention of facilitating the business system'. Every firm needs to determine some type of organizational structure, dividing the tasks and responsibilities among the organizational members, thereby instituting differing functions and units. Firms also require numerous organizational processes to link individual members to each other, to ensure that their separate tasks are coordinated into an integrated whole. And firms necessarily have organizational cultures, and sub-cultures, as organizational members interact with one another and build up joint beliefs, values and norms.

In Figure 4.2 the relationship between the business system and the major components of the organizational system is depicted. As this figure illustrates, the business system is 'supported' by the organizational system, with the organizational members 'at its base'. While each firm's business and organizational systems are essentially unique, their general configuration can be fairly similar to that of other firms. Where firms have a comparable business 'formula', it is said that they share the same business model. Likewise, where firms have a similar organizational 'form', they are said to subscribe to the same organizational model.

FIGURE 4.2   General view of the business system and the organizational system

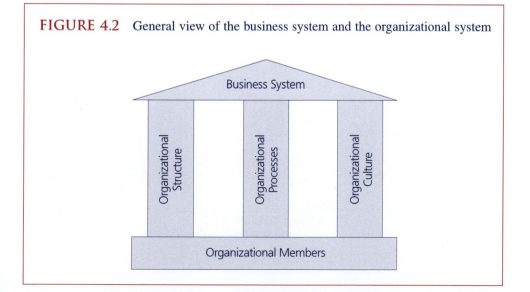

Both the business system and the organizational system can be further disaggregated into component parts and examined in more detail. With this aim in mind, the business system will be at the center of attention in Chapter 5. Here the organizational system will be further dissected. Actually, the term dissection conjures up images of the organizational system as 'corporate body', which is a useful metaphor for distinguishing the various components of an organizational system (Morgan, 1986). Following Bartlett and Ghoshal (1995) the organizational system can be divided into its anatomy (structure), physiology (processes) and psychology (culture). Each of these components, summarized in Figure 4.3, will be examined in the following sub-section.

Organizational structure.   Organizational structure refers to the clustering of tasks and people into smaller groups. All organizations need at least some division of labor in order to function efficiently and effectively, requiring them to structure the organization into smaller parts. The main question when determining the organizational structure is which criteria will be used to differentiate tasks and to cluster people into particular units. While there are numerous structuring (or decomposition) criteria, the most common ones are summarized in Figure 4.4. In a simple organization tasks might be divided according to just one criterion, but in most organizations multiple criteria are used (either sequentially or simultaneously).

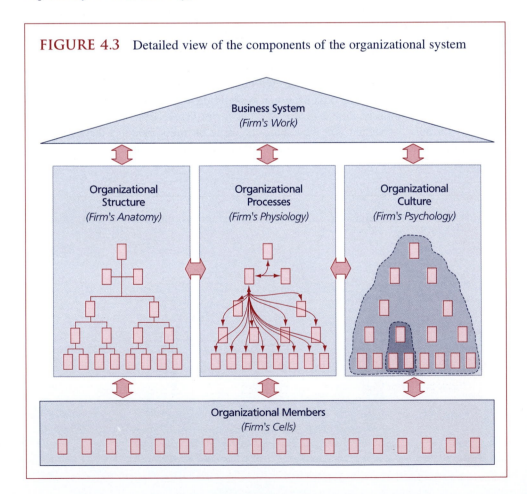

FIGURE 4.3   Detailed view of the components of the organizational system

Business System
(Firm's Work)

Organizational
Structure
(Firm's Anatomy)

Organizational
Processes
(Firm's Physiology)

Organizational
Culture
(Firm's Psychology)

Organizational Members
(Firm's Cells)

To balance this horizontal differentiation of tasks and responsibilities, all organizations also have integration mechanisms, intended to get the parts to function well within the organizational whole (Lawrence and Lorsch, 1967). While some of these integration mechanisms are found in the categories of organizational processes and culture, the most fundamental mechanism is usually built into the organizational structure – formal authority. In organizations, managers are appointed with the specific task of supervising the activities of various people or units and to report to managers higher up in the hierarchy. Depending on the span of control of each manager (the number of people or units reporting to him/her) an organizational structure will consist of one or more layers of management. At the apex of this vertical structure is the board of directors, with the ultimate authority to make decisions or ratify decisions made at lower levels in the hierarchy. The most important questions in this context are the number of management layers needed and the amount of authority delegated to lower levels of management. It should be noted that the organizational charts used to

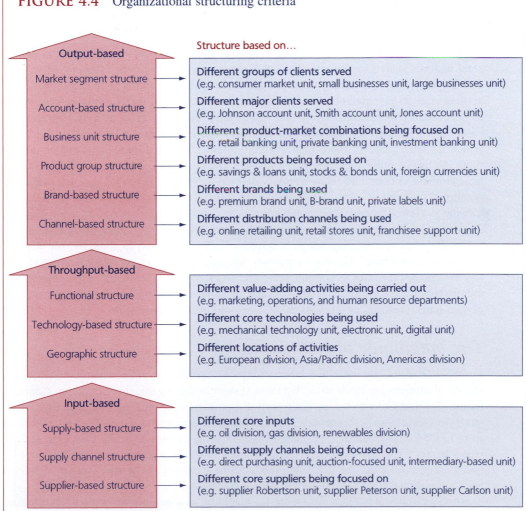

FIGURE 4.4   Organizational structuring criteria

Structure based on…

Output-based

Market segment structure → Different groups of clients served
(e.g. consumer market unit, small businesses unit, large businesses unit)

Account-based structure → Different major clients served
(e.g. Johnson account unit, Smith account unit, Jones account unit)

Business unit structure → Different product-market combinations being focused on
(e.g. retail banking unit, private banking unit, investment banking unit)

Product group structure → Different products being focused on
(e.g. savings & loans unit, stocks &. bonds unit, foreign currencies unit)

Brand-based structure → Different brands being used
(e.g. premium brand unit, B-brand unit, private labels unit)

Channel-based structure → Different distribution channels being used
(e.g. online retailing unit, retail stores unit, franchisee support unit)

Throughput-based

Functional structure → Different value-adding activities being carried out
(e.g. marketing, operations, and human resource departments)

Technology-based structure → Different core technologies being used
(e.g. mechanical technology unit, electronic unit, digital unit)

Geographic structure → Different locations of activities
(e.g. European division, Asia/Pacific division, Americas division)

Input-based

Supply-based structure → Different core inputs
(e.g. oil division, gas division, renewables division)

Supply channel structure → Different supply channels being focused on
(e.g. direct purchasing unit, auction-focused unit, intermediary-based unit)

Supplier-based structure → Different core suppliers being focused on
(e.g. supplier Robertson unit, supplier Peterson unit, supplier Carlson unit)

represent the formal structure of an organization (see Figure 4.3) need not be an accurate reflection of the informal organizational structure as it operates in reality.

Organizational processes.   Organizational processes refer to the arrangements, procedures and routines used to control and coordinate the various people and units within the organization. Some formalized processes span the entire organization, such as business planning and control procedures, and financial budgeting and reporting processes. Other control and coordination processes have a more limited scope, such as new product development meetings, yearly sales conferences, weekly quality circles, web-based expert panels and quarterly meetings with the board of directors. But not all organizational processes are institutionalized as ongoing integration mechanisms. Often, integration across units and departments is needed for a short period, making it useful to employ task forces, committees, working groups, project teams and even joint lunches as means for ensuring coordination.

While all of these processes are formalized to a certain degree, many more informal organizational processes exist, such as communicating via hallway gossip, building support through personal networking, influencing decision-making through informal negotiations and solving conflicts by means of impromptu meetings.

Organizational culture.   Organizational culture refers to the worldview and behavioral patterns shared by the members of the same organization (e.g. Schein, 1985; Trice and Beyer, 1993). As people within a group interact and share experiences with one another over an extended period of time, they construct a joint understanding of the world around them. This shared belief system will be emotionally charged, as it encompasses the values and norms of the organizational members and offers them an interpretive filter with which to make sense of the constant stream of uncertain and ambiguous events around them. As this common ideology grows stronger and becomes more engrained, it will channel members' actions into more narrowly defined patterns of behavior. As such, the organizational culture can strongly influence everything, from how to behave during meetings to what is viewed as ethical behavior.

As part of the organizational system, culture can act as a strong integration mechanism, controlling and coordinating people's behavior, by getting them to abide by 'the way we do things around here'. Having a common 'language', frame of reference and set of values also makes it easier to communicate and work together. However, an organizational culture is not always homogeneous – in fact, strongly divergent sub-cultures might arise in certain units, creating 'psychological' barriers within the organization.

The magnitude of change

Strategic change is by definition far-reaching. We speak of strategic change when fundamental alterations are made to the business system or the organizational system. Adding a lemon-flavored Coke to the product portfolio is interesting, maybe important, but not a strategic change, while branching out into bottled water was – it was a major departure from Coca-Cola's traditional business system. Hiring a new CEO, like Ben Vree at Smit (see Chapter 2), is also important, but is in itself not a strategic change, while his consequent reorganization of the firm into global business units was – it was a major shift from Smit's traditional regionalized organizational system.

Strategic renewal is often even more far-reaching, as a number of strategic changes are executed in a variety of areas to keep the firm aligned with market demands. But while the result of all of these strategic changes is far-reaching, this says nothing about the size of the steps along the way. The strategic renewal process might consist of a few large change steps or numerous small ones. This distinction is illustrated in Figure 4.5. The total amount of strategic change envisaged is measured along the Y-axis. Route A shows the change path taken by a firm that has implemented all changes in two big steps, while Route B shows the change path followed by a firm taking numerous smaller steps. Both organizations have completed the same renewal, but via distinctly different routes.

The size of the change steps is referred to as the magnitude of change. This issue of change magnitude can be divided into two component parts:

- Scope of change. The scope of change in a firm can vary from broad to narrow. Change is broad when many aspects and parts of the firm are altered at the same time. In the most extreme case the changes might be comprehensive, whereby the business system is entirely revised, and the organizational structure, processes, culture and people are changed in unison. However, change can also be much more narrowly focused on a specific organizational aspect (e.g. new product development processes) or department (e.g. marketing). If many changes are narrowly targeted, the total result will be a more piecemeal change process.

- Amplitude of organizational changes. The amplitude of change in firms can vary from high to low. The amplitude of change is high when the new business system, organizational culture, structure, processes or people are a radical departure from the previous situation. The amplitude of change is low when the step proposed is a moderate adjustment to the previous circumstances.

Where a change is comprehensive and radical, the magnitude of the change step is large. In Figure 4.5 this is represented as a large jump along the Y-axis. Where a change is narrow and moderate, the magnitude of the step is small. However, the above distinction also clarifies that there are two rather different types of medium-sized change steps – a focused radical change (narrow scope, high amplitude) and a comprehensive moderate change (broad scope, low amplitude). Both changes are 'mid-sized', yet significantly different to manage in practice.

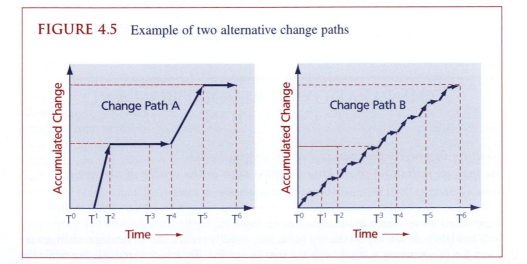

FIGURE 4.5 Example of two alternative change paths

The pace of change

Strategic renewal takes time. Yet, there is a variety of ways by which the strategic renewal process can take place over time. Strategic change measures can be evenly spread out over an extended period, allowing the organization to follow a relatively steady pace of strategic renewal. However, it is also possible to cluster all changes into a few short irregular bursts, giving the renewal process an unsteady, stop-and-go pace.

This distinction is seen in Figure 4.5 as well. The total time period needed for achieving a strategic change is measured along the X-axis. Route A shows the change path taken by a firm that has had an unsteady pace of change, while Route B tracks the path taken by a firm on a more steady change trajectory. Both organizations have completed the same strategic renewal process by T^3 and by T^6, but have distributed their change activities differently during the period.

In Figure 4.5 it can also be seen that the pace of organizational changes can be decomposed into two related parts:

- Timing of change. First, the pace of change depends on the moment at which changes are initiated. The timing of change can vary from intermittent to constant. Where change is intermittent, it is important for a firm to determine the right moment for launching a new initiative (for example, T^1 and T^4 in change path A). The need to 'wait for the right timing' is often a reason for spreading change activities unevenly over time. On the other hand, change can be constant, so that the exact moment for kicking off any new set of measures is less important, as long as there is no peak at any one moment in time (see change path B).

- Speed of change. The pace of change also depends on the time span within which changes take place. The speed of change can vary from high to low. Where a major change needs to be implemented within a short period of time, the speed of change must be high. A short burst of fast action can bring about the intended changes. In Figure 4.5, the speed can be seen by the slope of the arrow (in change path A, the speed between T^1 and T^2 is higher than between T^4 and T^5). On the other hand, where the change measures are less formidable and the time span for implementation is longer, the speed of change can be lower.

The variables of timing and speed of change, together with the variables of scope and amplitude of change, create a wide range of possible strategic renewal paths. Firms have many different ways of bringing about strategic change. Unavoidably, this raises the question of which route is best. Why should a firm choose one trajectory over another?

THE PARADOX OF REVOLUTION AND EVOLUTION

Nothing in progression can rest on its original plan.
We may as well think of rocking a grown man in the cradle of an infant.
Edmund Burke (1729–1797); Irish-born politician and man of letters

In selecting an approach to strategic change, most managers struggle with the question of how bold they should be. On the one hand, they usually realize that to fundamentally transform the organization a break with the past is needed. To achieve strategic renewal it is essential to turn away from the firm's heritage and to start with a clean slate. On the other hand, they also recognize the value of continuity, building on past experiences, investments and loyalties. To achieve lasting strategic renewal people in the organization will need time to learn, adapt and grow into a new organizational reality.

This distinction between disruptive change and gradual change has long been recognized in the strategic management and organizational behavior literature (e.g. Greiner, 1972; Tushman, Newman and Romanelli, 1986). Disruptive change is variably referred to as 'frame-breaking' (e.g. Baden-Fuller and Stopford, 1992; Grinyer, Mayes and McKiernan, 1987), 'radical' (e.g. Stinchcombe, 1965; Greenwood and Hinings, 1996) and 'revolutionary' (e.g. Gersick, 1991; Tushman and O'Reilly, 1996). Gradual change is variably referred to as 'incremental' (e.g. Quinn, 1980a; Johnson, 1987) and 'evolutionary' (e.g. Nelson and Winter, 1982; Tushman and O'Reilly, 1996). Here the labels revolutionary and evolutionary change will be used, in keeping with the terminology used by Greiner (1972) in his classic work.

It is widely accepted among researchers that firms need to balance revolutionary and evolutionary change processes. However, most authors see this as a balancing of strategic (revolutionary) change and operational (evolutionary) change. As strategic change is far-reaching, it is often automatically equated with radical means, while gradual means are reserved for smaller-scale operational changes. Yet, in the previous section it was made clear that a radical result (a strategic change) can be pursued by both revolutionary and evolutionary means (e.g. Hayes, 1985; Krüger, 1996; Nonaka, 1988b; Strebel, 1994).

While these two change processes are each other's opposites, and they seem to be at least partially contradictory, both approaches are needed within firms. In practice both change processes have valuable, but conflicting, qualities. The tension that this creates between revolution and evolution will be explored in the following sections.

The demand for revolutionary change processes

Revolution is a process whereby an abrupt and radical change takes place within a short period of time. Revolutionary change processes are those that do not build on the status quo, but overthrow it. 'Revolutionaries' revolt against the existing business system and organizational system, and attempt to push through changes that will reinvent the firm. Thus, revolution leads to a clear break with the past – a discontinuity in the firm's development path.

Such a 'big bang' approach to strategic change is generally needed when organizational rigidity is so deeply rooted that smaller pushes do not bring the firm into movement. If the firm threatens to become paralyzed by these inherited rigidities in the business system and organizational system, the only way to get moving can be to radically break with the past. Typical sources of organizational rigidity include:

- Psychological resistance to change. Many people resist change, because of the uncertainty and ambiguity that unavoidably accompanies any shift in the old way of doing business (e.g. Argyris, 1990; Pondy, Boland and Thomas, 1988). As people become accustomed to fixed organizational routines and established habits, their ability to learn and gradually adapt invariably recedes. New business methods or job descriptions are not seen as a challenging opportunity to learn, but as an unwelcome interference in the existing system. It can be necessary to break through this psychological resistance to change by imposing a new business system and/or organizational system on people (e.g. Hammer, 1990; Powell, 1991).

■ **Cultural resistance to change.** As discussed in Chapter 2, people can easily become immune to signals that their cognitive maps are outdated, especially if they are surrounded by others with the same flawed belief system. Once an organizational culture develops that perpetuates a number of obsolete assumptions about the market or the organization, it is very difficult for organizational members to challenge and gradually reshape the organizational belief system. It can be necessary to break through this cultural resistance to change by exposing the organization to a shocking crisis or by imposing a new organizational system (e.g. Tushman, Newman and Romanelli, 1986; Senge, 1990a).

■ **Political resistance to change.** Change is hardly ever to everyone's advantage, as Machiavelli pointed out at the start of this chapter. Each organizational change leads to a different constellation of winners and losers. Generally, the potential losers reject a strategic change, although they are likely to think of some seemingly objective reasons for their opposition. Even a situation in which a person or department thinks that it might run the risk of losing power to others can be enough to block a change. Since strategic changes invariably have a significant impact on all people within an organization, there will always be a number of open, and hidden, opponents. It can be necessary to break through this political resistance by imposing a new business system and reshuffling management positions (e.g. Allison, 1969; Krüger, 1996).

■ **Investment lock-in.** Once a firm has committed a large amount of money and time to a certain product portfolio, activity system or technology, it will find that this fixed investment locks the organization in. Any gradual movement away from the past investment will increase the risk of not earning back the sunk cost. Therefore, it can be necessary to break through the lock-in by radically restructuring or disposing of the investment (e.g. Ghemawat, 1991; Bower and Christensen, 1995).

■ **Competence lock-in.** The better a firm becomes at something, the more a firm becomes focused on becoming even better still – which is also known as the virtuous circle of competence-building. Once a competitive advantage has been built on a particular type of competence, the natural tendency of firms is to favor external opportunities based on these competences. New people are hired that fit with the corporate competence profile and R&D spending further hones the firm's skill. But if the firm's competence base threatens to become outdated due to market or technological changes, its former advantage could become its downfall – the firm could become caught in a vicious 'competence trap', unable to gradually shift the organization to an alternative set of competences, because the entire business system and organizational system have been aligned to the old set (e.g. Leonard-Barton, 1995; Teece, Pisano and Shuen, 1997). Changing the core competence of the corporation in a comprehensive and radical manner can be the only way to 'migrate' from one competence profile to another.

■ **System lock-in.** Firms can also become locked into an open standard (e.g. sizes in inches, GAAP accounting rules) or a proprietary system (e.g. Windows operating system, SAP enterprise resource planning software). Once the firm has implemented a standard or system, switching to another platform cannot be done gradually or at low cost. Therefore, the lock-in can usually only be overcome by a big bang transition to another platform (e.g. Arthur, 1996; Shapiro and Varian, 1998).

■ **Stakeholder lock-in.** Highly restrictive commitments can also be made towards the firm's stakeholders. Long-term contracts with buyers and suppliers, warranties, commitments to governments and local communities and promises to shareholders can all lock firms into a certain strategic direction. To break through the stakeholders' resistance to change it can be necessary to court a crisis and aim for a radical restructuring of the firm's external relationships (e.g. Freeman, 1984; Oliver, 1991).

Besides the use of revolutionary change to overcome organizational rigidity, such a radical approach to strategic renewal is often also necessary given the short time span available for a large change. The 'window of opportunity' for achieving a strategic change can be small for a number of reasons. Some of the most common triggers for revolutionary strategic change are:

- Competitive pressure. When a firm is under intense competitive pressure and its market position starts to erode quickly, a rapid and dramatic response might be the only approach possible. Especially when the organization threatens to slip into a downward spiral towards insolvency, a bold turnaround can be the only option left to the firm.

- Regulatory pressure. Firms can also be put under pressure by the government or regulatory agencies to push through major changes within a short period of time. Such externally imposed revolutions can be witnessed among public sector organizations (e.g. hospitals and schools) and highly regulated industries (e.g. utilities and telecommunications), but in other sectors of the economy as well (e.g. antitrust break-ups, public health regulations).

- First mover advantage. A more proactive reason for instigating revolutionary change, is to be the first firm to introduce a new product, service or technology and to build up barriers to entry for late movers. Especially for know-how that is dissipation-sensitive, or for which the patent period is limited, it can be important to cash in quickly before others arrive on the market (e.g. Kessler and Chakrabarthi, 1996; Lieberman and Montgomery, 1988, 1998).

To some extent all managers recognize that their organizations are prone to inertia, and most will acknowledge that it is often vital to move quickly, either in response to external pressures or to cash in on a potential first mover advantage. It should therefore come as no surprise that most managers would like their organizations to have the ability to successfully pull off revolutionary strategic changes.

The demand for evolutionary change processes

Evolution is a process whereby a constant stream of moderate changes gradually accumulates over a longer period of time. Each change is in itself small, but the cumulative result can be large. Evolutionary change processes take the current firm as a starting point, constantly modifying aspects through extension and adaptation. Some 'mutations' to the firm prove valuable and are retained, while other changes are discarded as dysfunctional. Thus, a new business system and/or organizational system can steadily evolve out of the old, as if the organization were shedding its old skin to grow a new one (e.g. Aldrich, 1999; Kagono et al., 1985).

This 'metamorphosis' approach to strategic change is particularly important where the strategic renewal hinges on widespread organizational learning. Learning is not a process that is easily compressed into a few short bursts of activity (as anyone who has studied knows). Learning is a relatively slow process, whereby know-how is accumulated over an extended period of time. It can take years to learn things, especially if the necessary knowledge is not readily available, but must be acquired 'on the job' (e.g. Agryris, 1990; Senge, 1990a). This is true for both individuals and firms. When groups of people in a firm need to develop new routines, new competences, new processes, as well as new ways of understanding the world, time is needed to experiment, reflect, discuss, test and internalize. Even in the circumstances where individuals or departments are merely asked to adjust their behaviors to new norms, the learning process is often protracted and difficult (e.g. Nelson and Winter, 1982; Pfeffer and Sutton, 1999a).

While the evolutionary nature of learning is a positive factor stimulating gradual change, the organizational reality is often also that power is too dispersed for revolutionary changes to be imposed upon the firm. Where no one has enough sway in the organization to push through radical changes, a more evolutionary approach can be the only viable route forward.

To some extent all managers recognize that their firms need to continuously learn and adapt, while most will acknowledge that they do not have the absolute power to impose revolutionary changes at will. For these reasons managers generally would like their organizations to have the ability to pursue evolutionary changes.

Yet, engaging in evolutionary change is the opposite of revolutionary change. On the one hand, being opposites might make revolution and evolution complementary. Some authors suggest that organizations should be 'ambidextrous', using both revolution and evolution, contingent upon internal and external conditions (e.g. Duncan, 1976; Krüger, 1996; Tushman and O'Reilly, 1996). On the other hand, the above discussion makes clear that the two are, to a certain extent, mutually incompatible. Once the one form of change has been chosen, this will seriously limit the ability of the strategist to simultaneously, or even subsequently, use the other. Hence, managers are once again faced with a paradox, between revolution and evolution.

EXHIBIT 4.1 SHORT CASE

ALLIANZ AND DRESDNER BANK: TAKING A RISK ON ALLFINANZ?

In April 2003 Michael Diekmann took over as the new CEO of Allianz, Europe's largest insurance company and Germany's most influential corporation. Although his predecessor's resignation had come as a surprise, the troubling situation leading up to his departure was widely known. Most visibly, the company's share price had tumbled from above €400 in January 2001 to a mere €52 in March 2003, while its credit rating had deteriorated to an A−. There were several external reasons that could be blamed for this dismal performance: the economic fallout from 9/11 and the Iraq war; expensive floods in Eastern Europe; asbestos claims in North America; and the 60% fall in value of the German stock market, reducing the

value of the equity portfolio of Allianz. But a significant self-inflicted wound was also apparent: the continuing huge losses incurred by Allianz from its newly acquired subsidiary, Dresdner Bank, Germany's second largest private bank by assets.

The strategy behind buying Dresdner Bank was to turn Allianz into a full range financial services company, where both retail and corporate customers could do their 'one stop shopping' for banking and insurance products. In this Allfinanz concept, a broad spectrum of products, ranging from savings and loans to investment services and insurance, would be distributed through the direct sales channel of Allianz, as well as through the extensive branch network of Dresdner. If this strategy could be made to work, sales per customer could be raised tremendously, significant cost savings could be attained, and unique financial products combining banking and insurance know-how could be introduced.

Until this Allfinanz vision was fully realized, however, Dresdner was a heavily loss-making bank, draining resources on a scale that was worrying even for a 'deep pocketed' company like Allianz: Dresdner lost €1.4 billion and consolidated Allianz lost €1.2 billion in 2002. In its corporate banking activities, Dresdner was suffering from the harsh economic climate in Germany, which was producing record numbers of bankruptcies, including headline-grabbing corporate failures, such as the collapse of the Kirch Group, Europe's formerly leading media empire. On the investment banking side, Dresdner had been clobbered by the downturn in the equity markets, and they were at any rate probably below critical size for international success. Finally, in the retail banking activities, the company was hurting from the chronic overcapacity in the German market.

Not that other German banks were doing any better. The 'big four' – Deutsche Bank, Commerzbank, HypoVereinsbank and Dresdner Bank – were all in sorry shape. Deutsche Bank, Germany's leading bank, was heavily hit by the downturn of the capital markets while aiming to turn itself into a global investment banking player, and was unable to keep its German retail and corporate banking activities profitable. In a bold strategic move, it had tried to rebrand its retail banking activities as Deutsche 24, shifting all its customers to this new outfit, but had lost a substantial amount of business in the process. Meanwhile, Commerzbank and HypoVereinsbank were both stuck in a positioning as universal bank, with no specific market focus or distinct competence profile. HypoVereinsbank had tried to fashion itself as the real estate specialist, only to run up huge losses in its portfolio. Virtually all attempts by all banks to launch telebanking, online-banking or discount banking also proved to be costly failures. To minimize losses, the big four shed 40 000 employees between 2001 and 2003, more than a fifth of their combined workforce, and sold assets left and right to strengthen their balance sheets. However, industry experts expected that more would be necessary, predicting that ultimately every third employee would have to leave the industry, and that every second bank branch would have to be closed.

The main reason for the extreme overcapacity in the German banking market was that the country was blessed with no less than four parallel banking systems. At the end of 1999 Germany had 62 000 banking branches (more than twice as many as bakeries, and almost four times the number of gas stations) resulting in the highest branch density in the world. Next to the regular private banking sector, there were (a) the mutual banks (the *Genossenschaftssektor*), formerly farmer-based and free from shareholder pressure, (b) the savings banks (the *Sparkassensektor*), owned by the *Länder* (states), cities and communities, and (c) the government-owned postal banking system. The savings banks had supervisory boards stuffed with local politicians, and operated under de facto state guarantees. The nonprivate alternative banking sectors could offer credits and services to consumers and small businesses at price levels unmatchable by the private banks, which needed to meet commercial return on capital targets. The result was that the big four had only a 14.4% share of the market, and total return on equity of the German banking system during the late 1990's boom years was still only a mere 6.6%. However, in 2000 the European Commission ordered the savings banks to discard their de facto state guarantees, forcing them to become profit-oriented and triggering a restructuring of the sector. Taking this cue, the mutual banks also rapidly started consolidating and professionalizing their operations. The postal system was privatized as well, along with its banking network.

On the corporate banking side the major problem was the web of shareholdings between the big financial institutions on the one hand and the largest German industrial groups on the other. In this system, collectively known as 'Deutschland AG' (Germany Inc.), the big four banks and the two large insurers, Allianz and Munich Re, had taken large stakes in many of the major German corporations in the post-war years, to finance the rebuilding of the economy. These long-term stakes in the engines of the German economic recovery served both sides well, far into the 1980s, and gave companies such as Allianz an enormous influence in the corporate world, although this power was always wielded ever so discretely. But with the onset of more sophisticated, global capital markets, German companies began to look abroad for advanced services, while the financial players became painfully aware that their returns were far below international standards. Both sides felt locked into an outdated system. So, in 2000 the law was changed to make it possible to sell corporate shareholdings without having to pay taxes on the hidden capital gains profits, thereby opening the way to unraveling the system.

Clearly, the German banking industry was finally changing shape, and it seemed that the time to move was now. A first attempt at restructuring was undertaken by Deutsche Bank, which tried to merge with Dresdner Bank in 2000. Integration teams had almost completed the job when the merger was called off because the investment banking units could not reach an agreement over leadership. Then in 2001, Allianz pounced on Dresdner, paying €18 billion, with the intention of bringing the Allfinanz concept to the German market.

For Michael Diekmann, who had previously headed the insurance operations of Allianz in the Americas, the new position as CEO came with a number of very pressing strategic questions. First, he had to ask himself whether he shared the same Allfinanz vision as his predecessor. If not, it seemed foolhardy to keep a bleeder like Dresdner in a business it did not fully understand. He could always choose to put Dresdner up for sale again, passing it on to someone better suited to adding value to its banking business and capable of pushing through the changes necessary to stem the losses. Actually, despite the awful results in 2002, the Allianz balance sheet was strong enough to do other deals if he thought they might be beneficial. Yet, if he did want to stick to the Allfinanz idea, the main issue was how he could bring about the strategic change necessary to make it work. Transforming the organization would then be the main challenge for the years to come.

Many advisors were urging Diekmann to move swiftly and decisively to implement the Allfinanz vision. In their view the crisis was actually an opportunity to break through the lingering resistance in both, rather conservative, organizations and roll out the new policy in full force. Being a new man was an advantage, for this would give him a honeymoon period with the employees and strong unions, allowing him to take firm actions and break down barriers between the two companies. He would have to determine to what extent the two would need to be integrated, but it might be better to really shake things up, to get bankers and insurers into common units, instead of keeping them on both sides of a divide. Especially when it came to the backbone of a modern financial service company, its IT system, it seemed he would have to go all out in integrating them, if banking and insurance products would need to be offered at the same time through the same channels. But other elements might also require integration, such as the sales forces, marketing and product development. Maybe even the brands would need to be merged. And these were points for which momentum was available now, not to mention that the hypercritical stock market was watching for tangible results, after the dismal results in 2002.

Yet, others pressed Diekmann to be measured and patient. Moving too rapidly might alienate employees and antagonize the unions, leaving the company inward-looking for years to come. Moreover, it was not inconceivable that major implementation bottlenecks might disrupt operations and that customers might be left bewildered by the sudden changes. Worse yet, it might turn out that Allfinanz did not work as intended and that things would need to be changed midstream. In the end, Allianz still had a rock-solid reputation to lose. Trust, solidity and reliability were long-term core assets in the market, far more important than short-term successes and ovations from the stock market.

Almost across the street from Allianz head office in Munich was the headquarters of Munich Re, the largest reinsurance company in the world. Munich Re had over the past years quietly, and without much fanfare, moved into other financial businesses. It had now become the second largest primary insurer in Germany after Allianz, and it owned two small minority holdings in Commerzbank and HypoVereinsbank, although through clever tactics these were actually controlling stakes. While Allianz was a German household name with a brand recognition close to a 100%, only a small well-informed circle of business people even knew of Munich Re's existence. Clearly, there were several paths to becoming an Allfinanz company and Michael Diekmann wondered whether Allianz had taken the right one.

Sources: *Financial Times*, November 5 2001, June 12 2002, November 22 2002; *The Economist*, August 17 and December 21 2002; company reports.

PERSPECTIVES ON STRATEGIC CHANGE

No great thing is created suddenly, any more than a bunch of grapes or a fig. If you tell me that you desire a fig, I answer that there must be time. Let it first blossom, then bear fruit, then ripen.
Epictetus (c. 60–120); Roman philosopher

Although the demand for both revolutionary and evolutionary change is clear, this does place managers in the difficult position of having to determine how these two must be combined and balanced in a process of ongoing strategic renewal. Revolutionary change is necessary to create *discontinuity* in the renewal process – radical and swift breaks with the past. Evolutionary change is necessary to ensure *continuity* in the renewal process – moderate and gradual metamorphosis from one state into another. In finding a balance between these two demands, the question is which of the two must play a leading role and what type of change path this leads to. Does successful strategic renewal hinge on a few infrequent big bangs, with some minor evolutionary changes in the intervening time span, or is successful strategic renewal essentially a gradual process of mutation and selection, where revolutionary changes are only used in case of emergency?

Yet, as in previous chapters, we see that the strategic management literature comes up with a wide variety of answers to this question. Both among business practitioners and strategy researchers, views differ sharply about the best way of dealing with the paradox of revolution and evolution. To gain insight into the major points of disagreement between people on the issue of strategic renewal, we will again outline the two diametrically opposed perspectives here.

At one end of the virtual continuum of views, are the strategists who argue that real strategic renewal can only be achieved by radical means. Revolutionary change, although difficult to achieve, is at the heart of renewal, while evolutionary changes can only figure in a supporting role. This point of view will be referred to as the 'discontinuous renewal perspective'. At the other end of the spectrum are the strategists who argue that real strategic renewal is not brought about by an 'axe', but must grow out of the existing firm, in a constant stream of small adjustments. Evolutionary change, although difficult to sustain, is at the heart of renewal, while revolutionary changes are a fall-back alternative, if all else fails. This point of view will be referred to as the 'continuous renewal perspective'.

The discontinuous renewal perspective

 According to advocates of the discontinuous renewal perspective, it is a common misconception that firms develop gradually. It is often assumed that organizations move fluidly from one state to the next, encountering minimal friction. In reality, however, strategic change is arduous and encounters significant resistance. Pressure must be exerted, and tension must mount, before a major shift can be accomplished. Movement, therefore, is not steady and constant, as a current in the sea, but abrupt and dramatic, as in an earthquake, where resistance gives way and tension is released in a short shock. In general, the more significant a change is, the more intense the shock will be.

Proponents of this perspective argue that people and organizations exhibit a natural reluctance to change. Humans have a strong preference for stability. Once general policy has been determined, most firms are inclined to settle into a fixed way of working. The organizational structure will solidify, formal processes will be installed, standard operating procedures will be defined, key competence areas will be identified, a distribution of power will emerge and a corporate culture will become established. The stability of an organization will be especially high if all of these elements form a consistent and cohesive configuration (e.g. Mintzberg, 1991; Waterman, Peters and Philips, 1980). Moreover, if a firm experiences a period of success, this usually strongly reinforces the existing way of working (e.g. Markides, 1998; Miller, 1990).

It must be emphasized that stability is not inherently harmful, as it allows people to 'get to work'. A level of stability is required to function efficiently (e.g. March and Simon, 1958; Thompson, 1967). Constant upheaval would only create an organizational mess. There would be prolonged confusion about tasks and authority, poorly structured internal communication and coordination, and a lack of clear standards and routines. The instability brought on by such continuously changing processes and structures would lead to widespread insecurity, political maneuvering and inter-departmental conflicts.

Advocates of the discontinuous renewal perspective, therefore, argue that long periods of relative stability are necessary for the proper functioning of firms. However, the downside of stability is rigidity – the unwillingness and/or inability to change, even when it is urgently required. To overcome rigidity and get the firm in motion, a series of small nudges will by no means be sufficient. A big shove will be needed. For strategic changes to really happen, measures must be radical and comprehensive. A coordinated assault is usually required to decisively break through organizational defenses and 'shock therapy' is needed to fundamentally change people's cognitive maps. Solving lock-in problems generally also demands a quick, firm-wide switchover to a new system. For instance, business process reengineering must involve all aspects of the value chain at once (e.g. Hammer, 1990; Hammer and Champy, 1993). However, proponents of the discontinuous renewal perspective emphasize that the period of turmoil must not take too long. People cannot be indefinitely confronted with high levels of uncertainty and ambiguity, and a new equilibrium is vital for a new period of efficient operations.

Therefore, the long-term pattern of strategic renewal is not gradual, but episodic. Periods of relative stability are interrupted by short and dramatic periods of instability, during which revolutionary changes take place (e.g. Greiner, 1972; Tushman, Newman and Romanelli, 1986). This pattern of development has been recognized in a variety of other sciences as well (Gersick, 1991). Following the natural historians Eldredge and Gould, this discontinuous pattern of strategic renewal is often called 'punctuated equilibrium' – stability punctuated by episodes of revolutionary change.

Some proponents of this view argue that episodes of revolutionary change are generally not chosen freely, but are triggered by crises. A major environmental jolt can be the reason for a sudden crisis (e.g. Meyer, 1982; Meyer, Brooks and Goes, 1990) – for example, the introduction of a new technology, a major economic recession, new government regulations, a novel market entrant or a dramatic event in international political affairs. However, often a misalignment between the firm and its environment grows over a longer period of time, causing a mounting sense of impending crisis (e.g. Johnson, 1988; Strebel, 1992). As tension increases, people in the firm become more receptive to submitting to the painful changes that are necessary. This increased willingness to change under crisis circumstances coincides with the physical law that 'under pressure things become fluid'. As long as the pressure persists, revolutionary change is possible, but as soon as the pressure lets up the firm will resolidify in a new form, inhibiting any further major changes (e.g. Lewin, 1947; Miller and Friesen, 1984). For this reason, managers often feel impelled to heighten and prolong the sense of crisis, to keep organization members receptive to the changes being pushed through. And where a crisis is lacking, some managers will induce one, to create the sense of urgency and determination needed to get people in the change mind-set.

Other authors argue that revolutionary changes are not always reactive responses to crisis conditions. Revolutionary change can also be proactively pursued to gain a competitive advantage, or even to change the rules of the game in the industry in which the firm is competing. If a firm decides to use a breakthrough technology or a new business model to improve its competitive position vis-à-vis rivals, this does entail that it will need to execute some major changes in a short period of time. Such innovations to the business system are inherently revolutionary. Creating novel products and developing a unique business formula requires a sharp break with the past. Old ways must be discarded before new methods can be adopted. This is the essence of what Schumpeter (1950) referred to as the process of 'creative destruction', inherent in the capitalist system. This process is not orderly and protracted, but disruptive and intense. Therefore, it is argued, to be a competitive success, firms must learn to master the skill of ongoing revolutionary change (e.g. D'Aveni, 1994; Hamel, 1996). Rapid implementation of system-wide change is an essential organizational capability – the firm needs to be able to run faster than its competitors.

It can be concluded that strategic changes, whether proactive or reactive, require an abrupt break with the status quo. Change management demands strong leadership to rapidly push through stressful, discomforting and risky shifts in the business and organizational system. Battling the sources of rigidity and turning crisis into opportunity are the key qualities needed by managers implementing strategic change. Ultimately, strategizing managers should know when to change and when it is more wise to seek stability – they should know when to trigger an 'earthquake' and when to avoid one.

EXHIBIT 4.2   THE DISCONTINUOUS RENEWAL PERSPECTIVE

CENTRICA: STEPPING ON THE GAS

In February 1997 British Gas was split into two companies – one for trading and retailing gas in the United Kingdom called Centrica, and one for producing and transporting gas (plus the international operations) called the BG Group. This radical move was a response to the pending liberalization of the residential market that the British government had planned for May 1998. British Gas had already been privatized in 1986 and had lost its monopoly for industrial and business customers in 1992, yet open competition in the household market for gas posed the biggest challenge the company had ever faced, requiring a separate company with an unequivocal focus on residential consumers.

At the moment of the split, Centrica inherited two main assets. It was given all the gas connections to British households and the brand name British Gas. However, the management of Centrica realized that both assets would rapidly decline in value within 24 months – they would have to give third parties access to their gas connections and new competitors were likely to introduce less staid brands and lower prices. Centrica's managers also recognized that along with these less than thrilling assets, the company had inherited the lumbering business practices of a giant former state-owned monopolist.

Centrica's reaction to this challenge was to radically redefine its business from simple gas provision to 'essential household services', and to rapidly transform the entire organization towards a client-centered service provider. The new 'essential household services' concept was based on the assumption that customers would value having a broad range of household services bundled into one package and paid for with one monthly bill. Within three years, Centrica expanded its product offering to include electricity, telecommunication services (mobile, fixed and internet), credit cards, consumer credit services (through its Goldfish brand), car repair services (through the AA, Automobile Association, which Centrica bought), insurance policies, home services (plumbing repair, home security services, kitchen appliance servicing) and various other services, such as Golf England and the delivery of fine wines.

By 2001, Centrica served 67% of the gas retail market (after having dropped to little over 50% shortly after liberalization) and had become the largest residential electricity supplier. More than 55% of its sales were in non-gas services, and it had a customer relationship with 90% of all British households. It had integrated customer relationship management across all its various businesses and worked on aggressively cross-selling its services. Centrica's slogan, 'taking care of the essentials', has also been true for the financial results, allowing the company to outperform the British FTSE stock index by about 200% between the demerger in 1997 and 2002.

Sources: Company reports; Hoovers Online; *European Utilities Sector Review*, Credit Suisse Equity Research, January 2002.

The continuous renewal perspective

According to proponents of the continuous renewal perspective, if firms shift by 'earthquake' it is usually their own 'fault'. The problem with revolution is that it commonly leads to the need for further revolution at a later time – discontinuous change creates its own boom-and-bust cycle. Revolutionary change is generally followed by a strong organizational yearning for stability. The massive, firm-wide efforts to implement agonizing changes can often only be sustained for a short period of time, after which change momentum collapses. Any positive inclination towards change among employees will have totally disappeared by the time the reorganizations are over. Consequently, the firm lapses back into a stable state in which only minor changes occur. This stable situation is maintained until the next round of shock therapy becomes necessary, to jolt the organization out of its ossified state.

To supporters of the continuous renewal perspective, the boom-and-bust approach to strategic change is like running a marathon by sprinting and then standing still to catch one's breath. Yet, marathons are not won by good sprinters, but by runners with endurance and persistence, who can keep a steady pace – runners who are more inspired by the tortoise than by the hare. The same is true for companies in the marathon of competition. Some companies behave like the hare in Aesop's fable, showing off their ability to take great leaps, but burdened by a short span of attention. Other companies behave more like the tortoise, moving gradually and undramatically, but unrelentingly and without interruption, focusing on the long-term goal. In the short run, the hares might dash ahead, suggesting that making big leaps forward is the best way to compete. But in the long run, the most formidable contenders will be the diligent tortoises, whose ability to maintain a constant speed will help them to win the race.

Therefore, the 'big ideas', 'frame-breaking innovations' and 'quantum leaps' that so mesmerize proponents of the discontinuous renewal perspective are viewed with suspicion by supporters of continuous renewal. Revolution not only causes unnecessary disruption and dysfunctional crises, but also is usually the substitute of diligence. If organizations do not have the stamina to continuously improve themselves, quick fix radical change can be used as a short-term remedy. Where firms do not exhibit the drive to permanently upgrade their capabilities, revolutionary innovations can be used as the short cut to renewed competitiveness. In other words, the lure of revolutionary change is that of short-term results. By abruptly and dramatically making major changes, managers hope to rapidly book tangible progress – and instantly win recognition and promotion (Imai, 1986).

To advocates of the continuous renewal perspective, a preference for revolution usually reflects an unhealthy obsession with the short term. Continuous renewal, on the other hand, is more long term in orientation. Development is gradual, piecemeal and undramatic, but as it is constantly maintained over a longer period of time, the aggregate level of change can still be significant. Three organizational characteristics are important for keeping up a steady pace of change. First, all employees within the firm should be committed to *continuously improve*. Everyone within the firm should be driven by constructive dissatisfaction with the status quo. This attitude, that things can always be done better, reflects a rejection of stability and the acceptance of bounded instability (e.g. Beinhocker, 1999; Stacey, 1993a) – everything is open to change.

Secondly, everyone in the firm must be motivated to *continuously learn*. People within the organization must constantly update their knowledge base, which not only means acquiring new information, but challenging accepted company wisdom as well. Learning goes hand in hand with unlearning – changing the cognitive maps shared within the organization. In this respect, it is argued that an atmosphere of crisis actually inhibits continuous renewal. In a situation of crisis, it is not a matter of 'under pressure things become fluid', but 'in the cold everything freezes'. Crisis circumstances might lower people's resistance to imposed change, but it also blunts their motivation for experimenting and learning, as they brace themselves for the imminent shock. Crisis encourages people to seek security and to focus on the short term, instead of opening up and working towards long-term development (e.g. Bate, 1994; Senge, 1990a).

Thirdly, everyone in the firm must be motivated to *continuously adapt*. Constant adjustment to external change and fluid internal realignment should be pursued. To this end, the organization must actively avoid inertia, by combating the forces of ossification. Managers should strive to create flexible structures and processes (e.g. Bartlett and Ghoshal, 1995; Eisenhardt and Brown, 1997), to encourage an open and tolerant corporate culture, and to provide sufficient job and career security for employees to accept other forms of ambiguity and uncertainty (e.g. Kagono et al., 1985; Nonaka, 1988b).

These three characteristics of an evolutionary firm – continuous improvement, learning and adaptation – have in common that basically everyone in the organization is involved. Revolutionary change can be initiated by top management, possibly assisted and urged on by a few external consultants, and carried by a handful of change agents or champions (e.g. Maidique, 1980; Day, 1994). Evolutionary change, on the other hand, requires a firm-wide effort. Leaders cannot learn on behalf of their organizations, nor can they orchestrate all of the small improvements and adaptations needed for continuous renewal. Managers must realize that evolution can be led from the top, but not imposed from the top. For strategizing managers to realize change, hands-on guidance of organizational developments is more important than commanding organizational actions.

EXHIBIT 4.3 THE CONTINUOUS RENEWAL PERSPECTIVE

McKINSEY: 'THE FIRM' REMAINS FIRM

Ise Jingu is Japan's most sacred Shinto shrine and in the eyes of many also its most aesthetically pure and serene one. The shrine compound consists of more than 200 buildings that are constructed using 14 000 Japanese cedar wood logs, special Kaya straw and not a single nail. Every 20 years, Ise Jingu is completely razed to the ground and the priests move to an exact replica that has been built in the meantime on a parallel site. Here they will stay for the next 20 years, until it is time to move back again. In 1993, the shrine was moved for the 61st time since the year 690, a ceremony that has been maintained with only one exception, in Japan's war-torn 16th century.

Why tear down such elaborate structures only to rebuild exact replicas? The high priests of Shinto realized at the time, that the only way to maintain the know-how for constructing the shrine was to rebuild it once every 20 years, thus handing down the skills from one generation to the next. By being continuously rebuilt, Ise Jingu remains eternally young – visitors enter brand new buildings that are 1300 years old. The symbolic importance of this ritual reaches very deep. As with the construction know-how of the shrine, insight into the Shinto belief system must also be passed on to the young. By making each new generation 'rebuild' it, the Shinto belief system evolves successfully with the challenges and opportunities of the present day, without changing what is at its core.

A similar approach to change can be observed at McKinsey & Co., the international management consulting company that has such a solid position in corporate markets that it is often simply referred to as 'the Firm'. McKinsey was founded in the 1930s by Marvin Bower, who remained active in the company until his death in January 2003. From the outset, Bower imprinted a set of principles and values to guide the functioning of McKinsey and these have remained virtually unchanged over the years. He also devised a business model that is basically the same today as it was 50 years ago. And this situation is not likely to change with the election in March 2003 of a new worldwide managing partner: Ian Davis, the head of the London office, who was voted into the top job, is seen as a stern follower of 'Bowerite' values and principles.

McKinsey's profile has remained fundamentally consistent, as the firm has grabbed a position of leadership across all continents, and all industries. A McKinsey consultant in Bombay today would easily recognize the Düsseldorf operations of the 1980s or New York of the 1970s. Similarly, the profile and image of McKinsey consultants has stayed remarkably stable, independent of time and place. But how can a company that does not seem to change continuously achieve the highest recognition across such a wide range of countries, industries and times? Doesn't the fast changing world require the firm to constantly reinvent itself? In reality, McKinsey does change, only fluidly, in a continuous stream of small steps.

One of its most notorious management practices bringing about that continuous renewal is McKinsey's 'up or out policy', or more politely its 'grow or go' system. This policy forces every consultant in the firm to constantly rise through the ranks, or else to leave. Even the speed at which each career step should be taken is fixed at about a year and a half, give or take a few months. The effect of this policy is that nobody in the company can ever build a nesting place. Even senior directors must move on, leaving an open space for a rising newcomer to occupy and to learn the necessary skills for this level anew. The effect is also that as an open space is reoccupied, it is reshaped to take account of the then somewhat different external business environment, different business cycle, and change in industry or shift in regional focus. Newcomers may be in the same slot as their predecessors, and they will adhere to the same McKinsey values of 'Client First, Firm Second, everything else Third', but their job will be a changed one. Since the long-term reliance on a fixed skill base is made impossible through the 'grow or go' system, the McKinsey consultants, and with them the entire company, evolve seamlessly over time and across borders, even while remaining the same at their core. Hence, while McKinsey often advises its clients to radically restructure, for itself the firm prefers a process of continual adjustment.

Sources: *The Economist*, March 1 2003; company documents; Ise-Jingu web site.

TOWARDS A SYNTHESIS

*Every act of creation is first of all
an act of destruction.*

Pablo Picasso (1881–1973); Spanish artist

Slow and steady wins the race.

The Hare and the Tortoise, Aesop
(c. 620–560 BC); Greek writer

So, how should managers go about renewing their organizations? Should managers strive
to bring about renewal abruptly, by emphasizing radical, comprehensive and dramatic
changes? Or should they try to make renewal a more continuous process, accentuating
ongoing improvement, learning and adaptation? As no consensus has yet developed within
the field of strategic management on how to balance revolution and evolution, it is once
again up to each individual to assess the arguments put forward in the debate and to form
their own opinion.

In Table 4.1 the main arguments of the two opposite poles in this debate have been summarized. As was argued in the previous chapters, the challenge for managers is to evaluate
the strengths and weaknesses of both sides and to seek a way to find the best combination
of the two, given the specific circumstances in which the organization finds itself. Drawing
a parallel with Aesop's fable of the hare and the tortoise, this challenge is like creating a
hybrid between the two animals, taking the speed of the one and the persistence of the
other. Developing such a hybrid would definitely not be an easy feat, but if done correctly
such an animal could be superior to both the hare and the tortoise, able to win the race,
'fast and steady'. In the spirit of this metaphor, it could be said that the challenge for managers is to actively engage in the 'cross-breeding' of the discontinuous and continuous
renewal perspectives, to come up with ever better approaches to the issue of strategic
renewal.

TABLE 4.1   Discontinuous renewal versus continuous renewal perspective

	Discontinuous renewal perspective	*Continuous renewal perspective*
Emphasis on	Revolution over evolution	Evolution over revolution
Strategic renewal as	Disruptive innovation/turnaround	Uninterrupted improvement
Strategic renewal process	Creative destruction	Organic adaptation
Magnitude of change	Radical, comprehensive and dramatic	Moderate, piecemeal and undramatic
Pace of change	Abrupt, unsteady and intermittent	Gradual, steady and constant
Lasting renewal requires	Sudden break with status quo	Permanent learning and flexibility
Reaction to external jolts	Shock therapy	Continuous adjustment
View of organizational crises	Under pressure things become fluid	In the cold everything freezes
Long-term renewal dynamics	Stable and unstable states alternate	Persistent transient state
Long-term renewal pattern	Punctuated equilibrium	Gradual development

FURTHER READING

Wisdom lies neither in fixity nor in change, but in the dialectic between the two.
Octavio Paz (1914–1998); Mexican poet and essayist

Many excellent writings on the topic of strategic change are available, although most carry other labels, such as innovation, entrepreneurship, reengineering, revitalization, rejuvenation and learning. For a good overview of the literature, readers can consult 'Environmental Jolts and Industry Revolutions: Organizational Responses to Discontinuous Change', by Alan Meyer, Geoffry Brooks and James Goes. Paul Strebel's book *Breakpoints: How Managers Exploit Radical Business Change* also provides broad introduction to much of the work on change.

In the discontinuous renewal literature, Larry Greiner's article 'Evolution and Revolution as Organizations Grow' is a classic well worth reading. Danny Miller and Peter Friesen's landmark book *Organizations: A Quantum View* is also stimulating, although not easily accessible. More readable books on radical change are *Rejuvenating the Mature Business* by Charles Baden-Fuller and John Stopford, *Sharpbenders: The Secrets of Unleashing Corporate Potential*, by Peter Grinyer, David Mayes and Peter McKiernan, and *Crisis and Renewal*, by David Hurst. More 'hands-on' is Rosabeth Moss Kanter's *When Giants Learn to Dance*, and of course *Reengineering the Corporation: A Manifesto for Business Revolution*, by Michael Hammer and James Champy.

On the topic of innovation, Jim Utterback's book *Mastering the Dynamics of Innovation* provides a good overview, as does *Managing Innovation: Integrating Technological, Market and Organizational Change*, by Joe Tidd, John Bessant and Keith Pavitt. An excellent collection of cases is provided by Charles Baden-Fuller and Martin Pitt in their book *Strategic Innovation*.

Literature taking a continuous renewal perspective is less abundant, but no less interesting. Masaaki Imai's book *Kaizen: The Key to Japan's Competitive Success* is highly recommended. A more academic work that explains the continuous renewal view in detail is 'The Art of Continuous Change: Linking Complexity Theory and Time-Paced Evolution in Relentlessly Shifting Organizations', by Kathleen Eisenhardt and Shona Brown. Their excellent book *Competing on the Edge: Strategy as Structured Chaos* (Brown and Eisenhardt, 1998) is also a good source. Another good academic work is *Strategic vs. Evolutionary Management: A US-Japan Comparison of Strategy and Organization*, by Tadao Kagono, Ikujiro Nonaka, Kiyonori Sakakibara and Akihiro Okumura. Ikujiro Nonaka's article 'Creating Organizational Order Out of Chaos: Self-Renewal in Japanese Firms' gives a good summary of this way of thinking.

Finally, the award-winning article 'Ambidextrous Organizations: Managing Evolutionary and Revolutionary Change', by Michael Tushman and Charles O'Reilly must be mentioned as a delightful article, in particular with regard to the way in which the authors explicitly wrestle with the paradox of revolution and evolution. Their book *Winning Through Innovation: A Practical Guide to Leading Organizational Change and Renewal* is equally stimulating.

STRATEGY CONTENT

Every generation laughs at the old fashions but religiously follows the new.
Henry David Thoreau (1817–1862); American philosopher

The output of the strategy process is a particular strategy that an organization follows – this is called the strategy content. 'Strategy content' is another way of saying 'the strategy itself, with all its specific characteristics'. While the strategy process section dealt with the questions of *how* strategy should be formed, *who* should be involved and *when* it should be made, the strategy content section deals with the question of *what* the strategy should be – what should be the course of action the firm should follow to achieve its purpose?

In determining what the strategy should be, two types of 'fit' are of central concern to managers. First, as discussed in Chapter 4, there needs to be a fit between the firm and its environment. If the two become misaligned, the firm will be unable to meet the demands of the environment and will start to underperform, which can eventually lead to bankruptcy or takeover. This type of fit is also referred to as 'external consonance'. At the same time, managers are also concerned with achieving an internal fit between the various parts of the firm. If various units become misaligned, the organization will suffer from inefficiency, conflict and poor external performance, which can eventually lead to its demise as well. This type of fit is also referred to as 'internal consistency'.

As external consonance and internal consistency are prerequisites for a successful strategy, they need to be achieved for each organizational unit. Most organizations have various levels, making it necessary to ensure internal and external fit at each level of aggregation within the firm. In Figure III.1 all these possible levels within a corporation have been reduced to just three general categories, and a fourth, supra-organizational level has been added. At each level the strategy followed should meet the requirements of external consonance and internal consistency:

- Functional level strategy. For each functional area, such as marketing, operations, finance, logistics, human resources, procurement and R&D, a strategy needs to be developed. At this level, internal consistency means having an overarching functional strategy that integrates various functional sub-strategies (e.g. a marketing strategy that aligns branding, distribution, pricing, product and communication strategies). External consonance means that the strategy must be aligned with the demands in the relevant external arena (e.g. the logistics or procurement environment).

- Business level strategy. At the business level, an organization can only be effective if it can integrate functional level strategies into an internally consistent whole. To achieve external consonance the business unit must be aligned with the specific demands in the relevant business area.

- Corporate level strategy. Where a company operates in two or more business areas, the business level strategies need to be aligned to form an internally consistent corporate level strategy. Between business and corporate levels there can also be divisions, but for most strategy purposes they can be approached as mini-corporations (both divisional and corporate level strategy are technically speaking 'multi-business level').

Achieving external consonance at this level of aggregation means that a corporation must be able to act as one tightly integrated unit or as many autonomous, differentiated units, depending on the demands of the relevant environment.

■ **Network level strategy.** Where various firms work together to create economic value, it sometimes is deemed necessary to align business and/or corporate level strategies to shape an internally consistent network level strategy. Such a network, or multi-company, level strategy can involve anywhere between two and thousands of companies. Here, too, the group must develop a strategy that fits with the demands in the relevant environment.

As the strategy content issues differ greatly depending on the level of aggregation under discussion, this section has been divided along the following lines. Chapter 5 will focus on business level strategy, Chapter 6 on corporate level strategy and Chapter 7 on network level strategy. Only the functional level strategies will be given no extensive coverage, as they are usually explored in great detail in functionally oriented books. It must be noted, however, that the aggregation levels used here are an analytical distinction and not an empirical reality that can always be found in practice – where one level stops and the other starts is more a matter of definition than of thick demarcation lines. Hence, when discussing strategy issues at any level, it is important to understand how they fit with higher and lower level strategy questions.

FIGURE III.1   The levels of strategy

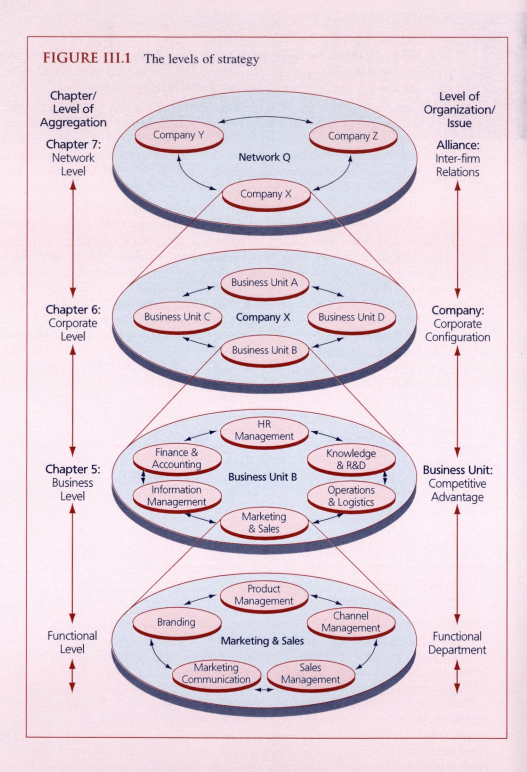

Chapter/
Level of
Aggregation

Chapter 7:
Network
Level

Chapter 6:
Corporate
Level

Chapter 5:
Business
Level

Functional
Level

Level of
Organization/
Issue

Alliance:
Inter-firm
Relations

Company:
Corporate
Configuration

Business Unit:
Competitive
Advantage

Functional
Department

Company Y   Company Z
Network Q
Company X

Business Unit A
Business Unit C   Company X   Business Unit D
Business Unit B

HR
Management
Finance &
Accounting   Knowledge
& R&D
Business Unit B
Information
Management   Operations
& Logistics
Marketing
& Sales

Product
Management
Branding   Channel
Management
Marketing & Sales
Marketing   Sales
Communication   Management

BUSINESS LEVEL STRATEGY

Advantage is a better soldier than rashness.
William Shakespeare (1564–1616); English dramatist and poet

INTRODUCTION

Strategic management is concerned with relating a firm to its environment in order to successfully meet long-term objectives. As both the business environment and individual firms are dynamic systems, constantly in flux, achieving a fit between the two is an ongoing challenge. Managers are continuously looking for new ways to align the current, and potential, strengths and weaknesses of the organization with the current, and potential, opportunities and threats in the environment.

Part of the difficulty lies in the competitive nature of the environment. To be successful, firms need to gain a competitive advantage over rival organizations operating in the same business area. Within the competitive arena chosen by a firm, it needs to accrue enough power to counterbalance the demands of buyers and suppliers, to outperform rival producers, to discourage new firms from entering the business and to fend off the threat of substitute products or services. Preferably this competitive advantage over other players in the business should be sustainable over a prolonged period of time. How firms should go about creating a (sustainable) competitive advantage in each business in which they operate is the central issue concerning managers engaged in business level strategy.

THE ISSUE OF COMPETITIVE ADVANTAGE

Whether a firm has a competitive advantage depends on the business system that it has developed to relate itself to its business environment. A business system is the configuration of resources (inputs), activities (throughput) and product/service offerings (output) intended to create value for customers – it is the way a firm conducts its business. In Figure 5.1 an overview is given of the components of a business system.

Competitive advantage can only be achieved if a business system creates superior value for buyers. Therefore, the first element in a successful business system is a superior 'value proposition'. A firm must be able to supply a product or service more closely fitted to client needs than rival firms. To be attractive, each element of a firm's 'product offering' needs to be targeted at a particular segment of the market and have a superior mix of attributes (e.g. price, availability, reliability, technical specifications, image, color, taste, ease of use, etc.). Secondly, a successful company must also have the ability to actually develop and supply the superior product offering. It needs to have the capability to perform the necessary value-adding activities in an effective and efficient manner. These value-adding activities, such as R&D, production, logistics, marketing and sales, are jointly referred to as a firm's activity system (or value chain). The third component of a business system consists of the resource base required to perform the value-adding activities. Resources such as know-how, patents, facilities, money, brands and relationships make up the stock of assets that can be employed to create the product offering. If these firm-specific assets are distinctive and useful, they can form the basis of a superior value proposition. To create a competitive advantage, alignment must be achieved between all three elements of a business system. In the following pages all three elements will be discussed in more detail.

Product offering

At the intersection between a firm and its environment, transactions take place whereby the firm supplies goods or performs services for clients in the market-place. It is here that the alignment of the firm and its environment is put to the test. If the products and services offered by the firm are more highly valued by customers than alternatives, a profitable transaction could take place. In other words, for sales to be achieved a firm must have a competitive value proposition – a cluster of physical goods, services and/or additional attributes with a superior fit to customer needs.

For the strategizing manager the key question is which products should be developed and which markets should be served. In many cases the temptation is to be everything to everybody – making a wide range of products and serving as many clients as possible.

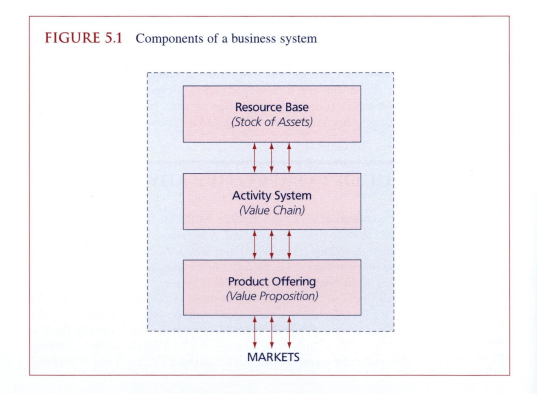

FIGURE 5.1   Components of a business system

However, a number of practical constraints inhibit companies from taking such an unfocused approach to the market. Companies that do not focus on a limited set of product–market combinations run the risk of encountering a number of major problems:

- **Low economies of scale.** Being unfocused is expensive, because of the low economies of scale that can be achieved. In general, the less specialized the company, the lower the opportunities to organize the activity system efficiently and leverage the resource base.

- **Slow organizational learning.** Being involved in a multitude of products and markets generally slows the organization's ability to build up specific knowledge and capabilities. In general, the less specialized the company, the lower the opportunity to develop a distinctive activity system and resource base.

- **Unclear brand image.** Unfocused companies have the added disadvantage of having a fuzzy image in the market. In general, companies that stand for everything tend to stand out in nothing.

- **Unclear corporate identity.** The lack of clear external image is usually compounded by a lack of internal identity within unfocused organizations. In general, a company with highly diversified activities will have difficulty explaining why its people are together in the same company.

- **High organizational complexity.** Highly diverse products and customers also create an exponential increase in organizational complexity. In general, the less specialized the company, the lower the opportunity to keep the organization simple and manageable.

- **Limits to flexibility.** Being all things to all people is often physically impossible due to the need to specify procedures, routines, systems and tools. In general, less specialized firms are often forced into certain choices due to operational necessity.

For these reasons, companies need to focus on a limited number of businesses and within each business on a limited group of customers and a limited set of products. This focus should not be arbitrary – the challenge for strategizing managers is to understand which businesses are (or can be made to be) structurally attractive and how their firm can gain a competitive advantage within each business, by offering specific value propositions to selected customer segments.

Determining a focus starts by looking for the 'boundaries' of a business – how can managers draw meaningful delineation lines in the environment, distinguishing one arena of competition from another, so that they can select some and ignore others? Ideally, the environment would be made up of neatly compartmentalized businesses, with clear borders separating them. In reality, however, the picture is much more messy. While there are usually certain clusters of buyers and suppliers interacting more intensely with one another, suggesting that they are operating in the same business, there are often numerous exceptions to any neat classification scheme. To explore how a business can be defined, it is first necessary to specify how a business differs from an 'industry' and a 'market'.

Delineating industries. An industry is defined as a group of firms making a similar type of product or employing a similar set of value-adding processes or resources. In other words, an industry consists of producers that are much alike – there is *supply side similarity* (Kay, 1993). The simplest way to draw an industry boundary is to use product similarity as the delineation criterion. For instance, British Airways can be said to be in the airline industry, along with many other providers of the same product, such as Singapore Airlines and Ryanair. However, an industry can also be defined on the basis of activity system similarity (e.g. consulting industry and mining industry) or resource similarity (e.g. information technology industry and oil industry).

Economic statisticians tend to favor fixed industry categories based on product similarity and therefore most figures available about industries are product-category based, often making use of Standard Industrial Classification (SIC) codes. Strategists, on the contrary, like to challenge existing definitions of an industry, for instance by regrouping them on the basis of underlying value-adding activities or resources. Take the example of Swatch – how did it conceptualize which industry it was in? If they had focused on the physical product and the production process, then they would have been inclined to situate Swatch in the watch industry. However, Swatch also viewed its products as fashion accessories, placing emphasis on the key value-adding activities of fashion design and marketing. On this basis, Swatch could just as well be categorized as a member of the fashion industry (Porac, Thomas and Baden-Fuller, 1989). For the strategizing manager, the realization that Swatch can be viewed in both ways is an important insight. As creating a competitive advantage often comes from doing things differently, rethinking the definition of an industry can be a powerful way to develop a unique product offering.

Figure 5.2 gives four examples of traditionally defined 'industry columns', which Porter (1980) draws not top-down, but left-right, using the term 'value system'. These columns start with upstream industries, which are involved in the extraction/growing of raw materials and their conversion into inputs for the manufacturing sector. Downstream industries take the output of manufacturing companies and bring them to clients, often adding a variety of services into the product mix. In practice, industry columns are not as simple as depicted in Figure 5.2, as each industry has many different industries as suppliers and usually many different industries as buyers.

A second limitation of the industry columns shown in Figure 5.2 is that they are materials-flow oriented – industry boundaries are drawn on the basis of product similarity, while strategists might want to take a different angle on defining the industry. The brown blocks are some examples of alternative industry definitions, but one can imagine many more; not only broader definitions, but also more narrow ones. For instance, it could be argued that clothing retailers with physical stores are in a distinct industry as opposed to internet/mail-order retailers.

A further downside of the industry column figure is that the 'materials-flow' angle does not really suit the two-thirds of the economy that is involved in services. Understanding who are the buyers and the suppliers of insurance, education, consultancy, advertising and healthcare requires a different way of conceiving the industry column than looking at the flow of goods. Generally, for each different type of service a different value system will exist, with a distinct web of suppliers and buyers.

Segmenting markets.   While economists see the market as a place where supply and demand meet, in the business world a market is usually defined as a group of customers with similar needs. In other words, a market consists of buyers whose demands are much alike – *demand side similarity*. For instance, there is a market for air transportation between London and Jamaica, which is a different market than for air transportation between London and Paris – the customer needs are different and therefore these products cannot be substituted for one another. But customers can substitute a British Airways London–Paris flight for one by Air France, indicating that both companies are serving the same market. Yet, this market definition (London–Paris air transport) might not be the most appropriate, if in reality many customers are willing to substitute air travel by rail travel, taking Le Shuttle through the channel tunnel, or by ferry. In this case, there is a

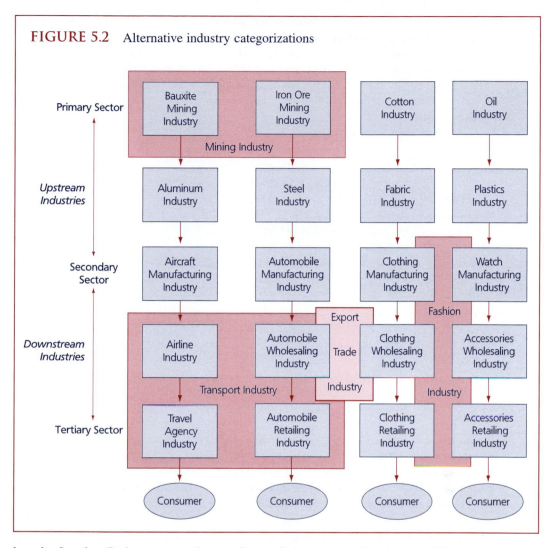

FIGURE 5.2   Alternative industry categorizations

broader London–Paris transportation market, and air transportation is a specific *market segment*. If many customers are willing to substitute physical travel by tele-conferencing or other telecommunications methods, the market might need to be defined as the 'London–Paris meeting market'.

As with industries, there are many ways of defining markets, depending on which buyer characteristics are used to make a clustering. In Figure 5.3, a number of examples are given of segmentation criteria. The first group of segmentation criteria is based on buyer attributes that are frequently thought to be important predictors of actual buying criteria and buyer behavior. Such customer characteristics are commonly used to group potential clients because this information is objective and easily available. However, the pitfall of segmenting on the basis of buyer attributes is that the causal link between characteristics and actual needs and behaviors is often rather tenuous – not all Canadians need hockey sticks and not all three-year-olds nag their parents while shopping. In other words, the market can be segmented on the basis of any demographic characteristic (e.g. income, family composition, employment), but this might not lead to meaningful groups of customers with similar needs and buying behavior.

FIGURE 5.3 Alternative market categorizations

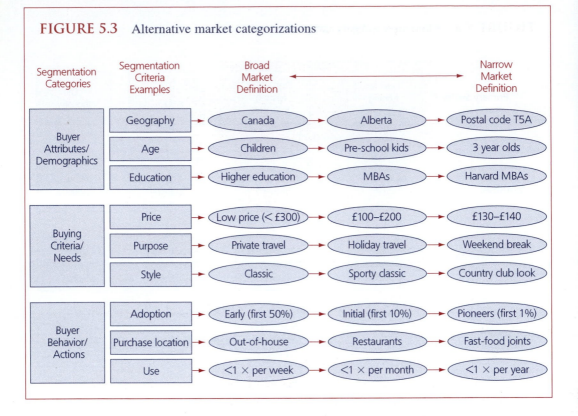

Therefore, instead of using buyer attributes as *indirect* – predictive – measures of what clients probably want, segments can also be *directly* defined on the basis of buying criteria employed and/or buyer behaviors exhibited. The advantage is that segments can then be identified with clearly similar wishes and/or behaviors. The disadvantage is that it is very difficult to gather and interpret information on what specific people want and how they really act.

For strategists, one of the key challenges is to look at existing categorizations of buyers and to wonder whether a different segmentation would offer new insights and new opportunities for developing a product offering specifically tailored to their needs. As with the redefining of industry boundaries, it is often in the reconceptualization of market segments that a unique approach to the market can be found.

Defining and selecting businesses. A business is as a set of related product–market combinations. The term 'business' refers neither to a set of producers nor a group of customers, but to the domain where the two meet. In other words, a business is a competitive arena where companies offering similar products serving similar needs rival against one another for the favor of the buyers. Hence, a business is delineated in both industry and market terms (see Figure 5.4). Typically, a business is narrower than the entire industry and the set of markets served is also limited. For instance, within the airline industry the charter business is usually recognized as rather distinct. In the charter business, a sub-set of the airline services is offered to a number of tourist markets. Cheap flights from London to Jamaica and from London to Barcelona fall within this business, while service levels will be different than in other parts of the airline industry. It should be noted, though, that just

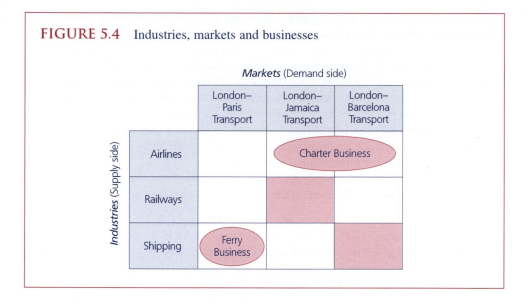

FIGURE 5.4   Industries, markets and businesses

as with industries and markets, there is no best way to define the boundaries of a business (Abell, 1980).

As stated earlier, companies cannot afford to be unfocused, operating superficially in a whole range of businesses. They must direct their efforts by focusing in two ways:

1 Selecting a limited number of businesses. The first constraint that companies need to impose on themselves is to choose a limited array of businesses within which they wish to be successful. This essential strategic challenge is referred to as the issue of corporate configuration and will be examined in more detail in Chapter 6 (multi-business level strategy). Here it suffices to say that firms need to analyze the structural characteristics of interesting businesses to be able to judge whether they are attractive enough for the firm, or can be made to be attractive (see Porter, 1980).

2 Focusing within each selected business. Even within the limited set of businesses selected, firms need to determine what they want to be and what they want to leave aside. To be competitive, it is necessary to choose a number of distinct market segments and to target a few special product offerings to meet these customers' needs. As illustrated in Figure 5.1, these specific product offerings in turn need to be aligned with a focused activity system and resource base.

This act of focusing the overall business system to serve the particular needs of a targeted group of buyers, in a way that distinguishes the firm vis-à-vis rivals, is called positioning. This positioning of the firm in the business requires a clearly tailored product offering (product positioning), but also an activity system and resource base that closely fit with the demands of the specific group of customers and competitors being targeted.

Positioning within a business.   Positioning is concerned with both the questions of 'where to compete' and 'how to compete' (Porter, 1980). Determining in which product–market combinations within a business a firm wants to be involved is referred to as the issue of competitive scope. Finding a way to beat rivals and win over customers for a product offering is the issue of competitive advantage. The two questions are tightly linked, because firms need to develop a specific advantage to be competitive within a specific product–market domain. If they try to use the same competitive advantage for too many dissimilar products and customers, they run the risk of becoming unfocused.

In selecting a competitive scope, firms can vary anywhere between being widely oriented and very tightly focused. Firms with a broad scope compete in a large number of segments within a business, with varied product offerings. Firms with a narrow scope target only one, or just a few, customer segments and have a more limited product line (see Figure 5.5). If there is a small part of the business with very specific demands, requiring a distinct approach, firms can narrowly focus on this niche as their competitive scope. In between these two extremes are firms with a segment focus and firms with a product focus, but in practice many other profiles are also possible.

In developing a competitive advantage, firms have many dimensions along which they can attempt to outdo their rivals. Some of the most important bases of competitive advantage are the following:

- **Price.** The most straightforward advantage a firm can have in a competitive situation is the ability to charge a lower price. All things being equal, buyers generally prefer to pay the lowest amount necessary. Hence, when purchasing a commodity product or service, most customers will be partial to the lowest priced supplier. And even when selecting among differentiated products, many customers will be inclined to buy the cheapest or at least the cheapest within a sub-group of more comparable products. For a firm wanting to compete on price, the essential point is that it should have a *low cost* product offering, activity system and resource base to match the price positioning. After all, in the long run a firm can only survive at a lower price level if it has developed a business system that can sustainably operate at a lower cost level.

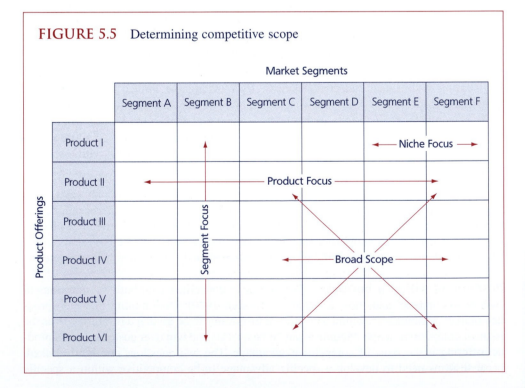

FIGURE 5.5   Determining competitive scope

- **Features.** Firms can also distinguish their product offerings by having different intrinsic functional characteristics than competing offerings. There are many ways to make a product or service different, for instance by changing its size, smell, taste, color, functionality, compatibility, content, design or style. An ice cream manufacturer can introduce a new flavor and more chunky texture, a motorcycle producer can design a special 'low rider' model for women, a pay TV company can develop special channels for dog owners and science fiction addicts, and a utility company can offer environmentally friendly electricity. To be able to compete on each of these product features, firms need to command different specialized resources and activity systems. In some cases, they require significant technological knowledge and a technically sophisticated activity system, while in other cases design capabilities, marketing prowess or a satellite infrastructure are essential to the functioning of the business system.

- **Bundling.** Another way to offer a uniquely different value proposition is to sell a package of products and/or services 'wrapped together'. By bundling a number of separate elements into a package, the customer can have the convenience of 'one stop shopping', while also having a family of related products and/or services that fit together well. So, for instance, many customers prefer to purchase their software from one supplier because this raises the chance of compatibility. In the chocolate industry, the leading manufacturer of chocolate making machines, Rademakers, was able to gain a competitive advantage by bundling its machines with various services, such as installation, repair, spare parts and financing.

- **Quality.** When competing with others, a firm's product offering doesn't necessarily have to be fundamentally different, it can just be better. Customers generally appreciate products and services that exhibit superior performance in terms of usability, reliability and durability, and are often willing to pay a premium price for such quality. Excellent quality can be secured on many fronts, for instance through the materials used, the people involved, the manufacturing process employed, the quality assurance procedures followed or the distribution system used.

- **Availability.** The method of distribution can in itself be the main competitive edge on which a firm bases its positioning. Having a product available at the right place, at the right moment and in the right way, can be much more important to customers than features and quality. Just ask successful ice cream manufacturers – most of their revenues are from out-of-doors impulse sales, so they need to have their products available in individually wrapped portions at all locations where people have the urge to indulge. In the same way, Avon's cosmetics are not primarily sold because of their uniqueness or low price, but because of the strength of their three million sales force, who can be at the right place at the right time.

- **Image.** In the competition for customers' preference, firms can also gain an advantage by having a more appealing image than their rivals. In business-to-consumer markets this is particularly clear when looking at the impact of brands. Consumers often feel attracted to brands that project a certain image of the company or the products it sells. Brands can communicate specific values that consumers want to be associated with (Nike's 'just do it'), or can help to build trust among consumers who have too little information on which to base their product choices (GE's 'we bring good things to life'). But even in business-to-business markets buyers often suffer from a shortage of information about the available product offerings or lack the time to research all possible suppliers. Therefore, the image of suppliers, mostly in terms of their standing ('a leading global player') and reputation ('high quality service') can be essential to be considered at all (to be 'shortlisted') and to be trusted as business partner.

- **Relations.** Good branding can give customers the impression that they know the supplier, without actually being in direct contact. Yet, having a direct relation with customers can in itself be a potent source of competitive advantage. In general, customers prefer to know their suppliers well, as this gives them a more intimate knowledge of the product offering being provided. Having a relationship with a supplier can also give the customer more influence on what is offered. But besides these rational points, customers often value the personal contact, the trust and the convenience of having a long-standing relationship as well. For suppliers this means that they might acquire a competitive edge by managing their customer relationships well. To do so, however, does imply that the activity system and resource base are fit to fulfill this task.

The type of competitive advantage that a firm chooses to pursue will be influenced by what the targeted group of buyers find important. These factors of importance to potential clients are referred to as 'value drivers' – they are the elements responsible for creating value in the eyes of the customer. Which value drivers a firm will want to base its value proposition on is a matter of positioning.

According to Porter (1980) all the specific forms of competitive advantage listed above can be reduced to two broad categories, namely lower cost and differentiation. On the one hand, firms can organize their business systems in such a manner that, while their products or services are largely the same as other manufacturers, their overall cost structure is lower, allowing them to compete on price. On the other hand, firms can organize their business systems to supply a product or service that has distinctive qualities compared to rival offerings. According to Porter, these two forms of competitive advantage demand fundamentally different types of business systems and therefore are next to impossible to combine. Firms that do try to realize both at the same time run the risk of getting 'stuck in the middle' – not being able to do either properly.

Treacy and Wiersema (1995) argue that there are actually three generic competitive advantages, each requiring a fundamentally different type of business system (they speak of three distinctive 'value disciplines'). They, too, warn firms to develop an internally consistent business system focused on one of these types of competitive advantage, avoiding a 'mix-and-match' approach to business strategy:

- **Operational excellence.** Firms striving for operational excellence meet the buyers' need for a reliable, low cost product offering. The activity system required to provide such no-frills, standardized, staple products emphasizes a 'lean and mean' approach to production and distribution, with simple service.

- **Product leadership.** Firms taking the route of product leadership meet the buyers' need for special features and advanced product performance. The activity system required to provide such differentiated, state-of-the-art products emphasizes innovation and the creative collaboration between marketing and R&D.

- **Customer intimacy.** Firms deciding to focus on customer intimacy meet the buyers' need for a tailored solution to their particular problem. The activity system required to provide such a client-specific, made-to-measure offering emphasizes flexibility and empowerment of the employees close to the customer.

Other strategy researchers, however, argue that there is no such thing as generic competitive strategies that follow from two or three broad categories of competitive advantage (e.g. Baden-Fuller and Stopford, 1992). In their view, there is an endless variety of ways in which companies can develop a competitive advantage, many of which do not fit into the categories outlined by Porter or Treacy and Wiersema – in fact, finding a new type of competitive advantage might be the best way of obtaining a unique position in a business.

Activity system

To be able to actually make what it wants to sell, a firm needs to have an activity system in place. An activity system is an integrated set of value creation processes leading to the supply of product and/or service offerings. Whether goods are being manufactured or services are being provided, each firm needs to perform a number of activities to successfully fill the customer's wants. As these value-adding activities need to be coordinated and linked together, this part of the business system is also frequently referred to as the 'value chain' (Porter, 1985).

Activity systems can vary widely from industry to industry. The activity system of a car manufacturer is quite distinct from that of an advertising agency. Yet even within an industry there can be significant differences. Most 'bricks and mortar' bookstores have organized their value chain differently than on-line book retailers like Amazon.com. The activity systems of most 'hub-and-spoke' airline companies hardly resemble that of 'no-frills' carriers such as Southwest in the United States and easyJet in Europe.

While these examples point to radically different activity systems, even firms that subscribe to the same basic model can apply it in their own particular way. Fast-food restaurants such as McDonald's and Burger King may employ the same basic model, but their actual activity systems differ in quite a few ways. The same goes for the PC manufacturers HP and IBM, which share a similar type of activity system, but which still differ on many fronts. 'On-line mass-customization' PC manufacturer Dell, on the other hand, has a different model and consequently a more strongly differing activity system than HP and IBM.

Having such a distinct activity system often provides the basis for a competitive advantage. A unique value chain allows a firm to offer customers a unique value proposition, by doing things better, faster, cheaper, nicer or more tailored than competing firms. Developing the firm's activity system is therefore just as strategically important as developing new products and services.

Although activity systems can differ quite significantly, some attempts have been made to develop a general taxonomy of value-adding activities that could be used as an analytical framework (e.g. Day, 1990; Norman and Ramirez, 1993). By far the most influential framework is Porter's value chain, which distinguishes primary activities and support activities (see Figure 5.6). Primary activities 'are the activities involved in the physical creation of the product and its sale and transfer to the buyer, as well as after-sale assistance' (Porter, 1985: 16). Support activities facilitate the primary process, by providing purchased inputs, technology, human resources and various firm-wide functions. The generic categories of primary activities identified by Porter are:

- Inbound logistics. Activities associated with receiving, storing, and disseminating inputs, including material handling, warehousing, inventory control, vehicle scheduling and returns to suppliers.
- Operations. Activities associated with transforming inputs into final products, including machining, packaging, assembly, equipment maintenance, testing, printing and facility operations.

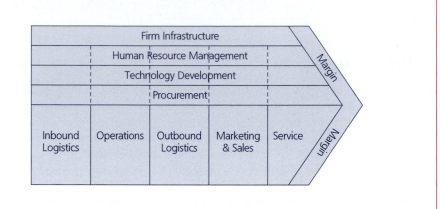

FIGURE 5.6 The generic value chain (Porter, 1985)

- **Outbound logistics.** Activities associated with collecting, storing and physically distributing products to buyers, including warehousing, material handling, delivery, order processing and scheduling.

- **Marketing and sales.** Activities associated with providing a means by which buyers can purchase the product and inducing them to do so, including advertising, promotion, sales force, quoting, channel selection, channel relations and pricing.

- **Service.** Activities associated with providing service to enhance or maintain the value of products, including installation, repair, training, parts supply and product adjustment.

For service industries Porter argues that the specific activities will be different, and might be performed in a different order, but can still be subdivided into these five generic categories. To ensure that the primary activities can be carried out, each firm also needs to organize four types of support activities:

- **Procurement.** Activities associated with the purchasing of inputs to facilitate all other activities, including vendor selection, negotiations, contracting and invoice administration.

- **Technology development.** Activities associated with the improvement of technologies throughout the firm, including basic research, product and process design, and procedure development.

- **Human resource management.** Activities associated with the management of personnel throughout the organization, including recruiting, hiring, training, development and compensation.

- **Firm infrastructure.** Firm infrastructure consists of all general activities that support the entire value chain, including general management, planning, finance, accounting, legal, government affairs and quality management.

The uniqueness of the activity system, and its strength as the source of competitive advantage, will usually not depend on only a few specialized activities, but on the extraordinary configuration of the entire activity system. An extraordinary configuration multiplies the distinctness of a particular activity system, while often raising the barrier to imitation (Porter, 1996; Amit and Zott, 2001).

Resource base

To carry out activities and to produce goods and services, firms need resources. A firm's resource base includes all means at the disposal of the organization for the performance of value-adding activities. Other authors prefer the term 'assets', to emphasize that the resources belong to the firm (e.g. Dierickx and Cool, 1989; Itami, 1987).

Under the broad umbrella of resource-based view of the firm, there has been much research into the importance of resources for the success and even existence of firms (e.g. Penrose, 1959; Wernerfelt, 1984; Barney, 1991). No generally accepted classification of firm resources has yet emerged in the field of strategic management, however the following major distinctions (see Figure 5.7) are commonly made:

- Tangible vs. intangible resources. Tangible resources are all means available to the firm that can physically be observed (touched), such as buildings, machines, materials, land and money. Tangibles can be referred to as the 'hardware' of the organization. Intangibles, on the other hand, are the 'software' of the organization. Intangible resources cannot be touched, but are largely carried within the people in the organization. In general, tangible resources need to be purchased, while intangibles need to be developed. Therefore, tangible resources are often more readily transferable, easier to price and usually are placed on the balance sheet.

- Relational resources vs. competences. Within the category of intangible resources, relational resources and competences can be distinguished. Relational resources are all of the means available to the firm derived from the firm's interaction with its environment (Lowendahl, 1997). The firm can cultivate specific relationships with individuals and organizations in the environment, such as buyers, suppliers, competitors and government agencies, which can be instrumental in achieving the firm's goals. As attested by the old saying, 'it's not what you know, but whom you know', relationships can often be an essential resource (see Chapter 7 for a further discussion). Besides direct relationships, a firm's reputation among other parties in the environment can also be an important resource. Competence, on the other hand, refers to the firm's fitness to perform in a particular field. A firm has a competence if it has the knowledge, capabilities and attitude needed to successfully operate in a specific area.

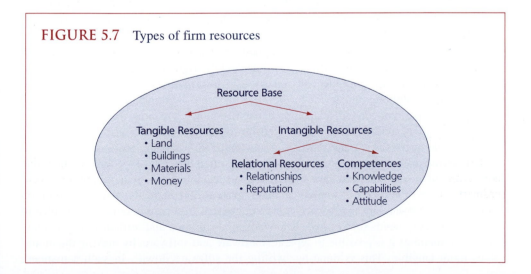

FIGURE 5.7 Types of firm resources

This description of competences is somewhat broad and therefore difficult to employ. However, a distinction between knowledge, capability and attitude (Durand, 1996) can be used to shed more light on the nature of competences:

- **Knowledge.** Knowledge can be defined as the whole of rules (know-how, know-what, know-where and know-when) and insights (know-why) that can be extracted from, and help make sense of, information. In other words, knowledge flows from, and influences, the interpretation of information (Dretske, 1981). Examples of knowledge that a firm can possess are market insight, competitive intelligence, technological expertise, and understanding of political and economic developments.

- **Capability.** Capability refers to the organization's potential for carrying out a specific activity or set of activities. Sometimes the term 'skill' is used to refer to the ability to carry out a narrow (functional) task or activity, while the term 'capability' is reserved for the quality of combining a number of skills. For instance, a firm's capability base can include narrower abilities such as market research, advertising and production skills, that if coordinated could result in a capability for new product development (Stalk, Evans and Shulman, 1992).

- **Attitude.** Attitude refers to the mind-set prevalent within an organization. Sometimes the terms 'disposition' and 'will' are used in the same sense, to indicate how an organization views and relates to the world. Although ignored by some writers, every sports coach will acknowledge the importance of attitude as a resource. A healthy body (tangible resource), insight into the game (knowledge), speed and dexterity (capabilities) – all are important, but without the winning mentality a team will not get to the top. Some attitudes may change rapidly within firms, yet others may be entrenched within the cultural fabric of the organization – these in particular can be important resources for the firm. A company's attitude can, for instance, be characterized as quality-driven, internationally oriented, innovation-minded and/or competitively aggressive.

It must be noted that the term 'competences' is used in many different ways, partially due to the ambiguous definition given by its early proponents (Prahalad and Hamel, 1990). It is often used as a synonym for capabilities, while Prahalad and Hamel seem to focus more on technologically oriented capabilities ('how to coordinate diverse production skills and integrate multiple streams of technologies'). Others (e.g. Durand, 1996) have suggested that a firm has a competence in a certain area, when the firm's underlying knowledge base, capabilities and attitude are all aligned. So, Honda's engine competence is built on specific knowledge, development capabilities and the right predisposition. Wal-Mart's inventory control competence depends on specific information technology knowledge, coordination capabilities and a conducive state of mind. Virgin's service competence combines customer knowledge, adaptation capabilities and a customer-oriented attitude.

As in the case of industries, markets and businesses, employing the concepts of tangible and intangible resources is quite difficult in practice. Two problems need to be overcome – resources are difficult to categorize, but worse yet, often difficult to recognize. The issue of categorization is a minor one. For some resources it is unclear how they should be classified. Are human resources tangible or intangible? Problematically, both. In humans, hardware and software are intertwined – if an engineer's expertise is required, the physical person usually needs to be hired. Knowledge, capabilities and attitudes need human carriers. Sometimes it is possible to separate hardware and software, by making the intangibles more tangible. This is done by 'writing the software down'. In such a manner, knowledge can be codified, for instance in a patent, a capability can be captured in a computer program and a relationship can be formalized in a contract. Sometimes intangibles become more tangible, as they become attached to physical carriers – for instance, attitude can be embodied by a person or a symbol, while reputation becomes attached to a brand.

More important is the problem of resource identification. Tangible resources, by their very nature, are relatively easy to observe. Accountants keep track of the financial resources, production managers usually know the quality of their machinery and stock levels, while the personnel department will have an overview of all people on the payroll. Intangible resources, on the other hand, are far more difficult to identify (e.g. Grant, 1991; Itami, 1987). With whom does the firm have a relationship and what is the state of this relationship? What is the firm's reputation? These relational resources are hard to pin down. Competences are probably even more difficult to determine. How do you know what you know? Even for an individual it is a formidable task to outline areas of expertise, let alone for a more complex organization. Especially the *tacit* (non-articulated) nature of much organizational knowledge makes it difficult to identify the firm's knowledge base (Polanyi, 1958; Nonaka and Konno, 1998). The same is true for a firm's capabilities, which have developed in the form of organizational routines (Nelson and Winter, 1982). Likewise, the firm's attitudes are difficult to discern, because all people sharing the same disposition will tend to consider themselves normal and will tend to believe that their outlook is 'a matter of common sense' (see Chapter 2). Hence, firms intent on identifying their competences find that this is not an easy task.

While an overview of the firm's resource base is important in itself, a strategizing manager will want to compare the firm's resources to other companies to determine their relative strength. In other words, are the firm's resources unique, superior to or inferior to the resources of (potential) competitors? This type of analysis is particularly difficult, as comparison requires insight into other firms' resource bases. Especially the identification of other firms' intangible resources can be quite arduous.

Sustaining competitive advantage

A firm has a competitive advantage when it has the means to edge out rivals when vying for the favor of customers. In the previous sub-sections it was argued that competitive advantage is rooted in a unique business system, whereby the resource base, activity system and product–market position are all aligned to provide goods and/or services with a superior fit to customer needs.

A competitive advantage is said to be sustainable if it cannot be copied, substituted or eroded by the actions of rivals, and is not made redundant by developments in the environment (Porter, 1980). In other words, sustainability depends on two main factors, competitive defendability and environmental consonance:

- Competitive defendability. Some competitive advantages are intrinsically easier to defend than others, either because they are difficult for rivals to imitate, or because rivals find it next to impossible to find an alternative route of attack. In general, a firm's competitive advantage is more vulnerable when it is based on only a limited number of distinct elements (e.g. a different packaging technology, a different delivery system or different product colors). For rivals, imitating or substituting a few elements is comparatively easy. If, however, a firm's business system has an entirely different configuration altogether, the barriers to imitation and substitution are much higher. In such a case, it is said that a firm has a distinct 'business model'. So, for instance, in the airline industry the traditional firms have tried to imitate some parts of the low cost service of Southwest in the United States, and Ryanair and easyJet in Europe, but have been largely unsuccessful because their business model as a whole is based on a different logic. Yet, many strategists note that the best defense is not to build walls around a competitive position to 'keep the barbarians out', but to have the ability to run faster than rivals – to be able to upgrade one's resources, activity system and product offering more rapidly than competitors. In this view, a competitive advantage is sustainable due to a company's capacity to stay one step ahead of rivals, *outpacing* them in a race to stay ahead (e.g. Gilbert and Strebel, 1989; Stalk, Evans and Shulman, 1992).

- **Environmental consonance.** The sustainability of a firm's competitive advantage is also threatened by developments in the market. Customer needs and wants are in constant flux, distribution channels can change, government regulations can be altered, innovative technologies can be introduced and new entrants can come into the competitive arena. All of these developments can undermine the fit between the firm's competitive advantage and the environment, weakening the firm's position (Rumelt, 1980).

Yet, these two factors for sustaining competitive advantage seem to pose opposite demands on the organization. Building a distinctive business system to fend off competition would suggest that a firm should remain true to its fundamental *strengths*, especially when it comes to unique resources and activities that it has built up over a prolonged period of time. On the other hand, environmental consonance requires a firm to continually adapt its business system to the demands and new *opportunities* in the market place. The tension created by these opposite pressures will be discussed in the following section.

THE PARADOX OF MARKETS AND RESOURCES

Sell where you can, you are not for all markets.
As You Like It, William Shakespeare (1564–1616); English dramatist and poet

There must be a fit between an organization and its environment. This point is often expressed in terms of the classic SWOT analysis tool, which suggests that a sound strategy should match a firm's strengths (S) and weaknesses (W) to the opportunities (O) and threats (T) encountered in the firm's environment. The key to success is *alignment* of the two sides. Yet, fitting internal strengths and weaknesses to external opportunities and threats is often frustrated by the fact that the two sides pull in opposite directions – the distinctive resource base and activity system of a firm can point in a totally different direction compared with the developments in their current markets. Take the example of Bally, in the 1990s the worldwide market leader in pinball machines. Their strength in the manufacturing of electromechanical games was no longer aligned with developments in the market, where young people were turning to video games produced by companies such as Nintendo, Sega and Sony. As sales of pinball machines were quickly deteriorating, it was clear that Bally had to find a new fit with the market to survive. On the one hand, this meant that there was a strong pressure on Bally to adapt to market developments, for instance by upgrading its technology to also produce video games. On the other hand, Bally felt a strong pressure to exploit its current strength in electromechanical manufacturing, instead of building a new competence base from scratch. It was not self-evident for Bally how the demands for market adaptation and resource leveraging could be met simultaneously, as they seemed to be tugging the firm in diametrically opposite directions.

This tension arising from the partially conflicting demands of market adaptation and resource leveraging is referred to as the paradox of markets and resources. In the following sub-sections both sides of the paradox will be examined in more detail.

The demand for market adaptation

While adaptation to the environment is a vital requirement for the success of any organization, Bally had been very slow in responding to external developments ever since the introduction of Pac-Man. Bally had not exhibited the ability to shift its product offering to follow changing customer preferences and to respond to new entrants in the gaming market. It had lost its leading position because it no longer fully understood 'the rules of the game' in its own market. As Bally drifted further and further away from developments in the market, the misalignment was threatening the survival of its business. 'Game over' was impending.

To counter this downward trend, Bally needed to identify an attractive market opportunity that it could exploit. Not a short-term sales opportunity, but a market position that could be defended against rival firms and potential new entrants over a longer period. Ideally, this market position would serve buyers willing and able to pay a premium price, and whose loyalty could be won, despite the efforts of the competition. This market position would also need to be largely immune to substitute products and should not make the firm overly dependent on strong suppliers. Once such an opportunity had been identified, it would be essential for Bally to reorganize itself to fully meet the demands of this new positioning.

Adapting to a new market position and subsequently following the many shifts in such factors as customer preferences, competitor moves, government regulations and distribution structures, can have a significant impact on a firm. It requires significant agility in changing the product offering, activity system and resource base to remain in constant alignment with the fluctuating external circumstances. For Bally, adapting to the digital technology and software environment of the current gaming industry would have had far-reaching consequences for its entire business system. Even if Bally decided to stick to electromechanical pinball machines and to target the home market of aging pinball wizards, the company would need to make significant alterations to its business system, getting to know new distribution channels and developing new marketing competences.

The demand for resource leveraging

Yet, for Bally it was essential to build on the resource base and activity system that it had already developed. It did not want to write off the investments it had made in building up a distinctive profile – it had taken years of acquiring and nurturing resources and fine-tuning the activity system to reach its level of expertise. Its strength in electromechanical manufacturing and the development of large 'moving parts' games was much too valuable to casually throw away just because video games were currently in fashion.

However, building a new area of competence, it was understood, should not be considered lightly. It would take a considerable amount of time, effort and money to shift the resource base and reconfigure the activity system, while there would be many risks associated with this transformation process as well. On the other hand, the danger of attempting to exploit the firm's current resources would be to excel at something of increasing irrelevance. The pinball machine might be joining the buggy whip and the vacuum tube as a museum exhibit, with a real threat that Bally too could become history.

Eventually, the solution found by Bally was to give up on pinball machines altogether and to redirect its existing resources towards a much more attractive market opportunity – slot machines. This move allowed Bally to exploit its electromechanical manufacturing capability and game-making expertise, while building a strong market position in a fast growing market. But while Bally was able to find a synthesis, reconciling the two conflicting demands, not all companies are as successful. Nor do all managers agree on how the paradox of markets and resources can best be tackled.

EXHIBIT 5.1 SHORT CASE

AVON: KEEP THOSE DOORBELLS RINGING?

Few powers in the world can field an army of three million, with the ability to reach each corner of the globe. Yet, one organization has such a legion, spread across 143 countries, equipped to engage in close-range encounters, toting little more than some cosmetics samples and a few brochures. This superpower is Avon, the world's largest direct seller of beauty-related products. With 2002 annual sales exceeding US$6 billion, of which more than 60% was outside of North America, Avon is a huge player in the global market for cosmetics, fragrances and toiletries. The New York-based company has a large presence in Europe (about US$2 billion sales) and Latin America (more than US$1 billion sales), with major growth coming from emerging markets such as China. While Avon is generally known for its beauty products, more than 20% of its sales come from fashion jewelry, accessories and apparel, with another 15% realized in the areas of gifts, decorative items and home entertainment.

From its start in 1886 as the California Perfume Company, the firm has been based on the concept of independent sales representatives selling directly to women. These sales reps are independent intermediaries, who buy from Avon at a discount and then resell to their clients at list price. While men are not excluded as sales people, only a small fraction of the 'Avon Ladies' are not female. In the early years most of the sales were done 'door-to-door', making the 1950s slogan 'Ding Dong, Avon Calling' quite appropriate. Since then, large numbers of women have shifted to paid employment in most of Avon's major markets and the company has followed them, making about a third of all sales at work. Yet, Avon's positioning has remained basically the same as at the outset – quality beauty products are provided to women of average and below average income at competitive prices, while offering personal attention and advice.

In 1999 Andrea Jung became Avon's CEO – the first female in the company's history to occupy the top job, but reflective of a management pyramid composed of more than 50% women. With years of experience in the company, Jung was acutely aware that Avon was facing a difficult battle on many fronts, particularly in its mature North American and Western European markets. On the competitive front, a number of early movers in the e-business domain, like Eve.com, ibeauty.com and women.com, had caught Avon off guard, by building up a strong direct sales channel over the Internet, while Avon had hardly taken any initiatives in this direction. At the same time, new cosmetics retailers were developing, such as the Sephora superstores in the United States, and in many countries the fragmented retailing sector was being consolidated and further professionalized. On the consumer front, Avon's brand was perceived as stale and down market, particularly by fashion-conscious younger women. Despite years of efforts to revitalize the brand, for many women Avon retained the connotation of the 1950s housewife. As Jung's predecessor, James Preston, confessed: 'I am well aware that there are many women who would not want to open their purses and pull out Avon lipstick.' To compound the image problem, Avon was finding it increasingly difficult to find new, younger recruits as Avon Ladies. For years the sales force in the mature markets had been shrinking, as younger women no longer had plenty of spare time to sell beauty products, or had better-paying alternatives open to them.

To counter these strategic weaknesses, Jung set out to bring about a 'thoughtful transformation' of Avon. Her first priority was to rejuvenate the Avon brand, and a new advertising campaign was launched around the slogan 'Let's Talk', a new tag line was added to the Avon logo ('The Company for Women'), packaging was upgraded, to create a Lancôme or Estee Lauder type luxury feel to the products and brochures were restyled to fit the new image. Jung also carried through some drastic business process redesign activities, streamlining production and logistics, indicating that she wanted to cut 8% of the workforce (3800 positions) by 2004.

Another important move Jung set out to implement was to strengthen the sales force, both in numbers and in quality. To improve the quality, Jung initiated the Beauty Advisor program, aimed at training tens of thousands of salespeople each year in the areas of beauty product knowledge and consultative selling skills. To increase the number of sales women was much more difficult since Avon, like most direct sales companies, experienced a nearly 100% turnover of its sales force each year. A core group of sales representatives – the President's Club – form the backbone of the system, generally selling full-time for many years, while the other 80% are part-timers that on average stay less than one year. To recruit more than two million salespeople each year is quite an effort, especially since Avon is not a 'network marketing' organization in which each sales representative can recruit their own resellers (multi-level sales structure). As Avon has a single level sales organization, more management time must be spent finding and training new recruits. To get the existing salespeople to assist with this task, Jung introduced a 'Sales Leadership' program, offering significant bonuses for contributing to the expansion of the sales force.

But with pressure to grow and to improve profitability, more was needed than these realignment measures. Jung was convinced that organic growth through the direct sales channels would be too limited in scale and would not catapult Avon into the top league. Therefore, Jung introduced the slogan, 'The brand is bigger than the channel', and started to look for ways to become a multichannel company. An early experiment was the initiative to start free-standing beauty kiosks in more than 50 shopping malls around the United States, to bring shoppers into contact with Avon products. In 2000, a hugely updated Avon.com was relaunched, which allowed each sales rep to run their personalized web site, making use of the Avon platform. Much more surprisingly, Avon announced that it would be moving into retail channels, launching an entirely new, upmarket product line called beComing in 125 Sears Roebuck stores in the United States in 2001. When Sears withdrew from this agreement because of a shift in strategy, Jung signed a deal with retailer J.C. Penney to have an Avon 'store-within-a-store' at 92 locations across the United States, all focusing on the beComing line of beauty products and fashion accessories. Jung emphasized that by developing a separate, premium product line, Avon would be able to access a group of consumers not yet served by the company, without conflicting with the interests of the direct sales channel.

Next to the new beComing product line, 2001 also saw the introduction of Avon Wellness, a line of health and wellness products, including vitamins, nutritional supplements, exercise and fitness items, and self-care and stress relief items. These products were placed in a separate brochure, but were intended to be sold through the existing direct sales channel, as well as in the retail outlets.

In 2002, Avon announced that it intended to target yet another difficult, but tantalizingly lucrative, market – teenage girls and young women. Noting that females between 16 and 24 in its top 20 markets spend US$200 billion on consumer goods annually, Avon outlined a plan to develop a line of several hundred different cosmetics and related products, under the new brand name 'mark', to be launched in the United States in 2003 and globally in 2004. An integral part of this plan was to recruit teenage girls and young women into the Avon sales force to be able to sell to the target group, as well as setting up a separate system of 'mark' salespeople, to visit colleges, high schools, shopping malls and other youth-oriented spots. To run this entire operation a new unit, Avon Future, was established.

By the beginning of 2003, things seemed to be going well for Avon. The economic downturn in many of its key markets in 2002 had actually largely worked in its favor, as many women turned to its lower priced products, while others looked for part-time employment as sales representative to prop up their sagging income. Then, fairly suddenly, Avon and J.C. Penney announced that they were ending their retail alliance, and Avon indicated that it would be selling its beComing product line exclusively through its certified Avon Beauty Advisors. According to Jung 'research confirms that consumer reaction to this prestige brand has been very positive. By offering beComing through our core business, we expect to accelerate sales of the brand, advance earnings of our Beauty Advisors, and attract new customers.' However, she denied that this meant the end of Avon's retail adventure: 'Avon remains committed to a multi-brand, multi-channel strategy and we will continue to pursue opportunities to reach new customer segments that prefer a retail shopping experience,' adding that Avon's retail president, Steve Bock, was not out of a job.

Yet, the company seemed at a crossroads. Some critical observers wondered out loud whether Avon had not overstretched itself, pursuing too many divergent growth directions at the same time. At the very least it seemed that Jung would have to set clear priorities for the coming period. On the one hand, Avon could focus on the challenge of expanding and upgrading its direct sales organization to carry two new brands (beComing and mark), reaching new market segments (more affluent women and younger women) and carrying new products (for instance Avon Wellness products). This would mean that in its core, Avon would remain a direct sales organization, building on this traditional strength. On the other hand, Avon could stay on the earlier track of becoming a multi-brand, multi-channel beauty company, to make optimal use of the market opportunities identified, but then the company would need to do some serious work to achieve this objective. Whichever focus was pursued, the challenges for the coming years seemed large, calling for some clear strategic choices, not merely a cosmetic touch up.

Sources: Avon annual reports 1997–2001; Avon.com; *Fortune*, October 15 2001; *Business Week*, August 20 2002 and January 13 2003.

PERSPECTIVES ON BUSINESS LEVEL STRATEGY

Always to be best, and to be distinguished above the rest.

The Iliad, Homer (8th century BC); Greek poet

Firms need to adapt themselves to market developments and they need to build on the strengths of their resource bases and activity systems. The main question dividing managers is 'who should be fitted to whom' – should an organization adapt itself to its environment or should it attempt to adapt the environment to itself? What should be the dominant factor driving a firm, its strengths or the opportunities? Should managers take the environment as the starting point, choose an advantageous market position and then build the resource base and activity system necessary to implement this choice? Or should managers take the organization's resource base (and possibly also its activity system) as the starting point, selecting and/or adapting an environment to fit with these strengths?

As before, the strategic management literature comes with strongly different views on how managers should proceed. The variety of opinions among strategy theorists is dauntingly large, with many incompatible prescriptions being given. Here the two diametrically opposed positions will be identified and discussed in order to show the richness of differing opinions. On the one side of the spectrum, there are those managers who argue that the market opportunities should be leading, while implying that the organization should adapt itself to the market position envisioned. This point of view is called the 'outside-in perspective'. At the other end of the spectrum, many managers believe that competition eventually revolves around rival resource bases and that firms must focus their strategies on the development of unique resources and activity systems. They argue that product–market positioning is a tactical decision that can be taken later. This view is referred to as the 'inside-out perspective'.

The outside-in perspective

 Managers with an outside-in perspective believe that firms should not be self-centered, but should continuously take their environment as the starting point when determining their strategy. Successful companies, it is argued, are externally oriented and market-driven (e.g. Day, 1990; Webster, 1994). They have their sights clearly set on developments in the market-place and are determined to adapt to the unfolding opportunities and threats encountered. They take their cues from customers and competitors, and use these signals to determine their own game plan (Jaworski and Kohli, 1993). For these successful companies, markets are leading, resources are following.

Therefore, for the outside-in directed manager, developing strategy begins with an analysis of the environment to identify attractive market opportunities. Potential customers must be sought, whose needs can be satisfied more adequately than currently done by other firms. Once these customers have been won over and a market position has been established, the firm must consistently defend or build on this position by adapting itself to changes in the environment. Shifts in customers' demands must be met, challenges from rival firms must be countered, impending market entries by outside firms must be rebuffed and excessive pricing by suppliers must be resisted. In short, to the outside-in manager the game of strategy is about market positioning and understanding and responding to external developments. For this reason, the outside-in perspective is sometimes also referred to as the 'positioning approach' (Mintzberg, Ahlstrand and Lampel, 1998).

Positioning is not short-term, opportunistic behavior, but requires a strategic perspective, because superior market positions are difficult to attain, but once conquered can be the source of sustained profitability. Some proponents of the outside-in perspective argue that in each market a number of different positions can yield sustained profitability. For instance, Porter suggests that companies that focus on a particular niche, and companies that strongly differentiate their product offering, can achieve strong and profitable market positions, even if another company has the lowest cost position (Porter, 1980, 1985). Other authors emphasize that the position of being market leader is particularly important (e.g. Buzzell and Gale, 1987). Companies with a high market share profit more from economies of scale, benefit from risk aversion among customers, have more bargaining power towards buyers and suppliers, and can more easily flex their muscles to prevent new entrants and block competitive attacks.

Unsurprisingly, proponents of the outside-in perspective argue that insight into markets and industries is essential. Not only the general structure of markets and industries needs to be analyzed, but also the specific demands, strengths, positions and intentions of all major forces need to be determined. For instance, buyers must be understood with regard to their needs, wants, perceptions, decision-making processes and bargaining chips. The same holds true for suppliers, competitors, potential market and/or industry entrants and providers of substitute products (Porter, 1980, 1985). Once a manager knows 'what makes the market tick' – sometimes referred to as the 'rules of the game' – a position can be identified within the market that could give the firm bargaining power vis-à-vis suppliers and buyers, while keeping competitors at bay. Of course, the wise manager will not only emphasize winning under the current rules with the current players, but will attempt to anticipate market and industry developments, and position the firm to benefit from these. Many outside-in advocates even advise firms to initiate market and industry changes, so that they can be the first to benefit from the altered rules of the game (this issue will be discussed further in Chapter 8).

Proponents of the outside-in perspective readily acknowledge the importance of firm resources and activities for cashing in on market opportunities the firm has identified. If the firm does not have, or is not able to develop or obtain, the necessary resources to implement a particular strategy, then specific opportunities will be unrealizable. Therefore, managers should always keep the firm's strengths and weaknesses in mind when choosing an external position, to ensure that it remains feasible. Yet, to the outside-in strategist, the firm's current resource base should not be the starting point when determining strategy, but should merely be acknowledged as a potentially limiting condition on the firm's ability to implement the best business strategy.

Actually, firms that are market-driven are often the first ones to realize that new resources and/or activities need to be developed and, therefore, are better positioned to build up a 'first mover advantage' (Lieberman and Montgomery, 1988, 1998). Where the firm does not have the ability to catch up with other firms' superior resources, it can always enter into an alliance with a leading organization, offering its partner a crack at a new market opportunity.

EXHIBIT 5.2 THE OUTSIDE-IN PERSPECTIVE

KODAK: REFOCUSING ON DIGITAL IMAGING

In 1888, inventor and entrepreneur George Eastman launched a new type of photographic camera that was pre-loaded with a roll of the light-sensitive film he had recently invented. This 'Kodak' camera marked the start of snapshot photography and ever since then the Kodak company has been inspired by Eastman's sales slogan, 'You push the button – we do the rest'. Kodak has been at the forefront of technological developments in photography, introducing color film, pocketsize cameras and photo-developing machines. Along the way, the company diversified into the related chemicals business, and from there into pharmaceuticals. By the beginning of the 1990s, Kodak was an unwieldy giant, with more than 100 000 employees, where innovation and market adaptation were slow, and growth and profitability were under pressure.

Then came the impending digital revolution. Kodak's picture-making technology was chemical-based, while the upcoming technology was IT-based, requiring different cameras and different 'information carriers'. The new digital imaging technologies promised to shake up the value system in the industry, as there would be no more need for film developers. For Kodak the initial question was how deeply its markets might be penetrated by the rival technology. Would digital imaging be largely confined to the high-end 'studio' market for professional photographers, or would it be equally successful among the midrange segment of photo-journalists and serious hobbyists? Or might it even invade the 'Point 'n Shoot' part of the market, where Kodak's 35mm film has a dominant position? Furthermore, Kodak needed to assess whether it could develop digital imaging capabilities of its own, strong enough to compete with such battle-hardened, digital savvy companies as Canon, Apple, Sony and Hewlett Packard. Not only would Kodak need to catch up technologically, but they would also need to adapt to their competitors' grueling pace of competence-building and new product development.

Alternatively, Kodak could ignore these new market developments and not step into the digital imaging 'free fighting' arena. Despite potential inroads that digital imaging might make, worldwide film sales were still predicted to grow slightly until 2000. Rather, it could look for ways to build on the chemical and printing competences it already possessed.

But this was not Kodak's perspective – they wanted to remain the world's leading imaging company, whatever competences and activity system that would require. So, ex-Motorola CEO, George Fischer was hired in 1993 and he set out to transform Kodak into a digital company. He divested Kodak's chemical and pharmaceutical businesses and poured most of the R&D budget into digital imaging technologies. Where key competences were lacking, alliances were established, for instance with Adobe (software), Hewlett Packard (inkjet printing), IBM (optical storage) and Wang (document architecture). The first digital camera for consumers was introduced in 1995, followed by a flood of new digital products and services since then. When in 2000 a successor to Fischer was sought, long-time Kodak insider Daniel Carp was selected, particularly because of his market-driven mentality.

According to Carp, 'the digital world opened up a treasure chest of possibilities . . . our strong business in traditional photography will allow us to fund our digital strategy for the long term'. In 2003 the company invested two-thirds of its US$900 million R&D budget in digital technology, stating that within the next decade about half of Kodak's revenues should come from the digital market. According to Carp: 'We are developing new tools and new software across all digital areas. These tools will give our customers what we call the "Digital Wow Factor".'

Sources: www.kodak.com; Kodak annual reports 2000–2002; *Photo Industry Reporter*, various issues 2002–2003; *Business Week*, August 2 1999 and January 8 2003.

The inside-out perspective

Managers adopting an inside-out perspective believe that strategies should not be built around external opportunities, but around a company's strengths. Successful companies, it is argued, build up a strong resource base over an extended period of time, which offers them access to unfolding market opportunities in the medium and short term. For such companies, the starting point of the strategy formation process is the question of which resource base it wants to have. The fundamental strategic issue is which difficult-to-imitate competences and exclusive assets should be acquired and/or further refined. Creating such a resource platform requires major investments and a long breath, and to a large extent will determine the culture and identity of the organization. Hence, it is of the utmost importance and should be the central tenet of a firm's strategy. Once the long-term direction for the building of the resource infrastructure has been set, attention can be turned to identifying market opportunities where these specific strengths can be exploited. To the inside-out oriented manager the issue of market positioning is essential, as only a strong competitive position in the market will result in above-average profitability. However, market positioning must take place within the context of the broader resource-based strategy and not contradict the main thrust of the firm – selected market positions must leverage the existing resource base, not ignore it. In other words, market positioning is vital, but tactical, taking place within the boundaries set by the resource-driven strategy. For success, resources should be leading, and markets following.

Many managers taking an inside-out perspective tend to emphasize the importance of a firm's competences over its tangible resources (physical assets). Their way of looking at strategy is referred to as the competence-based view (e.g. Prahalad and Hamel, 1990; Sanchez, Heene and Thomas, 1996) or capabilities-based view (e.g. Stalk, Evans and Shulman, 1992; Teece, Pisano and Shuen, 1997). These managers point out that it is especially the development of unique abilities that is such a strenuous and lengthy process, more so than the acquisition of physical resources, such as production facilities and computer systems. Some companies might be able to achieve a competitive advantage based on physical assets, but usually such tangible infrastructure is easily copied or purchased. However, competences are not readily for sale on the open market as 'plug-and-play' components, but need to be painstakingly built up by an organization through hard work and experience. Even where a company takes a short cut by buying another organization or engaging in an alliance, it takes significant time and effort to internalize the competences in such a way that they can be put to productive use. Hence, having distinctive competences can be a very attractive basis for competitive advantage, as rival firms generally require a long time to catch up (e.g. Collis and Montgomery, 1995; Barney, 1991). And even if competitors are successful at identifying embedded competences and imitating them, the company with an initial lead can work at upgrading its competences in a race to stay ahead – this is often referred to as the dynamic capabilities view (Teece, Pisano and Shuen, 1997).

To proponents of the inside-out perspective the 'dynamic capabilities' argument accentuates the importance of committing the organization to the long-term development of a limited set of competences in which it can stay ahead of rivals. The 'nightmare scenario' for inside-out oriented strategists is where the firm flexibly shifts from one market demand to the next, building up an eclectic collection of unrelated competences, none of which are distinctive compared to competence-focused companies. In this scenario, a firm is fabulously market-driven, adaptively responding to shifts in the environment, but incapable of concentrating itself on forming the distinctive competence base needed for a robust competitive advantage over the longer term.

Most inside-out oriented managers also recognize the 'shadow side' of competences – they are not only difficult to learn, but difficult to unlearn as well. The laborious task of building up competences makes it hard to switch to new competences, even if that is what the market demands (e.g. Christensen, 1997; Rumelt, 1996). Companies far down the route of competence specialization, find themselves locked in by the choices made in the past. In the same way as few concert pianists are able (and willing) to switch to playing saxophone when they are out of a job, few companies are able and willing to scrap their competence base, just because the market is taking a turn for the worse. Becoming a concert pianist not only costs years of practice but is a way of life, with a specific way of working, network and career path, making it very unattractive to make a mid-career shift towards a more marketable trade. Likewise, companies experience that their core competences can simultaneously be their core rigidities, locking them out of new opportunities (Leonard-Barton, 1995). From an inside-out perspective, both companies and concert pianists should therefore first try to build on their unique competences and attempt to find or create a more suitable market, instead of reactively adapting to the unpredictable whims of the current environment (see Figure 5.8).

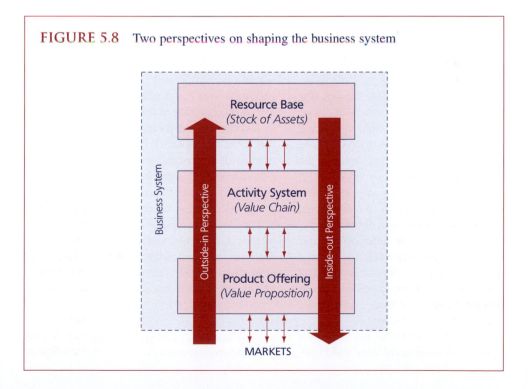

FIGURE 5.8   Two perspectives on shaping the business system

EXHIBIT 5.3 THE INSIDE-OUT PERSPECTIVE

RED BULL: BULLISH ABOUT ITS OWN WINGS

In the early 1980s, Dietrich Mateschitz, an Austrian traveling through South-East Asia, came across a local 'energy drink', containing ingredients such as taurine, caffeine and vitamins, and his entrepreneurial interest was directly spurred. Based on this example, he launched his own silver-canned energy drink, 'Red Bull', in 1987, starting an entirely new global beverage category. Soon, his little company seemed fueled by its own energy drink, and got wings. The company internationalized and experienced exponential growth throughout the 1990s. By 2001 Red Bull operated in more than 80 countries, including Japan, the United States, and most European countries, and had an estimated global market share of 70–90% in the quickly expanding energy drink category. Red Bull employed more than 1500 people, while selling 1.6 billion cans a year and realizing a turnover of €400 million.

The success of Red Bull did not go unnoticed. By the mid-1990s the first competitors entered the market with cheaper copycat products. More threatening was that the sleeping giants, Coca-Cola and PepsiCo, also awakened and moved into the branded energy drink business. Their frontal attack on Red Bull's market leadership pressured Mateschitz to explore ways to retain Red Bull's competitive advantage against the Goliaths. However, for many observers it seemed clear that Red Bull's only real option for not getting run over by the Coke and Pepsi steamrollers was to 'get out of the way' – to find a smaller, more defensible niche. Such a market positioning would have a large impact on the Red Bull organization, but it was suggested that in the long run it would be a more viable proposition than trying to take on two weighty sumo wrestlers.

However, Mateschitz was not perturbed by the prospect of taking on Coke and Pepsi, and in 2002 announced a two-pronged counter-attack. First, Mateschitz indicated that he would build further on Red Bull's existing distinctive competence, to create a slightly zany brand image and to market the experience instead of the product. To remain ahead of its lumbering competitors, Red Bull would be more agile and creative at boosting the brand. Mateschitz himself would be putting two days per week into 'generating wacky ideas' to promote Red Bull, particularly on the US home turf of Coke and Pepsi.

The second part of Red Bull's counter-attack would be to gain critical size, by introducing an entirely new drink to the market, called LunAqua. This drink, a natural spring water bottled during full moon, would be launched using the most important parts of Red Bull's resource base and activity system as its key ingredients. Crucially, Red Bull's international team of young and slightly contrarian brand-builders would cultivate an experience around LunAqua, including promotional stunts around 'full moon parties' and all types of sponsored events. Red Bull's carefully nurtured close relations with athletes and Red Bull fans would be leveraged to quickly bring LunAqua into the limelight. The Red Bull logo would also be put on the small bottle, to leverage brand awareness. Furthermore, the company would take advantage of its worldwide distribution network in retail, (sports)bars and nightclubs to get LunAqua flowing to potential customers.

By 2003 it was becoming clear that Red Bull's decision to build on its strengths and to give Coca-Cola and PepsiCo a run for their money was leading to positive results. Observers might have been right that Mateschitz and his team were 'lunatics', but obviously lunatics with wings.

Sources: *The Economist*, May 11 2002; www.red-bull.com; company reports.

TOWARDS A SYNTHESIS

One does not gain much by mere cleverness.

Marquis de Vauvenargues (1715–1747);
French soldier and moralist

Drive thy business; let it not drive thee.

Benjamin Franklin (1706–1790);
American writer and statesman

So, how can a sustainable competitive advantage be created? Should generals create a sustainable competitive advantage by first selecting a superior position in the environment (e.g. a mountain pass) and then adapt their military resources to this position, or should generals develop armies with unique resources and then try to let the battle take place where these resources can best be employed? Should football coaches first determine how they want the game to be played on the field and then attract and train players to fit with this style, or should coaches develop uniquely talented players and then adapt the team's playing style to make the best use of these resources? Whether a military, sports or business strategist, an approach to creating competitive advantage must be chosen.

As no consensus has yet developed within the field of strategic management on how to balance markets and resources, it is once again up to each individual to assess the arguments put forward in the debate and to form their own opinion.

In Table 5.1 the main arguments of the two opposite poles have been summarized. It is now up to the reader to turn these arguments 'inside-out' and 'outside-in' and to see whether they can be synthesized into an approach that combines the best of both worlds.

TABLE 5.1   Outside-in versus inside-out perspective

	Outside-in perspective	Inside-out perspective
Emphasis on	Markets over resources	Resources over markets
Orientation	Opportunity-driven (external potential)	Strength-driven (internal potential)
Starting point	Market demand and industry structure	Resource base and activity system
Fit through	Adaptation to environment	Adaptation of environment
Strategic focus	Attaining advantageous position	Attaining distinctive resources
Strategic moves	External positioning	Building resource base
Tactical moves	Acquiring necessary resources	External positioning
Competitive weapons	Bargaining power and mobility barriers	Superior resources and imitation barriers

FURTHER READING

Whoever is winning at the moment will always seem to be invincible.

George Orwell (1903–1950); English novelist

Although many textbooks give an overview of the variety of approaches to the topic of business level strategy, none of these introductions are as crisp as John Kay's book,

Foundations of Corporate Success: How Business Strategies Add Value, which can be highly recommended as further reading. For a clear summary of the competing perspectives on business level strategy, see Robert Hoskisson's article 'Theory and Research in Strategic Management: Swings of a Pendulum'.

Most of what has been published on the topic of business level strategy has implicitly or explicitly made reference to the work of Michael Porter. Therefore, any follow-up readings should include his benchmark works *Competitive Strategy* and *Competitive Advantage*. It is also interesting to see how his thinking has developed and has embraced some of the resource-based concepts. In particular his articles 'Towards a Dynamic Theory of Strategy', and 'What is Strategy?' are stimulating works. Also highly recommended is the book by Robert Buzzell and Bradley Gale, *The PIMS Principles: Linking Strategy to Performance*, which has had a big impact by clarifying how market share and profitability are closely linked.

For a better insight into the resource-based approach, readers might want to go back to Edith Penrose's classic book *The Theory of the Growth of the Firm*. For a more recent introduction, the follow-up to Jay Barney's classic article, 'Firm Resources and Sustained Competitive Advantage', is recommended. This article, written together with Mike Wright and David Ketchen, is titled 'The Resource-Based View of the Firm: Ten Years After 1991' and was part of an insightful special issue of the *Journal of Management*. David Collis and Cynthia Montgomery have also written an accessible article explaining the resource-based view, entitled 'Competing on Resources: Strategy in the 1990s'. Other important works that are more academically oriented are 'Dynamic Capabilities and Strategic Management' by David Teece, Garry Pisano and Amy Shuen, and 'The Cornerstones of Competitive Advantage: A Resource-Based View' by Margaret Peteraf. Two very stimulating articles bringing together outside-in and inside-out arguments are 'The Capabilities of Market-Driven Organizations', by George Day, and 'Strategic Integration: Competing in the Age of Capabilities', by Peter Fuchs, Kenneth Mifflin, Danny Miller and John Whitney.

Last, but not least, the works of Garry Hamel and C.K. Prahalad should be mentioned. Many of their articles in *Harvard Business Review*, such as 'Strategic Intent,' 'Strategy as Stretch and Leverage' and 'The Core Competence of the Corporation' (Prahalad and Hamel, 1990) have had a major impact, both on practitioners and academics, and are well worth reading. Many of the ideas expressed in these articles have been brought together in their book *Competing for the Future*, which is therefore highly recommended.

CORPORATE LEVEL STRATEGY

We are not all capable of everything.
Virgil (70–19 BC); Roman philosopher

INTRODUCTION

As firms seek growth, they have a number of directions in which they can expand. The most direct source of increased revenue is to enlarge their market share, selling more of their current product offerings in their current market segments. Besides this growth through focused market penetration, firms can also broaden their scope by extending their product range (product development) and/or move into neighboring market segments and geographic areas (market development). All of these growth options can be pursued while staying within the 'boundaries' of a single business (see Figure 6.1). However, firms can broaden their scope even further, venturing into other lines of business, thus becoming multi-business corporations. Some multi-business firms are involved in only two or three businesses, but there are numerous corporations spanning 20, 30, or more, business areas.

This chapter deals with the specific strategic questions facing firms as they work on determining their multi-business scope. At this level, strategists must not only consider how to gain a competitive advantage in each line of business the firm has entered, but also which businesses they should be in at all. Corporate level strategy is about selecting an optimal set of businesses and determining how they should be integrated into the corporate whole. This issue of deciding on the best array of businesses and relating them to one another is referred to as the issue of 'corporate configuration'.

THE ISSUE OF CORPORATE CONFIGURATION

All multi-business firms have a particular configuration, either intentionally designed or as the result of emergent formation. Determining the configuration of a corporation can be disentangled into two main questions: (a) What businesses should the corporation be active in? and (b) How should this group of businesses be managed? This first question of deciding on the business areas that will be covered by the company is called the topic of 'corporate composition'. The second question, of deciding on the organizational system necessary to run the cluster of businesses, is labeled as the issue of 'corporate management'. In the following pages both questions will be explored in more detail.

Corporate composition

A multi-business firm is composed of two or more businesses. When a corporation enters yet another line of business, either by starting up new activities (internal growth) or by buying another firm (acquisition), this is called diversification. There are two general categories of diversification moves, vertical and horizontal. Vertical diversification, usually called vertical integration, is when a firm enters other businesses upstream or downstream within its own industry column (see Chapter 5) – it can strive for backward integration by getting involved in supplier businesses or it can initiate forward integration by entering the businesses of its buyers. The firm can also integrate related businesses at the same tier in the industry column – an example of such horizontal integration is when a newspaper and magazine publisher moves into educational publishing, as Thomson did. If a firm expands outside of its current industry, the term 'integration' is no longer employed, and the step is referred to as straightforward (horizontal) diversification (see Figure 6.1).

The issue of corporate composition deals with the question of where the firm wants to have which level of involvement. Corporate level strategists must decide where to allocate resources, build up activities and try to achieve market sales. The issue of corporate composition can be further subdivided into two parts:

FIGURE 6.1   Corporate growth directions

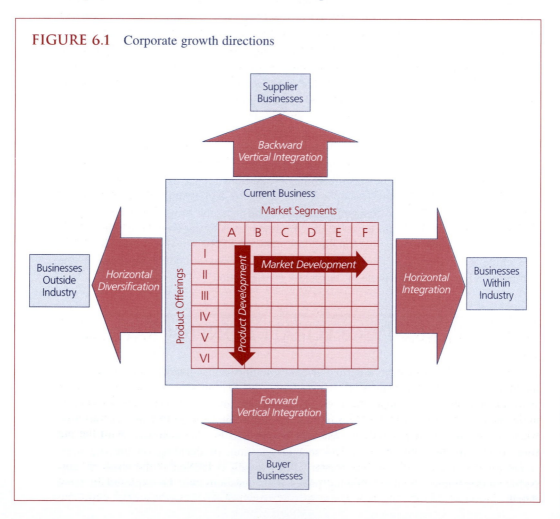

- Corporate scope. First, the composition of the corporation depends on the business areas selected. The more 'business components' chosen, the broader the scope of the corporation. Deciding on the corporate scope is not only a matter of choosing out of the diversification options depicted in Figure 6.1, but can also work in the opposite direction, as a firm can withdraw from a certain line of business, either by divesting, or closing down, its activities.

- Corporate distribution. The composition of the corporation also depends on the relative size of the activities in each business area covered. The distribution within the corporation is determined by the relative weight of each business component. Some corporations are equally active in all of their selected businesses, while other firms are more asymmetrical, placing more emphasis on just a few of their business activities. Deciding on the corporate distribution is a matter of determining which lines of business will receive more attention than others. Corporate level strategists need to decide which activities will be the focus of further growth and increased weight within the firm, allocating resources accordingly. However, they must also keep in mind that a certain balance within the corporation might be beneficial.

A common way of depicting the corporate composition is to plot all of the businesses in a 'portfolio matrix'. The term 'portfolio' refers to the set of business activities carried out by the corporation. In a portfolio matrix each business activity is represented as a 'bubble' in a two-dimensional grid, with the size of the bubble reflecting the revenue generated with that activity. The number of bubbles indicates the corporate scope, while the corporate distribution can be seen in the relative size of the bubbles. The intention of a portfolio matrix is not merely to give an overview of the corporate scope and distribution, but also to provide insight into the growth and profitability potential of each of the corporation's business activities and to judge the balance between the various business activities.

There are different types of portfolio matrices in use, the most well known of which (see Figure 6.2) are the Boston Consulting Group matrix (Hedley, 1977) and the General Electric business screen (Hofer and Schendel, 1978). All of these portfolio matrices are based on the same analytical format. Each business activity is mapped along two dimensions – one measuring the attractiveness of the business itself, the other measuring the strength of the corporation to compete in the business. In other words, one axis is a measure of external *opportunity*, while the other axis is a measure of internal *strength* in comparison to rival firms. The major difference between the portfolio matrices is which measures are used along the axes. The BCG matrix employs two simple variables: business growth to determine attractiveness and relative market share to reflect competitive strength. The GE business screen, on the other hand, uses composite measures: both industry attractiveness and competitive position are determined by analyzing and weighing a number of different factors. Industry attractiveness will be impacted by such variables as sales growth, demand cyclicality, buyer power, supplier power, the threat of new entrants, the threat of substitutes and competitive intensity. Competitive position often reflects such factors as market share, technological know-how, brand image, customer loyalty, cost structure and distinctive competences. Another difference between the two matrices is that in the BCG portfolio grid the bubbles represent the company's sales in a line of business, while in the GE business screen the bubbles reflect the total business size, with the pie slices indicating the firm's share of the business.

Deciding which portfolio of businesses to pursue, both in terms of corporate scope and corporate distribution, will depend on how the corporate strategist intends to create value – or as Porter (1987) puts it, how the corporate strategist wants to make 'the corporate

FIGURE 6.2   The BCG matrix and GE business screen

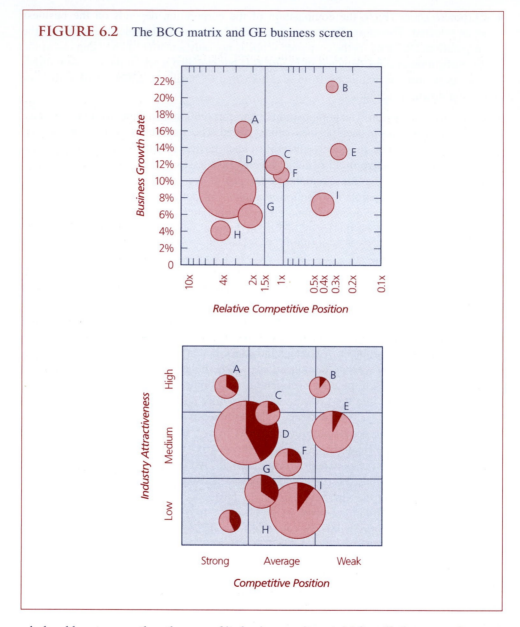

whole add up to more than the sum of its business unit parts.' After all, there must be some benefit to having the various business activities together in one corporation, otherwise each business activity could just as easily (and with less overhead) be carried out by autonomous firms. This added value of having two or more business activities under one corporate umbrella is called 'multi-business synergy' and it strongly determines the corporate composition the strategist will prefer. But before turning to the topic of synergy, the counterpart of corporate composition, namely corporate management, needs to be reviewed first.

Corporate management

It has become a widespread policy to organize multi-business firms into strategic business units (SBUs). Each strategic business unit is given the responsibility to serve the particular demands of one business area. The business units are labeled 'strategic', because each is driven by its own business level strategy.

This dominant approach to structuring multi-business firms does present managers with the issue of how to bring together the separate parts into a cohesive corporate whole. The corporation can be divided into business units with the intent of focusing each on separate business areas, but this *differentiation* must be offset by a certain degree of *integration* to be able to address common issues and realize synergies (Lawrence and Lorsch, 1967). The challenge for managers is to find the most effective and efficient forms of integration between two or more separate business units. Three key integration mechanisms can be distinguished:

- Centralization. The most straightforward form of integration is to bring resources and activities physically together into one organizational unit. In other words, where the 'division of labor' between the business units has not been applied, resources and activities will be kept together in one department. Such a centralized department can be situated at the corporate center, but can also reside at one of the business units or at another location.

- Coordination. Even where resources, activities and product offerings have been split along business unit lines, integration can be achieved by ensuring that coordination is carried out between business units. Such orchestration of work across business unit boundaries should result in the ability to operate as if the various parts were actually one unit.

- Standardization. Integration can also be realized by standardizing resources, activities and/or product offering characteristics across business unit boundaries. By having similar resources (e.g. technologies, people), standardized activities (e.g. R&D, human resource management) and common product features (e.g. operating system, high-tech positioning) such advantages as economies of scale and rapid competence development can be achieved without the need to physically centralize or continuously coordinate.

These three integration mechanisms are the tools available to managers to achieve a certain level of harmonization between the various parts of the corporate whole. Yet it is often the question who should take the initiative to realize integration – where in the management system is the responsibility vested to ensure that centralization, coordination and standardization are considered and carried out? If all business unit managers are looking after their own backyard, who is taking care of the joint issues and cross-business synergies? Basically there are two organizational means available to secure the effective deployment of the integration mechanisms (see Figure 6.3):

- Control. A straightforward way to manage activities that cross the boundaries of an individual business unit is to give someone the formal power to enforce centralization, coordination and standardization. Such a division level or corporate level manager can exert control in many ways. It can be by direct supervision (telling business units what to do), but often it is indirect, by giving business units objectives that must be met and discussing initiatives. The formal authority to secure integration does not always have to be given to a manager at the corporate center, but can be assigned to a manager within one of the business units as well. There are also various levels of authority that can be defined, ranging from full final decision-making power to 'coordinator' or 'liaison officer', who have only limited formal means at their disposal.

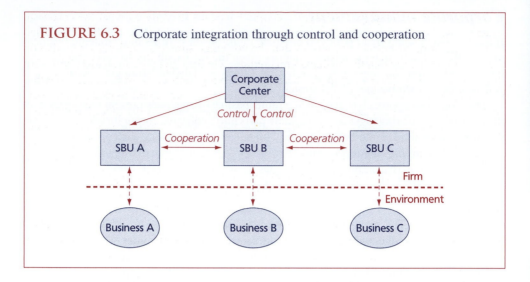

FIGURE 6.3 Corporate integration through control and cooperation

■ **Cooperation.** Centralization, coordination and standardization between business units can also be achieved without the use of hierarchical authority. Business units might be willing to cooperate because it is in their interest to do so, or because they recognize the overall corporate interests. If business units believe in the importance of certain joint activities, this can be a powerful impetus to collaborate. Corporate strategists interested in such integration by mutual adjustment will focus on creating the organizational circumstances under which such self-organization can take place (See Chapter 9 for a further discussion). For instance, they might strengthen formal and informal ties between the business units in order to enhance mutual understanding and encourage the exchange of ideas and joint initiatives. They may also support cross-business career paths and try to instill a corporation-wide culture, to facilitate the communication between business units (Eisenhardt and Galunic, 2000).

It is the task of the corporate level strategist to determine the mix of control and cooperation needed to manage the corporation. In their seminal research, Goold and Campbell (1987) distinguish three general corporate control styles, each emphasizing different levels of centralization, coordination and standardization:

■ **Financial control style.** In the financial control style the strategic business units are highly autonomous from the corporate center. Few activities are centralized or standardized (except for the financial reporting system) and the corporate center does not explicitly attempt to coordinate activities across business unit boundaries. Control is exerted by negotiating, setting and monitoring financial objectives.

■ **Strategic control style.** In the strategic control style the strategic business units have a closer relationship with the corporate center. A number of central services exist, some systems and activities are standardized and the corporate center explicitly tries to coordinate activities that reach beyond the boundaries of only one business unit. Control is exerted by negotiating, setting and monitoring strategic objectives.

■ **Strategic planning style.** In the strategic planning style the strategic business units have relatively little autonomy from the corporate center. Many key activities are centralized or standardized, and the corporate center is also heavily involved in securing cross-business coordination. Control is exerted by means of direct supervision.

Which corporate management style is adopted depends strongly on what the corporate strategist wishes to achieve. The preferred corporate management style will be determined by the type of multi-business synergies that the corporate strategist envisages, but also on the level of autonomy that the business units require. On the one hand, strategists will want to encourage integration to reap the benefits of having various business units together under one corporate roof and will therefore have a strong motivation to exert strong corporate center control and stimulate inter-business cooperation. On the other hand, strategists will be wary of heavy-handed head office intervention, blunt centralization, rigid standardization, paralyzing coordination meetings and excessive overhead. Recognizing that the business units need to be highly responsive to the specific demands of their own business area, corporate strategists will also be inclined to give business units the freedom to maneuver and to emphasize their own entrepreneurship. Yet, these two demands on the corporate level strategy – *multi-business synergy* and *business responsiveness* – are to a certain extent at odds with one another. How corporate strategists deal with the tension created by these conflicting demands will be examined more closely in the following section.

THE PARADOX OF RESPONSIVENESS AND SYNERGY

Nihil est ab omni parte beatum (nothing is an unmixed blessing).
Horace (65–8 BC); Roman poet

When Cor Boonstra took over as CEO of Philips Electronics in 1996, after a long career at the fast-moving consumer goods company Sara Lee, one of his first remarks to the business press was that Philips reminded him of 'a plate of spaghetti' – the company's more than 60 business units were intertwined in many different ways, sharing technologies, facilities, sales forces and customers, leading to excessive complexity, abundant bureaucracy, turf wars and a lack of accountability. To Boonstra the pursuit of multi-business synergy had spiraled into an overkill of centralization, coordination and standardization, requiring direct rectification. Thus Boonstra set out to restructure Philips into, in his own words, 'a plate of asparagus', with business units neatly lined up, one next to the other. Over a period of five years he disposed of numerous business units and made sure that the others were independent enough 'to hold up their own pants'. The result was a loss of some valuable synergies, but a significant increase in the business units' responsiveness to the demands in their own business. Then, in 2001, Boonstra handed over the reigns to a Philips insider, Gerard Kleisterlee, who during one of his first media encounters as new CEO stated that the business units within Philips had become too insular and narrowly focused, thereby missing opportunities to capture important synergies. Therefore, he indicated that it would be his priority to get Philips to work more like a team.

What this example of Philips illustrates is that corporate level strategists constantly struggle with the balance between realizing synergies and defending business unit responsiveness. To achieve synergies, a firm must to some extent integrate the activities carried out in its various business units. The autonomy of the business units must be partially limited, in the interest of concerted action. However, integration comes with a price tag. An extra level of management is often required, more meetings, extra complexity, potential conflicts of interest, additional bureaucracy – harmonization of operations costs money and diminishes a business unit's ability to precisely tailor its strategy to its specific business environment. Hence, for the corporate strategist the challenge is to realize more *value creation* through multi-business synergies than *value destruction* through the loss of business responsiveness (e.g. Campbell, Goold and Alexander, 1995; Prahalad and Doz, 1987).

This tension arising from the partially conflicting demands of business responsiveness and multi-business synergy is called the paradox of responsiveness and synergy. In the following sub-sections both sides of the paradox will be examined in more detail.

The demand for multi-business synergy

Diversification into new business areas can only be economically justified if it leads to value creation. According to Porter (1987) entering into another business (by acquisition or internal growth) can only result in increased shareholder value if three essential tests are passed:

- The attractiveness test. The business 'must be structurally attractive, or capable of being made attractive'. In other words, firms should only enter businesses where there is a possibility to build up a profitable competitive position (see Chapter 5). Each new business area must be judged in terms of its competitive forces and the opportunities available to the firm to sustain a competitive business model.

- The cost-of-entry test. 'The cost of entry must not capitalize all the future profits.' In other words, firms should only enter new businesses if it is possible to recoup the investments made. This is important for internally generated new business ventures, but even more so for external acquisitions. Many researchers argue that, on average, firms significantly overpay for acquisitions, making it next to impossible to compensate for the value given away during the purchase (e.g. Sirower, 1997).

- The better-off test. 'Either the new unit must gain competitive advantage from its link with the corporation or vice versa.' In other words, firms should only enter new businesses if it is possible to create significant synergies. If not, then the new unit would be better off as an independent firm or with a different parent company, and should be cut loose from the corporation.

It is this last test that reveals one of the key demands of corporate level strategy. Multi-business level firms need to be more than the sum of their parts. They need to create more added value than the extra costs of managing a more complex organization. They need to identify opportunities for synergy between business areas and manage the organization in such a way that the synergies can be realized.

But what are the sources of synergy? For quite some time, strategists have known that potential for synergy has something to do with 'relatedness' (Rumelt, 1974). Diversification moves that were unrelated (or 'conglomerate'), for example a food company's entrance into the bicycle rental business, were deemed to be less profitable, in general, than moves that were related (or 'concentric'), such as a car-maker's diversification into the car rental business (e.g. Chatterjee, 1986; Rumelt, 1982). However, the problem has been to determine the nature of 'relatedness'. Superficial signs of relatedness do not indicate that there is potential for synergy. Drilling for oil and mining might seem highly related (both are 'extraction businesses'), but Shell found out the hard way that they were not related, selling the acquired mining company Billiton to Gencor after they were unable to create synergy. Chemicals and pharmaceuticals seem like similar businesses (especially if pharmaceuticals are labeled 'specialty chemicals'), but ICI decided to split itself in two (into ICI and Zeneca), because it could not achieve sufficient synergy between these two business areas.

Strategy researchers have therefore attempted to pin down the exact nature of relatedness (e.g. Prahalad and Bettis, 1986; Ramanujam and Varadarajan, 1989). Following the business model framework outlined in Chapter 5, the areas of relatedness that have the potential for creating synergy can be organized into three categories (see Figure 6.4): resource relatedness, product offering relatedness and activity relatedness.

Synergy by leveraging resources.   The first area of relatedness is at the level of the businesses' resource bases. Two or more businesses are related if their resources can be productively shared between them. In principle, all types of resources can be shared, both the tangible and the intangible, although in practice some resources are easier to share than others – for example, it is easier to transfer money than knowledge. Such 'resource leveraging' (Hamel and Prahalad, 1993) can be achieved by physically reallocating resources from one business area to another, or by replicating them so they can be used in a variety of businesses simultaneously:

■   *Achieving resource reallocation.* Instead of leaving firm resources in the business unit where they happen to be located, a corporation can create synergy by transferring resources to other business units, where better use can be made of them. For instance, money and personnel are often shifted between business units, depending on where they are needed and the potential return is highest.

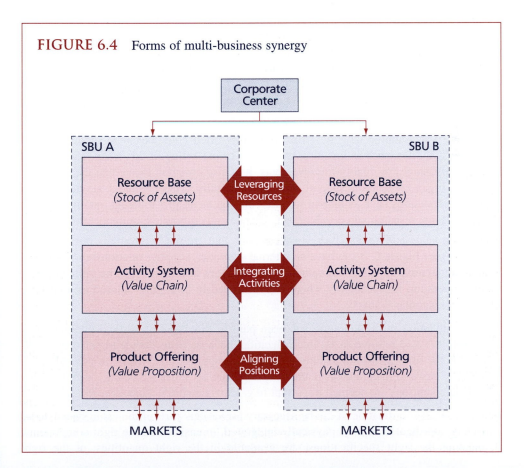

FIGURE 6.4   Forms of multi-business synergy

- Achieving resource replication. While physical resources can only be used in one place at a time, intangible resources can often be copied from one business unit to another, so that the same resource can be used many times over. This happens, for example, when knowledge and capabilities are copied and reused in other business units.

Synergy by aligning positions.   A second area of relatedness is at the level of product offerings. Two or more businesses are related if they can help each other by aligning their positioning in the market. Such coordination between product–market combinations can both improve the businesses' bargaining position vis-à-vis buyers, as well as improve the businesses' competitive position vis-à-vis rival firms:

- Improving bargaining position. Business units can improve their bargaining power vis-à-vis buyers by offering a broad package of related products and/or services to specific customer groups. Especially when the products being offered are complementary, share a common brand and have a comparable reputation, will they support each other in the market.

- Improving competitive position. Coordination of product offerings within one firm can also prevent a number of business units from fighting fiercely amongst one another, which might have happened if all units were independent companies. Moreover, it is even possible for multiple business units to support each other in attacking a third party, for example by setting a common standard or aggressively pricing selected products. Business units can team up to create barriers to entry into the industry/market as well.

Synergy by integrating activities.   The third area of relatedness is at the level of activity systems. Two or more businesses are related if an integration of their value chains is more efficient and/or more effective than if they were totally separated. Such integration of value-creation activities can focus on the sharing of similar activities or the linking up of sequential activities:

- Sharing value-adding activities. Business units often combine some of their value-adding activities, such as logistics, production or marketing, if this leads to significant scale advantages or quality improvements. It is also common to see that the corporate center organizes certain support activities centrally. These 'shared services' often include functions such as human resource management, procurement, quality control, legal affairs, research and development, finance and corporate communication.

- Linking value-adding activities. Business units that are not horizontally but vertically related (see Figure 6.1) can have an internal customer–supplier relationship. Such vertical integration of sequential value-adding activities in one firm can be more efficient than operating independently where supplies need to be highly tailored to a specific type of customer demand.

Much attention in the literature has been paid to this issue of vertical integration of activities. It is also referred to as 'internalization' because firms decide to perform activities inside the firm, instead of dealing with outside suppliers and buyers. In general, companies will strive to integrate upstream or downstream activities where one or more of the following conditions are deemed important (e.g. Harrigan 1985; Mahoney, 1992):

- Operational coordination. It can be necessary for various parts of the value system to be tightly coordinated or even physically integrated, to ensure that the right components, meeting the right specifications, are available in the right quantities, at the right moment, so that high quality, low cost and/or timely delivery can be achieved. To realize this level of coordination it can be necessary to gain control over a number of key activities in the value system, instead of trying to get suppliers and buyers to cooperate.

- **Avoidance of transaction costs.** Reaching a deal with a supplier or buyer and transferring the goods or services to the required location may be accompanied by significant direct costs. These contracting costs can include the expenses of negotiations, drawing up a contract, financial transfers, packaging, distribution and insurance. Add to these the search costs, required to locate and analyze potential new suppliers or buyers, as well as the policing costs, which are incurred to check whether the contract is being met according to expectations and to take actions against those parties not living up to their contractual responsibilities. If a firm vertically integrates, many of these costs can be avoided, leading to potential savings (Williamson, 1975).

- **Increased bargaining power.** If a firm is facing a supplier or buyer with a disproportionately high level of bargaining power (for instance, a monopolist), vertical integration can be used to weaken or neutralize such a party. By fully or partially performing the activities in-house, the firm can lessen its dependence on a strong buyer or supplier. The firm can also strive to acquire the other party, to avoid the bargaining situation altogether.

- **Learning curve advantages.** Where vertically linked business units work closely together, exchanging knowledge and personnel, they might also learn more quickly and more efficiently than if the business units were independent. Especially where they initiate joint R&D projects and collaborate on business process improvement efforts then significant learning curve advantages can be realized.

- **Implementing system-wide changes.** Besides continual operational coordination and ongoing learning, there may be a need to coordinate strategic changes throughout the value system. Switching over to new technologies, new production methods and new standards can sometimes only be implemented if there is commitment and a concerted effort in various parts of the value system. Sometimes even neighboring value systems need to be involved in the changes. Vertical integration and horizontal diversification can give a firm the formal control needed to push through such changes.

Corporate level strategy is about determining the corporate configuration that offers the best opportunities for synergy, and implementing a corporate management system capable of realizing the intended synergies. However, what types of synergies can realistically be achieved, without paying a heavier penalty in terms of integration costs? Recognizing the possible benefits of bringing together various businesses under one corporate umbrella is one thing, but developing a corporate management system that does not cost more than it yields is another. Therefore, corporate strategists need to carefully consider the potential downside of resource leveraging, activity integration and position alignment – the loss of business responsiveness.

The demand for business responsiveness

Responsiveness is defined as the ability to respond to the competitive demands of a specific business area in a timely and adequate manner. A business unit is responsive if it has the capability to tightly match its strategic behavior to the competitive dynamics in its business. If a business unit does not focus its strategy on the conditions in its direct environment and does not organize its value-adding activities and management systems to fit with the business characteristics, it will soon be at a competitive disadvantage compared to more responsive rivals. Business responsiveness is therefore a key demand for successful corporate level strategy.

Yet, in multi-business firms the responsiveness of the business units is constantly under pressure. Various scope disadvantages limit the ability of the corporation to ensure business responsiveness. The major problems encountered by multi-business firms are the following:

- **High governance costs.** Coordinating activities within a firm requires managers. Layers of management, and the bureaucratic processes that might entail, can lead to escalating costs.

- **Slower decision-making.** Business units must usually deal with more layers of management, more meetings for coordination purposes, more participants in meetings, more conflicts of interest and more political infighting. This not only increases governance costs, but also slows down decision-making and action.

- **Strategy incongruence.** The resource leveraging, activity integration and position alignment envisioned in the corporate strategy can be more suited to the conditions in some businesses than to others. Consequently, some business units might need to compromise, adapting their business strategy to fit with the corporate strategy. However, such internal adaptation might lead to a misfit with the business demands.

- **Dysfunctional control.** The corporate center might not have the specific business know-how needed to judge business unit strategies, activities and results. However, the corporate center might feel the need to exert some control over business units, potentially steering them in an inappropriate direction.

- **Dulled incentives.** Limited autonomy combined with the aforementioned problems can have a significant negative impact on the motivation to perform optimally. This dulled incentive to be entrepreneurial and to excel can be compounded by poorly delineated responsibilities, a lack of clear accountability and the existence of 'captive' internal customers. Together these factors limit the business units' drive to be responsive.

These threats make clear that multi-business firms must determine their composition and management systems in a way that enables business units to be responsive. Yet, simultaneously, corporate strategists need to strive towards the identification and realization of synergies. The question is how these two conflicting demands can be reconciled – how can corporate level strategists deal with the paradox of responsiveness and synergy?

EXHIBIT 6.1 SHORT CASE

GUCCI: AN AFFORDABLE LUXURY?

Most people do not associate the name Ford with luxury goods – but they should. Tom Ford is the widely admired creative director of Gucci, the Italian luxury goods group that designs, produces and distributes a broad array of leather goods, shoes, watches, jewelry, fragrances, cosmetics and high-end ready-to-wear apparel. He is a celebrity with rock-star status, providing the Gucci Group with a strong external profile, while he has simultaneously been able to create a clear identity for the brands in the company's portfolio. In Gucci he has been the driving force, together with CEO Domenico De Sole, ever since both men took charge of the floundering company in 1994. The Gucci Group spans a number of famous luxury brands, besides the core Gucci name, including Yves Saint Laurent (fragrances, cosmetics and apparel), Sergio Rossi and Bottega Veneta (footwear), Boucheron (jewelry and fragrances), Balenciaga (apparel) and Bédat (watches). In 2002 global sales totaled US$2.5 billion.

Gucci's origins are much more humble than its flashy image would suggest. In 1923 Guccio Gucci opened a small shop in Florence to sell leather goods. Not satisfied with the wares offered to him, he soon opened a workshop to manufacture his own bag and shoe designs. After World War II, Gucci rapidly developed into a prime international luxury brand, opening its first foreign shop in New York in 1953. Several stores followed in other US cities and later in Europe, plus, in the early 1970s, in Japan and Hong Kong. By that time, the red-and-green striped webbing and GG-logo had become part of the domain of celebrities such as Grace Kelly and Jacqueline Onasis.

Problems within the company began after the retirement of Guccio in the 1970s and lasted throughout the 1980s. Conflicts between Guccio's two sons, Aldo and Rodolfo, and later between Rodolfo's son Maurizio and other family members were often fought out in court. To make things worse, Aldo and Maurizio were convicted of tax evasion and fraud, leading to a spell in jail. These family matters were a strong distraction, leaving the company to grow without a clear sense of direction. Production became more scattered, the distribution network became a maze and the product portfolio became highly diversified. By the late 1980s, some 22 000 products, including tennis shoes, playing cards and cigarette holders, bore the Gucci name.

In the United States, De Sole, who was then managing director of Gucci America,

and one of the first professional managers in the family business, started rationalizing the operations and product portfolio. He expanded Gucci's control over distribution, by moving wholesale distribution in-house and by acquiring local franchises. Released from jail in 1989, Maurizio Gucci regained his post as chairman of Gucci and launched an ambitious restructuring program that proved to be too drastic – losses mounted and cash flow dried up. The image of the brand was also close to 'junk status'. 'No truly discerning luxury goods client would shop at Gucci at that time', says a Gucci manager. It was only when the Bahrain-based investment company Investcorp, which had acquired 50% of the Gucci shares in 1989, eventually replaced Maurizio in 1993 that the company's fortunes improved.

It was during this period that De Sole and Ford were given the reins, with the assignment to save the company. De Sole used his experience in the US market to revamp the Gucci business in other countries. As one Gucci manager explains: 'The company was never run as a united company, as one global brand. Each company was operating on its own . . . and no information was shared.' De Sole expanded the number of directly owned and operated stores from 65 in 1995 to 126 in 1998, to get a better grip on how the brand was presented to the outside world. He also sharply reduced distribution through duty-free shops and department stores. By 1999, two-thirds of Gucci's sales came from its own stores, with the intention of increasing this share even further. In order to regain control over product quality, De Sole selected an inner circle of 25 partner-suppliers, working exclusively for Gucci, to produce 70% of the total leather goods. The other 30% was provided by a group of about 60 non-exclusive suppliers, working on yearly production agreements. A program was installed for quality control and to provide financial support and training for all suppliers. For other products similar programs and rationalizations took place, resulting in a well-managed supplier base that was entirely Italian. Only the watches were sourced from Switzerland.

Ford had been lured away from the French fashion house Yves Saint Laurent with the promise of a free hand at restyling everything in the company – products, store interiors and advertising. He successfully rejuvenated the brand for a fashionable, modern, urban consumer with an aggressively glamorous edge. Advertising budgets were increased from 3% of sales in 1993 to 13% by 2000. Ford's goal was to 'create an arresting image of a world you wanted to be part of'. Gucci made it possible for a wider range of people to enter its world by offering accessory articles. Between 1994 and 1999, Gucci's sales increased by a staggering 35% annually, without any acquisitions, with 40% of the sales coming from Asia, 30% from the United States and 30% from Europe.

This formidable growth put Gucci back on the map in the US$60 billion luxury goods industry – but the industry was also rapidly transforming. Next to the traditional segment of 'high net worth individuals' (i.e. with investible assets of over US$1 million), the industry was increasingly catering to a new segment of 'wannabees', with less money, but a ferocious appetite for luxury goods. Serving this brand-sensitive, but not brand-loyal, segment required high advertising costs and a constant flow of new designs. As a consequence, deep pockets and professional management were becoming more and more important – something most of the traditional medium-sized family-owned companies, like Bulgari, Hermès, Prada and Chanel, had in short supply. To raise cash, many medium-sized players floated their stocks during the mid-1990s, as did Gucci in 1995. Yet this opened the door to being acquired by large, professionally run, multi-brand luxury conglomerates. Of these, the French LVMH, with brands like Louis Vuitton, Moët et Chandon, TAG Heuer and Christian Dior, and the Switzerland-based Richemont, with brands like Cartier, Dunhill and Piaget, were the most prominent examples. In 1999 LVMH attempted to take over Gucci, but as Gucci management did not relish the prospect of losing control to LVMH's domineering boss Bernard Arnault, they found a white knight willing to take over Gucci, yet leave them considerable strategic freedom. The white knight was the French retailing giant Pinault-Printemps-Redoute's (PPR), run by one of the richest people in France, François Pinault, who fought a long and bitter battle with Arnault, leading to an extremely high takeover price.

Seeing the developments in the industry, De Sole also believed that increased size and professionalism were vital. Yet, in his view the growth of the Gucci brand was reaching its limits: 'a luxury brand cannot be extended infinitely – if it becomes too common, it is devalued'. Therefore, he decided to follow the lead of LVMH and Richemont, to become a multi-brand corporation. As a first step, he acquired the French company Yves Saint Laurent (YSL) in 1999, which he split into YSL Couture for ready-to-wear clothing and accessories and YSL Beauté for fragrances and cosmetics. YSL catered for the more intelligent, chic and stylish segment, compared to the more sexy and flashy Gucci segment. After this, he added a number of other brands to the portfolio – Italian footwear designers Sergio Rossi and Bottega Veneta, French jewelry and fragrance company Boucheron, French ready-to-wear clothing house Balenciaga and the young Swiss watch house Bédat. With some of the acquisitions came a number of third party licenses as well, for fragrance and cosmetics brands like Van Cleef & Arpels and Oscar de la Renta. Furthermore he raided hip UK designers Alexander McQueen and Stella McCartney from competitors to develop their own brands within the Gucci group.

With the classic brands, like YSL, Boucheron and Balenciaga, De Sole hoped to rejuvenate them in the same way as he had done with Gucci. With the new brands, like Alexander McQueen, Stella McCartney and Bédat, De Sole aimed to stake out new segments, not properly served yet. However, there were also a few challenges, not least of which was that each brand needed a lot of investment and management attention to make it a success. Furthermore, the complexity of the company had multiplied, with each brand run from a different head office, scattered across Italy and France. Each brand also had a different distribution structure – some like YSL, Sergio Rossi and Boucheron, with their own stores, while others did not.

To balance responsiveness and synergy, De Sole developed a two-pronged approach to integrating the new acquisitions. On the one side, each brand was given a dedicated management team to run the 'front end' part of the business, including the brand image, product design, the store concept, sales and marketing, communications and PR, and licensing. On the other side, the 'group management' was given responsibility for the 'back end' part of the business, where synergies would need to be realized. This includes manufacturing, technical expertise for product development in accessories, ready-to-wear and shoes, warehousing and logistics, purchasing of media, packaging and fabrics, real estate, finance and back-office activities. From Florence, where the main company headquarters are situated, the group management would direct the integration of the back end business and Ford would oversee the creative development of the front end business. De Sole wanted all managers to focus on 'group success', while he also made explicit that he expected the brand management teams to be 'entrepreneurial – managers should run their business like they own it'.

By 2002, Gucci had expanded its sales to US$2.5 billion, up from US$1.2 billion in 1999. The Gucci brand represented 60% of group sales and YSL 27%. Accessories were 31% of the business, ready-to-wear 13%, shoes 12%, fragrances and cosmetics 22%, watches 9% and jewelry 5%. Yet, business was not going well and Gucci was forced to issue two profit warnings during the year. Clearly, the economic recession was hitting all luxury goods makers very hard, but Gucci was doing even worse. Except for YSL Beauté, none of the new brands were profitable and the situation for 2003 was not expected to improve.

De Sole faced the question, whether he had not overstretched the company by simultaneously adding a large number of new brands and new businesses. Had he overestimated the ability of the Gucci team to turn lingering brands into champions? Perhaps the synergy potential between the different brands had not yet been realized sufficiently. Could it also be that he had overestimated the synergy benefits of having multiple brands and businesses in one portfolio? Was there a bottom-line compelling logic, other than the growth imperative and the emergent industry behavior, for a multi-luxury brand corporation? De Sole had to make up his mind, whether and how to pursue a multi-brand strategy – and answer the question whether Gucci could afford the luxury of keeping all of its brands, or would need to sell off some of the family jewels.

Sources: *The Economist*, January 14 1999, January 10 2002 and February 8 2003; *Harvard Business School*, Case 9-701-037; *University College Dublin*, Note 301-025-5; www.guccigroup.com.

PERSPECTIVES ON CORPORATE LEVEL STRATEGY

We must indeed all hang together, or, most assuredly, we shall all hang separately.

Benjamin Franklin (1706–1790); American politician, inventor and scientist

Corporations need to capture multi-business synergies and they need to ensure each business unit's responsiveness to its competitive environment. In other words, corporations need to be integrated and differentiated at the same time – emphasizing the *whole* and respecting the *part*. Striving towards synergy is a centripetal force, pulling the firm together into an integrated whole, while being responsive to business demands is a centrifugal force, pulling the firm apart into autonomous market-focused units (Ghoshal and Mintzberg, 1994). The main question dividing strategists is whether a corporation should primarily be a collection of parts or an integrated whole. Should corporations be loose federations of business units or tightly knit teams? Should corporations be business groups made up of distinctive parts, where only modest synergies can be realized and business units should be accorded a large measure of leeway to be responsive to their specific market conditions? Or should corporations actually be unitary organizations, with the parts serving the whole, allowing for significant synergies to be achieved, with the challenge of being responsive enough to varied business demands.

As before, the strategic management literature comes with strongly different views on how strategists should proceed. Here the two diametrically opposed positions will be identified and discussed to show the richness of differing opinions. On the one side of the spectrum, there are those strategists who believe that multi-business firms should be viewed as portfolios of autonomous business units in which the corporation has a financial stake. They argue that business responsiveness is crucial and that only a limited set of financial synergies should be pursued. This point of view is referred to as the 'portfolio organization perspective'. At the other end of the spectrum, there are strategists who believe that corporations should be tightly integrated, with a strong central core of shared resources, activities and/or product offerings keeping the firm together. They argue that corporations built up around these strong synergy opportunities can create significantly more value than is lost through limitations to responsiveness. This point of view is referred to as the 'integrated organization perspective'.

The portfolio organization perspective

 In the portfolio organization perspective, responsiveness is strongly emphasized over synergy. Managers taking this perspective usually argue that each business has its own unique characteristics and demands. Firms operating in different businesses must therefore develop a specific strategy for each business and assign the responsibility for each business strategy to a separate strategic business unit. In this manner, the (strategic) business units can be highly responsive to the competitive dynamics in the business, while being a clear unit of accountability towards the corporate center. High responsiveness, however, requires freedom from corporate center interference and freedom from cross-business coordination. Hence, a high level of business unit autonomy is required, with the corporate center's influence limited to arm's length financial control.

In the portfolio organization perspective, the main reason for a number of highly autonomous business units to be in one firm is to leverage financial resources. The only synergies emphasized are financial synergies (e.g. Lubatkin and Chatterjee, 1994; Trautwein, 1990). Actually, the term 'portfolio' entered the business vocabulary via the financial sector, where it refers to an investor's collection of shareholdings in different companies, purchased to spread investment risks. Transferred to corporate strategy, the portfolio organization perspective views the corporate center as an active investor with financial stakes in a number of stand-alone business units. The role of the center is one of selecting a promising portfolio of businesses, keeping tight financial control, and allocating available capital – redirecting flows of cash from business units where prospects are dim ('cash cows' or 'dogs'), to other business units where higher returns can be expected ('stars' or 'question marks'). The strategic objective of each business unit is, therefore, also financial in orientation – grow, hold, milk or divest, depending on the business unit's position on the portfolio grid (e.g. Henderson, 1979; Hedley, 1977). A good corporate strategy strives for a balanced portfolio of mature cash producers and high potential ROI cash users, at an acceptable level of overall risk.

The financial synergies can be gained in a number of different ways (e.g. Chatterjee, 1986; Weston, Chung and Hoag, 1990). First, by having various businesses within one firm, the corporate center can economize on external financing. By internally shifting funds from one business unit to another the corporation can avoid the transaction costs and taxation associated with external capital markets. Secondly, the corporation can limit dependence on the whims of external capital providers, who might be less inclined to finance some ventures (e.g. new businesses or high risk turnarounds) at acceptable levels of capital cost. Thirdly, where the corporation does want to secure external financing, the firm's larger size, debt capacity and creditworthiness can improve its bargaining position in the financial markets. Finally, by having revenue and earning streams from two or more different businesses, the corporation can reduce its exposure to the risk of a single business. This risk balancing, or co-insurance, effect is largest where the portfolio is made up of counter-cyclical businesses. In turn, the stability and predictability of revenue and earning flows enable the corporation to plan and function more effectively and efficiently (e.g. Amit and Livnat, 1988; Seth, 1990).

The business units do not necessarily need to be 'related' in any other way than financial. In practice, the business units can be related, that is, there can be resource leveraging, activity integration and position alignment opportunities that are seized. The portfolio organization perspective does not reject the pursuit of other forms of synergy, but neither does it accommodate such efforts (Haspeslagh, 1982). Responsiveness is not compromised to achieve these synergy opportunities.

New businesses can be entered by means of internal growth, but the portfolio approach to corporate strategy is particularly well suited to diversification through acquisition. In a multi-business firm run on portfolio principles, acquired companies are simple to integrate into the corporation, because they can be largely left as stand-alone units and only need to be linked to corporate financial reporting and control systems. Proponents of the portfolio organization perspective argue that such 'non-synergistic' acquisitions can be highly profitable (Kaplan, 1989; Long and Ravenscraft, 1993). Excess cash can be routed to more attractive investment opportunities than the corporation has internally. Moreover, the acquiring corporation can shake up the management of the acquired company and can function as a strategic sounding board for the new people. In this way, the acquirer can release the untapped value potential of underperforming stand-alone businesses (Anslinger and Copeland, 1996).

The portfolio organization perspective is particularly well known for the analytical techniques that have been developed to support it. As was mentioned before, a large number of portfolio grids are in widespread use as graphical tools for visualizing corporate composition and for determining the position of each of the business units. These portfolio analysis tools have proven to be popular and much used (Goold and Lansdell, 1997), even among strategists who are not proponents of the portfolio organization perspective.

In conclusion, the basic assumption of the portfolio organization perspective is that business units must be responsible for their own competitive strategy. Business units are the main locus of strategic attention and the corporate center should understand their limited ability to get involved and stimulate synergy. Corporate centers should be modest in ambition and size, taking heed of the words of the famous 'business philosopher' Groucho Marx that 'the most difficult thing about business is minding your own'.

EXHIBIT 6.2 THE PORTFOLIO ORGANIZATION PERSPECTIVE

DEGUSSA: SPECIALTY CHEMICALS STORED SEPARATELY

Degussa is the world's largest producer of specialty chemicals, with global sales of €11.8 billion in 2002 and 48 000 employees. The company, which has its corporate headquarters in Düsseldorf, has a long industrial history in Germany, tracing its origin back to the year 1843 in Frankfurt am Main. Especially during the last ten years, Degussa has undergone an extensive series of mergers and consolidations, which have put the company at the forefront of its industry, both in terms of size and profitability (EBITDA in 2002 of 15.3%).

Degussa focuses almost exclusively on specialty chemicals because of the higher margins, lower cyclicality, higher growth rates, better differentiation, and greater value added for customers, when compared to bulk chemical suppliers. Every business of Degussa is expected to develop to be among the top three in its market. Degussa has aggressively divested every business unit that does not fit this preferred profile, amounting to more than €6 billion of divested sales between 2000 and 2002.

The key ingredient to success in the specialty chemicals market, according to Degussa, is the ability to solve problems for specific customers with specific needs. The company emphasizes as a key strategic goal to go one step further and to anticipate customer demands before customers are themselves aware of them. Responsiveness to customer demands is therefore the dominant paradigm throughout the company. In the words of the CEO, Prof. Dr. Utz-Hellmuth Felcht: 'Products, applications and processes must be developed very fast and in close cooperation with the customer. As a specialty chemicals company, there is therefore no alternative to a decentralized structure.'

Degussa has divided itself into 23 business units, with less than 150 staff members at corporate headquarters. Each business unit has global responsibility for operating results, with full control over all operating functions: sales and marketing, production, procurement, R&D and HRM. The business units (each consisting of one or more lines of business) are grouped into six divisions, which guide strategic development and are the first reporting level. There are also six global and ten site service centers providing some support activities such as IT. However, the business units are free to purchase these services from outside as well. The Figure shows their portfolio grid by line of business.

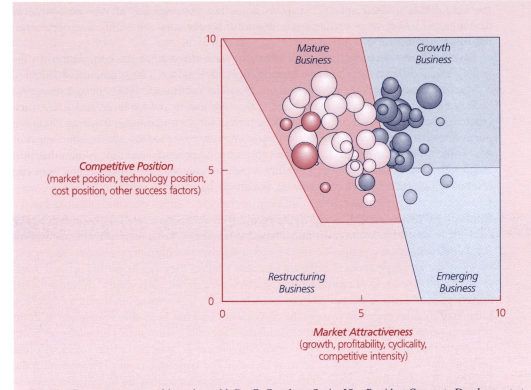

Sources: Company reports and interview with Dr. C. Grambow, Senior Vice President Corporate Development at Degussa.

The integrated organization perspective

The integrated organization perspective is fundamentally at odds with the portfolio organization perspective's minimalist interpretation of corporate level strategy. To proponents of the integrated organization perspective, a multibusiness firm should be more than a loose federation of businesses held together by a common investor. Actually, a corporation should be quite the opposite – a tightly knit team of business units grouped around a common core. Having various businesses together in one corporation, it is argued, can only be justified if the corporate center has a clear conception of how strategically relevant multi-business synergies can be realized. It is not enough to capture a few operational synergies here and there – a compelling logic must lie at the heart of the corporation, creating a significant competitive advantage over rivals who operate on a business-by-business basis. The multi-business synergies generated at the core of the organization should enable the corporation to beat its competitors in a variety of business areas.

As corporate level strategists 'lead from the center' (Raynor and Bower, 2001) and develop a joint competitive strategy together with business level strategists, they must make very clear which multi-business synergies they intend to foster as the nucleus of the corporation. It is their task to determine what the core of the organization should be and to take the lead in building it. To be successful, it is necessary for them to work closely together with business level managers, whose main task it is to apply the core strengths of the corporation to their specific business area. The consequence of this joint strategy development and synergy realization is that all business units are highly interdependent, requiring continual coordination.

Many different multi-business synergies can form the core of the corporation. In the strategic management literature one specific form has received a large amount of attention – the *core competence* centered corporation (Prahalad and Hamel, 1990). In such an organization a few competences are at the heart of the corporation and are leveraged across various business units. Prahalad and Hamel's metaphor for the corporation is not an investor's portfolio, but a large tree: 'the trunk and major limbs are core products, the smaller branches are business units, the leaves, flowers and fruit are end products; the root system that provides nourishment, sustenance and stability is the core competence.' Business unit branches can be cut off and new ones can grow on, but all spring from the same tree. It is the corporate center's role to nurture this tree, building up the core competences and ensuring that the firm's competence carriers can easily be redeployed across business unit boundaries. The strategic logic behind leveraging these intangible resources is that high investments in competence development can then be spread over a number of different businesses. Moreover, by using these competences in different business settings they can be further refined, leading to a virtuous circle of rapid learning, profiting the entire corporation. In line with the arguments of the inside-out perspective (see Chapter 5), it is pointed out that in the long run inter-firm rivalries are often won by the corporation who has been able to upgrade its competences fastest – skirmishes in particular markets are only battles in this broader war. From this angle, building the corporation's core competences is strategic, while engaging other corporations in specific business areas is tactical. The corporate center is therefore at the forefront of competitive strategy, instead of the business units, that are literally divisions in the overall campaign (e.g. Kono, 1999; Stalk, Evans and Shulman, 1992).

As all business units should both tap into, and contribute to, the corporation's core competences, the business units' autonomy is necessarily limited. Unavoidably, the responsiveness to the specific characteristics of each business does suffer from this emphasis on coordination. Yet, to advocates of the core competence model, the loss of business responsiveness is more than compensated for by the strategic benefits gained.

Besides competences as the core of the corporation, other synergies can also be at the heart of a multi-business firm. For instance, corporations can focus on aligning a variety of product offerings for a group of 'core customers'. Many professional service firms, such as PricewaterhouseCoopers and Cap Gemini Ernst & Young, are involved in a broad range of businesses, with the intention of offering an integrated package of services to their selected market segments. Another type of core is where a multi-business firm is built around shared activities. Many of the large airlines, for example, have one 'core process', flying planes, but operate in the very different businesses of passenger travel and cargo transport. Yet another central synergy can be the leveraging of the firm's 'software'. For instance, Disney is such a 'core content' corporation, letting Cinderella work hard selling Disney videos, luring families to Disney theme parks, getting kids to buy Disney merchandise and enticing people to watch the Disney channel. Whichever synergy is placed center stage, to the proponents of the integrated organization perspective it should not be trivial, as such minor value-creation efforts do not provide the driving motivation to keep a corporation together. The 'glue' of the corporation must be strong enough to convince all involved that they are much better off as part of the whole than on their own.

The flip side of having a tightly knit group of businesses arranged around a common core is that growth through acquisition is generally much more difficult than in the 'plug and play' set-up of a portfolio organization. To make an acquisition fit into the corporate family and to establish all of the necessary links to let the new recruits profit from, and contribute to, the core synergies, can be very challenging. Taking the previous metaphor a step further, the corporate center will find it quite difficult to graft oak roots and elm branches on to an existing olive tree. Consequently, acquisitions will be infrequent, as the firm will prefer internal growth.

EXHIBIT 6.3 THE INTEGRATED ORGANIZATION PERSPECTIVE

SONY: INTEGRATED HOME ENTERTAINMENT

In the late 1940s a small group of engineers came together on the third floor of a Tokyo department store and started a company that would become one of the world's most admired firms – Sony. In its first three decades, Sony grew into a worldwide leader in the consumer electronics industry, introducing such innovative products as the world's first transistor radio and the Walkman. It was Sony's disappointing introduction of the Betamax video cassette recorder that convinced CEO Akio Morita, that the successful launch of new consumer hardware products was strongly dependent on having accompanying software available: Betamax had lost out to Matsushita's VHS system because Sony was unable to convince the big studios to bring out enough movies in the Betamax format. As a consequence, Morita diversified into music and films, buying the US-based CBS records in 1988 and Columbia Pictures in 1989. According to Morita, 'with the development of software, new hardware products come to life. I hope Sony will develop its software business into a large-scale operation as well, including both sound and images.'

And so it did, but not without incurring heavy losses during the first years, as it tried to learn how to manage 'creative companies' in the United States within a more technology-oriented Japanese corporation. It also remained rather sketchy how the worlds of hardware and software would be brought together to create the anticipated synergy. So, when a successor to Morita was sought in 1995, more than a dozen senior managers were bypassed to make the outspoken Nobuyuki Idei the new CEO. Idei had a clear vision that Sony needed to evolve into an integrated home entertainment company, making use of the imminent emergence of broadband networks. Instead of seeing software ('content') as a supporting ingredient for selling more stand-alone gadgets, Idei's vision was that people's enjoyment of the software content should be central and that different types of devices for accessing this content should be networked into an integrated system. Through broadband networks, content such as music, films and games could be shared between various terminals, such as personal computers, televisions, game consoles, personal digital assistants, cellphones or any other imaginable device.

To make this happen, Idei stressed that 'collaboration between our technology and content businesses are most crucial . . . Sony as a group must work together as a single entity to create an appealing broadband environment.' To facilitate the process of transforming Sony into what had become labeled as the 'Personal Broadband Network Solutions Company', Idei reorganized Sony in 2001 into five pillars; electronics, entertainment, games, internet/communication services and financial services. While each of these pillars remained 'in charge of devising their own strategy to accomplish their mission', a strong global hub was also established, with the responsibility for 'strategically unifying the group's resources and activities for the five key business pillars'. In Idei's words, what he wanted to achieve was 'integrated, decentralized management' – only corporate strategy and some critical support services, such as accounting, finance, human resources, legal affairs, intellectual copyright, public relations, external affairs and design were centralized, but many other, decentralized, activities were closely coordinated.

Since then, Sony has made considerable steps towards providing an integrated package for the broadband networking era. Most of its new hardware products are network based, such as the Airboard, a wireless panel that can be used to watch television, send e-mail or surf the internet. To its Vaio computers it has added a RoomLink device, which can send photos, videos or music wirelessly to other devices around the house. When it comes to products and services linking hardware and software, the first steps have also been taken. For instance,

through Sony's Clié personal digital assistant, people can log on to the Clié Plaza web site, to listen to music or watch a movie video. They can also play EverQuest, an on-line PlayStation2-based computer game, played by over 360 000 subscribers worldwide. Another electronics unit developed the supporting Memory Stick, which can be used to store digital data by virtually any Sony device.

As Sony's COO Kunitake Ando reiterated: 'For many years, Sony has sought to derive synergies from its manufacturing and entertainment businesses. Now, in an era when networks allow an increase in these synergies between hardware and entertainment content, more than ever our assets are uniquely suited to create new value.'

Sources: *Time Online* (www.time.com); *The Economist*, March 1 2003; www.sony.com.

TOWARDS A SYNTHESIS

Consider the little mouse, how sagacious an animal it is which never entrusts its life to one hole only.
Plautus (254–184 BC); Roman playwright

None ever got ahead of me except the man of one task.
Azariah Rossi (1513–1578); Italian physician

So, how should the corporate configuration be determined? Should corporate strategists limit themselves to achieving financial synergies, leaving SBU managers to 'mind their own business'? Or should corporate strategists strive to build a multi-business firm around a common core, intricately weaving all business units into a highly integrated whole? As before, the strategic management literature does not offer a clear-cut answer to the question of which corporate level strategies are the most successful. Many points of views have been put forward on how to reconcile the opposing demands of responsiveness and synergy, but no common perspective has yet emerged. Therefore, it is up to individual strategists to form their own opinion once again.

In Table 6.1 the main arguments of the two opposite poles in the debate have been summarized. The challenge now is to judge whether elements of the thesis and antithesis can be 'merged' into a synthesis, or whether one of the two views must simply be 'divested'. While integrating these two perspectives might not be easy, the potential synergy between them justifies giving it a try.

TABLE 6.1 Portfolio organization versus integrated organization perspective

	Portfolio organization perspective	Integrated organization perspective
Emphasis on	Responsiveness over synergy	Synergy over responsiveness
Conception of corporation	Collection of business shareholdings	Common core with business applications
Corporate composition	Potentially unrelated (diverse)	Tightly related (focused)
Key success factor	Business unit responsiveness	Multi-business synergy
Focal type of synergy	Cash flow optimization and risk balance	Integrating resources, activities and positions
Corporate management style	Exerting financial control	Joint strategy development
Primary task corporate center	Capital allocation and performance control	Setting direction and managing synergies
Position of business units	Highly autonomous (independent)	Highly integrated (interdependent)
Coordination between BUs	Low, incidental	High, structural
Growth through acquisitions	Simple to accommodate	Difficult to integrate

FURTHER READING

Growth for the sake of growth is the ideology of the cancer cell.
Edward Abbey (1927–1989); American author

Readers who would like to gain a better overview of the literature on the topic of corporate level strategy have a number of good sources from which to choose. Two scholarly reviews are 'Strategy and Structure in the Multiproduct Firm' by Charles Hill and Robert Hoskisson, and 'Research on Corporate Diversification: A Synthesis', by Vasudevan Ramanujam and P. Varadarajan, although both have become somewhat dated. A more recent review is 'Why Diversify? Four Decades of Management Thinking', by Michael Goold and Kathleen Luchs. Mark Sirower's book *The Synergy Trap: How Companies Lose the Acqusition Game* also has an excellent overview of the literature as an appendix.

Much of the strategy literature taking a portfolio organization perspective is from the end of the 1970s and the beginning of the 1980s. Bruce Henderson's popular book, *On Corporate Strategy*, which explains the basic principles of the portfolio organization perspective, is from this period. However, a better review of the portfolio approach, and especially portfolio techniques, is given by Charles Hofer and Dan Schendel in *Strategy Formulation: Analytical Concepts*. Recently, there has been renewed interest in viewing the corporation as investor and restructurer. In this crop, the article 'Growth Through Acquisitions: A Fresh Look', by Patricia Anslinger and Thomas Copeland is particularly provocative.

For further reading on the integrated organization perspective, Gary Hamel and C.K. Prahalad's book *Competing for the Future* is an obvious choice. The literature on the resource-based view of the firm mentioned in the 'Further reading' section at the end of Chapter 5 is also interesting in the context of this chapter. Highly stimulating is Hiroyuki Itami's book *Mobilizing Invisible Assets*, in which he also argues for sharing intangible resources throughout a multi-business firm.

More generally, the recent book by Alexander Campbell and Michael Goold, *Synergy: Why Links Between Business Units Often Fail and How to Make Them Work*, does an excellent job at reviewing various types of synergies and the practical problems of getting a more integrated organization to function effectively.

On the topic of acquisitions, a good overview of the arguments and quantitative research is provided by Anju Seth, in his article 'Value Creation in Acquisitions: A Re-Examination of Performance Issues'. Mark Sirower's earlier mentioned book is also an excellent choice. When it comes to issues in the area of post-acquisition integration, Philippe Haspeslagh and David Jemison's book *Managing Acquisitions: Creating Value Through Corporate Renewal* is a good start. The more recent book by Michael Hitt, J. Harrison, and R. Ireland, *Mergers and Acquisitions: A Guide to Creating Value for Shareholders*, is also well worth reading.

On the role of the corporate center, *Corporate-Level Strategy: Creating Value in the Multibusiness Company*, by Michael Goold, Andrew Campbell and Marcus Alexander, is highly recommended. Also stimulating is Charles Hill's article 'The Functions of the Headquarters Unit in Multibusiness Firms'. For a more academic analysis, readers are advised to turn to Vijay Govindarajan's article 'A Contingency Approach to Strategy Implementation at the Business-Unit Level: Integrating Administrative Mechanisms with Strategy'.

NETWORK LEVEL STRATEGY

Alliance, n. In international politics, the union of two thieves who have their hands so deeply inserted in each other's pocket that they cannot separately plunder a third.

The Devil's Dictionary, Ambrose Bierce (1842–1914); American columnist

INTRODUCTION

A business unit can have a strategy, while a group of business units can also have a strategy together – this joint course of action at the divisional or corporate level was discussed in the previous chapter. What has not been examined yet is whether a group of companies can also have a strategy together. Is it possible that companies do not develop their strategies in 'splendid isolation', but rather coordinate their strategies to operate as a team? And is it a good idea for firms to link up with others for a prolonged period of time to try to achieve shared objectives together?

Where two or more firms move beyond a mere transactional relationship and work jointly towards a common goal, they form an alliance, partnership or network. Their shared strategy is referred to as a network level strategy. In such a case, strategy is not only 'concerned with relating a firm to its environment', as was stated in Chapter 5, but also with relating a network to its broader environment.

The existence of networks does raise a range of questions, not the least of which is whether they make strategic sense or not. Is it beneficial to engage in long-term collaborative relationships with other firms or is it more advantageous for firms to 'keep their distance' and to interact with one another in a more market-like, transactional way? Is it viable to manage a web of partnership relations or is it preferable to keep it simple, by having the firm operate more or less independently? To address these questions is to raise the issue of inter-organizational relationships – what should be the nature of the relationship between a firm and other organizations in its surroundings? This issue will be the focus of the further discussion in this chapter.

THE ISSUE OF INTER-ORGANIZATIONAL RELATIONSHIPS

No firm exists that is autarchic. All firms must necessarily interact with other organizations (and individuals) in their environment and therefore they have inter-organizational (or inter-firm) relationships. These relationships can evolve without any clear strategic intent or tactical calculation, but most managers agree that actively determining the nature of their external relations is a significant part of what strategizing is about. Even avoiding relations with some external parties can be an important strategic choice.

To gain a better understanding of the interaction between firms, four aspects are of particular importance and will be reviewed here – the who, why, what and how of inter-organizational relationships (see Figure 7.1). The first aspect is the question of who – who are the potential counterparts with whom a firm can actually have a relationship? This is referred to as the topic of 'relational actors'. The second aspect is the question of why – why do the parties want to enter into a relationship with one another? This is referred to as the topic of 'relational objectives'. The third aspect is the question of what – what type of influences determine the nature of the relationship? This is referred to as the topic of 'relational factors'. The fourth aspect is the question of how – how can relationships be structured into a particular organizational form to let them function in the manner intended? This is referred to as the topic of 'relational arrangements'.

Relational actors

In Figure 7.2 an overview is given of the eight major groups of external parties with whom the firm can, or must, interact. A distinction has been made between industry and contextual actors. The industry actors are those individuals and organizations that perform value-adding activities and/or consume the outputs of these activities. The contextual actors are those parties whose behavior, intentionally or unintentionally, sets the conditions under which the industry actors must operate. The four main categories of relationships between the firm and other industry parties are the following (e.g. Porter, 1980; Reve, 1990):

- **Upstream vertical (supplier) relations.** Every company has suppliers of some sort. In a narrow definition these include the providers of raw materials, parts, machinery and business services. In a broader definition the providers of all production factors (land, capital, labor, technology, information and entrepreneurship) can be seen as suppliers, if they are not part of the firm itself. All these suppliers can either be the actual producers of the input, or an intermediary (distributor or agent) trading in the product or service. Beside the suppliers with which the firm transacts directly (first-tier suppliers), the firm may also have relationships with suppliers further upstream in the industry. All these relationships are traditionally referred to as upstream vertical relations, because economists commonly draw the industry system as a column.

- **Downstream vertical (buyer) relations.** On the output side, the firm has relationships with its customers. These clients can either be the actual users of the product or serv-

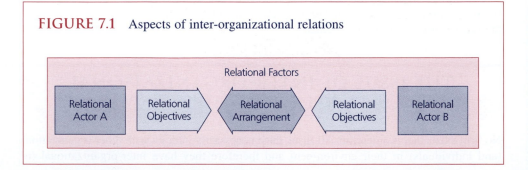

FIGURE 7.1   Aspects of inter-organizational relations

ice, or intermediaries trading the output. Besides the buyers with which the firm transacts directly, it may also have relationships with parties further downstream in the industry column.

■ Direct horizontal (industry insider) relations. This category includes the relations between the firm and other industry incumbents. Because these competitors produce similar goods or services, they are said to be at the same horizontal level in the industry column.

■ Indirect horizontal (industry outsider) relations. Where a firm has a relationship with a company outside its industry, this is referred to as an indirect horizontal relation. Commonly, companies will have relationships with the producers of complementary goods and services (e.g. hardware manufacturers with software developers). Such a relationship can develop with the producer of a substitute good or service, either as an adversary or as an ally. A relation can also exist between a firm and a potential industry entrant, whereby the incumbent firm can assist or attempt to block the entry of the industry outsider. Furthermore, a firm can establish a relationship with a firm in another industry, with the intention of diversifying into that, or a third, industry. In reality, where industry boundaries are not clear, the distinction between direct and indirect horizontal relations is equally blurry.

Besides relationships with these industry actors, there can be many contacts with condition-setting parties in the broader environment. Employing the classic SEPTember distinction, the following rough categories of contextual actors can be identified:

■ Socio-cultural actors. Individuals or organizations that have a significant impact on societal values, norms, beliefs and behaviors may interact with the firm. These could

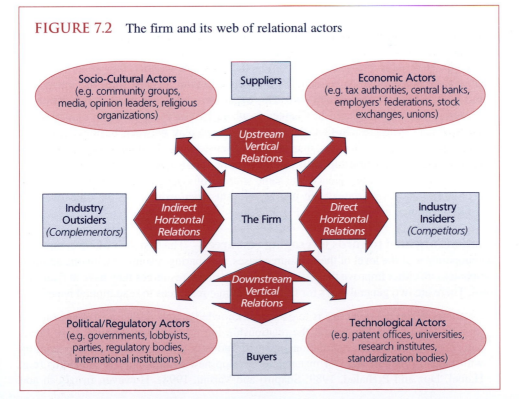

FIGURE 7.2 The firm and its web of relational actors

include the media, community groups, charities, religious organizations and opinion leaders.

- Economic actors. There can also be organizations influencing the general economic state of affairs, with which the firm interacts. Among others, tax authorities, central banks, employers' federations, stock exchanges and unions may be of importance.

- Political/legal actors. The firm may also interact with organizations setting or influencing the regulations under which companies must operate. These could include governments, political parties, special interest groups, regulatory bodies and international institutions.

- Technological actors. There are also many organizations that influence the pace and direction of technological development and the creation of new knowledge. Among others, universities, research institutes, patent offices, government agencies and standardization bodies may be important to deal with.

As Figure 7.2 visualizes, companies can choose, but are often also forced, to interact with a large number of organizations and individuals in the environment. This configuration of external actors with which the organization interacts is referred to as the company's group of 'external stakeholders'.

Relational objectives

How organizations deal with one another is strongly influenced by what they hope to achieve (e.g. Dyer and Singh, 1998; Preece, 1995). Both parties may have clear, open and mutually beneficial objectives, but it is also possible that one or both actors have poorly defined intentions, hidden agendas and/or mutually exclusive goals. Moreover, it is not uncommon that various people within an organization have different, even conflicting, objectives and expectations with regard to an external relationship (e.g. Allison, 1969; Doz and Hamel, 1998).

Where two or more firms seek to work together with one another, they generally do so because they expect some value added – they assume more benefit from the interaction than if they had proceeded on their own. This expectation of value creation as a driver for cooperation was also discussed in Chapter 6, where two or more business units worked together to reap synergies. In fact, the same logic is at play between business units and between companies. In both cases, managers are oriented towards finding sources of added value in a potential relationship with another – either across business unit boundaries or across company boundaries. Hence, the same sources of synergy identified in the discussion on corporate level strategy are just as relevant when examining the objectives for inter-organizational cooperation (see Figure 7.3).

Relations oriented towards leveraging resources.   The first area where companies can cooperate is at the level of their resource bases. By sharing resources with one another, companies can either improve the quantity or quality of the resources they have at their disposal. There are two general ways for firms to leverage resources to reap mutual benefit:

- Learning. When the objective is to exchange knowledge and skills, or to engage in the joint pursuit of new know-how, the relationship is said to be learning-oriented. Firms can enter into new learning relationships with industry outsiders, but can also team up with industry incumbents, for instance to develop new technologies or standards (e.g. Hamel, Doz and Prahalad, 1989; Shapiro and Varian, 1998). However, firms can add

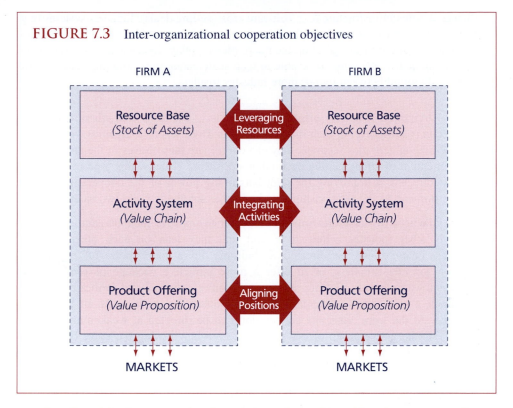

FIGURE 7.3   Inter-organizational cooperation objectives

a learning objective to an already existing relationship with a buyer or supplier as well.

■ Lending. Where one firm owns specific resources that it cannot make full use of, or another firm can make better use of, it can be attractive for both to lend the resource to the other. Lending relationships happen frequently in the areas of technology, copyrights and trademarks, where licensing is commonplace. But physical resources can also be lent, usually in the form of lease contracts. In all cases the benefit to lenders can be financial or they receive other resources in return.

Relations oriented towards integrating activities.   The second area where companies can cooperate is at the level of their activity systems. Few companies can span an entire industry column from top to bottom and excel at every type of activity. Usually, by integrating their value chains with other organizations, firms can be much more efficient and effective than if they were totally separated. There are two general ways for firms to integrate their activities with others:

■ Linking. The most common type of relationship in business is the vertical link between a buyer and a seller. All relationships in which products or services are exchanged fall into this category. Most firms have many linking relationships, both upstream and downstream, because they want to focus on only a limited number of value-adding activities, but need a variety of inputs, as well as clients to purchase their finished goods.

■ Lumping. Where firms bring together their similar activities to gain economies of scale, the relationship is said to be oriented towards lumping. Sharing operations (e.g. airline alliances), sales infrastructure (e.g. software cross-selling deals), logistics systems (e.g. postal partnerships) or payment facilities (e.g. inter-bank settlement agreements) are examples of where firms can lump their activities together. Because the activities need to be more or less the same to be able to reap scale economies, lumping relationships are usually found between two or more industry insiders.

Relations oriented towards aligning positions.   The third area where companies can cooperate is at the level of their market positions. Even where companies want to keep their value-adding activities separate, they can coordinate their moves in the environment with the intention of strengthening each other's position. Usually, this type of coalition-building is directed at improving the joint bargaining power of the cooperating parties. These position-enhancing relationships can be further subdivided into two categories:

- Leaning. Where two or more firms get together to improve their bargaining position vis-à-vis other industry actors, it is said that they lean on each other to stand stronger. Leaning can be directed at building up a more powerful negotiation position towards suppliers, or to offer a more attractive package of products and services towards buyers. Getting together with other companies to form a consortium to launch a new industry standard can also bolster the position of all companies involved. At the same time, the cooperation can be directed at weakening the position of an alternative group of companies or even heightening the entry barriers for interested industry outsiders.

- Lobbying. Firms can also cooperate with one another with the objective of gaining a stronger position vis-à-vis contextual actors. Such lobbying relationships are often directed at strengthening the firms' voice towards political and regulatory actors, such as governments and regulatory agencies. However, firms can get together to put pressure on various other contextual actors, such as standard setting bodies, universities, tax authorities and stock exchanges as well.

In practice, cooperative relationships between organizations can involve a number of these objectives simultaneously. Moreover, it is not uncommon for objectives to shift over time and for various participants in the relationship to have different objectives.

Relational factors

How inter-organizational relationships develop is strongly influenced by the objectives pursued by the parties involved. However, a number of other factors also have an impact on how relationships unfold. These relational factors can be grouped into four general categories (e.g. Mitchell, Agle and Wood, 1997; Gulati, 1998):

- Legitimacy. Relationships are highly impacted by what is deemed to be legitimate. Written and unwritten codes of conduct give direction to what is viewed as acceptable behavior. Which topics are allowed on the agenda, who has a valid claim, how interaction should take place and how conflicts should be resolved, are often decided by what both parties accept as 'the rules of engagement'. There is said to be 'trust', where it is expected that the other organization or individual will adhere to these rules. However, organizations do not always agree on 'appropriate behavior', while what is viewed as legitimate can shift over time as well. It can also be (seen as) advantageous to act opportunistically by not behaving according to the unwritten rules (e.g. Gambetta, 1988; Williamson, 1991).

- Urgency. Inter-organizational relations are also shaped by the factor 'timing'. Relationships develop differently when one or both parties are under time pressure to achieve results, as opposed to a situation where both organizations can interact without experiencing a sense of urgency (e.g. Pfeffer and Salancik, 1978; James, 1985).

- Frequency. Inter-organizational relations also depend on the frequency of interaction and the expectation of future interactions. Where parties expect to engage in a one-off transaction they usually behave differently than when they anticipate a more structural relationship extending over multiple interactions. Moreover, a relationship with a low rate of interaction tends to develop differently than one with a high regularity of interaction (e.g. Axelrod, 1984; Dixit and Nalebuff, 1991).

- Power. Last but not least, relations between organizations are strongly shaped by the power held by both parties. Power is the ability to influence others' behavior and organizations can have many sources of power. Most importantly for inter-organizational relationships, a firm can derive power from having resources that the other organization requires. In relationships with a very high level of resource dependence, firms tend to behave differently towards each other than when they are interdependent or relatively independent of one another (e.g. Pfeffer and Salancik, 1978; Porter, 1980).

Especially the impact of power differences on inter-organizational relationships is given extensive attention in the strategic management literature. Many authors (e.g. Chandler, 1990; Kay, 1993; Pfeffer and Salancik, 1978; Porter, 1980; Schelling, 1960) stress that for understanding the interaction between firms it is of the utmost importance to gain insight into their relative power positions. One way of measuring relative power in a relationship is portrayed in Figure 7.4, where a distinction is made between the closeness of the relationship (loose vs. tight) and the distribution of power between the two parties involved (balanced vs. unbalanced). This leads to a categorization of four specific types of inter-firm relationships from the perspective of relative power position. These four categories (adapted from Ruigrok and van Tulder, 1995) are:

FIGURE 7.4   Relative power positions in inter-organizational relationships

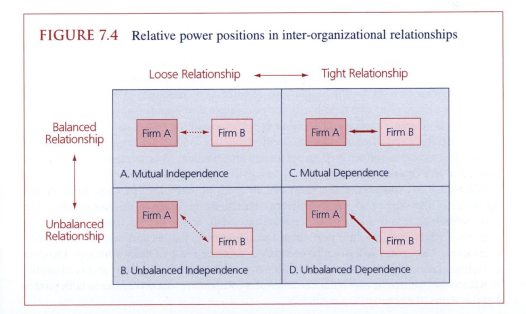

A Mutual independence. Organizations are independent in a relationship if they have full freedom to act according to their own objectives. Independence in an inter-organizational relationship means that organizations will only interact on their own terms and that they have the ability to break off the relationship without any penalty. In a situation of mutual independence, neither organization has significant influence over the other.

B Unbalanced independence. When two organizations work together in a loose relationship, one side (Firm A) can have more power than the other (Firm B). In such a case, it is said that Firm A is more independent than Firm B – Firm A's power gives it more freedom to act, while Firm B can be influenced by the powerful Firm A. This situation is called unbalanced independence, as both sides are independent, but one more so than the other.

C Mutual dependence. Two organizations can have a tight relationship, in which they are mutually dependent, while having an equal amount of sway over their counterpart. This type of situation, where there is a substantial, yet balanced, relationship between two or more parties, is also called interdependence.

D Unbalanced dependence. Where a tight relationship is characterized by asymmetrical dependence, one party will be able to dominate the other. In this situation of unbalanced dependence, the organization with the lower level of dependence will have more freedom to maneuver and impose its conditions than its counterpart.

The first category, mutual independence, is what is typically expected of a normal *market* relationship, although it is not strange to also witness market relationships that fit more in the second category, unbalanced independence. At the other extreme, unbalanced dependence is very close to the situation that would occur if the dominant firm acquired its counterpart. Whether acquired or fully dependent, the dominant firm controls its behavior. For this reason it is said that in cases of unbalanced dependence the inter-organizational relationship comes close to resembling the *hierarchy*-type relationship found within a firm. Interdependence seems to be somewhere between market and hierarchy-type relationships. What this means for the structuring of these relationships will be examined below.

Relational arrangements

In the classic dichotomy, the firm and its environment are presented as rather distinct entities. Within a firm coordination is achieved by means of direct control, leading transaction cost economists to refer to this organizational form as a 'hierarchy' (Williamson, 1975, 1985). In a hierarchy a central authority governs internal relationships and has the formal power to coordinate strategy and solve inter-departmental disputes. In the environment, relationships between firms are non-hierarchical, as they interact with one another without any explicit coordination or dispute settlement mechanism. This organizational form is referred to as a 'market'.

In Chapter 6 it was argued that there are all types of activities that companies should not want to internalize and run themselves, but should leave up to the market-place. In many situations, it is much more efficient to buy inputs in the market than to make them yourself – where activities are performed by autonomous parties and outputs are sold in the market-place, costs will often be lowest. As summarized by Ouchi (1980, p. 130), 'in a market relationship, the transaction takes place between the two parties and is mediated by a price mechanism in which the existence of a competitive market reassures both parties that the terms of exchange are equitable'.

Integration of activities into the firm is only necessary where 'markets do not function properly' – where doing it yourself is cheaper or better. The firm must internalize activities, despite the disadvantages of hierarchy, where the 'invisible hand' of the market cannot be trusted to be equitable and effective. Control over activities by means of formal authority – the 'visible hand' – is needed under these conditions. This is particularly true of all of the synergy advantages mentioned in Chapter 6, that the corporation would not be able to reap if the various business activities were not brought together under one 'corporate roof'.

In reality, however, there are many organizational forms between markets and hierarchies (e.g. Håkansson and Johanson, 1993; Powell, 1990; Thorelli, 1986). These are the networks, partnerships, or alliances introduced at the start of this chapter. In networks, strategies are coordinated and disputes resolved, not through formal top-down power, but by mutual adaptation. To extend the above metaphor, networks rely neither on the visible nor invisible hand to guide relationships, but rather employ the 'continuous handshake' (Gerlach, 1992).

The organizations involved in networks can employ different sorts of collaborative arrangements to structure their ties with one another. In Figure 7.5, an overview of a number of common types of collaborative arrangements is presented. Two major distinctions are made in this overview. First, between bilateral arrangements, which only involve two parties, and multilateral arrangements, which involve three or more. Commonly, only the multilateral arrangements are referred to as networks, although here the term is employed to cover all groupings of two or more cooperating firms. The second distinction is between non-contractual, contractual and equity-based arrangements. Non-contractual arrangements are cooperative agreements that are not binding by law, while contractual arrangements do have a clear legal enforceability. Both, however, do not involve taking a financial stake in each other or in a new joint venture, while the equity-based arrangements do.

FIGURE 7.5   Examples of collaborative arrangements

	Non-Contractual Arrangements	Contractual Arrangements	Equity-based Arrangements
Multilateral Arrangements	• Lobbying coalition (e.g. European Roundtable of Industrialists) • Joint standard setting (e.g. Linux coalition) • Learning communities (e.g. Strategic Management Society)	• Research consortium (e.g. Symbian in PDAs) • International marketing alliance (e.g. Star Alliance in airlines) • Export partnership (e.g. Netherlands Export Combination)	• Shared payment system (e.g. Visa) • Construction consortium (e.g. Eurotunnel) • Joint reservation system (e.g. Galileo)
Bilateral Arrangements	• Cross-selling deal (e.g. between pharmaceutical firms) • R&D staff exchange (e.g. between IT firms) • Market information sharing agreement (e.g. between hardware and software makers)	• Licensing agreement (e.g. Disney and Coca-Cola) • Co-development contract (e.g. Disney and Pixar in movies) • Co-branding alliance (e.g. Coca-Cola and McDonald's)	• New product joint venture (e.g. Sony and Ericsson in cellphones) • Cross-border joint venture (e.g. Daimler Chrysler and Beijing Automotive) • Local joint venture (e.g. CNN Turk in Turkey)

The intent of these collaborative arrangements is to profit from some of the advantages of vertical and horizontal integration, without incurring their costs. Networks are actually hybrid organizational forms that attempt to combine the benefits of hierarchy with the benefits of the market. The main benefits of hierarchy are those associated with the structural coordination of activities. In non-market relational arrangements, all parties collaborate on a more long-term basis with the intent of realizing a common goal. They will organize procedures, routines and control systems to ensure effective and efficient functioning of their joint activities and a smooth transition at their organizational interfaces. The benefits of the market that these collaborative arrangements retain are flexibility and motivation. By not being entirely locked into a fixed hierarchy, individual firms can flexibly have multiple relationships, of varying length and intensity, and can change these relationships more easily where circumstances require adaptation. The market also provides the motivation to be efficient and to optimize the pursuit of the organization's self-interest. This entrepreneurial incentive can be a strong spur for risk-taking, innovation and change.

A significant advantage of collaborative arrangements is that such relationships facilitate the process of 'co-specialization'. Much of humanity's economic progress is based on the principle of specialization by means of a division of labor. As people and firms focus more closely on performing a limited set of value-adding activities, they become more effective and efficient in their work. This division of labor assumes, however, that the value-adding activities that are outsourced by one become the specialization of another, hence co-specialization. Yet, many activities cannot be outsourced to outsiders on the basis of normal market relations, either due to the risk of dependence or because of the need for the structural coordination of activities. Under these conditions, collaborative arrangements can act as a synthesis of hierarchy and market relations, thus catalyzing the process of specialization (e.g. Best, 1990; Axelsson and Easton, 1992).

Such co-specialization can progress to such an extent that clusters of firms work together in more of less permanent networks. Such symbiotic groups of collaborating firms can actually function as 'virtual corporations' (e.g. Chesbrough and Teece, 1996; Quinn, 1992). In such networks, the relationships between the participating firms are often very tight and durable, based on a high level of trust and perceived mutual interest. While each organization retains its individual identity, the boundaries between them become fuzzy, blurring the clear distinction between 'the organization' and 'its environment'. When a high level of trust and reciprocity has been achieved, relations can move far beyond simple contractual obligations. The collaborative relations can become more open-ended, with objectives, responsibilities, authority and results not fully determined in advance in a written contract, but evolving over time, given all parties' sincere willingness to 'work on their relationship' (e.g. Jarillo, 1988; Kanter, 1994).

While the intention of collaborative arrangements may be to blend the advantages of hierarchy with the qualities of the market, it is also possible that the weaknesses of both are actually combined. The main weakness of hierarchy is bureaucracy – creating red tape, unnecessary coordination activities and dulling the incentive to perform. In reality, collaborative arrangements might be mechanisms for structuring static relationships and dampening entrepreneurial behavior. A further danger is that the mutual dependence might become skewed, shifting the balance of power to one of the partners. Under such conditions, one or more organizations can become dependent on a dominant party, without much influence (voice) or the possibility to break off the relationship (exit). Such unbalanced dependency relationships (see Figure 7.4) might be a great benefit for the stronger party, but can easily lead to the predominance of its interests over the interests of the weaker partners (e.g. Oliver and Wilkinson, 1988; Ruigrok and van Tulder, 1995).

Simultaneously such partnerships are vulnerable to the main disadvantage of the market, namely opportunism. Companies run the risk of opportunism, that is (according to Williamson, 1985: 47):

> *self-interest seeking with guile. This includes but is scarcely limited to more blatant forms, such as lying, stealing and cheating . . . More generally, opportunism refers to the incomplete or distorted disclosure of information, especially to calculated efforts to mislead, distort, disguise, obfuscate, or otherwise confuse.*

Such behavior can be limited by clearly defining objectives, responsibilities, authority and expected results ahead of time, preferably in an explicit contract. Even then collaborative arrangements expose companies to the risk of deception, the abuse of trust and the exploitation of dependence, making their use by no means undisputed.

THE PARADOX OF COMPETITION AND COOPERATION

We have no eternal allies and we have no perpetual enemies. Our interests are eternal and perpetual, and those interests it is our duty to follow.
Lord Palmerston (Henry John Temple) (1784–1865); British prime minister

When former CEO of KLM Royal Dutch Airlines, Pieter Bouw, teamed up with Northwest Airlines in 1989, he was thrilled to have the first major transatlantic strategic alliance in the industry, involving joint flights, marketing and sales activities, catering, ground handling, maintenance and purchasing. Northwest was the fourth largest American carrier at that time, but was in 'Chapter 11', balancing on the verge of bankruptcy, and in dire need of cash. To help their new ally out, KLM gave a US$400 million capital injection, in return for 20% of the shares and the option to increase this to a majority stake within a few years. KLM and Northwest were on their way to becoming a virtual transatlantic company – a marriage 'made in the heavens'.

Commercially the deal was a success, but relationally the alliance was a Shakespearean drama. KLM gave up its hopes of an alliance with Swissair, SAS and Delta, to remain loyal to Northwest, but as soon as Northwest emerged from Chapter 11, it blocked KLM's efforts to increase its shareholding. In the resulting two-year legal shooting match between 1995 and 1997, relations deteriorated sharply and the goose laying the golden eggs threatened to be killed in the cross fire. Disappointed and dismayed, Bouw decided to give in, selling Northwest back its shares, in return for a prolongation of the alliance, after which he immediately resigned. His successor, and current CEO, Leo van Wijk, has managed the alliance since then and it is still 'up in the air', in both senses of the expression. His most important conclusion has been that a collaborative alliance is not only about working together towards a common interest, but equally about being assertive with regard to one's own interests. Alliances are not only *cooperative*, but also have *competitive* aspects.

What this example of KLM and Northwest illustrates is that firms constantly struggle with the tension created by the need to work together with others, while simultaneously needing to pursue their own interests. Firms cannot isolate themselves from their environments, but must actively engage in relationships with suppliers and buyers, while selectively teaming up with other firms inside and outside their industry to attain mutual benefit. But while they are collaborating to create joint value, firms are also each other's rivals when it comes to dividing the benefits. These opposite demands placed on organizations are widely referred to as the pressures for competition and cooperation (e.g. Brandenburger and Nalebuff, 1996; Lado, Boyd and Hanlon, 1997). In the following sections both pressures will be examined in more detail.

The demand for inter-organizational competition

Competition can be defined as the act of working against others, where two or more organizations' goals are mutually exclusive. In other words, competition is the rivalry behavior exhibited by organizations or individuals where one's win is the other's loss.

Organizations need to be competitive in their relationships with others. As the interests and/or objectives of different organizations are often mutually exclusive, each organization needs to be determined and assertive in pursuing its own agenda. Each organization needs to be willing to confront others to secure its own interests. Without the will to engage in competitive interaction, the organization will be at the mercy of more aggressive counterparts – e.g. suppliers will charge excessively for products, buyers will express stiff demands for low prices, governments will require special efforts without compensation, and rival firms will poach among existing customers. Taking a competitive posture towards these external parties means that the organization is determined to assert its own interests and fight where necessary.

The resulting competitive relations can vary between open antagonism and conflict on the one hand, and more subtle forms of friction, tension and strain on the other. Blatant competitive behavior is often exhibited towards organizations whose objectives are fully in conflict – most clearly other producers of the same goods, attempting to serve the same markets (aptly referred to as 'the competition'). Highly competitive behavior can also be witnessed where a supplier and a buyer confront each other for dominance in the industry value chain (e.g. Porter, 1980; Van Tulder and Junne, 1988). A more restrained competitive stance can be observed where organizations' objectives are less at odds, but assertiveness is still important to protect the organization's interests. Negotiation and bargaining will commonly be employed under these circumstances.

To be competitive an organization must have the power to overcome its rivals and it must have the ability and will to use its power. Many factors shape the power of an organization, but its relative level of resource dependence is one of the most important determining elements. The more independent the organization, and the more others are dependent on it, the more power the organization will wield. In competitive relationships maneuvering the other party into a relatively dependent position is a common approach. In general, calculation, bargaining, maneuvering, building coalitions and outright conflict are all characteristic for the competitive interaction between organizations.

The demand for inter-organizational cooperation

Cooperation can be defined as the act of working together with others, where two or more organizations' goals are mutually beneficial. In other words, cooperation is the collaborative behavior exhibited by organizations or individuals where both sides need each other to succeed.

Organizations need to be cooperative in their relationships with others. The interests and/or objectives of different organizations are often complementary and working together can be mutually beneficial. Therefore, organizations must be willing to behave as partners, striving towards their common good. Without the will to engage in cooperative interaction, the organization will miss the opportunity to reap the advantages of joint efforts – e.g. developing new products together with suppliers, creating a better service offering together with buyers, improving the knowledge infrastructure together with government and setting new technical standards together with other firms in the industry. Taking a cooperative posture towards these external parties means that the organization is determined to leverage its abilities through teamwork.

The resulting cooperative relations can vary between occasional alliances on the one hand, to tight-knit, virtual integration on the other. Strongly cooperative behavior can be witnessed where the long-term interests of all parties are highly intertwined. This type of symbiotic relationship can be found between the producers of complementary goods and services, where success by one organization will positively impact its partners – aptly referred to as the 'network effect' (Arthur, 1994; Shapiro and Varian, 1998). Highly cooperative behavior can also be observed where suppliers and buyers face a joint challenge (such as government regulation, an innovative technology or a new market entrant) that can only be tackled by significant mutual commitment to a shared objective.

More restrained cooperative behavior is common where there is potential for a 'positive sum game', but some parties seek to optimize their own returns to the detriment of others. Under such circumstances, exhibiting cooperative behavior does not mean being naive or weak, but creating conditions under which the long-term shared interests prevail over the short-term temptation by some to cheat their partners. An important ingredient for overcoming the lure of opportunism is to build long-term commitment to one another, not only in words and mentality, but also practically, through a high level of interdependence. Where organizations are tightly linked to one another, the pay-off for cooperative behavior is usually much more enticing than the possibility to profit from the dependence of one's partner. But to be willing to commit to such a high level of interdependence, people on both sides of a relationship need to trust each other's intentions and actions, while there must be coordination and conflict-resolution mechanisms in place to solve evolving issues (e.g. Dyer, Kale and Singh, 2001; Simonin, 1997).

EXHIBIT 7.1 SHORT CASE

MERCK: A MEDICINE AGAINST ANOREXIA?

Name an industry in which the average product takes 10 years to develop, at a cost of US$500 million a shot. Aerospace? Robotics? Logical choices, but the right answer is pharmaceuticals. Developing new drugs does not come easily or cheaply. The R&D budgets of the large pharmaceutical companies are approximately 18% of sales, placing some of them among the biggest R&D spenders in the world. With such high investments and long lead times, the pharmaceutical industry is a competitive arena that should be avoided by the short-winded and faint-hearted. Ray Gilmartin, however, does not need to reach for Prilosec, a heartburn drug – he only needs to sell the product and is doing so quite well. Since 1994, Gilmartin has been CEO of Merck & Co., the fourth largest pharmaceutical company in the world, after Pfizer, GlaxoSmithKline, and Johnson & Johnson, with sales in 2002 of US$21.4 billion and a net profit of US$6.8 billion. Merck employs more than 60 000 people around the world, many of them working in the 11 research facilities the company has in seven different countries.

Merck has competed in this high-stakes industry for more than 100 years, initially as the US subsidiary of the German company Merck. During World War I the Merck subsidiary became separated from its parent company in Darmstadt, and to this day both companies use the Merck name (the German E. Merck has sales of approximately €8 billion, half of which is in pharmaceuticals). For decades, the pharmaceutical industry has enjoyed double-digit revenue growth and recession-proof high profitability, making it a stock market favorite despite the risk involved in the drug development process. But since the end of the 1990s, the industry conditions have taken a turn for the worse. After years of unchallenged price hikes, governments have started to look at the drug firms as partially responsible for the soaring cost of healthcare, threatening the industry with price regulations. In the United States, the rise of 'managed care' organizations that can buy in bulk has further enhanced the bargaining power of buyers, placing more pressure on prices. In many other countries, the healthcare insurance companies have been major players in searching for ways to clamp down on spiraling pharmaceutical expenditures.

At the same time, the highly profitable 'monopoly' period after the launch of a new drug is becoming ever shorter – successful products are soon joined by competitors' me-too products, which skillfully circumvent patent protection. And as soon as the patents actually expire, aggressive generic drug manufacturers quickly enter the market with products at cut-rate prices, often largely wiping out the sales of the patent holder. To extend their monopoly period, the research-based pharmaceutical companies have tried to devise all types of ways of getting new patents for modifications to existing drugs – only 15% of newly approved major drugs are based on 'new chemical entities' or treat illnesses in novel ways. However, some generic drug companies

have responded by making court battles a 'standard operating procedure', sometimes fighting up to 100 cases a year. Most research-based drug companies realize that their best defense is to forge ahead and develop new blockbuster products. The result has been a significant growth in R&D investments, yet the stream of new products has slowed, dropping by 35% between 1997 and 2002, reaching the lowest level in 20 years. And for many companies, the product development pipeline does not seem to offer enough potential to compensate for the older products due to lose patent protection.

The US$500 million price tag and 8–15 year time span for getting the scientists' chemical compounds out of the test tube and on to the pharmacists' shelves is only partially attributable to the process of actually discovering a potential new drug. In general it takes about one to three years for a new preparation to be synthesized and tested. But once a preparation is in the pipeline, many further steps need to be taken before it becomes a sellable product. First, the preparation enters the pre-clinical development phase, which might involve animal testing. If, after a few years of tests, the results are promising, permission can be gained to proceed with clinical trials on human volunteers. At first, these are conducted on small groups, but if successful, they are enlarged to full-scale tests. The clinical trials can take five to ten years before a drug is approved for broader use and sales can begin. On average, of the 20 preparations entering pre-clinical development, only one comes out of the pipeline as a marketable drug. Obviously, pharmaceutical companies would like to increase this yield and shorten the process, but this is not proving to be easy.

Merck has followed the industry trend by investing more heavily in R&D, raising its budget for 2002 to more than US$2.7 billion; double what it was just eight years before. The company seems to be spending this money well, as its scientists hold the lead in obtaining patents – between 1996 and 2002, Merck patented no less than 1933 new compounds, 400 more than second-place Pharmacia and also at the lowest cost, of 'just' US$6 million per patent. As a result, Merck claims its pipeline of upcoming new drugs is among the strongest ever. This has allowed Merck to go against another industry trend, which is to seek more intensive cooperation with others, either through alliances or mergers. Many of Merck's competitors have merged in the past few years, such as Pfizer with Pharmacia (together now number one), and Glaxo Wellcome with SmithKline Beecham (together now number two), with the intention of obtaining economies of scale in marketing and R&D. Gilmartin has been quite adamant that he prefers organic growth, seeing no value in such mega-mergers, as they only bring bureaucracy and infighting, not the innovative new products that are needed for above-average performance.

Merck has also been reluctant to join the strong movement towards all sorts of alliances, both with major pharmaceutical competitors and with small start-ups. Merck has a few joint ventures and licensing arrangements, but all on a relatively small scale. Only in 2002 did Merck's vice president and CFO, Judy Lewent, announce that the company would consider more alliances with small biotech companies, both in R&D and marketing. But the company's approach is hesitant and its philosophy towards new product development has remained largely 'do-it-yourself'. Not more than 5% of Merck's total research spending ends up outside of its own laboratories. This emphasis on doing most R&D in-house contrasts sharply with the direction being taken by the rest of the industry. All of Merck's rivals reserve between 10% and 20% of their R&D budgets for external work. In some cases only the laborious task of conducting clinical trials is outsourced, but increasingly the pharmaceutical giants are contracting out the development of new drugs to specialist firms, or licensing in the new products created by small biotech start-ups. Some analysts are predicting that the proportion of R&D performed outside of the big companies could reach 80%. Sir Richard Sykes, head of GlaxoSmithKline, has even suggested that the major drug firms will increasingly become 'virtual' companies, as they concentrate on the marketing of drugs developed by the legions of small independent biotech firms.

The enthusiasm of Merck's competitors for alliances with the creative independents has been based on the view 'if you can't beat them, join them'. Despite going through a funding crisis after the bursting of the internet bubble, the number of small biotech firms has grown rapidly – in the United States alone there are more than 1800 firms active, with approximately the same number scattered around the rest of the world. All of these firms are so specialized, that at any one moment at least one of them will be ahead of any given big firm in any given technology. Most pharmaceutical giants believe that it is wise to tap into this source of new products, especially if this speeds up the process of getting newly developed drugs into their pipeline. Moreover, licensing in new drugs from the small biotech firms can usually be achieved at a fraction of the cost of doing it in-house. Most biotech firms do not have the financial stamina to shepherd their products through the years of development and trials, nor do they have the marketing and distribution infrastructure needed to reap the benefits of their labors. This gives the big firms the negotiating position to snap up promising products for considerably less than they are worth. During the past few years, hundreds of deals have been struck between small biotech firms and big pharmaceutical companies, and the number of alliances and joint ventures is still rising.

Merck, however, is strongly opposed to this policy of hollowing out. It thinks that the type of 'R&D anorexia' that its rivals are suffering from might end up being fatal. Without first class in-house scientific talent a drug firm will have problems to rapidly identify the best biotech ideas worth buying. In Merck's view, competitors are taking the easy route of shopping for new products simply because they are not clever enough to come up with their own. The president of Merck Research Laboratories, Peter Kim, has indicated that if Merck does lack certain key knowledge, he would prefer to selectively acquire smaller companies and integrate them into his research community. For example, in 2001 Merck purchased Rosetta Inpharmatics, a leading informational genomics company, to fill in a gap in its portfolio of technologies.

Of course, the question is whether Gilmartin and his team are right, while the rest of the industry is wrong. Is it necessary to keep all key activities in-house and to remain largely self-contained and independent from the outside world? Or are Merck's competitors right when they argue that the pharmaceutical industry will come to resemble Hollywood, where the big studios are focusing more on marketing and distribution, while the films are increasingly being made by small production companies? Time will tell who is right, but maybe Gilmartin should keep a bottle of Prilosec handy, just in case.

Sources: www.merck.com; *The Economist*, October 24 2002, February 13 2003; www.ims-global.com.

PERSPECTIVES ON NETWORK LEVEL STRATEGY

Concordia discors (discordant harmony).
Horace (65–8 BC); Roman poet

Firms need to be able to engage in competition and cooperation simultaneously, even though these demands are each other's opposites. Firms need to exhibit a strongly cooperative posture to reap the benefits of collaboration, and they need to take a strongly competitive stance to ensure that others do not block their interests. Some theorists conclude that what is required is 'co-opetition' (Brandenburger and Nalebuff, 1996). But while a catchy word, managers are still left with the difficult question of how to deal with these conflicting demands. To meet the pressure for cooperation, firms must actually become part of a broader 'team', spinning a web of close collaborative relationships. But to meet the pressure for competition, firms must not become too entangled in restrictive relationships, but rather remain free to maneuver, bargain and attack, with the intention of securing their own interests. In other words, firms must be *embedded* and *independent* at the same time – embedded in a network of cooperative interactions, while independent enough to wield their power to their own advantage.

The question dividing strategizing managers is whether firms should be more embedded or more independent. Should firms immerse themselves in broader networks to create strong groups, or should they stand on their own? Should firms willingly engage in long-term interdependence relationships or should they strive to remain as independent as possible? Should firms develop network level strategies at all, or should the whole concept of multi-firm strategy-making be directed to the garbage heap?

While strategy writers generally agree about the need to manage the paradox of competition and cooperation, they come to widely differing prescriptions on how to do so.

Views within the field of strategic management are strongly at odds with regard to the best approach to inter-organizational relations. As before, here the two diametrically opposed positions will be identified and discussed, to show the scope of differing ideas. On the one side of the spectrum, there are strategists who believe that it is best for companies to be primarily competitive in their relationships to all outside forces. They argue that firms should remain independent and interact with other companies under market conditions as much as possible. As these strategists emphasize the discrete boundaries separating the firm from its 'competitive environment', this point of view is called the 'discrete organization perspective'. At the other end of the spectrum, there are strategists who believe that companies should strive to build up more long-term cooperative relationships with key organizations in their environment. They argue that firms can reap significant benefits by surrendering a part of their independence and developing close collaborative arrangements with a group of other organizations. This point of view will be referred to as the 'embedded organization perspective'.

The discrete organization perspective

Managers taking the discrete organization perspective view companies as independent entities competing with other organizations in a hostile market environment. In line with neoclassical economics, this perspective commonly emphasizes that individuals, and the organizations they form, are fundamentally motivated by aggressive self-interest and therefore that competition is the natural state of affairs. Suppliers will try to enhance their bargaining power vis-à-vis buyers with the aim of getting a better price, while conversely buyers will attempt to improve their negotiation position to attain better quality at lower cost. Competing firms will endeavor to gain the upper hand against their rivals if the opportunity arises, while new market entrants and manufacturers of substitute products will consistently strive to displace incumbent firms (e.g. Porter, 1980, 1985).

In such a hostile environment it is a strategic necessity for companies to strengthen their competitive position in relation to the external forces. The best strategy for each organization is to obtain the market power required to get good price/quality deals, ward off competitive threats, limit government demands and even determine the development of the industry. Effective power requires independence and therefore heavy reliance on specific suppliers, buyers, financiers or public organizations should be avoided.

The label 'discrete organization' given to this perspective refers to the fact that each organization is seen as being detached from its environment, with sharp boundaries demarcating where the outside world begins. The competitive situation is believed to be *atomistic*, that is, each self-interested firm strives to satisfy its own objectives, leading to rivalry and conflict with other organizations. Vertical interactions between firms in the industry column tend to be transactional, with an emphasis on getting the best possible deal. It is generally assumed that under such market conditions the interaction will be of a zero-sum nature, that is, a fight for who gets how much of the pie. The firm with the strongest bargaining power will usually be able to appropriate a larger portion of the 'economic rent' than will the less potent party. Therefore, advocates of the discrete organization perspective emphasize that the key to competitive success is the ability to build a powerful position and to wield this power in a calculated and efficient manner. This might sound Machiavellian to the faint-hearted, but it is the reality of the market-place that is denied at one's own peril.

Essential for organizational power is the avoidance of resource dependence. Where a firm is forced to lean on a handful of suppliers or buyers, this can place the organization in a precariously exposed position. To managers taking a discrete organization perspective, such dependence on a few external parties is extremely risky, as the other firm will be tempted to exploit their position of relative power to their own advantage. Wise firms will therefore not let themselves become overly dependent on any external organization, certainly not for any essential resources. This includes keeping the option open to exit from the relationship at will – with low barriers to exit the negotiating position of the firm is significantly stronger. Therefore the firm must never become so entangled with outsiders that it cannot rid themselves of them at the drop of a hat. The firm must be careful that in a web of relationships it is the spider, not the fly (e.g. Pfeffer & Salancik, 1978; Ruigrok and van Tulder, 1995).

Keeping other organizations at arm's-length also facilitates clear and business-like interactions. Where goods and services are bought or sold, distinct organizational boundaries help to distinguish tasks, responsibilities, authority and accountability. But as other firms will always seek to do as little as possible for the highest possible price, having clear contracts and a believable threat to enforce them, will serve as a method to ensure discipline. Arm's-length relations are equally useful in avoiding the danger of vital information leaking to the party with whom the firm must (re)negotiate.

In their relationships with other firms in the industry it is even clearer that companies' interests are mutually exclusive. More market share for one company must necessarily come at the expense of another. Coalitions are occasionally formed to create power blocks, if individual companies are not strong enough to compete on their own. Such tactical alliances bring together weaker firms, not capable of doing things independently. But 'competitive collaboration' is usually short lived – either the alliance is unsuccessful and collapses, or it is successful against the common enemy, after which the alliance partners become each other's most important rivals.

Proponents of the discrete organization perspective argue that collaborative arrangements are always second best to doing things independently. Under certain conditions, weakness might force a firm to choose an alliance, but it is always a tactical necessity, never a strategic preference. Collaborative arrangements are inherently risky, fraught with the hazard of opportunism. Due to the ultimately competitive nature of relationships, allies will be tempted to serve their own interests to the detriment of the others, by maneuvering, manipulating or cheating. The collaboration might even be a useful ploy, to cloak the company's aggressive intentions and moves. Collaboration, it is therefore concluded, is merely 'competition in a different form' (Hamel, Doz and Prahalad, 1989). Hence, where collaboration between firms really offers long-term advantages, a merger or acquisition is preferable to the uncertainty of an alliance.

Where collaboration is not the tool of the weak, it is often a conspiracy of the strong to inhibit competition. If two or more formidable companies collaborate, chances are that the alliance is actually ganging up on a third party – for instance on buyers. In such cases the term 'collaboration' is just a euphemism for collusion and not in the interest of the economy at large.

Worse yet, collaboration is usually also bad for a company's long-term health. A highly competitive environment is beneficial for a firm, because it provides the necessary stimulus for companies to continually improve and innovate. Strong adversaries push companies towards competitive fitness. A more benevolent environment, cushioned by competition-inhibiting collaboration, might actually make a firm more content and less eager to implement tough changes. In the long run this will make firms vulnerable to more aggressive companies, battle-hardened by years of rivalry in more competitive environments.

In conclusion, the basic assumption of the discrete organization perspective is that companies should not develop network level strategies, but should strive for 'strategic self-sufficiency'. Collaborative arrangements are a tactical tool, to be selectively employed. The sentiment of this perspective has been clearly summarized by Porter (1990a; 224): 'alliances are rarely a solution . . . no firm can depend on another independent firm for skills and assets that are central to its competitive advantage . . . Alliances tend to ensure mediocrity, not create world leadership.'

EXHIBIT 7.2 THE DISCRETE ORGANIZAION PERSPECTIVE

McCAIN: NO SMALL FRY

Which *Belgian* invention was spread around the world by *American* fast-food restaurants and is dominated by a *Canadian* multinational? Well, a product English-speakers accidentally call *French* fries. The Canadian firm leading the international market for this golden crispy delicacy is McCain, headquartered in the small town of Florenceville in the province of New Brunswick. With worldwide sales of more than US$6 billion in 2002 and 18 000 employees scattered around the globe, McCain is no 'small fry'. The company is both in the B2C and B2B markets, selling chilled and frozen fries through supermarkets and to restaurants.

Producing French fries is a low margin, high volume business with demanding customers, particularly in the B2B market. Achieving a stable supply of potatoes at a uniform quality level is key to keeping customers happy and margins up – which is easier said than done, as potatoes are highly susceptible to the influences of the weather and natural pests. The first step in getting a good supply of quality potatoes is in breeding 'seed potatoes' that are free of diseases and suited to local growing conditions. The second step is the actual growing and harvesting of the edible potatoes. Then come the industrialized processing steps of grading, skinning, slicing and packaging. Most companies in the industry column are specialized in either breeding, growing or processing, as each step requires significantly different competences. Breeding is highly R&D intensive, oriented towards developing new, patented varieties that taste different, or have lower growing or processing costs. Potato growing has also become increasingly high-tech, but can still be carried out efficiently by relatively small-sized farms. Potato processing is an industrialized process, with high economies of scale.

In striking contrast with its specialized competitors, McCain's strategy has long been to control the entire value chain. Or as one key manager recently put it, McCain's perspective is that 'competitive strength comes from having control over every aspect of the business'. While its competitors are dependent on others in the value chain for their success, McCain has gained a high level of independence by building a substantial power base in all stages of the industry column. At the breeding stage, McCain develops its own varieties, which ensures its independence from external breeders. The company also seeks to buy patents of promising varieties before others get access to them. At the growing stage, McCain maintains a limited in-house farming capacity, yet 'outsources' most production to low cost suppliers, because potato growing has low economies of scale and a high level of risk, due to unpredictable harvests. This outsourcing is done via 'pre-harvest' contracts, on conditions very favorable to McCain – most potato growers are relatively small-scale farmers, giving McCain a powerful bargaining position. To secure uniform, high quality supplies for its factories, tightly specified contracts are used that set standards and strict delivery times. Furthermore, the firm has an 'agronomy' team that closely monitors and supports contract farmers on a day-to-day basis. Besides these contract suppliers, McCain also purchases additional supplies on the post-harvest spot market, in which large price fluctuations can occur. For this reason (but also to keep in touch with the art of potato production), McCain grows a relatively small part of its own potato supply – just enough to counter speculative 'trade strikes' by growers and traders. Well-timed 'trade strikes', whereby suppliers refuse to sell their produce, can drive up the spot market potato price, just when processors need new supplies to keep their French fry factories running.

The discrete organization perspective, which drives McCain's vertical relationships (within the value chain) is also at the basis of their horizontal relationships (with competitors and trade associations). McCain prefers to stand alone – avoiding any dependence on the trade associations that populate the potato industry. These associations, jointly paid and run by the competing firms, are mainly aimed to promote common interests vis-à-vis national and supranational (e.g. European Union) regulatory agencies and pressure groups. Apart from the occasional short-term coalition, McCain has sought to pursue its interests on its own.

Sources: *Rademakers*, 1999; www.mccain.com.

The embedded organization perspective

Strategists taking an embedded organization perspective are fundamentally at odds with the assumption that competition is the predominant factor determining the interaction between organizations. Business isn't war, so to approach all interactions from an antagonistic angle is seen as overly pessimistic, even cynical. On the contrary, it is argued that business is about value creation, which is inherently a positive-sum activity. Creating value brings together organizations towards a common goal, as they can achieve more by working together than by behaving autistically. In the modern economy, no organization can efficiently perform all activities in-house, as the division of labor has encouraged companies to specialize and outsource as many non-core activities as possible. Companies are necessarily cogs in the larger industrial machine and they can achieve little without working in unison with the other parts of the system. In the embedded organization perspective, atomistic competition is a neoclassical theoretical abstraction that seriously mischaracterizes the nature of relationships between organizations. In reality, cooperation is the predominant factor determining inter-organizational relations. Symbiosis, not aggression, is the fundamental nature of economic functioning (e.g. Jarillo, 1988; Moore, 1996).

A company can always find many organizations in its environment with which it shares an interest and whose objectives are largely parallel to its own (Child and Faulkner, 1998). A company might want to develop new products together with its buyers, optimize the logistical system together with its suppliers, expand the industry's potential together with other manufacturers, link technological standards with other industries and improve employment conditions together with the government. In general, most organizations have a stronger interest in increasing the size of the pie, than in deciding who gets what – keeping the focus on making a success of value creation eases the process of finding an equitable solution to the issue of value distribution.

The label 'embedded organization' given to this perspective refers to the fact that firms are becoming increasingly integrated into webs of mutually dependent organizations (e.g. Gnyawali and Madhavan, 2001; Granovetter, 1985). As companies strive to focus on a limited set of core competences and core business processes, they have moved to outsource as many non-core activities as possible. But as firms have attempted to further specialize by outsourcing activities that are close to their core business, they have become more vulnerable to outside suppliers and the need for explicit coordination of activities has often remained high. The outsourcing of such essential and coordination-intensive activities can only take place where the other party can be trusted to closely collaborate with the joint interests in mind. Of course, a company will not quickly move to such dependence on an outside supplier. But as experience and trust build over time, a strategic partnership can develop, where both sides come to accept the value of the close cooperation (e.g. Axelsson and Easton, 1992; Lorenzoni and Baden-Fuller, 1995).

For a firm to willingly surrender a part of its independence, it must be certain that its partners are also willing to invest in the relationship and will not behave opportunistically. Ideally, therefore, durable partnerships are based on mutual dependence and reciprocity. Both sides of the relationship must need each other, which gives an important incentive for both to find solutions to the disputes that will inevitably pop up. A balance in the benefits to be gained and the efforts to be exerted will also contribute to the success of a long-term collaborative relationship.

While such close collaborative relationships place a firm in a position of resource dependence, the benefits are much larger. By specializing in a certain area, the firm can gain scale and experience advantages much faster. Specialization helps the firm to focus on a more limited set of core competences, which can be developed more efficiently and rapidly than if the firm were a 'conglomerate' of activities. At the same time the firm can tap into the complementary resources (Richardson, 1972) developed by its co-specialized partners. These complementary resources will usually be of higher quality and lower price than if the firm had built them up independently.

Specialized firms also use collaborative arrangements to quickly combine their resources with industry outsiders, to create new products and services. As product and business innovation is high paced and usually requires the combination of various types of resources, developing everything in isolation is unworkable for most firms. By teaming up with other firms that have complementary resources, a company can make the most of its own resource base, without having to build up other resources from scratch. But again trust is needed to engage in such a joint venture, as there are significant downside risks that the firm needs to take into account.

So, from the embedded organization perspective, collaboration is not competition in disguise, but a real alternative means of dealing with other organizations (e.g. Contractor and Lorange, 1988; Piore and Sabel, 1984). Successful firms embed themselves in webs of cooperative relationships, developing strategies together with their partners. These networks might compete against other networks (e.g. Gomes-Casseres, 1994; Hamilton and Woolsey Biggart, 1988; Weidenbaum and Hughes, 1996), but even here the relationships need not be fundamentally antagonistic. Proponents of the embedded organization perspective do not believe that firms should become obsessed with 'putting the competition out of business', as this again reduces business to a win-lose, zero-sum game. Firms should be focused on creating value and avoiding direct confrontation with other manufacturers, emphasizing the opportunity for a win-win, positive-sum game (e.g. Kim and Mauborgne, 1999; Moore, 1996). With this approach, firms in the same industry will recognize that they often have parallel interests as well. Setting industry standards, lobbying the government, finding solutions to joint environmental problems, improving the image of the industry, investing in fundamental research and negotiating with the unions are just a few of the issues where cooperation can be fruitful.

EXHIBIT 7.3 THE EMBEDDED ORGANIZATION PERSPECTIVE

HANDSPRING: WEB-ENABLED

In 1992, Jeff Hawkins teamed up with Donna Dubinsky and Ed Colligan to start Palm Computing, leading to the launch of the PalmPilot personal digital assistant (PDA) in 1995. The PalmPilot soon became the standard of the handheld computing industry, but Hawkins, Dubinsky and Colligan lost control of Palm to 3Com in the process, so they left to start all over again, founding Handspring in 1998. Within a year the company launched its first product, the Visor, which strongly resembled the PalmPilot, with one revolutionary distinction – the Springboard expansion slot. This feature allowed users to plug in extra modules, to add additional functions. The Springboard modules included hardware (e.g. modem, cellular phone, GPS system, voice recorder, digital camera and mp3 player) and software (e.g. e-books, games and advanced calculators). By the end of 2000, Handspring had sold over one million Visors, grabbing a 15% share of the market.

Crucial to this success has been Handspring's policy of embedding itself in a network of partnerships. According to Colligan: 'There was a huge time-to-market advantage to getting right back into the game. We knew we had to build a business quickly.' Therefore, Handspring decided to focus on a few key activities itself and to involve a broad range of companies into the launch of the Visor, letting each partner contribute a different set of competences. First, Handspring went back to Palm to license its operating system. For Palm this deal with a new competitor was slightly risky, yet preferable to Handspring opting for

Windows CE or Psion's EPOC operating system and thus threatening the dominance of the Palm operating system in the market. Another important choice for Handspring was to stay away from manufacturing itself. Realizing that its core strengths were in design and marketing, Handspring outsourced manufacturing to Flextronics in Malaysia and Solectron in Mexico. Having two manufacturing partners added complexity to the system, but as Dubinsky noted, 'doing business with both helped keep each of them on their toes'. But while comparing prices and best practices, Handspring's policy was also to ensure that both partners shared in the benefits of any cost savings.

In the same way, Dubinsky went back to suppliers she knew from her days at Palm, to strike some good deals, but with a strong emphasis on fostering a win-win situation. As Colligan puts it: 'We have regular partner meetings where execs come in from various suppliers and tell us what we're doing wrong, what we're doing right and what we can do better ... We're aggressive about making sure they feel included.' The same cooperative approach is taken to relationships with the developers of the Springboard plug-in modules. From the outset, Handspring made it highly attractive for independent developers to create modules, by making all code and specifications available free-of-charge on the Handspring web site, and providing engineering support. Customer support was also outsourced, as was order fulfillment, although Handspring was forced to switch the latter partner in 2000, due to performance shortfalls.

Reflecting on their approach to partnerships, Dubinsky says:

We've always been a little cynical and skeptical about 'Strategic Partnerships' in capital letters. We see a lot of this in our industry: big announcements about big partnerships. We've seen a lot of them through the years be very ill defined and unsuccessful and very difficult to implement . . . At Handspring, we try to distinguish between what are real delivering partnerships and real day-to-day working partnerships, as opposed to . . . 'Barney partnerships' – a lot of 'I love you and you love me' and nothing ever happens.

At the same time, the Handspring team also wanted to avoid their Palm experience with Casio and Sharp. According to Colligan:

We were totally dependent on them – shipping, selling, marketing, doing

everything. And they didn't execute, and they didn't care. It was a tiny little piece of their business. When they didn't do it, we were left holding the bag. Those were really bad partnerships.

As for the success factors of an embedded company, Dubinsky concludes: 'In structuring a relationship, know what the other party gets out of it, and understand how to structure that relationship for success for both parties, as opposed to just worrying about what it means to you.' But she also notes: 'We may get people to partner with us to execute pieces of our vision, but we're going to make it very clear that it's our vision and our direction.'

Sources: *The Economist*, September 16 1999, March 8 2001; www.handspring.com; Feldstein, Flanagan and Holloway, 2001.

TOWARDS A SYNTHESIS

The strong one is most powerful alone.
Friedrich von Schiller (1759–1805); German writer

All for one, one for all.
The Three Musketeers,
Alexandre Dumas Jr. (1824–1895);
French novelist

So, should managers form network level strategies or not? Should firms consciously embed themselves in a web of durable collaborative relationships, emphasizing the value of cooperative inter-organizational interactions for realizing their long-term aims? Or should firms try to remain as independent as possible, emphasizing the value of competitive power in achieving their strategic objectives? Is it 'all for one, one for all' or must the strong truly stand alone?

The debate on this issue within the field of strategy is far from being concluded. Many perspectives exist on how to reconcile the conflicting demands of competition and cooperation, and many 'best practices' have been put forward, but no consensus has thus far emerged. Therefore, individual strategists are once again in the position of needing to determine their own point of view.

In Table 7.1 the main arguments of the two opposite poles in this debate have been summarized. As before, the challenge for the strategizing manager is not to take sides in this debate, selecting one position over the other, but rather to seek a way of combining the advantages of both perspectives, blending them into a more effective synthesis. While it is far from simple to find a virtuous form of 'competitive cooperation' or 'cooperative competition', it might be well worth the effort to try to get the best of both worlds.

TABLE 7.1   Discrete organization versus embedded organization perspective

	Discrete organization perspective	Embedded organization perspective
Emphasis on	Competition over cooperation	Cooperation over competition
Preferred position	Independence	Interdependence
Environment structure	Discrete organizations (atomistic)	Embedded organizations (networked)
Firm boundaries	Distinct and defended	Fuzzy and open
Inter-organizational relations	Arm's-length and transactional	Close and structural
Interaction outcomes	Mainly zero-sum (win/lose)	Mainly positive-sum (win/win)
Interaction based on	Bargaining power and calculation	Trust and reciprocity
Network level strategy	No	Yes
Use of collaboration	Temporary coalitions (tactical alliance)	Durable partnerships (strategic alliance)
Collaborative arrangements	Limited, well-defined, contract-based	Broad, open, relationship-based

FURTHER READING

Do as adversaries in law, strive mightily, but eat and drink as friends.

William Shakespeare (1564–1616); English dramatist and poet

No one who wishes to delve more deeply into the topic of organizational boundaries and inter-organizational relationships can avoid running into references to the classic in this area. Oliver Williamson's *Markets and Hierarchies: Analysis and Antitrust Implications*. Williamson's writings have inspired many researchers, especially economists. Others have remarked that Williamson's transaction cost economics largely ignores the political, social and psychological aspects of business relationships. As an antidote to Williamson's strongly rationalist view of the world, another classic can be recommended. Jeffrey Pfeffer and Gerald Salancik's *The External Control of Organizations: A Resource Dependency Perspective* is an excellent book that emphasizes the political aspects of inter-organizational relationships. However, both books are quite academic and not for the faint-hearted.

A more accessible overview of the topic of inter-organizational cooperation is provided by Yves Doz and Gary Hamel in their book *The Alliance Advantage: The Art of Creating Value Through Partnering*. A very good hands-on, practitioner-oriented book is *Smart Alliances: A Practical Guide to Repeatable Success*, by John Harbison and Peter Pekar. For further reading on the subject of vertical relationships, Michael Best's *The New Competition*, and Carlos Jarillo's 'On Strategic Networks', are both excellent choices. For horizontal relationships a good starting point would be *Strategic Alliances: Formation, Implementation and Evolution*, by Peter Lorange and Johan Roos, or *The Knowledge Link: How Firms Compete Through Strategic Alliances*, by J. Badaracco. If the reader is interested in a broader view of the business ecosystem, then James Moore's book, *The Death of Competition: Leadership and Strategy in the Age of Business Ecosystems*, can also be recommended.

All of the above works are positively inclined towards collaboration, largely adopting the embedded organization perspective. For a more critical appraisal of networks, alliances and close relationships, by authors taking the discrete organization perspective, readers are advised to start with the article 'Outsourcing and Industrial Decline', by Richard Bettis, Stephen Bradley and Gary Hamel. Other critical accounts are John Hendry's article 'Culture, Community and Networks: The Hidden Cost of Outsourcing', and S. MacDonald's 'Too Close for Comfort?: The Strategic Implications of Getting Close to the Customer'.

For a more thorough understanding of networks within the Japanese context, Michael Gerlach's *Alliance Capitalism: The Social Organization of Japanese Business* is a good book to begin with. T. Nishiguchi's book *Strategic Industrial Sourcing: The Japanese Advantage* is particularly interesting on the topic of Japanese supplier relationships. For the Chinese view on networks, Murray Weidenbaum and Samuel Hughes book, *The Bamboo Network: How Expatriate Chinese Entrepreneurs Are Creating a New Economic Superpower in Asia*, is recommended, as is S. Redding's *The Spirit of Chinese Capitalism*. For an overview of European views, Ronnie Lessem and Fred Neubauer's *European Management Systems* is an excellent book, but also Roland Calori and Philippe de Woot's collection, *A European Management Model: Beyond Diversity*, provides challenging insights.

STRATEGY CONTEXT

Circumstances? I make circumstances!

Napoleon Bonaparte (1769–1821); French emperor

The strategy context is the set of circumstances surrounding strategy-making – the conditions under which both the strategy process and the strategy content are formed. It could be said that strategy context is concerned with the *where* of strategy – where (i.e. in which firm and which environment) the strategy process and strategy content are embedded.

Most strategizing managers have an ambivalent relationship with their strategy context. On the one hand, strategizing is about creating something new, and for this a healthy level of disregard, or even disrespect, for the present circumstances is required. Much like Napoleon, managers do not want to hear about current conditions limiting their capability to shape the future – they want to create their own circumstances. On the other hand, managers recognize that many contextual limitations are real and that wise strategists must take these circumstances into account. In this section, this fundamental tension between *shaping* the context and *adapting* to it will be at the center of attention.

As visualized in Figure IV.1, the strategy context can be dissected along two different dimensions: industry versus organization, and national versus international. This gives the three key contexts that will be explored in Chapters 8, 9 and 10:

- **The industry context.** The key issue here is how industry development takes place. Can the individual firm influence its industry and to what extent does the industry context dictate particular types of firm behavior?

- **The organizational context.** The key issue here is how organizational development takes place. Can strategizing managers influence their own organizational conditions and to what extent does the organizational context determine particular types of firm behavior?

- **The international context.** The key issue here is how the international context is developing. Must firms adapt to ongoing global convergence or will international diversity remain a characteristic with which firms will need to cope?

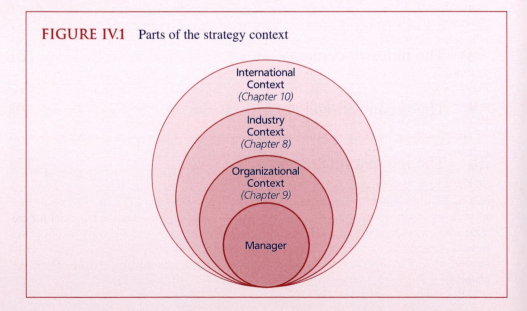

FIGURE IV.1 Parts of the strategy context

International
Context
(Chapter 10)

Industry
Context
(Chapter 8)

Organizational
Context
(Chapter 9)

Manager

THE INDUSTRY CONTEXT

Know the other and know yourself: Triumph without peril.
Know nature and know the situation: Triumph completely.

Sun Tzu (5th century BC); Chinese military strategist

INTRODUCTION

If strategic management is concerned with relating a firm to its environment, then it is essential to know this environment well. In the previous chapters the factors and actors that shape the external context of the firm have been thoroughly reviewed. While the entire outside world was taken into consideration, emphasis was placed on the direct environment in which a firm needs to compete – its industry context. It was concluded that an understanding of competitors, buyers, suppliers, substitutes and potential new entrants, as well as the structural factors that influence their behavior, is invaluable for determining a successful strategy.

A constant theme in the strategy process and strategy content sections was industry change. Knowing the current industry context, it became clear, is not enough to secure an ongoing alignment between a firm and its environment. Strategizing managers need to recognize in which direction the industry is developing to be able to maintain a healthy fit. However, what was not addressed in these discussions is how industry development actually takes place. Important questions such as 'what are the drivers propelling industry development?' and 'what patterns of development do industries exhibit?' have not yet been examined. Nor has it been established whether industries develop in the same way and at the same speed, and whether change is always accompanied by the same opportunities and threats. In this chapter, these questions surrounding the issue of industry development will be at the center of attention.

For strategizing managers, however, the most important question linked to the issue of industry development is how a firm can move beyond *adapting* to *shaping*. How can a firm, or a group of collaborating firms, modify the structure and competitive dynamics in their industry to gain an advantageous position? How can the industry's evolutionary path be proactively diverted into a particular direction? If a firm would be capable of shaping its industry environment instead of following it, this would give them the potential for creating a strong competitive advantage – they could 'set the rules of the competitive game' instead of having to 'play by the rules' set by others. This topic of industry leadership – shaping events as opposed to following them – will be the key focus throughout this chapter.

THE ISSUE OF INDUSTRY DEVELOPMENT

When strategists look at an industry, they are interested in understanding 'the rules of the game' (e.g. Prahalad and Doz, 1987; Hamel, 1996). The industry rules are the demands dictated to the firm by the industry context, which limit the scope of potential strategic behaviors. In other words, industry rules stipulate what must be done to survive and thrive in the chosen line of business – they determine under what conditions the competitive game will be played. For example, an industry rule could be 'must have significant scale economies', 'must have certain technology' or 'must have strong brand'. Failure to adhere to the rules leads to being selected out.

The industry rules arise from the structure of the industry (e.g. Porter, 1980; Tirole, 1988). All of Porter's five forces can impose constraints on a firm's freedom of action. Where the rules are strict, the degrees of freedom available to the strategist are limited. Strict rules imply that only very specific behavior is allowed – firms must closely follow the rules of the game or face severe consequences. Where the rules are looser, firms have more room to maneuver and exhibit distinctive behavior – the level of managerial discretion is higher (e.g. Hambrick and Abrahamson, 1995; Carpenter and Golden, 1997).

As industries develop, the rules of competition change – vertical integration becomes necessary, certain competences become vital or having a global presence becomes a basic requirement. To be able to play the competitive game well, strategizing managers need to identify which characteristics in the industry structure and which aspects of competitive interaction are changing. This is the topic of 'dimensions of industry development', which will be reviewed in more detail below. To determine their response, it is also essential to understand the nature of the change. Are the industry rules gradually shifting or is there a major break with the past? Is the industry development more evolutionary or more revolutionary? A process of slow and moderate industry change will demand a different strategic reaction than a process of sudden and dramatic disruption of the industry rules. This topic of 'paths of industry development' will also be examined more closely.

As strategists generally like to have the option to shape instead of always being shaped, they need to recognize the determinants of industry development as well. What are the factors that cause the industry rules to change? This subject can be divided into two parts. First, the question of what the drivers of industry development are, pushing the industry in a certain direction. Secondly, the question of what the inhibitors of industry development are, placing a brake on changes. Together, these forces of change and forces for stability will determine the actual path of development that the industry will follow. How these four topics are interrelated is outlined in Figure 8.1.

Dimensions of industry development

Industry development means that the structure of the industry changes. In Chapter 5, the key aspects of the industry structure have already been discussed. Following Porter (1980), five important groups of industry actors were identified (i.e. competitors, buyers, suppliers, new entrants and substitutes) and the underlying factors determining their behavior were reviewed. Industry development is the result of a change in one or more of these underlying factors.

As Porter already indicates, the industry structure can be decomposed into dozens of elements, each of which can change, causing a shift in industry rules. Here it is not the intention to go through all of these elements, but to pick out a number of important structural

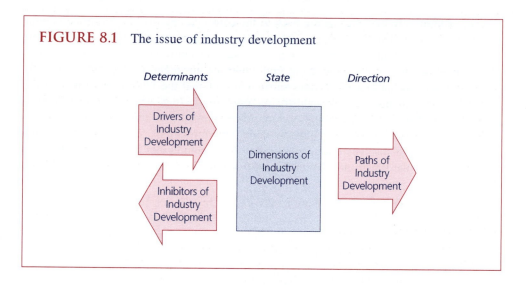

FIGURE 8.1   The issue of industry development

characteristics that require special attention. Each one of these structural characteristics represents a dimension along which significant industry developments can take place:

- Convergence–divergence. Where the business models that firms employ increasingly start to resemble each other, the industry is said to be moving towards convergence (e.g. insurance and airline industries). In contrast, where many firms introduce new business models, the industry is said to be developing towards more diversity (e.g. car retailing and restaurant industries). Higher diversity can be due to the 'mutation' of existing firms, as they strive to compete on a different basis, or the result of new entrants with their own distinct business model. Convergence is the consequence of adaptation by less successful firms to a 'dominant design' in the industry and the selecting out of unfit firms incapable of adequate and timely adaptation (e.g. Hannan and Freeman, 1977; Porter, 1980). Generally, patterns of divergence and convergence can be witnessed in all industries, although the amount of mutation and the pressure for convergence can greatly differ, as can the overall cycle time of an 'evolutionary phase' of mutation and selection (e.g. Aldrich, 1999; Baum and Singh, 1994).

- Concentration–fragmentation. Where an increasing share of the market is in the hands of only a few companies, the industry is said to be developing towards a more concentrated structure (e.g. aircraft and food retailing industries). Conversely, where the average market share of the largest companies starts to decrease, the industry is said to be moving towards a more fragmented structure (e.g. airline and telecom services industries). Concentration can be due to mergers and acquisitions, or the result of companies exiting the business. Fragmentation can happen when new companies are formed and grab a part of the market, or through the entry of existing companies into the industry. In a concentrated industry it is much more likely that only one or two firms will be dominant than in a fragmented industry, but it is also possible that the industry structure is more balanced.

- Vertical integration–fragmentation. Where firms in the industry are becoming involved in more value-adding activities in the industry column, the industry is said to be developing towards a more vertically integrated structure (e.g. media and IT service providers). Conversely, where firms in the industry are withdrawing from various value-adding activities and 'going back to the core', the industry is said to be moving towards a more, disintegrated, layered or vertically fragmented structure (e.g. telecom and automotive industries). It is even possible that the entire vertical structure changes if a new business model has major consequences upstream and/or downstream. In recent years, technological changes surrounding IT and the internet have triggered a number of such instances of industry reconfiguration (e.g. travel and encyclopedia industries). However, even though we are now equipped with more fashionable terms (e.g. 'deconstruction'), such industry-wide transformations of the value-creation process are in themselves not new (e.g. PCs and the computer industry in the 1980s; airplanes and the travel industry in the 1950s) (e.g. Evans and Wurster, 1997; Porter, 2001).

- Horizontal integration–fragmentation. Where the boundaries between different businesses in an industry become increasingly fuzzy, the industry is said to be developing towards a more horizontally integrated structure (e.g. consumer electronics and defense industries). Conversely, where firms become more strictly confined to their own business, the industry is said to be moving towards a more segmented or horizontally fragmented structure (e.g. construction and airline industries). Links between businesses can intensify or wane, depending on the mobility barriers and potential cross-business synergies. However, horizontal integration and fragmentation are not limited to the intra-industry domain. Inter-industry integration between two or more industries can also increase, creating a more or less open competitive space (Hamel and Prahalad, 1994) with few mobility barriers (e.g. the digital industries). Inter-industry integration can also occur where the producers of different products and services are complementary and/or converge on a common standard or platform (e.g. Palm OS and Linux), making them 'complementors' (e.g. Cusumano and Gawer, 2002; Moore, 1996). Yet, the opposite trend is possible as well, whereby an industry becomes more isolated from neighboring sectors (e.g. accountancy).

- International integration–fragmentation. Where the international boundaries separating various geographic segments of an industry become increasingly less important, the industry is said to be developing towards a more internationally integrated structure (e.g. food retailing and business education industries). Conversely, where the competitive interactions in an industry are increasingly confined to a region (e.g. Europe) or country, the industry is said to be moving towards a more internationally fragmented structure (e.g. satellite television and internet retailing). These developments will be more thoroughly examined in Chapter 10, which deals with the international context.

- Expansion–contraction. Industries can also differ with regard to the structural nature of the demand for their products and/or services. Where an industry is experiencing an ongoing increase in demand, the industry is said to be in growth or expansion. Where demand is constantly receding, the industry is said to be in decline or contraction. If periods of expansion are followed by periods of contraction, and vice versa, the industry is said to be cyclical. A prolonged period of expansion is usually linked to the growth phase of the industry life cycle (e.g. Moore, 2000; Porter, 1980), while contraction is linked to the decline phase, but often it is rather difficult to apply the 'life cycle' concept to an entire industry (as opposed to a product or technology). As industry growth (expansion) can easily follow a period of industry decline (contraction), the life cycle model has little descriptive value – what does it mean to be mature? – and even less predictive value.

Paths of industry development

The development of an industry can be mapped along any one of the dimensions listed above. The most popular is to track the pattern of expansion and contraction, to gain some indication of the life cycle phase in which the industry might have arrived. Another frequently analyzed characteristic is the level of concentration, commonly using a concentration index to measure the market share of the four or eight largest companies. But it is equally viable to trace the trajectory of vertical, horizontal or international integration. In Figure 8.2 examples of these paths of industry development are given.

In Figure 8.3 one particular element of the convergence–divergence dimension has been selected for further magnification. As discussed above, in the development of an industry a particular business model can become the dominant design around which the rest of the industry converges. A strategically relevant development occurs when the dominant business model is replaced by a new business model that offers customers higher value. In Figure 8.3, four generic patterns of industry development are outlined, each describing a different type of transition from the old dominant model to the new (Burgelman and Grove, 1996; D'Aveni, 1999):

- **Gradual development.** In an industry where one business model is dominant for a long period of time and is slowly replaced by an alternative that is a slight improvement, the development process is gradual. The firms adhering to the dominant design will generally have little trouble adapting to the new rules of the game, leading to a situation of relative stability. Competition can be weak or fierce, depending on the circumstances, but will take place on the basis of the shared rules of the game. In this type of environment, companies with an established position have a strong advantage.

- **Continuous development.** In an industry where changes to the dominant business model are more frequent, but still relatively modest in size, the development process is continuous. While firms need not have difficulties adjusting to each individual change to the rules of the game, they can fall behind if they do not keep up with the pace of improvement. In this type of environment, rapid adaptation to developments will strengthen the competitive position of firms vis-à-vis slow movers.

- **Discontinuous development.** In an industry where one business model is dominant for a long period of time and is then suddenly displaced by a radically better one, the

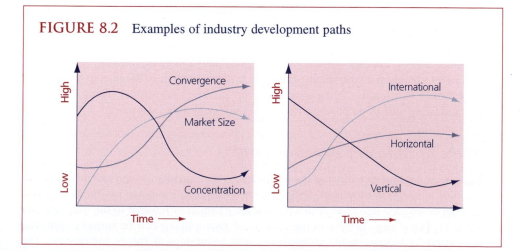

FIGURE 8.2 Examples of industry development paths

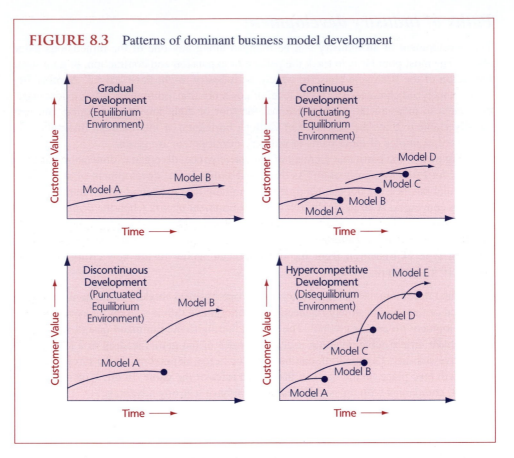

FIGURE 8.3   Patterns of dominant business model development

development process is discontinuous. The firms riding the wave of the new business model will generally have a large advantage over the companies that need to adjust to an entirely different set of industry rules. Where industry incumbents are themselves the 'rule breakers' (Hamel, 1996), they can strongly improve their position vis-à-vis the 'rule takers' in the industry. But the business model innovator can also be an industry outsider, who gains entrance by avoiding competition with established players on their terms (e.g. Bower and Christensen, 1995; Slywotsky, 1996).

■ Hypercompetitive development. In an industry where business models are frequently pushed aside by radically better ones, the development process is hypercompetitive (D'Aveni, 1994). The rules of the game are constantly changing, making it impossible for firms to build up a sustainably dominant position. The only defense in this type of environment is offense – being able to outrun existing competitors, being innovative first and being able to outperform new rule breakers at their own game.

Drivers of industry development

There is an endless list of factors in the environment that can change and can influence the direction of industry development. Following the categorization made in Chapter 7, these factors can be divided into change drivers that are external or internal to the industry (see Figure 8.4). The change drivers in the contextual environment can be roughly split into socio-cultural, economic, political/regulatory and technological forces for change. The

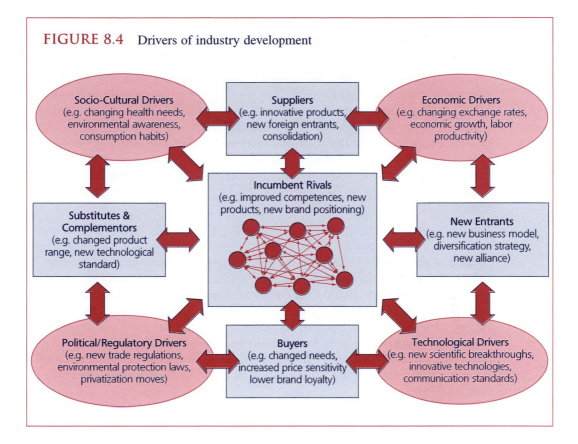

FIGURE 8.4 Drivers of industry development

change drivers in the industry environment can be divided into groups surrounding suppliers, buyers, incumbent rivals, new entrants, and substitutes and complementors.

As the arrows indicate, change in a complex system like an industry does not always start in one discernible part and then reverberate throughout the whole. Rather, change can also be the result of the interplay of various elements in the system, without any clear start or ending point. Yet, for the discussion on shaping industry development it is important to recognize the distinction between industry changes that are largely triggered by an individual firm, as opposed to broader, system-wide changes, for which no one actor can claim responsibility. Where one firm is the major driver of industry development, it can claim industry leadership. But if there is no industry leader and the evolution of the industry is due to the complex interaction of many different change drivers, it is said that the industry dynamics determine the path of industry development.

Inhibitors of industry development

Forces of change do not always go unopposed. In the discussion on strategic change in Chapter 4, the sources of organizational rigidity were reviewed, each of which acts as an inhibitor to organizational change. In the same way, there are many sources of industry rigidity, making the industry rules much more difficult to bend or break. Industry rigidity can be defined as the lack of susceptibility to change. If an industry is rigid, the rules of the game cannot be altered and competitive positions are relatively fixed. The opposite term is industry plasticity – an industry's susceptibility to change.

A large number of factors can contribute to rigidity, thereby inhibiting industry development. Some of the most important ones are the following:

- **Underlying conditions.** Basically, some rules might be immutable because the underlying industry conditions cannot be changed. In some industries economies of scale are essential (e.g. airplane manufacturing, merchant shipping), where in others economies of scale are not of importance (e.g. wedding services, dentistry services). In some industries buyers are fragmented (e.g. newspapers, moving services), while in others they are highly concentrated (e.g. defense systems, harbor construction). In some industries buyers value product differentiation (e.g. clothing, restaurants), while in others bulk producers must compete on price (e.g. chemicals, general construction). Many of these structural factors are inherent to the industry and defy any attempts to change them (e.g. Bain, 1959; Porter, 1980).

- **Industry integration.** Besides the limited plasticity of individual aspects of the industry context, it is also important to recognize that some industries are particularly rigid because of the complex linkages between various aspects of the industry. For example, to be a rule breaking music company not only requires developing new delivery methods via the internet, but also getting electronics manufacturers to adopt the new standards, finding ways to safeguard copyrights, working together with governments to find new policing methods, and not least to change the buying behavior of consumers. Such interrelations between various elements of the industry can make it particularly difficult to actually influence the direction of events over time. The industry can become 'locked in' to a specific structure for a long period of time (e.g. Arthur, 1994; Shapiro and Varian, 1998).

- **Power structures.** The industry rules can also be kept in place by those who feel they are better off with the status quo. Powerful industry incumbents often have little to gain and much to lose. They have established positions and considerable sunk costs, in the form of historical investments in technology, competencies, facilities and relationships, which makes them reluctant to support changes to the rules of the game. Hence, rule changers are usually vehemently resisted by existing firms and denied support by potential suppliers and buyers. For example, rivals might attack a rule breaker by lowering prices, launching a media campaign, or even lobbying government regulators to impose legal rules. Especially where a rule breaker needs allies to secure supplies, distribution or a new standard it will be vulnerable to the countermoves of parties with a vested interest in the current structure (e.g. Ghemawat, 1991; Moore, 2000).

- **Risk averseness.** Challenging the industry rules is not only a risky step for the rule breaker, but also for many other parties involved. Customers might be hesitant about a new product or service until it has a firmer track record. Suppliers and distributors might worry whether the initial investments will pay off and what the countermoves will be of the established companies. The more risk averse the parties in the industry, the more rigid will be the industry rules (e.g. Christensen, 1997; Parolini, 1999).

- **Industry recipes.** An industry recipe is a widely held perception among industry incumbents regarding the actual rules of the game in the industry. In other words, an industry recipe is the cognitive map shared by industry incumbents about the structure and demands of an industry. Such a common understanding of the rules of the game can develop over time through shared experiences and interaction – the longer people are in the industry and converse with each other, the greater the chance that a consensus will grow about 'what makes the industry tick'. Thus, the industry recipe can limit people's openness to rule changers who challenge the industry orthodoxy (e.g. Baden-Fuller and Stopford, 1992; Spender, 1989).

■ **Institutional pressures.** While the industry recipe is a shared understanding of how the industry actually functions, industry incumbents usually also share norms of what constitutes socially acceptable economic behavior. Companies experience strong pressures from government, professional associations, customers, consultants, trade unions, pressure groups and other industry incumbents prescribing permissible strategies and actions, and generally internalize these behavioral standards. Such conformity to institutional pressures gives companies legitimacy, but makes them less willing to question industry conventions, let alone work together with a maverick rule breaker (e.g. Aldrich and Fiol, 1994; Oliver, 1997).

Taken together, these historically determined factors inhibit developments in the industry. It is said that industry evolution is path dependent – the path that the industry has traveled in the past will strongly limit how and in which direction it can develop in the future. In other words, 'history matters', setting bounds on the freedom to shape the future.

THE PARADOX OF COMPLIANCE AND CHOICE

When people are free to do as they please, they usually imitate each other.
Eric Hoffer (1902–1983); American philosopher

Yet, the question is whether firms should attempt to shape their industries at all, given the required effort and apparent risk of failure. There might be attractive rewards if a firm can lead industry developments, but trying to break industry rules that turn out to be immutable can be a quick way to achieve bankruptcy. Being an industry leader might sound very proactive, and even heroic, but it is potentially suicidal if the industry context defies being shaped.

This duality of wanting to change the industry rules that are malleable, while needing to adapt to the industry rules that are fixed, is the tension central to dealing with the industry context. On the one hand, managers must be willing to irreverently transgress widely acknowledged industry rules, going against what they see as the industry recipe. On the other hand, managers must respectfully accept many characteristics of the industry structure and play according to existing rules of the competitive game. Yet, these conflicting demands of being irreverent and respectful towards the industry rules are difficult for strategists to meet at the same time.

Where firms cannot influence the structure of their industry, *compliance* to the rules of the game is the strategic imperative. Under these circumstances, the strategic demand is for managers to adapt the firm to the industry context. Where firms do have the ability to manipulate the industry structure, they should exercise their freedom of *choice* to break the industry rules. In such a case, the strategic demand is for managers to try to change the terms of competition in their own favor.

This tension between compliance and choice has been widely acknowledged in the strategic management literature (e.g. Porter, 1980; Hrebiniak and Joyce, 1985). The pressure for compliance has usually been presented as a form of environmental determinism, as the industry developments force firms to adapt or be selected out (e.g. Astley and

Van der Ven, 1983; Wilson, 1992). The freedom of choice has often been labeled as organizational voluntarism, to convey the notion that industry developments can be the result of the willful actions of individual organizations (e.g. Bettis and Donaldson, 1990; Child, 1972). In the following sections both compliance and choice will be further examined.

The demand for firm compliance

It goes almost without saying that organizations must, to a large extent, adapt themselves to their environments. No organization has the ability to shape the entire world to fit its needs. Therefore, to be successful, all organizations need to understand the context in which they operate and need to play by most of the rules of the game.

After all, the alternative of ignoring the rules is fraught with danger. Probably the most common cause of 'corporate death' is misalignment between the organization and its environment. And misalignment can happen very quickly, as most industries are constantly in flux. Companies can misinterpret the direction of the changes, can fail to take appropriate corrective action, or can be plainly self-centered, paying insufficient attention to external developments. Most companies have enough difficulty just staying attuned to the current rules of the competitive game, let alone anticipating how the industry context will change in the future.

To achieve compliance with the industry rules, firms must develop structures, processes and a culture in which listening and adapting to the environment becomes engrained. Firms must learn to become customer and market-oriented, reacting to the 'pull' of the market, instead of 'pushing' their standard approach and pet projects at an unwilling audience. Firm compliance means avoiding the pitfall of organizational arrogance – knowing better than the market and imposing an approach that no one is waiting for (e.g. Miller, 1990; Whitley, 1999).

The demand for strategic choice

While compliance to the industry rules can be very beneficial, contradicting them can also be strategically valuable. If firms only play by the current rules, it is generally very difficult for them to gain a significant competitive advantage over their rivals. After all, adapting to the current industry structure means doing business in more or less the same way as competitors, with few possibilities to distinguish the organization. In other words, 'compliance' might be another way of saying 'follow a me-too strategy'.

To be unique and develop a competitive advantage, firms need to do something different, something that does not fit within the current rules of the game. The more innovative the rule breaker, the larger will be the competitive advantage over rivals stuck with outdated business models. The more radical the departure from the old industry recipe, the more difficult it will be for competitors to imitate and catch up. Where companies are capable of constantly leading industry developments, they will have the benefit of capturing attractive industry positions before less proactive competitors eventually follow. In other words, there is a strong pressure for firms to attempt to shape the industry rules.

To achieve organizational choice, firms must find ways of escaping the pitfall of organizational conformity – the strict adherence to current industry rules. Firms must develop structures, processes and a culture in which the current industry recipe is constantly questioned, challenged and changed. Managers must come to see that in the long run the easy path of following the industry rules will be less productive than the rocky road of innovation and change (e.g. Hamel and Prahalad, 1994; Kim and Mauborgne, 1999).

EXHIBIT 8.1 SHORT CASE

PALM: WAVING PALMS OR SWEATY PALMS?

The name 'Palm' engenders different connotations depending to whom you speak. Some people will picture white sand, turquoise water and waving palm trees, while others will picture white foam, brown ale and waving customers, trying to order another round of Belgium's famous Palm beer. Yet others will think of PDAs – personal digital assistants – small handheld computers for minor administrative tasks, such as jotting down notes, making a 'to do' list, performing calculations, updating a calendar, keeping track of expenses and filing telephone numbers and addresses. Palm was not the first company to introduce a PDA to the market, but it was the first company to do so successfully, launching the PalmPilot in 1996. Within four years, Palm's annual revenues soared to US$564 million, with a 70% share of the 10 million PDAs sold around the world, making the company just as well known as the trees and more profitable than the beer.

The company was established in 1992 by Jeff Hawkins, a software designer, and he was soon joined by ex-Apple director, Donna Dubinsky. They entered an industry that was already littered with the broken dreams of many high-tech firms. Since the late 1980s, various companies from the computer and consumer electronics industries, including Apple, Microsoft, Sony, IBM, Motorola, Psion and Sharp, had tried to introduce PDAs to the presumed technology-hungry masses. Yet, all attempts had failed, some silently, others with a big bang. And in each case the flop could be attributed to more or less the same problem – companies were selling a brick. The PDAs were too large and heavy, or too expensive, or both. Moreover, none had found a convenient data entry method, instead using impossibly small keyboards or primitive handwriting recognition software. At the basis of these failures was an implicit belief that the device should be a small-sized substitute for the notebook computer. This belief was rooted in an evolutionary logic – first there was the mainframe, then the personal computer, then came the notebook computer and next would obviously be the handheld computer. However, neither the technology, nor the customer, seemed ready for the industry envisioned.

Initially, Palm followed this industry recipe as well. In 1993, its first device, the Zoomer, zoomed to an early death soon after its market launch. Unlike its companions in misfortune, however, Palm was triggered by the debacle to fundamentally rethink its assumptions about the industry during a full year of investigations. The result was a new insight that was simple, but revolutionary. Instead of striving to produce a substitute for a notebook computer, Palm devised a substitute for paper and pencil, which could be used as a complement to any PC. This insight led to the development of the PalmPilot: a small, fast and affordable PDA, with a simple operating system and a stylus as data entry tool.

To quickly build on its early success and establish a dominant position in the PDA industry, Palm set a high pace of new product introductions, grabbing the limelight as innovation leader. Sales were aggressive, distributing products via all possible channels – through distributors to large retailers, directly to retailers, directly via an online store to consumers and via a direct sales force to business customers. The success of the PalmPilot hardware also paved the way for Palm's Operating System (OS) software to become the industry standard, with a market share of more than 80% in 2001.

But the juicy PDA market, which was forecast to grow to 30 million units per year by 2004, was much too attractive to remain Palm's private domain for long. Many competitors saw PDAs as the future mobile access points to the internet and at the very least as a device for controlling many networked machines around the house and in the office. One formidable contender lured in by this promising future was Microsoft. In 1998, Microsoft stepped up its attempts to extend Windows to the PDA environment, launching Windows CE 2.0. At the same time, Microsoft introduced the Palm PC, and later the Pocket PC, which looked very similar to Palm's PDAs and had about the same price as well. The result was that Palm started to lose market share to Microsoft, made worse by a slow down in Palm's new model releases after founders Hawkins and Dubinsky left to start Handspring.

Compounding the looming problems, another competitor, Psion, released the EPOC operating system, which combined PDA and wireless communications technology. Via a coalition called Symbian, EPOC was successfully promoted among the world's largest cellular telephone manufacturers, including Nokia, Ericsson and Motorola. These giants wanted to enhance their cell phones by adding PDA functions, thus creating 'smartphones', and ultimately making conventional PDAs obsolete.

The introduction of the Windows CE and EPOC operating systems caused quite a few sweaty palms at the headquarters of Palm in Santa Clara, California. Palm's strategy was to keep its operating system to itself, as the main competitive advantage of its PDAs. But with such powerful rivals as Microsoft, Nokia and Motorola, many were worried that Palm might suffer the same fate as Apple – being the owner of a proprietary operating system with insufficient critical mass to attract application software developers and a large community of interconnected users. To be able to stay at the forefront of the PDA industry, Palm would have to convince software developers that its large and growing group of users would

make it profitable to keep on creating new applications based on Palm OS. Simultaneously, Palm would need to convince consumers that its PDAs would remain the industry standard, ensuring a steady stream of compatible new applications and facilitating the future exchange of data between Palm PDAs and other devices. Therefore, Palm decided to defend its 'network effect' advantage by licensing its operating system to other hardware manufacturers, including IBM, Sony, Handspring, Dell and Sun Microsystems. Palm also made a deal with Qualcomm and Samsung to incorporate Palm OS into their cellular phones, while Symbol Technologies started using it for process control devices. As a consequence, in 2000 more than 50 000 developers had signed up with Palm.

By 2003 it had become clear that Palm's licensing strategy was working – Palm OS had retained its leading position, being incorporated into three-quarters of all PDAs being sold. The downside, however, was that Palm's hardware had taken a beating, dropping to less than 40% market share and slipping fast. Yet, Palm's handhelds were still responsible for 95% of the company's revenues, while licensing only brought in a meager 5%. This did not bode well for Palm's long-term viability vis-à-vis larger manufacturers of computers and consumer electronics, with their scale economies and huge R&D budgets. Especially the fact that new PDAs were being introduced that actually did resemble genuine handheld PCs was rather worrying, as this conflicted with Palm's focus on simplicity, speed, reliability and style as distinguishing factors. It also seemed to suggest that the domains of PCs and PDAs were finally starting to converge, tilting the field in favor of Microsoft's Windows CE that from the start was intended to bridge these two worlds. Other industry watchers were even more pessimistic, predicting the end of the PDA device in its current form altogether. They pointed to emerging customer preferences to combine many of the functions of cell phones, PDAs, PCs and game consoles into one 'smartphone' gadget. If this trend continued to gather momentum, the members of the Symbian alliance (Psion and the cellular phone manufacturers) would be best positioned to profit.

Palm's response to these threats was three-fold. First, Palm decided to spin off its operating system activities to raise cash. The new company, Palm Source, would continue to focus on building powerful, but simple and fault-free, operating systems to prolong its leading position in the industry. Secondly, to fight back in the segment for business people and the techno savvy, Palm decided to follow the trend towards highly advanced PDAs with PC-like applications and the latest features including wireless communication. Thirdly, the company decided to broaden Palm's appeal beyond current segments, branching out to serve non-conventional customers. By tapping into new markets that were less technology-oriented, such as 'busy suburban moms', Palm would be able to play its old game of offering a simple, small and affordable

PDA. Contrary to its competitors, these PDAs would not be sold through electronics shops, but via department stores, supermarkets and gasoline stations.

Not everyone was confident that Palm's new strategy would work. Some analysts feared that Palm's response was 'too little, too late' – much too compliant with the current rules of the game to really gain a significant competitive advantage vis-à-vis the circling scavengers. Palm would have to come up with a path breaking innovation to regain control over its own destiny. Others observed that, as the PDA industry had become mature, no such new breakthroughs could be expected, and that Palm would be wise to find ways to remain competitive without hoping for a miracle. Palm should adjust to the well-known rules of a maturing hardware industry and get ready to survive, and perhaps take advantage of, the coming shakeout. Clearly, Palm still had some tough choices to make – no time for waving palms, only for sweaty palms, at the moment.

Sources: *The Economist*, June 2 2001; *Financial Times*, August 9 2002; Yoffie and Kwak (2001); *FEM Business*, April 5 2003; www.palm.com.

PERSPECTIVES ON THE INDUSTRY CONTEXT

A wise man will make more opportunity than he finds.

Francis Bacon (1561–1624); Lord Chancellor of England

Once again the strategizing manager seems 'stuck between a rock and a hard place'. The pressures for both compliance and choice are clear, but as opposites they are at least partially incompatible. Developing an organizational culture, structure and processes attuned to compliance will to some extent be at odds with the culture, structure and processes needed to shape an industry. An organization well rehearsed in the art of adaptation and skillful imitation is usually quite different than one geared towards business innovation and contrarian behavior. How should managers actually deal with the issue of industry development – should they lead or follow?

In the strategic management literature many answers to this question are given – unfortunately, many contradictory ones. The views among management theorists differ sharply, as they emphasize a different balance between the need to comply and the need to choose.

To gain a better overview of the range of conflicting opinions, here the two diametrically opposed positions will be identified and discussed. On the one hand, there are strategists who argue that industry development is an autonomous process, which individual firms can hardly hope to shape. They believe that compliance to shifting industry characteristics is mandatory – adjust or risk being selected out. This point of view will be referred to as the 'industry dynamics perspective'. On the other hand, many strategists believe that the industry context can be shaped in an infinite variety of ways by innovative firms. Therefore, industry development can be driven by firms willing and able to take a leading role. This point of view will be referred to as the 'industry leadership perspective'.

The industry dynamics perspective

 To those taking an industry dynamics perspective, the popular notion that individual firms have the power to shape their industry is an understandable, but quite misplaced, belief. Of course, the illusion of control is tempting – most people, especially managers, would like to control their own destiny. Most individuals assume they have a free will and can decide their own future. Many governments suppose that they can shape society and many cultures assume that they control nature. In the same way, it is seductive to believe that the individual firm can matter, by influencing the development of its industry.

Unfortunately, this belief is largely a fallacy, brought on by a poor understanding of the underlying industry dynamics. In reality, according to advocates of the industry dynamics perspective, industries are complex systems, with a large number of forces interacting simultaneously, none of which can significantly direct the long-term development of the whole. Firms are relatively small players in a very large game – their behaviors may have some impact on industry development, but none can fundamentally shape the direction of changes. On the contrary, as industries evolve, all firms that do not meet the changing demands of the environment are weeded out. Firms not suited to the new circumstances die, while firms complying with the changing rules prosper. Hence, through selection the industry context determines the group of industry survivors and through the pressures for adaptation the behavior of the remaining firms is determined. In short, the industry shapes the firm, not the other way around.

The industry dynamics perspective is often also referred to as the industry evolution perspective, due to the strong parallel with biological evolution. Both evolutionary processes, it is argued, share a number of basic characteristics. In nature, as in business, the survival and growth of entities depends on their fit with the environment. Within each environment variations to a successful theme might come about. These new individuals will thrive, as long as they suit the existing circumstances, but as the environment changes, only those that meet the new demands will not be selected out. Hence, Darwin's well-known principle of 'survival of the fittest' is based on a cycle of variation and environmental selection. Many proponents of the industry dynamics perspective think that this biological view of evolution is a good model for what happens in industries – new organizations arise as mutations and only the fittest mutations survive. However, it is usually pointed out that in a business environment, organizations do not vary 'at random', but purposefully, and they possess the ability to adapt to selection pressures during the evolution process (e.g. Nelson and Winter, 1982; Baum and Singh, 1994). Therefore, organizations have much more flexibility to evolve along with the unfolding industry dynamics than life forms generally do. This process of mutual adaptation and development between entities in the system is called 'co-evolution' (e.g. Aldrich, 1999; Moore, 1996). To proponents of the industry dynamics perspective, the objective of a firm should be to co-evolve with its environment, instead of trying to conquer it.

Supporters of the industry dynamics perspective do not deny that every once in a while a rule breaker comes along, turning an industry upside down and spawning dozens of case studies by admiring business professors and hours of television interviews. But these successes must be put into perspective, just as a lottery winner should not encourage everyone to invest their life savings into buying lottery tickets. Yes, some business innovators are successful, but we have no idea of how many challengers were weeded out along the way – only the most spectacular failures make it into the media, but most go unreported. This is called the 'survivor's bias', and the emphasis on case-based reasoning in the field of strategy makes theorists and practitioners equally susceptible to fall into this trap. But even where a firm has been able to pull off a major industry change once, this does not make them the industry leader going into the future. They might have been the right company in the right place at the right time, able to push the industry in a certain direction once, but to assume that they will win the lottery twice is not particularly realistic.

The conclusion drawn by advocates of the industry dynamics perspective is that 'winning big' by changing the rules of the game sounds easy, fast and spectacular – but isn't. If one thing has been learnt from the internet bubble, it is that changing the rules of the game is extremely difficult, slow and hazardous, and should be left up to those 'high rollers' willing to play for 'high stakes' with only a low chance of success (i.e. venture capitalists and entrepreneurs). For regular companies, such an approach cannot be the mainstay of their strategy. Their basic approach must be to stick close to the shifting currents in their industry, which is challenging enough in most cases. Competitive advantage can be sought, but through hard work within the rules of the game.

The bad news is that this leaves limited freedom to maneuver and that the general level of profitability that a firm can achieve is largely predetermined. Once in a poor industry, a firm's growth and profit potential are significantly limited (Porter, 1980). The good news is that this still leaves plenty of room for a firm to score above the industry average, by positioning better than competitors, but also by adapting better to the ongoing industry changes, or even anticipating changes more skillfully and reacting appropriately.

EXHIBIT 8.2 THE INDUSTRY DYNAMICS PERSPECTIVE

WESTJET: GO WITH THE FLOW

Everyone visiting the world's largest rodeo, the Calgary Stampede, knows that it doesn't matter who gets out of the gate first – the winner is who stays on the wild horse's back longest. This lesson has not been lost on the entrepreneurs David Neeleman and Clive Beddoe, who started their airline, WestJet, in Calgary in 1996. WestJet was by no means the first Southwest Airlines clone in Canada, offering low-fare, no-frills, point-to-point air travel. But while they were not first movers, and did not attempt to rewrite the rules of the game in the airline industry, they are still on the bronco's back, while many of their competitors have been sent flying to the ground. Within only a few years, WestJet has become Canada's second largest, and most profitable, airline, not by being more innovative than its rivals, but by steadfastly rolling out its business model in accordance with the emerging industry rules.

WestJet did not take off immediately. In the first few years, WestJet was a small pioneering outfit, with three Boeing 737–200s, struggling to overcome initial barriers, such as strict safety-related licensing regulations and a lack of capital. It also needed time to build up a good reputation and a route structure. But WestJet's growth was disciplined, and after 1999 expansion started to accelerate, to 35 aircraft in 2002, and plans to operate 94 modern Boeing 737–700s by 2008.

In 2002, one of WestJet's main competitors, Canada 3000, went bankrupt. It propelled WestJet into the position of Canada's second largest airline. Air Canada, the country's largest airline, used the collapse of Canada 3000 to quickly capture 80% of the domestic market. Industry stakeholders, disliking Air Canada's dominance, started to court WestJet. Medium-sized cities came begging for WestJet's service to break Air Canada's stranglehold, foreign airlines looked for alternatives to Air Canada's steep rates for connecting flights and the international airline alliance Oneworld started to court WestJet, hoping to get a Canadian partner to complement their international network. However, WestJet was cautious about overextending itself under these favorable market circumstances. The company decided that it was not ready to internationalize yet, and turned down Oneworld and its foreign carrier suitors. WestJet did, however, join the global distribution system Sabre in 2002. CEO Beddoe explained: 'We did not want to do that, but gradually we found that we had to give it a try.' Sabre rapidly represented a significant portion of WestJet's bookings.

Looking back over the past few years, it can be seen that WestJet's business model has evolved along with the developments in the industry. Starting as a straightforward Southwest Airlines clone, WestJet has gradually moved away from point-to-point services, towards the hub-and-spoke model typical of the industry incumbents. Its home base, Calgary, already was a mini-hub and nearby Edmonton was soon given the same function. Another change, whereby WestJet has moved along with shifting external circumstances, has been to refocus on more long-haul routes. Initially WestJet had targeted car travelers, luring them to switch to air travel for shorter distances. But with a new security charge of C$24 on each round-trip imposed by the Canadian government, short hops have become less competitive compared to driving. At the same time, WestJet's new Boeing 737s have opened up new longer-haul opportunities.

The skies looked bright for WestJet. Clearly, the rules of the game in the domestic airline industry had tilted in favor of low-costs no-frills carriers. Even the industry leader, Air Canada, had shifted capacity to its in-house no-frills brand Tango and was about to launch Zip, another low-cost carrier. Referring to Air Canada's latest move, Beddoe stated: 'Imitation is the greatest form of flattery.' He should know, as WestJet was no stranger to the practice of flattering the right examples.

Sources: *Financial Times*, August 2 and 26 2002, October 21 2002; *Airline Business*, October 1 2002.

The industry leadership perspective

Strategists taking an industry leadership perspective fundamentally disagree with the determinism inherent in the industry dynamics perspective. Even in biology, breeders and genetic engineers consistently attempt to shape the natural world. Of course, in industries, as in biology, some rules are immutable. Certain economic, technological, social and political factors have to be accepted as hardly changeable. But the remaining environmental factors that can be manipulated leave strategists with an enormous scope for molding the industry of the future. This belief is reflected in the remark by the Dutch poet Jules Deelder that 'even within the limits of the possible, the possibilities are limitless'. It is up to the strategist to identify which rules of the game must be respected and which can be ignored in the search for new strategic options. The strategist must recognize both the limits on the possible and the limitless possibilities.

Advocates of the industry leadership perspective do not deny that in many industries the developments are largely an evolutionary result of industry dynamics. For an understanding of the development paths of these 'leaderless' industries, the industry dynamics perspective offers a powerful explanatory 'lens' – many industries do evolve without a clear industry leader. However, these industries only followed this path because no firm was creative and powerful enough to actively shape the direction of change. A lack of leadership is not the 'natural state of affairs', but simply weakness on behalf of the industry incumbents. Industry developments can be shaped, but it does require innovative companies willing to take on the leadership role (e.g. Baden-Fuller and Stopford, 1992; Hamel and Prahalad, 1994).

A leadership role, supporters of this perspective argue, starts with envisioning what the industry of tomorrow might look like. The firm's strategists must be capable of challenging the existing industry recipe and building a new conception of how the industry could function in the future. They must test their own assumptions about which industry rules can be changed and must, in fact, think of ways of 'destroying their current business'. Hamel and Prahalad (1994) refer to this as intellectual leadership, noting that smart strategists also develop 'industry foresight', anticipating which trends are likely to emerge, so that they can be used to the firm's advantage.

Not only must a firm have the intellectual ability to envision the industry's future, but it must also be able to communicate this vision in a manner that other firms and individuals will be willing to buy in. If a vision of the industry of tomorrow is compelling enough, people inside and outside the company will start to anticipate, and will become committed to, that future, making it a self-fulfilling prophecy. This 'inevitableness' of an industry vision can be important in overcoming risk averseness and resistance from industry incumbents (e.g. Levenhagen, Porac and Thomas, 1993; Moore, 2000).

To actually change the rules of the competitive game in an industry, a firm must move beyond a compelling vision, and work out a new competitive business model. If this new business model is put into operation and seems to offer a competitive advantage, this can attract sufficient customers and support to gain 'critical mass' and break through as a viable alternative to the older business models. To shape the industry, the firm will also need to develop the new competences and standards required to make the new business model function properly. The better the firm is at building new competences and setting new standards, alone or in cooperation with others, the more power it will have to determine the direction of industry development (e.g. D'Aveni, 1999; Hamel, 1996).

All of the above points together add up to quite a considerable task. But then, industry leadership is not easy and changing the industry rules rarely happens overnight. Rather, it can take years, figuring out which rules can be broken and which cannot. It can be a marathon, trying to get the business model right, while building competences and support. Therefore, organizations require perseverance and commitment if they are to be successful as industry shapers (Hamel and Prahalad, 1994).

EXHIBIT 8.3 THE INDUSTRY LEADERSHIP PERSPECTIVE

AUTONATION: DRIVEN TO RULE

Wayne Huizenga has a reputation for being a serial rule breaker. When as a young man he first got involved in the waste disposal business in the United States, he was struck by the conservatism and lack of entrepreneurship in the industry. Companies were satisfied to remain relatively small and keep on working as they had done for years, which to Huizenga seemed like the ideal type of competitors to have. Garbage smelt like a great opportunity and Huizenga went on to make his fortune building up a more innovative, large-scale company, Waste Management. But instead of retiring early and taking up golf, Huizenga started to look for other industries populated by small, unimaginative companies, stuck in an old business model. This eventually brought him to the video rental business, with its many 'Mom and Pop' stores. Here too, Huizenga swept through the industry, creating a large-scale professional organization, Blockbuster Video. Yet, even after this adventure, the golf course did not beckon. Huizenga once again went hunting for a fragmented industry wedded to outdated business recipes, and he found car retailing.

When Huizenga spotted the US car retailing industry in the mid-1990s, total revenues in the sector exceeded US$1 trillion per year. But while the sales were enormous, individual car retailers were comparatively small. Most car dealers were local or regional, and carried only one or two brands. This industry structure had suited the car manufacturers well, as they had more or less dedicated sales channels, which had limited bargaining power to extract a high margin from the car producers. This is where Huizenga saw an opportunity to change the rules of the game. By establishing a large-scale professional retailing organization, Huizenga believed

that he could gain significant purchasing power vis-à-vis the car manufacturers, while creating a more appealing service offering towards consumers. So, in 1996 he started AutoNation and within only four years became the largest car retailer in the United States.

The business model of AutoNation is based on a branded value proposition of high service at a relatively low price. Key to the high service perception is the 'one-price, no-hassle' car selling process, removing many buyers' frustration of having to deal with high-pressure salespeople. AutoNation also offers multiple brands at each location, saving consumers the trouble of needing to drive around town to many dealerships. In addition, AutoNation's car service departments offer longer hours, completion of work within the agreed budget, and free service if work is not finished on time. AutoNation also does more than other car retailers to develop its own brand into a trusted household name.

Keeping prices low means keeping costs low, which in turn requires economies of scale. AutoNation's approach has been to strive for at least a 15% share of each local market, allowing them to run large retailing outlets, attract more expensive professional management and have a larger marketing budget than rivals, while still having a competitive cost structure. To gain such a large market share quickly, AutoNation market entry has been through the acquisition of the top two or three car dealerships, predominantly in the most lucrative market areas in the United States. Generally, these dealerships already had the best management teams, good reputations, excellent market knowledge, reasonable retail capabilities, and clean operations, making it easier for AutoNation to quickly accelerate. Additional benefits of this acquisition policy have been that no extra capacity has been added to the market spoiling prices and that potential copycats will have to settle for buying the third or fourth best dealerships if they want to take on AutoNation.

'We feel we have found the approach that will change the automobile retailing industry,' says Huizenga, and the results seem to back up this assertion. By 2003 AutoNation owned and operated more than 400 outlets, employing about 30 000 people. The firm's sales of new vehicles (60% of total), used cars (20% of total), and service, financing and insurance (20% of total) were approximately US$20 billion, with the highest profitability in the industry. The question on everyone's mind now is whether Huizenga will finally head for the golf course, or whether other industries are on his list to be re-created.

Sources: Sexton (2001); http://corp.AutoNation.com.

TOWARDS A SYNTHESIS

The pilot cannot mitigate the billows or calm the winds.

Plutarch (c. 46–c. 120);
Greek biographer and philosopher

The reasonable man adapts himself to the world; the unreasonable one persists in trying to adapt the world to himself. Therefore, all progress depends on the unreasonable man.

George Bernard Shaw (1856–1950);
Irish playwright and critic

So, how should managers deal with the industry context? Should they concentrate on adapting to the dynamics in the industry, honing their ability to respond to changing demands and to adjust their business model to meet new requirements? Or should they take a more proactive role in shaping the future of the industry, changing the rules of the competitive game to suit their own needs? As the views within the field of strategic management are so far apart and no consensus seems to be emerging, managers must once again determine their own view on the topic.

In Table 8.1 the main arguments of the two opposite poles in this debate have been summarized. The next step could be to let the two views on the nature of the industry context

TABLE 8.1   Industry dynamics versus industry leadership perspective

	Industry dynamics perspective	Industry leadership perspective
Emphasis on	Compliance over choice	Choice over compliance
Industry development	Uncontrollable evolutionary process	Controllable creation process
Change dynamics	Environment selects fit firms	Firm creates fitting environment
Firm success due to	Fitness to industry demands	Manipulation of industry demands
Ability to shape industry	Low, slow	High, fast
Normative implication	Play by the rules (adapt)	Change the rules (innovate)
Development path	Convergence towards dominant design	Divergence, create new design
Firm profitability	Largely industry-dependent	Largely firm-dependent

compete with one another, allowing for 'survival of the fittest'. However, as in previous chapters, it is a much more fruitful challenge to 'cross-breed' the two perspectives, to come up with an even more 'fit' approach. The question should be how the strengths of the industry dynamics perspective and the industry leadership perspective – the thesis and the antithesis – can be combined into a more robust synthesis. Or, to paraphrase George Bernard Shaw, how can managers blend reasonableness and unreasonableness to achieve real progress?

FURTHER READING

How many things are looked upon as quite impossible until they have been actually effected.
Pliny the Elder (23–79); Roman writer

For a good academic overview of the debate on 'who shapes whom' readers are advised to consult the special edition of *Academy of Management Review* (July 1990) that focused on this issue. In particular, the article 'Market Discipline and the Discipline of Management' by Richard Bettis and Lex Donaldson is very insightful. For a broader discussion on the issue of determinism and voluntarism, good readings are 'Central Perspective and Debates in Organization Theory', by W. Graham Astley and Andrew van der Ven, and 'Organizational Adaptation: Strategic Choice and Environmental Determinism', by Lawrence Hrebiniak and William Joyce. Also useful is the recent work on managerial discretion, which attempts to measure how much leeway top managers have in shaping the future of their firm in different industries. Of these, the article 'Managerial Discretion: A Bridge Between Polar Views of Organizational Outcomes', by Donald Hambrick and Sydney Finkelstein, is interesting for its theoretical base, while 'Assessing the Amount of Managerial Discretion in Different Industries: A Multi-Method Approach', by Donald Hambrick and Eric Abrahamson is interesting for its analysis of various industry environments. All of these studies, it should be mentioned, do not have an audience of practitioners in mind.

The same is true for all further literature taking an industry dynamics perspective. A good book outlining the population ecology view of industry and firm development is the classic *Organizational Ecology* by Michael Hannan and John Freeman. For an excellent overview of the work in the area of industry and organizational evolution see Howard Aldrich's recent book, *Organizations Evolving*. Other constraints on the freedom of firms to shape their own fate are brought forward by institutional theory and resource dependence theory, both of which have not been represented in this debate. Christine Oliver gives a good overview of these two approaches in her article 'Strategic Responses to Institutional Processes'. The classic in the field of institutional theory is Paul DiMaggio and Walter Powell's article 'The Iron Cage Revisited: Institutional Isomorphism and Collective Rationality in Organizational Fields', while Scott's book *Institutions and Organizations* is a good, more recent work. The classic in the field of resource dependence is Jeffrey Pfeffer and Gerald Salancik's book *The External Control of Organizations*.

Readers interested in the industry leadership perspective might want to start by looking at J.-C. Spender's book *Industry Recipe: An Enquiry into the Nature and Sources of Managerial Judgement*. Charles Baden-Fuller and John Stopford's book, *Rejuvenating the Mature Business*, is also excellent follow-up reading. The same is true of Gary Hamel and

C.K. Prahalad's book *Competing for the Future*. In this context, Richard D'Aveni's book *Hypercompetition* is also worth reviewing, as is Geoffrey Moore's book *Living on the Fault Line*, which goes more deeply into adapting strategies according to the product life cycle.

For those who want to understand what happened during the internet bubble and whether there was anything to the New Economy, we advise starting with Michael Porter's article 'Strategy and the Internet'. Also valuable is Michael Cusumano and Annabelle Gawer's article 'The Elements of Platform Leadership' which describes the functioning of industry standards, as does Carl Shapiro and Hal Varian's excellent book, *Information Rules*.

THE ORGANIZATIONAL CONTEXT

We shape our environments, then our environments shape us.

Winston Churchill (1874–1965); British statesman and writer

INTRODUCTION

In organizations, just as in families, each new generation does not start from scratch but inherits properties belonging to their predecessors. In families, a part of this inheritance is in the form of genetic properties, but other attributes are also passed down such as family traditions, myths, habits, connections, feuds, titles and possessions. People might think of themselves as unique individuals, but to some degree they are an extension of the family line, and their behavior is influenced by this inheritance. In firms the same phenomenon is observable. New top managers may arrive on the scene, but they inherit a great deal from the previous generation. They inherit traditions and myths in the form of an organizational culture. Habits are passed along in the form of established organizational processes, while internal and external relationships and rivalries shape the political constellation in which new managers must function. They are also handed the family jewels – brands, competences and other key resources.

In Chapter 4 it was pointed out that such inheritance is often the source of organizational rigidity and inertia (e.g. Hannan and Freeman, 1977; Rumelt, 1996). Inheritance limits 'organizational plasticity' – the capacity of the organization to change shape. As such, organizational inheritance can partially predetermine a firm's future path of development – which is referred to as path dependency, or sometimes simply summed up as 'history matters' (e.g. Aldrich, 1999; Nelson and Winter, 1982). Therefore, it was concluded that for strategic renewal to take place, some inherited characteristics could be preserved, but others needed to be changed, by either evolutionary or revolutionary means.

What was not discussed in Chapter 4 was *who* should trigger the required strategic changes. Who should initiate adaptations to the firm's business system and who should take steps to reshape the organizational system? Typically, managers will have some role to play in all developments in the organizational context, but the question is what role. It is unlikely that any manager will have complete influence over all organizational developments, or would even want to exert absolute control. Inheritance and other organizational factors limit 'organizational malleability' – the capacity of the organization to be shaped by someone. As such, managers need to determine what power they do have and where this power should be applied to achieve the best results. At the same time, managers will generally also look for opportunities to tap into the capabilities of other people in the firm to contribute to ongoing organizational adaptation.

So, the question can be summarized as 'what is the role of managers in achieving a new alignment with the environment and what input can be garnered from other organizational members?'. This question is also referred to as the issue of organizational development and will be the central topic of further discussion in this chapter.

THE ISSUE OF ORGANIZATIONAL DEVELOPMENT

When it comes to realizing organizational development, managers generally acknowledge that they have some type of leadership role to play. Leadership refers to the act of influencing the views and behaviors of organizational members with the intention of accomplishing a particular organizational aim (e.g. Selznick, 1957; Bass, 1990). Stated differently, leadership is the act of getting organizational members to follow. From this definition it can be concluded that not all managers are necessarily leaders, and not all leaders are necessarily managers. Managers are individuals with a formal position in the organizational hierarchy, with associated authority and responsibilities. Leaders are individuals who have the ability to sway other people in the organization to get something done.

To be able to lead organizational developments, managers need power. Power is the capability to influence. They also need to know how to get power, and how and where to exert it. In the following sections, these three topics will be examined in more detail. First, the sources of leadership influence will be described, followed by the levers of leadership influence. Finally, the arenas of leadership influence will be explored.

Sources of leadership influence

To lead means to use power to influence others. Leaders can derive their potential influence from two general sources – their position and their person (Etzioni, 1961). 'Position power' comes from a leader's formal function in the organization. 'Personal power' is rooted in the specific character, knowledge, skills and relationships of the leader. Managers always have some level of position power, but they do not necessarily have the personal power needed to get organizational members to follow them. These two main types of power can be further subdivided into the following categories (French and Raven, 1959):

- Legitimate power. Legitimate power exists when a person has the formal authority to determine certain organizational behaviors and other employees agree to comply with this situation. Examples of legitimate power are the authority to assign work, spend money and demand information.

- Coercive power. People have coercive power when they have the capability to punish or withhold rewards to achieve compliance. Examples of coercive power include giving a poor performance review, withholding a bonus and dismissing employees.

- Reward power. Reward power is derived from the ability to offer something of value to a person in return for compliance. Examples of reward power include giving praise, awarding wage raises and promoting employees.

- Expert power. Expert power exists when organizational members are willing to comply because of a person's superior knowledge or skills in an important area. Such expert power can be based on specific knowledge of functional areas (e.g. marketing, finance), technologies (e.g. pharmaceuticals, information technology), geographic areas (e.g. South-East Asia, Florida) and/or businesses (e.g. mining, automotive).

- Referent power. When organizational members let themselves be influenced by a person's charismatic appeal, this is called referent power. This personal attraction can be based on many attributes, such as likeableness, forcefulness, persuasiveness, visionary qualities and image of success.

The first three types of power are largely determined by the organizational position of leaders and their willingness to exert them – coercive and reward capabilities without the credibility of use are not a viable source of power. The last two sources of power, expert and referent power, are largely personal in nature, and also more subjective. Whether someone is seen as an expert and therefore accorded a certain level of respect and influence depends strongly on the perceptions of the people being lead. Expert power can be made more tangible by wearing a white lab coat, putting three pens in your breast pocket or writing a book, but still perceived expertise will be in the eyes of the beholder. The same is true for referent power, as people do not find the same characteristics equally charismatic. What is forceful to one follower might seem pushy to someone else; what is visionary to one person might sound like the murmurings of a madman to others (e.g. Klein and House, 1998; Waldman and Yammarino, 1999).

In practice, leaders will employ a mix of all five types of power to achieve the influence they desire. However, leadership styles can differ greatly depending on the relative weight placed on the various sources of power within the mix.

Levers of leadership influence

The sources of power available to the leader need to be used to have influence. There are three generic ways for leaders to seek influence, each focused on a different point in the activities of the people being influenced. These levers of leadership influence are:

- Throughput control. Leaders can focus their attention directly at the actions being taken by others in the organization. Throughput control implies getting involved hands-on in the activities of others, either by suggesting ways of working, engaging in a discussion on how things should be done, leading by example or simply by telling others what to do. This form of direct influence does require sufficiently detailed knowledge about the activities of others to be able to point out what should be done.

- Output control. Instead of directly supervising how things should be done, leaders can set objectives that should be met. Output control implies reaching agreement on certain performance targets and then monitoring how well they are being lived up to. The targets can be quantitative or qualitative, financial or strategic, simple or complex, realistic or stretch-oriented. And they can be arrived at by mutual consent or imposed by the leader. The very act of setting objectives can have an important influence on people in the organization, but the ability to check ongoing performance and to link results with punishment and rewards can further improve a person's impact.

- Input control. Leaders can also choose to influence the general conditions under which activities are carried out. Input control implies shaping the circumstances preceding and surrounding the actual work. Before activities start a leader can influence who is assigned to a task, which teams are formed, who is hired, where they will work and in what type of environment. During the execution of activities the leader can supply physical and financial resources, mobilize relationships and provide support. Not unimportantly, the leader can also be a source of enthusiasm, inspiration, ambition, vision and mission.

Of these three, throughput control is the most direct in its impact and input control the least. However, throughput control offers the lowest leverage and input control the highest, allowing a leader to influence many people over a longer period of time, while leaving more room for organizational members to take on their own responsibilities as well. In practice, leaders can combine elements of all three of the above, although leadership styles differ greatly with regard to the specific mix.

Arenas of leadership influence

As leaders attempt to guide organizational development, there are three main organizational arenas where they need to direct their influence to achieve strategic changes. These three overlapping arenas are the parts in the organization most resistant to change – they are the sub-systems of the firm where organizational inheritance creates its own momentum, resisting a shift into another direction (e.g. Miller and Friesen, 1980; Tushman, Newman and Romanelli, 1986):

- The political arena. While most top managers have considerable position power with which they can try to influence the strategic decision-making process within their organization, very few top managers can impose their strategic agenda on the organization without building widespread political support. Even the most autocratic CEO will need to gain the commitment and compliance of key figures within the organization to be able to successfully push through significant changes. In practice, however, there are not many organizations where the 'officers and the troops' unquestioningly follow the general into battle. Usually, power is more dispersed throughout organizations, with different people and units having different ideas and interests, as well as the assertiveness to pursue their own agenda. Ironically, the more leaders that are developed throughout the organization, the more complex it becomes for any one leader to get the entire organization to follow – broad leadership can easily become fragmented leadership, with a host of strong people all pointing in different directions. For top management to gain control of the organization they must therefore build coalitions of supporters, not only to get favorable strategic decisions made, but also to ensure acceptance and compliance during the period of implementation. Otherwise strategic plans will be half-heartedly executed, opposed or silently sabotaged. However, gaining the necessary political support in the organization can be very difficult if the strategic views and interests of powerful individuals and departments differ significantly. Cultural and personality clashes can add to the complexity. Yet, top managers cannot recoil from the political arena, for it is here that new strategic directions are set (e.g. Allison, 1969; Pfeffer, 1992).

- The cultural arena. Intertwined with the process of gaining political influence in the organization, there is the process of gaining cultural influence. After all, to be able to change the organization, a leader must be able to change people's beliefs and associated behavioral patterns. Yet, affecting cultural change is far from simple. A leader must be capable of questioning the shared values, ideas and habits prevalent in the organization, even though the leader has usually been immersed in the very same culture for years. Leaders must also offer an alternative worldview and set of behaviors to supercede the old. All of this requires exceptional skills as visionary – to develop a new image of a desired future state for the firm – and as missionary – to develop a new set of beliefs and values to guide the firm. Furthermore, the leader needs to be an excellent teacher to engage the organizational members in a learning process to adapt their beliefs, values and norms to the new circumstances. In practice, this means that leaders often have to 'sell' their view of the new culture, using a mix of rational persuasion, inspirational appeal, symbolic actions, motivational incentives and subtle pressure (e.g. Senge, 1990a; Ireland and Hitt, 1999).

- The psychological arena. While leaders need to influence the political process and the cultural identity of the organization, attention also needs to be paid to the psychological needs of individuals. To affect organizational change, leaders must win both the hearts and minds of the members of the organization. People must be willing to, literally, 'follow the leader' – preferably not passively, but actively, with commitment, courage and even passion (e.g. Bennis and Nanus, 1985; Kelley, 1988). To achieve such 'followership', leaders must gain the respect and trust of their colleagues. Another important factor in winning people over is the ability to meet their emotional need for certainty, clarity and continuity, to offset the uncertainties, ambiguities and discontinuities surrounding them (e.g. Argyris, 1990; Pfeffer and Sutton, 1999b).

Even where political, cultural and psychological processes make the organization difficult to lead, managers might still be able to gain a certain level of control over their organizations. Yet, there will always remain aspects of the organizational system that managers cannot control, and should not even want to control, and this will be discussed in the following section.

THE PARADOX OF CONTROL AND CHAOS

Of all men's miseries the bitterest is this, to know so much and to have control over nothing.
Herodotus (5th century BC); Greek historian

In general, managers like to be in control. Managers like to be able to shape their own future, and by extension, to shape the future of their firm. Managers do not shy away from power – they build their power base to be able to influence events and steer the development of their organization. In short, to be a manager is to have the desire to be in charge.

Yet, at the same time, most managers understand that their firms do not resemble machines, where one person can sit at the control panel and steer the entire system. Organizations are complex social systems, populated by numerous self-thinking human beings, each with their own feelings, ideas and interests. These people need to decide and act for themselves on a daily basis, without the direct intervention of the manager. They must be empowered to weigh situations, take initiatives, solve problems and grab opportunities. They must be given a certain measure of autonomy to experiment, do things differently and even constructively disagree with the manager. In other words, managers must also be willing to 'let go' of some control for the organization to function at its best.

Moreover, managers must accept that in a complex system, like an organization, trying to control everything would be a futile endeavor. With so many people and so many interactions going on in a firm, any attempt to run the entire system top-down would be an impossible task. Therefore, letting go of some control is a pure necessity for normal organizational functioning.

This duality of wanting to control the development of the organization, while understanding that letting go of control is often beneficial, is the key strategic tension when dealing with the organizational context. On the one hand, managers must be willing to act as benevolent 'philosopher kings', autocratically imposing on the company what they see as best. On the other hand, managers must be willing to act as constitutional monarchs, democratically empowering organizational citizens to take their own responsibilities and behave more as entrepreneurs. The strategic paradox arises from the fact that the need for top-down *imposition* and bottom-up *initiative* are conflicting demands that are difficult for managers to meet at the same time.

On one side of this strategy paradox is 'control', which can be defined as the power to direct and impose order. On the other side of the paradox is the need for 'chaos', which can be defined as disorder or the lack of fixed organization. The paradox of control and chaos is a recurrent theme in the literature on strategy, organization, leadership and governance. In most writings the need for control is presented as a pressure for a directive leadership style and/or an autocratic governance system (e.g. Tannenbaum and Schmidt, 1958; Vroom and Jago, 1988). The need for chaos is presented as a pressure for a participative leadership style and/or a democratic governance system (e.g. Ackoff, 1980; Stacey, 1992). In the following sub-sections both control and chaos will be further examined.

The demand for top management control

As Herodotus remarked, it would be bitter indeed to have control over nothing. Not only would it be a misery for the frustrated managers, who would be little more than mere administrators or caretakers. It would also be a misery for their organizations, which would need to constantly adjust course without a helmsman to guide the ship. Managers cannot afford to let their organizations drift on the existing momentum. It is a manager's task and responsibility to ensure that the organization changes in accordance to the environment, so that the organizational purpose can still be achieved.

Top management cannot realize this objective without some level of control. They need to be able to direct developments in the organization. They need to have the power to make the necessary changes in the organizational structure, processes and culture, to realign the organization with the demands of the environment. This power, whether positional or personal, needs to be applied towards gaining sufficient support in the political arena, challenging existing beliefs and behaviors in the cultural arena, and winning the hearts and minds of the organizational members in the psychological arena.

The control that top management needs is different from the day-to-day control built in to the organizational structure and processes – they need *strategic control* as opposed to *operational control*. While operational control gives managers influence over activities within the current organizational system, strategic control gives managers influence over changes to the organizational system itself (e.g. Goold and Quinn, 1990; Simons, 1994). It is this power that managers require to be able to steer the development of their organization.

The demand for organizational chaos

To managers the term 'chaos' sounds quite menacing – it carries connotations of rampant anarchy, total pandemonium and a hopeless mess. Yet, chaos only means disorder, coming from the Greek term for the unformed original state of the universe. In the organizational context chaos refers to situations of disorder, where phenomena have not yet been organized, or where parts of an organizational system have become 'unfreezed'. In other words, something is chaotic if it is unformed or has become 'disorganized'.

While this still does not sound particularly appealing to most managers, it should, because a period of disorganization is often a prerequisite for strategic renewal. Unfreezing existing structures, processes, routines and beliefs, and opening people up to different possibilities might be inefficient in the short run, as well as making people feel uncomfortable, but it is usually necessary to provoke creativity and to invent new ways of seeing and doing things. By allowing experimentation, skunk works, pilot projects and out-of-the-ordinary initiatives, managers accept a certain amount of disorder in the organization, which they hope will pay off in terms of organizational innovations.

But the most appealing effect of chaos is that it encourages 'self-organization'. To illustrate this phenomenon, one should first think back to the old Soviet 'command economy', which was based on the principle of control. It was believed that a rational, centrally planned economic system, with strong top-down leadership, would be the most efficient and effective way to organize industrial development. In the West, on the other hand, the 'market economy' was chaotic – no one was in control and could impose order. Everyone could go ahead and start a company. They could set their own production levels and even set their own prices! As entrepreneurs made use of the freedom offered to them, the economy 'self-organized' bottom-up. Instead of the 'visible hand' of the central planner controlling and regulating the economy, it was the 'invisible hand' of the market that created relative order out of chaos.

As the market economy example illustrates, chaos does not necessarily lead to pandemonium, but can result in a self-regulating interplay of forces. A lack of top-down control frees the way for a rich diversity of bottom-up ventures. Managers who also want to release the energy, creativity and entrepreneurial potential pent up in their organizations must therefore be willing to let go and allow some chaos to exist. In this context, the role of top management is comparable to that of governments in market economies – creating suitable conditions, encouraging activities and enforcing basic rules.

EXHIBIT 9.1 SHORT CASE

LE MÉRIDIEN: CHARGE OF THE FIVE STAR GENERAL?

On September 8 2001 a press release was sent to the international media: 'The independent luxury hotel group Le Méridien, announces a widespread £850 million (US$1204 million) global investment program designed to dramatically upgrade its facilities and catapult the brand to the top of the hotel industry rankings in three years.' Le Méridien, with such hotels as The Ritz in Madrid and Barcelona, The Eden in Rome and Le Parker Méridien in New York, ambitiously, yet confidently, declared that they would push through major changes to become the leader in the five star segment of the hotel business. Just three days later came 9/11. For hotels around the world the shock was enormous. Occupancy rates dropped, followed by profitability.

Yet Jürgen Bartels, CEO of Le Méridien, was not pessimistic. He believed that gains could be made in any market: 'My bottom line is that there are winners and losers in all conditions . . . it is not that everyone loses equally in a holding pattern.' Jürgen Bartels was known as JB to the industry, and his voice counted. A veteran of the hospitality business, with more than 40 years of experience, JB was known to be as eccentric as he was successful. He founded Renaissance Hotels, was CEO of Carlson Hospitality, and moved on to become CEO and chairman of the Westin Hotels and Resorts. Under his leadership, the group staged its impressive growth in the 1990s and merged with Starwood Hotels and ITT Sheraton Hotels and Resorts.

Eventually JB was lured away by Guy Hands of the Principal Finance Group (PFG), a subsidiary of the Japanese bank Nomura, to help with the acquisition of Le Méridien. After a bidding war with the Marriott Hotel Group, Le Méridien was purchased by PFG in July 2001 for £1.9 billion, which was quite expensive for a company with annual sales of just over £1 billion. Yet JB was bullish, even putting in £10 million of his own money. His goal was not merely to shake up Le Méridien, but to establish a new benchmark for modern luxury hotels. The global investment program he had planned would be the 'largest R&D effort . . . ever undertaken in the industry'.

The challenge facing JB was quite formidable, even without the events of 9/11. With 140 Le Méridien hotels in 55 countries, JB had gained formal control over a very diverse family of hotels, often with long histories and idiosyncratic practices. In each hotel different conditions, customer demands and business habits had grown into differing local market approaches. In Japan, for example, the wedding market is a major income earner for a hotel, and therefore an in-house chapel and wedding package are essential. In Barcelona, on the other hand, weekend travelers are an important market segment, while in Dubai more emphasis is needed for the stopover traveler. Yet, the differences between the hotels ran much deeper than distinctive client profiles, seasonal cycles of supply and demand, local labor force issues, government regulations, municipal sanitary conditions and local food supplies – many hotels had unique personalities, strongly rooted in their local environment.

The diversity of Le Méridien's hotels was matched by its diversity of ownership. The company had changed hands four times in only seven years, from Air France to the British Forte Group, then to the Granada Group, then to the catering giant Compass Group, and then to PFG. Every owner had left its own imprint on the company. Furthermore, Le Méridien held many hotel properties under an operating license only, with the actual hotel owner being a real estate or other type of investor. These license agreements came in many different shapes and forms, giving the owners varying degrees of influence on management practice and strategic direction.

In response to the variety of local conditions, the managing directors of the individual hotels had generally been granted far-reaching autonomy. Both the pricing in the local market, the management of the local work force, and the need to respond immediately to customers' requests required the entrepreneurial talents of local bosses. But even they had only one pair of eyes and hands, and needed to sleep at night, relying on their organizations to create the luxury experience, 365 days and nights around the clock. Unlike in a manufacturing environment, in hotels product reworking is not possible – lousy service to guests cannot be undone. Managers have to rely on the organizational systems in the hotel, and the improvisation skills of their staff, to get things right the first time, every time.

Yet, despite the autonomy given to local managing directors, the financial performance of Le Méridien was below par, even before the economic downturn. While industry leader Four Seasons managed a 36% earnings margin on sales in 2000, Le Méridien achieved only 15%. The brand also lacked the pulling power required in the five star segment of the market, which the Ritz Carltons or the Mandarin Orientals for instance had. Therefore, it was JB's task as new CEO to reinvigorate the company and to make the whole worth more than the sum of its individual locations. As a private equity investor, PFG had set the financial targets high for JB, in effect requiring Le Méridien to outperform the industry within three years. In order to achieve these ambitious goals, JB developed a two-pronged strategy: one was called 'Art & Tech', and the other was called 'treasure hunting'.

Art & Tech was based on JB's vision to combine the power of a worldwide brand with the avant-garde appeal of local boutique hotels. Approximately 5000 of the 40 000 hotel rooms at Le Méridien would be converted to this concept, and the others would contain several elements of it. The 'Tech' part of the concept consisted of such features as a 42 inch plasma TV screen, high speed dataport/internet access in the room, showering and bathing facilities with thick water jets, specially engineered beds 'providing the ultimate sleep experience in crisp white cotton duvets' and 'advanced lighting technologies electronically controlled to create a series of different moods'. The 'Art' component included various artistic elements throughout the room, creating a 'space that will not only provide luxury accommodation but an environment that will engage, surprise and intrigue Le Méridien's guests'. Each hotel would have specially commissioned photographs and art themes inspired from the locality of the hotel, nearby museums or their collections. In all, 'the Art & Tech room is designed to offer today's increasingly sophisticated traveler the ultimate in innovative luxury'.

The second prong of JB's strategy was the treasure hunt. The moneymaking parts of a hotel are its rooms and its conference facilities. But inside a typical hotel, a lot of space is used as staff rooms, management offices and apartments, which do not directly contribute to hotel revenue. In JB's view, these could be converted into rooms, and cheaper space could be rented outside of the main building for the administrative and supply functions. Likewise, low-income space usages such as swimming pools, fit-ness areas, shopping malls and restaurants could be reduced to the minimum, using the surplus space as conference facilities. In this way, JB believed that he could significantly increase the revenue potential for a given piece of real estate, adding a total of 1600 bedrooms and more than 2000 square meters of conferencing rooms throughout the group at comparatively minor cost.

Once JB arrived in July 2001, he lost no time starting to implement his strategy. Top management was almost completely replaced by hand-picked recruits, who were often industry outsiders. For instance, his new marketing chief came from American Express, which JB hoped would bring fresh ideas into the company. Even the designer responsible for fashioning the Art & Tech look was an unconventional outside choice, with a background in museum design.

However, by early 2003, half way into JB's three-year plan, not much could yet be seen of Le Méridien climbing to the top. Given the overall economic climate, this was hardly surprising. Times were such that mere survival was reason to celebrate. The business travel market that Le Méridien was targeting was the hardest hit of all. Of the £850 million investment program that had been announced in September of 2001, little had actually been spent – most of the money had been pledged by the hotel property owners to convert hotels to the Art & Tech concept and few were inclined to proceed with this plan after 9/11.

While putting on a brave face, this situation was a severe blow to JB's ambitions. With only a year and a half left to achieve the above-average profitability needed to pay off its high debts, JB could not afford to sit back and wait for the world economy to rebound. To many people around him it was now the moment of truth – to see whether JB had the leadership abilities to take decisive action and to pilot the organization into a safe haven. In particular, Le Méridien's owner, PFG, was very anxious to see whether JB, with all his industry experience and wealth of contacts, could push through the measures necessary to improve the company's long-term, and short-term prospects.

Other observers, however, were doubtful whether JB's strategy would have worked, even without 9/11. In their view, JB's top-down approach to rejuvenating the company was bound to run into the sand anyway, due to the complexity and diversity of the organization. Local managing directors were unlikely to be very thrilled with wild ideas coming from headquarters that paid scant attention to local conditions and the uniqueness of each hotel. Even where they broadly agreed with

JB, it would not have been easy to get local owners, staff and management to accept all the required changes and implement them in such a short period of time.

For JB, with a career and £10 million at stake, the pressing question was what he could still do to revitalize Le Méridien. Should he charge forward, leading the 40 000 troops, or were there more effective ways to keep himself, and the hotels, occupied?

Sources: *Financial Times*, March 25, April 3, May 24 and September 27 2002; Company reports; 'Four Seasons goes to Paris', *Academy of Management Executive*, 2002, Vol. 16 No. 4.

PERSPECTIVES ON THE ORGANIZATIONAL CONTEXT

I claim not to have controlled events, but confess plainly that events have controlled me.

Abraham Lincoln (1809–1865); American president

While the pressures for both control and chaos are clear, this does leave managers with the challenging question of how they must reconcile two opposite, and at least partially incompatible, demands. Gaining a considerable level of top management control over the development of the organization will to some extent be at odds with a policy of accepting, or even encouraging, organizational chaos. To control or not to control, that is the question.

And yet again managers should not hope to find widespread consensus in the strategic management literature on what the optimal answer is for dealing with these two conflicting pressures. For among strategy academics and business practitioners alike, opinions differ strongly with regard to the best balance between control and chaos. Although many writers do indicate that there may be different styles in dealing with the paradox and that these different styles might be more effective under different circumstances (e.g. Strebel, 1994; Vroom and Jago, 1988), most authors still exhibit a strong preference for a particular approach – which is duly called the 'modern' or 'new' style, or better yet, '21st century practices' (Ireland and Hitt, 1999).

Following the dialectical inquiry method used in previous chapters, here the two diametrically opposed positions will be identified and discussed. On the one hand, there are those who argue that top managers should lead from the front. Top managers should dare to take on the responsibility of imposing a new strategic agenda on the organization and should be at the forefront in breaking away from organizational inheritance where necessary. This point of view, with its strong emphasis on control and leading top-down, will be referred to as the 'organizational leadership perspective'. This view is also known as the strategic leadership perspective (e.g. Cannella and Monroe, 1997; Rowe, 2001), but to avoid confusion with the industry leadership perspective discussed in Chapter 8, here the prefix 'organizational' is preferred. On the other hand, there are people who believe that managers rarely have the ability to shape their organizations at will, but rather that organizations develop according to their own dynamics. These strategists argue that in most organizations no one is really in control and that managers should not focus their energy on attempting to impose developments top-down, but rather focus on facilitating processes of self-organization. This point of view, with its strong emphasis on chaos and facilitating bottom-up processes, will be referred to as the 'organizational dynamics perspective'.

The organizational leadership perspective

 To proponents of the organizational leadership perspective, top management can – and should – take charge of the organization. In their view, organizational inertia and a growing misfit between the organization and its environment are not an inevitable state of affairs, but result from a failure of leadership. Bureaucracy, organizational fiefdoms, hostile relationships, inflexible corporate cultures, rigid competences and resistance to change – all of these organizational diseases exist, but they are not unavoidable facts of organizational life. 'Healthy' organizations guard against falling prey to such degenerative illnesses, and when symptoms do arise it is a task of the leader to address them. If organizations do go 'out of control', it is because weak leadership has failed to deal with a creeping ailment. The fact that there are many sick, poorly controllable companies does not mean that sickness should be accepted as the natural condition.

At the basis of the organizational leadership perspective lies the belief that if people in organizations are left to 'sort things out' by themselves, this will inevitably degenerate into a situation of strategic drift (see Chapter 4). Without somebody to quell political infighting, set a clear strategic direction, force through tough decisions, and supervise disciplined implementation, the organization will get bogged down in protracted internal bickering. Without somebody to champion a new vision, rally the troops and lead from the front, the organization will never get its heavy mass in motion. Without somebody who radiates confidence and cajoles people into action, the organization will not be able to overcome its risk averseness and conservatism. In short, leaders are needed to counteract the inherent inertia characteristic of human organization.

As organizational order and direction do not happen spontaneously, the 'visible hand' of management is indispensable for the proper functioning of the organization (e.g. Child, 1972; Cyert, 1990). And this hand must be firm. Managers cannot afford to take a *laissez-faire* attitude towards their task as leader – to lead means to get the organizational members to follow, and this is usually plain hard work (e.g. Bennis and Nanus, 1985; Kelley, 1988). To convince people in the organization to let themselves be led, managers cannot simply fall back on their position power. To be able to steer organizational developments managers need considerable personal power. To be successful, managers must be trusted, admired and respected. The forcefulness of their personality and the persuasiveness of their vision must be capable of capturing people's attention and commitment. And as leaders, managers must also be politically agile, able to build coalitions where necessary to get their way.

Of course, not all managers have the qualities needed to be effective leaders – either by nature or nurture. Some theorists emphasize the importance of 'nature', arguing that managers require specific personality traits to be successful leaders (e.g. House and Aditya,

1997; Tucker, 1968). Yet, other theorists place more emphasis on 'nurture', arguing that most effective leadership behavior can be learned if enough effort is exerted (e.g. Kotter, 1990; Nanus, 1992). Either way, the importance of having good leadership makes finding and developing new leaders one of the highest priorities of the existing top management team.

To proponents of the organizational leadership perspective, being a leader does not mean engaging in simple top-down, command-and-control management. There are circumstances where the CEO or the top management team design strategies in isolation and then impose them on the rest of the organization. This type of direct control is sometimes necessary to push through reorganizations or to make major acquisitions. In other circumstances, however, the top managers can control organizational behavior more indirectly. Proposals can be allowed to emerge bottom-up, as long as top management retains its power to approve or terminate projects as soon as they become serious plans (e.g. Bourgeois and Brodwin, 1983; Quinn, 1980b). Some authors suggest that top management might even delegate some decision-making powers to lower level managers, but still control outcomes by setting clear goals, developing a conducive incentive system and fostering a particular culture (e.g. Senge, 1990a; Tichy and Cohen, 1997).

What leaders should not do, however, is to relinquish control over the direction of the organization. The strategies do not have to be their own ideas, nor do they have to carry out everything themselves. But they should take upon themselves the responsibility for leading the organization in a certain direction and achieving results. If leaders let go of the helm, organizations will be set adrift, and will be carried by the prevailing winds and currents in directions unknown. Someone has to be in control of the organization, otherwise its behavior will be erratic. Leadership is needed to ensure that the best strategy is followed.

In conclusion, the organizational leadership perspective holds that the upper echelons of management can, and should, control the strategy process and by extension the strategy content. The CEO, or the top management team (e.g. Finkelstein and Hambrick, 1996; Hambrick and Mason, 1984), should have a grip on the organization's process of strategy formation and should be able to impose their will on the organization. Leaders should strive to overcome organizational inertia and adapt the organization to the strategic direction they intend. This type of controlled strategic behavior is what Chandler (1962) had in mind when he coined the aphorism 'structure follows strategy' – the organizational structure should be adapted to the strategy intended by the decision-maker. In the organizational leadership perspective it would be more fitting to expand Chandler's maxim to 'organization follows strategy' – all aspects of the company should be matched to the strategist's intentions.

EXHIBIT 9.2 THE ORGANIZATIONAL LEADERSHIP PERSPECTIVE

NISSAN: NEW DRIVER AT THE WHEEL

In 1998 car-maker Nissan was heading for a brick wall at high speed. Its market share in Japan had been sliding for 26 years straight, and while its key domestic rivals Honda and Toyota were reporting record profits, Nissan had not been able to make a profit for seven of the eight previous years. Daimler Chrysler had declined to buy Nissan, even for the symbolic amount of one dollar, while Ford, too, had lost interest. Eventually it was French car-maker Renault who took the opportunity to gain a controlling stake in March 1999. Just three years later, Nissan was one of the most profitable automobile manufacturers in the world, even surpassing Toyota, and was set to recapture the number two market share position in Japan. Seldom has a turnaround been so dramatic, so complete and so attributable to one person – Carlos Ghosn.

Between 1992 and 1998, three different presidents had been behind the wheel at Nissan, but none were able to get the skidding company under control. No fewer than four restructuring plans were announced, but nothing seemed capable of avoiding the imminent crash. So when Renault eventually stepped in and sent the 45-year-old, non-Japanese speaking, Brazil-born French/Lebanese Carlos Ghosn to take control of Nissan in summer 1999, his task was widely hailed as 'Mission Impossible'. Later in that year, this assessment was toned down to 'Mission Improbable', and in 2002 *Fortune* named Carlos Ghosn 'Asia's Businessman of the Year'. What did he do that predecessors were incapable of doing?

According to one senior executive at Nissan, 'Ghosn stresses action, speed and results. He follows up closely. If there are any deviations he goes after them immediately. He is relentless in following up.' In his own words at the time:

I have one goal, that Nissan will be profitable in 2001. . . This is not like buying a Persian rug: the guy says he wants 100, but if he gets 50 he will be happy. We want 100, and we are going to get 100. If we do not get it in 2001, that's it, we will resign . . . From now on, financial objectives will entail accountability.

Accountability is Ghosn's credo. He sees no value in business relationships that are not characterized by clear and controllable targets. Starting at the top, the number of directors on the board was reduced from

43 to nine. The traditional lifetime employment and seniority-based reward system was completely revamped. Several hundred key managers received stock options instead. Promotion and rewards were linked to performance against an annual set of objectives. Ghosn created six program directors with worldwide profit responsibility for a range of cars under their management. Externally, by the end of 2002, Nissan's 67 equity investments in Keiretsu (group) companies were reduced to 25, while all 1400 cross-shareholdings with other Japanese companies were undone. The 300 global banking relationships were centralized into a single treasury function. The number of suppliers was reduced by half to 600, with each remaining supplier committing to at least a 20% cost reduction over three years.

The pressure was equally fierce inside the company. Headcount was reduced by almost 20%, dropping from 148 000 to 127 000 employees, and five manufacturing plants were closed. Yet, at the same time Ghosn planned to introduce 28 new car models within three years. In order to achieve all that, one of Ghosn's first actions in office was to install nine cross-functional teams with up to ten middle managers and hundreds of sub-team members, to work out the entire 'Nissan Revival Plan' within only two months. Team members were not responsible for implementation, but their recommendations had to be aggressive, specific, backed up by numbers and not respectful towards current practices. Any team that did not live up to these targets was sent straight back to work.

In May 2002, having achieved the turnaround one year ahead of schedule, Ghosn unveiled the new Nissan 180 plan – by 2005, Nissan would increase car sales almost 40%, from 2.6 to 3.6 million vehicles, reach 8% operating profit on sales (top of the industry), and have reduced net automotive debt to zero. To industry insiders, this sounded like 'Mission Impossible' all over again, but if anyone could pull off this assignment, it would be Carlos Ghosn.

Sources: *Business Week,* January 18 2000, June 21 2001, January 13 2003; Interview with Carlos Ghosn in *Harvard Business Review*, January–February 2002; Yoshino, 2002.

The organizational dynamics perspective

To proponents of the organizational dynamics perspective, such an heroic depiction of leadership is understandable, but usually more myth than reality. There might be a few great, wise, charismatic managers that rise to the apex of organizations, but unfortunately, all other organizations have to settle for regular mortals. Strong leaders are an exception, not the norm, and even their ability to mold the organization at will is highly exaggerated – good stories for best-selling (auto)biographies, but legend nevertheless (e.g. Chen and Meindl, 1991; Kets de Vries, 1994). Yet, the belief in the power of leadership is quite popular, among managers and the managed alike (e.g. Meindl, Ehrlich and Dukerich, 1985; Pfeffer, 1977). Managers like the idea that as leaders of an organization or organizational unit, they can make a difference. To most, 'being in control' is what management is all about. They have a penchant for attributing organizational results to their own efforts (e.g. Calder, 1977; Sims and Lorenzi, 1992). As for 'the managed', they too often ascribe organizational success or failure to the figurehead leader, whatever that person's real influence has been – after all, they too like the idea that somebody is in control. In fact, both parties are subscribing to a seductively simple 'great person model' of how organizations work. The implicit assumption is that an individual leader, by the strength of personality, can steer large groups of people, like a present-day Alexander the Great.

However seductive, this view of organizational functioning is rarely a satisfactory model. A top manager does not resemble a commander leading the troops into battle, but rather a diplomat trying to negotiate a peace. The top manager is not like a jockey riding a thoroughbred horse, but more like a cowboy herding mules. Organizations are complex social systems, made up of many 'stubborn individuals' with their own ideas, interests and agendas (e.g. Greenwood and Hinings, 1996; Stacey, 1993a). Strategy formation is therefore an inherently political process, that leaders can only influence depending on their power base. The more dispersed the political power, the more difficult it is for a leader to control the organization's behavior. Even if leaders are granted, or acquire, significant political power to push through their favored measures, there may still be considerable resistance and guerilla activities. Political processes within organizations do not signify the derailment of strategic decision-making – politics is the normal state of affairs and few leaders have real control over these political dynamics.

Besides such political limitations, a top manager's ability to control the direction of a company is also severely constrained by the organization's culture. Social norms will have evolved, relationships will have been formed, aspirations will have taken root and cognitive maps will have been shaped. A leader cannot ignore the cultural legacy of the organization's history, as this will be deeply etched into the minds of the organization's members. Any top manager attempting to radically alter the direction of a company will find out that changing the underlying values, perceptions, beliefs and expectations is extremely difficult, if not next to impossible. As Weick (1979) puts it, an organization does not have a culture, it is a culture – shared values and norms are what make an organization. And just as it is difficult to change someone's identity, it is difficult to change an organization's culture (e.g. Schein, 1993; Smircich and Stubbart, 1985). Moreover, as most top managers rise through the ranks to the upper echelons, they themselves are a product of the existing organizational culture. Changing your own culture is like pulling yourself up by your own bootstraps – a great trick, too bad that nobody can do it.

In Chapters 5 and 6, a related argument was put forward, as part of the resource-based view of the firm. One of the basic assumptions of the resource-based view is that building up competences is an arduous task, requiring a relatively long period of time. Learning is a slow process under the best of circumstances, but even more difficult if learning one thing means unlearning something else. The stronger the existing cognitive maps (knowledge), routines (capabilities) and disposition (attitude), the more challenging it is to 'teach an old dog new tricks'. The leader's power to direct and speed up such processes, it was argued, is quite limited (e.g. Barney, 1991; Leonard-Barton, 1995).

Taken together, the political, cultural and learning dynamics leave top managers with relatively little direct power over the system they want to steer. Generally, they can react to this limited ability to control in one of two basic ways – they can squeeze tighter or let go. Many managers follow the first route, desperately trying to acquire more power, to gain a tighter grip on the organization, in the vain attempt to become the heroic leader of popular legend. Such a move to accumulate more power commonly results in actions to assert control, including stricter reporting structures, more disciplined accountability, harsher punishment for non-conformists and a shakeout among managers. In this manner, control comes to mean restriction, subordination or even subjugation. Yet, such a step towards authoritarian management will still not bring managers very much further towards having a lasting impact on organizational development.

The alternative route is for managers to accept that they cannot, but also should not try to, tightly control the organization. As they cannot really control organizational dynamics, all heavy-handed control approaches will have little more result than making the organization an unpleasant and oppressive place to work. If managers emphasize control, all they will do is run the risk of killing the organization's ability to innovate and learn. Innovation and learning are very difficult to control, especially the business innovation and learning happening outside of R&D labs. Much of this innovation and learning is sparked by organizational members, out in the markets or on the work floor, questioning the status quo. New ideas often start 'in the margins' of the organization and grow due to the room granted to offbeat opinions. Fragile new initiatives often need to be championed by their owners lower down in the hierarchy and only survive if there is a tolerance for unintended 'misfits' in the organization's portfolio of activities. Only if employees have a certain measure of freedom and are willing to act as intrapreneurs, will learning and innovation be an integral part of the organization's functioning (e.g. Amabile, 1998; Quinn, 1985).

In other words, if managers move beyond their instinctive desire for control and recognize the creative and entrepreneurial potential of self-organization, they will not bemoan their lack of control. They will see that a certain level of organizational chaos can create the conditions for development (e.g. Levy, 1994; Stacey, 1993a). According to the organizational dynamics perspective, the task for managers is to use their limited powers to facilitate self-organization (e.g. Beinhocker, 1999; Wheatley and Kellner-Rogers, 1996). Managers can encourage empowerment, stimulate learning and innovation, bring people together, take away bureaucratic hurdles – all very much like the approach by most governments in market economies, who try to establish conditions conducive to entrepreneurial behavior instead of trying to control economic activity. Managers' most important task is to ensure that the 'invisible hand of self-organization' functions properly, and does not lead to 'out-of-hand disorganization'.

So, does the manager matter? Yes, but in a different sense than is usually assumed. The manager cannot shape the organization – it shapes itself. Organizational developments are the result of complex internal dynamics, which can be summarized as strategy follows organization, instead of the other way around. Managers can facilitate processes of self-organization and thus indirectly influence the direction of development, but at the same time managers are also shaped by the organization they are in.

EXHIBIT 9.3 THE ORGANIZATIONAL DYNAMICS PERSPECTIVE

SEMCO: PUMPING SUCCESS

When Ricardo Semler took over his father's pump-making business in 1980, Semco was a US$4 million company, focused on the domestic Brazilian market, and heading for bankruptcy in a severe recession that was to last for most of the decade. By 2003, Semco had expanded beyond pumps to dishwashers, digital scanners, cooling units and mixers for anything from bubble gum to rocket fuel, operating as a federation of ten businesses, with revenues totaling US$160 million and about 3000 employees. While a fascinating business success, Semco's turnaround is all the more interesting because it was achieved without the leadership of a charismatic CEO – actually, it was achieved without having a CEO at all.

Semco has no traditional organizational hierarchy for decision-making and control. Major decisions affecting the entire organization, such as the purchase of a new plant site or an acquisition, are put to a democratic vote, while other decisions are taken consensually by all employees involved. There are no internal audit groups, no controls on travel expenses, and inventory and storage rooms remain unlocked – but all information is made available to everyone, encouraging self-control. According to Semler: 'Freedom is no easy thing. It does not make life carefree – because it introduces difficult choices.' To stimulate infor-

mation exchange, the offices have no walls and all memos must be kept to one page, without exception. Furthermore, everyone is trained to read financial statements, and everybody knows the profit and loss statements of the company and their business unit.

The alternative organizational configuration of Semco is made up of four concentric circles. The innermost circle consists of six Counselors, who serve as the executive team and take turns as chairperson every six months. Despite being the 90% owner of the company, Semler is only one of these six. Around the Counselors is a circle of Partners, who act as business unit managers. Around them is a circle of Coordinators, who function as first-line supervisors. Everybody else is in the fourth circle, and is called Associate. Additionally there are 'Nucleuses of Technology Innovation', which are 'no-boss' temporary project teams who are freed from their day-to-day work in order to focus on some kind of business improvement project, a new product, a cost reduction program, a new business plan or the like.

The members of Semco decide among themselves what their pay will be. The amount is made transparent to all others by regular participation in salary surveys, thus everybody knows what the pay is of everyone else. Furthermore, every member is part of the company-wide profit sharing program that pays out 23% of a business unit's profits per quarter to the employees. In fact, the payout ratio of 23% was also decided by the employees. Members of a Nucleus of Technology Innovation receive royalties on the achievements of their projects.

At any given moment, who belongs to the Semco company and who doesn't, can be rather fuzzy. Semler explains:

When we walk through our plants, we rarely even know who works for us. Some of the people in the factory are full-time employees; some work for us part-time; some work for themselves and supply Semco with components or services; some work for themselves under contract to outside companies (even competitors); and some of them work for each other. We could decide to find out which is which and who is who, but . . . we think it is all useless information.

As for strategy, Semco has no grand design. Semler readily admits that he has no idea what the company will be making in ten years time: 'I think that strategic planning and vision are often barriers to suc-

cess.' Semco's approach is largely to let strategy emerge on the basis of opportunities identified by employees close to the market. Where new initiatives can muster enough support among colleagues, they are awarded more time and money to bring them to fruition. In this way, Semco can make the best possible use of the engagement and entrepreneurship of its employees.

Summing up the Semco philosophy, Semler told the *Financial Times*:

At Semco, the basic question we work on is: how do you get people to come to work on a gray Monday morning? This is the only parameter we care about, which is a 100% motivation issue. Everything else – quality, profits, growth – will fall into place, if enough people are interested in coming to work on Monday morning.

Sources: Semler (1994); *Financial Times*, May 15 1997; *Guardian Unlimited*, April 17 2003; Semler (1995, 2003).

TOWARDS A SYNTHESIS

An institution is the lengthened shadow of one man.

Ralph Waldo Emerson (1803–1882);
American essayist and poet

Chaos often breeds life, when order breeds habit.

Henry Brooks Adams (1838–1919);
American writer and historian

So, how should organizational development be encouraged? Can the top management of a firm shape the organization to fit with their intended strategy or does the organizational context determine the strategy that is actually followed? And should top management strive to have a tight grip on the organization, or should they leave plenty of room for self-organization?

As before, views differ strongly, both in business practice and in academia; not only in the field of strategy, but also in neighboring fields such as organizational behavior, human resource management and innovation management. And not only in the management sciences, but more broadly in the humanities, including sociology, economics, political science and psychology as well. The economic sociologist Duesenberry once remarked that 'economics is all about how people make choices; sociology is all about how they don't have any choices to make'. Although half in jest, his comment does ring true. Much of the literature within the field of economics assumes that people in organizations can freely make choices and have the power to shape their strategy, while possible restraints on their freedom usually come from the environment. Sociological literature, but also psychological and political science work, often features the limitations on individual's freedom. These different disciplinary inclinations are not absolute, but can be clearly recognized in the debate.

With so many conflicting views and incompatible prescriptions on the issue of organizational development, it is again up to each individual strategist to form their own opinion on how best to deal with the paradox of control and chaos. In Table 9.1 the main arguments of the two opposite poles in this debate have been summarized. As before, the challenge for managers is not to choose one over the other, but to find a synthesis that is the most powerful given their specific circumstances.

TABLE 9.1　Organizational leadership versus organizational dynamics perspective

	Organizational leadership perspective	Organizational dynamics perspective
Emphasis on	Control over chaos	Chaos over control
Organizational development	Controllable creation process	Uncontrollable evolutionary process
Development metaphor	The visible hand	The invisible hand
Development direction	Top-down, imposed organization	Bottom-up, self-organization
Decision-making	Authoritarian (rule of the few)	Democratic (rule of the many)
Change process	Leader shapes new behavior	New behavior emerges from interactions
Change determinants	Leader's vision and skill	Political, cultural and learning dynamics
Organizational malleability	High, fast	Low, slow
Development driver	Organization follows strategy	Strategy follows organization
Normative implication	Strategize, then organize	Strategizing and organizing intertwined

FURTHER READING

So long as men worship the Caesars and Napoleons, Caesars and Napoleons will duly arise and make them miserable.
Aldous Huxley (1894–1963); English novelist

Readers interested in pursuing the topics of leadership and organizational dynamics have a rich body of literature from which to choose. An excellent overview of the subject is provided by Sydney Finkelstein and Donald Hambrick, in their book *Strategic Leadership: Top Executives and Their Effects on Organizations*. Also recommended as overview of the leadership literature is Yukl's *Leadership in Organizations*. In the category of more academically oriented works, the special issue of *Organization Studies* entitled 'Interpreting Organizational Leadership', and edited by Susan Schneider gives a rich spectrum of ideas. The same is true for the special edition of the *Strategic Management Journal* entitled 'Strategic Leadership', and edited by Donald Hambrick.

For more specific readings taking an organizational leadership perspective, the classics with which to start are John Kotter's *The General Managers* and Gordon Donaldson and Jay Lorsch's *Decision Making at the Top: The Shaping of Strategic Direction*. Good follow-up readings are the book by Warren Bennis, *On Becoming a Leader*, and the book by Burt Nanus, *Visionary Leadership: Creating a Compelling Sense of Direction for Your Organization*. For leadership literature further away from the 'control pole', readers are advised to turn to Peter Senge's book *The Fifth Discipline: The Art and Practice of the Learning Organization* and Edward Schein's *Organizational Culture and Leadership*. The book by Henry Sims and Peter Lorenzi, *The New Leadership Paradigm: Social Learning and Cognition in Organizations*, is also a challenging book, but not easy to read.

For a critical reaction to the leadership literature, Manfred Kets de Vries has many excellent contributions. His article 'The Leadership Mystique' is very good, as are his books with Danny Miller, entitled *The Neurotic Organization* and *Unstable at the Top*. Miller also has many thought-provoking works to his name, of which *The Icarus Paradox: How Excellent Companies Can Bring About Their Own Downfall* is highly recommended. In the more academic literature, stimulating commentaries are given in the articles 'The Romance of Leadership' by James Meindl, S. Ehrlich and J. Dukerich, and in 'The Ambiguity of Leadership', by Jeffrey Pfeffer. A more recent book by Pfeffer, together with Robert Sutton, is *The Knowing-Doing Gap*, which is quite accessible and a very interesting view on organizational dynamics.

For a good reading highlighting the importance of organizational dynamics for both strategy process and strategy content, Ralph Stacey's book *Strategic Management and Organizational Dynamics* is a good place to start. Gerry Johnson's *Strategic Change and the Management Process* also provides provocative ideas about the relationship between strategy and the organizational context. Richard Pascale's *Managing on the Edge: How Successful Companies Use Conflict to Stay Ahead* is also stimulating reading. Finally, for the academically more adventurous, Joel Baum and Jitendra Singh's volume, *Evolutionary Dynamics of Organizations*, gives plenty of food for thought, as does Howard Aldrich's recent *Organizations Evolving*.

THE INTERNATIONAL CONTEXT

There never were, since the creation of the world, two cases exactly parallel.

Philip Dormer Stanhope (1694–1773); English Secretary of State

INTRODUCTION

As firms move out of their domestic market on to the international stage, they are faced with differing business arenas. The nations they expand to can vary with regard to consumer behavior, language, legal system, technological infrastructure, business culture, educational system, labor relations, political ideology, distribution structures and fiscal regime, to name just a few. At face value, the plurality of the international context can seem daunting. Yet, the question is how important the international differences are for firms operating across borders. Do firms need to adapt to the international diversity encountered, or can they find ways of overcoming the constraints imposed by distinct national systems, structures and behaviors? This matter of understanding and dealing with international variety is one of the key topics for managers operating across borders.

A second question with regard to the international context is that of international linkages – to what extent do events in one country have an impact on what happens in other countries? When a number of nations are tightly linked to one another in a particular area, this is referred to as a case of international integration. If, on the other hand, there are very weak links between developments in one country and developments elsewhere, this is referred to as a situation of international fragmentation. The question for managers is how tightly linked nations around the world actually are. Countries might be quite different, yet developments in one nation might significantly influence developments elsewhere. For instance, if interest rates rise in the United States, central bankers in most other countries cannot ignore this. If the price of oil goes down on the spot market in Rotterdam, this will have a 'spill over effect' towards most other nations. And if a breakthrough chip technology is developed in Taiwan, this will send a shockwave through the computer industry around the world. If nations are highly integrated, the manager must view all countries as part of the same system – as squares on a chessboard, not to be judged in isolation.

When looking at the subjects of international variety and linkages, it is also important to know in which direction they have been moving, and will develop further, over time. Where a development towards lower international variety and tighter international linkages on a worldwide scale can be witnessed, a process of globalization is at play. Where a movement towards more international variety and a loosening of international linkages is apparent, a process of localization is taking place.

For managers operating in more than one nation, it is vital to understand the nature of the international context. Have their businesses been globalizing or localizing, and what can be expected in future? Answers to these questions should guide strategizing managers in choosing which countries to be active in and how to manage their activities across borders. Taken together, these international context questions constitute the issue of international configuration, and will be the focus of the further discussion in this chapter.

THE ISSUE OF INTERNATIONAL CONFIGURATION

How a firm configures its activities across borders is largely dependent on how it deals with the fundamental tension between the opposite demands of globalization and localization. To understand these forces, pulling the organization in contrary directions, it is first necessary to further define them. Globalization and localization are terms used by many, but explained by few. This lack of uniform definition often leads to an unfocused debate, as different people employ the same terms, but actually refer to different phenomena. Therefore, this discussion will start with a clarification of the concepts of globalization and localization. Subsequently, attention will turn to the two central questions facing the international manager: which countries should the firm be active in and how should this array of international activities be managed? This first question, of deciding on which geographic areas the organization should be involved in, is the issue of international composition. The second question, of deciding on the organizational structure and systems needed to run the multi-country activities, is the issue of international management.

Dimensions of globalization

Clearly, globalization refers to the process of becoming more global. But what is global? Although there is no agreement on a single definition, most writers use the term to refer to one or more of the following elements (see Figure 10.1):

■ Worldwide scope. 'Global' can simply be used as a geographic term. A firm with operations around the world can be labeled a global company, to distinguish it from firms that are local (not international) or regional in scope. In such a case, the term 'global' is primarily intended to describe the *spatial* dimension – the broadest possible international scope is to be global. When this definition of global is employed, globalization is the process of international expansion on a worldwide scale (e.g. Patel and Pavitt, 1991).

■ Worldwide similarity. 'Global' can also refer to homogeneity around the world. For instance, if a company decides to sell the same product in all of its international markets, it is often referred to as a global product, as opposed to a locally tailored product. In such a case, the term 'global' is primarily intended to describe the *variance* dimension – the ultimate level of worldwide similarity is to be global. When this definition of global is employed, globalization is the process of declining international variety (e.g. Levitt, 1983).

■ Worldwide integration. 'Global' can also refer to the world as one tightly linked system. For instance, a global market can be said to exist if events in one country are significantly impacted by events in other geographic markets. This as opposed to local markets, where price levels, competition, demand and fashions are hardly influenced by

FIGURE 10.1 Internationalization and globalization of the firm

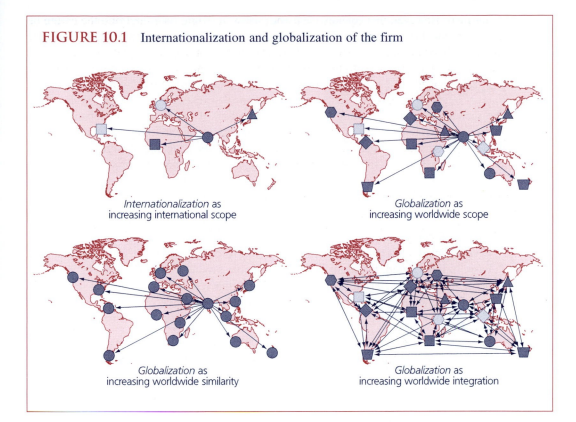

Internationalization as
increasing international scope

Globalization as
increasing worldwide scope

Globalization as
increasing worldwide similarity

Globalization as
increasing worldwide integration

developments in other nations. In such a case, the term 'global' is primarily intended to describe the *linkages* dimension – the ultimate level of worldwide integration is to be global. When this definition of global is employed, globalization is the process of increasing international interconnectedness (e.g. Porter, 1986).

So, is for example McDonald's a global company? That depends along which of the above three dimensions the company is measured. When judging the international scope of McDonald's, it can be seen that the company is globalizing, but far from global. The company operates in approximately half the countries in the world, but in many of these only in one or a few large cities. Of McDonald's worldwide revenues, more than half is still earned in the United States. This predominance of the home country is even stronger if the composition of the company's top management is looked at (Ruigrok and Van Tulder, 1995). However, when judging McDonald's along the dimension of international similarity, it is simple to observe that the company is relatively global, as it takes a highly standardized approach to most markets around the world. Although, it should be noted that on some aspects as menu and interior design there is leeway for local adaptation. Finally, when judging McDonald's along the dimension of international integration, the company is only slightly global, as it is not very tightly linked around the world. Some activities are centralized or coordinated, but in general there is relatively little need for concerted action.

As for localization – the opposite of the process of globalization – it is characterized by decreasing international scope, similarity and integration. From the angle of international strategy the most extreme form of localness is when firms operate in one country and there is no similarity or integration between countries (e.g. the hairdressing and driving school businesses). However, this equates local with national, while firms and businesses can be even more local, all the way down to the state/province/department/district and municipal playing fields.

Levels of globalization

The second factor complicating a clear understanding of the concept of globalization is that it is applied to a variety of subjects, while the differences are often not made explicit. Some people discuss globalization as a development in the economy at large, while others debate globalization as something happening to industries, markets, products, technologies, fashions, production, competition and organizations. In general, debates on globalization tend to concentrate on one of three levels of analysis:

- **Globalization of companies.** Some authors focus on the micro level, debating whether individual companies are becoming more global. Issues are the extent to which firms have a global strategy, structure, culture, workforce, management team and resource base. In more detail, the globalization of specific products and value-adding activities is often discussed. Here it is of particular importance to acknowledge that the globalization of one product or activity (e.g. marketing) does not necessarily entail the globalization of all others (e.g. Prahalad and Doz, 1987; Bartlett and Ghoshal, 1987).

- **Globalization of businesses.** Other authors are more concerned with the *meso* level, debating whether particular businesses are becoming more global. Here it is important to distinguish those who emphasize the globalization of markets, as opposed to those accentuating the globalization of industries (see Chapter 5 for this distinction). The issue of globalizing markets has to do with the growing similarity of worldwide customer demand and the growing ease of worldwide product flows (e.g. Levitt, 1983; Douglas and Wind, 1987). For example, the crude oil and foreign currency markets are truly global – the same commodities are traded at the same rates around the world. The markets for accountancy and garbage collection services, on the other hand, are very local – demand differs significantly, there is little cross-border trade and consequently prices vary sharply. The globalization of industries is quite a different issue, as it has to do with the emergence of a set of producers that compete with one another on a worldwide scale (e.g. Prahalad and Doz, 1987; Porter, 1990a, 1990b). So, for instance, the automobile and consumer electronics industries are quite global – the major players in most countries belong to the same set of companies that compete against each other all around the world. Even the accountancy industry is relatively global, even though the markets for accountancy services are very local. On the other hand, the hairdressing and retail banking industries are very local – the competitive scene in each country is relatively uninfluenced by competitive developments elsewhere.

- **Globalization of economies.** Yet other authors take a macro level of analysis, arguing whether or not the world's economies in general are experiencing a convergence trend. Many authors are interested in the macroeconomic dynamics of international integration and its consequences in terms of growth, employment, inflation, productivity, trade and foreign direct investment (e.g. Kay, 1989; Krugman, 1990). Others focus more on the political realities constraining and encouraging globalization (e.g. Klein, 2000; McGrew and Lewis, 1992). Yet others are interested in the underlying dynamics of technological, institutional and organizational convergence (e.g. Dunning, 1986; Kogut, 1993).

Ultimately, the question in this chapter is not only whether economies, businesses and companies are actually globalizing, but also whether these developments are a matter of choice. In other words, is global convergence or continued international diversity an uncontrollable evolutionary development to which firms (and governments) must comply, or can managers actively influence the globalization or localization of their environment?

International composition

An international firm operates in two or more countries. When a firm starts up value-adding activities in yet another country, this process is called internationalization. In Figure 10.2 an overview is presented of the most common forms of internationalization. One of the earliest international growth moves undertaken by firms is to sell their products to foreign buyers, either directly (internet or telephone sales), through a traveling sales-person, or via a local agent or distributor. Such types of export activities are generally less taxing for the organization than the establishment of a foreign sales subsidiary (or sales unit). Serving a foreign market by means of a sales subsidiary often requires a higher level of investment in terms of marketing expenditures, sales force development and after-sales service provision. A firm can also set up a foreign production subsidiary (or 'off-shore' production unit), whose activities are focused on manufacturing goods to be exported back to the firm's other markets. Alternatively, a firm can begin an integrated foreign subsidiary that is responsible for a full range of value-adding activities, including production and sales. In practice, there are many variations to these basic forms of internationalization, depending on the specific value-adding activities carried out in different countries. For example, some subsidiaries have R&D, assembly and marketing their portfolio of activities, while others do not (Birkenshaw and Hood, 1998).

When establishing a foreign subsidiary the internationalizing firm must decide whether to purchase an existing local company (entry by acquisition) or to start from scratch (greenfield entry). In both cases the firm can work independently or by means of a joint

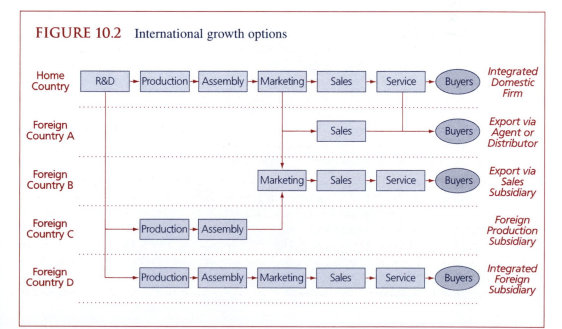

FIGURE 10.2 International growth options

venture with a local player or foreign partner. It is also possible to dispense with the establishment of a subsidiary at all, by networking with local manufacturers, assemblers, sales agents and distributors (as discussed in Chapter 7).

The issue of international composition deals with the question of where the firm wants to have a certain level of involvement. The firm's strategists must decide where to allocate resources, build up activities and try to achieve results. The issue of international composition can be further subdivided into two parts:

- **International scope.** The international composition of the firm depends first of all on the countries selected to do business in. The geographic spectrum covered by the firm is referred to as its international scope. The firm's strategists must decide how many countries they want to be active in, and which countries these should be.

- **International distribution.** The international composition of the firm also depends on how it has distributed its value-adding activities across the countries selected. In some firms all national subsidiaries carry out similar activities and are of comparable size. However, in many firms activities are distributed less symmetrically, with, for example, production, R&D and marketing concentrated in only a few countries (Porter, 1986). Commonly some countries will also contribute much more revenue and profits than others, but these might not be the countries where new investments can best be made. It is the task of the firm's strategists to determine how activities can best be distributed and how resources can best be allocated across the various countries.

Just as a corporation's portfolio of businesses could be visualized by means of a portfolio grid, so too can a business's portfolio of foreign sales markets be displayed using such a matrix. In Figure 10.3 a fictitious example is given of a firm's international sales portfolio using the GE business screen as analysis tool. Instead of industry attractiveness

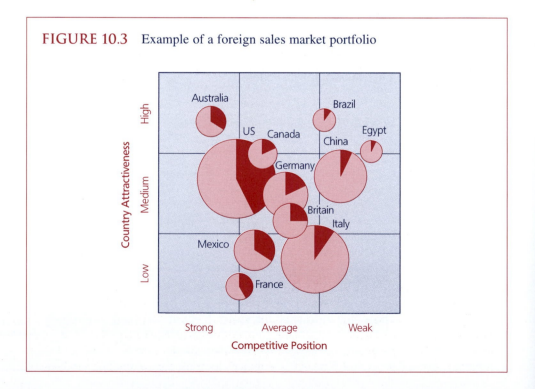

FIGURE 10.3   Example of a foreign sales market portfolio

along the vertical axis, country attractiveness is used, calculating items such as market growth, competitive intensity, buyer power, customer loyalty, government regulation and operating costs. Following a similar logic, firms can also evaluate their international portfolios of, for instance, production locations and R&D facilities.

Deciding which portfolio of countries to be active in, both in terms of international scope and distribution, will largely depend on the strategic motives that have stimulated the firm to enter the international arena in the first place. After all, there must be some good reasons why a firm is willing to disregard the growth opportunities in its home market and to enter into uncertain foreign adventures. There must be some advantages to being international that offset the disadvantages of foreignness and distance. These advantages of having activities in two or more countries – cross-border synergies – will be discussed in more detail, after an account of the second international configuration question, the issue of international management.

International management

A firm operating in two or more countries needs to find some way of organizing itself to deal with its border-spanning nature. As managing across borders is difficult and costly, the simplest solution would be to organize all operations on a country-by-country basis, and to leave all country units as autonomous as possible. Yet, internationalization is only economically rational if 'the international whole is more than the sum of the country parts' (see Chapter 6). In other words, internationalization only makes sense if enough cross-border synergies can be reaped to offset the extra cost of foreignness and distance.

Therefore, the firm needs to have international integration mechanisms to facilitate the realization of cross-border synergies. The three most important integration mechanisms used in international management are:

- Standardization. An easy way to reap cross-border synergies is to do the same thing in each country, without any costly adaptation. Such standardization can be applied to all aspects of the business model (see Chapter 5) – the product offerings, value-adding activities and resources employed. Standardization is particularly important for achieving economies of scale (e.g. Hout, Porter and Rudden, 1982; Levitt, 1983), but can be equally valuable for serving border-crossing clients who want to encounter a predictable offering (e.g. Hamel and Prahalad, 1985; Yip, 1993).

- Coordination. Instead of standardizing products or activities, international firms can also align their varied activities in different countries by means of cross-border coordination. Getting the activities in the various countries aligned is often inspired by the need to serve border-crossing clients in a coordinated manner (e.g. global service level agreements), or to counter these clients' policy of playing off the firm's subsidiaries against one another (e.g. cross-border price shopping). International coordination can be valuable when responding to, or attacking, competitors as well. A coordinated assault on a few markets, financed by the profits from many markets (i.e. cross-subsidization), can sometimes lead to competitive success (Prahalad and Doz, 1987).

- Centralization. Of course, activities within the firm can also be integrated at one central location, either in the firm's home country or elsewhere. Such centralization is often motivated by the drive for economies of scale (e.g. Buckley and Casson, 1985; Dunning, 1981), but might be due to the competitive advantage of a particular country as well. For example, production costs might be much lower, or quality much higher, in a certain part of the world, making it a logical location for centralized production.

Centralization of knowledge intensive activities is sometimes also needed, to guard quality or to ensure faster learning than could be attained with decentralized activities (e.g. Porter, 1990b; Dunning, 1993).

It is up to the firm's strategists to determine the most appropriate level of standardization, coordination and centralization needed to function efficiently and effectively in an international context. The level chosen for each of these three characteristics will largely determine the organizational model adopted by the international firm.

In their seminal research, Bartlett and Ghoshal (1989) distinguish four generic organizational models for international firms, each with its own mix of standardization, coordination and centralization (see Figure 10.4):

■ Decentralized federation. In a decentralized federation, the firm is organized along geographic lines, with each full-scale country subsidiary largely self-sufficient and autonomous from international headquarters in the home country. Few activities are centralized and little is coordinated across borders. The level of standardization is also low, as the country unit is free to adapt itself to the specific circumstances in its national environment. Bartlett and Ghoshal refer to this organizational model as 'multinational'. Another common label is 'multi-domestic' (e.g. Prahalad and Doz, 1987; Stopford and Wells, 1972).

FIGURE 10.4   Generic organizational models for international firms (adapted from Bartlett and Ghoshal,1995)

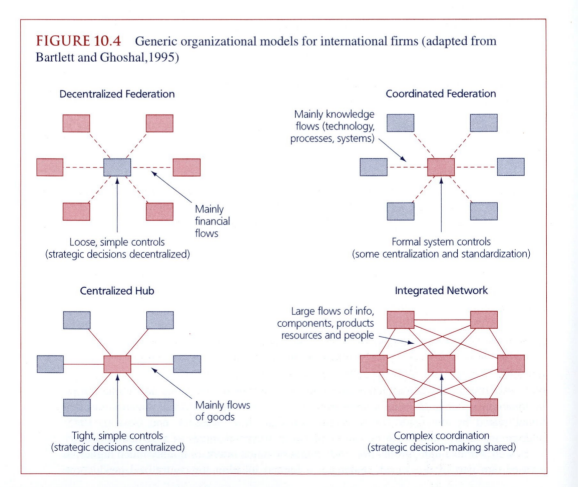

- **Coordinated federation.** In a coordinated federation, the firm is also organized along geographic lines, but the country subsidiaries have a closer relationship with the international headquarters in the home country. Most of the core competences, technologies, processes and products are developed centrally, while other activities are carried out locally. As a consequence, there is some standardization and coordination, requiring some formalized control systems (i.e. planning, budgeting, administration). Another name employed by Bartlett and Ghoshal to refer to this organizational model is 'international'.

- **Centralized hub.** In a centralized hub, national units are relatively unimportant, as all main activities are carried out in the home country. Generally a highly standardized approach is used towards all foreign markets. As centralization and standardization are high, foreign subsidiaries are limited to implementing headquarters' policies in the local markets. Coordination of activities across countries is made easy by the dominance of headquarters. Bartlett and Ghoshal use the term 'global' to describe this organizational model.

- **Integrated network.** In an integrated network, the country subsidiaries have a close relationship with international headquarters, just as in the coordinated federation, but also have a close relationship with each other. Very little is centralized at the international headquarters in the home country, but each national unit can become the worldwide center for a particular competence, technology, process or product. Thus subsidiaries need to coordinate the flow of components, products, knowledge and people between each other. Such a networked organization requires a certain level of standardization to function effectively. Another name used by Bartlett and Ghoshal for this organizational model is 'transnational'.

Which international organizational model is adopted depends strongly on what the corporate strategist wishes to achieve. The preferred international management structure will be largely determined by the type of cross-border synergies that the strategists envisage. This topic of multi-country synergies will be examined more closely in the following section.

THE PARADOX OF GLOBALIZATION AND LOCALIZATION

The axis of the earth sticks out visibly through the center of each and every town or city.

Oliver Wendell Holmes (1809–1894); American physician, poet and essayist

It requires almost no argumentation that internationally operating companies are faced with a tension between treating the world as one market and acknowledging national differences. During the last few decades, achieving a balance between international uniformity and meeting local demands has been the dominant theme in the literature on international management. All researchers have recognized the tension between international standardization and local adaptation. The key question has been whether international firms have the *liberty* to standardize or face the *pressure* to adapt.

However, since the mid-1980s, this standardization-adaptation discussion has progressed significantly as strategy researchers have moved beyond the organizational design question, seeking the underlying strategic motives for standardization and adaptation (e.g. Bartlett and Ghoshal, 1987; Porter, 1986; Prahalad and Doz, 1987). It has been acknowledged that international standardization is not a matter of organizational convenience that companies naturally revert to when the market does not demand local adaptation. Rather, international standardization is a means for achieving cross-border synergies. A firm can achieve cross-border synergies by leveraging resources, integrating activities and aligning product offerings across two or more countries. Creating additional value in this way is the very *raison d'être* of the international firm. If internationalizing companies would fully adapt to local conditions, without leveraging a homegrown quality, they would have no advantage over local firms, while they would be burdened by the extra costs of international business (e.g. overcoming distance and foreignness). Therefore, international companies need to realize at least enough cross-border synergies to compensate for the additional expenses of operating in multiple countries.

Much of the theoretical discourse has focused on the question which cross-border synergies can be achieved on the ultimate, global scale. Most researchers identify various potential opportunities for worldwide synergy, yet recognize the simultaneous demands to meet the specific conditions in each local market (e.g. Dicken, 1992; Yip, 1993). These possibilities for reaping global synergy will be examined first, followed by the countervailing pressures for local responsiveness.

The demand for global synergy

Striving for cross-border synergies on as large a scale as possible can be an opportunity for an international firm to enhance its competitive advantage. However, realizing global synergies is often less an opportunity than a competitive demand. If rival firms have already successfully implemented a global strategy, there can be a severe pressure to also reap the benefits of globalization through standardization, coordination and/or centralization.

There are many different types of cross-border synergies. In accordance with the business model framework described in Chapter 5, these synergies can be organized into three categories: aligning product offerings, integrating activities and leveraging resources (see Figure 10.5).

Synergy by aligning positions.   The first way to create cross-border synergies is to align market positions in the various countries in which the firm operates. Taking a coordinated approach to different national markets can be necessary under two circumstances – namely to provide a concerted cross-border product offering to customers and to stage a concerted cross-border attack on competitors:

- Dealing with cross-border customers. An international firm is ideally placed to offer border-crossing customers an internationally coordinated product and/or service offering. Whether it is for a tourist who wants to have the same hotel arrangements around the world, or for an advertiser who wants to stage a globally coordinated new product introduction, it can be important to have a standardized and coordinated offering across various nations. It might be equally necessary to counter the tactics of customers shopping around various national subsidiaries for the best deals, or to meet the customer's demand to aggregate all global buying via one central account.

- Dealing with cross-border competition. An international firm is also in an ideal position to successfully attack locally oriented rivals, if it does not spread its resources too thinly around the world, but rather focuses on only a few countries at a time. By coordinating

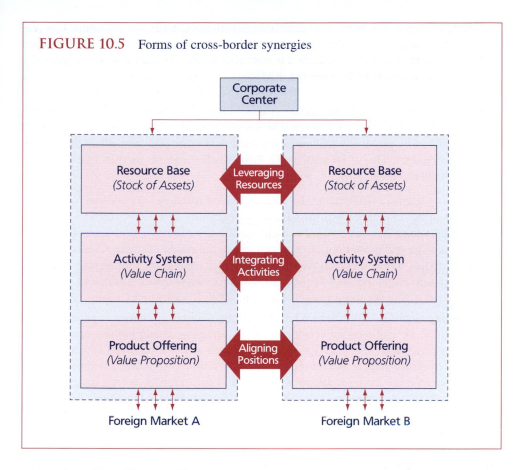

FIGURE 10.5   Forms of cross-border synergies

its competitive efforts and bringing its global power to bear on a few national markets, an international firm can push back or even defeat local rivals country-by-country. Of course, an international company must also have the capability of defending itself against such a globally coordinated attack by a rival international firm.

Synergy by integrating activities.   Cross-border synergies can also be achieved by linking the activity systems of the firm in its various national markets. Integrating the value-creation processes across borders can be useful to realize economies of scale and to make use of the specific competitive advantages of each nation:

■ Reaping scale advantages. Instead of organizing the international firm's activity system on a country-by-country basis, certain activities can be pooled to reap economies of scale. Commonly this means that activities must be centralized at one or a few locations, and that a certain level of product and/or process standardization must be accepted. Economies of scale can be realized for many activities, most notably production, logistics, procurement and R&D. However, scale advantages might be possible for all activities of the firm. Although scale advantages are often pursued by means of centralization, it is often possible to achieve economies by standardizing and coordinating activities across borders (e.g. joint procurement, joint marketing campaigns).

■ Reaping location advantages. For some activities certain locations are much more suited than others, making it attractive to centralize these activities in the countries that possess a particular competitive advantage. A national competitive advantage can consist of inexpensive or specialist local inputs, such as raw materials, energy, physical infrastructure or human resources, but can also be due to the presence of attractive buyers and related industries (Porter, 1990a).

Synergy by leveraging resources.   A third manner in which cross-border synergies can be realized is by sharing resources across national markets. Such resource leveraging can be achieved by physically reallocating resources to other countries where they can be used more productively, or by replicating them so they can be used in many national markets simultaneously:

- Achieving resource reallocation. Instead of leaving resources in countries where they happen to be, international firms have the opportunity to transfer resources to other locations, where they can be used to more benefit. For example, money, machinery and people can be reallocated out of countries where the return on these resources is low, into countries where they can reap a higher return. Managers specializing in market development might be sent to new subsidiaries, while older machinery might be transferred to less advanced markets (Vernon, 1966; Buckley and Casson, 1976).

- Achieving resource replication. While leveraging tangible resources requires physical reallocation or sharing (see reaping scale advantages), intangible resources can be leveraged by means of replication. Intangibles such as knowledge and capabilities can be copied across borders and reused in another country. This allows international companies to leverage their know-how with regard to such aspects as technology, production, marketing, logistics and sales (Kogut and Zander, 1993; Liebeskind, 1996).

For all of these cross-border synergies it holds that the wider the geographic scope, the greater the potential benefit. Where possible, realizing these synergies on a global scale would result in the highest level of value creation.

These opportunities for global synergy represent a strong demand on all companies, both international and domestic. If a company can reap these synergies more quickly and successfully than its competitors, this could result in a strong offensive advantage. If other companies have a head start in capturing these global synergies, the firm must move quickly to catch up. Either way, there is a pressure on companies to seek out opportunities for global synergy and to turn them to their advantage.

The demand for local responsiveness

Yet the pressure to pursue global synergies is only half the equation. Simultaneously, companies must remain attuned to the specific demands of each national market and retain the ability to respond to these particular characteristics in a timely and adequate manner. In other words, firms must have the capability to be responsive to local conditions. If they lose touch with the distinct competitive dynamics in each of their national markets, they might find themselves at a competitive disadvantage compared to more responsive rivals.

While business responsiveness is always important, it becomes all the more pressing when the differences between various national markets are large. The more dissimilar the national markets, the more pressure on the international firm to be attuned to these distinct characteristics. The most important differences between countries include:

- Differences in market structure. Countries can differ significantly with regard to their competitive landscape. For example, in some national markets there are strong local competitors, requiring the international firm to respond differently than in countries where it encounters its 'regular' international rivals. Another difference is that in some countries there are only a few market parties, while in other countries the market is highly fragmented among numerous competitors. There can also be large differences from country to country in the background of competitors – in some countries conglomerates dominate the business scene, while in other countries single business competitors are more frequent.

- Differences in customer needs. Customers in each national market can have needs that are significantly different than the needs exhibited in other countries. The nature of these customer differences can vary from divergent cultural expectations and use circumstances, to incompatible technical systems and languages employed.

- Differences in buying behavior. Not only the customers' needs can differ across countries, but so can their buying behavior. For example, customers can be different with regard to the way they structure buying decisions, the types of information they consider and the relationship they wish to have with their suppliers.

- Differences in substitutes. National markets can also differ with regard to the types of indirect competition that needs to be faced. In some countries, for instance, beer brewers have to deal with wine as an important rival product, while in other markets tea or soft drinks might be the most threatening substitutes.

- Differences in distribution channels. Countries can exhibit remarkable differences in the way their distribution channels work. For example, countries can vary with regard to the kinds of distribution channels available, the number of layers in the distribution structure, their level of sophistication, their degree of concentration and the negotiating power of each player.

- Differences in media structure. National markets can have very different media channels available for marketing communication purposes. In the area of television, for instance, countries vary widely with regard to the number of stations on the air (or on the cable), the types of regulation imposed, the amount of commercial time available, and its cost and effectiveness. In the same way, all other media channels may differ.

- Differences in infrastructure. Many products and services are heavily dependent on the type of infrastructure available in a country. For example, some products rely on a digital telephone system, high-speed motorways, 24-hour convenience stores, or a national healthcare system. Some services require an efficient postal service, poor public transport, electronic banking or cable television.

- Differences in supply structure. If a company has local operations, the differences between countries with regard to their supply structures can also force the company to be more locally responsive. Not only the availability, quality and price of raw materials and components can vary widely between countries, but the same is true for other inputs such as labor, management, capital, facilities, machinery, research, information and services.

- Differences in government regulations. As most government regulations are made on a country-by-country basis, they can differ significantly. Government regulations can affect almost every aspect of a company's operations, as they range from antitrust and product liability legislation, to labor laws and taxation rules.

Responsiveness to these local differences is not only a matter of adaptation. Simple adaptation can be reactive and slow. Being responsive means that the firm has to have the ability to be proactive and fast. As each market develops in a different way and at a different pace, the international firm needs to be able to respond quickly and adequately to remain in tune.

It is clear that international managers cannot afford to neglect being responsive to local conditions. Yet, at the same time, they need to realize cross-border synergies to create additional value. Unfortunately for managers, these two key demands placed on the international firm are, at least to some extent, in conflict with one another. Striving for cross-border synergies on a global scale will interfere with being locally responsive and vice versa. Therefore, the question is how these two conflicting demands can be reconciled – how can the international manager deal with the paradox of globalization and localization?

EXHIBIT 10.1 SHORT CASE

WAL-MART: ANOTHER BRICK IN THE WALL?

Bentonville, Arkansas. Small-town America. On one side of the street is Colleen's Beauty Chalet; on the other is a three-story warehouse with a brick facade. Although rather unremarkable, this is the headquarters of the largest company in the world, Wal-Mart. By reaching revenues exceeding US$246 billion in 2002, Wal-Mart overtook General Motors and Exxon-Mobil, which had previously topped the global sales list. Drawn by rock-bottom prices and friendly service, 100 million customers push their shopping carts through the aisles of Wal-Mart's stores every week. There they can find everything, ranging from food and clothing to hardware, electronics and medicine. At the same time they can do their banking, have their weekend's pictures developed, get their eyes checked and have the oil changed in their car. The company that started as a humble discount retailer in small-town America now operates some 4400 stores in ten countries, employing 1.4 million people, also making it the largest private employer in the world.

Sam Walton and his brother James 'Bud' Walton opened up their first Discount City Store in 1962, selling a broad range of general merchandise and soon started adding new stores to this chain. While most of their American rivals in the 'low price department store' category, like K-Mart and Target, focused on urban areas, Wal-Mart stores were typically located in small and medium-sized towns, where they faced only fragmented competition and profited from lower operating costs. As the Walton brothers offered prices equal to, or lower than, prices in nearby cities, this made them very popular among local shoppers. Sam Walton, who died in 1992, was an ambitious man: whenever his wife pressed him to stop building new stores, his answer was always 'just one more, dear'. To keep on growing, Wal-Mart eventually broadened beyond its rural base, expanding into metropolitan areas. Wal-Mart also expanded into grocery retailing, by creating Wal-Mart Supercenters, which combine the inventories of a discount store with a full-line supermarket. Furthermore, Wal-Mart set up a chain of membership-based warehouse stores focused on bulk sales, called Sam's Clubs.

By the beginning of the 1990s Wal-Mart had become the largest retailer in the United States, and started to look to foreign markets to sustain the 30% annual growth rate that it had averaged throughout the 1980s. Not only capital markets had come to expect this pace of growth, but so did Wal-Mart's employees, many of whom have significant amounts of shares through the company's stock purchase plan. The first step abroad was into Mexico in 1991, where the company started a 50–50 joint venture with

Mexico's largest retailer, Cifra, and then to Puerto Rico in 1992. The following moves showed that Wal-Mart wanted to have the large markets in the Americas as its initial international focus – in 1994 a 60–40 joint venture was established with Lojas Americana in Brazil, followed later in the year by the acquisition and rebranding of 122 Woolco stores in Canada, and a greenfield entry into Argentina in 1995. By 1996 Wal-Mart felt confident enough to shift its expansion focus to Asia, first entering China, and in 1998 South Korea, both by means of joint ventures with local players. To the surprise of many, Wal-Mart also signaled that it wanted to break into the more mature European markets, acquiring the 21-store Wertkauf chain in Germany in 1998, quickly followed up by the purchase of 74 German Interspar grocery stores in 1999. In the same year Wal-Mart rolled into Britain, taking over the 229-outlet ASDA supermarket group. After a short pause, Wal-Mart again surprised many by taking a minority stake in the Japanese retailer Seiyu in 2002, with the option of increasing its stake to 66.7% before 2008. By the end of 2002 Wal-Mart had more than 1200 stores outside of the United States, employing 300 000 people and generating revenues exceeding US$35 billion. It also had plans to invest about US$2 billion in 2003 to renovate existing stores abroad and to open about 130 new ones.

In this international expansion, Wal-Mart has attempted to replicate the competitive advantages it had already developed in its home market. At the heart of Wal-Mart's success has been its enormous bargaining power with multinational suppliers, which has helped it to sell branded products at 'everyday low prices', undercutting all other discount retailers. But there is much more to the Wal-Mart business model than buying and selling cheaply. On the buying side, Wal-Mart requires vendors to hook-up to its supply chain management system, to keep order entry and processing costs low, while keeping stock buffers in the supply chain to a bare minimum. Most merchandise is then shipped to Wal-Mart's advanced distribution centers, which have been tactically placed to be able to serve between 150 and 200 stores within a day's drive. These highly automated distribution centers operate 24 hours per day, using cross-docking techniques, whereby goods received at one end are quickly used to fill orders at the other. Wal-Mart's own fleet of trucks then supply the stores. This distribution and logistics infrastructure saves Wal-Mart transportation costs (only full truck loads are sent), while still ensuring that all the shelves are stocked, with a minimum of back-room inventory. At the same time, the sales and inventory data per store are analyzed to understand trends, to anticipate growing needs and to avoid being stuck with slow-moving stocks. Furthermore, Wal-Mart is known for having a dedicated and highly productive workforce that provides outstanding customer service. It achieves this loyalty and effectiveness by such policies as profit sharing, incentive bonuses, performance-based promotion from within and team building.

Yet, from the beginning of its international expansion the question has been whether the Wal-Mart formula is exportable to all countries around the world. According to Craig Herkert, Chief of Operations of Wal-Mart International, there can be no doubt: 'Every day low prices, quality assortment and exceptional service are Wal-Mart principles that transcend borders, language and cultural differences.' Many analysts agree, pointing to Wal-Mart's many successes so far in transplanting its corporate DNA to other nations. In Canada, for instance, Wal-Mart was able to quickly turn around the acquired Woolco chain, increasing sales per square foot three-fold in only three years and increasing market share from roughly 20% to over 50%, making them the largest retailer in the country, with more than 200 stores. In Mexico, Wal-Mex operates approximately 600 stores, making them the largest retailer and private employer around. As one local put it, 'this idea that the customer comes first is a great gringo strategy'.

In entering foreign markets, Wal-Mart has been cautious not to bluntly apply its US store formats and range of merchandise. For example, in China the company experimented with a number of different store sizes (supercenters and smaller satellite stores) and added a range of local delicacies to the cooked food section. It also quickly became clear to the company that you can't sell electric stoves to Mexicans (they cook with natural gas), golf clubs to Brazilians (too few people are rich enough to play) or tenderized T-bone steaks to Argentineans (they prefer specially-cut rump steaks). Yet, the thrust of Wal-Mart's approach has been to 'standardize unless'. Mexicans have been turned in to avid bagel eaters, while donuts have been a runaway success in China. As a *Newsweek* reporter put it, 'the Wal-Mart effect is already homogenizing global consumer tastes. Sam Walton built his chain on the idea that you could sell the same stuff everywhere, and major Wal-Mart suppliers such as Proctor & Gamble and Heinz now often deliver the same sauces and soaps to Berlin, Mexico City and Houston.'

However, Wal-Mart's internationalization track record is not all fame and glory. Take its operations in Germany, where since its entry in 1997 the firm has suffered five consecutive years of negative results, losing US$100–200 million per year on sales of about US$3 billion. The first blow was that Wal-Mart encountered much stiffer competition than expected from another global retailing chain, Metro, which was on its home-turf, but equally from tough local chains such as Aldi and Lidl, who were trying to gain a larger share of a stagnant market with low prices and no-frills service. Moreover, the German managers running

Wertkauf and Interspar were not amused by American 'mentors' telling them how to run their business when they didn't even speak German or know the German market. To make things worse, suppliers did not take kindly to being forced to switch to a new supply system and to send merchandise to Wal-Mart's new centralized warehouses, leaving Wal-Mart's shelves regularly empty. To start exerting pressure on suppliers, Wal-Mart would need to triple its market share to 6% and double the number of stores, but to their despair they have found that regulations protecting small neighborhood stores can add five or more years to the launching of a new hypermarket. Other rules are just as limiting, including store closing hours and labor laws. Wal-Mart also collided with fair-competition regulators, who forced them to raise prices on milk, butter and some other staples, which it was selling below cost. Top management had to concede they underestimated the challenge: 'We just walked in and said "we're going to lower prices, we're going to add people to the stores and we're going to remodel the stores, because inherently, that's correct", and it wasn't', Wal-Mart's CEO, Lee Scott, admitted.

To improve its international performance, Scott hired John Menzer as chief of Wal-Mart's International Division in 2000. Menzer hired a German as country head and delegated more authority in buying, logistics, building design and other operational decisions, not only in Germany, but across the board, cutting the international staff in Bentonville from 450 to less than 150 people. 'We could get very specific on what should be on an end cap [a store display at the end of an aisle] ... I think we've matured', says Scott. In Germany, Wal-Mart is working with suppliers to boost centralized distribution efforts. Instead of the expensive renovations to 'Walmartize' 24 stores in 2000, the company switched to more modest facelifts and opened two new stores in 2001, instead of the intended 50.

Says Menzer: 'We set ourselves back a few years, and now we're rebounding.'

Others are not convinced, wondering whether Wal-Mart's internationalization has not hit a brick wall: 'We don't see Wal-Mart as a threat anymore', says Hong Sun Sang of E-Mart, a 35-store chain in South Korea, indicating that Wal-Mart's 'headquarters knows best' mind-set is their Achilles' heel. With few top managers that aren't American and few people around that speak more than one language, critics point out that it will be difficult for Wal-Mart to ever become more than a US company with an international division. Moreover, critics argue that Wal-Mart might be able to enter less developed retailing markets like China, but are in for trouble in mature markets such as Europe and Japan. And even in China, Wal-Mart will need to become more Chinese to withstand the pressure of copycat competitors, while at the same time being up against more experienced international competitors such as Carrefour, Tesco, Ahold and Metro.

As Wal-Mart wants to keep up its pace of international expansion, a key question for Scott and Menzer is where the 'Wal-Martians' should land next – what should be the next brick in the wall? But just as important is the question of how the company should manage itself internationally, to gain a strong competitive position in each country of operation. Despite all international problems, both inside and outside the company, one thing was clear to Scott: 'The chances this company has to grow are as big as it ever had in the past.' If Sam Walton were still around, he certainly would agree.

Sources: *Business Week*, September 3 2001; *Newsweek*, May 20 2002; *Fortune*, May 13 2002; Wal-Mart Annual Report 2002; Govindarajan and Gupta, 1999; www.walmartstores.com.

PERSPECTIVES ON THE INTERNATIONAL CONTEXT

Nothing is more dangerous than an idea, when you have only one idea.

Alain (Emile-Auguste Chartier) (1868–1951); French poet and philosopher

When doing business in an international context, it is generally accepted that the challenge for firms is to strive for cross-border synergies, while simultaneously being responsive to the local conditions. It is acknowledged that international managers need to weigh the specific characteristics of their business when reconciling the paradox of globalization and localization – some businesses are currently more suited for a global approach than others. Where opinions start to diverge is on the question of which businesses will become more global, or can be made more global, in the near future. To some managers it is evident that countries are rapidly becoming increasingly similar and more closely interrelated. To them globalization is already far advanced and will continue into the future, wiping out the importance of nations as it progresses. Therefore, they argue that it is wise to anticipate, and even encourage, a 'nationless' world, by focusing on global synergies over local responsiveness. Other managers, however, are more skeptical about the speed and impact of globalization. In their view, much so-called globalization is quite superficial, while at a deeper level important international differences are not quickly changing and cross-border integration is moving very slowly. They also note that there are significant counter-currents creating more international variety, with the potential of loosening international linkages.

Therefore, wise managers should remain highly responsive to the complex variety and fragmentation that characterizes our world, while only carefully seeking out selected cross-border synergy opportunities.

These differing opinions among international strategists are reflected in differing views in the strategic management literature. While there is a wide spectrum of positions on the question of how the international context will develop, here the two opposite poles in the debate will be identified and discussed. On the one side of the spectrum, there are the managers who believe that globalization is bringing Lennon's dream of the 'world living as one' closer and closer. This point of view is called the 'global convergence perspective'. At the other end of the spectrum are the managers who believe that deep-rooted local differences will continue to force firms to 'do in Rome as the Romans do'. This point of view is referred to as the 'international diversity perspective'.

The global convergence perspective

 According to proponents of the global convergence perspective, the growing similarity and integration of the world can be argued by pointing to extensive economic statistics, showing significant rises in foreign direct investment and international trade. Yet, it is simpler to observe things directly around you. For instance, are you wearing clothing unique to your country, or could you mingle in an international crowd without standing out? Is the television you watch, the vehicle you drive, the telephone you use and the timepiece you wear specific to your nation, or based on the same technology and even produced by the same companies as those in other countries? Is the music you listen to made by local bands, unknown outside your country, or is this music equally popular abroad? Is the food you eat unique to your region, or is even this served in other countries? Now compare your answers to what your parents would have answered 30 years ago – the difference is due to global convergence.

Global convergence, it is argued, is largely driven by the ease, low cost and frequency of international communication, transport and travel. This has diminished the importance of distance. In the past world of large distances, interactions between countries were few and international differences could develop in relative isolation. But the victory of technology over distance has created a 'global village', in which goods, services and ideas are easily exchanged, new developments spread quickly and the 'best practices' of one nation are rapidly copied in others. Once individuals and organizations interact with one another as if no geographic distances exist, an unstoppable process towards cultural, political, technological and economic convergence is set in motion – countries will become more closely linked to one another and local differences will be superseded by new global norms.

Of course, in the short run there will still be international differences and nations will not be fully integrated into a 'world without borders'. Managers taking a global convergence perspective acknowledge that such fundamental and wide-ranging changes take time. There are numerous sources of inertia – e.g. vested interests, commitment to existing systems, emotional attachment to current habits and fear of change. The same type of change inhibitors could be witnessed during the industrial revolution, as well. Yet, these change inhibitors can only slow the pace of global convergence, not reverse its direction – the momentum caused by the shrinking of distance can only be braked, but not stopped. Therefore, firms thinking further than the short term, should not let themselves be guided too much by current international diversity, but rather by the emerging global reality (Ohmae, 1990).

For individual firms, global convergence is changing the rules of the competitive game. While in the past most countries had their own distinct characteristics, pressuring firms to be locally responsive, now growing similarity offers enormous opportunities for leveraging resources and sharing activities across borders – e.g. production can be standardized to save costs, new product development can be carried out on an international scale to reduce the total investments required, and marketing knowledge can easily be exchanged to avoid reinventing the wheel in each country. Simultaneously, international integration has made it much easier to centralize production in large-scale facilities at the most attractive locations and to supply world markets from there, unrestrained by international borders. In the same manner, all types of activities, such as R&D, marketing, sales and procurement, can be centralized to profit from worldwide economies of scale.

An equally important aspect of international integration is that suppliers, buyers and competitors can also increasingly operate as if there are no borders. The ability of buyers to shop around internationally makes the world one global market, in which global bargaining power is very important. The ability of suppliers and competitors to reap global economies of scale and sell everywhere around the world creates global industries, in which competition takes place on a worldwide stage, instead of in each nation separately. To deal with such global industries and global markets, the firm must be able to align its market activities across nations.

These demands of standardization, centralization and coordination require a global firm, with a strong center responsible for the global strategy, instead of a federation of autonomous national subsidiaries focused on being responsive to their local circumstances. According to proponents of the global convergence perspective, such global organizations, or 'centralized hubs' (Bartlett and Ghoshal, 1995), will become increasingly predominant over time. And as more companies switch to a global strategy and a global organizational form, this will in turn speed up the general process of globalization. By operating in a global fashion, these firms will actually contribute to a further decrease of international variety and fragmentation. In other words, globalizing companies are both the consequence and a major driver of further global convergence.

EXHIBIT 10.2 THE GLOBAL CONVERGENCE PERSPECTIVE

SIX CONTINENTS: 'THE WORLD'S MOST GLOBAL HOTEL GROUP'

In the summer of 1951, Kemmons Wilson, the founder of Holiday Inn, took his family on 'the road trip that changed the world'. Unable to find lodgings for his family at an affordable price, Wilson decided to enter the hotel business himself. Now, some 50 years later, more travelers have stayed at a Holiday Inn than at any other hotel chain, making it the most recognized name in mid-range lodging around the world. Together with the luxurious InterContinental hotel chain and the business-class Crowne Plaza, Holiday Inn is now part of the Six

Continents hotel group, which owns 3300 hotels in some 100 countries, selling 28 million hotel nights per year. 'Six Continents is a name which emphasizes the global spread of the company', according to Tim Clarke, chief executive of Six Continents Holding. Yet, worldwide scope is not the only thing that makes the hotel group global in character.

The distinct policy of Six Continents Hotels is that its ethos, culture and services should transcend national boundaries. With the mission of 'building the world's preferred places to meet, relax, and dream', Six Continents wants to offer its guests the same experience irrespective of the continent that they happen to be on. 'Our aim is to make our hotels the preferred choice of our guests, so that they return again and again, finding exactly the same level of service and the amenities they want, wherever they are', says Thomas Oliver, chairman and CEO of Six Continents Hotels. To achieve this level of conformity every hotel goes through the same service quality award program – 'our Quality Excellence Award sets the standard for all Six Continents hotels around the world', according to the Annual Report 2001. Guests can also make use of the global reservation system, Holidex, become members of the global loyalty program, Priority Club, and watch the same television programs around the world, provided by a global uniform broadcasting platform.

Behind the scenes, the company's global offerings are complemented by an impressive global infrastructure, managed from the company's headquarters in Atlanta and London. For instance, all Six Continents hotels make use of the same property management system, OPERA, reap the benefits of the corporation's alliances with product and service providers, and are able to make use of procurement systems that allow large-scale purchasing around the world. Marketing is often executed on a global scale as well. For instance, when the InterContinental in Hong Kong was refurbished, hotels such as the ones in Beirut, Chicago, London, New York, São Paulo and Tokyo had to join in for a fix up launch, supported by a US$25 million marketing campaign around the world. Taken together, this level of international service standardization and back-office coordination and centralization seems to justify Six Continents' claim to be the 'most global hotel group in the world'.

Sources: *Financial Times*, November 8 2002; Annual Report 2001; www.6c.com.

The international diversity perspective

To managers taking an international diversity perspective, the 'brave new world' outlined in the previous sub-section is largely science fiction. People around the world might be sporting a Swatch or a Rolex, munching Big Macs and drinking Coke, while sitting in their Toyota or Nissan, but to conclude that these are symptoms of global convergence is a leap of faith. Of course, there are some brand names and products more or less standardized around the world, and their numbers might actually be increasing. The question is whether these manufacturers are globalizing to meet increasing worldwide similarity, or whether they are actually finally utilizing the similarities between countries that have always existed. The actual level of international variety may really be quite consistent.

It is particularly important to recognize in which respects countries remain different. For instance, the world might be drinking the same soft drinks, but they are probably doing it in different places, at different times, under different circumstances and for different reasons in each country. The product might be standardized worldwide, but the cultural norms and values that influence its purchase and use remain diverse across countries. According to proponents of the international diversity perspective, it is precisely these fundamental aspects of culture that turn out to be extremely stable over time – habits change slowly, but cultural norms and values are outright rigid. Producers might be lucky to find one product that fits in with such cultural diversity, but it would be foolish to interpret this as worldwide cultural convergence.

Other national differences are equally resilient against the tides of globalization. No countries have recently given up their national language in favor of Esperanto or English. On the contrary, there has been renewed emphasis on the local language in many countries (e.g. Ireland and the Baltic countries) and regions (e.g. Catalonia and Quebec). In the same way, political systems have remained internationally diverse, with plenty of examples of localization, even within nations. For instance, in Russia and the United States the shift of power to regional governments has increased policy diversity within the country. Similar arguments can be put forward for legal systems, fiscal regimes, educational systems and technological infrastructure – each is extremely difficult to change due to the lock-in effects, vested interests, psychological commitment and complex decision-making processes.

For each example of increasing similarity, a counter-example of local initiatives and growing diversity could be given. Some proponents of the international diversity perspective argue that it is exactly this interplay of divergence and convergence forces that creates a dynamic balance preserving diversity. While technologies, organizing principles, political trends and social habits disperse across borders, resulting in global convergence, new developments and novel systems in each nation arise causing international divergence (Dosi and Kogut, 1993). Convergence trends are usually easier to spot than divergence – international dispersion can be more simply witnessed than new localized developments. To the casual observer, this might suggest that convergence trends have the upper hand, but after more thorough analysis, this conclusion must be cast aside.

Now add to this enduring international diversity the reality of international economic relations. Since World War II attempts have been made to facilitate the integration of national economies. There have been some regional successes (e.g. the North American Free Trade Association and the European Union) and some advances have been made on a worldwide scale (e.g. the World Trade Organization). However, progress has been slow and important political barriers remain.

The continued existence of international diversity and political obstacles, it is argued, will limit the extent to which nations can become fully integrated into one borderless world. International differences and barriers to trade and investment will frustrate firms' attempts to standardize and centralize, and will place a premium on firms' abilities to adapt and decentralize. Of course, there will be some activities for which global economies of scale can be achieved and for which international coordination is needed, but this will not become true for all activities. Empowering national managers to be responsive to specific local conditions will remain an important ingredient for international success. Balancing globalization and localization of the firm's activities will continue to be a requirement in the future international context.

Ideally, the internationally operating company should neither deny nor regret the existence of international diversity, but regard it as an opportunity that can be exploited. Each country's unique circumstances will pose different challenges, requiring the development of different competences. Different national 'climates' will create opportunities for different innovations. If a company can tap into each country's opportunities and leverage the acquired competences and innovations to other countries, this could offer the company an important source of competitive advantage. Naturally, these locally leveraged competences and innovations would subsequently need to be adapted to the specific circumstances in other countries. This balancing act would require an organization that combined strong local responsiveness with the ability to exchange and coordinate internationally, even on a worldwide scale. International organizations blending these two elements are called 'transnational' (Bartlett and Ghoshal, 1995), or 'heterarchical' (Hedlund, 1986). However, in some businesses the international differences will remain so large that an even more locally responsive organizational form might be necessary, operating on a federative basis.

EXHIBIT 10.3 THE INTERNATIONAL DIVERSITY PERSPECTIVE

HSBC: THE WORLD'S LOCAL BANK

When Scotsman Thomas Sutherland arrived in Hong Kong in 1865, he soon realized that the growing trade between China and Europe was creating considerable demand for local banking services, so he founded the Hongkong and Shanghai Banking Corporation (HSBC). As international trade grew and spread, so did HSBC, establishing offices around South-East Asia. By the 1950s, HSBC began to acquire subsidiaries farther afield, such as the Imperial Bank of Persia, the Cyprus Popular Bank, New York's Marine Midland Bank and CCF, one of France's largest banks. Nowadays the HSBC Group has some 7000 offices worldwide, employing 170 000 people, serving over 30 million customers in 81 countries. In 2002, HSBC ranked second in the world and first in Europe in terms of market capitalization, and received the 'Best Global Bank Award'.

HSBC is headed by Sir John Bond, a distinguished Hong Kong Anglo-Saxon, who has been with the bank since he was 19. When he became group chairman of HSBC Holding in 1998, he started a review of the firm's international strategy, questioning whether a globally standardized approach was the best route for the future. He wanted to blend the company's many acquisitions and subsidiaries into an integrated worldwide organization that could deliver high quality services around the globe, yet also strongly believed that the bank needed to embrace local cultures and conform to different regulatory regimes. To quote Bond:

Success for HSBC means operating in a globalizing world . . . but we don't want to Americanize the world; we want to enjoy the world in all its diversity. If globalization is about cultural hegemony, we disapprove. If it is about better products and services for host countries, and it benefits the citizens of a country, then we are for it.

In 2002 HSBC started a marketing campaign, positioning itself as the 'World's Local Bank'. The company's international strategy is 'to be a Chinese bank in China, a Brazilian bank in Brazil and a French bank in France', while still sharing core values around the world and creating a global back-office infrastructure. At the group's head office in London a global digital network, Hexagon, is at the core of HSBC's transaction, data and communication traffic. All staff members around the world are also trained to use common operating platforms and conform to internal standards, based on 'a cast-iron set of universal values which we practice wherever we are in the world'. Within these boundaries, the various local subsidiaries are encouraged to develop products and services tailored to local circumstances by local staff. For instance, for countries with large Muslim populations HSBC has created an Islamic banking unit that conducts business according to the principle in the Koran, forbidding the charging of interest. Another example is that in Saudi Arabia women-only branches have been opened. Summing up HSBC's philosophy, Bond has remarked that 'we need to be constantly aware that we view the world through the distorting lens or our own culture, and that sometimes we need to change our perspective. In our business we aim to adjust to cultural requirements wherever needed.'

Sources: *Business Week*, September 20 1999; *The Banker*, September 1 2002; www.HSBC.com.

TOWARDS A SYNTHESIS

You may say I'm a dreamer,
but I'm not the only one;
I hope some day you'll join us,
and the world will live as one.

John Lennon (1940–1980);
British musician and songwriter

When I am at Milan,
I do as they do at Milan;
but when I go to Rome,
I do as Rome does.

St. Augustine (354–430);
Roman theologian and philosopher

So, is the international context moving towards increased similarity and integration, or will it remain as diverse and fragmented as at the moment? And what does this mean for the international configuration of firms? Should managers anticipate and encourage global convergence by emphasizing global standardization, centralization and coordination? In that case, they would choose to place more emphasis on realizing value creation by means of global synergies, accepting some value destruction due to a loss of local responsiveness. Or should managers acknowledge and exploit international diversity by emphasizing local adaptation, decentralization and autonomy? If so, they would then focus on being locally responsive, accepting that this will frustrate the realization of cross-border synergies.

Again, the strategic management literature does not provide a uniform answer to the question of which international strategy firms can best pursue. On the contrary, the variety of opinions among strategy theorists is dauntingly large, with many incompatible prescriptions being given. At the core of the debate within the field of strategy is the paradox of globalization and localization. Many points of view have been expounded on how to reconcile these opposing demands, but no common perspective has yet emerged. Hence, it is up to individual managers to judge for themselves whether the vision of a global village is an emerging reality or merely a fata morgana.

In Table 10.1 the main arguments of the two opposite poles in this debate have been summarized. As in previous chapters the real challenge for managers is not to gravitate to one of these extreme poles. Rather, the internationally minded manager should weigh the arguments presented by both sides and seek ways to unite the best of both worlds. Such a synthesis of the global convergence and international diversity perspectives should go further than merely reciting the cliché 'Think global, act local'. Managers should search for

TABLE 10.1   Global convergence versus international diversity perspective

	Global convergence perspective	International diversity perspective
Emphasis on	Globalization over localization	Localization over globalization
International variety	Growing similarity	Remaining diversity
International linkages	Growing integration	Remaining fragmentation
Major drivers	Technology and communication	Cultural and institutional identity
Diversity and fragmentation	Costly, convergence can be encouraged	Reality, can be exploited
Strategic focus	Global-scale synergies	Local responsiveness
Organizational preference	Standardize/centralize unless	Adapt/decentralize unless
Innovation process	Center-for-global	Locally leveraged
Organizational structure	Global (centralized hub)	Transnational (integrated network)

tangible ways to combine global synergies and local responsiveness in one and the same approach. But what such a 'glocal' style should be like, given the specific circumstances of a firm, remains the issue for the strategizing manager to tackle.

FURTHER READING

A truth on this side of the Pyrenees, a falsehood on the other.
Montaigne (1533–1592); French moralist and essayist

There have been few writers as radical in their global convergence stance as Theodore Levitt, in his well-known article, 'The Globalization of Markets'. Other good places to start for readers interested in the global convergence perspective would be Kenichi Ohmae's *The Borderless World: Power and Strategy in the Interlinked Economy* and George Yip's *Total Global Strategy*. For a stronger balancing of perspectives, the reader should turn to *The Multinational Mission*, by C.K. Prahalad and Yves Doz, and *Competition in Global Industries* by Michael Porter. For a critical review of the globalization literature, *The Logic of International Restructuring* by Winfried Ruigrok and Rob van Tulder makes for stimulating reading.

Most of this literature emphasizes strategy content issues, while largely neglecting strategy process aspects. A well-known exception is the article 'Strategic Planning for a Global Business' by Balaji Chakravarthy and Howard Perlmutter. With regard to the management of large international companies, *Managing Across Borders: The Transnational Solution*, by Christopher Bartlett and Sumantra Ghoshal, is highly recommended.

PURPOSE

ORGANIZATIONAL PURPOSE

*Corporation, n. An ingenious device for obtaining individual profit
without individual responsibility.*

The Devil's Dictionary, Ambrose Bierce (1842–1914); American columnist

INTRODUCTION

At the beginning of this book, strategy was defined as a course of action for achieving
an organization's purpose. Subsequently, nine chapters were spent looking at strategy
from many different angles, but scant attention was paid to the organizational purposes that
firms want to achieve. How to set a course for the organizational vessel through turbulent
waters was discussed, but the question of why the journey was being undertaken in the first
place was hardly raised – the focus was on means, not on ends. This lack of attention to
the subject of organizational purpose is a notable feature of the strategic management literature. This might be due to the widespread assumption that it is obvious why business
organizations exist. Some writers might avoid the topic because it is highly value-laden
and somehow outside the realm of strategic management.

Yet, in practice, managers must constantly make choices and seek solutions based on
an understanding of what their organization is intended to achieve. It is hardly possible for
strategizing managers to avoid taking a stance on what they judge to be the purpose of their
organization. They are confronted with many different claimants who believe that the firm
exists to serve their interests. Demands are placed on the firm by shareholders, employees,
suppliers, customers, governments and communities, forcing managers to weigh whose
interests should receive priority over others. Even when explicit demands are not voiced,
managers must still determine who will be the main beneficiary of the value-creation
activities of the firm.

Where managers have a clear understanding of their organization's purpose, this can
provide strong guidance during processes of strategic thinking, strategy formation and
strategic change. The organizational purpose can function as a fundamental principle,
against which strategic options can be evaluated. Yet, while of central importance, organizations can be guided by more principles than organizational purpose alone. For example,
they can be strongly influenced by certain business philosophies and values. The broader
set of fundamental principles giving direction to strategic decision-making, of which
organizational purpose is the central element, is referred to as the 'corporate mission'.

Determining the corporate mission is a challenging task, not least because there are so
many different views on how it should be done. In this chapter, the issue of corporate mission

will be explored in more detail, with the intention of uncovering the conflicting perspectives on the subject of organizational purpose that lie at the heart of the divergent opinions.

THE ISSUE OF CORPORATE MISSION

Corporate mission is a rather elusive concept, often used to refer to the wooly platitudes on the first few pages of annual reports. To many people, mission statements are lists of lofty principles that have potential public relations value, but have little bearing on actual business, let alone impact on the process of strategy formation. Yet, while frequently employed in this hollow manner, a corporate mission can be very concrete and play an important role in determining strategic actions.

A good way to explain the term's meaning is to go back to its etymological roots. 'Mission' comes from the Latin word *mittere*, which means 'to send' (Cummings and Davies, 1994). A mission is some task, duty or purpose that 'sends someone on their way' – a motive or driver propelling someone in a certain direction. Hence, 'corporate mission' can be understood as the basic drivers sending the corporation along its way. The corporate mission consists of the fundamental principles that mobilize and propel the firm in a particular direction.

The corporate mission contributes to 'sending the firm in a particular direction' by influencing the firm's strategy. To understand how a mission impacts strategy, two topics require closer attention. First, it is necessary to know what types of 'fundamental principles' actually make up a corporate mission. These elements of corporate mission will be described below. Secondly, it needs to be examined what types of roles are played by a corporate mission in the strategy formation process. These functions of corporate mission will also be described (see Figure 11.1).

Besides the 'what' of corporate mission, it is equally important to explore the 'who' – who should determine a corporate mission. In the previous chapters the implicit assumption has consistently been that managers are the primary 'strategic actors' responsible for

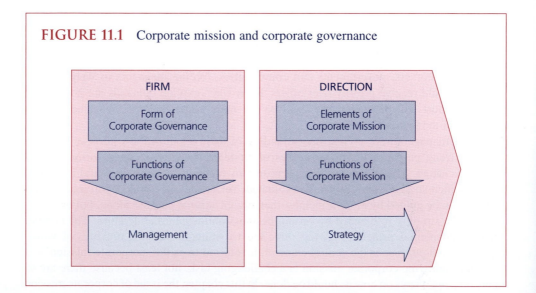

FIGURE 11.1   Corporate mission and corporate governance

FIRM
- Form of Corporate Governance
- Functions of Corporate Governance
- Management

DIRECTION
- Elements of Corporate Mission
- Functions of Corporate Mission
- Strategy

setting the direction of the firm. But in fact, their actions are formally monitored and controlled by the board of directors. In this way, the direction of the firm must be understood as a result of the interaction between management ('the executives') and the board of directors. As the name would imply, directors have an important influence on direction.

The activities of the board of directors are referred to as 'corporate governance' – directors govern the strategic choices and actions of the management of a firm. And because they have such an important role in setting the corporate mission and strategy, their input will be examined here as well. First, an overall review will be presented of the various functions of corporate governance. Then it will be examined what the different forms of corporate governance are, as this can significantly influence the eventual mission and strategy that are followed (see Figure 11.1).

Elements of corporate mission

Organizational purpose can be defined as the reason for which an organization exists. It can be expected that the perception that managers have of their organization's purpose will give direction to the strategy process and influence the strategy content (e.g. Bartlett and Ghoshal, 1994; Campbell and Tawadey, 1990). Sometimes strategizing managers consciously reflect on, or question, the organizational purpose as they make strategic choices. However, more often their view of the organization's purpose will be a part of a broader set of business principles that steers their strategic thinking. This enduring set of fundamental principles, that forms the base of a firm's identity and guides its strategic decision-making, is referred to as the corporate mission.

While the purpose of an organization is at the heart of the corporate mission, three other components can also be distinguished (see Figure 11.2):

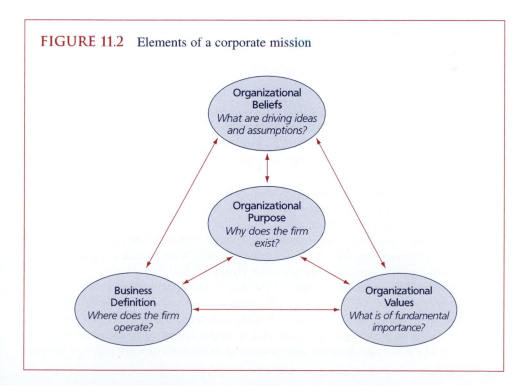

FIGURE 11.2   Elements of a corporate mission

- **Organizational beliefs.** All strategic choices ultimately include important assumptions about the nature of the environment and what the firm needs to do to be successful in its business. If people in a firm do not share the same fundamental strategic beliefs, joint decision-making will be very protracted and conflictual – opportunities and threats will be interpreted differently and preferred solutions will be very divergent (see Chapter 2). To work swiftly and in unison, a common understanding is needed. The stronger the set of shared beliefs subscribed to by all organizational members, the easier communication and decision-making will become, and the more confident and driven the group will be. Where researchers refer to the organizational ideology ('system of ideas') as their 'collective cognitive map' (Axelrod, 1976), 'dominant logic' (Prahalad and Bettis, 1986) or 'team mental model' (Klimoski and Mohammed, 1994), companies themselves usually simply speak of their beliefs or philosophy.

- **Organizational values.** Each person in an organization can have their own set of values, shaping what they believe to be good and just. Yet, when an organization's members share a common set of values, determining what they see as worthwhile activities, ethical behavior and moral responsibilities, this can have a strong impact on the strategic direction (e.g. Falsey, 1989; Hoffman, 1989). Such widely embraced organizational values also contribute to a clear sense of organizational identity, attracting some individuals, while repelling others. Although it can be useful to explicitly state the values guiding the organization, to be influential they must become embodied in the organization's culture (e.g. McCoy, 1985; Collins and Porras, 1994).

- **Business definition.** For some firms, any business is good business, as long as they can make a reasonable return on investment. Yet, if any business is fine, the firm will lack a sense of direction. In practice, most firms have a clearer identity, which they derive from being active in a particular line of business. For these firms, having a delimiting definition of the business they wish to be in strongly focuses the direction in which they develop. Their business definition functions as a guiding principle, helping to distinguish opportunities from diversions (e.g. Abell, 1980; Pearce, 1982). Of course, while a clear business definition can focus the organization's attention and efforts, it can lead to shortsightedness and the missing of new business developments (e.g. Ackoff, 1974; Levitt, 1960).

The strength of a corporate mission will depend on whether these four elements fit together and are mutually reinforcing (Campbell and Yeung, 1991). Where a consistent and compelling corporate mission is formed, this can infuse the organization with a sense of mission, creating an emotional bond between organizational members and energizing them to work according to the mission.

A concept that is often confused with mission is vision. Individuals or organizations have a vision if they picture a future state of affairs they wish to achieve (from the Latin *vide* – to see; Cummings and Davies, 1994). While the corporate mission outlines the fundamental principles guiding strategic choices, a strategic vision outlines the desired future at which the company hopes to arrive. In other words, vision provides a business aim, while mission provides business principles (see Figure 11.3).

Generally, a strategic vision is a type of aim that is less specific than a short-term target or longer-term objective. Vision is usually defined as a broad conception of a desirable future state, of which the details remain to be determined (e.g. Senge, 1990b; Collins and Porras, 1996). As such, strategic vision can play a similar role as corporate mission, pointing the firm in a particular direction and motivating individuals to work together towards a shared end.

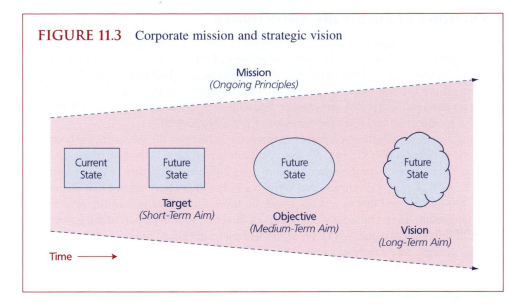

FIGURE 11.3   Corporate mission and strategic vision

Functions of corporate mission

The corporate mission can be articulated by means of a mission statement, but in practice not everything that is called a mission statement meets the above criteria (e.g. David, 1989; Piercy and Morgan, 1994). However, firms can have a mission, even if it has not been explicitly written down, although this does increase the chance of divergent interpretations within the organization.

In general, paying attention to the development of a consistent and compelling corporate mission can be valuable for three reasons. A corporate mission can provide:

- Direction. The corporate mission can point the organization in a certain direction, by defining the boundaries within which strategic choices and actions must take place. By specifying the fundamental principles on which strategies must be based, the corporate mission limits the scope of strategic options and sets the organization on a particular heading (e.g. Bourgeois and Brodwin, 1983; Hax, 1990).

- Legitimization. The corporate mission can convey to all stakeholders inside and outside the company that the organization is pursuing valuable activities in a proper way. By specifying the business philosophy that will guide the company, the chances can be increased that stakeholders will accept, support and trust the organization (e.g. Klemm, Sanderson and Luffman, 1991; Freeman and Gilbert, 1988).

- Motivation. The corporate mission can go a step further than legitimization, by actually inspiring individuals to work together in a particular way. By specifying the fundamental principles driving organizational actions, an *esprit de corps* can evolve, with the powerful capacity to motivate people over a prolonged period of time (e.g. Campbell and Yeung, 1991; Peters and Waterman, 1982).

Especially these last two functions of a corporate mission divide both management theorists and business practitioners. What is seen as a legitimate and motivating organizational purpose is strongly contested. What the main factors of disagreement are will be examined in a later section of this chapter.

Functions of corporate governance

The subject of corporate governance, as opposed to corporate management, deals with the issue of governing the strategic choices and actions of top management. Popularly stated, corporate governance is about managing top management – building in checks and balances to ensure that the senior executives pursue strategies that are in accordance with the corporate mission. Corporate governance encompasses all tasks and activities that are intended to supervise and steer the behavior of top management.

In the common definition, corporate governance 'addresses the issues facing boards of directors' (Tricker, 1994: xi). In this view, corporate governance is the task of the directors and therefore attention must be paid to their roles and responsibilities (e.g. Cochran and Wartick, 1994; Keasey, Thompson and Wright, 1997). Others have argued that this definition is too narrow, and that in practice there are more forces that govern the activities of top management. In this broader view, boards of directors are only a part of the governance system. For instance, regulation by local and national authorities, as well as pressure from societal groups, can function as the checks and balances limiting top management's discretion (e.g. Mintzberg, 1984; Demb and Neubauer, 1992).

Whether employing a narrow or broad definition, three important corporate governance functions can be distinguished (adapted from Tricker, 1994):

- Forming function. The first function of corporate governance is to influence the forming of the corporate mission. The task of corporate governance is to shape, articulate and communicate the fundamental principles that will drive the organization's activities. Determining the purpose of the organization and setting priorities among claimants are part of the forming function. The board of directors can conduct this task by, for example, questioning the basis of strategic choices, influencing the business philosophy, and explicitly weighing the advantages and disadvantages of the firm's strategies for various constituents (e.g. Freeman and Reed, 1983; Yoshimori, 1995).

- Performance function. The second function of corporate governance is to contribute to the strategy process with the intention of improving the future performance of the corporation. The task of corporate governance is to judge strategy initiatives brought forward by top management and/or to actively participate in strategy development. The board of directors can conduct this task by, for example, engaging in strategy discussions, acting as a sounding board for top management, and networking to secure the support of vital stakeholders (e.g. Baysinger and Hoskisson, 1990; Donaldson and Davis, 1995; Zahra and Pearce, 1989).

- Conformance function. The third function of corporate governance is to ensure corporate conformance to the stated mission and strategy. The task of corporate governance is to monitor whether the organization is undertaking activities as promised and whether performance is satisfactory. Where management is found lacking, it is a function of corporate governance to press for changes. The board of directors can conduct this task by, for example, auditing the activities of the corporation, questioning and supervising top management, determining remuneration and incentive packages, and even appointing new managers (e.g. Parkinson, 1993; Spencer, 1983).

These functions give the board of directors considerable influence in determining and realizing the corporate mission. As such, they have the ultimate power to decide on the organizational purpose. Therefore, it is not surprising that the question to whom these functions should be given is extremely important.

Forms of corporate governance

There is considerable disagreement on how boards of directors should be organized and run. Currently, each country has its own system of corporate governance and the international differences are large. Yet even within many countries, significant disagreements are discernible. In designing a corporate governance regime, three characteristics of boards of directors are of particular importance (adapted from Tricker, 1994):

■ Board structure. Internationally, there are major differences between countries requiring a two-tier board structure (e.g. Germany, the Netherlands and Finland), countries with a one-tier board (e.g. United States, Britain and Japan), and countries in which companies are free to choose (e.g. France and Switzerland). In a two-tier system there is a formal division of power, with a management board made up of the top executives and a distinct supervisory board made up of non-executives with the task of monitoring and steering the management board. In a one-tier (or unitary) board system, executive and non-executive (outside) directors sit together on one board (see Figure 11.4).

■ Board membership. The composition of boards of directors can vary sharply from company to company and from country to country. Some differences are due to legal requirements that are not the same internationally. For instance, in Germany by law half of the membership of a supervisory board must represent labor, while the other half represents the shareholders. In French companies labor representatives are given observer status on the board. In other countries there are no legal imperatives, yet differences have emerged. In some cases outside (non-executive) directors from other companies are common, while in other nations fewer outsiders are involved. Even within countries, differences can be significant, especially with regard to the number, stature and independence of outside (non-executive) directors.

■ Board tasks. The tasks and authority of boards of directors also differ quite significantly between companies. In some cases boards meet infrequently and are merely asked to vote on proposals put in front of them. Such boards have little formal or informal power to contradict the will of the CEO. In other companies, boards meet regularly and play a more active role in corporate governance, by formulating proposals, proactively

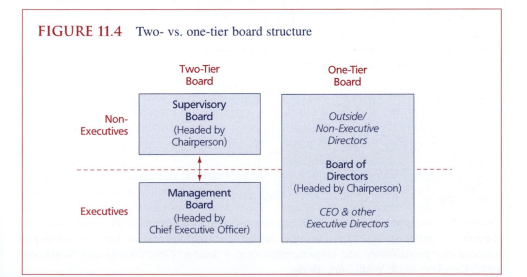

FIGURE 11.4   Two- vs. one-tier board structure

selecting new top managers, and determining objectives and incentives. Normally, the power of outside (non-executive) directors to monitor and steer a company only partly depends on their formally defined tasks and authority. To a large degree their impact is determined by how proactive they define their own role.

The question in the context of this chapter is how a board of directors should be run to ensure that the organization's purpose is best achieved. What should be the structure, membership and tasks of the board of directors, to realize the ends for which the organization exists?

THE PARADOX OF PROFITABILITY AND RESPONSIBILITY

Property has its duties as well as its rights.
Thomas Drummond (1797–1840); English public administrator

Discussions on what firms should strive to achieve are not limited to the field of strategic management. Given the influential position of business organizations in society, the purpose they should serve is also discussed by theorists in the fields of economics, political science, sociology, ethics and philosophy. Since the industrial revolution, and the rise of the modern corporation, the role of business organizations within the 'political economic order' has been a central theme in many of the social sciences. It has been the topic that has filled libraries of books, inspired society-changing theories and stirred deep-rooted controversies.

The enormous impact of corporations on the functioning of society has also attracted political parties, labor unions, community representatives, environmentalists, the media and the general public to the debate. All take a certain position on the role that business organizations should play within society and the duties that they ought to shoulder. Here, too, the disagreements can be heated, often spilling over from the political arena and negotiating tables into the streets.

In countries with a market economy, it is generally agreed that companies should pursue strategies that ensure economic profitability, but that they have certain social responsibilities that must be fulfilled as well. But this is where the consensus ends. Opinions differ sharply with regard to the relative importance of profitability and responsibility. Some people subscribe to the view that profitability is the very purpose of economic organizations and that the only social responsibility of a firm is to pursue profitability within the boundaries of the law. However, other people argue that business corporations are not only economic entities, but also social institutions, embedded in a social environment, which brings along heavy social responsibilities. In this view, organizations are morally obliged to behave responsibly towards all parties with a stake in the activities of the firm, and profitability is only a means to fulfill this duty.

Most managers accept that both economic profitability and social responsibility are valuable goals to pursue. Yet, as organizational purpose, profitability and responsibility are at least partially contradictory. If managers strive towards profit maximization, shareholders might be enamored, but this will bring managers into conflict with the optimization of benefits for other stakeholders. In other words, to a certain extent there is a tension between the profitability and responsibility (e.g. Cannon, 1992; Demb and Neubauer, 1992; Drucker, 1984; Yoshimori, 1995).

The demand for economic profitability

It is clear that business organizations must be profitable to survive. Yet simple profitability, that is having higher income than costs, is not sufficient. To be an attractive investment, a company must earn a higher return on the shareholders' equity than could be realized if the money were deposited in the bank. Put differently, investors must have a financial incentive to run a commercial risk; otherwise they could just as well bring their money to the bank or buy low risk government bonds.

Yet, offsetting the risk carried by investors is but a small part of the larger picture. Once a corporation has established a track record of profitability, this inspires trust among financiers. Such trust makes it much easier to raise new capital, either through borrowing (at more attractive rates) or by issuing new shares. And of course, new capital can be used to further the competitive objectives of the organization. Where companies have not been particularly profitable in the past, and cannot authoritatively project an attractive level of profitability in the future, they will find it difficult or virtually impossible to find new financing. This can significantly weaken the position of the firm and undermine its long-term competitiveness.

For publicly traded corporations strong profitability is usually reflected in higher share prices, which is not only beneficial to the shareholders at that moment, but also makes it easier to acquire other firms and to pay with shares. Moreover, a high share price is the best defense against a hostile takeover and the best negotiating chip for a friendly one. In both publicly and privately held companies, retained profits can also be an important source of funds for new investments.

In short, profitability is not only a *result*, but also a *source*, of competitive power. Profitability provides a company with the financial leeway to improve its competitive position and pursue its ambitions.

The demand for social responsibility

As economic entities engaging in formalized arrangements with employees, suppliers, buyers and government agencies, corporations have the legal responsibility to abide by the stipulations outlined in their contracts. Equally, they are bound to stay within the 'letter of the law' in each jurisdiction in which they operate. However, being good corporate citizens entails more than just staying out of court.

Companies are more than just 'economic machines' regulated by legal contracts. They are also networks of people, working together towards a common goal. And as members of a social group, people within a company need to develop a sense of 'community' if they are to function properly. One of the most basic needs is to build a level of trust among people – a feeling of security that each individual's interests will be taken into account. Trust evolves where people feel certain that others will behave in a socially responsible manner, instead of letting their own self-interest prevail without limitation. Once there is enough trust between people, they can engage in productive teamwork and invest in their mutual relationships.

Hence, social responsibility – that is, acting in the interest of others, even when there is no legal imperative – lies at the basis of trust. And where there is trust, people are generally willing to commit themselves to the organization, both emotionally and practically. Emotionally, they will become involved with, and can become strongly connected to, the organization, which can lead to a sense of pride and loyalty. Practically, they will be willing to invest years acquiring firm-specific knowledge and skills, and in building a career.

Such commitments make people dependent on the organization, as they will be less able and inclined to job-hop. It is therefore vital that the organization rewards such commitment by acting responsibly, even where this hurts profitability; otherwise the bond of trust can be seriously damaged.

Acting in the interest of all employees is a limited form of social responsibility. Just as it is beneficial for trust to evolve within organizations, it is important for trust to develop between the organization and its broader environment of buyers, suppliers, governments, local communities and activist groups. Therefore, it is important that these organizations also come to trust that the organization is willing to act in a socially responsible way, even when this entails sacrificing profitability.

EXHIBIT 11.1 SHORT CASE

GOLDMAN SACHS: HITTING THE JACKPOT?

Freud probably would have had a good explanation why the name Goldman Sachs exerts such a strong pull on university graduates. However, an alternative explanation is that Goldman Sachs is the world's premier investment bank and working there is the ultimate career ambition of many 'high potentials'. Despite the fact that its employees are reputed to work the hardest and the longest in the industry, the prestige of Goldman Sachs encourages many of the top people to try to get a job with the firm. By 2002, the company employed over 20 000 employees in 20 offices around the world, with the reputation of being the very best analysts, traders and associates around.

Goldman Sachs is active in the areas of investment banking, asset management and securities services, with a particular strength in initial public offerings (IPOs) and mergers and acquisitions (M&A). Since its establishment in 1869, the firm has added many of the world's blue chip companies to its client list. A typical aspect of its culture is that it combines a strongly proactive attitude towards fulfilling its clients' needs with a cautious stance towards the financial markets. A famous saying within the firm is: 'Good companies worry about their competition, great companies worry about their clients.' This way of thinking translates into high levels of client commitment and client care, with a strong emphasis on preserving relationships and reputation. To insiders it came as no surprise that Goldman Sachs' cautious stance helped it to stay away from the reckless behavior that got its competitors like Merrill Lynch, Lehman Brothers and Morgan Stanley into difficulties in the 1980s.

In hiring new employees, the firm has (quoting its web site) a specific approach:

Although our activities are measured in billions of dollars, we select our people one by one. In a service business we know that without the best people we cannot be the best firm . . . so we aggressively recruit the very best professionals. But where we differ most from some of the other Wall Street firms is in the attention we pay to retention. Goldman's standards of care of its professionals are simply the best in the industry.

Which might be true, but in practice the firm's most powerful tool for retaining professionals has always been the prospect of partnership. These top-of-class professionals have been willing to work 14–18 hour days for 10–15 years at salaries often lower than they could earn elsewhere, in the hope of hitting the jackpot – becoming a partner in the firm. This jackpot has consisted of an eight-figure compensation package and the prestige of belonging to an exclusive club. Of course, only the happy few have made it to the top of this pyramid scheme, but those who have, have shared in the yearly profits. And these profits, a newspaper once remarked, have regularly surpassed the national income of a country like Tanzania, but have only needed to be distributed among approximately 200 people. Over the course of their careers, Goldman Sachs partners have had the prospect of earning at least US$25 million.

By the 1990s, this partnership structure made Goldman Sachs the odd-man out on Wall Street, where all other investment banks had long before become public companies. But the pros and cons of the partnership model were hotly debated in the firm. On the one hand, many partners argued that 'if it ain't broke, don't fixed it'. They felt that for more than 100 years the partnership structure had ensured a high commitment of the partners to work towards maximizing the firm's value – partners could only cash in their shares after a number of years and therefore had a strong incentive to keep the value of the shares high. These partners also felt little need to share their hard-earned profits with outside shareholders. On the other hand, many partners were increasingly worried about the risks that the partners needed to bare. As they became more and more reliant on trading to boost profitability, they also became more exposed to the risk of a single trader losing millions in a day, as happened at Barings. Furthermore, the partnership was vulnerable to groups of partners leaving and taking their equity with them, as happened during the 1994 bond crash. At the same time, competitors were merging and getting bigger, often becoming a part of a large financial service conglomerate. It was believed that these dinosaurs had little extra

competitive power, but would be better placed to survive the next shakeout during a prolonged bear market. This left many partners feeling small and vulnerable. Finally, it was argued that for Goldman Sachs to grow by acquisition, it would be much easier to pay in shares than in cash.

A first move by Goldman Sachs to find a solution to the downsides of the partnership structure was to switch to a limited liability partnership status. The firm also extended the period that partners had to wait before being allowed to sell their shares, to slow the cash drain, as well as limiting the number of people entitled to a share of the profits. But then disaster hit. Goldman Sachs was accused of IPO spinning – giving special IPO allocations to key clients in exchange for investment bank business. This led to an investigation into conflicts of interest by the Securities and Exchange Commission (SEC) and ended up costing the firm a significant fine and a dented reputation.

With the SEC threatening further probes, the partners started to feel ever more vulnerable. With each one of them having so much of their personal wealth tied up in the company, partners felt overexposed to the threat of one big mistake wiping out the company. So, after ample discussion, the partners decided to float a small part of their company (12.6%) on the stock market. In November 1999, the initial public offering was made, raking in US$3.6 billion and valuing the entire company at US$33 billion – a healthy four times book value. Approximately 50% of the equity capital was still owned by the 221 former partners, making them worth an average of US$75 million per person. Another 20% of the shares were owned by non-partner employees, with the remaining shares in the hands of retired partners and other long-time investors.

The fear that the partners-turned-employees would be less eager to pursue financial success now they had to share it with thousands of outside shareholders has not yet been borne out. The market circumstances have been rather difficult since 2001, leading the new top management team to fire some employees and push through pay cuts, but the financial results of Goldman Sachs have still been respectable. In 2002, revenues were down for the second year in a row (from US\$16.5 to US\$14 billion), as were earnings (from US\$3 to US\$2 billion), but the firm was doing well compared to the carnage around it. In a letter to the shareholders the board wrote 'this performance also reflected, as it has throughout the 133 years since the firm's founding, in good and bad times, the quality of the people of Goldman Sachs and their ability to develop and execute business'.

Which 'people of Goldman Sachs' the board saw as responsible for the reasonable performance became clear soon after the presentation of the 2002 annual report. In a mandatory annual statement of information to shareholders, a new compensation plan was announced for the company's 29 most senior employees, in which each was promised a bonus of up to 1% of before-tax profits, on top of their multi-million dollar base salaries. To avoid the appearance of excess, the bonuses would be limited to US\$35 million per executive. The rationale for the compensation plan according to the company was 'to perpetuate the sense of partnership'. Over 2002, the CEO, Henry Paulson, had earned US\$10 million, but this amount was deemed to be inadequate for the purpose of 'the perpetuation of the sense of partnership', hence the need to introduce more stimulating bonuses. In justifying Paulson's pay for 2002, the compensation committee of the board of management called him a 'strong voice for Goldman Sachs and the industry as a whole' and praised him for taking steps to restore trust in the integrity of corporate management.

The question on the minds of many shareholders and employees was whether this compensation plan was a necessary investment to ensure the future success of the company, or whether it was more the reflection of the true purpose of the firm – to make its partners/executives rich. With the old partners still in power, it seemed as if they were still running the show primarily to serve their own interests. To many it seemed that the 'sense of partnership' was another way to say 'a continued partnership, but by another means'. For many shareholders, this was not what they had expected of a publicly traded company. And for many employees, especially those sacked or whose pay had been cut, this was not the type of responsibility they had hoped would come with the demise of the partnership pyramid. But then, were their expectations justified? After all, whose company is it in the first place?

But for the Goldman Sachs top management team, these gripes sounded odd. To most insiders it was clear that Goldman Sachs would continue to be run by its partners, for its partners, with a few public shareholders allowed to climb aboard for the ride. As one manager summarized it: 'We're going to let you in. Now shut up and sit back and we'll let you know how much you made.'

Sources: *The Economist*, April 4 1999 and March 20 2003; *Business Week*, May 19 1999; Goldman Sachs web site.

PERSPECTIVES ON ORGANIZATIONAL PURPOSE

Perfection of means and confusion of goals . . . characterize our age.
Albert Einstein (1879–1955); German-American physicist

Firms require a certain measure of economic profitability if they want to compete and survive, and they need to exhibit a certain amount of social responsibility if they are to retain the trust and support of key stakeholders. In itself, this creates a tension, as the two demands can be at odds with one another. Often, socially responsible behavior costs money, which can only be partially recouped by the increased 'social dividend' it brings. But if profitability and responsibility are both seen as the ultimate purpose of business firms, then the tension is even stronger, as optimizing the one will be in conflict with maximizing the other. Emphasizing profitability means subjecting all investments to an economic rationale – socially responsible behavior should only be undertaken if the net present value of such an investment is attractive or there is no legal way of avoiding compliance. Emphasizing responsibility means subjecting all activities to a moral and/or political rationale – asking who has a legitimate and pressing claim to be included as a beneficiary of the activities being undertaken, which can severely depress profitability.

Hence, it is not surprising to find that the paradox of profitability and responsibility strongly divides people across many walks of life, not only business managers and management theorists. The main point of contention is whether firms should primarily be run for the financial benefit of the legal owners, or for the broader benefit of all parties with a significant interest in the joint endeavor. Should it be the purpose of firms to serve the interests of their shareholders or of their stakeholders? Should profitability be emphasized because economic organizations belong to the providers of risk capital, or should responsibility be emphasized because organizations are joint ventures bringing together various resource providers by means of a social contract?

While there are many points of view on the 'right' organizational purpose in the strategy literature, here the two diametrically opposed positions will be identified and discussed. At the one pole of the debate are those people who argue that corporations are established to serve the purposes of their owners. Generally, it is in the best interest of a corporation's shareholders to see the value of their stocks increase through the organization's pursuit of profitable business strategies. This point of view is commonly referred to as the 'shareholder value perspective'. At the other end of the spectrum are those people who argue that corporations should be seen as joint ventures between shareholders, employees, banks, customers, suppliers, governments and the community. All of these parties hold a stake in the organization and therefore can expect that the corporation will take as its responsibility to develop business strategies that are in accordance with their interests and values. This point of view will be referred to as the 'stakeholder values perspective'.

The shareholder value perspective

To proponents of the shareholder value perspective it is obvious that companies belong to their owners and therefore should act in accordance with the interests of the owners. Corporations are instruments whose purpose it is to create economic value on behalf of those who invest risk-taking capital in the enterprise. This clear purpose should drive companies, regardless of whether they are privately or publicly held. According to Rappaport (1986, p. xiii), 'the idea that business strategies should be judged by the economic value they create for shareholders is well accepted in the business community. After all, to suggest that companies be operated in the best interests of their owners is hardly controversial.'

There is some disagreement between advocates of this perspective with regard to the best way of advancing the interests of the shareholders, particularly in publicly held companies. Many people taking this point of view argue that the well-being of the shareholders is served if the strategy of a company leads to higher share prices and/or higher dividends (e.g. Hart, 1995; Rappaport, 1986). Others are less certain of the stock markets' ability to correctly value long-term investments, such as R&D spending and capital expenditures. In their view, stock markets are excessively concerned with the short term and therefore share prices myopically overemphasize current results and heavily discount investments for the future. To avoid being pressured into short-termism, these people advocate that strategists must keep only one eye on share prices, while the other is focused on the long-term horizon (e.g. Charkham, 1994; Sykes, 1994).

According to supporters of the shareholder value perspective, one of the major challenges in large corporations is to actually get top management to pursue the shareholders' interests. Where ownership and managerial control over a company have become separated, it is often difficult to get the managers to work on behalf of the shareholders, instead of letting managers' self-interest prevail. This is known as the principal-agent problem (e.g. Jensen and Meckling, 1976; Eisenhardt, 1989) – the managers are agents, working to further the interests of their principals, the shareholders, but are tempted to serve their own interests, even when this is to the detriment of the principals. This has led to a widespread debate in the academic and business communities, especially in Britain and the United States, about the best form of corporate governance. The most important players in corporate governance are the outside, or non-executive, members on the board of directors. It is one of the tasks of these outsiders to check whether the executives are truly running the company in a way that maximizes the shareholders' wealth. For this reason, many proponents of the shareholder value perspective call for a majority of independent-minded outside directors on the board, preferably owning significant amounts of the company's stock themselves.

The emphasis placed on profitability as the fundamental purpose of firms does not mean that supporters of the shareholder value perspective are blind to the demands placed on firms by other stakeholders. On the contrary, most exponents of this view argue that it is in the interest of the shareholders to carry out a 'stakeholder analysis' and even to actively manage stakeholder relations. Knowing the force field of stakeholders constraining the freedom of the company is important information for the strategy process. It is never advisable to ignore important external claimants such as labor unions, environmental activists, bankers, governmental agencies and community groups. Few strategists would doubt that proactive engagement is preferable to 'corporate isolationism'. However, recognizing that it is expedient to pay attention to stakeholders does not mean that it is the corporation's purpose to serve them. If parties have a strong bargaining position, a firm might be forced into all types of concessions, sacrificing profitability, but this has little to do with any moral responsibility of the firm towards these other powers. The only duty of a company is to maximize shareholder value, within the boundaries of what is legally permissible.

The important conclusion is that in this perspective it might be in the interest of shareholders to treat stakeholders well, but that there is no moral obligation to do so. For instance, it might be a good move for a troubled company not to lay off workers if the resulting loyalty and morale improve the chances of recovery and profitability later on. In this case the decision not to fire workers is based on profit-motivated calculations, not on a sense of moral responsibility towards the employees. Generally, proponents of the shareholder value perspective argue that society is best served by this type of economic rationale. By pursuing enlightened self-interest and maintaining market-based relationships between the firm and all stakeholders, societal wealth will be maximized. Responsibility for employment, local communities, the environment, consumer welfare and social developments are not an organizational matter, but issues for individuals and governments (Friedman, 1970).

EXHIBIT 11.2 THE SHAREHOLDER VALUE PERSPECTIVE

GENERAL ELECTRIC: YOUR COMPANY

Few companies are as widely known and admired as General Electric. In 2002 it was elected 'The World's Most Respected Company' for the fifth consecutive year by a panel of 1000 CEOs from around the globe. This impressive achievement is all the more surprising given the fact that GE defies the conventional industry wisdom that conglomerates should have become extinct. With its US$132 billion in sales coming from such businesses as airplane engines, television broadcasting, medical equipment, household appliances, plastics, locomotives and financial services, GE is a highly diversified company, but without the 'conglomerate discount' applied to its share price. On the contrary, for years GE shares have traded at a very high price/earnings level, to the envy of many focused competitors.

Much of the popularity of GE has been due to the man who was at the helm of the company from 1981 to 2001, Jack Welch. After taking over as CEO in 1981, Welch quickly acquired his nickname, Neutron Jack, due to his hard-nosed approach to restructuring, in which he was said to have the same impact as a neutron bomb – the buildings were left standing, but all of the people were gone. During these early years of his tenure, he thoroughly shook up the company, introducing the rule that GE should exit any business in which it could not be number one or two, on the premise that only these two top spots hold the promise of superior profitability. Subsequently, he drove the company hard, with one clear focus: maximizing shareholder value. His style at the corporate center was that of a very demanding and challenging sparring partner for the business units, constantly setting high financial targets for each to achieve.

Welch's impact has been enormous. GE is characterized by a results-oriented culture, in which financial performance is the name of the game. The clear sense of purpose within the company has made a mission statement redundant – it is engrained in the firm that success means giving the shareholders 10%-plus earnings growth per year and 20%-plus return on total capital per year. Executive compensation packages are strongly tied to financial performance, to encourage them to pursue what is best for the shareholders. And to further motivate employees to serve the interests of the owners, GE has stimulated widespread share ownership within the company, which currently totals approximately 10% of the company's stock.

Welch's relentless focus on shareholder value has been very beneficial for this group. During his reign the market capitalization of GE grew 23% annually (rising 62-fold). GE was one of the few companies to consistently outperform the S&P 500, which rose on average 15% per year in the same period. Furthermore, in 2002 the company raised its annual dividend for the

27th consecutive year – an unparalleled performance. In 2003, GE was one of the nine companies left in the world holding the prized triple-A credit rating.

The focus on shareholder value has not meant that GE has disregarded its employees or other stakeholders. For instance, GE has recognized that investing in human resources is an important means for achieving the purpose of shareholder value creation. Similarly, GE has been at the forefront of the development of environment-friendly technologies, particularly in engines and turbines, but with the clear objective of making money by pleasing customers.

When in 2001 Jeffrey Immelt took on the daunting task of filling Welch's shoes, he emphasized continuity of goals and management practices. It is clear that he plans to follow the same type of shareholder value-driven strategy as Welch. Yet, things have not been easy for Immelt, with an economic downturn and a scandal surrounding the extravagant retirement perks of Welch. In 2002, GE shares underperformed the S&P 500, and analysts and shareholders have started arguing whether there is enough reason to keep the industrial and financial businesses of GE together in one company. But whatever happens next, Immelt has promised GE shareholders that 'your GE team' is committed to maximizing the value of 'your company'.

Sources: www.ge.com; *The Economist*, May 4 2002.

The stakeholder values perspective

 Advocates of the stakeholder values perspective do not see why the supplier of one ingredient in an economic value-creation process has a stronger moral claim on the organization than the providers of other inputs. They challenge the assumption that individuals with an equity stake in a corporation have the right to demand that the entire organization work on their behalf. In the stakeholder values perspective, a company should not be seen as the instrument of shareholders, but as a coalition between various resource suppliers, with the intention of increasing their common wealth. An organization should be regarded as a joint venture in which the suppliers of equity, loans, labor, management, expertise, parts and service all participate to achieve economic success. As all groups hold a stake in the joint venture and are mutually dependent, it is argued that the purpose of the organization is to serve the interests of all parties involved (e.g. Berle and Means, 1932; Freeman and Reed, 1983).

According to endorsers of the stakeholder values perspective, shareholders have a legitimate interest in the firm's profitability. However, the emphasis shareholders place on stock price appreciation and dividends must be balanced against the legitimate demands of the other partners. These demands are not only financial, as in the case of the shareholders, but also qualitative, reflecting different values held by different groups (e.g. Clarke, 1998; Freeman, 1984). For instance, employees might place a high value on job security, occupational safety, holidays and working conditions, while a supplier of parts might prefer secure demand, joint innovation, shared risk-taking and prompt payment. Of course, balancing these interests is a challenging task, requiring an on-going process of negotiation and compromise. The outcome will in part depend on the bargaining power of each stakeholder – how essential is its input to the economic success of the organization? However, the extent to which a stakeholder's interests are pursued will depend on the perceived legitimacy of their claim as well. For instance, employees usually have a strong moral claim because they are heavily dependent on the organization and have a relatively low mobility, while most shareholders have a spread portfolio and can 'exit the corporation with a phone call' (Stone, 1975).

In this view of organizational purpose, managers must recognize their responsibility towards all constituents (e.g. Clarkson, 1995; Alkhafaji, 1989). Maximizing shareholder value to the detriment of the other stakeholders would be unjust. Managers in the firm have a moral obligation to consider the interests and values of all joint venture partners. Managing stakeholder demands is not merely a pragmatic means of running a profitable business – serving stakeholders is an end in itself. These two interpretations of stakeholder management are often confused. Where it is primarily viewed as an approach or technique for dealing with the essential participants in the value-adding process, stakeholder management is *instrumental*. But if it is based on the fundamental notion that the organization's purpose is to serve the stakeholders, then stakeholder management is *normative* (e.g. Buono and Nichols, 1985; Donaldson and Preston, 1995).

Most proponents of the stakeholder values perspective argue that, ultimately, pursuing the joint interests of all stakeholders it is not only more just, but also more effective for organizations (e.g. Jones, 1995; Solomon, 1992). Few stakeholders are filled with a sense of mission to go out and maximize shareholder value, especially if shareholders bear no responsibility for the other stakeholders' interests (e.g. Campbell and Yeung, 1991; Collins and Porras, 1994). It is difficult to work as a motivated team if it is the purpose of the organization to serve only one group's interests. Furthermore, without a stakeholder values perspective, there will be a deep-rooted lack of trust between all of the parties involved in the enterprise. Each stakeholder will assume that the others are motivated solely by self-interest and are tentatively cooperating in a calculative manner. All parties will perceive a constant risk that the others will use their power to gain a bigger slice of the pie, or even rid themselves of their 'partners'. The consequence is that all stakeholders will vigorously guard their own interests and will interact with one another as adversaries. To advocates of the stakeholder values perspective, this 'every person for themselves' model of organizations is clearly inferior to the partnership model in which sharing, trust and symbiosis are emphasized. Cooperation between stakeholders is much more effective than competition (note the link with the embedded organization perspective in Chapter 7).

Some exponents of the stakeholder values perspective argue that the narrow economic definition of stakeholders given above is too constrictive. In their view, the circle of stakeholders with a legitimate claim on the organization should be drawn more widely. Not only should the organization be responsible to the direct participants in the economic value-creation process (the 'primary stakeholders'), but also to all parties affected by the organization's activities. For example, an organization's behavior might have an impact on local communities, governments, the environment and society in general, and therefore these groups have a stake in what the organization does as well. Most supporters of the stakeholder values perspective acknowledge that organizations have a moral responsibility towards these 'secondary stakeholders' (e.g. Carroll, 1993; Langtry, 1994). However, opinions differ whether it should actually be a part of business organizations' purpose to serve this broader body of constituents.

The implication of this view for corporate governance is that the board of directors should be able to judge whether the interests of all stakeholders are being justly balanced. This has led some advocates of the stakeholder values perspective to call for representatives of the most important stakeholder groups to be on the board (e.g. Guthrie and Turnbull, 1994). Others argue more narrowly for a stronger influence of employees on the choices made by organizations (e.g. Bucholz, 1986; Blair, 1995). Such co-determination of the corporation's strategy by management and workers can, for instance, be encouraged by establishing work councils (a type of organizational parliament or senate), as is mandatory for larger companies in most countries of the European Union. Yet others emphasize measures to strengthen corporate social responsibility in general. To improve corporate social performance, it is argued, companies should be encouraged to adopt internal policy processes that promote ethical behavior and responsiveness to societal issues (e.g. Epstein, 1987; Wartick and Wood, 1998). Corporate responsibility should not be, to quote Ambrose Bierce's sarcastic definition, 'a detachable burden easily shifted to the shoulders of God, Fate, Fortune, Luck, or one's neighbor'.

EXHIBIT 11.3 THE STAKEHOLDER VALUES PERSPECTIVE

MEDTRONIC: FULL VALUE THROUGH FULL LIFE

When opening the annual shareholders' meeting each year, William George, chairman of Medtronic is crystal clear: 'Medtronic is not in the business of maximizing shareholder value. We are in the business of maximizing value to the patients we serve.' And nobody doubts for one moment that he means what he is saying – Medtronic lives by this principle. As the world's leading medical device company for all types of inner organs, with sales in 2001 exceeding US$5.5 billion, Medtronic is driven by its purpose of bringing medical technology to a higher level and improving the quality of life of its patients.

Illustrative is Medtronic's Mission and Medallion Ceremony, which has been conducted since the founding of the company in the early 1960s, where George meets every new employee personally to review the mission of the company and to present them with a bronze medallion. The medallion has a picture of a person rising off an operating table, with the words 'towards full life' inscribed around the perimeter. The employees are urged to put the medallion on their desk and to remind themselves that they work at Medtronic not just to make money for themselves or the company, but to restore people to fuller lives. After completing five major acquisitions in 1998/99, George personally conducted Mission and Medallion Ceremonies for more than 9000 employees around the world.

In 2001 George was named 'Executive of the Year' by the US-based Academy of Management. In his address to the Academy members he outlined his view that many corporations espouse lofty values, such as serving customers, quality, integrity, respect for employees and good citizenship, but what matters is what you actually live by. Values have to be constantly reinforced and consistently reflected in the actions of management at all levels. At Medtronic, all employees are asked each year to sign a detailed compliance statement, confirming that they have behaved in accordance with the company's values. Individuals who deviate from this statement or falsify their responses are asked to leave the company immediately.

According to George, long-term success requires companies to be driven by an inspiring purpose, to have a strong set of shared values at the core of the organization, and to have an adaptable business strategy. The real flaw in having the maximization of shareholder value as sole purpose, argues George, is the inability to motivate a large group of employees to exceptional performance. The shareholder value theme has little or no meaning, even if the employees benefit from the stock performance. Instead, employees should be inspired by a mission that motivates them to achieve superior performance in serving their customers. Innovative product ideas will be copied by competitors, but an organization of highly motivated people is extremely difficult to duplicate.

The intensive attention to stakeholders produces tangible results. *The Economist* labels Medtronic as 'the most innovative and market-savvy firm in the medical device industry and Mr. George is one of the best strategists in healthcare'. Medtronic is introducing new medical devices at breakneck speed – it wants to have 70% of its revenues coming from products launched in the previous two years. Lead times for developing medical devices are a mere 18 months.

And the shareholders? From 1986 to 2001, the company's revenues grew from US$363 million to US$5.5 billion, an 18% compound annual growth rate. Earnings per share went from US$0.04 in 1985 to US$1.05 in 2001, and shareholder value grew in that period from US$1.1 billion to US$60 billion (having peaked at US$70 billion in 2000), representing a 37% compound annual growth rate. Even in the worldwide recession year 2002, Medtronic reported an increase in earnings per share to US$1.21. Shareholders, it seems, are also enjoying a full life at Medtronic.

Sources: *Academy of Management Executive*, 2001, Vol. 15, No. 4; company reports; *The Economist*, August 31 2000.

TOWARDS A SYNTHESIS

The business of America is business.

Calvin Coolidge (1872–1933); American president

A business that makes nothing but money is a poor kind of business.

Henry Ford (1863–1947); American industrialist

So, what should be the purpose of a firm? Should managers strive to maximize shareholder value or stakeholder values? Should it be the purpose of business organizations to pursue profitability on behalf of their owners, or should firms serve the interests and promote the values of all of their stakeholders in a balanced way?

In Table 11.1 the main arguments of the two opposite poles in this debate have been summarized. The debate has been going on for some time now, made all the more relevant by the mounting political pressure in many countries to reform their system of corporate governance. The proponents of the shareholder value perspective are lobbying for more receptiveness to the interests of the shareholders on the part of the board, to increase top management accountability and to curb perceived executive self-enrichment at the expense of shareholders. The advocates of the stakeholder values perspective are vying for a system that would bring more receptiveness to the interests of stakeholders, to ensure that firms do not become more myopically 'bottom line' oriented. While both sides do agree on one or two points (e.g. corporate governance is generally too weak), on the whole, little consensus can be found on how to deal with the paradox of profitability and responsibility. Therefore, again, managers cannot look to the strategy literature to glean the best practice and apply it to their own situation, but will need to determine their own point of view on what they believe should be the purpose of the organization. The question that must be posed is whether these two views are unbridgeable. Are they based on such fundamentally conflicting principles, that the 'twain shall never meet'? Or can the two perspectives cross-fertilize each other, leading to hybrid views on organizational purpose? It remains a vexing question, both in theory and in society at large. But also at the level of

TABLE 11.1   Shareholder value versus stakeholder values perspective

	Shareholder value perspective	Stakeholder values perspective
Emphasis on	Profitability over responsibility	Responsibility over profitability
Organizations seen as	Instruments	Joint ventures
Organizational purpose	To serve owner	To serve all parties involved
Measure of success	Share price and dividends (shareholder value)	Satisfaction among stakeholders
Major difficulty	Getting agent to pursue principal's interests	Balancing interests of various stakeholders
Corporate governance through	Independent outside directors with shares	Stakeholder representation
Stakeholder management	Means	End and means
Social responsibility	Individual, not organizational matter	Both individual and organizational
Society best served by	Pursuing self-interest (economic efficiency)	Pursuing joint-interests (economic symbiosis)

each individual manager, the issue is whether behavior should be guided by profitability, responsibility or both. It might not be possible to give a definitive solution to this paradox, but it is possible to accept the challenge of searching for ways to get the best of both worlds – high profitability and high responsibility at the same time.

FURTHER READING

I am I plus my surroundings, and if I do not preserve the latter I do not preserve myself.
José Ortega y Gasset (1883–1955); Spanish writer and philosopher

Readers interested in delving deeper into the topic of organizational purpose have a richness of sources from which to choose. A good introductory work is the textbook *International Corporate Governance* by Robert Tricker, which also contains many classic readings and a large number of interesting cases. One of the excellent readings reprinted in Tricker's book is Henry Mintzberg's article 'Who Should Control the Corporation?', which provides a stimulating insight into the basic questions surrounding the topic of organizational purpose. Another good overview of the issues and literature in the area of corporate governance is presented in the book *Strategic Leadership: Top Executives and Their Effects on Organizations* by Sydney Finkelstein and Donald Hambrick.

Other worthwhile follow-up readings on the topic of corporate governance include the book by Ada Demb and Friedrich Neubauer, *The Corporate Board: Confronting the Paradoxes*, and an excellent comparison of five national governance systems given in the book *Keeping Good Company*, by Jonathan Charkham. Recent edited volumes well worth reading are *Capital Markets and Corporate Governance*, by Nicolas Dimsdale and Martha Prevezer, and *Corporate Governance: Economic, Management and Financial Issues*, by Kevin Keasey, Steve Thompson and Mike Wright.

For further reading on the topic of shareholder value, Alfred Rappaport's book *Creating Shareholder Value* is the obvious place to start. A good follow-up reading is Michael Jensen's article 'Corporate Control and the Politics of Finance'. For a very fundamental point of view, Milton Friedman's classic article 'The Social Responsibility of Business is to Increase Its Profits', is also highly recommended. For a stinging attack on the stakeholder concept, readers are directed to 'The Defects of Stakeholder Theory', by Elaine Sternberg.

For a more positive view of stakeholder theory, Edward Freeman's *Strategic Management: A Stakeholder Approach* is still the book at which to begin. Only recently has stakeholder theory really attracted significant academic attention. Excellent works in this new crop include 'Instrumental Stakeholder Theory: A Synthesis of Ethics and Economics', by Thomas Jones, and 'The Stakeholder Theory of the Corporation: Concepts, Evidence, and Implications', by Thomas Donaldson and Lee Preston.

On the topic of corporate social responsibility, there are a number of good books that can be consulted. Archie Carroll's, *Business and Society: Ethics and Stakeholder Management* can be recommended, while the book *International Business and Society*, by Steven Wartick and Donna Wood, has a stronger international perspective. Good articles include 'The Corporate Social Policy Process: Beyond Business Ethics, Corporate Social Responsibility and Corporate Social Responsiveness', by Edwin Epstein, and the more academic 'A Stakeholder Framework For Analyzing and Evaluating Corporate Social Performance', by Max Clarkson.

For an explicit link between strategy and ethics, the book *Corporate Strategy and the Search For Ethics*, by Edward Freeman and Daniel Gilbert, provides a good point of entry. The more recent article 'Strategic Planning As If Ethics Mattered', by LaRue Hosmer, is also highly recommended. Many books on the general link between ethics and business, such as Thomas Donaldson's *Ethics in International Business*, deal with major strategy issues as well.

Finally, on the topic of corporate mission a very useful overview of the literature is given in the reader *Mission and Business Philosophy*, edited by Andrew Campbell and Kiran Tawadey. Good follow-up works not in this reader are Derek Abell's classic book *Defining the Business: The Starting Point of Strategic Planning*, and the article 'Mission Analysis: An Operational Approach', by Nigel Piercy and Neil Morgan. An interesting book emphasizing the importance of vision is *Built To Last: Successful Habits of Visionary Companies*, by James Collins and Jerry Porras.

READINGS

Unless a variety of opinions are laid before us, we have
no opportunity of selection, but are bound of necessity
to adopt the particular view which may have been brought
forward. The purity of gold cannot be ascertained by
a single specimen; but when we have carefully compared it
with others, we are able to fix upon the finest ore.

Herodotus (5th century BC); Greek historian

In the preceding sections a 'variety of opinions' has been 'laid before us', so that we could 'fix upon the finest ore'. Yet, the debates were held between virtual contestants, not real ones. The proponents of the opposing perspectives did not 'speak' for themselves; their arguments were summarized for them. We took a large body of literature and condensed it into a manageable format and we made explicit what is often left implicit. This streamlined representation of the strategy perspectives made the debates more structured and understandable, but it also came at a cost: in a summary, a bit of the original style and character gets filtered out. In a second-hand rendition of someone's views, elements of the original are lost.

Therefore, in this last section of the book, it is the intention to give readers a first-hand impression of the debates by introducing the original works of leading theorists. For each of the ten debates, two readings are reprinted here, each representing one of the two poles in each debate. Some of these readings are well-known classics, while others are relatively new or less known. The key consideration for selecting these 20 readings has been that they are such clear and powerful advocates of one of the strategy perspectives. To keep the size of the book within acceptable limits, most readings have been reduced in length, while extensive footnotes and references have been dropped. At all times this editing has been guided by the principle that the authors' key ideas and arguments should be preserved intact.

In this section, the readings will be organized into groups of two, following the order of the previous chapters. To make it easy to see which reading belongs to which chapter, each reading is numbered to correspond with the chapter and position it is meant to illustrate. So, Reading 2.1 corresponds with Chapter 2, pole 1, which is the rational reasoning perspective, while Reading 2.2 represents the generative reading perspective. Preceding each pair of readings, a short introduction will be given, placing the readings in a broader context. It is then up to the reader to 'fix upon the finest ore' – or maybe to recognize that the one 'ore' is gold, while the other is diamond, and that it might be possible to combine the two into an even more valuable synthesis.

READINGS ON STRATEGIC THINKING

Selecting the first reading, to represent the rational reasoning perspective, was not easy, as few authors make a point of arguing their rational leanings. The position of logical thinking is so entrenched in much of the management literature, that most writers adopt the rational reasoning perspective without making this choice explicit. Hence, it has not proved possible to present a vocal defender of this perspective to get a nicely polarized debate going. Instead, as the first reading, a classic work has been selected that is a good example of the rational approach to strategic thinking. This reading, 'The Concept of Corporate Strategy', by Kenneth Andrews, has been drawn from one of the most influential textbooks in the field of strategy, *Business Policy: Text and Cases* (Christensen, Andrews, et al, 1987). Andrews is arguably one of the godfathers of strategic management and this chapter from his book has had considerable impact on theorists and practitioners alike. True to the rational reasoning perspective, Andrews argues that strategy analysis and formulation should be conducted consciously, explicitly and rationally. In his view, strategic reasoning is a 'logical activity', while subsequent strategy implementation 'comprises a series of subactivities that are primarily administrative'. It should be noted that in this article Andrews is positioning himself in opposition to strategic incrementalists (see Chapter 3), not vis-à-vis proponents of the generative reasoning perspective. Therefore, he does not counter any of the major arguments raised by advocates of this perspective.

The second reading, highlighting the views of the generative reasoning perspective, is 'The Mind of the Strategist', by Kenichi Ohmae. Ohmae, formerly head of McKinsey's Tokyo office, is one of Japan's most well-known strategy authors. In this reading, taken from the book of the same name, Ohmae argues that the mind of the strategist is not dominated by linear, logical thinking. On the contrary, a strategist's thought processes are 'basically creative and intuitive rather than rational'. In his view, 'great strategies . . . originate in insights that are beyond the reach of conscious analysis'. He does not dismiss logic as unnecessary, but notes that it is insufficient for arriving at innovative strategies. Yet, he observes that in most large companies creative strategists 'are being pushed to the sidelines in favor of rational, by-the-numbers strategic and financial planners', leading to a withering of strategic thinking ability.

READING

2.1

The concept of corporate strategy

By Kenneth Andrews[1]

What strategy is

Corporate strategy is the pattern of decisions in a company that determines and reveals its objectives, purposes, or goals, produces the principal policies and plans for achieving those goals, and defines the range of business the company is to pursue, the kind of economic and human organization it is or intends to be, and the nature of the economic and noneconomic contribution it intends to

[1]Source: This article was adapted with permission from Chapter 2 of *The Concept of Corporate Strategy*, 1987, McGraw-Hill Companies Inc.

make to its shareholders, employees, customers, and communities. In an organization of any size or diversity, *corporate strategy* usually applies to the whole enterprise, while *business strategy*, less comprehensive, defines the choice of product or service and market of individual businesses within the firm. Business strategy is the determination of how a company will compete in a given business and position itself among its competitors. Corporate strategy defines the businesses in which a company will compete, preferably in a way that focuses resources to convert distinctive competence into competitive advantage. Both are outcomes of a continuous process of strategic management that we will later analyze in detail.

The strategic decision contributing to this pattern is one that is effective over long periods of time, affects the company in many different ways, and focuses and commits a significant portion of its resources to the expected outcomes. The pattern resulting from a series of such decisions will probably define the central character and image of a company, the individuality it has for its members and various publics, and the position it will occupy in its industry and markets. It will permit the specification of particular objectives to be attained through a timed sequence of investment and implementation decisions and will govern directly the deployment or redeployment of resources to make these decisions effective.

Some aspects of such a pattern of decisions may be in an established corporation unchanging over long periods of time, like a commitment to quality, or high technology, or certain raw materials, or good labor relations. Other aspects of a strategy must change as or before the world changes, such as a product line, manufacturing process, or merchandising and styling practices. The basic determinants of company character, if purposefully institutionalized, are likely to persist through and shape the nature of substantial changes in product-market choices and allocation of resources.

It would be possible to extend the definition of strategy for a given company to separate a central character and the core of its special accomplishment from the manifestations of such characteristics in changing product lines, markets, and policies designed to make activities profitable from year to year. *The New York Times*, for example, after many years of being shaped by the values of its owners and staff, is now so self-conscious and respected an institution that its nature is likely to remain unchanged, even if the services it offers are altered drastically in the direction of other outlets for its news-processing capacity.

It is important, however, not to take the idea apart in another way, that is, to separate goals from the policies designed to achieve those goals. The essence of the definition of strategy I have just recorded is pattern. The interdependence of purposes, policies, and organized action is crucial to the particularity of an individual strategy and its opportunity to identify competitive advantage. It is the unity, coherence, and internal consistency of a company's strategic decisions that position the company in its environment and give the firm its identity, its power to mobilize its strengths, and its likelihood of success in the marketplace. It is the interrelationship of a set of goals and policies that crystallizes from the formless reality of a company's environment a set of problems an organization can seize upon and solve.

What you are doing, in short, is never meaningful unless you can say or imply what you are doing it for: the quality of administrative action and the motivation lending it power cannot be appraised without knowing its relationship to purpose. Breaking up the system of corporate goals and the character-determining major policies for attainment leads to narrow and mechanical conceptions of strategic management and endless logic chopping.

We should get on to understanding the need for strategic decisions and for determining the most satisfactory pattern of goals in concrete instances. Refinement of definition can wait, for you will wish to develop definition in practice in directions useful to you.

Summary statements of strategy

Before we proceed to clarification of this concept by application, we should specify the terms in which strategy is usually expressed. A summary statement of strategy will characterize the product line and services offered or planned by the company, the markets and market segments for which products and services are now or will be designed, and the channels through which these markets will be reached. The means by which the operation is to be financed will be specified, as will the profit objectives and the emphasis to be placed on the safety of capital versus level of return. Major policy in central functions such as marketing, manufacturing, procurement, research and development, labor relations, and personnel, will be stated where they distinguish the company from others, and usually the intended size, form, and climate of the organization will be included.

Each company, if it were to construct a summary strategy from what it understands itself to be aiming at, would have a different statement with different categories of decision emphasized to indicate what it wanted to be or do.

Reasons for not articulating strategy

For a number of reasons companies seldom formulate and publish a complete strategy statement. Conscious planning of the long-term development of companies has been until recently less common than individual executive responses to environmental pressure, competitive threat, or entrepreneurial opportunity. In the latter mode of development, the unity or coherence of corporate effort is unplanned, natural, intuitive, or even nonexistent. Incrementalism in practice sometimes gives the appearance of consciously formulated strategy, but may be the natural result of compromise among coalitions backing contrary policy proposals or

skillful improvisatory adaptation to external forces. Practicing managers who prefer muddling through to the strategic process would never commit themselves to an articulate strategy.

Other reasons for the scarcity of concrete statements of strategy include the desirability of keeping strategic plans confidential for security reasons and ambiguous to avoid internal conflict or even final decision. Skillful incrementalists may have plans in their heads that they do not reveal, to avoid resistance and other trouble in their own organization. A company with a large division in an obsolescent business that it intends to drain of cash until operations are discontinued could not expect high morale and cooperation to follow publication of this intent. In a dynamic company, moreover, where strategy is continually evolving, the official statement of strategy, unless couched in very general terms, would be as hard to keep up to date as an organization chart. Finally, a firm that has internalized its strategy does not feel the need to keep saying what it is, valuable as that information might be to new members.

Deducing strategy from behavior

In your own company you can do what most managements have not done. In the absence of explicit statements and on the basis of your experience, you may deduce from decisions observed what the pattern is and what the company's goals and policies are, on the assumption that some perhaps unspoken consensus lies behind them. Careful examination of the behavior of competitors will reveal what their strategy must be. At the same time none of us should mistake apparent strategy visible in a pattern of past incremental decisions for conscious planning for the future. What will pass as the current strategy of a company may almost always be deduced from its behavior, but a strategy for a future of changed circumstances may not always be distinguishable from performance in the present. Strategists who do not look beyond present behavior to the future are vulnerable to surprise.

Formulation of strategy

Corporate strategy is an organization process, in many ways inseparable from the structure, behavior, and culture of the company in which it takes place. Nevertheless, we may abstract from the process two important aspects, interrelated in real life but separable for the purposes of analysis. The first of these we may call formulation, the second implementation. Deciding what strategy should be may be approached as a rational undertaking, even if, as in life, emotional attachments (to metal skis or investigative reporting) may complicate choice among future alternatives (for ski manufacturers or alternative newspapers). The principle subactivities of strategy formulation as a logical activity include indentifying opportunities and threats in the company's environment and attaching some estimate of risk to the discernible alternatives. Before a choice can be made, the company's strengths and weaknesses should be appraised together with the resources on hand and available. Its actual or potential capacity to take advantage of perceived market needs or to cope with attendant risks should be estimated as objectively as possible. The strategic alternative that results from matching opportunity and corporate capability at an acceptable level of risk is what we may call an *economic strategy*.

The process described thus far assumes that strategists are analytically objective in estimating the relative capacity of their company and the opportunity they see or anticipate in developing markets. The extent to which they wish to undertake low or high risk presumably depends on their profit objectives. The higher they set the latter, the more willing they must be to assume a correspondingly high risk that the market opportunity they see will not develop or that the corporate competence required to excel competition will not be forthcoming.

So far we have described the intellectual processes of ascertaining what a company *might do* in terms of environmental opportunity, of deciding what it *can do* in terms of ability and power, and of bringing these two considerations together in optimal equilibrium. The determination of strategy also requires consideration of what alternatives are preferred by the chief executive and perhaps by his or her immediate associates as well, quite apart from economic considerations. Personal values, aspirations and ideals do, and in our judgment quite properly should, influence the final choice of purposes. Thus what the executives of a company *want to do* must be brought into the strategic decision.

Finally strategic choice has an ethical aspect – a fact much more dramatically illustrated in some industries than in others. Just as alternatives may be ordered in terms of the degree of risk they entail, so may they be examined against the standards of responsiveness to the expectations of society the strategist elects. Some alternatives may seem to the executive considering them more attractive than others when the public good or service to society is considered. What a company *should do* thus appears as a fourth element of the strategic decision.

The ability to identify the four components of strategy – (a) market opportunity, (b) corporate competence and resources, (c) personal values and aspirations, and (d) acknowledged obligations to segments of society other than stockholders – is easier to exercise than the art of reconciling their implications in a final choice of purpose. Taken by itself each consideration might lead in a different direction.

If you put the various aspirations of individuals in your own organization against this statement you will see what I mean. Even in a single mind contradictory aspirations can survive a long time before the need to calculate trade-offs and integrate divergent inclinations becomes clear. Growth opportunity attracted many companies to the computer business after World War II. The decision to diversify out of typewriters and calculators was encouraged by growth opportunity and excitement that captivated the managements of RCA, General Electric, and Xerox, among others. But the financial, technical, and marketing requirements of this business exceeded the capacity of most of the competitors of IBM. The magnet of opportunity and the incentive of desire obscured the calculations of what resources and competence were required to succeed. Most crucially, where corporate capability leads, executives do not always want to go. Of all the components of strategic choice, the combination of resources and competence is most crucial to success.

The implementation of strategy

Since effective implementation can make a sound strategic decision ineffective or a debatable choice successful, it is as important to examine the processes of implementation as to weigh the advantages of available strategic alternatives. The implementation of strategy comprises a series of subactivities that are primarily administrative. If purpose is determined, then the resources of a company can be mobilized to accomplish it. An organizational structure appropriate for the efficient performance of the required tasks must be made effective by information systems and relationships permitting coordination of subdivided activities. The organizational processes of performance measurement, compensation, management development – all of them enmeshed in systems of incentives and controls – must be directed toward the kind of behavior required by organizational purpose. The role of personal leadership is important and sometimes decisive in the accomplishment of strategy. Although we know that organizational structure and processes of compensation, incentives, control, and management development influence and constrain the formulation of strategy, we should look first at the logical proposition that structure should follow strategy in order to cope later with the organizational reality that strategy also follows

structure. When we have examined both tendencies, we will understand and to some extent be prepared to deal with the interdependence of the formulation and implementation of corporate purpose. Figure 2.1.1 may be useful in understanding the analysis of strategy as a pattern of interrelated decisions.

Criteria for evaluation

How is the actual or proposed strategy to be judged? How are we to know that one strategy is better than another? A number of important questions can regularly be asked. As is already evident, no infallible indicators are available. With practice they will lead to reliable intuitive discriminations.

- Is the strategy indentifiable and has it been made clear either in words or in practice? The degree to which attention has been given to the strategic alternatives available to a company is likely to be basic to the soundness of its strategic decision. To cover in empty phrases ('Our policy is planned profitable growth in any market we can serve well') an absence of analysis of opportunity or actual determination of corporate strength is worse than to remain silent, for it conveys the illusion of a commitment when none has been made. The unstated strategy cannot be tested or contested and is likely therefore to be weak. If it is implicit in the intuition of a strong leader, the organization is likely to be weak and the demands the strategy makes upon it are likely to remain unmet. A strategy must be explicit to be effective and specific enough to require some actions and exclude others.

- Does the strategy exploit fully domestic and international environmental opportunity? The relation between market opportunity and organizational development is a critical one in the design of future plans. Unless growth is incompatible with the resources of an organization or the aspirations of its management, it is likely that a strategy that does

FIGURE 2.1.1 The strategy process

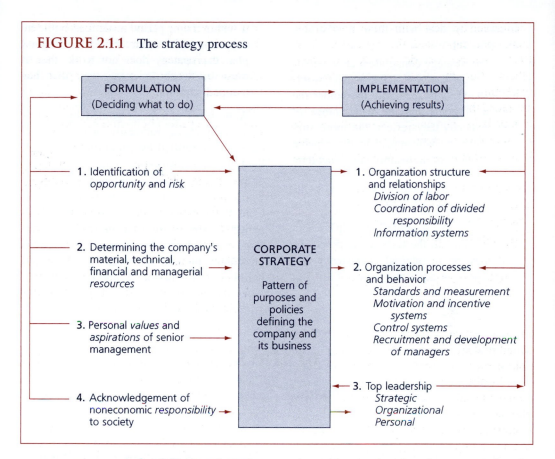

not purport to make full use of market opportunity will be weak also in other aspects. Vulnerability to competition is increased by lack of interest in market share.

- Is the strategy consistent with corporate competence and resources, both present and projected? Although additional resources, both financial and managerial, are available to companies with genuine opportunity, the availability of each must be finally determined and programmed along a practicable time scale. This may be the most difficult question in this series.

- Are the major provisions of the strategy and the program of major policies of which it is comprised internally consistent? One advantage of making as specific a statement of strategy as is practicable is the resultant availability of a careful check on fit, unity, coherence, compatibility, and synergy – the state in which the whole of

anything can be viewed as greater than the sum of its parts.

- Is the chosen level of risk feasible in economic and personal terms? The riskiness of any future plan should be compatible with the economic resources of the organization and the temperament of the managers concerned.

- Is the strategy appropriate to the personal values and aspirations of the key managers? Conflict between personal preferences, aspirations, and goals of the key members of an organization and the plan for its future is a sign of danger and a harbinger of mediocre performance or failure.

- Is the strategy appropriate to the desired level of contribution to society? To the extent that the chosen economic opportunity of the firm has social costs, such as air or water pollution, a statement of intention to deal with these is desirable and prudent.

■ **Does the strategy constitute a clear stimulus to organizational effort and commitment?** Generally speaking, the bolder the choice of goals and the wider range of human needs they reflect, the more successfully they will appeal to the capable membership of a healthy and energetic organization.

■ **Are there early indications of the responsiveness of markets and market segments to the strategy?** A strategy may pass with flying colors all the tests so far proposed, and may be in internal consistency and uniqueness an admirable work of art. But

if within a time period made reasonable by the company's resources and the original plan the strategy does not work, then it must be weak in some way that has escaped attention.

A business enterprise guided by a clear sense of purpose rationally arrived at and emotionally ratified by commitment is more likely to have a successful outcome, in terms of profit and social good, than a company whose future is left to guesswork and chance. Conscious strategy does not preclude brilliance of improvisation or the welcome consequences of good fortune. Its cost is principally thought and work for which it is hard but not impossible to find time.

READING 2.2

The mind of the strategist

By Kenichi Ohmae[1]

As a consultant I have had the opportunity to work with many large Japanese companies. Among them are many companies whose success you would say must be the result of superb strategies. But when you look more closely, you discover a paradox. They have no big planning staffs, no elaborate, gold-plated strategic planning processes. Some of them are painfully handicapped by lack of the resources – people, money, and technology – that seemingly would be needed to implement an ambitious strategy. Yet despite all these handicaps, they are outstanding performers in the marketplace. Year after year, they manage to build share and create wealth.

How do they do it? The answer is easy. They may not have a strategic planning staff, but they do have a strategist of great natural

talent: usually the founder or chief executive. Often – especially in Japan, where there is no business school – these outstanding strategists have had little or no formal business education, at least at the college level. They may never have taken a course or read a book on strategy. But they have an intuitive grasp of the basic elements of strategy. They have an idiosyncratic mode of thinking in which company, customers, and competition merge in a dynamic interaction out of which a comprehensive set of objectives and plans for action eventually crystallizes.

Insight is the key to this process. Because it is creative, partly intuitive, and often disruptive of the status quo, the resulting plans might not even hold water from the analyst's point of view. It is the creative element in these plans and the drive and will of the mind that con-

[1]Source: This article was adapted with permission from the Introduction, and Chapters 1 and 17 of *The Mind of the Strategist: The Art of Japanese Business*, McGraw-Hill New York, 1982.

ceived them that give these strategies their extraordinary competitive impact.

Both in Japan and in the West, this breed of natural or instinctive strategist is dying out or at least being pushed to the sidelines in favor of rational, by-the-numbers strategic and financial planners. Today's giant institutions, both public and private, are by and large not organized for innovation. Their systems and processes are all oriented toward incremental improvement – doing better what they are doing already. In the United States, the pressure of innumerable social and governmental constraints on corporate activities – most notably, perhaps, the proliferation of government regulations during the 1960s and 1970s – has put a premium on the talent for adaptation and reduced still further the incentive to innovate. Advocates of bold and ambitious strategies too often find themselves on the sidelines, labeled as losers, while the rewards go to those more skilled at working within the system. This is especially true in mature industries, where actions and ideas often move in narrow grooves, forcing out innovators. Conversely, venture capital groups tend to attract the flexible, adaptive minds.

In all times and places, large institutions develop cultures of their own, and success is often closely tied to the ability to conform. In our day, the culture of most business corporations exalts logic and rationality; hence, it is analysts rather than innovators who tend to get ahead. It is not unreasonable to say that many large US corporations today are run like the Soviet economy. In order to survive, they must plan ahead comprehensively, controlling an array of critical functions in every detail. They specify policies and procedures in meticulous detail, spelling out for practically everyone what can and what cannot be done in particular circumstances. They establish hurdle rates, analyze risks, and anticipate contingencies. As strategic planning processes have burgeoned in these companies, strategic thinking has gradually withered away.

My message, as you will have guessed by now, is that successful business strategies result not from rigorous analysis but from a particular state of mind. In what I call the mind of the strategist, insight and a consequent drive for achievement, often amounting to a sense of mission, fuel a thought process which is basically creative and intuitive rather than rational. Strategists do not reject analysis. Indeed they can hardly do without it. But they use it only to stimulate the creative process, to test the ideas that emerge, to work out their strategic implications, or to ensure successful execution of high potential 'wild' ideas that might otherwise never be implemented properly. Great strategies, like great works of art or great scientific discoveries, call for technical mastery in the working out but originate in insights that are beyond the reach of conscious analysis.

If this is so – if the mind of the strategist is so deeply at odds with the culture of the corporation – how can an already institutionalized company recover the capacity to conceive and execute creative business strategies? In a book entitled *The Corporate Strategist* that was published in Japan in 1975, I attempted to answer that question in a specifically Japanese context.

In Japan, a different set of conditions from those in the West inhibits the creation of bold and innovative strategies. In the large Japanese company, promotion is based on tenure; there is no fast track for brilliant performers. No one reaches a senior management post before their mid-fifties, and chief executives are typically over 60 – well past the age when they are likely to be able to generate dynamic strategic ideas. At the same time, the inventive, often aggressive younger people have no means of contributing in a significant way to the strategy of the corporation. The result: strategic stagnation or the strong probability of it.

How, I asked myself, could the mind of the strategist, with its inventive élan, be reproduced in this kind of corporate culture? What were the ingredients of an excellent strategist, and how could they be reproduced in the Japanese context? These were the questions I addressed in my book. The answer I came up with involved the formation within the corporation of a group of young 'samurais' who would play a dual role. On the one hand they would function as real strategists, giving free rein to their imagination and entrepreneurial flair in order to come up with bold and innovative strategic ideas. On the other hand they would serve as staff analysts, testing out, digesting, and assigning priorities to the ideas, and providing staff assistance to line managers in implementing the approved strategies. This 'samurai' concept has since been adopted in several Japanese firms with great success.

Such a solution would not fit the circumstances of the typical American or European company. Yet it seems to me that the central notion of my book and of a sequel published in Japan 18 months later is relevant to the problem of strategic stagnation in any organization. There are ways in which the mind of the strategist can be reproduced, or simulated, by people who may lack a natural talent for strategy. Putting it another way, although there is no secret formula for inventing a successful strategy, there are some specific concepts and approaches that can help anyone develop the kind of mentality that comes up with superior strategic ideas. Thus the reader will find in this reading no formulas for successful business strategy. What I will try to supply in their place is a series of hints that may help him or her develop the capacity for and the habit of strategic thinking.

Analysis: The starting point

Analysis is the critical starting point of strategic thinking. Faced with problems, trends, events, or situations that appear to constitute a harmonious whole or come packaged as a whole by the common sense of the day, the strategic thinker dissects them into their constituent parts. Then, having discovered the significance of these constituents, he reassembles them in a way calculated to maximize his advantage.

In business as on the battlefield, the object of strategy is to bring about the conditions most favorable to one's own side, judging precisely the right moment to attack or withdraw and always assessing the limits of compromise correctly. Besides the habit of analysis, what marks the mind of the strategist is an intellectual elasticity or flexibility that enables him to come up with realistic responses to changing situations, not simply to discriminate with great precision among different shades of gray.

In strategic thinking, one first seeks a clear understanding of the particular character of each element of a situation and then makes the fullest possible use of human brainpower to restructure the elements in the most advantageous way. Phenomena and events in the real world do not always fit a linear model. Hence the most reliable means of dissecting a situation into its constituent parts and reassembling them in the desired pattern is not a step-by-step methodology such as systems analysis. Rather, it is that ultimate nonlinear thinking tool, the human brain. True strategic thinking thus contrasts sharply with the conventional mechanical systems approach based on linear thinking. But it also contrasts with the approach that stakes everything on intuition, reaching conclusions without any real breakdown or analysis (Figure 2.2.1).

No matter how difficult or unprecedented the problem, a breakthrough to the best possible solution can come only from a combination of rational analysis, based on the real nature of things, and imaginative reintegration of all the different items into a new pattern, using nonlinear brainpower. This is always the most effective approach to devising strategies for dealing successfully with challenges and opportunities, in the market arena as on the battlefield.

Determining the critical issue

The first stage in strategic thinking is to pinpoint the critical issue in the situation. Everyone facing a problem naturally tries in his or her own way to penetrate to the key

FIGURE 2.2.1 Three kinds of thinking process

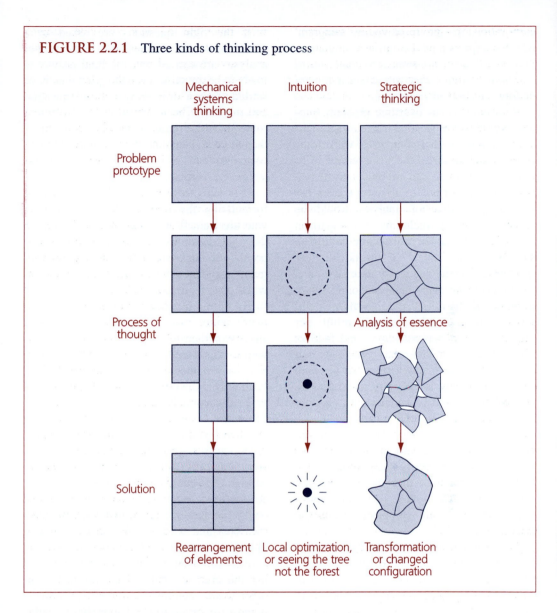

issue. Some may think that one way is as good as another and that whether their efforts hit the mark is largely a matter of luck. I believe it is not a question of luck at all but of attitude and method. In problem solving, it is vital at the start to formulate the question in a way that will facilitate the discovery of a solution.

Suppose, for example, that overtime work has become chronic in a company, dragging down profitability. If we frame the question as What should be done to reduce overtime?, many answers will suggest themselves:

- work harder during the regular working hours;
- shorten the lunch period and coffee breaks;
- forbid long private telephone conversations.

Such questioning is often employed by companies trying to lower costs and improve product quality by using zero defect campaigns and quality control (QC) circles that involve the participation of all employees. Ideas are gathered, screened, and later incorporated in the improvement program. But this approach has an intrinsic limitation. *The questions are not framed to point toward a solution; rather, they are directed toward finding remedies to symptoms.*

Returning to our overtime problem, suppose we frame the question in a more solution-oriented way: Is this company's work force large enough to do all the work required? To this question there can be only one of two answers – yes or no. To arrive at the answer yes, a great deal of analysis would be needed, probably including a comparison with other companies in the same industries, the historical trend of workload per employee, and the degree of automation and computerization and their economic effectiveness. On the other hand, if – after careful perusal of the sales record, profit per employee, ratio between direct and indirect labor, comparison with other companies, and so on – the answer should turn out to be no (i.e. the company is currently understaffed), this in itself would be tantamount to a solution of the original problem. This solution – an increase in personnel – will be validated by all the usual management indicators. And if the company adopts this solution, the probability increases that the desired outcome will actually follow. This way, objective analysis can supplant emotional discussions.

That is not the only way the question could have been formulated, however. We might have asked it this way: Do the capabilities of the employees match the nature of the work? This formulation, like the previous one, is oriented toward deriving a possible solution. Here too, a negative answer would imply a shortage of suitable personnel, which would in turn suggest that the solution should be sought either in staff training or in recruiting capable staff from elsewhere. On the other hand, if the answer is yes, this indicates that the problem of chronic overtime lies not in the nature of the work but in the amount of the workload. Thus, not training but adding to the work force would then be the crucial factor in the solution.

If the right questions are asked in a solution-oriented manner, and if the proper analyses are carried out, the final answer is likely to be the same, even though it may have started from a differently phrased question and may have been arrived at by a different route. In either case, a question concerning the nature and amount of work brings the real issue into focus and makes it easy to arrive at a clear-cut verdict.

It is hard to overstate the importance of formulating the question correctly. People who are trained and motivated to formulate the right questions will not offer vague proposals for 'improvements', as are seen in many suggestion boxes. They will come up with concrete, practical ideas.

By failing to grasp the critical issues, too many senior managers today impose great anxiety on themselves and their subordinates, whose efforts end in failure and frustration. Solution-oriented questions can be formulated only if the critical issue is localized and grasped accurately in the first place. A clear common understanding of the nature of a problem that has already been localized provides a critical pressure to come up with creative solutions. When problems are poorly defined or vaguely comprehended, one's creative mind does not work sharply. The greater one's tolerance for lukewarm solutions, half measures and what the British used to call muddling through, the more loosely the issue is likely to be defined. For this reason, isolating the crucial points of the problem – in other words, determining the critical issue – is most important to the discovery of a solution. The key at this initial stage is to *narrow down the issue by studying the observed phenomena closely.*

Figure 2.2.2 illustrates one method often used by strategists in the process of abstraction, showing how it might work in the case of a large, established company faced with the problem of declining competitive vigor.

The first step in the abstraction process is to use such means as brainstorming and opinion polls to assemble and itemize the respects in which the company is at a disadvantage

FIGURE 2.2.2 Narrowing down the issue

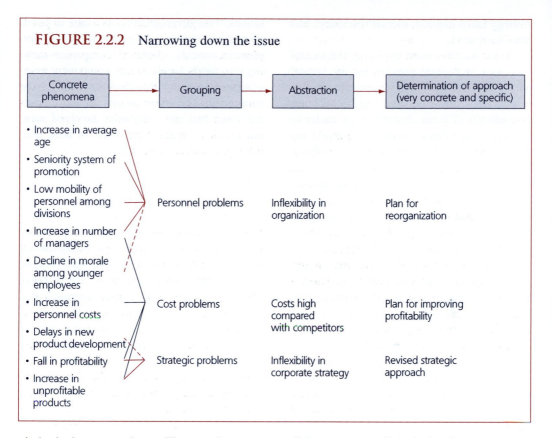

Concrete phenomena	Grouping	Abstraction	Determination of approach (very concrete and specific)
• Increase in average age • Seniority system of promotion • Low mobility of personnel among divisions • Increase in number of managers • Decline in morale among younger employees	Personnel problems	Inflexibility in organization	Plan for reorganization
• Increase in personnel costs • Delays in new product development	Cost problems	Costs high compared with competitors	Plan for improving profitability
• Fall in profitability • Increase in unprofitable products	Strategic problems	Inflexibility in corporate strategy	Revised strategic approach

vis-à-vis its competitors. These points can then be classified under a smaller number of headings (shown in Figure 2.2.2 as Concrete Phenomena) according to their common factors.

Next, phenomena sharing some common denominator are themselves combined into groups. Having done this, we look once again at each group as a unit and ask ourselves what crucial issue each unit poses. The source of the problem must be understood before any real solution can be found, and the process of abstraction enables us to bring the crucial issues to light without the risk of overlooking anything important.

Once the abstraction process has been completed, we must next decide on the right approach to finding a solution. Once we have determined the solution in principle, there remains the task of working out implementation programs and then compiling detailed action plans. No solution, however perfectly it may address the critical issue, can be of the slightest use until it is implemented. Too many companies try to short-circuit the necessary steps between identification of critical issues and line implementation of solutions by skipping the intermediate steps: planning for operational improvement and organizing for concrete actions. Even the most brilliant line manager cannot translate an abstract plan into action in a single step.

The art of strategic thinking

Most of us are familiar with Thomas Alva Edison's recipe for inventive genius: '1 percent inspiration, 99 percent perspiration.' The same ratio holds true for creativity in any endeavor, including the development of business strategy. Don't be misled by the ratio. That spark of insight *is* essential. Without it, strategies disintegrate into stereotypes. But to bring insight to fruition as a successful strategy takes method, mental discipline, and plain hard work.

So far we have been exploring the mental processes or thought patterns for the 'grunt' part of the strategy. When we come to creative inspiration, however, our task becomes exceedingly difficult. Insight is far easier to recognize than define. Perhaps we might say that creative insight is the ability to combine, synthesize, or reshuffle previously unrelated phenomena in such a way that you get more out of the emergent whole than you have put in.

What does this all mean to the strategist? Can creativity be taught? Perhaps not. Can it be cultivated consciously? Obviously I believe so, or I wouldn't have written this article. Inventive geniuses such as Thomas Edison or Edwin Land are by definition rare exceptions. For most of us, creative insight is a smoldering ember that must be fanned constantly to glow. I strongly believe that when all the right ingredients are present – sensitivity, will, and receptiveness – they can be nurtured by example, direction, and conditioning. In short, creativity cannot be taught, but it can be learned.

Putting it more prosaically, we need to identify and stimulate those habits or conditions which nurture creativity and at the same time to crystallize the constraints or boundaries defining our probability of success. In my experience, there are at least three major constraints to which the business strategist needs to be sensitive. I think of them as the essential Rs: reality, ripeness, and resources.

Let's begin with *reality*. Unlike scientific conceptualizers or creative artists, business strategists must always be aware of the customer, the competition, and the company's field of competence. *Ripeness*, or timing, is the second key consideration that the business strategist must address. Unless the time is ripe for the proposed strategy, it is virtually certain to fail. *Resources*, my third R, constitute such an obvious constraint that it is amazing that they should be ignored or neglected by strategists. Yet examples abound of strategies that failed because their authors were not sensitive to their own resource limi-tations. Take diversification as a case in point. Few food companies trying to move into pharmaceuticals, chemical companies moving into foods, or electronic component manufacturers moving into final assembly have succeeded. The basic reason in most cases has been that the companies involved were not sensitive to the limitations of their own internal resources and skills.

Conditions of creativity

Being attuned to the three Rs is a necessary precondition of creative insight, but in itself it will not fan the spark of creative power within us. For that, other elements are needed. Obviously, there is no single approach that will dependably turn anyone into a super-strategist, but there are certain things we can consciously do to stretch or stimulate our creative prowess. Most important, I believe, we need to cultivate three interrelated conditions – an initial charge, directional antennae, and a capacity to tolerate static.

Call it what you will – vision, focus, inner drive – the initial charge must be there. It is the mainspring of intuitive creativity. We have seen how Yamaha, originally a wood-based furniture company, was transformed into a major force in the leisure industry by just such a vision, born of one man's desire to bring positive enrichment into the lives of the work-oriented Japanese. From this vision he developed a totally new thrust for Yamaha.

An entire family of musical instruments and accessories – organs, trumpets, cornets, trombones, guitars, and so on – was developed to complement Yamaha's pianos. These were followed by stereo equipment, sporting goods, motorcycles and pleasure boats. Music schools were established. Then came the Yamaha Music Camp, complete with a resort lodge complex, a game reserve, an archery range, and other leisure-oriented pursuits. Today, Yamaha plans concerts and is involved with concert hall management as well, reaping profits while enriching the lives of millions of Japanese.

If the initial charge provides the creative impetus, directional antennae are required to recognize phenomena which, as the saying goes, are in the air. These antennae are the component in the creative process that uncovers and selects, among a welter of facts and existing conditions, potentially profitable ideas that were always there but were visible only to eyes not blinded by habit.

Consider how these directional antennae work for Dr Kazuma Tateishi, founder and chairman of Omron Tateishi Electronics. Tateishi has an uncanny flair for sensing phenomena to which the concept of flow can be applied. He perceived the banking business as a flow of cash, traffic jams and congested train stations as blocked flows of cars and people, and production lines as a physical flow of parts. From these perceptions evolved the development of Japan's first automated banking system, the introduction of sequence controllers that automatically regulate traffic according to road conditions and volume, and the evolution of the world's first unmanned railroad station based on a completely automatic system that can exchange bills for coins, issue tickets and season passes, and adjust fares and operate turnstiles. Today, Omron's automated systems are used in many industrial operations from production to distribution. Dr Tateishi is a remarkable example of a man whose directional antennae have enabled him to implement his youthful creed: 'Man should do only what only man can do.'

Creative concepts often have a disruptive as well as a constructive aspect. They can shatter set patterns of thinking, threaten the status quo, or at the very least stir up people's anxieties. Often when people set out to sell or implement a creative idea, they are taking a big risk of failing, losing money, or simply making fools of themselves. That is why the will to cope with criticism, hostility, and even derision, while not necessarily a condition of creative thinking, does seem to be an important characteristic of successful innovative strategists. To squeeze the last drop out of my original metaphor, I call this the static-tolerance component of creativity.

Witness the static that Soichiro Honda had to tolerate in order to bring his clean-engine car to market. Only corporate insiders can tell how much intracompany interference he had to cope with. That the government vainly brought severe pressure on him to stay out of the auto market is no secret, however. Neither is the public ridicule he bore when industry experts scoffed at his concept.

Dr Koji Kobayashi of NEC tolerated static of a rather different kind. Despite prevailing industry trends, he clung fast to his intuitive belief (some 20 years ahead of its time) that computers and telecommunications would one day be linked. To do so, he had to bear heavy financial burdens, internal dissension, and scorn. All this leads me to a final observation. Strategic success cannot be reduced to a formula, nor can anyone become a strategic thinker merely by reading a book. Nevertheless, there are habits of mind and modes of thinking that can be acquired through practice to help you free the creative power of your subconscious and improve your odds of coming up with winning strategic concepts.

The main purpose of this contribution is to encourage you to do so and to point out the directions you should pursue. The use of Japanese examples to illustrate points and reinforce assertions may at times have given it an exotic flavor, but that is ultimately of no importance. Creativity, mental productivity and the power of strategic insight know no national boundaries. Fortunately for all of us, they are universal.

READINGS ON STRATEGY FORMATION

As opening reading in the debate on strategy formation, 'Managing the Strategy Process', by Balaji Chakravarthy and Peter Lorange, has been selected to represent the strategic planning perspective. Lorange is one of the most well-known writers on the topic of formal planning systems (Lorange, 1980; Lorange and Vancil, 1977) and this reading is taken from the textbook he co-authored with Chakravarthy, entitled *Managing the Strategy Process: A Framework for a Multibusiness Firm*. As most proponents of the strategic planning perspective, Chakravarthy and Lorange do not actively defend their assumption that formal planning is beneficial. Rather, basing themselves on this supposition, they concentrate on outlining a framework for effectively structuring strategic planning activities. Their ideal is an extensive strategic planning system, comprised of a number of distinct steps, procedures, mechanisms and roles. However, they go further than just structuring strategic planning. In their view, a formal planning system will not lead to effective strategy formation if it is not linked to other organizational systems. In particular, the strategic planning system needs to interact with the monitoring, control, and learning system, the incentives system and the staffing system. As such, Chakravarthy and Lorange champion a highly comprehensive and structured approach to strategic planning.

As spokesman for the strategic incrementalism perspective, James Brian Quinn has been chosen. Together with Henry Mintzberg, Quinn has been one of the most influential pioneers on the topic of emergent strategy. Quinn's article, 'Logical Incrementalism', reprinted here, and his subsequent book *Strategies for Change* (1980), are widely accepted as having been instrumental in developing the strategic incrementalism perspective. In his reading, Quinn explains some of the key shortcomings of formal strategic planning and goes on to make a case for strategic incrementalism. Important in his argumentation is that strategic incrementalism is distinguished from muddling through. Incrementalism is a proactive approach to strategy formation – managers can intentionally choose to let unintended strategies emerge. Muddling through is also incremental in nature, but reactive and ad hoc – improvised decisions are made to deal with unplanned and poorly controllable circumstances. To make this distinction more explicit, Quinn refers to the proactive strain of incremental behavior as 'logical incrementalism'. By 'logical' he means 'reasonable and well-considered'. However, logical incrementalism is not always logical by the definition used in Chapter 2 – incremental behavior is not necessarily 'dictated by formal logic'. Therefore, for the sake of accuracy and clarity, the term strategic incrementalism is used in this book instead of logical incrementalism.

Managing the strategy process

By Balaji Chakravarthy and Peter Lorange[1]

There are five distinct steps in the strategy process (see Figure 3.1.1). The first three steps involve the strategic planning system; the final two steps cover the role of the monitoring, control, and learning system and the incentives and staffing systems, respectively.

[1]Source: This article was adapted from Chapter 1 of B.S. Chakravarty and P. Lorange, *Managing the Strategy Process: A Framework for a Multibusiness Firm,* © 1991, reprinted by permission of Pearson Education, Inc., Upper Saddle River, NJ.

FIGURE 3.1.1   The strategy process

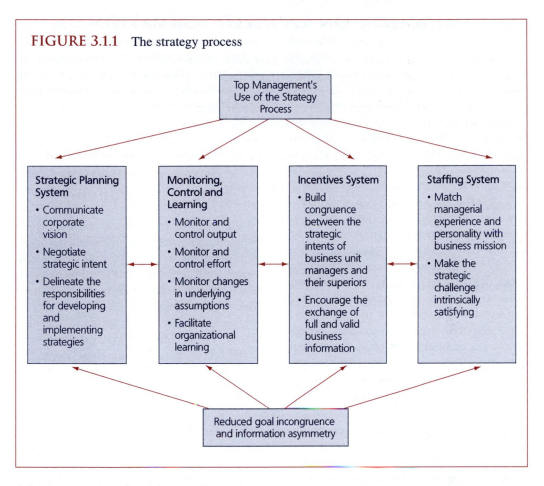

The strategic planning system

The purpose of the first step in the planning system, *objectives setting*, is to determine a strategic direction for the firm and each of its divisions and business units. Objectives setting calls for an open-ended reassessment of the firm's business environments and its strengths in dealing with these environments. At the conclusion of this step, there should be agreement at all levels of the organization on the goals that should be pursued and the strategies that will be needed to meet them. It is worth differentiating here between objectives and goals. Objectives refer to the strategic intent of the firm in the long run. Goals, on the other hand, are more specific statements of the achievements targeted for certain deadlines – goals can be accomplished, and when that happens the firm moves closer to

meeting its objectives. Objectives represent a more enduring challenge.

The second step, *strategic programming*, develops the strategies identified in the first step and defines the cross-functional programs that will be needed to implement the chosen strategies. Cross-functional cooperation is essential to this step. At the end of the strategic programming step a long-term financial plan is drawn up for the firm as a whole and each of its divisions, business units, and functions. On top of the financial projections from existing operations, the long-term financial plan overlays both the expenditures and revenues associated with the approved strategic programs of an organizational unit. The time horizon for these financial plans is chosen to cover the typical lead times that are required to implement the firm's strategic programs. A five-year financial plan is, however, very common. The purpose of the five-year financial plan is to ensure that the approved strategic programs can be funded through either the firm's internally generated resources or externally financed resources.

The third step, *budgeting*, defines both the strategic and operating budgets of the firm. The strategic budget helps identify the contributions that the firm's functional departments, business units, and divisions will be expected to make in a given fiscal year in support of the firm's approved strategic programs. It incorporates new product/market initiatives. The operating budget, on the other hand, provides resources to functional departments, business units, and divisions so that they can sustain their existing momentum. It is based on projected short-term activity levels, given past trends. Failure to meet the operating budget will hurt the firm's short-term performance, whereas failure to meet the strategic budget will compromise the firm's future.

The monitoring, control, and learning system

The fourth step in the strategy process is *monitoring, control, and learning*. Here the emphasis is not on output but on meeting key milestones in the strategic budget and on adhering to planned spending schedules. Strategic programs, like strategic budgets, are monitored for the milestones reached and for adherence to spending schedules. In addition, the key assumptions underlying these programs are validated periodically. As a natural extension to this validation process, even the agreed-on goals at various levels are reassessed in the light of changes to the resources of the firm and its business environment.

The incentives and staffing systems

The fifth and final step in the strategy process is *incentives and staffing*. One part of this is the award of incentives as contracted to the firm's managers. If the incentives system is perceived to have failed in inducing the desired performance, redesigning the incentives system and reassessing the staffing of key managerial positions are considered at this step.

Linking organizational levels and steps in strategic planning

An effective strategy process must allow for interactions between the organizational levels and iterations between the process steps. Figure 3.1.2 describes some of the interactions and iterations in the strategic planning steps. The formal interactions in the process are shown in the figure by the solid line that weaves up and down through the organizational levels and across the three steps. The informal interactions that complement the formal interactions are shown by dotted loops.

Objectives setting

The first formal step of the strategy process commences soon after top management reaffirms or modifies the firm's objectives at the beginning of each fiscal year. Embedded in these objectives should be the vision of the chief executive officer (CEO) and his or her top management team. Top management's vision helps specify what will make the firm great. An elaboration of this vision can be done through a formal statement of objectives. However, it is not the formality of a firm's objectives but rather the excitement and challenge that top management's vision can bring to a firm's managers that is important to the strategy process.

Along with its communication of corporate objectives, top management must provide a forecast on key environmental factors. Assumptions on exchange rates, inflation, and other economic factors – as well as projections on the political risks associated with each country – are best compiled centrally so as to ensure

FIGURE 3.1.2 Steps in the strategy process

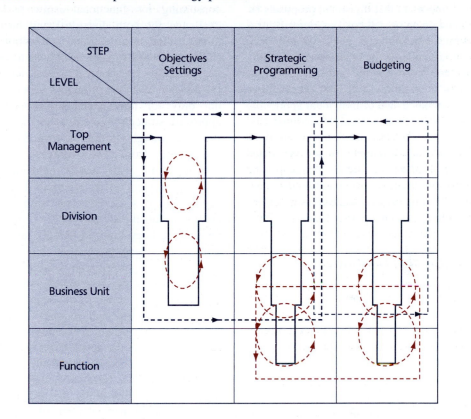

objectivity and consistency. These objectives and forecasts are then discussed with a firm's divisional and business unit managers.

Once the corporate objectives are decided, top management negotiates, for each division and business unit in the firm, goals that are consistent with these objectives. The nature of these negotiations can vary. In some firms, top management may wish to set goals in a top-down fashion; in others, it may invite subordinate managers to participate in the goal-setting process. Managers are encouraged to examine new strategies and modify existing ones in order to accomplish their goals. The proposed strategies are approved at each higher level in the organizational hierarchy, then eventually by top management. Top management tries to make certain that the strategies as proposed are consistent with the firm's objectives and can be supported with the resources available

to the firm. Modifications, where necessary, are made to the objectives, goals, and strategies in order to bring them in alignment. Another important outcome of the objectives-setting step is to build a common understanding across the firm's managerial hierarchy of the goals and strategies that are intended for each organizational unit.

The objectives-setting step in Figure 3.1.2 does not include the functional departments. As we observed earlier, the primary role of these departments is a supporting one. They do not have a profit or growth responsibility, and their goals cannot be decided until the second step, when strategic programs in support of approved business unit goals begin to be formed. It is not uncommon, however, for key functional managers to be invited to participate in the objectives-setting step either as experts in a corporate task force or, more informally, as participants in the deliberations that are held at the business unit level.

It is important that divisional proposals be evaluated on an overall basis as elements of a corporate portfolio and not reviewed in a sequential mode. In the latter case, the resulting overall balance in the corporate portfolio would be more or less incidental, representing the accumulated sum of individual approvals. It makes little sense to attempt to judge in isolation whether a particular business family or business strategy is attractive to the corporate portfolio. That will depend on a strategy's fit with the rest of the portfolio and on the competing investment opportunities available to the firm in its business portfolio.

Strategic programming

The second step in the process has two purposes:

1   To forge an agreement between divisional, business unit, and functional managers on the strategic programs that have to be implemented over the next few years.

2   To deepen the involvement of functional managers in developing the strategies that were tentatively selected in the first step.

The strategic programming step begins with a communication from top management about the goals and strategies that were finally approved for the firm's divisions and business units. The divisonal manager then invites his or her business unit and functional managers to identify program alternatives in support of the approved goals and strategies. Examples of strategic programs include increasing market share for an existing product, introducing a new product, and launching a joint marketing campaign for a family of divisional products. As in these examples, a strategic program typically requires the cooperation of multiple functional departments.

However, the functional specialties within a firm often represent different professional cultures that do not necessarily blend easily. Further, day-to-day operating tasks can be so demanding that the functional managers may simply find it difficult to participate in the time-consuming cross-functional teamwork. A key challenge for both divisional and business managers is to bring about this interaction.

The proposed strategic programs travel up the hierarchy for approval at each level. At the division level, the programs are evaluated not only for how well they support the approved strategies but also for how they promote synergies within the firm. Synergies can come from two sources: through economies of scale and/or economies of scope. The creation of synergies based on economies of scale calls for a sharing of common functional activities – such as research and development (R&D), raw materials procurement, production, and distribution – so as to spread over a larger volume the overhead costs associated with these functions. The creation of economies of scope, on the other hand, requires a common approach to the market. Examples of such an approach include the development of a common trademark, the development of products/services that have a complementary appeal to a customer group, and the ability to offer a common regional service organization for the firm's diverse businesses.

At the corporate level, the proposed strategic programs provide an estimate of the resources that will be required to support the divisional and business unit goals. These goals, as well as their supporting strategies, are once again reassessed; and where needed, modifications are sought in the proposed strategic programs. As noted earlier, a long-term financial plan is drawn up at this stage for the firm as a whole and each of its organizational units. The approved strategic programs are communicated to the divisions, business units, and functional departments at the beginning of the budgeting cycle.

Budgeting

When top management decides on the strategic programs that the firm should pursue, it has de facto allocated all of the firm's human, technological, and financial resources that are available for internal development. This allocation influences the strategic budgets that may be requested at each level in the organizational hierarchy.

The strategic budgets, together with the operating budgets of the various organizational units, are consolidated and sent up for top management approval. When top management finally approves the budgets of the various organizational units, before the start of a new budget year, it brings to a close what can be a year-long journey through the three steps of the strategy-making subprocess. The strategy implementation subprocess is then set into motion. Even though the two subprocesses are described sequentially here, it is important to mention that even as the budget for a given year is being formed, the one for the prior year will be under implementation. Midcourse corrections to the prior year's budget can have an

impact on the formulation of the current budget.

If the actual accomplishments fall short of the strategic budget, in particular, the negative variance may suggest that the firm's managers failed to implement its chosen strategy efficiently. But it can also suggest that the strategic programs that drive this budget may have been ill conceived or even that the goals underlying these programs may have been specified incorrectly. The monitoring, control, and learning system provides continuous information on both the appropriateness of a strategic budget and the efficiency with which the budget is implemented. This information, based on the implementation of the prior year's strategic budget, can trigger another set of iterations between the three strategy-making steps, calling into question the goals and strategies on which the current year's budget are based. These iterations are shown by the dotted rectangles in Figure 3.1.2.

READING	# Logical incrementalism
3.2	*By James Quinn*[1]

When I was younger I always conceived of a room where all these [strategic] concepts were worked out for the whole company. Later I didn't find any such room . . . . The strategy [of the company] may not even exist in the mind of one man. I certainly don't know where it is written down. It is simply transmitted in the series of decisions made.

Interview quote

Introduction

When well-managed major organizations make significant changes in strategy, the approaches they use frequently bear little resemblance to the rational-analytical systems so often touted in the planning literature. The full strategy is rarely written down in any one place. The processes used to arrive at the total strategy are typically fragmented, evolutionary, and largely intuitive. Although one can usually find embedded in these fragments some very refined pieces of formal strategic

[1] Source: This article was originally published as 'Strategic Change: Logical Incrementalism' in *Sloan Management Review*, Fall, 1978, pp. 7–21. Reproduced by permission.

analysis, the real strategy tends to evolve as internal decisions and external events flow together to create a new, widely shared consensus for action among key members of the top management team. Far from being an abrogation of good management practice, the rationale behind this kind of strategy formulation is so powerful that it perhaps provides the normative model for strategic decision making, rather than the step-by-step 'formal systems planning' approach so often espoused.

The formal systems planning approach

A strong normative literature states what factors should be included in a systematically planned strategy and how to analyze and relate these factors step-by-step. The main elements of this 'formal' planning approach include:

- analyzing one's own internal situation: strengths, weaknesses, competencies, problems;

- projecting current product lines, profits, sales, investment needs into the future;

- analyzing selected external environments and opponents' actions for opportunities and threats;

- establishing broad goals as targets for subordinate groups' plans;

- identifying the gap between expected and desired results;

- communicating planning assumptions to the divisions;

- requesting proposed plans from subordinate groups with more specific target goals, resource needs, and supporting action plans;

- occasionally asking for special studies of alternatives, contingencies, or longer-term opportunities;

- reviewing and approving divisional plans and summing these for corporate needs;

- developing long-term budgets presumably related to plans;

- implementing plans;

- monitoring and evaluating performance (presumably against plans, but usually against budgets).

While this approach is excellent for some purposes, it tends to focus unduly on measurable quantitative factors and to underemphasize the vital qualitative, organizational, and power-behavioral factors that so often determine strategic success in one situation versus another. In practice, such planning is just one building block in a continuous stream of events that really determine corporate strategy.

The power-behavioral approach

Other investigators have provided important insights on the crucial psychological, power, and behavioral relationships in strategy formulation. Among other things, these have enhanced understanding about: the multiple goal structures of organizations, the politics of strategic decisions, executive bargaining and negotiation processes, 'satisficing' (as opposed to maximizing) in decision making, the role of coalitions in strategic management, and the practice of 'muddling' in the public sphere. Unfortunately, however, many power-behavioral studies have been conducted in settings far removed from the realities of strategy formulation. Others have concentrated solely on human dynamics, power relationships, and organizational processes and ignored the ways in which systematic data analysis shapes and often dominates crucial aspects of strategic decisions. Finally, a few have offered much normative guidance for the strategist.

The study

Recognizing the contributions and limitations of both approaches, I attempted to document the dynamics of actual strategic change processes in some 10 major companies as perceived by those most knowledge-ably and intimately involved in them. Several important findings have begun to emerge from these investigations:

- Neither the power-behavioral nor the formal systems planning paradigm adequately characterizes the way successful strategic processes operate.

- Effective strategies tend to emerge from a series of 'strategic subsystems,' each of which attacks a specific class of strategic issue (e.g. acquisitions, divestitures, or major reorganizations) in a disciplined way, but which blends incrementally and opportunistically into a cohesive pattern that becomes the company's strategy.

- The logic behind each subsystem is so powerful that to some extent it may serve as a normative approach for formulating these key elements of strategy in large companies.

- Because of cognitive and process limits, almost all of these subsystems – and the formal planning activity itself – must be managed and linked together by an approach best described as logical incrementalism.

- Such incrementalism is not muddling. It is a purposeful, effective, proactive management technique for improving and integrating both the analytical and behavioral aspects of strategy formulation.

This article will document these findings, suggest the logic behind several important subsystems for strategy formulation, and outline some of the management and thought processes executives in large organizations use to synthesize them into effective corporate strategies. Such strategies embrace those patterns of high-leverage decisions (on major goals, policies, and action sequences) that affect the viability and direction of the entire enterprise or determine its competitive posture for an extended time period.

Critical strategic issues

Although certain 'hard data' decisions (e.g. on product-market position or resource allocations) tend to dominate the analytical literature, executives identified other 'soft' changes that have at least as much importance in shaping their concern's strategic posture. Most often cited were changes in the company's

- overall organizational structure or its basic management style;
- relationships with the government or other external interest groups;
- acquisition, divestiture, or divisional control practices;
- international posture and relationships;
- innovative capabilities or personnel motivations as affected by growth;
- worker and professional relationships reflecting changed social expectations and values;
- past or anticipated technological environments.

When executives were asked to 'describe the processes through which their company arrived at its new posture' *vis-à-vis* each of these critical domains, several important points emerged. First, a few of these issues lent themselves to quantitative modeling techniques or perhaps even formal financial analyses. Second, successful companies used a different subsystem to formulate strategy for each major class of strategic issues, yet these subsystems were quite similar among companies even in very different industries. Finally, no single formal analytical process could handle all strategic variables simultaneously on a planned basis. Why?

Precipitating events

Often external or internal events over which managements had essentially no control would precipitate urgent, piecemeal, interim decisions that inexorably shaped the company's future strategic posture. One clearly observes this phenomenon in the decisions forced on General Motors by the 1973–74 oil crisis; the shift in posture pressed upon Exxon by sudden nationalizations; or the dramatic opportunities allowed for Haloid Corporation and Pilkington Brothers Ltd by the unexpected inventions of xerography and float glass.

In these cases, analyses from earlier formal planning cycles did contribute greatly, as long as the general nature of the contingency had been anticiapted. They broadened the information base available (as in Exxon's case), extended the options considered (Haloid-Xerox), created shared values to guide decisions about precipitating events in consistent directions (Pilkington), or built up resource bases, management flexibilities, or active search routines for opportunities whose specific nature could not be defined in advance (General Mills, Pillsbury). But no organization – no matter how brilliant, rational, or imaginative – could possibly foresee the timing, severity, or even the nature of all such precipitating events. Further, when these events did occur there might be neither time, resources, nor information enough to undertake a full formal strategic analysis of all possible options and their consequences. Yet early decisions made under stress conditions often meant new thrusts, precedents, or lost opportunities that were difficult to reverse later.

An incremental logic

Recognizing this, top executives usually consciously tried to deal with precipitating events in an incremental fashion. Early commitments were kept broadly formative, tentative, and subject to later review. In some cases neither the company nor the external players could understand the full implications of alternative actions. All parties wanted to test assumptions and have an opportunity to learn from and adapt to the others' responses. For example: Neither the potential producer nor user of a completely new product or process (like xerography or float glass) could fully conceptualize its ramifications without inter-

active testing. All parties benefited from procedures that purposely delayed decisions and allowed mutual feedback. Some companies, like IBM or Xerox, have formalized this concept into 'phase program planning' systems. They make concrete decisions only on individual phases (or stages) of new product developments, establish interactive testing procedures with customers, and postpone final configuration commitments until the latest possible moment.

Similarly, even under pressure, most top executives were extremely sensitive to organizational and power relationships and consciously mananged decision processes to improve these dynamics. They often purposely delayed initial decisions, or kept such decisions vague, in order to encourage lower-level participation, to gain more information from specialists, or to build commitment to solutions. Even when a crisis atmosphere tended to shorten time horizons and make decisions more goal oriented than political, perceptive executives consciously tried to keep their options open until they understood how the crisis would affect the power bases and needs of their key constituents.

Incrementalism in strategic subsystems

One also finds that an incremental logic applies in attacking many of the critical subsystems of corporate strategy. Those subsystems for considering diversification moves, divestitures, major reorganizations, or government-external relations are typical and will be described here. In each case conscious incrementalism helps to

1 cope with both the cognitive and process limits on each major decision;
2 build the logical-analytical framework these decisions require;
3 create the personal and organizational awareness, understanding, acceptance, and commitment needed to implement the strategies effectively.

The diversification subsystem

Strategies for diversification, either through research and development (R&D) or acquisitions, provide excellent examples. The formal analytical steps needed for successful diversification are well documented. However, the precise directions that R&D may project the company can only be understood step-by-step as scientists uncover new phenomena, make and amplify discoveries, build prototypes, reduce concepts to practice, and interact with users during product introductions. Similarly, only as each acquisition is sequentially identified, investigated, negotiated for, and integrated into the organization can one predict its ultimate impact on the total enterprise.

A step-by-step approach is clearly necessary to guide and assess the strategic fit of each internal or external diversification candidate. Incremental processes are also required to manage the crucial psychological and power shifts that ultimately determine the program's overall direction and consequences. These processes help unify both the analytical and behavioral aspects of diversification decisions. They create the broad conceptual consensus, the risk-taking attitudes, the organizational and resource flexibilities, and the adaptive dynamism that determine both the timing and direction of diversification strategies. Most important among these processes are:

- Generating a genuine, top-level psychological commitment to diversification. General Mills, Pillsbury, and Xerox all started their major diversification programs with broad analytical studies and goal-setting exercises designed both to build top-level consensus around the need to diversify and to establish the general directions for diversification. Without such action, top-level bargaining for resources would have continued to support only more familiar (and hence apparently less risky) old lines, and this could delay or undermine the entire diversification endeavor.

- Consciously preparing to move opportunistically. Organizational and fiscal resources must be built up in advance to exploit candidates as they randomly appear. And a 'credible activist' for ventures must be developed and backed by someone with commitment power. All successful acquirers created the potential for profit centered divisions within their organizational structures, strengthened their financial controllership capabilities, took action to create low-cost capital access, and maintained the shortest possible communication lines from the acquisitions activist to the resource-committing authority. All these actions integrally determined which diversifications actually could be made, the timing of their accession, and the pace at which they could be absorbed.

- Building a 'comfort factor' for risk taking. Perceived risk is largely a function of one's knowledge about a field. Hence well-conceived diversification programs should anticipate a trial-and-error period during which top managers reject early proposed fields or opportunities until they have analyzed enough trial candidates to 'become comfortable' with an initial selection. Early successes tend to be 'sure things' close to the companies' past (real or supposed) expertise. After a few successful diversifications, managements tend to become more confident and accept other candidates – farther from traditional lines – at a faster rate. Again, the way this process is handled affects both the direction and pace of the actual program.

- Developing a new ethos. If new divisions are more successful than the old – as they should be – they attract relatively more resources and their political power grows. Their most effective line managers move into corporate positions, and slowly the company's special competency and ethos change. Finally, the concepts and products that once dominated the company's culture may decline in importance or even disappear. Acknowledging these ultimate consequences to the organization at the beginning of a diversification program would clearly be impolitic, even if the manager both desired and could predict the probable new ethos. These factors must be handled adaptively, as opportunities present themselves and as individual leaders and power centers develop.

Each of the above processes interacts with all others (and with the random appearance of diversification candidates) to affect action sequences, elapsed time, and ultimate results in unexpected ways. Complexities are so great that few diversification programs end up as initially envisioned. Consequently, wise managers recognize the limits to systematic analysis in diversification, and use formal planning to build the 'comfort levels' executives need for risk taking and to guide the program's early directions and priorities. They then modify these flexibly, step-by-step, as new opportunities, power centers, and developed competencies merge to create new potentials.

The divestiture subsystem

Similar practices govern the handling of divestitures. Divisions often drag along in a less-than-desired condition for years before they can be strategically divested. In some cases, ailing divisions might have just enough yield or potential to offer hoped-for viability. In others, they might represent the company's vital core from earlier years, the creations of a powerful person nearing retirement, or the psychological touchstones of the company's past traditions.

Again, in designing divestiture strategies, top executives had to reinforce vaguely felt concerns with detailed data, build up managers' comfort levels about issues, achieve participation in and commitment to decisions, and move opportunistically to make actual changes. In many cases, the precise nature of the decision was not clear at the outset. Executives often made seemingly unrelated personnel shifts or appointments that changed the value set of critical groups, or started a series of staff studies that generated awareness

or acceptance of a potential problem. They might then instigate goal assessment, business review, or 'planning' programs to provide broader forums for discussion and a wider consensus for action. Even then they might wait for a crisis, a crucial retirement, or an attractive sale opportunity to determine the timing and conditions of divestiture. In some cases, decisions could be direct and analytical. But when divestitures involved the psychological centers of the organization, the process had to be much more oblique and carefully orchestrated.

The major reorganization subsystem

It is well recognized that major organizational changes are an integral part of strategy. Sometimes they constitute a strategy themselves, sometimes they precede and/or precipitate a new strategy, and sometimes they help to implement a strategy. However, like many other important strategic decisions, macro-organizational moves are typically handled incrementally and outside of formal planning processes. Their effects on personal or power relationships preclude discussion in open forums and reports of such processes.

In addition, major organizational changes have timing imperatives (or 'process limits') all their own. In making any significant shifts, executives must think through the new roles, capabilities, and probable individual reactions of the many principals affected. They may have to wait for the promotion or retirement of a valued colleague before consummating any change. They then frequently have to bring in, train, or test new people for substantial periods before they can staff key posts with confidence. During this testing period they may substantially modify their original concept of the reorganization, as they evaluate individuals' potentials, their performance in specific roles, their personal drives, and their relationships with other team members.

Because this chain of decisions affects the career development, power, affluence, and self-image of so many, executives tend to keep close counsel in their discussions, negotiate individually with key people, and make final commitments as late as possible in order to obtain the best matches between people's capabilities, personalities, and aspirations and their new roles. Typically, all these events do not come together at one convenient time, particularly the moment annual plans are due. Instead executives move opportunistically, step-by-step, selectively moving people toward a broadly conceived organizational goal, which is constantly modified and rarely articulated in detail until the last pieces fit together.

The government-external relations subsystem

Almost all companies cited government and other external activist groups as among the most important forces causing significant changes in their strategic postures during the periods examined. However, when asked 'How did your company arrive at its own strategy *vis-à-vis* these forces?' it became clear that few companies had cohesive strategies (integrated sets of goals, policies, and programs) for government-external relations, other than lobbying for or against specific legislative actions. To the extent that other strategies did exist, they were piecemeal, *ad hoc* and had been derived in a very evolutionary manner. Yet there seemed to be very good reasons for such incrementalism. The following are two of the best short explanations of the way these practices develop:

We are a very large company, and we understand that any massive overt action on our part could easily create more public antagonism than support for our viewpoint. It is also hard to say in advance exactly what public response any particular action might create. So we tend to test a number of different approaches on a small scale with only limited or local company identification. If one approach works, we'll test it further and amplify its use. If another bombs, we try to keep it from being used again.

Slowly we find a series of advertising, public relations, community relations actions that seem to help. Then along comes another issue and we start all over again. Gradually the successful approaches merge into a pattern of actions that becomes our strategy.

I [the president] start conversations with a number of knowledgeable people . . . I collect articles and talk to people about how things get done in Washington in this particular field. I collect data from any reasonable source. I begin wide-ranging discussions with people inside and outside the corporation. From these a pattern eventually emerges. It's like fitting together a jigsaw puzzle. At first the vague outline of an approach appears like the sail of a ship in a puzzle. Then suddenly the rest of the puzzle becomes quite clear. You wonder why you didn't see it all along. And once it's crystallized, it's not difficult to explain to others.

In this realm, uncontrollable forces dominate. Data are very soft, often can be only subjectively sensed, and may be costly to quantify. The possible responses of individuals and groups to different stimuli are difficult to determine in advance. The number of potential opponents with power is very high, and the diversity in their viewpoints and possible modes of attack is so substantial that it is physically impossible to lay out probabilistic decision diagrams that would have much meaning. Results are unpredictable and error costs extreme. Even the best intended and most rational-seeming strategies can be converted into disasters unless they are thoroughly and interactively tested.

Formal planning in corporate strategy

What role do classical formal planning techniques play in strategy formulation? All companies in the sample do have formal planning procedures embedded in their management direction and control systems. These serve certain essential functions. In a process sense, they

- provide a discipline forcing managers to take a careful look ahead periodically;
- require rigorous communications about goals, strategic issues, and resource allocations;
- stimulate longer-term analyses than would otherwise be made;
- generate a basis for evaluating and integrating short-term plans;
- lengthen time horizons and protect long-term investments such as R&D;
- create a psychological backdrop and an information framework about the future against which managers can calibrate short-term or interim decisions.

In a decision-making sense, they

- fine-tune annual commitments;
- formalize cost-reduction programs;
- help implement strategic changes once decided on (for example, coordinating all elements of Exxon's decision to change its corporate name).

Formal plans also 'increment'

Although individual staff planners were often effective in identifying potential problems and bringing them to top management's attention, the annual planning process itself was rarely (if ever) the initiating source of really new key issues or radical departures into new product/market realms. These almost always came from precipitating events, special studies, or conceptions implanted through the kinds of 'logical incremental' processes described above.

In fact, formal planning practices actually institutionalize incrementalism. There are two reasons for this. First, in order to utilize specialized expertise and to obtain executive involvement and commitment, most planning

occurs from the bottom up in response to broadly defined assumptions or goals, many of which are longstanding or negotiated well in advance. Of necessity, lower-level groups have only a partial view of the corporation's total strategy, and command only a fragment of its resources. Their power bases, identity, expertise, and rewards also usually depend on their existing products or processes. Hence, these products or processes, rather than entirely new departures, should and do receive their primary attention. Second, most managements purposely design their plans to be 'living' or 'evergreen.' They are intended only as frameworks to guide and provide consistency for future decisions made incrementally. To act otherwise would be to deny that further information could have a value. Thus, properly formulated formal plans are also a part of an incremental logic.

Special studies

Formal planning was most successful in stimulating significant change when it was set up as a special study on some important aspect of corporate strategy. For example, when it became apparent that Pilkington's new float glass process would work, the company formed a Directors' Float Glass Committee consisting of all internal directors associated with float glass 'to consider the broad issues of float glass [strategy] in both the present and the future.' The committee did not attempt detailed plans. Instead, it tried to deal in broad concepts, identify alternate routes, and think through the potential consequences of each route some 10 years ahead. Of some of the key strategic decisions it was later remarked, 'It would be difficult to identify an exact moment when the decision was made . . . Nevertheless, over a period of time a consensus crystallized with great clarity.'

Such special strategic studies represent a subsystem of strategy formulation distinct from both annual planning activities and the other subsystems exemplified above. Each of these develops some important aspect of strategy, incrementally blending its conclusions with those of other subsystems, and it would be virtually impossible to force all these together to crystallize a completely articulated corporate strategy at any one instant.

Total posture planning

Occasionally, however, managements do attempt very broad assessments of their companies' total posture. Shortly after becoming CEO of General Mills, James McFarland decided that his job was 'to take a very good company and move it to greatness,' but that it was up to his management group, not himself alone, to decide what a great company was and how to get there. Consequently he took some 35 of the company's topmost managers away for a three-day management retreat. On the first day, after agreeing to broad financial goals, the group broke up into units of six to eight people. Each unit was to answer the question 'What is a great company?' from the viewpoints of stockholders, employees, suppliers, the public, and society. Each unit reported back at the end of the day, and the whole group tried to reach a consensus through discussion.

On the second day the groups, in the same format, assessed the company's strengths and weaknesses relative to the defined posture of 'greatness.' The third day focused on how to overcome the company's weaknesses and move it toward a great company. This broad consensus led, over the next several years, to the surveys of fields for acquisition, the building of management's initial comfort levels with certain fields, and the acquisition-divestiture strategy that characterized the McFarland era at General Mills.

Yet even such a major endeavor is only a portion of a total strategic process. Values that had been built up over decades stimulated or constrained alternatives. Precipitating events, acquisitions, divestitures, external relations, and organizational changes developed important segments of each strategy incrementally. Even the strategies articulated left key elements to be defined as new information became available, polities permitted, or particular opportuni-

ties appeared. Major product thrusts proved unsuccessful. Actual strategies therefore evolved as each company overextended, consolidated, made errors, and rebalanced various thrusts over time. And it was both logical and expected that this would be the case.

Logical incrementalism

All of the above suggest that strategic decisions do not lend themselves to aggregation into a single massive decision matrix where all factors can be treated relatively simultaneously in order to arrive at a holistic optimum. Many have spoken of the cognitive limits that prevent this. Of equal importance are the process limits – that is, the timing and sequencing imperatives necessary to create awareness, build comfort levels, develop consensus, select and train people, and so forth – that constrain the system yet ultimately determine the decision itself. Unlike the preparation of a fine banquet, it is virtually impossible for the manager to orchestrate all internal decisions, external environmental events, behavioral and power relationships, technical and informational needs, and actions of intelligent opponents so that they come together at any precise moment.

Can the process be managed?

Instead, executives usually deal with the logic of each subsystem of strategy formulation largely on its own merits and usually with a different subset of people. They try to develop or maintain in their own minds a consistent pattern among the decisions made in each subsystem. Knowing their own limitations and the unknowability of the events they face, they consciously try to tap the minds and psychic drives of others. They often purposely keep questions broad and decisions vague in early stages to avoid creating undue rigidities and to stimulate others' creativity. Logic, of course, dictates that they make final commitments *as late as possible* consistent with the information they have.

Consequently, many successful executives will initially set only broad goals and policies that can accommodate a variety of specific proposals from below, yet give a sense of guidance to the proposers. As they come forward the proposals automatically and beneficially attract the support and identity of their sponsors. Being only proposals, the executives can treat these at less politically charged levels, as specific projects rather than as larger goal or policy precedents. Therefore, they can encourage, discourage, or kill alternatives with considerably less political exposure. As events and opportunities emerge, they can incrementally guide the pattern of escalated or accepted proposals to suit their own purposes without getting prematurely committed to a rigid solution set that unpredictable events might prove wrong or that opponents find sufficiently threatening to coalesce against.

A strategy emerges

Successful executives link together and bring order to a series of strategic processes and decisions spanning years. At the beginning of the process it is literally impossible to predict all the events and forces that will shape the future of the company. The best executives can do is to forecast the forces most likely to impinge on the company's affairs and the ranges of their possible impact. They then attempt to build a resource base and a corporate posture so strong in selected areas that the enterprise can survive and prosper despite all but the most devastating events. They consciously select market/technological/product segments the concern can dominate given its resource limits, and place some side bets in order to decrease the risk of catastrophic failure or to increase the company's flexibility for future options.

They then proceed incrementally to handle urgent matters, start longer-term sequences whose specific future branches and consequences are perhaps murky, respond to unforeseen events as they occur, build on successes, and brace up or cut losses on failures. They constantly reassess the future, find new congruencies as events unfurl, and blend the organization's skills and resources into new balances of dominance and risk aversion as various forces intersect to suggest better – but never perfect – alignments. The process is dynamic, with neither a real beginning nor end.

Strategy deals with the unknowable, not the uncertain. It involves forces of such great number, strength, and combinatory powers that one cannot predict events in a probabilistic sense. Hence logic dictates that one proceed flexibly and experimentally from broad concepts toward specific commitments, making the latter concrete as late as possible in order to narrow the bands of uncertainty and to benefit from the best available information. This is the process of logical incrementalism.

READINGS ON STRATEGIC CHANGE

As the opening reading on the topic of strategic change, Michael Hammer's 'Reengineering Work: Don't Automate, Obliterate' has been selected to represent the discontinuous renewal perspective. This paper was published in *Harvard Business Review* in 1990 and was followed in 1993 by the highly influential book *Reengineering the Corporation: A Manifesto for Business Revolution*, that Hammer co-authored with James Champy. In this article, Hammer explains the concept of reengineering in much the same way as in the best-selling book: 'At the heart of reengineering,' he writes, 'is the notion of discontinuous thinking – of recognizing and breaking away from the outdated rules and fundamental assumptions that underlie operations.' In his view, radically redesigning business processes 'cannot be planned meticulously and accomplished in small and cautious steps. It's an all-or-nothing proposition with an uncertain result.' He exhorts managers to 'think big', by setting high goals, taking bold steps and daring to accept a high risk.

In short, he preaches business revolution, and the tone of his article is truly that of a manifesto – impassioned, fervent, with, here and there, 'a touch of fanaticism'.

Equally impassioned is the argumentation in the second reading, 'Kaizen', by Masaaki Imai, which has been selected to represent the continuous renewal perspective. This article has been taken from Imai's famous book *Kaizen: The Key to Japan's Competitive Success*. Kaizen (pronounced Ky'zen) is a Japanese term that is best translated as continuous improvement. Imai argues that it is this continuous improvement philosophy that best explains the competitive strength of so many Japanese companies. In his view, Western companies have an unhealthy obsession with one-shot innovations and revolutionary change. They are fixated on the great leap forward, while disregarding the power of accumulated small changes. Imai believes that innovations are also important for competitive success, but that they should be embedded in an organization that is driven to continuously improve.

Reengineering work: Don't automate, obliterate

By Michael Hammer[1]

Despite a decade or more of restructuring and downsizing, many US companies are still unprepared to operate in the 1990s. In a time of rapidly changing technologies and ever-shorter product life cycles, product development often proceeds at a glacial pace. In an age of the customer, order fulfillment has high error rates and customer inquiries go unanswered for weeks. In a period when asset utilization is critical, inventory levels exceed many months of demand.

The usual methods for boosting performance – process rationalization and automation – haven't yielded the dramatic improvements companies need. In particular, heavy investments in information technology have delivered disappointing results – largely because companies tend to use technology to mechanize old ways of doing business. They leave the existing processes intact and use computers simply to speed them up.

But speeding up those processes cannot address their fundamental performance deficiencies. Many of our job designs, work flows, control mechanisms, and organizational structures came of age in a different competitive environment and before the advent of the computer. They are geared toward efficiency and control. Yet the watchwords of the new decade are innovation and speed, service and quality.

It is time to stop paving the cow paths. Instead of embedding outdated processes in silicon and software, we should obliterate them and start over. We should 'reengineer' our businesses: use the power of modern information technology to radically redesign our business processes in order to achieve dramatic improvements in their performance.

Every company operates according to a great many unarticulated rules. 'Credit decisions are made by the credit department.'

[1]Source: This article was adapted by permission of *Harvard Business Review*. From 'Reengineering Work: Don't Automate, Obliterate' by M. Hammer, July/August 1990, Vol. 68. © 1990 by the Harvard Business School Publishing Corporation, all rights reserved.

'Local inventory is needed for good customer service.' 'Forms must be filled in completely and in order.' Reengineering strives to break away from the old rules about how we organize and conduct business. It involves recognizing and rejecting some of them and then finding imaginative new ways to accomplish work. From our redesigned processes, new rules will emerge that fit the times. Only then can we hope to achieve quantum leaps in performance.

Reengineering cannot be planned meticulously and accomplished in small and cautious steps. It's an all-or-nothing proposition with an uncertain result. Still, most companies have no choice but to muster the courage to do it. For many, reengineering is the only hope for breaking away from the antiquated processes that threaten to drag them down. Fortunately, managers are not without help. Enough businesses have successfully reengineered their processes to provide some rules of thumb for others.

What Ford and MBL did

Japanese competitors and young entrepreneurial ventures prove every day that drastically better levels of process performance are possible. They develop products twice as fast, utilize assets eight times more productively, respond to customers ten times faster. Some large, established companies also show what can be done. Businesses like Ford Motor Company and Mutual Benefit Life Insurance have reengineered their processes and achieved competitive leadership as a result. Ford has reengineered its accounts payable processes, and Mutual Benefit Life its processing of applications for insurance.

In the early 1980s, when the American automotive industry was in a depression, Ford's top management put accounts payable – along with many other departments – under the microscope in search of ways to cut costs. Accounts payable in North America alone employed more than 500 people. Management thought that by rationalizing

processes and installing new computer systems, it could reduce the head count by some 20 percent.

Ford was enthusiastic about its plan to tighten accounts payable – until it looked at Mazda. While Ford was aspiring to a 400-person department, Mazda's accounts payable organization consisted of a total of five people. The difference in absolute numbers was astounding, and even after adjusting for Mazda's smaller size, Ford figured that its accounts payable organization was five times the size it should be. The Ford team knew better than to attribute the discrepancy to callisthenics, company songs, or low interest rates.

Ford managers ratcheted up their goal: accounts payable would perform with not just a hundred but many hundreds fewer clerks. It then set out to achieve it. First, managers analyzed the existing system. When Ford's purchasing department wrote a purchase order, it sent a copy to accounts payable. Later, when material control received the goods, it sent a copy of the receiving document to accounts payable. Meanwhile, the vendor sent an invoice to accounts payable. It was up to accounts payable, then, to match the purchase order against the receiving document and the invoice. If they matched, the department issued payment.

The department spent most of its time on mismatches, instances where the purchase order, receiving document, and invoice disagreed. In these cases, an accounts payable clerk would investigate the discrepancy, hold up payment, generate documents, and all-in-all gum up the works.

One way to improve things might have been to help the accounts payable clerk investigate more efficiently, but a better choice was to prevent the mismatches in the first place. To this end, Ford instituted 'invoiceless processing.' Now when the purchasing department initiates an order, it enters the information into an on-line database. It doesn't send a copy of the purchase order to anyone. When the goods arrive at the receiving dock, the receiving clerk checks the database to see if they correspond to an outstanding purchase order. If so, he or she accepts them and enters the transaction into the computer system. (If receiving can't find a database entry for the received goods, it simply returns the order.)

Under the old procedures, the accounting department had to match 14 data items between the receipt record, the purchase order, and the invoice before it could issue payment to the vendor. The new approach requires matching only three items – part number, unit of measure, and supplier code – between the purchase order and the receipt record. The matching is done automatically, and the computer prepares the check, which accounts payable sends to the vendor. There are no invoices to worry about since Ford has asked its vendors not to send them.

Ford didn't settle for the modest increases it first envisioned. It opted for radical change – and achieved dramatic improvement. Where it has instituted this new process, Ford has achieved a 75 percent reduction in head count, not the 20 percent it would have gotten with a conventional program. And since there are no discrepancies between the financial record and the physical record, material control is simpler and financial information is more accurate.

Mutual Benefit Life, the country's eighteenth largest life carrier, has reengineered its processing of insurance applications. Prior to this, MBL handled customers' applications much as its competitors did. The long, multistep process involved credit checking, quoting, rating, underwriting, and so on. An application would have to go through as many as 30 discrete steps, spanning five departments and involving 19 people. At the very best, MBL could process an application in 24 hours, but more typical turnarounds ranged from five to 25 days – most of the time spent passing information from one department to the next. (Another insurer estimated that while an application spent 22 days in process, it was actually worked on for just 17 minutes.)

MBL's rigid, sequential process led to many complications. For instance, when a customer wanted to cash in an existing policy and purchase a new one, the old business department first had to authorize the treasury department to issue a check made payable to MBL. The check would then accompany the paperwork to the new business department.

The president of MBL, intent on improving customer service, decided that this nonsense had to stop and demanded a 60 percent improvement in productivity. It was clear that such an ambitious goal would require more than tinkering with the existing process. Strong measures were in order, and the management team assigned to the task looked to technology as a means of achieving them. The team realized that shared databases and computer networks could make many different kinds of information available to a single person, while expert systems could help people with limited experience make sound decisions. Applying these insights led to a new approach to the application-handling process, one with wide organizational implications and little resemblance to the old way of doing business.

MBL swept away existing job definitions and departmental boundaries and created a new position called a case manager. Case managers have total responsibility for an application from the time it is received to the time a policy is issued. Unlike clerks, who performed a fixed task repeatedly under the watchful gaze of a supervisor, case managers work autonomously. No more handoffs of files and responsibility, no more shuffling of customer inquiries.

Case managers are able to perform all the tasks associated with an insurance application because they are supported by powerful PC-based workstations that run an expert system and connect to a range of automated systems on a mainframe. In particularly tough cases, the case manager calls for assistance from a senior underwriter or physician, but these specialists work only as consultants and advisers to the case manager, who never relinquishes control.

Empowering individuals to process entire applications has had a tremendous impact on operations. MBL can now complete an application in as little as four hours, and average turnaround takes only two to five days. The company has eliminated 100 field office positions, and case managers can handle more than twice the volume of new applications the company previously could process.

The essence of reengineering

At the heart of reengineering is the notion of discontinuous thinking – of recognizing and breaking away from the outdated rules and fundamental assumptions that underlie operations. Unless we change these rules, we are merely rearranging the deckchairs on the Titanic. We cannot achieve breakthroughs in performance by cutting fat or automating existing processes. Rather, we must challenge old assumptions and shed the old rules that made the business underperform in the first place.

Every business is replete with implicit rules left over from earlier decades. 'Customers don't repair their own equipment.' 'Local warehouses are necessary for good service.' 'Merchandising decisions are made at headquarters.' These rules of work design are based on assumptions about technology, people, and organizational goals that no longer hold. The contemporary repertoire of available information technologies is vast and quickly expanding. Quality, innovation, and service are now more important than cost, growth, and control. A large portion of the population is educated and capable of assuming responsibility, and workers cherish their autonomy and expect to have a say in how the business is run.

It should come as no surprise that our business processes and structures are outmoded and obsolete: our work structures and processes have not kept pace with the changes in technology, demographics, and business objectives. For the most part, we have organized work as a sequence of separate tasks and employed complex mechanisms to track its progress. This arrangement can be traced to the Industrial Revolution, when specialization of labor and economies of scale promised to overcome the inefficiencies of cottage industries. Businesses disaggregated work into narrowly defined tasks, reaggregated the people performing those tasks into departments, and installed managers to administer them.

Our elaborate systems for imposing control and discipline on those who actually do the work stem from the postwar period. In that halcyon period of expansion, the main concern was growing fast without going broke, so businesses focused on cost, growth, and control. And since literate, entry-level people were abundant but well-educated professionals hard to come by, the control systems funneled information up the hierarchy to the few who presumably knew what to do with it.

These patterns of organizing work have become so ingrained that, despite their serious drawbacks, it's hard to conceive of work being accomplished any other way. Conventional process structures are fragmented and piecemeal, and they lack the integration necessary to maintain quality and service. They are breeding grounds for tunnel vision, as people tend to substitute the narrow goals of their particular department for the larger goals of the process as a whole. When work is handed off from person to person and unit to unit, delays and errors are inevitable. Accountability blurs, and critical issues fall between the cracks. Moreover, no one sees enough of the big picture to be able to respond quickly to new situations. Managers desperately try, like all the king's horses and all the king's men, to piece together the fragmented pieces of business processes.

Managers have tried to adapt their processes to new circumstances, but usually in ways that just create more problems. If, say, customer service is poor, they create a mechanism to deliver service but overlay it on the existing organization. Bureaucracy thickens, costs rise, and enterprising competitors gain market share.

In reengineering, managers break loose from outmoded business processes and the design principles underlying them and create new ones. Ford had operated under the old rule that 'We pay when we receive the invoice.' While no one had ever articulated or recorded it, that rule determined how the accounts payable process was organized. Ford's reengineering effort challenged and ultimately replaced the rule with a new one: 'We pay when we receive the goods.'

Reengineering requires looking at the fundamental processes of the business from a cross-functional perspective. Ford discovered that reengineering only the accounts payable department was futile. The appropriate focus of the effort was what might be called the goods acquisition process, which included purchasing and receiving as well as accounts payable.

One way to ensure that reengineering has a cross-functional perspective is to assemble a team that represents the functional units involved in the process being reengineered and all the units that depend on it. The team must analyze and scrutinize the existing process until it really understands what the process is trying to accomplish. The point is not to learn what happens to form 73B in its peregrinations through the company but to understand the purpose of having form 73B in the first place. Rather than looking for opportunities to improve the current process, the team should determine which of its steps really add value and search for new ways to achieve the result.

The reengineering team must keep asking Why? and What if? Why do we need to get a manager's signature on a requisition? Is it a control mechanism or a decision point? What if the manager reviews only requisitions above $500? What if he or she doesn't see them at all? Raising and resolving heretical questions can separate what is fundamental to the process from what is superficial. The regional offices of an East Coast insurance company had long produced a series of reports that they regularly sent to the home office. No one in the field realized that these reports were simply filed and never used. The process outlasted the circumstances that had created the need for it. The reengineering study team should push to discover situations like this.

In short, a reengineering effort strives for dramatic levels of improvement. It must break away from conventional wisdom and the constraints of organizational boundaries and should be broad and cross-functional in scope. It should use information technology not to automate an existing process but to enable a new one.

Principles of reengineering

Creating new rules tailored to the modern environment ultimately requires a new conceptualization of the business process – which comes down to someone having a great idea. But reengineering need not be haphazard. In fact, some of the principles that companies have already discovered while reengineering their business processes can help jump start the effort for others.

Organize around outcomes, not tasks

This principle says to have one person perform all the steps in a process. Design that person's job around an objective or outcome instead of a single task. The redesign at Mutual Benefit Life, where individual case managers perform the entire application approval process, is the quintessential example of this.

The redesign of an electronics company is another example. It had separate organizations performing each of the five steps between selling and installing the equipment. One group determined customer requirements, another translated those requirements into internal product codes, a third conveyed that information to various plants and warehouses, a fourth received and assembled the components, and a fifth delivered and installed the equipment. The process was based on the centuries-old notion of specialized labor and on the limitations inherent in paper files. The departments each possessed a specific set of skills, and only one department at a time could do its work.

The customer order moved systematically from step to step. But this sequential processing caused problems. The people getting the information from the customer in step one had to get all the data anyone would need throughout the process, even if it wasn't needed until step five. In addition, the many handoffs were responsible for numerous errors and misunderstandings. Finally, any questions about customer requirements that arose late in the process had to be referred back to the people doing step one, resulting in delay and rework.

When the company reengineered, it eliminated the assembly-line approach. It compressed responsibility for the various steps and assigned it to one person, the 'customer service representative.' That person now oversees the whole process – taking the order, translating it into product codes, getting the components assembled, and seeing the product delivered and installed. The customer service rep expedites and coordinates the process, much like a general contractor. And the customer has just one contact, who always knows the status of the order.

Have those who use the output of the process perform the process

In an effort to capitalize on the benefits of specialization and scale, many organizations established specialized departments to handle specialized processes. Each department does only one type of work and is a 'customer' of other groups' processes. Accounting does only accounting. If it needs new pencils, it goes to the purchasing department, the group specially equipped with the information and expertise to perform that role. Purchasing finds vendors, negotiates price, places the order, inspects the goods, and pays the invoice – and eventually the accountants get their pencils. The process works (after a fashion), but it's slow and bureaucratic.

Now that computer-based data and expertise are more readily available, departments, units, and individuals can do more for themselves. Opportunities exist to reengineer processes so that the individuals who need the result of a process can do it themselves. For example, by using expert systems and databases, departments can make their own purchases without sacrificing the benefits of specialized purchasers. One manufacturer has reengineered its purchasing process along just these lines. The company's old system, whereby the operating departments submitted requisitions and let purchasing do the rest, worked well for controlling expensive and important items like raw materials and capital equipment. But for inexpensive and non-strategic purchases, which constituted some 35 percent of total orders, the system was slow and cumbersome; it was not uncommon for the cost of the purchasing process to exceed the cost of the goods being purchased.

The new process compresses the purchase of sundry items and pushes it on to the customers of the process. Using a database of approved vendors, an operating unit can directly place an order with a vendor and charge it on a bank credit card. At the end of the month, the bank gives the manufacturer a tape of all credit card transactions, which the company runs against its internal accounting system.

When an electronics equipment manufacturer reengineered its field service process, it pushed some of the steps of the process on to its customers. The manufacturer's field service had been plagued by the usual problems: technicians were often unable to do a particular repair because the right part wasn't on the van, response to customer calls was slow, and spare-parts inventory was excessive.

Now customers make simple repairs themselves. Spare parts are stored at each customer's site and managed through a computerized inventory-management system. When a problem arises, the customer calls the manufacturer's field-service hot line and describes the symptoms to a diagnostician, who accesses a diagnosis support system. If the problem appears to be something the customer can fix, the diagnostician tells the customer what part to replace and how to install it. The old part is picked up and a new part left in its place at a later time. Only for complex problems is a service technician dispatched to the site, this time without having to make a stop at the warehouse to pick up parts.

When the people closest to the process perform it, there is little need for the overhead associated with managing it. Interfaces and liaisons can be eliminated, as can the mechanisms used to coordinate those who perform the process with those who use it. Moreover, the problem of capacity planning for the process performers is greatly reduced.

Subsume information-processing work into the real work that produces the information

The previous two principles compress linear processes. This principle suggests moving work from one person or department to another. Why doesn't an organization that produces information also process it? In the past, people didn't have the time or weren't trusted to do both. Most companies established units to do nothing but collect and process information that other departments created. This arrangement reflects the old rule about specialized labor and the belief that people at lower organizational levels are incapable of acting on information they generate. An accounts payable department collects information from purchasing and receiving and reconciles it with data that the vendor provides. Quality assurance gathers and analyzes information it gets from production.

Ford's redesigned accounts payable process embodies the new rule. With the new system, receiving, which produces the information about the goods received, processes this information instead of sending it to accounts payable. The new computer system can easily compare the delivery with the order and trigger the appropriate action.

Treat geographically dispersed resources as though they were centralized

The conflict between centralization and decentralization is a classic one. Decentralizing a resource (whether people, equipment, or inventory) gives better service to those who use it, but at the cost of redundancy, bureaucracy, and missed economies of scale. Companies no longer have to make such trade-offs. They can use databases, telecommunications networks, and standardized processing systems to get the benefits of scale and coordination while maintaining the benefits of flexibility and service.

At Hewlett-Packard, for instance, each of the more than 50 manufacturing units had its own separate purchasing department. While this arrangement provided excellent responsiveness and service to the plants, it prevented H-P from realizing the benefits of its scale, particularly with regard to quantity discounts. H-P's solution is to maintain the divisional purchasing organizations and to introduce a corporate unit to coordinate them. Each purchasing unit has access to a shared database on vendors and their performance and issues its own purchase orders. Corporate purchasing maintains this database and uses it to negotiate contracts for the corporation and to monitor the units. The payoffs have come in a 150 percent improvement in on-time deliveries, 50 percent reduction in lead times, 75 percent reduction in failure rates, and a significantly lower cost of goods purchased.

Link parallel activities instead of integrating their results

H-P's decentralized purchasing operations represent one kind of parallel processing in which separate units perform the same function. Another common kind of parallel processing is when separate units perform different activities that must eventually come together. Product development typically operates this way. In the development of a photocopier, for example, independent units develop the various subsystems of the copier. One group works on the optics, another on the mechanical paperhandling device, another on the power supply, and so on. Having people do development work simultaneously saves time, but at the dreaded integration and testing phase, the pieces often fail to work together. Then the costly redesign begins.

Or consider a bank that sells different kinds of credit – loans, letters of credit, asset-based financing – through separate units. These groups may have no way of knowing whether another group has already extended credit to a particular customer. Each unit could extend the full $10 million credit limit.

The new principle says to forge links between parallel functions and to coordinate them while their activities are in process rather than after they are completed. Communications networks, shared databases, and teleconferencing can bring the independent groups together so that coordination is ongoing. One large electronics company has cut its product development cycle by more than 50 percent by implementing this principle.

Put the decision point where the work is performed, and build control into the process

In most organizations, those who do the work are distinguished from those who monitor the work and make decisions about it. The tacit assumption is that the people actually doing the work have neither the time nor the inclination to monitor and control it and that they lack the knowledge and scope to make decisions about it. The entire hierarchical management structure is built on this assumption. Accountants, auditors, and supervisors check, record, and monitor work. Managers handle any exceptions.

The new principle suggests that the people who do the work should make the decisions and that the process itself can have built-in controls. Pyramidal management layers can therefore be compressed and the organization flattened.

Information technology can capture and process data, and expert systems can to some extent supply knowledge, enabling people to make their own decisions. As the doers become self-managing and self-controlling, hierarchy – and the slowness and bureaucracy associated with it – disappears.

When Mutual Benefit Life reengineered the insurance application process, it not only compressed the linear sequence but also eliminated the need for layers of managers. These two kinds of compression – vertical and horizontal – often go together; the very fact that a worker sees only one piece of the process calls for a manager with a broader vision. The case managers at MBL provide end-to-end management of the process, reducing the need for traditional managers. The managerial role is changing from one of controller and supervisor to one of supporter and facilitator.

Capture information once and at the source

This last rule is simple. When information was difficult to transmit, it made sense to collect information repeatedly. Each person, department, or unit had its own requirements and forms. Companies simply had to live with the associated delays, entry errors, and costly overhead. But why do we have to live with those problems now? Today when we collect a piece of information, we can store it in an on-line database for all who need it. Bar coding, relational databases, and electronic data interchange (EDI) make it easy to collect, store, and transmit information. One insurance company found that its application review process required that certain items be entered into 'stovepipe' computer systems supporting different functions as many as five times. By integrating and connecting these systems, the company was able to eliminate this redundant data entry along with the attendant checking functions and inevitable errors.

Think big

Reengineering triggers changes of many kinds, not just of the business process itself. Job designs, organizational structures, management systems – anything associated with the process must be refashioned in an integrated way. In other words, reengineering is a tremendous effort that mandates change in many areas of the organization.

When Ford reengineered its payables, receiving clerks on the dock had to learn to use computer terminals to check shipments, and they had to make decisions about whether to accept the goods. Purchasing agents also had to assume new responsibilities – like making sure the purchase orders they entered into the database had the correct information about where to send the check. Attitudes toward vendors also had to change: vendors could no longer be seen as adversaries; they had to become partners in a shared business process. Vendors too had to adjust. In many cases, invoices formed the basis of their accounting systems. At least one Ford supplier adapted by continuing to print invoices, but instead of sending them to Ford threw them away, reconciling cash received against invoices never sent.

The changes at Mutual Benefit Life were also widespread. The company's job-rating scheme could not accommodate the case manager position, which had a lot of responsibility but no direct reports. MBL had to devise new job-rating schemes and compensation policies. It also had to develop a culture in which people doing work are perceived as more important than those supervising work. Career paths, recruitment and training programs, promotion policies – these and many other management systems are being revised to support the new process design.

The extent of these changes suggests one factor that is necessary for reengineering to succeed: executive leadership with real vision. No one in an organization wants reengineering. It is confusing and disruptive and affects everything people have grown accustomed to. Only if top-level managers back the effort and outlast the company cynics will people take reengineering seriously. As one wag at an electronics equipment manufacturer has commented, 'Every few months, our senior managers find a new religion. One time it was quality, another it was customer service, another it was flattening the organization. We just hold our breath until they get over it and things get back to normal.' Commitment, consistency – maybe even a touch of fanaticism – are needed to enlist those who would prefer the status quo.

Considering the inertia of old processes and structures, the strain of implementing a reengineering plan can hardly be overestimated. But by the same token, it is hard to overestimate the opportunities, especially for established companies. Big, traditional organizations aren't necessarily dinosaurs doomed to extinction, but they are burdened with layers of unproductive overhead and armies of unproductive workers. Shedding them a layer at a time will not be good enough to stand up against sleek startups or streamlined Japanese companies. US companies need fast change and dramatic improvements.

We have the tools to do what we need to do. Information technology offers many options for reorganizing work. But our imaginations must guide our decisions about technology – not the other way around. We must have the boldness to imagine taking 78 days out of an 80-day turnaround time, cutting 75 percent of overhead, and eliminating 80 percent of errors. These are not unrealistic goals. If managers have the vision, reengineering will provide a way.

READING 4.2

READING 4.2 Kaizen

By Masaaki Imai[1]

Back in the 1950s, I was working with the Japan Productivity Center in Washington, D.C. My job mainly consisted of escorting groups of Japanese businessmen who were visiting American companies to study 'the secret of American industrial productivity.' Toshiro Yamada, now Professor Emeritus of the Faculty of Engineering at Kyoto University, was a member of one such study team visiting the United States to study the industrial-vehicle industry. Recently, the members of his team gathered to celebrate the silver anniversary of their trip.

At the banquet table, Yamada said he had recently been back to the United States in a 'sentimental journey' to some of the plants he had visited, among them the River Rouge steelworks in Dearborn, Michigan. Shaking his head in disbelief, he said, 'You know, the plant was exactly the same as it had been 25 years ago.'

These conversations set me to thinking about the great differences in the ways Japanese and Western managers approach their work. It is inconceivable that a Japanese plant would remain virtually unchanged for over a quarter of a century.

I had long been looking for a key concept to explain these two very different management approaches, one that might also help explain why many Japanese companies have come to gain their increasingly conspicuous competitive edge. For instance, how do we explain the fact that while most new ideas come from the West and some of the most advanced plants, institutions, and technologies are found there, there are also many plants there that have changed little since the 1950s?

Change is something which everybody takes for granted. Recently, an American executive at a large multinational firm told me his company chairman had said at the start of an executive committee meeting: 'Gentlemen, our job is to manage change. If we fail, we must change management.' The executive smiled and said, 'We all got the message!'

In Japan, change is a way of life, too. But are we talking about the same change when we talk about managing change or else changing management? It dawned on me that there might be different kinds of change: gradual and abrupt. While we can easily observe both gradual and abrupt changes in Japan, gradual change is not so obvious a part of the Western way of life. How are we to explain this difference?

This question led me to consider the question of values. Could it be that differences between the value systems in Japan and the West account for their different attitudes toward gradual change and abrupt change? Abrupt changes are easily grasped by everyone concerned, and people are usually elated to see them. This is generally true in both Japan and the West. Yet what about the gradual changes? My earlier statement that it is inconceivable that a Japanese plant would remain unchanged for years refers to gradual change as well as abrupt change.

Thinking all this over, I came to the conclusion that the key difference between how change is understood in Japan and how it is viewed in the West lies in the Kaizen concept – a concept that is so natural and obvious to many Japanese managers that they often do not even realize that they possess it! The Kaizen concept explains why companies can-

---

[1]Source: This article was adapted with permission from Chapters 1 and 2 of *Kaizen: The Key to Japan's Competitive Success*, McGraw-Hill, New York, 1986.

not remain the same for long in Japan. Moreover, after many years of studying Western business practices, I have reached the conclusion that this Kaizen concept is non-existent, or at least very weak, in most Western companies today. Worse yet, they reject it without knowing what it really entails. It's the old 'not invented here' syndrome. And this lack of Kaizen helps explain why an American or European factory can remain exactly the same for a quarter of a century.

The essence of Kaizen is simple and straightforward: Kaizen means improvement. Moreover, Kaizen means ongoing improvement involving everyone, including both managers and workers. The Kaizen philosophy assumes that our way of life – be it our working life, our social life, or our home life – deserves to be constantly improved.

In trying to understand Japan's postwar 'economic miracle,' scholars, journalists, and businesspeople alike have dutifully studied such factors as the productivity movement, total quality control (TQC), small-group activities, the suggestion system, automation, industrial robots, and labor relations. They have given much attention to some of Japan's unique management practices, among them the lifetime employment system, seniority-based wages, and enterprise unions. Yet I feel they have failed to grasp the very simple truth that lies behind the many myths concerning Japanese management.

The essence of most 'uniquely Japanese' management practices – be they productivity improvement, TQC (Total Quality Control) activities, QC (Quality Control) circles, or labor relations – can be reduced to one word: Kaizen. Using the term Kaizen in place of such words as productivity, TQC, ZD (Zero Defects), *kamban*, and the suggestion system paints a far clearer picture of what has been going on in Japanese industry. Kaizen is an umbrella concept covering most of those 'uniquely Japanese' practices that have recently achieved such world-wide fame.

The implications of TQC or CWQC (Company-Wide Quality Control) in Japan have been that these concepts have helped Japanese companies generate a process-oriented way of thinking and develop strategies that assure continuous improvement involving people at all levels of the organizational hierarchy. The message of the Kaizen strategy is that not a day should go by without some kind of improvement being made somewhere in the company.

The belief that there should be unending improvement is deeply ingrained in the Japanese mentality. As the old Japanese saying goes, 'If a man has not been seen for three days, his friends should take a good look at him to see what changes have befallen him.' The implication is that he must have changed in three days, so his friends should be attentive enough to notice the changes.

After World War II, most Japanese companies had to start literally from the ground up. Every day brought new challenges to managers and workers alike, and every day meant progress. Simply staying in business required unending progress, and Kaizen has become a way of life. It was also fortunate that the various tools that helped elevate this Kaizen concept to new heights were introduced to Japan in the late 1950s and early 1960s by such experts as W.E. Deming and J.M. Juran. However, most new concepts, systems, and tools that are widely used in Japan today have subsequently been developed in Japan and represent qualitative improvements upon the statistical quality control and total quality control of the 1960s.

Kaizen and management

Figure 4.2.1 shows how job functions are perceived in Japan. As indicated, management has two major components: maintenance and improvement. Maintenance refers to activities directed toward maintaining current technological, managerial, and operating standards; improvement refers to those directed toward improving current standards.

Under its maintenance functions, management performs its assigned tasks so that

---

FIGURE 4.2.1 Japanese perceptions of job functions

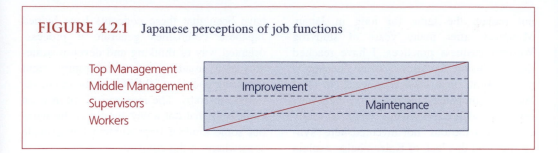

---

everybody in the company can follow the established SOP (Standard Operating Procedure). This means that management must first establish policies, rules, directives, and procedures for all major operations and then see to it that everybody follows SOP. If people are able to follow the standard but do not, management must introduce discipline. If people are unable to follow the standard, management must either provide training or review and revise the standard so that people can follow it.

In any business, an employee's work is based on existing standards, either explicit or implicit, imposed by management. Maintenance refers to maintaining such standards through training and discipline. By contrast, improvement refers to improving the standards. The Japanese perception of management boils down to one precept: maintain and improve standards.

The higher up the manager is, the more he is concerned with improvement. At the bottom level, an unskilled worker working at a machine may spend all his time following instructions. However, as he becomes more proficient at his work, he begins to think about improvement. He begins to contribute to improvements in the way his work is done, either through individual suggestions or through group suggestions.

Ask any manager at a successful Japanese company what top management is pressing for, and the answer will be, 'Kaizen' (improvement). Improving standards means establishing higher standards. Once this is done, it becomes management's maintenance job to see that the new standards are observed. Lasting improvement is achieved only when

people work to higher standards. Maintenance and improvement have thus become inseparable for most Japanese managers.

What is improvement? Improvement can be broken down between Kaizen and innovation. Kaizen signifies small improvements made in the status quo as a result of ongoing efforts. Innovation involves a drastic improvement in the status quo as a result of a large investment in new technology and/or equipment. Figure 4.2.2 shows the breakdown among maintenance, Kaizen, and innovation as perceived by Japanese management.

On the other hand, most Western managers' perceptions of job functions are as shown in Figure 4.2.2. There is little room in Western management for the Kaizen concept.

Sometimes, another type of management is found in the high-technology industries. These are the companies that are born running, grow rapidly, and then disappear just as rapidly when their initial success wanes or markets change.

The worst companies are those which do nothing but maintenance, meaning there is no internal drive for Kaizen or innovation, change is forced on management by market conditions and competition and management does not know where it wants to go.

Implications of QC for Kaizen

While management is usually concerned with such issues as productivity and quality, the thrust of this article is to look at the other side of the picture – at Kaizen.

The starting point for improvement is to recognize the need. This comes from recognition of a problem. If no problem is recog-

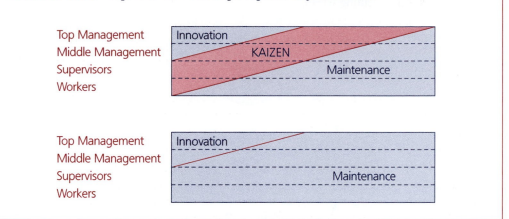

FIGURE 4.2.2   Japanese vs. Western perceptions of job functions

nized, there is no recognition of the need for improvement. Complacency is the archenemy of Kaizen. Therefore, Kaizen emphasizes problem-awareness and provides clues for identifying problems.

Once identified, problems must be solved. Thus Kaizen is also a problem-solving process. In fact, Kaizen requires the use of various problem-solving tools. Improvement reaches new heights with every problem that is solved. In order to consolidate the new level, however, the improvement must be standardized. Thus Kaizen also requires standardization.

Such terms as QC (Quality Control), SQC (Statistical Quality Control), QC circles, and TQC (or CWQC) often appear in connection with Kaizen. To avoid unnecessary confusion, it may be helpful to clarify these terms here. The word *quality* has been interpreted in many different ways, and there is no agreement on what actually constitutes quality. In its broadest sense, quality is anything that can be improved. In this context, quality is associated not only with products and services but also with the way people work, the way machines are operated, and the way systems and procedures are dealt with. It includes all aspects of human behavior. This is why it is more useful to talk about Kaizen than about quality or productivity.

The English term *improvement* as used in the Western context more often than not means improvement in equipment, thus excluding the human elements. By contrast, Kaizen is generic and can be applied to every aspect of everybody's activities. This said, however, it must be admitted that such terms as quality and quality control have played a vital role in the development of Kaizen in Japan.

In March 1950, the Union of Japanese Scientists and Engineers (JUSE) started publishing its magazine *Statistical Quality Control*. In July of the same year, W.E. Deming was invited to Japan to teach statistical quality control at an eight-day seminar organized by JUSE. Deming visited Japan several times in the 1950s, and it was during one of those visits that he made his famous prediction that Japan would soon be flooding the world market with quality products.

Deming also introduced the 'Deming cycle,' one of the crucial QC tools for assuring continuous improvement, to Japan. The Deming cycle is also called the Deming wheel or the PDCA (Plan-Do-Check-Action) cycle. (See Figure 4.2.3.) Deming stressed the importance of constant interaction among research, design, production, and sales in order for a company to arrive at better quality that satisfies customers. He taught that this wheel should be rotated on the ground of quality-first perceptions and quality-first responsibility. With this process, he argued, the company could win consumer confidence and acceptance and prosper.

FIGURE 4.2.3   Deming wheel

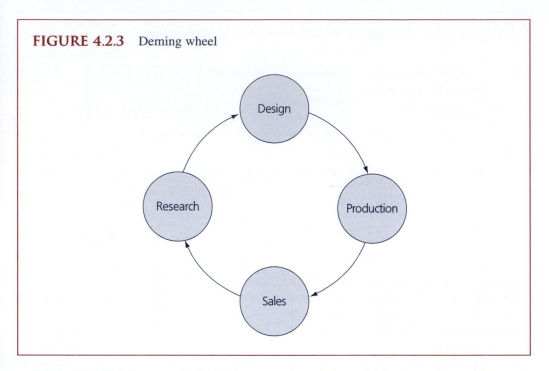

In July 1954, J.M. Juran was invited to Japan to conduct a JUSE seminar on quality-control management. This was the first time QC was dealt with from the overall management perspective.

In 1956, Japan Shortwave Radio included a course on quality control as part of its educational programming. In November 1960, the first national quality month was inaugurated. It was also in 1960 that Q-marks and Q-flags were formally adopted. Then in April 1962 the magazine *Quality Control for the Foreman* was launched by JUSE, and the first QC circle was started that same year.

A QC circle is defined as a small group that *voluntarily* performs quality-control activities within the shop. The small group carries out its work continuously as part of a company-wide program of quality control, self-development, mutual education, and flow-control and improvement within the workshop. The QC circle is only *part* of a company-wide program; it is never the whole of TQC or CWQC.

Those who have followed QC circles in Japan know that they often focus on such areas as cost, safety, and productivity, and that their activities sometimes relate only indirectly to product-quality improvement. For the most part, these activities are aimed at making improvements in the workshop.

There is no doubt that QC circles have played an important part in improving product quality and productivity in Japan. However, their role has often been blown out of proportion by overseas observers who believe that QC circles are the mainstay of TQC activities in Japan. Nothing could be further from the truth, especially when it comes to Japanese management. Efforts related to QC circles generally account for only 10 percent to 30 percent of the overall TQC effort in Japanese companies.

What is less visible behind these developments is the transformation of the term quality control, or QC, in Japan. As is the case in many Western companies, quality control initially meant quality control applied to the manufacturing process, particularly the inspections for rejecting defective incoming material or defective outgoing products at the end of the production line. But very soon the realization set in that inspection alone does nothing to improve the quality of the product, and that product quality should be built at the production stage. 'Build quality into the process' was (and still is) a popular phrase in Japanese quality control. It is at this stage that control charts and the other tools for statistical quality control were introduced after Deming's lectures.

Juran's lectures in 1954 opened up another aspect of quality control: the managerial approach to quality control. This was the first time the term QC was positioned as a vital management tool in Japan. From then on, the term QC has been used to mean both quality control and the tools for overall improvement in managerial performance.

At a later stage, other industries started to introduce QC for such products as consumer durables and home appliances. In these industries, the interest was in building quality in at the design stage to meet changing and increasingly stringent customer requirements. Today, management has gone beyond the design stage and has begun to stress the importance of quality product development, which means taking customer-related information and market research into account from the very start.

All this while, QC has grown into a full-fledged management tool for Kaizen involving everyone in the company. Such company-wide activities are often referred to as TQC (total quality control) or CWQC (company-wide quality control). No matter which name is used, TQC and CWQC mean company-wide Kaizen activities involving everyone in the company, managers and workers alike. Over the years, QC has been elevated to SQC and then to TQC or CWQC, improving managerial performance at every level. Thus it is that such words as QC and TQC have come to be almost synonymous with Kaizen. This is also why I constantly refer to QC, TQC, and CWQC in explaining Kaizen.

On the other hand, the function of quality control in its original sense remains valid. Quality assurance remains a vital part of management, and most companies have a QA (quality assurance) department for this. To confuse matters, TQC or CWQC activities are sometimes administered by the QA depart-

ment and sometimes by a separate TQC office. Thus it is important that these QC-related words be understood in the context in which they appear.

Kaizen and TQC

Considering the TQC movement in Japan as part of the Kaizen movement gives us a clearer perspective on the Japanese approach. First of all, it should be pointed out that TQC activities in Japan are not concerned solely with quality control. People have been fooled by the term 'quality control' and have often construed it within the narrow discipline of product-quality control. In the West, the term QC is mostly associated with inspection of finished products, and when QC is brought up in discussion, top managers, who generally assume they have very little to do with quality control, lose interest immediately.

It is unfortunate that in the West TQC has been dealt with mainly in technical journals when it is more properly the focus of management journals. Japan has developed an elaborate system of Kaizen strategies as management tools within the TQC movement. These rank among this century's most outstanding management achievements. Yet because of the limited way in which QC is understood in the West, most Western students of Japanese QC activities have failed to grasp their real significance and challenge. At the same time, new TQC methods and tools are constantly being studied and tested.

TQC in Japan is a movement centered on the improvement of managerial performance at all levels. As such, it has typically dealt with:

1   quality assurance;

2   cost reduction;

3   meeting production quotas;

4   meeting delivery schedules;

5   safety;

6   new-product development;

7   productivity improvement;

8   supplier management.

More recently, TQC has come to include marketing, sales, and service as well. Furthermore, TQC has dealt with such crucial management concerns as organizational development, cross-functional management, policy deployment, and quality deployment. In other words, management has been using TQC as a tool for improving overall performance.

Those who have closely followed QC circles in Japan know that their activities are often focused on such areas as cost, safety and productivity, and that their activities may only indirectly relate to product-quality improvement. For the most part, these activities are aimed at making improvements in the workplace.

Management efforts for TQC have been directed mostly at such areas as education, systems development, policy deployment, cross-functional management and, more recently, quality deployment.

Kaizen and the suggestion system

Japanese management makes a concerted effort to involve employees in Kaizen through suggestions. Thus, the suggestion system is an integral part of the established management system, and the number of workers' suggestions is regarded as an important criterion in reviewing the performance of these workers' supervisor. The manager of the supervisors is in turn expected to assist them so that they can help workers generate more suggestions.

Most Japanese companies active in Kaizen programs have a quality-control system and a suggestion system working in concert. The role of QC circles may be better understood if we regard them collectively as a group-oriented suggestion system for making improvements.

One of the outstanding features of Japanese management is that it generates a great number of suggestions from workers and that management works hard to consider these suggestions, often incorporating them into the overall Kaizen strategy. It is not uncommon for top management of a leading Japanese company to spend a whole day listening to presentations of activities by QC circles, and giving awards based on predetermined criteria. Management is willing to give recognition to employees' efforts for improvements and makes its concern visible wherever possible. Often, the number of suggestions is posted individually on the wall of the work-place in order to encourage competition among workers and among groups.

Another important aspect of the suggestion system is that each suggestion, once implemented, leads to a revised standard. For instance, when a special foolproof device has been installed on a machine at a worker's suggestion, this may require the worker to work differently and, at times, more attentively.

However, inasmuch as the new standard has been set up by the worker's own volition, he takes pride in the new standard and is willing to follow it. If, on the contrary, he is told to follow a standard imposed by management, he may not be as willing to follow it.

Thus, through suggestions, employees can participate in Kaizen in the workplace and play a vital role in upgrading standards. In a recent interview, Toyota Motor chairman Eiji Toyoda said, 'One of the features of the Japanese workers is that they use their brains as well as their hands. Our workers provide 1.5 million suggestions a year, and 95 percent of them are put to practical use. There is an almost tangible concern for improvement in the air at Toyota.'

Kaizen vs. innovation

There are two contrasting approaches to progress: the gradualist approach and the great-leap-forward approach. Japanese companies generally favor the gradualist approach and Western companies the great-leap approach – an approach epitomized by the term 'innovation'.

Western management worships at the altar of innovation. This innovation is seen as major changes in the wake of technological breakthroughs, or the introduction of the latest management concepts or production techniques. Innovation is dramatic, a real attention-getter. Kaizen, on the other hand, is often undramatic and subtle, and its results are seldom immediately visible. While Kaizen is a continuous process, innovation is generally a one-shot phenomenon.

In the West, for example, a middle manager can usually obtain top management support for such projects as CAD (computer-aided design), CAM (computer-aided manufacture), and MRP (materials requirements planning), since these are innovative projects that have a way of revolutionizing existing systems. As such, they offer ROI (return on investment) benefits that managers can hardly resist.

However, when a factory manager wishes, for example, to make small changes in the way his workers use the machinery, such as working out multiple job assignments or realigning production processes (both of which may require lengthy discussions with the union as well as reeducation and retraining of workers), obtaining management support can be difficult indeed.

Table 4.2.1 compares the main features of Kaizen and of innovation. One of the beautiful things about Kaizen is that it does not necessarily require sophisticated technique or state-of-the-art technology. To implement Kaizen, you need only simple, conventional techniques. Often, common sense is all that is needed. On the other hand, innovation usually requires highly sophisticated technology, as well as a huge investment.

Kaizen is like a hotbed that nurtures small and ongoing changes, while innovation is like magma that appears in abrupt eruptions from time to time. One big difference between Kaizen and innovation is that while Kaizen does not necessarily call for a large investment to implement it, it does call for a great deal of continuous effort and commitment. The difference between the two opposing concepts may thus be likened to that of a staircase and a slope. The innovation strategy is supposed to bring about progress in a staircase progression. On the other hand, the Kaizen strategy brings about gradual progress. I say the innovation strategy 'is supposed to' bring about progress in

TABLE 4.2.1 Features of Kaizen and innovation

	Kaizen	Innovation
1. Effect	Long-term and long-lasting but undramatic	Short-term but dramatic
2. Pace	Small steps	Big steps
3. Timeframe	Continuous and incremental	Intermittent and non-incremental
4. Change	Gradual and constant	Abrupt and volatile
5. Involvement	Everybody	Select few 'champions'
6. Approach	Collectivism, group efforts, systems approach	Rugged individualism, individual ideas and efforts
7. Mode	Maintenance and improvement	Scrap and rebuild
8. Spark	Conventional know-how and state of the art	Technological break-throughs, new inventions, new theories
9. Practical requirements	Requires little investment but great effort to maintain it	Requires large investment but little effort to maintain it
10. Effort orientation	People	Technology
11. Evaluation criteria	Process and efforts for better results	Results and profits
12. Advantage	Works well in slow-growth economy	Better suited to fast-growth economy

a staircase progression, because it usually does not. Instead of following the staircase pattern, the actual progress achieved through innovation will generally follow the pattern shown in Figure 4.2.4, if it lacks the Kaizen strategy to go along with it. This happens because a system, once it has been installed as a result of new innovation, is subject to steady deterioration unless continuing efforts are made first to maintain it and then to improve on it.

In reality, there can be no such thing as a static constant. All systems are destined to deteriorate once they have been established. One of the famous Parkinson's Laws is that an organization, once it has built its edifice, begins its decline. In other words, there must be a continuing effort for improvement to even maintain the status quo.

When such effort is lacking, decline is inevitable (see Figure 4.2.4). Therefore, even when an innovation makes a revolutionary standard of performance attainable, the new performance level will decline unless the standard is constantly challenged and upgraded. Thus, whenever an innovation is achieved, it must be followed by a series of Kaizen efforts to maintain and improve it (see Figure 4.2.5).

Whereas innovation is a one-shot deal whose effects are gradually eroded by intense

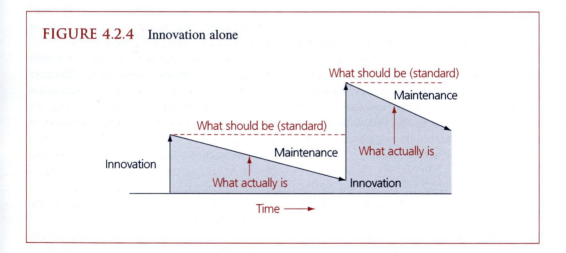

FIGURE 4.2.4 Innovation alone

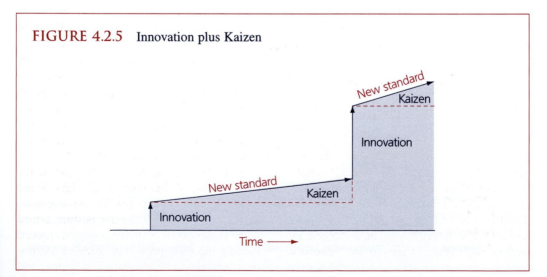

FIGURE 4.2.5 Innovation plus Kaizen

competition and deteriorating standards, Kaizen is an ongoing effort with cumulative effects marking a steady rise as the years go by. If standards exist only in order to maintain the status quo, they will not be challenged so long as the level of performance is acceptable. Kaizen, on the other hand, means a constant effort not only to maintain but also to upgrade standards. Kaizen strategists believe that standards are by nature tentative, akin to stepping stones, with one standard leading to another as continuing improvement efforts are made. This is the reason why QC circles no sooner solve one problem than they move on to tackle a new problem. This is also the reason why the so-called PDCA (plan-do-check-action) cycle receives so much emphasis in Japan's TQC movement.

Another feature of Kaizen is that it requires virtually everyone's personal efforts. In order for the Kaizen spirit to survive, management must make a conscious and continuous effort to support it. Such support is quite different from the fanfare recognition that management accords to people who have achieved a striking success or breakthrough. Kaizen is concerned more with the process than with the result. The strength of Japanese management lies in its successful development and implementation of a system that acknowledges the ends while emphasizing the means.

Thus Kaizen calls for a substantial management commitment of time and effort. Infusions of capital are no substitute for this investment in time and effort. Investing in Kaizen means investing in people. In short, Kaizen is people-oriented, whereas innovation is technology- and money-oriented.

Finally, the Kaizen philosophy is better suited to a slow-growth economy, while innovation is better suited to a fast-growth economy. While Kaizen advances inch-by-inch on the strength of many small efforts, innovation leaps upward in hopes of landing at a much higher plateau in spite of gravitational inertia and the weight of investment costs. In a slow-growth economy characterized by high costs of energy and materials, overcapacity, and stagnant markets, Kaizen

often has a better payoff than innovation does. As one Japanese executive recently remarked, 'It is extremely difficult to increase sales by 10 percent. But it is not so difficult to cut manufacturing costs by 10 percent to even better effect.'

I argued that the concept of Kaizen is nonexistent or at best weak in most Western companies today. However, there was a time, not so long ago, when Western management also placed a high priority on Kaizen-like improvement-consciousness. Older executives may recall that before the phenomenal economic growth of the late 1950s and early 1960s, management attended assiduously to improving all aspects of the business, particularly the factory. In those days, every small improvement was counted and was seen as effective in terms of building success.

People who worked with small, privately owned companies may recall with a touch of nostalgia that there was a genuine concern for improvement 'in the air' before the company was bought out or went public. As soon as that happened, the quarterly P/L (profit/loss) figures suddenly became the most important criterion, and management became obsessed with the bottom line, often at the expense of pressing for constant and unspectacular improvements.

For many other companies, the greatly increased market opportunities and technological innovations that appeared during the first two decades after World War II meant that developing new products based on the new technology was much more attractive or 'sexier' than slow, patient efforts for improvement. In trying to catch up with the ever-increasing market demand, managers boldly introduced one innovation after another, and they were content to ignore the seemingly minor benefits of improvement.

Most Western managers who joined the ranks during or after those heady days do not have the slightest concern for improvement. Instead, they take an offensive posture, armed with professional expertise geared toward making big changes in the name of innovation, bringing about immediate gains, and winning instant recognition and promotion. Before they knew it, Western managers had lost sight of improvement and put all their eggs in the innovation basket.

Another factor that has abetted the innovation approach has been the increasing emphasis on financial controls and accounting. By now, the more sophisticated companies have succeeded in establishing elaborate accounting and reporting systems that force managers to account for every action they take and to spell out the precise payout or ROI of every managerial decision. Such a system does not lend itself to building a favorable climate for improvement.

Improvement is by definition slow, gradual, and often invisible, with effects that are felt over the long run. In my opinion, the most glaring and significant shortcoming of Western management today is the lack of improvement philosophy. There is no internal system in Western management to reward efforts for improvement; instead, everyone's job performance is reviewed strictly on the basis of results. Thus it is not uncommon for Western managers to chide people with, 'I don't care what you do or how you do it. I want the results – and now!' This emphasis on results has led to the innovation-dominated approach of the West. This is not to say that Japanese management does not care about innovation. But Japanese managers have enthusiastically pursued Kaizen even when they were involved in innovation.

READINGS ON BUSINESS LEVEL STRATEGY

The first reading on the topic of business level strategy, 'Competitive Strategy', has been taken from Michael Porter's 1985 book, *Competitive Advantage*, but its central concepts were originally introduced in his 1980 book, *Competitive Strategy*. Since Porter is considered by all to be the most important theorist in the positioning tradition, it is only logical to start with him as representative of the outside-in perspective. In his contribution, Porter argues that 'two central questions underlie the choice of competitive strategy'. First, managers must select a competitive domain with attractive characteristics and then they must position the firm vis-à-vis the five competitive forces encountered. These five forces impinging on the firm's profit potential are 'the entry of new competitors, the threat of substitutes, the bargaining power of buyers, the bargaining power of suppliers, and the rivalry among the existing competitors'. Long run, above-average performance results from selecting one of the three defensible positions available to the strategist: cost leadership, differentiation or focus. According to Porter, these three options, or 'generic strategies', are the only feasible ways of achieving a sustainable competitive advantage. A firm that does not make a clear choice between one of the three generic strategies, is 'stuck in the middle' and will suffer below-average performance. For the debate it is important to note that Porter does not explicitly advocate an exclusively outside-in approach. However, he strongly emphasizes competitive positioning as a leading strategy principle and treats the development of firm resources as a derivative activity. Indirectly, therefore, his message to managers is that in the game of strategy it is essential to be focused on the external dynamics.

As representative of the inside-out perspective, a recent article by Danny Miller, Russell Eisenstat and Nathaniel Foote has been selected, with the telling title 'Strategy From the Inside Out: Building Capability-Creating Organizations'. In this reading the authors start by emphasizing the value of 'skills, knowledge, processes, relationships, or outputs an organization possesses or produces' that are unique and difficult for competitors to copy or acquire – which in this book are called 'resources', but Miller, Eisenstat and Foote prefer to call 'asymmetries', to accentuate that they encompass all differences, even those that have not yet been turned to economic use. The thrust of the authors' argumentation is that 'by continually identifying and building on asymmetries, by nurturing and exploiting these within a complementary organizational design, and by leveraging them via an appropriate market focus, companies may be able to aspire realistically to attain sustainable competitive advantage'. To make this inside-out approach work they believe that companies must do three things well. First, they must be able to discover asymmetries and to recognize their potential. Secondly, these asymmetries must be developed into a cohesive set of capabilities. Thirdly, market opportunities must be pursued that build on and leverage these capabilities. On this last point Miller, Eisenstat and Foote recognize that in the tension between markets and resources one cannot fully dominate over the other: 'Managers need to find opportunities tailored to their capabilities. Opportunities also must ultimately shape capabilities.' Yet, while they underline the value of mutual adjustment between markets and resources, they do reiterate that asymmetries and capabilities should be the drivers of this processes, not created somewhere along the line on the basis of a perceived opportunity. An important additional point brought up by the authors is that capabilities can be leveraged across two or more business units. This makes capability-based approaches to strategy equally relevant to corporate level strategy as to business level strategy (in readings linked to Chapter 6, Prahalad and Hamel will pick up on this issue).

READING

5.1

Competitive strategy

By Michael Porter[1]

Competition is at the core of the success or failure of firms. Competition determines the appropriateness of a firm's activities that can contribute to its performance, such as innovations, a cohesive culture, or good implementation. Competitive strategy is the search for a favorable competitive position in an industry, the fundamental arena in which competition occurs. Competitive strategy aims to establish a profitable and sustainable position against the forces that determine industry competition.

Two central questions underlie the choice of competitive strategy. The first is the attractiveness of industries for long-term profitability and the factors that determine it. Not all industries offer equal opportunities for sustained profitability, and the inherent prof-

itability of its industry is one essential ingredient in determining the profitability of a firm. The second central question in competitive strategy is the determinants of relative competitive position within an industry. In most industries, some firms are much more profitable than others, regardless of what the average profitability of the industry may be.

Neither question is sufficient by itself to guide the choice of competitive strategy. A firm in a very attractive industry may still not earn attractive profits if it has chosen a poor competitive position. Conversely, a firm in an excellent competitive position may be in such a poor industry that it is not very profitable, and further efforts to enhance its position will be of little benefit. Both questions are dynamic; industry attractiveness and competitive position change. Industries become more or less attractive over time, and competitive position reflects an unending battle among competitors. Even long periods of stability can be abruptly ended by competitive moves.

Both industry attractiveness and competitive position can be shaped by a firm, and this is what makes the choice of competitive strategy both challenging and exciting. While industry attractiveness is partly a reflection of factors over which a firm has little influence, competitive strategy has considerable power to make an industry more or less attractive. At the same time, a firm can clearly improve or erode its position within an industry through its choice of strategy. Competitive strategy, then, not only responds to the environment but also attempts to shape that environment in a firm's favor.

The structural analysis of industries

The first fundamental determinant of a firm's profitability is industry attractiveness. Competitive strategy must grow out of a sophisticated understanding of the rules of competition that determine an industry's attractiveness. The ultimate aim of competitive strategy is to cope with and, ideally, to change those rules in the firm's favor. In any industry, whether it is domestic or international or produces a product or a service, the rules of competition are embodied in five competitive forces: the entry of new competitors, the threat of substitutes, the bargaining power of buyers, the bargaining power of suppliers, and the rivalry among the existing competitors.

The collective strength of these five competitive forces determines the ability of firms in an industry to earn, on average, rates of return on investment in excess of the cost of capital. The strength of the five forces varies from industry to industry, and can change as an industry evolves. The result is that all industries are not alike from the standpoint of inherent profitability. In industries where the five forces are favorable, such as pharmaceu-

ticals, soft drinks, and database publishing, many competitors earn attractive returns. But in industries where pressure from one or more of the forces is intense, such as rubber, steel, and video games, few firms command attractive returns despite the best efforts of management. Industry profitability is not a function of what the product looks like or whether it embodies high or low technology, but of industry structure. Some very mundane industries such as postage meters and grain trading are extremely profitable, while some more glamorous, high-technology industries such as personal computers and cable television are not profitable for many participants.

The five forces determine industry profitability because they influence the prices, costs, and required investment of firms in an industry – the elements of return on investment. Buyer power influences the prices that firms can charge, for example, as does the threat of substitution. The power of buyers can also influence cost and investment, because powerful buyers demand costly service. The bargaining power of suppliers determines the costs of raw materials and other inputs. The intensity of rivalry influences prices as well as the costs of competing in areas such as plant, product development, advertising, and sales force. The threat of entry places a limit on prices, and shapes the investment required to deter entrants.

The strength of each of the five competitive forces is a function of *industry structure*, or the underlying economic and technical characteristics of an industry. Its important elements are shown in Figure 5.1.1. Industry structure is relatively stable, but can change over time as an industry evolves. Structural change shifts the overall and relative strength of the competitive forces, and can thus positively or negatively influence industry profitability. The industry trends that are the most important for strategy are those that affect industry structure.

If the five competitive forces and their structural determinants were solely a function of intrinsic industry characteristics, then

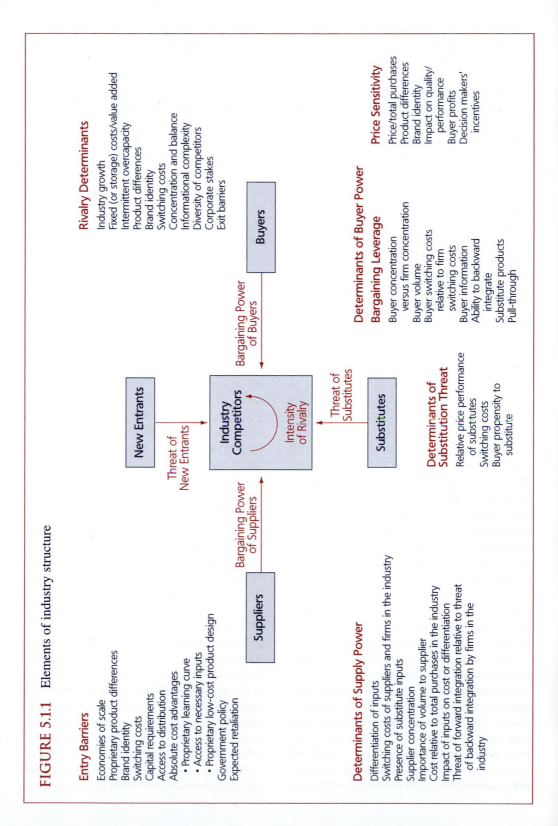

FIGURE 5.1.1 Elements of industry structure

Entry Barriers

Economies of scale
Proprietary product differences
Brand identity
Switching costs
Capital requirements
Access to distribution
Absolute cost advantages
  • Proprietary learning curve
  • Access to necessary inputs
  • Proprietary low-cost product design
Government policy
Expected retaliation

Rivalry Determinants

Industry growth
Fixed (or storage) costs/value added
Intermittent overcapacity
Product differences
Brand identity
Switching costs
Concentration and balance
Informational complexity
Diversity of competitors
Corporate stakes
Exit barriers

Determinants of Buyer Power

Bargaining Leverage

Buyer concentration
versus firm concentration
Buyer volume
Buyer switching costs
relative to firm
switching costs
Buyer information
Ability to backward
integrate
Substitute products
Pull-through

Price Sensitivity

Price/total purchases
Product differences
Brand identity
Impact on quality/
performance
Buyer profits
Decision makers'
incentives

Determinants of Supply Power

Differentiation of inputs
Switching costs of suppliers and firms in the industry
Presence of substitute inputs
Supplier concentration
Importance of volume to supplier
Cost relative to total purchases in the industry
Impact of inputs on cost or differentiation
Threat of forward integration relative to threat
of backward integration by firms in the
industry

Determinants of Substitution Threat

Relative price performance
of substitutes
Switching costs
Buyer propensity to
substitute

New Entrants

Suppliers

Industry Competitors

Intensity of Rivalry

Buyers

Substitutes

Threat of New Entrants

Bargaining Power of Suppliers

Bargaining Power of Buyers

Threat of Substitutes

competitive strategy would rest heavily on picking the right industry and understanding the five forces better than competitors. But while these are surely important tasks for any firm, and are the essence of competitive strategy in some industries, a firm is usually not a prisoner of its industry's structure. Firms, through their strategies, can influence the five forces. If a firm can shape structure, it can fundamentally change an industry's attractiveness for better or for worse. Many successful strategies have shifted the rules of competition in this way.

Figure 5.1.1 highlights all the elements of industry structure that may drive competition in an industry. In any particular industry, not all of the five forces will be equally important and the particular structural factors that are important will differ. Every industry is unique and has its own unique structure. The five-forces framework allows a firm to see through the complexity and pinpoint those factors that are critical to competition in its industry, as well as to identify those strategic innovations that would most improve the industry's – and its own – profitability. The five-forces framework does not eliminate the need for creativity in finding new ways of competing in an industry. Instead, it directs managers' creative energies toward those aspects of industry structure that are most important to long-run profitability. The framework aims, in the process, to raise the odds of discovering a desirable strategic innovation.

Strategies that change industry structure can be a double-edged sword, because a firm can destroy industry structure and profitability as readily as it can improve it. A new product design that undercuts entry barriers or increases the volatility of rivalry, for example, may undermine the long-run profitability of an industry, though the initiator may enjoy higher profits temporarily. Or a sustained period of price cutting can undermine differentiation. In the tobacco industry, for example, generic cigarettes are a potentially serious threat to industry structure. Generics may enhance the price sensitivity of buyers, trigger price competition, and erode the high advertising barriers that have kept out new entrants. Joint ventures entered into by major aluminum producers to spread risk and lower capital cost may have similarly undermined industry structure. The majors invited a number of potentially dangerous new competitors into the industry and helped them overcome the significant entry barriers to doing so. Joint ventures also can raise exit barriers because all the participants in a plant must agree before it can be closed down.

Often firms make strategic choices without considering the long-term consequences for industry structure. They see a gain in the competitive position if a move is successful, but they fail to anticipate the consequences of competitive reaction. If imitation of a move by major competitors has the effect of wrecking industry structure, then everyone is worse off. Such industry 'destroyers' are usually second-tier firms that are searching for ways to overcome major competitive disadvantages, firms that have encountered serious problems and are desperately seeking solutions, or 'dumb' competitors that do not know their costs or have unrealistic assumptions about the future. In the tobacco industry, for example, the Liggett Group (a distant follower) has encouraged the trend toward generics.

The ability of firms to shape industry structure places a particular burden on industry leaders. Leaders' actions can have a disproportionate impact on structure, because of their size and influence over buyers, suppliers, and other competitors. At the same time, leaders' large market shares guarantee that anything that changes overall industry structure will affect them as well. A leader, then, must constantly balance its own competitive position against the health of the industry as a whole. Often leaders are better off taking actions to improve or protect industry structure rather than seeking greater competitive advantage for themselves. Such industry leaders as Coca-Cola and Campbell's Soup appear to have followed this principle.

Industry structure and buyer needs

It has often been said that satisfying buyer needs is at the core of success in business endeavor. How does this relate to the concept of industry structural analysis? Satisfying buyer needs is indeed a prerequisite to the viability of an industry and the firms within it. Buyers must be willing to pay a price for a product that exceeds its cost of production, or an industry will not survive in the long run.

Satisfying buyer needs may be a prerequisite for industry profitability, but in itself is not sufficient. The crucial question in determining profitability is whether firms can capture the value they create for buyers, or whether this value is competed away to others. Industry structure determines who captures the value. The threat of entry determines the likelihood that new firms will enter an industry and compete away the value, either passing it on to buyers in the form of lower prices or dissipating it by raising the costs of competing. The power of buyers determines the extent to which they retain most of the value created for themselves, leaving firms in an industry only modest returns. The threat of substitutes determines the extent to which some other product can meet the same buyer needs, and thus places a ceiling on the amount a buyer is willing to pay for an industry's product. The power of suppliers determines the extent to which value created for buyers will be appropriated by suppliers rather than by firms in an industry. Finally, the intensity of rivalry acts similarly to the threat of entry. It determines the extent to which firms already in an industry will compete away the value they create for buyers among themselves, passing it on to buyers in lower prices or dissipating it in higher costs of competing.

Industry structure, then, determines who keeps what proportion of the value a product creates for buyers. If an industry's product does not create much value for its buyers, there is little value to be captured by firms regardless of the other elements of structure. If the product creates a lot of value, structure becomes crucial. In some industries such as automobiles and heavy trucks, firms create enormous value for their buyers but, on average, capture very little of it for themselves through profits. In other industries such as bond rating services, medical equipment, and oil field services and equipment, firms also create high value for their buyers but have historically captured a good proportion of it. In oil field services and equipment, for example, many products can significantly reduce the cost of drilling. Because industry structure has been favorable, many firms in the oil field service and equipment sector have been able to retain a share of these savings in the form of high returns. Recently, however, the structural attractiveness of many industries in the oil field services and equipment sector has eroded as a result of falling demand, new entrants, eroding product differentiation, and greater buyer price sensitivity. Despite the fact that products offered still create enormous value for the buyer, both firm and industry profits have fallen significantly.

Industry structure and the supply/demand balance

Another commonly held view about industry profitability is that profits are a function of the balance between supply and demand. If demand is greater than supply, this leads to high profitability. Yet, the long-term supply/demand balance is strongly influenced by industry structure, as are the consequences of a supply/demand imbalance for profitability. Hence, even though short-term fluctuations in supply and demand can affect short-term profitability, industry structure underlies long-term profitability.

Supply and demand change constantly, adjusting to each other. Industry structure determines how rapidly competitors add new supply. The height of entry barriers underpins the likelihood that new entrants will enter an industry and bid down prices. The intensity of rivalry plays a major role in determining whether existing firms will expand capacity aggressively or choose to maintain profitability. Industry structure also determines how rapidly competitors will retire excess supply. Exit barriers keep firms from leaving an industry when there is too much capacity, and prolong periods of excess capacity. In oil tanker shipping, for example, the exit barriers are very high because of the specialization of assets. This has translated into short peaks and long troughs of prices. Thus industry structure shapes the supply/demand balance and the duration of imbalances.

The consequences of an imbalance between supply and demand for industry profitability also differs widely depending on industry structure. In some industries, a small amount of excess capacity triggers price wars and low profitability. These are industries where there are structural pressures for intense rivalry or powerful buyers. In other industries, periods of excess capacity have relatively little impact on profitability because of favorable structure. In oil tools, ball valves, and many other oil field equipment products, for example, there has been intense price cutting during the recent sharp downturn. In drill bits, however, there has been relatively little discounting. Hughes Tool, Smith International, and Baker International are good competitors operating in a favorable industry structure. Industry structure also determines the profitability of excess demand. In a boom, for example, favorable structure allows firms to reap extraordinary profits, while a poor structure restricts the ability to capitalize on it. The presence of powerful suppliers or the presence of substitutes, for example, can mean that the fruits of a boom pass to others. Thus industry structure is fundamental to both the speed of adjustment of supply to demand and the relationship between capacity utilization and profitability.

Generic competitive strategies

The second central question in competitive strategy is a firm's relative position within its industry. Positioning determines whether a firm's profitability is above or below the industry average. A firm that can position itself well may earn high rates of return even though industry structure is unfavorable and the average profitability of the industry is therefore modest.

The fundamental basis of above-average performance in the long run is *sustainable competitive advantage*. Though a firm can have a myriad strengths and weaknesses *vis-à-vis* its competitors, there are two basic types of competitive advantage a firm can possess: low cost or differentiation. The significance of any strength or weakness a firm possesses is ultimately a function of its impact on relative cost or differentiation. Cost advantage and differentiation in turn stem from industry structure. They result from a firm's ability to cope with the five forces better than its rivals.

The two basic types of competitive advantage combined with the scope of activities for which a firm seeks to achieve them lead to three *generic strategies* for achieving above-average performance in an industry: cost leadership, differentiation, and focus. The focus strategy has two variants, cost focus and differentiation focus. The generic strategies are shown in Figure 5.1.2.

Each of the generic strategies involves a fundamentally different route to competitive advantage, combining a choice about the type of competitive advantage sought with the scope of the strategic target in which competitive advantage is to be achieved. The cost leadership and differentiation strategies seek competitive advantage in a broad range of industry segments, while focus strategies aim at cost advantage (cost focus) or differentiation (differentiation focus) in a narrow segment. The specific actions required to implement each generic strategy vary widely from industry to industry, as do the feasible

FIGURE 5.1.2   Three generic strategies

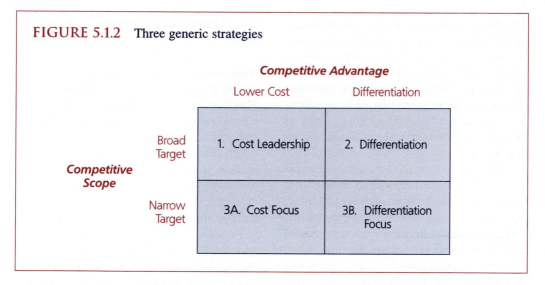

generic strategies in a particular industry. While selecting and implementing a generic strategy is far from simple, they are the logical routes to competitive advantage that must be probed in any industry.

The notion underlying the concept of generic strategies is that competitive advantage is at the heart of any strategy, and achieving competitive advantage requires a firm to make a choice – if a firm is to attain a competitive advantage, it must make a choice about the type of competitive advantage it seeks to attain and the scope within which it will attain it. Being all things to all people is a recipe for strategic mediocrity and below-average performance, because it often means that a firm has no competitive advantage at all.

Cost leadership

Cost leadership is perhaps the clearest of the three generic strategies. In it, a firm sets out to become *the* low-cost producer in its industry. The firm has a broad scope and serves many industry segments, and may even operate in related industries – the firm's breadth is often important to its cost advantage. The sources of cost advantage are varied and depend on the structure of the industry. They may include the pursuit of economies of scale, proprietary technology, preferential access to raw materials, and other factors. In TV sets, for example, cost leadership requires efficient-size picture tube facilities, a low-cost design, automated assembly, and global scale over which to amortize research and development (R&D). In security guard services, cost advantage requires extremely low overhead, a plentiful source of low-cost labor, and efficient training procedures because of high turnover. Low-cost producer status involves more than just going down the learning curve. A low-cost producer must find and exploit all sources of cost advantage. Low-cost producers typically sell a standard, or no-frills, product and place considerable emphasis on reaping scale or absolute cost advantages from all sources.

If a firm can achieve and sustain overall cost leadership, then it will be an above-average performer in its industry provided it can command prices at or near the industry average. At equivalent or lower prices than its rivals, a cost leader's low-cost position translates into higher returns. A cost leader, however, cannot ignore the bases of differentiation. If its product is not perceived as comparable or acceptable by buyers, a cost leader will be forced to discount prices well below competitors' to gain sales. This may nullify the benefits of its favorable cost position. Texas Instruments (in watches) and Northwest Airlines (in air transportation) are two low-cost firms that fell into this trap. Texas Instruments could not overcome its disadvantage in differentiation and exited the watch industry. Northwest Airlines recognized its problem in time, and has instituted efforts to improve marketing, passenger service, and service to travel agents to make its product more comparable to those of its competitors.

A cost leader must achieve *parity or proximity* in the bases of differentiation relative to its competitiors to be an above-average performer, even though it relies on cost leadership for its competitive advantage. Parity in the bases of differentiation allows a cost leader to translate its cost advantage directly into higher profits than competitors'. Proximity in differentiation means that the price discount necessary to achieve an acceptable market share does not offset a cost leader's cost advantage and hence the cost leader earns above-average returns.

The strategic logic of cost leadership usually requires that a firm be *the* cost leader, not one of several firms vying for this position. Many firms have made serious strategic errors by failing to recognize this. When there is more than one aspiring cost leader, rivalry among them is usually fierce because every point of market share is viewed as crucial. Unless one firm can gain a cost lead and 'persuade' others to abandon their strategies, the consequences for profitability (and long-run industry structure) can be disastrous, as has been the case in a number of petrochemical industries. Thus cost leadership is a strategy particularly dependent on pre-emption, unless major technological change allows a firm to radically change its cost position.

Differentiation

The second generic strategy is differentiation. In a differentiation strategy, a firm seeks to be unique in its industry along some dimensions that are widely valued by buyers. It selects one or more attributes that many buyers in an industry perceive as important, and uniquely positions itself to meet those needs. It is rewarded for its uniqueness with a premium price.

The means for differentiation are peculiar to each industry. Differentiation can be based on the product itself, the delivery system by which it is sold, the marketing approach, and a broad range of other factors. In construction equipment, for example, Caterpillar Tractor's differentiation is based on product durability, service, spare parts availability, and an excellent dealer network. In cosmetics, differentiation tends to be based more on product image and the positioning of counters in the stores.

A firm that can achieve and sustain differentiation will be an above-average performer in its industry if its price premium exceeds the extra costs incurred in being unique. A differentiator, therefore, must always seek ways of differentiating that lead to a price premium greater than the cost of differentiating. A differentiator cannot ignore its cost position, because its premium prices will be nullified by a markedly inferior cost position. A differentiator thus aims at cost parity or proximity relative to its competitors by reducing cost in all areas that do not affect differentiation.

The logic of the differentiation strategy requires that a firm choose attributes in which to differentiate itself that are *different* from its rivals'. A firm must truly be unique at something or be perceived as unique if it is to expect a premium price. In contrast to cost leadership, however, there can be more than one successful differentiation strategy in an industry if there are a number of attributes that are widely valued by buyers.

Focus

The third generic strategy is focus. This strategy is quite different from the others because it rests on the choice of a narrow competitive scope within an industry. The focuser selects a segment or group of segments in the industry and tailors its strategy to serving them to the exclusion of others. By optimizing its strategy for the target segments, the focuser seeks to achieve a competitive advantage in its target segments even though it does not possess a competitive advantage overall.

The focus strategy has two variants. In *cost focus* a firm seeks a cost advantage in its target segment, while in *differentiation focus* a firm seeks differentiation in its target segment. Both variants of the focus strategy rest on *differences* between a focuser's target segments and other segments in the industry. The target segments must either have buyers with unusual needs or else the production and delivery system that best serves the target segment must differ from that of other industry segments. Cost focus exploits differences in cost behavior in some segments, while differentiation focus exploits the special needs of buyers in certain segments. Such differences imply that the segments are poorly served by broadly targeted competitors who serve them at the same time as they serve others. The focuser can thus achieve competitive advantage by dedicating itself to the segments exclusively. Breadth of target is clearly a matter of degree, but the essence of focus is the exploitation of a narrow target's differences from the balance of the industry. Narrow focus in and of itself is not sufficient for above-average performance.

A good example of a focuser who has exploited differences in the production process that best serves different segments is Hammermill Paper. Hammermill has increasingly been moving toward relatively low-volume, high-quality speciality papers, where the larger paper companies with higher volume machines face a stiff cost penalty for short production runs. Hammermill's equipment is more suited to shorter runs with frequent setups.

A focuser takes advantage of suboptimization in either direction by broadly targeted competitors. Competitors may be *underperforming* in meeting the needs of a particular segment, which opens the possibility for differentiation focus. Broadly targeted competitors may also be *overperforming* in meeting the needs of a segment, which means that they are bearing higher than necessary cost in serving it. An opportunity for cost focus may be present in just meeting the needs of such a segment and no more.

If a focuser's target segment is not different from other segments, then the focus strategy will not succeed. In soft drinks, for example, Royal Crown has focused on cola drinks, while Coca-Cola and Pepsi have broad product lines with many flavored drinks. Royal Crown's segment, however, can be well served by Coke and Pepsi at the same time they are serving other segments. Hence Coke and Pepsi enjoy competitive advantages over Royal Crown in the cola segment due to the economies of having a broader line.

If a firm can achieve sustainable cost leadership (cost focus) or differentiation (differentiation focus) in its segment and the segment is structurally attractive, then the focuser will be an above-average performer in its industry. Segment structural attractiveness is a necessary condition because some segments in an industry are much less profitable than others. There is often room for several sustainable focus strategies in an industry, provided that focusers choose different target segments. Most industries have a variety of segments, and each one that involves a different buyer need or a different optimal production or delivery system is a candidate for a focus strategy.

Stuck in the middle

A firm that engages in each generic strategy but fails to achieve any of them is 'stuck in the middle.' It possesses no competitive advantage. This strategic position is usually a recipe for below-average performance. A firm that is stuck in the middle will compete at a disadvantage because the cost leader, differentiators, or focusers will be better positioned to compete in any segment. If a firm that is stuck in the middle is lucky enough to discover a profitable product or buyer, competitors with a sustainable competitive advantage will quickly eliminate the spoils. In most industries, quite a few competitors are stuck in the middle.

A firm that is stuck in the middle will earn attractive profits only if the structure of its industry is highly favorable, or if the firm is fortunate enough to have competitors that are also stuck in the middle. Usually, however, such a firm will be much less profitable than rivals achieving one of the generic strategies. Industry maturity tends to widen the performance differences between firms with a generic strategy and those that are stuck in the middle, because it exposes ill-conceived strategies that have been carried along by rapid growth.

Becoming stuck in the middle is often a manifestation of a firm's unwillingness to make *choices* about how to compete. It tries for competitive advantage through every means and achieves none, because achieving different types of competitive advantage usually requires inconsistent actions. Becoming stuck in the middle also afflicts successful firms, who compromise their generic strategy for the sake of growth or prestige. A classic example is Laker Airways, which began with a clear cost-focus strategy based on no-frills operation in the North Atlantic market, aimed at a particular segment of the traveling public that was extremely price sensitive. Over time, however, Laker began adding frills, new services, and new routes. It blurred its image, and suboptimized its service and delivery system. The consequences were disastrous, and Laker eventually went bankrupt.

The temptation to blur a generic strategy, and therefore become stuck in the middle, is particularly great for a focuser once it has dominated its target segments. Focus involves deliberately limiting potential sales volume. Success can lead a focuser to lose sight of the reasons for its success and compromise its focus strategy for growth's sake. Rather than compromise its generic strategy, a firm is usually better off finding new industries in which to grow where it can use its generic strategy again or exploit interrelationships.

Pursuit of more than one generic strategy

Each generic strategy is a fundamentally different approach to creating and sustaining a competitive advantage, combining the type of competitive advantage a firm seeks and the scope of its strategic target. Usually a firm must make a choice among them, or it will become stuck in the middle. The benefits of optimizing the firm's strategy for a particular target segment (focus) cannot be gained if a firm is simultaneously serving a broad range of segments (cost leadership or differentiation). Sometimes a firm may be able to create two largely separate business units within the same corporate entity, each with a different generic strategy. A good example is the British hotel firm Trusthouse Forte, which operates five separate hotel chains each targeted at a different segment. However, unless a firm strictly separates the units pursuing different generic strategies, it may compromise the ability of any of them to achieve its competitive advantage. A suboptimized approach to competing, made likely by the spillover among units of corporate policies and culture, will lead to becoming stuck in the middle.

Achieving cost leadership and differentiation is also usually inconsistent, because differentiation is usually costly. To be unique and command a price premium, a differentiator deliberately elevates costs, as Caterpillar has done in construction equipment. Conversely, cost leadership often requires a firm to forego some differentiation by standardizing its product, reducing marketing overhead, and the like.

Reducing cost does not always involve a sacrifice in differentiation. Many firms have discovered ways to reduce cost not only without hurting their differentiation but while actually raising it, by using practices that are both more efficient and effective or employing a different technology. Sometimes dramatic cost savings can be achieved with no impact on differentiation at all if a firm has not concentrated on cost reduction previously. However, cost reduction is not the same as achieving a cost advantage. When faced with capable competitors also striving for cost leadership, a firm will ultimately reach the point where further cost reduction requires a sacrifice in differentiation. It is at this point that the generic strategies become inconsistent and a firm must make a choice.

If a firm can achieve cost leadership and differentiation simultaneously, the rewards are great because the benefits are additive – differentiation leads to premium prices at the same time that cost leadership implies lower costs. An example of a firm that has achieved both a cost advantage and differentiation in its segments is Crown Cork and Seal in the metal container industry. Crown has targeted the so-called hard-to-hold uses of cans in the beer, soft drink, and aerosol industries. It manufactures only steel cans rather than both steel and aluminum. In its target segments, Crown has differentiated itself based on service, technological assistance, and offering a full line of steel cans, crowns, and canning machinery. Differentiation of this type would be much more difficult to achieve in other industry segments that have different needs. At the same time, Crown has dedicated its facilities to producing only the types of cans demanded by buyers in its chosen segments and has aggressively invested in modern two-piece steel-canning technology. As a result, Crown has probably also achieved low-cost producer status in its segments.

Sustainability

A generic strategy does not lead to above-average performance unless it is sustainable *vis-à-vis* competitors, though actions that improve industry structure may improve industrywide profitability even if they are imitated. The sustainability of the three generic strategies demands that a firm's competitive advantage resist erosion by competitor behavior or industry evolution. Each generic strategy involves different risks, which are shown in Table 5.1.1.

The sustainability of a generic strategy requires that a firm possess some barriers that make imitation of the strategy difficult. Since barriers to imitation are never insurmountable, however, it is usually necessary for a firm to offer a moving target to its competitors by investing in order to continually improve its position. Each generic strategy is also a potential threat to the others – as Table 5.1.1 shows, for example, focusers must worry about broadly targeted competitors and vice versa.

Table 5.1.1 can be used to analyze how to attack a competitor that employs any of the generic strategies. A firm pursuing overall differentiation, for example, can be attacked by firms that open up a large cost gap, narrow the extent of differentiation, shift the differentiation desired by buyers to other dimensions, or focus. Each generic strategy is vulnerable to different types of attacks.

In some industries, industry structure or the strategies of competitors eliminate the possibility of achieving one or more of the generic strategies. Occasionally no feasible way for one firm to gain a significant cost advantage exists, for example, because several firms are equally placed with respect to scale economies, access to raw materials, or other cost drivers. Similarly, an industry with few segments or only minor differences among segments, such as low-density polyethylene, may offer few opportunities for focus. Thus the mix of generic strategies will vary from industry to industry.

In many industries, however, the three generic strategies can profitably coexist as long as firms pursue different ones or select different bases for differentiation or focus. Industries in which several strong firms are pursuing differentiation strategies based on different sources of buyer value are often particularly profitable. This tends to improve industry structure and lead to stable industry competition. If two or more firms choose to pursue the same generic strategy on the same basis, however, the result can be a protracted and unprofitable battle. The worst situation is where several firms are vying for overall cost

TABLE 5.1.1 Risks of the generic strategies

Risks of cost leadership	Risks of differentiation	Risks of focus
Cost leadership is not sustained ■ competitors imitate ■ technology changes ■ other bases for cost leadership erode	Differentiation is not sustained ■ competitors imitate ■ bases for differentiation become less important to buyers	The focus strategy is imitated The target segment becomes structually unattractive ■ structure erodes ■ demand disappears
Proximity in differentiation is lost	Cost proximity is lost	Broadly targeted competitors overwhelm the segment ■ the segment's differences from other segments narrow ■ the advantages of a broad line increase
Cost focusers achieve even lower cost in segments	Differentiation focusers achieve even greater differentiation in segments	New focusers subsegment the industry

leadership. The past and present choice of generic strategies by competitors, then, has an impact on the choices available to a firm and the cost of changing its position.

The concept of generic strategies is based on the premise that there are a number of ways in which competitive advantage can be achieved, depending on industry structure. If all firms in an industry followed the principles of competitive strategy, each would pick different bases for competitive advantage. While not all would succeed, the generic strategies provide alternate routes to superior performance. Some strategic planning concepts have been narrowly based on only one route to competitive advantage, most notably cost. Such concepts not only fail to explain the success of many firms, but they can also lead all firms in an industry to pursue the same type of competitive advantage in the same way – with predictably disastrous results.

READING

5.2

Strategy from the inside out: Building capability-creating organizations

By Danny Miller, Russell Eisenstat and Nathaniel Foote[1]

For Citibank CEO John Reed, 1991 was a very tough year. Citi's stock had plummeted, in no small part because of its trouble-ridden global coporate bank. Some problems, such as non-performing Latin American loans, were shared by competitors. However, Citi was especially hobbled. Paradoxically, although it had banks in over 100 countries, many of these were weak. Local rivals with better ties to customers and government were strangling Citi's revenues and eroding its margins.

The choices confronting Reed seemed bleak. On the one hand, he could try to strengthen Citi's presence in lucrative markets such as Germany or Japan by copying regional rivals like Deutsche Bank. He might, for example, try to build deeper relationships with local businesses. However, Citi would always be at a disadvantage vis-à-vis local rivals, who had better government and industry contacts – relationships that for historical and political reasons Citi was unlikely to duplicate. A more feasible strategy would be to offer new services and try to become more efficient. However, there was nothing to stop competitors from following suit and neutralizing Citi's efforts. Reed, like so many of today's CEOs, was facing a quandary.

Citibank (now Citigroup) and some two dozen other firms we studied have managed, quite craftily, to escape this predicament of how to grow sustainable capabilities. They began not be emulating best practices, but by delving constantly within themselves to discover and build on their unique, hard-to-copy assets, knowledge, relationships, and experiences. We call these emergent, potential, or hidden resources 'asymmetries'. Over time, the firms we studied evolved a set of explicit organizational processes and designs to find these asymmetries, turn them into capabilities, and leverage them across the appropriate market opportunities.

At Citi, John Reed realized that his extensive network of international banks could be of immense service to large multinationals (MNCs). This was no commonplace observation as the scattered network was at the time a liability in serving MNCs. Citi's local banks gave service priority to local clients, offered products unsuitable to MNCs, and did not cooperate to facilitate cross-border business. Nor were MNCs the most profitable customers. However, Reed had a three-pronged epiphany. He realized first that no rival had Citi's global reach or could attain it easily. He also saw that by redesigning his organization, processes, and performance management systems he could make the network more responsive to MNCs. Finally, he envisioned how the international bank network could be re-deployed to great advantage to serve not local firms but large clients doing extensive – and lucrative – cross-border business. In short, Reed saw how his bank was different, figured out how to make that difference an asset, and found a market that would most value that asset.

It is vital to point out that it is not only large firms such as Citi that may have potentially valuable asymmetries. The example of Shana Corp. (Exhibit 5.2.1) shows a very similar path of asymmetry identification and

[1] Source: This article © 2002, by the Regents of the University of California. Adapted from the *California Management Review*, Vol. 44, No. 3. By permission of the Regents. All rights reserved.

EXHIBIT 5.2.1

MOLEHILLS INTO MOUNTAINS: THE CASE OF SHANA CORP.

Shana Corp is a private Canadian software company. Some of Shana's product development efforts, combined with a few technologically related contracts, had allowed the company, over several years, to develop special expertise. It acquired the capability to create sophisticated forms completion software that was compatible between two popular operating systems. This occurred, quite fortuitously, because of the kinds of jobs Shana had worked on. However, the top managers of Shana soon became quite conscious of this emerging capability. Their firm, they realized, had learned to artfully and economically do some valuable kinds of work that its competitors simply could not do as well or as fast. Also, some natural affinities began to occur among the software developers as each began to realize more fully one another's strengths and weaknesses, and each began to specialize on certain sub-routines. What had been a work group became a real team, with all of the synergies and efficiencies that entails. Soon Shana's managers began to develop training routines, work procedures, and compensation and incentive policies to further improve team performance. Shana also began to use its growing body of specialized knowledge and its effective development teams to concentrate on particular clients that required its special abilities. These were clients that used the two popular operating systems but wanted the same forms software for both. The new market focus and additional product development and marketing experience it brought sharpened Shana's expertise still further, widening the skill gap between it and its rivals. This gradual convergence of the company around its capabilities and target market helped to focus new selection and training programs, project management protocols, and marketing campaigns. These allowed Shana to exploit and extend its competitive advantage.

Note that Shana did not set out to master a special capability. Nor did it perform a competitive analysis to look for promising niches. Rather, Shana's managers noticed retrospectively what their firm was unusually good at, reflected on and developed it, and pursued those clients that would most benefit from Shana's emerging talents. The firm, moreover, did not set out to emulate the competitive advantages and competencies of its most successful rivals. First, it did not have the financial or technological wherewithal to accomplish this, nor could it reasonably expect to develop it. Second, even if Shana were able to develop those competencies, by the time it did its competitors most likely would have moved ahead. Shana's managers realized that emulation would cede to rivals product and market leadership – no competitor was a sitting target. Finally, had it attempted to do what its rivals do well, Shana would have had to share a market with a host of other imitators.

capability development unfolding even within a small and new firm with nowhere near the assets or relationships of a Citigroup.

The lessons from Citi and Shana are much the same: competitive advantage comes not from imitation but from using organizational processes and designs to identify emerging asymmetries and build them into capabilities. Again, asymmetries are hard-to-copy ways in which a firm differs from its rivals – ways that may ultimately bring advantage (see Exhibit 5.2.2 for the definitions of our key terms).

EXHIBIT 5.2.2

THE TERMS OF OUR ANALYSIS

Asymmetries are skills, knowledge, processes relationships, proper ties, or outputs an organization possesses or produces that its motivated competitors are unlikely to acquire or copy in a cost or time-effective way. Typically, these do not currently produce any economic advantages but have potential to be transformed into valuable resources or capabilities.

Capability configurations are systems of reinforcing elements incorporating core capabilities and the organizational design infrastructures in which they are embedded and that renew, adapt, and support these capabilities.

They may consist of outputs (such as products or solutions), relationships and alliances, systems (such as Citi's global network or contacts), processes and routines, and nascent skills and knowledge (such as Shana's) – all provided that rivals cannot imitate these within practical time and cost constraints. In fact, asymmetries, because of their subtlety or uniqueness, confer a head start and discourage imitation – and that sustains their edge.

Another advantage is their accessibility. Due to accidents of history and normal variations in the skills and experiences of organizations, many companies will find that they possess asymmetries. While the capabilities or best practices of other enterprises may be almost impossible to duplicate, managers begin the hunt for asymmetries in their own back yard.

Unfortunately, *asymmetries are not resources or core competencies*. Like personal characteristics such as shyness or aggressiveness, they can serve as advantages or disadvantages. As with Citi's network they tend to be under-explored, under-funded, and unconnected to a firm's engine of value creation. However, where carefully fostered and directed, asymmetries may come to underlie the most important capabilities in a firm's competitive arsenal. By continually identifying and building on asymmetries, by nurturing and exploiting these within a complementary organizational design, and by leveraging them via an appropriate market focus, companies may be able to aspire realistically to attain sustainable advantage.

Paradoxically, a continual and intimate connection with the market environment is vital to this 'inside-out approach'. First, firms have to understand their rivals in order to know how they themselves are unique. More importantly, they need to track market reactions to discover which asymmetries are relevant. It is this ongoing ability to find the intersection between a firm's emerging asymmetries and the opportunities in the environment that is the fundamental strength of the organizations we describe here.

The three imperatives of inside-out strategy

Three imperatives are especially central to our approach. Although our presentation is necessarily linear, the process of developing inside-out strategy is emergent – full of trial and error, iteration between imperatives, and exploitation of chance.

Imperative 1: Discover asymmetries and their potential

To do well, firms need to develop important capabilities or resources that their rivals cannot. As indicated, however, it is hard for them to develop these resources unless they already have some realized or potential edge. The first step is *discovering* the asymmetries that underlie that edge, as unrecognized resources or capabilities are of little advantage.

Asymmetries can arise in a number of ways. Some, such as Citi's banking network, develop as a result of the vagaries of corporate history. Others, such as long-term contracts and distinctive patents, are consciously created. In all cases, asymmetries serve as useful starting points for creating advantage precisely because they cannot be easily copied. The search for asymmetries is the search for these inimitable differences.

The inimitability of an asymmetry may be due to legal barriers, as in the case of patents. More often, however, it is because asymmetries represent subtle and interrelated attributes and skills that have co-evolved over a significant interval – as in the case of Shana. The subtle and tacit nature of these attributes, and in some cases their lack of connection to success, keeps these asymmetries beneath the radar screens of rivals (and sometimes those of the firm itself).

Because of this subtlety, the search for asymmetries cannot be a casual process. It demands thorough and persistent inquiry across the breadth of an organization. The search must lead to an understanding of how a firm differs from its competitors in the assets it possesses, the execution processes it uses, and the combinations of these things. It should also provide insights into how these asymmetries are currently generating or may potentially generate the resources or capabilities that produce advantage. Having discovered these resources, they must be evaluated for their potential contributions to performance.

Outside search.   A good place to begin the search for internal asymmetries is to find the more obvious *external* ones – the kinds of clients and business that gravitate to a firm rather than its competitors. Managers might look for the kinds of opportunities they can capture that their competitors cannot. The types of customers and the peculiarities of their product and service demands are key clues. Asymmetries can also be spotted by asking why a company beats its rivals in capturing a particular client or market. Answers may be found in the breadth of offerings or geographic reach, reputation with a client, or intimate market knowledge.

Learning demands action as well as reflection. In fact, one of the surest ways of revealing valuable asymmetries is to launch a set of entrepreneurial initiatives, determine which ones show promise, and then try to discover why. These can be viewed as experiments and may include broaching new kinds of customers or market segments, combining existing products with services, and altering the mix of products. Such experiments bring out new fans of the firm and make clearer *emerging* asymmetries. Shana's particular talents became clearer to its managers both as it pursued different clients and new software projects. In fact, in highly emergent contexts – in e-commerce, for example, or a newly deregulated industry – required capabilities are highly ambiguous and first mover advantages are central to ultimate success. Here firms are better off moving quickly to seize opportunities. Only after carrying out their market experiments can they determine where their advantages lie.

Inside search.   Search also must take place inside a company. In many cases, the most useful asymmetries are buried deep within a firm and have to be traced back from surface abilities. Willamette Inc. is a successful medium-sized paper manufacturer. One of Willamette's apparent strengths was its ability to track the paper market by making the right grade of paper at the right time. However, the knowledge of what to make is widely available – many competitors have it. The most basic capability is ability to convert production processes quickly and cheaply enough to take advantage of industry price changes. The reason Willamette could do this was because of its flexible equipment. The reason it had such equipment when its competitors did not was because of the experience Willamette's engineers had built up over the years converting the dilapidated plants of rivals into some of the most flexible and efficient factories in the industry. Willamette's fundamental asymmetry and its primary source of advantage was its state-of-the-art plant conversion and operating capabilities – capabilities, it turned out, that usually could not even be duplicated by the nation's top engineering consultants. It was this profound recognition of its capabilities that then allowed Willamette to allocate the human and financial resources and gear its hiring, training, promotion, and compensation approaches to support them.

Discovering asymmetries that represent *latent* resources or capabilities is particularly challenging. The case of Citigroup's global relationship banking unit was instructive because its crucial asymmetry – unrivaled geographic presence – for many years represented as much a liability as an asset. By 1980, Citi had developed a system of banks in 100 countries. Its nearest rival, Hong Kong Shanghai Bank Corp., had offices in 40 countries. However, many of Citi's banks were weak, and margins were being squeezed in developed countries by competing local banks with better ties to customers and government. Meanwhile in developing countries, market volatility and political instability were real and costly hazards. Despite these problems, then-CEO John Reed realized that the international network could *potentially* put it in a unique position to do business with far-flung multinationals that desired further globalization. Also, it was unlikely that rivals could easily imitate this resource.

Thus, asymmetry identification can take at least two forms. The first is a re-framing insight, spotting pre-existing but unexploited assets – as at Citi. The second is evolutionary and requires managers to recognize an emerging edge, frequently in intangible assets such as knowledge, relationships, and reputation. This was the case at Shana and Willamette.

Table 5.2.1 provides suggestions on how a firm can identify its own key asymmetries and capabilities. An Assessment Audit is available from the authors to guide this process.

Imperative 2: Create capability configurations – by design

Asymmetries evolve into sustainable core capabilities largely through organization design – which builds and supports capabilities by embedding them in a cohesive configuration. Design also energizes these configurations by setting up 'virtuous circles' of capability enhancement.

There are two aspects to capability configurations. First, they are made up of a *cohesive combination of resources and capabilities* that is hard to imitate. Simple resources such as patents or proprietary processes can be contrasted with more complex bundles of elements such as a distribution system. Citi's bank network, for example, encompassed a set of mutually reinforcing elements that made it easier to serve multinational clients – many banks in many countries, business and political contacts connected to and shared among the banks, and a set of common product and service standards across banks. Such resource or capability configurations tend to be far more powerful, distinctive, and tough to copy than single capabilities. Advantages of capability configurations include:

1 Configurations develop powerful complementarities around core capabilities and among resources, often by using an array of design levers.

2 Configurations embed and empower resources within a design, thereby more firmly capturing those resources, and making them more valuable to an organization than to its rivals (a condition economists call asset specificity).

3 Configurations organize capabilities into socially complex systems that are difficult for rivals to imitate.

4 Configurations embody virtuous cycles that enhance capabilities.

5 Points 2 to 4 all help to turn capabilities into sustainable competitive advantages.

TABLE 5.2.1   Discovering asymmetries and capabilities

Questions	Information sought	Possible data sources
What are the differences in observable outputs between a firm and its rivals: where is the firm superior? Hints from: ■ What kinds of customers are more apt to choose this firm than its rivals and why? ■ What do they ask from the firm – and value most from its offerings?	Comparison of outputs along dimensions such as design attractiveness or functionality, service, price, solutions tailoring, reputation, guarantees, and quality. Also relevant may be the scale, scope, and reach of the firm and its EDI and logistical connections to clients.	Market facing units or key account managers; customer reactions; and data on kinds of clients drawn to firm and their reactions to firm. Indexes of performance and quality by product, geography, and plant.
Which resources and capabilities appear to underlie the above sources of superiority – and where in the firm do they reside? Which asymmetries between a firm and its rivals ultimately can be *built* into sources of superiority?	**Resources** may include those that are *property-based*: patents, control over unique supplies or channels, talent under long-term contract; *knowledge-based*: unique information about customers, segments, and tecnologies; and *relationship-based*: partnerships, alliances, reputation, and customer ties. **Capabilities** include process and product design, product development, operations, value chain integration, all aspects of marketing and customer service, and organization design.	Managers in product and process development units, market and client-facing units, and geographic units.
Which resources and capabilities would be hardest for rivals to nullify?	Target for analysis especially those resources and competencies identified above.	Market-facing managers and customers, studies of rivals' products, communications, and what is written about them.
Which capabilities and resources are most central now and for the future to a firm's competitive advantage?	Consider the degree to which each of the resources and capabilities are sustainable, drive growth and profitability, underlie other capabilities, complement other capabilities, can be enhanced and developed, and can be leveraged across a wide range of market opportunities.	Managers from different functions and SBUs.

However, capability configurations have an even more valuable property – they are *embedded within a design infrastructure that* leverages, sustains, and develops them. At Citicorp, the international bank network at first was just a *potentially* valuable resource, not an actual one. The network only became a sustainable capability within the context of a supportive organizational design. As long as Citi was organized as a set of geographically based profit centers, local managers refused to give good service to multinationals that demanded bargain interest rates and service fees. John Reed was only able to unlock the value of the international network for multinationals through a new organization design. The design incorporated a group of very powerful key account managers and the multifunctional, multi-product teams needed to serve them. A flexible resource allocation system was set up to provide human, product, and knowledge resources to each multinational client – to serve that client in a globally coordinated and integrated way anywhere in the world, for a vast array of products and on demand. Reed reinforced the configuration with information systems that give all key account team members access to all client information and with a dynamic planning process that makes team members commit to specific objectives for each customer. He extracted support from local managers by having them assessed and rewarded against their ability to serve the multinationals. At Citi, then, the design of the organization was a core enabler and key component of the capability configuration (Table 5.2.2), one that dramatically enhanced its business with multinationals.

The Citi case is a good example of a firm that identified a key asymmetry (the international bank system and web of connections), realized that it could be an important resource, and developed that resource into a capability configuration by embedding it in an effective organization design. Without the configuration, the bank system resource could not be exploited or leveraged. In fact, the reason so many potentially valuable resources go undetected is because they only take on value when deployed within a complementary design configuration.

Building molehills into mountains: Virtuous cycles that enhance capabilities.

One of the most advantageous aspects of design configurations is that they create 'virtuous cycles' of capability enhancement – cycles that turn the potential of an asymmetry into a real and growing capability. Virtuous cycles are simply chains of influence in which one good outcome promotes another. Companies, for example, may possess a capability that attracts talented new employees and partners whose enlistment then augments that capability. Well-managed capabilities also raise performance, which in turn fuels them with additional resources and attention.

The emergence of Denmark's International Service System (ISS), illustrates the powerful role of virtuous circles in building what is now one of the largest service firms in the world. Early in its history, ISS began to accept contracts for cleaning slaughterhouses. This was a demanding task as equipment had to be disassembled for cleaning, and it was necessary to use special detergents and pressurized cleaning techniques to eradicate harmful bacteria. Also needed was expertise in testing for sterility. The experience gained with various types of clients allowed ISS to develop highly effective and efficient routines for doing the work, as well as enough financial expertise to be able to cost and price cleaning services by the machine, square meter, type of food, and so on. The proprietary technical knowledge gained in food hygiene enabled ISS to form partnerships with customers to jointly develop techniques for new products and evolving types of bacteria. This enhanced ISS's skills still further, giving them an even greater competitive advantage and an expanding client base. Eventually, ISS's expertise grew to encompass related hygiene-food businesses, including poultry and fish.

Such virtuous cycles do not happen by themselves. Design and leaders play a key role. At ISS, both executive action and the levers of design convert experience gained in a capability into policy priorities and market targets, codified knowledge, and efficient routines – which in turn extend those capabilities. For example, ISS's leadership strives to acquire 'customer density' in various segments. Scale in a segment leads not only to buying power but greater specialization, with resulting learning and customer intimacy advantages. Leaders also prioritize new opportunities that are becoming realizable because of growing skills or reputation. Information systems then build databases on

TABLE 5.2.2 How designs build and exploit capability

Design enablers	Leadership/ governance	Values and culture	Structural mechanisms	Systems and policies
Embedding capabilities within the organization	Leaders create context to prioritize, fund, and build strategy around capabilities. TMT ensures synergy among resources and capabilities. TMT establishes policies to bring front and back units together to develop and adapt capabilities.	Corporate culture celebrates capabilities and accords prestige to units and people most central in creating those capabilities. Collaborative culture to bring together front and back units. Emphasis is on knowledge building and knowledge sharing among units.	Capability-based units such as task forces and cross-SBU teams are established to create and share knowledge. Multi-SBU, multi-function coordinating committees build and adapt capabilities. High-level management committees oversee long-term development of a specific capability.	Information and planning systems target and track capabilities by unit versus competitors. HR systems select, reward, and promote based on capabilities. Knowledge systems codify proprietary information on technologies, customers, and so on.
Enhancing capabilities	Governance bodies describe a trajectory for core capability extension and leveraging.	Informal networks bring front and back units and people together to develop capabilities.	Multi-unit teams and strategic alliances build knowledge. Communities of practice grow capabilities.	Information systems feed learning efforts: e.g., report results according to segments and customers. Training programs.
Shaping capabilities to market opportunities	Leaders link capabilities to target markets and define policy parameters for identification and sequencing of opportunities.	Entrepreneurial culture encourages managers to identify opportunities that exploit capabilities.	Opportunity-based units help shape capabilities to market segments.	HR, planning, and incentive systems create resources that can be easily leveraged across opportunities. Rewards based on firm-wide objectives to get front and back to collaborate.

costs and customers that facilitate better pricing, costing, and scheduling: this improves the capture rate of the most prized kinds of customers. Also, human resource systems codify criteria for selection and training, thereby sharpening the most important capabilities. Finally, structural mechanisms bring managers together to share knowledge across clients so that additional services can be sold to existing clients and ideas are shared around picking up additional business. Each of these design levers shapes the virtuous cycle as they help accumulate 'stocks of assets' such as reputation, technical, managerial and customer knowledge, cohesive teams and team skills, and distinctive systems and infrastructures.

Virtuous cycles have a number of things in common. They engender good performance and thus create resources to plow back into capability development. They enhance reputation, which brings opportunities. They elicit positive feedback from the market that reinforces the right kinds of people, skills, and products. Design serves as a powerful governor and amplifier of these cycles in identifying and prioritizing a capability; in assembling and coordinating the resources, people, systems, and mechanisms to develop it; in disseminating the capability within the organization; and in leveraging the capability across the right market opportunities.

Imperative 3: Pursue market opportunities that build on and leverage capabilities

The deepest capabilities and most integrated configurations are of no value unless they extract superior returns. So they have to satisfy the needs of a large enough audience who will pay amply to have that done. At the same time, emerging capabilities must be constantly unearthed and evaluated so they can be leveraged across a wider audience and set of opportunities.

A market can be looked at as a set of niches and opportunities that a firm must choose from to best leverage its capabilities. Managers must ask not only where are the opportunities, but also why should their firm be able to capture and exploit them better than potential competitors. The attractiveness of a niche must be evaluated in the context of a firm's uniqueness and the capabilities it can attain more readily than its rivals.

It is also vital that *market niches and opportunities be related or complementary in that they benefit from the same kinds of capabilities*. This consideration guided some of

our most successful firms. Citi's global corporate clients, for example, are similar in that they are large, do plenty of cross-border business, and benefit from Citi's global presence and international banking services. In fact, Citi changed its pricing strategy to attract *only* those types of clients. Without this relatedness, Citi's capabilities would be underutilized or underdeveloped. Note that it is not similarity of outputs or industry boundaries that define complementarity: Citi's global clients were in many different industries and locations, and Citi sold lots of different products. Rather, complementarity is defined in terms of the ability of different opportunities to benefit from the same asymmetries and capabilities.

Citi also pursued complementarity among opportunities in developing multi-product international banking solutions tailored to specific industries. It created product packages or 'industry templates' that would appeal to *many* clients within an industry – and thus give Citi economies of product development and market knowledge. Citi's product packages built not only on the similar needs of global clients in the same industry, but also on its banking contacts and expertise in foreign exchange, global cash management, and investment banking.

Inevitably, managers will have to shape capabilities according to such related opportunities. Recall that Citi made many changes to render its international bank network valuable to global clients – for example, abolishing regional profit centers to get local managers to serve multinationals. Citi also organized its global bank into industry groups to develop its tailored product solutions and increase market penetration. Because market focus was so clear, the bank could afford to develop industry- and client-based planning and information systems. These incorporated detailed information on *each* targeted client's potential banking business, which enabled representatives to home in on the best business opportunities and develop tailored approaches to capture that business. As the examples show, when adapting asymmetries and capabilities to market opportunities, the design configuration again plays a central role.

Leveraging capabilities across new opportunities. Capabilities are especially valuable when they can be leveraged across a broadening set of market opportunities. Such leveraging must become a never-ending process. Here again virtuous cycles are useful. They strengthen current capabilities, but they also push asymmetries and capabilities into new areas. As learning occurs, a firm is able to employ capabilities or resources garnered in one situation to serve a different one. This can happen in several ways.

- The same capabilities can be applied across different products and industries. ISS leveraged its special capabilities in cleaning and sterilizing slaughterhouses to enter the hospital services field. A deep knowledge of bacteria, chemicals, sterilization, cleaning, and testing techniques allowed ISS to enter a completely different industry, with similar capability requirements.

- Customer-related expertise and reputation developed around one output can be used to sell others to the same customer. ISS-Mediclean used the reputation and customer-specific knowledge it garnered in cleaning a given hospital to get other types of service contracts with that same institution. 'Knowledge of a specific customer and a broader range of services gains Mediclean access to the customer's senior management.... It is this access that leads to the deepening and expanding of the relationship.'

- Segment-related expertise developed with one customer can be used with others in the same segment. ISS leveraged its knowledge across different health care institutions based on its extensive segment-specific knowledge. The company is successful in part because it thoroughly understands the needs of the British hospital customer, and because its capabilities span a comprehensive array of hospital

cleaning and facilitates management services.

ISS excels at all three kinds of leverage, in part because of an organization design that encompasses entrepreneurial, opportunity-seeking leadership as well as systems that gather and disseminate information on both capabilities and market opportunities. ISS's culture ensures that knowledge is easily shared across organizational boundaries, and its flexible administrative structure can manage capabilities and exploit new opportunities.

Ultimately, most capabilities become obsolete. Major sources of obsolescence include rival imitators eroding value, product lines reaching maturity, and major transformations in industry technology. The threat of imitation can often be countered by our virtuous cycles that build on capabilities fast enough to stay ahead of competitors. The threat of product obsolescence can be reduced by leveraging capabilities across new or related product areas. However, the only way to deal with technological or knowledge obsolescence is to continually look for *new* asymmetries that can be developed into capabilities that can be connected with a new set of opportunities (Christensen, 1997). This involves all three of our imperatives.

Implications for managers

In pursuing strategy from the inside out managers must learn both to pursue and trade off seeming opposites. Specifically, in discovering, building and leveraging capability they must balance reflection and action, selection and variation, resources and opportunities. Moreover, to make these tradeoffs in a quick and superior way, firms must make organizational design their source of competitive advantage. They must significantly empower their units to discover and develop the right capabilities and leverage them across the right opportunities; and they must create strong leadership and infrastructure at the center to get those units to collaborate to do this rapidly and effectively.

Three tradeoffs

Balance reflection and action: Discovering asymmetries and capabilities.

Knowledge about capabilities comes in part from reflection. Managers must critically evaluate their resources and talents in looking for hidden gems – trying to determine which are the best employees, which people and units work together best, which technologies show promise, what types of projects and products succeed, and what sorts of customers are attracted to the firm. The best outcomes of reflection are imaginative 're-framings' of the value of different resources, experiences, and relationships. At Shana, for example, they led managers to see that the really valuable capabilities were not in building forms software but in bridging operating systems.

Reflection, however, is not enough. True self-knowledge demands action and experimentation. Asymmetries and capabilities are always changing and the best way to keep track is by trying things and assessing the results. At ISS experiments might include working with different types of customers, trying a new process, or changing offerings for a new market segment. These experiments provide good information on what works – cues that then can be used to shape more focused experiments that converge on capabilities and launch virtuous circles.

Given the job pressures, managers must put time aside to reflect on capabilities and initiate experiments. They might launch quarterly sessions with top management, venture teams, or 'capability teams' to explore emerging competencies and the opportunities they bring. These discussions may work especially well when members of different business or technical units or functions get together. 'Outsider' units often see creative uses for resources their counterparts deem commonplace. Gathering to address a specific market challenge or opportunity may bring some urgency to the task of surfacing capabilities.

Balance variation and selection: Developing and embedding capabilities.

Leaders must determine *which* emerging capabilities are most promising and then 'select' or embed them as priorities for development. If the targeted set of capabilities is overly large or varied, resources will be too thinly spread to achieve critical mass and competitive superiority. Core or fundamental capabilities must take the lion's share of funds, talent, and visibility – even where this hurts other activities. However, to commandeer resources from 'secondary' activities, priorities must be reflected in accountabilities, performance criteria, rewards and promotions, and also in dedicated units and teams and in planning and information systems. ISS and Willamette use their planning and resource-allocation processes to drive resources towards the most promising asymmetries and capabilities. They also designate top priority capabilities and constitute teams that are appraised and rewarded according to capability development.

Variation in capabilities must also be restricted over time. Core capabilities have the highest yields when developed cumulatively over the long run and varied 'around the edges'. This requires top-level, long-term resource planning, coupled with regular follow-ups to determine how to elaborate, adapt, and fund a capability. In many of our firms, multi-functional, multi-SBU units and top-management committees assured continuity in developing longstanding capabilities. At the same time, firms searched for and experimented with capability variations – emerging but related relationships, client knowledge, expertise, and technologies. Without this exploration and 'playfulness' at the edges, a capability set narrows and loses relevance.

Balance capabilities and opportunities: Leveraging capabilities in the market.

Managers need to find opportunities tailored to their capabilities. Opportunities also must ultimately shape capabilities. The faster these mutual adjustments occur, the more likely the virtuous circles, and the longer a firm is able to sustain competitive advantage. Of course, such speed is only possible when organizational designs and processes foster an ongoing, enriching dialogue between capability managers and opportunity managers.

Advantage by design

Different parts of the firm bring to bear different perspectives in building capabilities and making these tradeoffs. Units dealing with customers and markets ('front-end' units) look to leverage asymmetries in customer relationships, perhaps by broadening the product set. Units charged with engineering, R&D, and operations ('back-end' units) seek to leverage functional capabilities or products across different market opportunities. Both these pursuits are essential. Unfortunately, some product variations will unduly stretch capabilities, and some capabilities will not find a market. It is only by getting the front and back of an organization to work together that complementarity can be quickly realized between capabilities and market opportunities. This calls for organizational designs that not only empower front- and back-end units to develop opportunities and capabilities, but also create a strong center and infrastructure to get these units to collaborate.

Strong front, strong back. Back-end units must have fungible resources: flexible resources they can use to discover and develop capabilities, and ones that are free from the day-to-day pull of operations. They also require the clout to call upon resources from the front to discover the needs of customers and the strengths of the competition. Typically, this requires that some front-end resources be accountable for capability development. Front-end units also need fungible resources to identify and pursue opportunities. Moreover, they need access to resources from the back to help them adapt capabilities

to the new opportunities. Back-end resources, therefore, may have to be made accountable for realizing front-end opportunities. At Citi, for example, back-end functional and product specialists were appraised according to their service to large clients.

Strong-center: Leadership and collaborative infrastructure. A strong center is needed to make front and back collaborate. This involves myriad organizational levers and processes (see Table 5.2.2), with strong leadership being primary. Leaders must establish objectives, policies, and even transfer prices for determining how front and back can work together. They need to prioritize capabilities and opportunities, or at least delineate their scope. Leaders also may act as final arbiters in disputes between front and back, the way John Reed was called to do at Citi.

However, firms do even better where front and back can work together without a leader's intervention. This is more apt to happen where corporate cultures encourage collaboration, as at Willamette, or where extensive informal networks exist, as at Citi and ISS. Such cultures are fostered by strong and clear corporate values and by grapevines that widely disseminate reputational information so that managers can assemble effective teams. Other useful integrators are clear conflict resolution protocols, job rotation and training programs that reduce parochialism, and even virtual communities on the Internet.

Structural mechanisms such as multi-functional, multi-SBU task forces, standing committees, and integrative positions and roles can also bring together front and back. Finally, in all of the firms we studied, important roles were played by a variety of organizational systems and processes. Information and resource allocation systems, for example, identified the best human resources to serve capabilities and opportunities. Incentive systems rewarded organization-wide goals rather than departmental goals, and ensured that collaboration around capabilities and opportunities would be in the long-run interests of the firm.

Final words

Well-conceived organization processes and designs can help managers constantly identify asymmetries and potential capabilities, embed these in a configuration that grows and exploits them, and leverage those capabilities across complementary sets of market opportunities. Indeed, effective design provides the vehicle for bringing together developing resources and emerging opportunities in an ongoing process that sustains advantage.

READINGS ON CORPORATE LEVEL STRATEGY

To open the debate on behalf of the portfolio organization perspective, Barry Hedley's article 'Strategy and the Business Portfolio' has been selected. Hedley was an early proponent of the portfolio perspective, together with other consultants from the Boston Consulting Group (BCG), such as Bruce Henderson (1979). In this article, he explains the strategic principles underlying the famed growth-share grid that is commonly known as the BCG matrix. His argument is based on the premise that a complex corporation can be viewed as a portfolio of businesses, in which each have their own competitive arena to which they must be responsive. By disaggregating a corporation into its business unit components, separate strategies can be devised for each. The overarching role of the corporate level can then be defined as that of portfolio manager. The major task of the corporate headquarters is to manage the allocation of scarce financial resources over the business units, to achieve the highest returns at an acceptable level of risk. Each business unit can be given a strategic mission to grow, hold or milk, depending on their prospects compared to the businesses in the corporate portfolio. This is where portfolio analysis comes in. Hedley argues that the profit and growth potential of each business unit depends on two key variables: the growth rate of the total business and the relative market share of the business unit within its business. When these two variables are put together in a grid, this forms the BCG matrix. For the discussion here, the precise details of the BCG portfolio technique are less relevant than the basic corporate strategy perspective that Hedley advocates – running the multi-business firm as a hands-on investor.

Selecting a representative for the integrated organization perspective was a simple choice. In 1990, C.K. Prahalad and Gary Hamel published an article in *Harvard Business Review* with the title 'The Core Competence of the Corporation'. This article has had a profound impact on the debate surrounding the topic of corporate level strategy, and has inspired a considerable amount of research and writing investigating resource-based synergies. In this article, and in their subsequent book, *Competing for the Future* (Hamel and Prahalad, 1994) the authors explicitly dismiss the portfolio organization perspective as a viable approach to corporate strategy. Prahalad and Hamel acknowledge that diversified corporations have a portfolio of businesses, but they do not believe that this implies the need for a portfolio organization approach in which the business units are highly autonomous. In their view, 'the primacy of the SBU – an organizational dogma for a generation – is now clearly an anachronism'. Drawing mainly on Japanese examples, they carry on to argue that corporations should be built around a core of shared competences. Business units should use and help to further develop these core competences. The consequence is that the role of corporate level management is much more far-reaching than in the portfolio organization perspective. The corporate center must 'establish objectives for competence building' and must ensure that this 'strategic architecture' is carried through.

READING 6.1

READING

6.1

Strategy and the business portfolio

By Barry Hedley[1]

All except the smallest and simplest companies comprise more than one business. Even when a company operates within a single broad business area, analysis normally reveals that it is, in practice, involved in a number of product-market segments which are distinct economically. These must be considered separately for purposes of strategy development.

The fundamental determinant of strategy success for each individual business segment is relative competitive position. As a result of the experience curve effect the competitor with high market share in the segment relative to competition should be able to develop the lowest cost position and hence the highest and most stable profits. This will be true regardless of changes in the economic environment. Hence relative competitive position in the appropriately defined business segment forms a simple but sound strategic goal. Almost invariably, any company which reviews its various businesses carefully in this light will discover that they occupy widely differing relative competitive positions. Some businesses will be competitively strong already, and may appear to present no strategic problem; others will be weak, and the company must face the question of whether it would be worthwhile to attempt to improve their position, making whatever investments might be required to achieve this; if this is not done, the company can only expect poor performance from the business and the best option economically will be divestment.

Even in quite small companies, the total number of possible combinations of individual business strategies can be extremely large. The difficulty of making a firm final choice on strategy for each business is normally compounded by the fact that most companies must operate within constraints established by limited resources, particularly cash resources.

The business portfolio concept

At its most basic, the importance of growth in shaping strategy choice is twofold. First, the growth of a business is a major factor influencing the likely ease – and hence cost – of gaining market share. In low-growth businesses, any market share gained will tend to require an actual volume reduction in competitors' sales. This will be very obvious to the competitors and they are likely to fight to prevent the throughput in their plants dropping. In high-growth businesses, on the other hand, market share can be gained steadily merely by securing the largest share of the growth in the business: expanding capacity earlier than the competitors, ensuring product availability and effective selling support despite the strains imposed by the *growth*, and so forth. Meanwhile competitors may even be unaware of their share loss because their actual volume of throughput has been well maintained. Even if aware of their loss of share, the competitors may be unconcerned by it given that their plants are still well loaded. This is particularly true of competitors who do not understand the strategic importance of market share for long term profitability resulting from the experience curve effect.

An unfortunate example of this is given by the history of the British motorcycle industry.

[1]Source: This article was adapted from B. Hedley, 'Strategy and the Business Portfolio', *Long Range Planning*, February 1977, Vol. 10, No. 1, pp. 9–15, © 1977. With permission from Elsevier.

British market share was allowed to erode in motorcycles world-wide for more than a decade, throughout which the British factories were still fairly full: British motorcycle production volumes held up at around 80,000 units per year throughout the sixties; in sharp contrast, Japanese export volumes leapt from only about 60,000 in 1960 to 2.5 million in 1973; their total production volumes roughly tripled in the same period. The long term effect was that while Japanese real costs were falling rapidly British costs were not: somewhat oversimplified, this is why the British motorcycle industry faced bankruptcy in the early seventies.

The second important factor concerning growth is the opportunity it provides for investment. Growth businesses provide the ideal vehicles for investment, for ploughing cash into a business in order to see it compound and return even larger amounts of cash at a later point in time. Of course this opportunity is also a need: the faster a business grows, the more investment it will require just to maintain market share. Yet the experience curve effect means that this is essential if its profitability is not to decline over time.

Whilst these growth considerations affect the rate at which a business will use cash, the relative competitive position of the business will determine the rate at which the business will generate cash: the stronger the company's position relative to its competitors the higher its margins should be, as a result of the experience curve effect. The simplest measure of relative competitive position is, of course, relative market share. A company's relative market share in a business can be defined as its market share in the business divided by that of the largest other competitor. Thus only the biggest competitor has a relative market share greater than one. All the other competitors should enjoy lower profitability and cash generation than the leader.

The growth–share matrix

Individual businesses can have very different financial characteristics and face different strategic options depending on how they are placed in terms of growth and relative competitive position. Businesses can basically fall into any one of four broad strategic categories, as depicted schematically in the growth–share matrix in Figure 6.1.1.

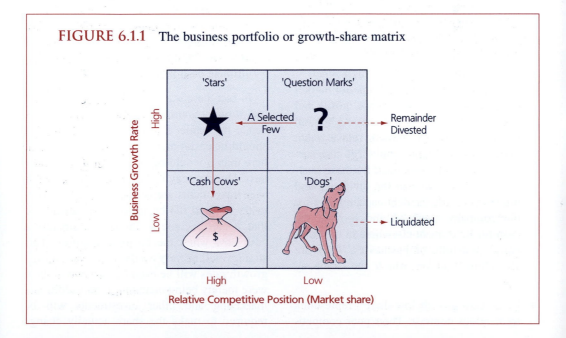

FIGURE 6.1.1 The business portfolio or growth-share matrix

- **Stars.** High growth, high share – are in the upper left quadrant. Growing rapidly, they use large amounts of cash to maintain position. They are also leaders in the business, however, and should generate large amounts of cash. As a result, star businesses are frequently roughly in balance on net cash flow, and can be self-sustaining in growth terms. They represent probably the best profit growth and investment opportunities available to the company, and every effort should therefore be made to maintain and consolidate their competitive position. This will sometimes require heavy investment beyond their own generation capabilities and low margins may be essential at times to deter competition, but this is almost invariably worthwhile for the longer term: when the growth slows, as it ultimately does in all businesses, very large cash returns will be obtained if share has been maintained so that the business drops into the lower left quadrant of the matrix, becoming a cash cow. If star businesses fail to hold share, which frequently happens if the attempt is made to net large amounts of cash from them in the short and medium term (e.g. by cutting back on investment and raising prices, creating an 'umbrella' for competitors), they will ultimately become dogs (lower right quadrant). These are certain losers.

- **Cash cows.** Low growth, high share – should have an entrenched superior market position and low costs. Hence profits and cash generation should be high, and because of the low growth reinvestment needs should be light. Thus large cash surpluses should be generated by these businesses. Cash cows pay the dividends and interest, provide the debt capacity, pay for the company overhead and provide the cash for investment elsewhere in the company's portfolio of businesses. They are the foundation on which the company rests.

- **Dogs.** Low growth, low share – represent a tremendous contrast. Their poor competitive position condemns them to poor profits. Because the growth is low, there is little potential for gaining sufficient share to achieve a viable cost position at anything approaching a reasonable cost. Unfortunately, the cash required for investment in the business just to maintain competitive position, though low, frequently exceeds that generated, especially under conditions of high inflation. The business therefore becomes a 'cash trap' likely to absorb cash perpetually unless further investment in the business is rigorously avoided. The colloquial term dog describing these businesses, though undoubtedly pejorative, is thus rather apt. A company should take every precaution to minimize the proportion of its assets that remain in this category.

- **Question marks.** High growth, low share – have the worst cash characteristics of all. In the upper right quadrant, their cash needs are high because of their growth, but their cash generation is small because of their low share. If nothing is done to change its market share, the question mark will simply absorb large amounts of cash in the short term and later, as the growth slows, become a dog. Following this sort of strategy, the question mark is a cash loser throughout its existence. Managed this way, a question mark becomes the ultimate cash trap.

In fact there is a clear choice between only two strategy alternatives for a question mark, hence the name. Because growth is high, it should be easier and less costly to gain share here than it would be in a lower growth business. One strategy is therefore to make whatever investments are necessary to gain share, to try to fund the business to dominance so that it can become a star and, ultimately a cash cow when the business matures. This strategy will be very costly in the short term – growth rates will be even higher than if share were merely being maintained, and additional marketing and other investments will be required to make the share actually change hands – but it offers the only way of developing a sound business from the question mark over the long term. The only logical alternative is divestment. Outright sale is preferable; but if this is not possible, then a firm decision must be taken not to invest further in the business and it must be allowed simply to generate whatever cash it can while none is reinvested. The business will then decline, possibly quite rapidly if market growth is high, and will have to be shut down at some point. But it will produce cash in the short term and this is greatly preferable to the error of sinking cash into it perpetually without improving its competitive position.

These then, are the four basic categories to which businesses can belong. Some companies tend to fit almost entirely into a single quadrant. General Motors and English China Clays are examples of predominantly cash cow companies. Chrysler, by comparison, is a dog which compounded its fundamental problem of low share in its domestic US market by acquiring further mature low share competitors in other countries (e.g. Rootes which became Chrysler UK). IBM in computers, Xerox in photocopiers, BSR in low cost record autochangers, are all examples of predominantly star businesses. Xerox's computer operation, XDS, was clearly a question mark, however, and it is not surprising that Xerox recently effectively gave it away free to Honeywell, and considered itself lucky to escape at that price! When RCA closed down its computer operation, it had to sustain a write-off of about $490m. Question marks are costly.

Portfolio strategy

Most companies have their portfolio of businesses scattered through all four quadrants of the matrix. It is possible to outline quite briefly and simply what the appropriate overall portfolio strategy for such a company should be. The first goal should be to maintain position in the cash cows, but to guard against the frequent temptation to reinvest in them excessively. The cash generated by the

cash cows should be used as a first priority to maintain or consolidate position in those stars which are not self-sustaining. Any surplus remaining can be used to fund a selected number of question marks to dominance. Most companies will find they have inadequate cash generation to finance market share-gaining strategies in all their question marks. Those which are not funded should be divested either by sale or liquidation over time.

Finally, virtually all companies have at least some dog businesses. There is nothing reprehensible about this, indeed on the contrary, an absence of dogs probably indicates that the company has not been sufficiently adventurous in the past. It is essential, however, that the fundamentally weak strategic position of the dog be recognized for what it is. Occasionally it is possible to restore a dog to viability by a creative business segmentation strategy, rationalizing and specializing the business into a small niche which it can dominate. If this is impossible, however, the only thing which could rescue the dog would be an increase in share taking it to a position comparable to the leading competitors in the segment. This is likely to be unreasonably costly in a mature business, and therefore the only prospect for obtaining a return from a dog is to manage it for cash, cutting off all investment in the business. Management should be particularly wary of expensive 'turn around' plans developed for a dog if these do not involve a significant change in fundamental competitive position. Without this, the dog is a sure loser. An indictment of many corporate managements is not the fact that their companies have dogs in the portfolio, but rather that these dogs are not managed according to logical strategies. The decision to liquidate a business is usually even harder to take than that of entering a new business. It is essential, however, for the long-term vitality and performance of the company overall that it be prepared to do both as the need arises.

Thus the appropriate strategy for a multi-business company involves striking a balance in the portfolio such that the cash generated by the cash cows, and by those question marks and dogs which are being liquidated, is sufficient to support the company's stars and to fund the selected question marks through to dominance. This pattern of strategies is indicated by the arrows in Figure 6.1.1. Understanding this pattern conceptually is, however, a far cry from being able to implement it in practice. What any company should do with its own specific businesses is of course a function of the precise shape of the company's portfolio, and the particular opportunities and problems it presents. But how can a clear picture of the company's portfolio be developed?

The matrix quantified

Based on careful analysis and research it is normally possible to divide a company into its various business segments appropriately defined for purposes of strategy development. Following this critical first step, it is usually relatively straightforward to determine the overall growth rate of each individual business (i.e. the growth of the market, not the growth of the company within the market),

and the company's size (in terms of turnover or assets) and relative competitive position (market share) within the business.

Armed with these data it is possible to develop a precise overall picture of the company's portfolio of businesses graphically. This can greatly facilitate the identification and resolution of the key strategic issues facing the company. It is a particularly useful approach where companies are large, comprising many separate businesses. Such complex portfolios often defy description in more conventional ways.

The nature of the graphical portfolio display is illustrated by the example in Figure 6.1.2. In this chart, growth rate and relative competitive position are plotted on continuous scales. Each circle in the display represents a single business or business segment, appropriately defined. To convey an impression of the relative significance of each business, size is indicated by the area of the circle, which can be made proportional to either turnover or assets employed. Relative competitive position is plotted on a logarithmic scale, in order to be consistent with the experience curve effect, which implies that profit margin or rate of cash generation dif-

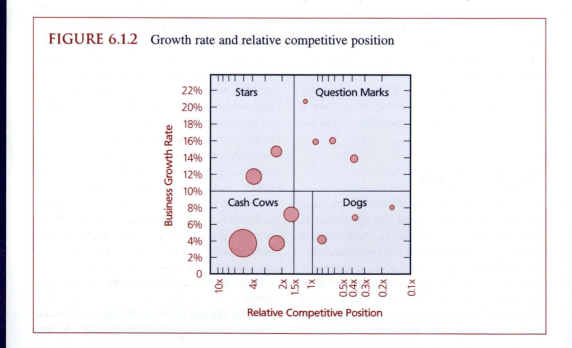

FIGURE 6.1.2 Growth rate and relative competitive position

ferences between competitors will tend to be related to the ratio of their relative competitive positions (market shares). A linear axis is used for growth, for which the most generally useful measure is volume growth of the business concerned, as, in general, rates of cash use should be directly proportional to growth.

The lines dividing the portfolio into four quadrants are inevitably somewhat arbitrary. 'High growth', for example, is taken to include all businesses growing in excess of 10 percent per annum in volume terms. Certainly, above this growth rate market share tends to become fairly fluid and can be made to change hands quite readily. In addition many companies have traditionally employed a figure of 10 percent for their discount rate in times of low inflation, and so this also tends to be the growth rate above which investment in market share becomes particularly attractive financially.

The line separating areas of high and low relative competitive position is set at 1.5 times. Experience in using this display has been that in high-growth businesses relative strengths of this magnitude or greater are necessary in order to ensure a sufficiently dominant position that the business will have the characteristic of a star in practice. On the other hand, in low-growth businesses acceptable cash generation characteristics are occasionally, but not always, observed at relative strengths as low as 1 times; hence the addition of a second separating line at 1 times in the low growth area, to reflect this. These lines should, of course, be taken only as approximate guides in characterizing businesses in the portfolio as dogs and question marks, cash cows and stars. In actuality, businesses cover a smooth spectrum across both axes of the matrix. There is obviously no 'magic' which transforms a star into a cash cow as its growth declines from 10.5 to 9.5 percent. It is undeniably useful, however, to have some device for broadly indicating where the transition points occur within the matrix, and the lines suggested here have worked well in practical applications of the matrix in a large number of companies.

Portfolio approaches in practice

The company shown in Figure 6.1.2 would be a good example of a potentially well-balanced portfolio. With a firm foundation in the form of two or three substantial cash cows, this company has some well-placed stars to provide growth and to yield high cash returns in the future when they mature. The company also has some question marks, at least two of which are probably sufficiently well placed that they offer a good chance of being funded into star positions at a reasonable cost, not out of proportion to the company's resources. The company is not without dogs, but properly managed there is no reason why these should be a drain on cash.

The sound portfolio, unsoundly managed

Companies with an attractive portfolio of this kind are not rare in practice. In fact Figure 6.1.2 is a disguised version of a representation of an actual UK company analyzed in the course of a Boston Consulting Group assignment. What is much rarer, however, is to find that the company has made a clear assessment of the matrix positioning and appropriate strategy for each business in the portfolio.

Ideally, one would hope that the company in Figure 6.1.2 would develop strategy along the following lines. For the stars, the key objectives should be the maintenance of market share; current profitability should be accorded a lower priority. For the cash cows, however, current profitability may well be the primary goal. Dogs would not be expected to be as profitable as the cash cows, but would be expected to yield cash. Some question marks would be set objectives in terms of increased market share; others, where gaining dominance appeared too costly, would be managed instead for cash.

The essence of the portfolio approach is therefore that strategy objectives must vary between businesses. The strategy developed for each business must fit its own matrix position and the needs and capabilities of the company's overall portfolio of businesses. In practice, however, it is much more common to find all businesses within a company being operated with a common overall goal in mind. 'Our target in this company is to grow at 10 percent per annum and achieve a return of 10 percent on capital.' This type of overall target is then taken to apply to every business in the company. Cash cows beat the profit target easily, though they frequently miss on growth. Nevertheless, their managements are praised and they are normally rewarded by being allowed to plough back what only too frequently amounts to an excess of cash into their 'obviously attractive' businesses. Attractive businesses, yes: but not for growth investment. Dogs on the other hand rarely meet the profit target. But how often is it accepted that it is in fact unreasonable for them ever to hit the target? On the contrary, the most common strategic mistake is that major investments are made in dogs from time to time in hopeless attempts to turn the business around without actually shifting market share. Unfortunately, only too often question marks are regarded very much as dogs, and get insufficient investment funds ever to bring them to dominance. The question marks usually do receive some investment, however, possibly even enough to maintain share. This is throwing money away into a cash trap. These businesses should either receive enough support to enable them to achieve segment dominance, or none at all.

These are some of the strategic errors which are regularly committed even by companies which have basically sound portfolios. The result is a serious sub-optimization of potential performance in which some businesses (e.g. cash cows) are not being called on to produce the full results of which they are actually capable, and resources are being mistakenly squandered on other businesses (dogs, question marks) in an attempt to make them achieve performance of which they are intrinsically incapable without a fundamental improvement in market share.

Where mismanagement of this kind becomes positively dangerous, is when it is applied within the context of a basically unbalanced portfolio.

The unbalanced portfolio

The disguised example in Figure 6.1.3 is another actual company. This portfolio is seriously out of balance. As shown in Figure 6.1.3(a), the company has a very high proportion of question marks in its portfolio, and an inadequate base of cash cows. Yet at the time of investigation this company was in fact taking such cash as was being generated by its mature businesses and spreading it out amongst all the high-growth businesses, only one of which was actually receiving sufficient investment to enable it even to maintain share! Thus the overall relative competitive position of the portfolio was on average declining. At the same time, the balance in the portfolio was shifting: as shown in the projected portfolio in Figure 6.1.3(b), because of the higher relative growth of the question marks their overall weight in the portfolio was increasing, making them even harder to fund from the limited resources of the mature businesses.

If the company continued to follow the same strategy of spreading available funds between all the businesses, then the rate of decline could only increase over time leading ultimately to disaster.

This company was caught in a vicious circle of decline. To break out of the circle would require firm discipline and the strength of will to select only one or two of the question marks and finance those, whilst cutting off investment in the remainder. Obviously the choice of which should receive investment involves rather more than selection at random from the portfolio chart. It requires careful analysis of the actual nature of the businesses concerned and particularly the characteristics and behavior of the competitors faced in those businesses. However, the nature of the strategic choice facing the company is quite clear, when viewed in portfolio

FIGURE 6.1.3 An unbalanced portfolio

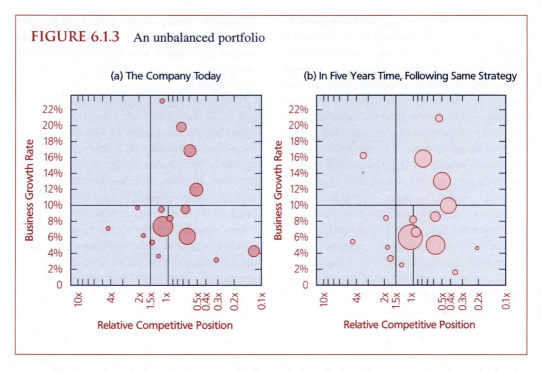

(a) The Company Today

(b) In Five Years Time, Following Same Strategy

terms. Without the clarity of view provided by the matrix display, which focuses on the real fundamentals of the businesses and their relationships to each other within the portfolio, it is impossible to develop strategy effectively in any multibusiness company.

READING

6.2

The core competence of the corporation

By C.K. Prahalad and Gary Hamel[1]

The most powerful way to prevail in global competition is still invisible to many companies. During the 1980s, top executives were judged on their ability to restructure, declutter, and delayer their corporations. In the 1990s, they'll be judged on their ability to identify, cultivate, and exploit the core competencies that make growth possible – indeed, they'll have to rethink the concept of the corporation itself.

Rethinking the corporation

Once, the diversified corporation could simply point its business units at particular

[1]Source: This article was reprinted by permission of *Harvard Business Review*. From 'The Core Competence of the Corporation' by C.K. Prahalad and G. Hamel, May–June 1990, Vol. 68. © 1990 by the Harvard Business School Publishing Corporation, all rights reserved.

end-product markets and admonish them to become world leaders. But with market boundaries changing ever more quickly, targets are elusive and capture is at best temporary. A few companies have proven themselves adept at inventing new markets, quickly entering emerging markets, and dramatically shifting patterns of customer choice in established markets. These are the ones to emulate. The critical task for management is to create an organization capable of infusing products with irresistible functionality or, better yet, creating products that customers need but have not yet even imagined.

This is a deceptively difficult task. Ultimately, it requires radical change in the management of major companies. It means, first of all, that top managements of western companies must assume responsibility for competitive decline. Everyone knows about high interest rates, Japanese protectionism, outdated antitrust laws, obstreperous unions, and impatient investors. What is harder to see, or harder to acknowledge, is how little added momentum companies actually get from political or macroeconomic 'relief.' Both the theory and practice of western management have created a drag on our forward motion. It is the principles of management that are in need of reform.

The roots of competitive advantage

In the short run, a company's competitiveness derives from the price/performance attributes of current products. But the survivors of the first wave of global competition, western and Japanese alike, are all converging on similar and formidable standards for product cost and quality – minimum hurdles for continued competition, but less and less important as sources of differential advantage. In the long run, competitiveness derives from an ability to build, at lower cost and more speedily than competitors, the core competencies that spawn unanticipated products. The real sources of advantage are to be found in man-

agement's ability to consolidate corporate-wide technologies and production skills into competencies that empower individual businesses to adapt quickly to changing opportunities.

Senior executives who claim that they cannot build core competencies either because they feel the autonomy of business units is sacrosanct or because their feet are held to the quarterly budget fire should think again. The problem in many western companies is not that their senior executives are any less capable than those in Japan or that Japanese companies possess greater technical capabilities. Instead, it is their adherence to a concept of the corporation that unnecessarily limits the ability of individual businesses to fully exploit the deep reservoir of technological capability that many American and European companies possess.

The diversified corporation is a large tree. The trunk and major limbs are core products, the smaller branches are business units; the leaves, flowers, and fruit are end products. The root system that provides nourishment, sustenance, and stability is the core competence. You can miss the strength of competitors by looking only at their end products, in the same way you miss the strength of a tree if you look only at its leaves (see Figure 6.2.1).

Core competencies are the collective learning in the organization, especially how to coordinate diverse production skills and integrate multiple streams of technologies. Consider Sony's capacity to miniaturize or Philips's optical-media expertise. The theoretical knowledge to put a radio on a chip does not in itself assure a company the skill to produce a miniature radio no bigger than a business card. To bring off this feat, Casio must harmonize know-how in miniaturization, microprocessor design, materials science, and ultrathin precision casing – the same skills it applies in its miniature card calculators, pocket TVs, and digital watches.

If core competence is about harmonizing streams of technology, it is also about the organization of work and the delivery of

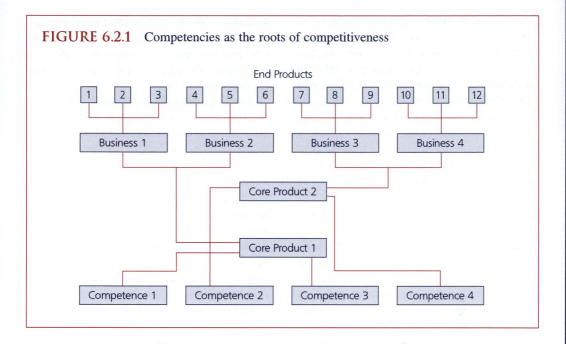

FIGURE 6.2.1 Competencies as the roots of competitiveness

value. Among Sony's competencies is miniaturization. To bring miniaturization to its products, Sony must ensure that technologists, engineers, and marketers have a shared understanding of customer needs and of technological possibilities. The force of core competence is felt as decisively in services as in manufacturing. Citicorp was ahead of others investing in an operating system that allowed it to participate in world markets 24 hours a day. Its competence in systems has provided the company with the means to differentiate itself from many financial service institutions.

Core competence is communication, involvement, and a deep commitment to working across organizational boundaries. It involves many levels of people and all functions. World-class research in, for example, lasers or ceramics can take place in corporate laboratories without having an impact on any of the businesses of the company. The skills that together constitute core competence must coalesce around individuals whose efforts are not so narrowly focused that they cannot recognize the opportunities for blending their functional expertise with those of others in new and interesting ways.

Core competence does not diminish with use. Unlike physical assets, which do deteriorate over time, competencies are enhanced as they are applied and shared. But competencies still need to be nurtured and protected; knowledge fades if it is not used. Competencies are the glue that binds existing businesses. They are also the engine for new business development. Patterns of diversification and market entry may be guided by them, not just by the attractiveness of markets.

Consider 3M's competence with sticky tape. In dreaming up businesses as diverse as 'Post-it' note pads, magnetic tape, photographic film, pressure-sensitive tapes, and coated abrasives, the company has brought to bear widely shared competencies in substrates, coatings, and adhesives and devised various ways to combine them. Indeed, 3M has invested consistently in them. What seems to be an extremely diversified portfolio of businesses belies a few shared core competencies.

In contrast, there are major companies that have had the potential to build core competencies but failed to do so because top management was unable to conceive of the company as anything other than a collection of discrete businesses. General Electric sold much of its consumer electronics business to Thomson of France, arguing that it was becoming increasingly difficult to maintain its competitiveness in this sector. That was undoubtedly so, but it is ironic that it sold several key businesses to competitors who were already competence leaders – Black & Decker in small electrical motors, and Thomson, which was eager to build its competence in microelectronics and had learned from the Japanese that a position in consumer electronics was vital to this challenge.

Management trapped in the strategic business unit (SBU) mind-set almost inevitably finds its individual businesses dependent on external sources for critical components, such as motors or compressors. But these are not just components. They are core products that contribute to the competitiveness of a wide range of end products. They are the physical embodiments of core competencies.

How not to think of competence

Since companies are in a race to build the competencies that determine global leadership, successful companies have stopped imagining themselves as bundles of businesses making products. Canon, Honda, Casio, or NEC may seem to preside over portfolios of businesses unrelated in terms of customers, distribution channels, and merchandising strategy. Indeed, they have portfolios that may seem idiosyncratic at times: NEC is the only global company to be among leaders in computing, telecommunications, and semiconductors *and* to have a thriving consumer electronics business.

But looks are deceiving. In NEC, digital technology, especially VLSI and systems integration skills, is fundamental. In the core competencies underlying them, disparate businesses become coherent. It is Honda's core competence in engines and power trains that gives it a distinctive advantage in car, motorcycle, lawn mower, and generator businesses. Canon's core competencies in optics,

imaging, and microprocessor controls have enabled it to enter, even dominate, markets as seemingly diverse as copiers, laser printers, cameras, and image scanners. Philips worked for more than 15 years to perfect its optical-media (laser disc) competence, as did JVC in building a leading position in video recording. Other examples of core competencies might include mechantronics (the ability to marry mechanical and electronic engineering), video displays, bioengineering, and microelectronics. In the early stages of its competence building, Philips could not have imagined all the products that would be spawned by its optical-media competence, nor could JVC have anticipated miniature camcorders when it first began exploring videotape technologies.

Unlike the battle for global brand dominance, which is visible in the world's broadcast and print media and is aimed at building global 'share of mind,' the battle to build world-class competencies is invisible to people who aren't deliberately looking for it. Top management often tracks the cost and quality of competitors' products, yet how many managers untangle the web of alliances their Japanese competitors have constructed to acquire competencies at low cost? In how many western boardrooms is there an explicit, shared understanding of the competencies the company must build for world leadership? Indeed, how many senior executives discuss the crucial distinction between competitive strategy at the level of a business and competitive strategy at the level of an entire company?

Let us be clear. Cultivating core competence does not mean outspending rivals on research and development. In 1983, when Canon surpassed Xerox in world-wide unit market share in the copier business, its R&D budget in reprographics was but a small fraction of Xerox's. Over the past 20 years, NEC has spent less on R&D as a percentage of sales than almost all of its American and European competitors.

Nor does core competence mean shared costs, as when two or more SBUs use a common facility – a plant, service facility, or sales force – or share a common component. The gains of sharing may be substantial, but the search for shared costs is typically a post hoc effort to rationalize production across existing businesses, not a premeditated effort to build the competencies out of which the businesses themselves grow.

Building core competencies is more ambitious and different than integrating vertically, moreover. Managers deciding whether to make or buy will start with end products and look upstream to the efficiencies of the supply chain and downstream toward distribution and customers. They do not take inventory of skills and look forward to applying them in nontraditional ways. (Of course, decisions about competencies *do* provide a logic for vertical integration. Canon is not particularly integrated in its copier business, except in those aspects of the vertical chain that support the competencies it regards as critical.)

Identifying core competencies – and losing them

At least three tests can be applied to identify core competencies in a company. First, a core competence provides potential access to a wide variety of markets. Competence in display systems, for example, enables a company to participate in such diverse businesses as calculators, miniature TV sets, monitors for laptop computers, and automotive dashboards – which is why Casio's entry into the handheld TV market was predictable. Second, a core competence should make a significant contribution to the perceived customer benefits of the end product. Clearly, Honda's engine expertise fills this bill.

Finally, a core competence should be difficult for competitors to imitate. And it will be difficult if it is a complex harmonization of individual technologies and production skills. A rival might acquire some of the technologies that comprise the core competence, but it will find it more difficult to duplicate the more-or-less comprehensive pattern of internal coordination and learning. JVC's decision in the early 1960s to pursue the development of a videotape competence passed the three tests outlined here. RCA's decision in the late 1970s to develop a stylus-based video turntable system did not.

Few companies are likely to build world leadership in more than five or six fundamental competencies. A company that compiles a list of 20 to 30 capabilities has probably not produced a list of core competencies. Still, it is probably a good discipline to generate a list of this sort and to see aggregate capabilities as building blocks. This tends to prompt the search for licensing deals and alliances through which the company may acquire, at low cost, the missing pieces.

Most western companies hardly think about competitiveness in these terms at all. It is time to take a tough-minded look at the risks they are running. Companies that judge competitiveness, their own and their competitors', primarily in terms of the price/performance of end products are courting the erosion of core competencies – or making too little effort to enhance them. The embedded skills that give rise to the next generation of competitive products cannot be 'rented in' by outsourcing and original equipment manufacturer (OEM) supply relationships. In our view, too many companies have unwittingly surrendered core competencies when they cut internal investment in what they mistakenly thought were just 'cost centers' in favor of outside suppliers.

Of course, it is perfectly possible for a company to have a competitive product line up but be a laggard in developing core competencies – at least for a while. If a company wanted to enter the copier business today, it would find a dozen Japanese companies more than willing to supply copiers on the basis of an OEM private label. But when fundamental technologies changed or if its supplier decided to enter the market directly and become a competitor, that company's product line, along with all of its investments in marketing and distribution, could be vulnerable.

Outsourcing can provide a shortcut to a more competitive product, but it typically contributes little to building the people-embodied skills that are needed to sustain product leadership.

Nor is it possible for a company to have an intelligent alliance or sourcing strategy if it has not made a choice about where it will build competence leadership. Clearly, Japanese companies have benefited from alliances. They've used them to learn from western partners who were not fully committed to preserving core competencies of their own. Learning within an alliance takes a positive commitment of resources – travel, a pool of dedicated people, test-bed facilities, time to internalize and test what has been learned. A company may not make this effort if it doesn't have clear goals for competence building.

Another way of losing is forgoing opportunities to establish competencies that are evolving in existing businesses. In the 1970s and 1980s, many American and European companies – like General Electric, Motorola, GTE, Thorn, and General Electric Company (GEC) – chose to exit the color television business, which they regard as mature. If by 'mature' they meant that they had run out of new product ideas at precisely the moment global rivals had targeted the TV business for entry, then yes, the industry was mature. But it certainly wasn't mature in the sense that all opportunities to enhance and apply video-based competencies had been exhausted.

In ridding themselves of their television businesses, these companies failed to distinguish between divesting the business and destroying their video media-based competencies. They not only got out of the TV business but they also closed the door on a whole stream of future opportunities reliant on video-based competencies.

There are two clear lessons here. First, the costs of losing a core competence can be only partly calculated in advance. The baby may be thrown out with the bath water in divestment decisions. Second, since core competencies are built through a process of continuous improvement and enhancement that may span a decade or longer, a company that has failed to invest in core competence building will find it very difficult to enter an emerging market, unless, of course, it will be content simply to serve as a distribution channel.

American semiconductor companies like Motorola learned this painful lesson when they elected to forgo direct participation in the 256k generation of DRAM chips. Having skipped this round, Motorola, like most of its American competitors, needed a large infusion of technical help from Japanese partners to rejoin the battle in the 1-megabyte generation. When it comes to core competencies, it is difficult to get off the train, walk to the next station, and then reboard.

From core competencies to core products

The tangible link between identified core competencies and end products is what we call the core products – the physical embodiments of one or more core competencies. Honda's engines, for example, are core products, linchpins between design and development skills that ultimately lead to a proliferation of end products. Core products are the components or subassemblies that actually contribute to the value of the end products. Thinking in terms of core products forces a company to distinguish between the brand share it achieves in end product markets (for example, 40 percent of the US refrigerator market) and the manufacturing share it achieves in any particular core product (for example, five percent of the world share of compressor output).

It is essential to make this distinction between core competencies, core products, and end products because global competition is played out by different rules and for different stakes at each level. To build or defend leadership over the long term, a corporation will probably be a winner at each level. At the level of core competence, the goal is to build world leadership in the design and development of a particular class of product functionality – be it compact data storage and retrieval, as with Philips's optical-media competence, or compactness and ease of use, as with Sony's micromotors and microprocessor controls.

To sustain leadership in their chosen core competence areas, these companies *seek to maximize their world manufacturing share in core products*. The manufacture of core products for a wide variety of external (and internal) customers yields the revenue and market feedback that, at least partly, determines the pace at which core competencies can be enhanced and extended. This thinking was behind JVC's decision in the mid-1970s to establish VCR supply relationships with leading national consumer electronics companies in Europe and the United States. In supplying Thomson, Thorn, and Telefunken (all independent companies at that time) as well as US partners, JVC was able to gain the cash and the diversity of market experience that ultimately enabled it to outpace Philips and Sony. (Philips developed videotape competencies in parallel with JVC, but it failed to build a world-wide network of OEM relationships that would have allowed it to accelerate the refinement of its videotape competence through the sale of core products.)

JVC's success has not been lost on Korean companies like Goldstar, Samsung, Kia, and Daewoo, who are building core product leadership in areas as diverse as displays, semiconductors, and automotive engines through their OEM-supply contracts with western companies. Their avowed goal is to capture investment initiative away from potential competitors, often US companies. In doing so, they accelerate their competence-building efforts while 'hollowing out' their competitors. By focusing on competence and embedding it in core products, Asian competitors have built up advantages in component markets first and have then leveraged off their superior products to move downstream to build brand share. And they are not likely to remain the low-cost suppliers forever. As

their reputation for brand leadership is consolidated, they may well gain price leadership. Honda has proven this with its Acura line, and other Japanese carmakers are following suit.

Control over core products is critical for other reasons. A dominant position in core products allows a company to shape the evolution of applications and end markets. Such compact audio disc-related core products as data drives and lasers have enabled Sony and Philips to influence the evolution of the computer-peripheral business in optical-media storage. As a company multiplies the number of application arenas for its core products, it can consistently reduce the cost, time, and risk in new product development. In short, well-targeted core products can lead to economies of scale and scope.

The tyranny of the SBU

The new terms of competitive engagement cannot be understood using analytical tools devised to manage the diversified corporation of 20 years ago, when competition was primarily domestic (GE versus Westinghouse, General Motors versus Ford) and all the key players were speaking the language of the same business schools and consultancies. Old prescriptions have potentially toxic side effects. The need for new principles is most obvious in companies organized exclusively according to the logic of SBUs. The implications of the two alternate concepts of the corporation are summarized in Table 6.2.1.

Obviously, diversified corporations have a portfolio of products and a portfolio of businesses. But we believe in a view of the company as a portfolio of competencies as well. United States companies do not lack the technical resources to build competencies, but their top management often lacks the vision to build them and the administrative means for assembling resources spread across multiple businesses. A shift in commitment will inevitably influence patterns of diversification, skill deployment, resource allocation

TABLE 6.2.1 Two concepts of the corporation

	SBU	Core competence
Basis for competition	Competiveness of today's products	Interfirm competition to build competencies
Corporate structure	Portfolio of businesses related in product-market terms	Portfolio of competencies, core products, and businesses
Status of the business unit	Autonomy is sacrosanct; the SBU 'owns' all resources other than cash	SBU is a potential reservoir of core competencies
Resource allocation	Discrete businesses are the unit of analysis; capital is allocated business by business	Businesses and competencies are the unit of analysis: top management allocates capital and talent
Value added of top management	Optimizing corporate returns through capital allocation trade-offs among businesses	Enunciating strategic architecture and building competencies to secure the future

priorities, and approaches to alliances and outsourcing.

We have described the three different planes on which battles for global leadership are waged: core competence, core products, and end products. A corporation has to know whether it is winning or losing on each plane. By sheer weight of investment, a company might be able to beat its rivals to blue-sky technologies yet still lose the race to build core competence leadership. If a company is winning the race to build core competencies (as opposed to building leadership in a few technologies), it will almost certainly outpace rivals in new business development. If a company is winning the race to capture world manufacturing share in core products, it will probably outpace rivals in improving product features and the price/performance ratio.

Determining whether one is winning or losing end-product battles is more difficult because measures of product market share do not necessarily reflect various companies' underlying competitiveness. Indeed, companies that attempt to build market share by relying on the competitiveness of others, rather than investing in core competencies and world core-product leadership, may be treading on quicksand. In the race for global brand dominance, companies like 3M, Black & Decker, Canon, Honda, NEC, and Citicorp have built global brand umbrellas by proliferating products out of their core competencies. This has allowed their individual businesses to build image, customer loyalty, and access to distribution channels.

When you think about this reconceptualization of the corporation, the primacy of the SBU – an organizational dogma for a generation – is now clearly an anachronism. Where the SBU is an article of faith, resistance to the seductions of decentralization can seem heretical. In many companies, the SBU prism means that only one plane of the global competitive battle, the battle to put competitive products on the shelf *today*, is visible to top management. What are the costs of this distortion?

Underinvestment in developing core competencies and core products

When the organization is conceived of as a multiplicity of SBUs, no single business may feel responsible for maintaining a viable position in core products or be able to justify the investment required to build world leadership in some core competence. In the absence of a more comprehensive view imposed by corporate management, SBU managers will tend to underinvest. Recently, companies such as Kodak and Philips have recognized this as a potential problem and have begun searching for new organizational forms that will allow them to develop and manufacture core products for both internal and external customers.

SBU managers have traditionally conceived of competitors in the same way they've seen themselves. On the whole, they've failed to note the emphasis Asian competitors were placing on building leadership in core products or to understand the critical linkage between world manufacturing leadership and the ability to sustain development pace in core competence. They've failed to pursue OEM-supply opportunities or to look across their various product divisions in an attempt to identify opportunities for coordinated initiatives.

Imprisoned resources

As an SBU evolves, it often develops unique competencies. Typically, the people who embody this competence are seen as the sole property of the business in which they grew up. The manager of another SBU who asks to borrow talented people is likely to get a cold rebuff. SBU managers are not only unwilling to lend their competence carriers but they may actually hide talent to prevent its redeployment in the pursuit of new opportunities. This may be compared to residents of an underdeveloped country hiding most of their cash under their mattresses. The benefits of competencies, like the benefits of the money supply, depend on the velocity of their circulation as well as on the size of the stock the company holds.

Western companies have traditionally had an advantage in the stock of skills they possess. But have they been able to reconfigure them quickly to respond to new opportunities? Canon, NEC, and Honda have had a lesser stock of the people and technologies that compose core competencies but could move them much quicker from one business unit to another. Corporate R&D spending at Canon is not fully indicative of the size of Canon's core competence stock and tells the casual observer nothing about the velocity with which Canon is able to move core competencies to exploit opportunities.

When competencies become imprisoned, the people who carry the competencies do not get assigned to the most exciting opportunities, and their skills begin to atrophy. Only by fully leveraging core competencies can small companies like Canon afford to compete with industry giants like Xerox. How strange that SBU managers, who are perfectly willing to compete for cash in the capital budgeting process, are unwilling to compete for people – the company's most precious asset. We find it ironic that top management devotes so much attention to the capital budgeting process yet typically has no comparable mechanism for allocating the human skills that embody core competencies. Top managers are seldom able to look four or five levels down into the organization, identify the people who embody critical competencies, and move them across organizational boundaries.

Bounded innovation

If core competencies are not recognized, individual SBUs will pursue only those innovation opportunities that are close at hand – marginal product-line extensions or geographic expansions. Hybrid opportunities like fax machines, laptop computers, handheld televisions, or portable music keyboards will emerge only when managers take off their SBU blinkers. Remember, Canon appeared to be in the camera business at the time it was preparing to become a world leader in copiers. Conceiving of the corporation in terms of core competencies widens the domain of innovation.

Developing strategic architecture

The fragmentation of core competencies becomes inevitable when a diversified company's information systems, patterns of communication, career paths, managerial rewards, and processes of strategy development do not transcend SBU lines. We believe that senior management should spend a significant amount of its time developing a corporate-wide strategic architecture that establishes objectives for competence-building. A strategic architecture is a road map of the future that identifies which core competencies to build and their constituent technologies.

By providing an impetus for learning from alliances and a focus for internal development efforts, a strategic architecture like NEC's C&C (computers and communication) can dramatically reduce the investment needed to secure future market leadership. How can a company make partnerships intelligently without a clear understanding of the core competencies it is trying to build and those it is attempting to prevent from being unintentionally transferred?

Of course, all of this begs the question of what a strategic architecture should look like. The answer will be different for every company. But it is helpful to think again of that tree, of the corporation organized around core products and, ultimately, core competencies. To sink sufficiently strong roots, a company must answer some fundamental questions: How long could we preserve our competitiveness in this business if we did not control this particular core competence? How central is this core competence to perceived customer benefits? What future opportunities would be foreclosed if we were to lose this particular competence?

The architecture provides a logic for product and market diversification, moreover. An SBU manager would be asked: Does the new market opportunity add to the overall goal of becoming the best player in the world? Does it exploit or add to the core competence? At Vickers, for example, diversification options

have been judged in the context of becoming the best power and motion control company in the world.

The strategic architecture should make resource allocation priorities transparent to the entire organization. It provides a template for allocation decisions by top management. It helps lower-level managers understand the logic of allocation priorities and disciplines senior management to maintain consistency. In short, it yields a definition of the company and the markets it serves. 3M, Vickers, NEC, Canon, and Honda all qualify on this score. Honda knew it was exploiting what it had learned from motorcycles – how to make high-revving, smooth-running, lightweight engines – when it entered the car business. The task of creating a strategic architecture forces the organization to identify and commit to the technical and production linkages across SBUs that will provide a distinct competitive advantage.

It is consistency of resource allocation and the development of an administrative infrastructure appropriate to it that breathes life into a strategic architecture and creates a managerial culture, teamwork, a capacity to change, and a willingness to share resources, to protect proprietary skills, and to think long term. That is also the reason the specific architecture cannot be copied easily or overnight by competitors. Strategic architecture is a tool for communicating with customers and other external constituents. It reveals the broad direction without giving away every step.

Redeploying to exploit competencies

If the company's core competencies are its critical resource and if top management must ensure that competence carriers are not held hostage by some particular business, then it follows that SBUs should bid for core competencies in the same way they bid for capital. We've made this point glancingly. It is important enough to consider more deeply.

Once top management (with the help of divisional and SBU managers) has identified overarching competencies, it must ask businesses to identify the projects and people closely connected with them. Corporate officers should direct an audit of the location, number, and quality of the people who embody competence.

This sends an important signal to middle managers: core competencies are corporate resources and may be reallocated by *corporate* management. An individual business doesn't own anybody. SBUs are entitled to the services of individual employees so long as SBU management can demonstrate that the opportunity it is pursuing yields the highest possible payoff on the investment in their skills. This message is further underlined if each year in the strategic planning or budgeting process, unit managers must justify their hold on the people who carry the company's core competencies.

Also, reward systems that focus only on product-line results and career paths that seldom cross SBU boundaries engender patterns of behavior among unit managers that are destructively competitive. At NEC, divisional managers come together to identify next-generation competencies. Together they decide how much investment needs to be made to build up each future competence and the contribution in capital and staff support that each division will need to make. There is also a sense of equitable exchange. One division may make a disproportionate contribution or may benefit less from the progress made, but such short-term inequalities will balance out over the long term.

Incidentally, the positive contribution of the SBU manager should be made visible across the company. An SBU manager is unlikely to surrender key people if only the other business (or the general manager of that business who may be a competitor for promotion) is going to benefit from the redeployment. Cooperative SBU managers should be celebrated as team players. Where priorities are clear, transfers are less likely to be seen as idiosyncratic and politically motivated.

Transfers for the sake of building core competence must be recorded and appreciated in the corporate memory. It is reasonable to expect a business that has surrendered core skills on behalf of corporate opportunities in other areas to lose, for a time, some of its competitiveness. If these losses in performance bring immediate censure, SBUs will be unlikely to assent to skills transfers next time.

Finally, there are ways to wean key employees off the idea that they belong in perpetuity to any particular business. Early in their careers, people may be exposed to a variety of businesses through a carefully planned rotation program.

Competence carriers should be regularly brought together from across the corporation to trade notes and ideas. The goal is to build a strong feeling of community among these people. To a great extent, their loyalty should be to the integrity of the core competence area they represent and not just to particular businesses. In traveling regularly, talking frequently to customers, and meeting with peers, competence carriers may be encouraged to discover new market opportunities.

Core competencies are the wellspring of new business development. They should constitute the focus for strategy at the corporate level. Managers have to win manufacturing leadership in core products and capture global share through brand-building programs aimed at exploiting economies of scope. Only if the company is conceived of as a hierarchy of core competencies, core products, and market-focused business units will it be fit to fight.

Nor can top management be just another layer of accounting consolidation, which it often is in a regime of radical decentralization. Top management must add value by enunciating the strategic architecture that guides the competence acquisition process. We believe an obsession with competence building will characterize the global winners of the 1990s. With the decade underway, the time for rethinking the concept of the corporation is already overdue.

READINGS ON NETWORK LEVEL STRATEGY

To open on behalf of the discrete organization perspective, the reading by Michael Porter reprinted under the business level strategy heading (Reading 5.1) could easily have been selected here as well. In this reading, Porter states that 'the essence of strategy formulation is coping with competition', and that there are five sources of competitive pressure, all impinging on a firm's profit potential. These competitive forces are the threat of new entrants, powerful buyers and suppliers, rivalry among existing competitors and the threat of substitute products. Porter asserts that a company's profitability depends on how well it is able to defend itself against these 'opponents'. It is this view of the firm, as a lone organization surrounded by hostile forces, which places this reading clearly within the discrete organization perspective. While Porter does not denounce or warn against cooperative arrangements in this reading (as he does elsewhere; Porter, 1990a), neither does he recognize cooperation as a possibility. His message is that of *realpolitik* – in inter-organizational relationships, conflict and power are the name of the game.

Because Porter's reading is already reprinted under the business level strategy heading, here another classic, 'Collaborate with Your Competitors – and Win', has been selected as the opening article to represent the discrete organization perspective. In this piece, the authors, Gary Hamel, Yves Doz and C.K. Prahalad, basically take the same stance as Porter, in assuming that inter-firm relations are largely competitive and governed by power and calculation. However, while Porter makes little mention of, or is apprehensive about, collaboration with other organizations, Hamel, Doz and Prahalad see collaboration as a useful tool for improving the firm's competitive profile. They argue that alliances with competitors 'can strengthen both companies against outsiders even if it weakens one partner vis-à-vis the other', and therefore that the net result can be positive. Yet they emphasize that companies should not be naive about the real nature of alliances – 'collaboration is competition in a different form'. An alliance is 'a constantly evolving bargain', in which each firm will be fending for itself, trying to learn as much as possible from the other, while attempting to limit the partner's access to its knowledge and skills. The authors advise firms to precede cautiously with alliances, only when they have clear objectives of what they wish to learn from their allies, a well-developed capacity to learn, and defenses against their allies' probing of their skills and technologies. While Hamel, Doz and Prahalad only focus on horizontal relationships in this reading, their message is similar to that of Porter – competition in the environment is paramount and cooperation is merely an opportunistic move in the overall competitive game.

As representative of the embedded organization perspective, a reading by Gianni Lorenzoni and Charles Baden-Fuller has been selected, entitled 'Creating a Strategic Center to Manage a Web of Partners'. Lorenzoni and Baden-Fuller are particularly interested in how companies structure their vertical relationships, balancing pressures for competition and cooperation. In their view, where a group of firms works together closely, they can form a 'virtual company'. This type of network can benefit from most of the benefits of being a large vertically integrated company, while avoiding most of the disadvantages of integration. But Lorenzoni and Baden-Fuller articulate that it is necessary for a network of firms to have a strategic center that can act as builder and coordinator. As builder, the strategic center can deliberately design and assemble the network components, and as coordinator it can regulate activities and resolve disputes. The authors carry on to specify the conditions under which a network of firms can be an advantageous organizational form and what is required to make them work. Overall, their main message is that durable partnerships between multiple firms are not easy, but if this interdependence can be managed well, it can give the group a strong competitive edge against others.

READING

7.1

Collaborate with your competitors – and win

By Gary Hamel, Yves Doz and C.K. Prahalad[1]

Collaboration between competitors is in fashion. General Motors and Toyota assemble automobiles, Siemens and Philips develop semiconductors, Canon supplies photocopiers to Kodak, France's Thomson and Japan's JVC manufacture videocassette recorders. But the spread of what we call 'competitive collaboration' – joint ventures, outsourcing agreements, product licensings, cooperative research – has triggered unease about the long-term consequences. A strategic alliance can strengthen both companies against outsiders even as it weakens one partner *vis-à-vis* the other. In particular, alliances between Asian companies and western rivals seem to work against the western partner. Cooperation becomes a low-cost route for new competitors to gain technology and market access.

Yet the case for collaboration is stronger than ever. It takes so much money to develop new products and to penetrate new markets that few companies can go it alone in every situation. ICL, the British computer company, could not have developed its current generation of mainframes without Fujitsu. Motorola needs Toshiba's distribution capacity to break into the Japanese semiconductor market. Time is another critical factor. Alliances can provide shortcuts for western companies racing to improve their production efficiency and quality control.

We have spent more than five years studying the inner workings of 15 strategic alliances and monitoring scores of others. Our research involves cooperative ventures between competitors from the United States and Japan, Europe and Japan, and the United States and Europe. We did not judge the success or failure of each partnership by its longevity – a common mistake when evaluating strategic alliances – but by the shifts in competitive strength on each side. We focused on how companies use competitive collaboration to enhance their internal skills and technologies while they guard against transferring competitive advantages to ambitious partners.

There is no immutable law that strategic alliances *must* be a windfall for Japanese or Korean partners. Many western companies do give away more than they gain – but that's because they enter partnerships without knowing what it takes to win. Companies that benefit most from competitive collaboration adhere to a set of simple but powerful principles.

- **Collaboration is competition in a different form.** Successful companies never forget that their new partners may be out to disarm them. They enter alliances with clear strategic objectives, and they also understand how their partners' objectives will affect their success.

- **Harmony is not the most important measure of success.** Indeed, occasional conflict may be the best evidence of mutually beneficial collaboration. Few alliances remain win-win undertakings forever. A partner may be content even as it unknowingly surrenders core skills.

- **Cooperation has limits.** Companies must defend against competitive compromise. A strategic alliance is a constantly evolving bargain whose real terms go beyond the legal agreement or the aims of top management. What information gets traded is determined day to day, often by engineers and operating managers. Successful companies inform employees at all levels about what skills and technologies are off-limits to the partner and monitor what the partner requests and receives.

■ Learning from partners is paramount. Successful companies view each alliance as a window on their partners' broad capabilities. They use the alliance to build skills in areas outside the formal agreement and systematically diffuse new knowledge throughout their organizations.

Why collaborate?

Using an alliance with a competitor to acquire new technologies or skills is not devious. It reflects the commitment and capacity of each partner to absorb the skills of the other. We found that in every case in which a Japanese company emerged from an alliance stronger than its western partner, the Japanese company had made a greater effort to learn.

Strategic intent is an essential ingredient in the commitment to learning. The willingness of Asian companies to enter alliances represents a change in competitive tactics, not competitive goals. NEC, for example, has used a series of collaborative ventures to enhance its technology and product competences. NEC is the only company in the world with a leading position in telecommunications, computers, and semiconductors – despite its investing less in research and development (R&D) (as a percentage of revenues) than competitors like Texas Instruments, Northern Telecom, and L.M. Ericsson. Its string of partnerships, most notably with Honeywell, allowed NEC to leverage its in-house R&D over the last two decades.

Western companies, on the other hand, often enter alliances to avoid investments. They are more interested in reducing the costs and risks of entering new businesses or markets than in acquiring new skills. A senior US manager offered this analysis of his company's venture with a Japanese rival: 'We complement each other well – our distribution capability and their manufacturing skill. I see no reason to invest upstream if we can find a secure source of product. This is a comfortable relationship for us.'

An executive from this company's Japanese partner offered a different perspective: 'When it is necessary to collaborate, I go to my employees and say, "This is bad, I wish we had these skills ourselves. Collaboration is second best. But I will feel worse if after four years we do not know how to do what our partner knows how to do." We must digest their skills.'

The problem here is not that the US company wants to share investment risk (its Japanese partner does too) but that the US company has no ambition beyond avoidance. When the commitment to learning is so one-sided, collaboration invariably leads to competitive compromise.

Many so-called alliances between western companies and their Asian rivals are little more than sophisticated outsourcing arrangements. General Motors buys cars and components from Korea's Daewoo. Siemens buys computers from Fujitsu. Apple buys laser printer engines from Canon. The traffic is almost entirely one way. These original equipment manufacturer (OEM) deals offer Asian partners a way to capture investment initiative from western competitors and displace customer-competitors from value-creating activities. In many cases this goal meshes with that of the western partner: to regain competitiveness quickly and with minimum effort.

Consider the joint venture between Rover, the British automaker, and Honda. Some 25 years ago, Rover's forerunners were world leaders in small car design. Honda had not even entered the automobile business. But in the mid-1970s, after failing to penetrate foreign markets, Rover turned to Honda for technology and product development support. Rover has used the alliance to avoid investments to design and build new cars. Honda has cultivated skills in European styling and marketing as well as multinational manufacturing. There is little doubt which company will emerge stronger over the long term.

Troubled laggards like Rover often strike alliances with surging latecomers like Honda. Having fallen behind in a key skills area (in this case, manufacturing small cars), the laggard attempts to compensate for past failures. The latecomer uses the alliance to close a specific skills gap (in this case, learning to build cars for a regional market). But a laggard that forges a partnership for short-term gain may find itself in a dependency spiral: as it contributes fewer and fewer distinctive skills, it must reveal more and more of its internal operations to keep the partner interested. For the weaker company, the issue shifts from, 'Should we collaborate?' to 'With whom should we collaborate?' to 'How do we keep our partner interested as we lose the advantages that made us attractive to them in the first place?'

There's a certain paradox here. When both partners are equally intent on internalizing the other's skills, distrust and conflict may spoil the alliance and threaten its very survival. That's one reason joint ventures between Korean and Japanese companies have been few and tempestuous. Neither side wants to 'open the kimono.' Alliances seem to run most smoothly when one partner is intent on learning and the other is intent on avoidance – in essence, when one partner is willing to grow dependent on the other. But running smoothly is not the point; the point is for a company to emerge from an alliance more competitive than when it entered it.

One partner does not always have to give up more than it gains to ensure the survival of an alliance. There are certain conditions under which mutual gain is possible, at least for a time:

- **The partners' strategic goals converge while their competitive goals diverge.** That is, each partner allows for the other's continued prosperity in the shared business. Philips and Du Pont collaborate to develop and manufacture compact discs, but nei-

ther side invades the other's market. There is a clear upstream/downstream division of effort.

- **The size and market power of both partners is modest compared with industry leaders.** This forces each side to accept that mutual dependence may have to continue for many years. Long-term collaboration may be so critical to both partners that neither will risk antagonizing the other by an overtly competitive bid to appropriate skills or competences. Fujitsu's 1 to 5 size disadvantage with IBM means it will be a long time, if ever, before Fujitsu can break away from its foreign partners and go it alone.

- **Each partner believes it can learn from the other and at the same time limit access to proprietary skills.** JVC and Thomson, both of whom make VCRs, know that they are trading skills. But the two companies are looking for very different things. Thomson needs product technology and manufacturing prowess; JVC needs to learn how to succeed in the fragmented European market. Both sides believe there is an equitable chance for gain.

How to build secure defenses

For collaboration to succeed, each partner must contribute something distinctive: basic research, product development skills, manufacturing capacity, access to distribution. The challenge is to share enough skills to create advantage *vis-à-vis* companies outside the alliance while preventing a wholesale transfer of core skills to the partner. This is a very thin line to walk. Companies must carefully select what skills and technologies they pass to their partners. They must develop safeguards against unintended, informal transfers of information. The goal is to limit the transparency of their operations.

The type of skill a company contributes is an important factor in how easily its partner can internalize the skills. The potential for transfer is greatest when a partner's contribution is easily transported (in engineering drawings, on computer tapes, or in the heads of a few technical experts); easily interpreted (it can be reduced to commonly understood equations or symbols); and easily absorbed (the skill or competence is independent of any particular cultural context).

Western companies face an inherent disadvantage because their skills are generally more vulnerable to transfer. The magnet that attracts so many companies to alliances with Asian competitors is their manufacturing excellence – a competence that is less transferable than most. Just-in-time inventory systems and quality circles can be imitated, but this is like pulling a few threads out of an oriental carpet. Manufacturing excellence is a complex web of employee training, integration with suppliers, statistical process controls, employee involvement, value engineering, and design for manufacture. It is difficult to extract such a subtle competence in any way but a piecemeal fashion.

So companies must take steps to limit transparency. One approach is to limit the scope of the formal agreement. It might cover a single technology rather than an entire range of technologies; part of a product line rather than the entire line; distribution in a limited number of markets or for a limited period of time. The objective is to circumscribe a partner's opportunities to learn.

Moreover, agreements should establish specific performance requirements. Motorola, for example, takes an incremental, incentive-based approach to technology transfer in its venture with Toshiba. The agreement calls for Motorola to release its microprocessor technology incrementally as Toshiba delivers on its promise to increase Motorola's penetration in the Japanese semiconductor market. The greater Motorola's market share, the greater Toshiba's access to Motorola's technology.

Many of the skills that migrate between companies are not covered in the formal terms of collaboration. Top management puts together strategic alliances and sets the legal parameters for exchange. But what actually gets traded is determined by day-to-day interactions of engineers, marketers, and product developers: who says what to whom, who gets access to what facilities, who sits on what joint committees. The most important deals ('I'll share this with you if you share that with me') may be struck four or five organizational levels below where the deal was signed. Here lurks the greatest risk of unintended transfers of important skills.

Consider one technology-sharing alliance between European and Japanese competitors. The European company valued the partnership as a way to acquire a specific technology. The Japanese company considered it a window on its partner's entire range of competences and interacted with a broad spectrum of its partner's marketing and product development staff. The company mined each contact for as much information as possible.

For example, every time the European company requested a new feature on a product being sourced from its partner, the Japanese company asked for detailed customer and competitor analyses to justify the request. Over time, it developed a sophisticated picture of the European market that would assist its own entry strategy. The technology acquired by the European partner through the formal agreement had a useful life of three to five years. The competitive insights acquired informally by the Japanese company will probably endure longer.

Limiting unintended transfers at the operating level requires careful attention to the role of gatekeepers, the people who control what information flows to a partner. A gatekeeper can be effective only if there are a limited number of gateways through which a partner can access people and facilities. Fujitsu's many partners all go through a single office, the 'collaboration section,' to request information and assistance from different divisions. This way the company can monitor and control access to critical skills and technologies.

We studied one partnership between European and US competitors that involved several divisions of each company. While the

US company could only access its partner through a single gateway, its partner had unfettered access to all participating divisions. The European company took advantage of its free rein. If one division refused to provide certain information, the European partner made the same request of another division. No single manager in the US company could tell how much information had been transferred or was in a position to piece together patterns in the requests.

Collegiality is a prerequisite for collaborative success. But *too much* collegiality should set off warning bells to senior managers. CEOs or division presidents should expect occasional complaints from their counterparts about the reluctance of lower level employees to share information. That's a sign that the gatekeepers are doing their jobs. And senior management should regularly debrief operating personnel to find out what information the partner is requesting and what requests are being granted.

Limiting unintended transfers ultimately depends on employee loyalty and self-discipline. This was a real issue for many of the western companies we studied. In their excitement and pride over technical achievements, engineering staffs sometimes shared information that top management considered sensitive. Japanese engineers were less likely to share proprietary information.

There are a host of cultural and professional reasons for the relative openness of western technicians. Japanese engineers and scientists are more loyal to their company than to their profession. They are less steeped in the open give-and-take of university research since they receive much of their training from employers. They consider themselves team members more than individual scientific contributors. As one Japanese manager noted, 'We don't feel any need to reveal what we know. It is not an issue of pride for us. We're glad to sit and listen. If we're patient we usually learn what we want to know.'

Controlling unintended transfers may require restricting access to facilities as well as to people. Companies should declare sensitive laboratories and factories off-limits to their partners. Better yet, they might house the collaborative venture in an entirely new facility. IBM is building a special site in Japan where Fujitsu can review its forthcoming mainframe software before deciding whether to license it. IBM will be able to control exactly what Fujitsu sees and what information leaves the facility.

Finally, which country serves as 'home' to the alliance affects transparency. If the collaborative team is located near one partner's major facilities, the other partner will have more opportunities to learn – but less control over what information gets traded. When the partner houses, feeds, and looks after engineers and operating managers, there is a danger they will 'go native.' Expatriate personnel need frequent visits from headquarters as well as regular furloughs home.

Enhance the capacity to learn

Whether collaboration leads to competitive surrender or revitalization depends foremost on what employees believe the purpose of the alliance to be. It is self-evident: to learn, one must want to learn. Western companies won't realize the full benefits of competitive collaboration until they overcome an arrogance borne of decades of leadership. In short, western companies must be more receptive.

We asked a senior executive in a Japanese electronics company about the perception that Japanese companies learn more from their foreign partners than vice versa. 'Our western partners approach us with the attitude of teachers,' he told us. 'We are quite happy with this, because we have the attitude of students.'

Learning begins at the top. Senior management must be committed to enhancing their companies' skills as well as to avoiding financial risk. But most learning takes place at the lower levels of an alliance. Operating employees not only represent the front lines in an effective defense but also play a vital role in acquiring knowledge. They must be well briefed on the partner's strengths and weaknesses and understand how acquiring particular skills will bolster their company's competitive position.

This is already standard practice among Asian companies. We accompanied a Japanese development engineer on a tour through a partner's factory. This engineer dutifully took notes on plant layout, the number of production stages, the rate at which the line was running, and the number of employees. He recorded all this despite the fact that he had no manufacturing responsibility in his own company, and that the alliance didn't encompass joint manufacturing. Such dedication greatly enhances learning.

Collaboration doesn't always provide an opportunity to fully internalize a partner's skills. Yet just acquiring new and more precise benchmarks of a partner's performance can be of great value. A new benchmark can provoke a thorough review of internal performance levels and may spur a round of competitive innovation. Asking questions like, 'Why do their semiconductor logic designs have fewer errors than ours?' and 'Why are they investing in this technology and we're not?' may provide the incentive for a vigorous catch-up program.

Competitive benchmarking is a tradition in most of the Japanese companies we studied. It requires many of the same skills associated with competitor analysis: systematically calibrating performance against external targets; learning to use rough estimates to determine where a competitor (or partner) is better, faster, or cheaper; translating those estimates into new internal targets; and recalibrating to establish the rate of improvement in a competitor's performance. The great advantage of competitive collaboration is that proximity makes benchmarking easier.

Indeed, some analysts argue that one of Toyota's motivations in collaborating with GM in the much-publicized NUMMI venture is to gauge the quality of GM's manufacturing technology. GM's top manufacturing people get a close look at Toyota, but the reverse is true as well. Toyota may be learning whether its giant US competitor is capable of closing the productivity gap with Japan.

Competitive collaboration also provides a way of getting close enough to rivals to predict how they will behave when the alliance unravels or runs its course. How does the partner respond to price changes? How does it measure and reward executives? How does it prepare to launch a new product? By revealing a competitor's management orthodoxies, collaboration can increase the chances of success in future head-to-head battles.

Knowledge acquired from a competitor-partner is only valuable after it is diffused through the organization. Several companies we studied had established internal clearinghouses to collect and disseminate information. The collaborations manager at one Japanese company regularly made the rounds of all employees involved in alliances. He identified what information had been collected by whom and then passed it on to appropriate departments. Another company held regular meetings where employees shared new knowledge and determined who was best positioned to acquire additional information.

Proceed with care – but proceed

After World War II, Japanese and Korean companies entered alliances with western rivals from weak positions. But they worked steadfastly toward independence. In the early 1960s, NEC's computer business was one-quarter the size of Honeywell's, its primary foreign partner. It took only two decades for NEC to grow larger than Honeywell, which eventually sold its computer operations to an alliance between NEC and Group Bull of France. The NEC experience demonstrates that dependence on a foreign partner doesn't automatically condemn a company to also-ran status. Collaboration may sometimes be unavoidable; surrender is not.

Managers are too often obsessed with the ownership structure of an alliance. Whether a company controls 51 percent or 49 percent of a joint venture may be much less important than the rate at which each partner learns from the other. Companies that are confident of their ability to learn may even prefer some ambiguity in the alliance's legal structure. Ambiguity creates more potential to acquire skills and technologies. The challenge for western companies is not to write tighter legal agreements but to become better learners.

Running away from collaboration is no answer. Even the largest western companies can no longer outspend their global rivals. With leadership in many industries shifting toward the East, companies in the United States and Europe must become good borrowers – much like Asian companies did in the 1960s and 1970s. Competitive renewal depends on building new process capabilities and winning new product and technology battles. Collaboration can be a low-cost strategy for doing both.

READING 7.2

Creating a strategic center to manage a web of partners

By Gianni Lorenzoni and Charles Baden-Fuller[1]

Strategic alliances and inter-firm networks have been gaining popularity with many firms for their lower overhead costs, increased responsiveness and flexibility, and greater efficiency of operations. Networks that are *strategically guided* are often fast-growing and on the leading edge. In 10 years, Sun Microsystems (founded in 1982) grew to $3.2 billion in sales and $284 million in profits. This remarkable growth has been achieved by Sun's strategic direction of a web of alliances.

Few would expect such rapid growth and technological success in an older and mature industry such as textiles. Yet Benetton, the famous global textile empire, is in many ways like Sun. Founded in 1964, it had by 1991 achieved more than $2 billion in sales and $235 million in profits. Benetton is widely admired in Europe and the Far East for its rapid growth and ability to change the industry's rules of the game through its strategy of 'mass fashion to young people.'

What creates and guides the successful, innovative, leading-edge interfirm network? Most research into inter-firm networks has emphasized how they can reconcile the flexibility of market relationships with the long-term commitment of hierarchically centralized management. Although all networks reflect the conscious decisions of some managers, it is becoming increasingly apparent that those networks that are not guided strategically by a 'center' are unable to meet the demanding challenges of today's markets. In this reading, we are concerned with those strategic centers that have had a very significant impact on their sectors, especially as regards innovation. They are not confined to just a few isolated sectors, but have been observed in a wide variety of circumstances, some of which are listed in Table 7.2.1.

In this reading, we examine three dimensions of the strategic center:

TABLE 7.2.1 Some central firms and their activities

Name of company and its industry	Activities of strategic center	Activities of the network
Apple (computers)	■ Hardware design ■ Software design ■ Distribution	■ Principal subcontractors manufacture ■ 3,000 software developers
Benetton (apparel)	■ Designing collections ■ Selected production ■ Developing new technology systems	■ 6,000 shops ■ 400 subcontractors in production ■ Principal joint ventures in Japan, Egypt, India, and others
Corning (glass, medical products and optical fibers)	■ Technology innovation ■ Production	■ More than 30 joint ventures world-wide
Genentech (biotechnology/DNA)	■ Technology innovation	■ J.V.s with drug companies for production and distribution, licensing in from universities
McDonald's (fast food)	■ Marketing ■ Prototyping technology and systems	■ 9,000 outlets, joint ventures in many foreign countries
McKesson (drug distribution)	■ Systems ■ Marketing ■ Logistics ■ Consulting advice	■ Thousands of retail drug outlets, and ties with drug companies, and government institutions
Nike (shoes and sportswear)	■ Design ■ Marketing	■ Principal subcontractors world-wide
Nintendo (video games)	■ Design ■ Prototyping ■ Marketing	■ 30 principal hardware subcontractors ■ 150 software developers
Sun (computers and computer systems)	■ Innovation of technology ■ Software ■ Assembly	■ Licensor/licensees for software and hardware
Toyota (automobiles)	■ Design ■ Assembly ■ Marketing	■ Principal subcontractors for complex components ■ Second tier for other components ■ Network of agents for distribution

■ as a creator of value for its partners;

■ as leader, rule setter, and capability builder;

■ as simultaneously structuring and strateg-izing.

The role of the strategic center

The strategic center (or central firm) plays a critical role as a creator of value. The main features of this role are:

- Strategic outsourcing. Outsource and share with more partners than the normal broker and traditional firm. Require partners to be more than doers, expect them to be problemsolvers and initiators.

- Capability. Develop the core skills and competencies of partners to make them more effective and competitive. Force members of the network to share their expertise with others in the network, and with the central firm.

- Technology. Borrow ideas from others which are developed and exploited as a means of creating and mastering new technologies.

- Competition. Explain to partners that the principle dimension of competition is between value chains and networks. The network is only as strong as its weakest link. Encourage rivalry between firms inside the network, in a positive manner.

From subcontracting to strategic outsourcing

All firms that act as brokers or operate networks play only a limited role in undertaking the production and delivery of the good or service to the markets in which the system is involved. What distinguishes central firms is both the extent to which they subcontract, and the way that they collect together partners who contribute to the whole system and whose roles are clearly defined in a positive and creative way.

Many organizations see their subcontractors and partners as passive doers or actors in their quest for competitive advantage. They typically specify exactly what they want the partners to do, and leave little to the creative skills of others. They reserve a special creative role for only a few 'critical' partners. In strategic networks, it is the norm rather than an exception for partners to be innovators.

Typically each of these partnerships extends beyond a simple subcontracting relationship. Strategic centers expect their partners to do more than follow the rules, they

expect them to be creative. For example, Apple worked with Canon and Adobe to design and create a laser jet printer which then gave Apple an important position in its industry. In all the cases we studied, the strategic center looked to the partners to be creative in solving problems and being proactive in the relationships. They demanded more – and obtained more – from their partners than did their less effective counterparts that used traditional subcontracting.

Developing the competencies of the partners

How should the central firm see its own competencies *vis-à-vis* its partners? Most writers ague that current competencies should guide future decisions. Many have warned of the dangers in allowing the other partners in a joint venture or alliance to exploit the skills of the host organization. For example, Reich and Mankin (1986) noted that joint ventures between Japanese and US firms often result in one side (typically the Japanese) gaining at the expense of the other. Bleeke and Ernst (1991) found similar disappointment in that in only 51 percent of the cases they studied did both firms gain from alliances. In a study of cross border alliances, Hamel (1991) found that the unwary partner typically found that its competencies were 'hollowed out' and that its collaborator became a more powerful competitor. Badaracco (1991) examined the experiences of GM and IBM, who have signed multiple agreements, and explored the difficulties they face.

Traditional brokers and large integrated firms do not 'hand out' core skills, but the central firms we studied have ignored this advice and won. While keeping a very few skills and assets to themselves, the central firms were remarkable in their desire to transfer skill and knowledge adding value to their partners. Typically, they set out to build up the partners' ability and competencies. At Benetton, site selection and sample selection were skills which Benetton would offer to the new retail partners, either directly or through the agents. Skill transfers were also evident in the machinery networks and at Apple.

Nike brings its partners to its research site at Beaverton to show them the latest developments in materials, product designs, technologies, and markets. Sometimes the partners share some of the costs, but the prime benefit is to shorten cycle times and create a more vibrant system. Toyota's subcontractors may receive training from Toyota and are helped in their development of expertise in solving problems pertaining to their particular component. Not only does this encourage them to deliver better quality parts to the Toyota factories, but it also allows the Toyota system to generate an advantage over other car manufacturers.

In contrast to these companies, the less successful organizations we studied did not have groups of specialists to transfer knowledge to partners – nor, it seems, did they appreciate its importance. They did not enlist all their suppliers and customers to fight a common enemy. Moreover, their experiences did not encourage exploration of this approach. They spoke of past difficulties in alliances. Skill transfers between parties did not always result in mutual benefit. One defense contractor explained that their experience of skill transfers nearly always meant that the partner was strengthened and became a stronger rival.

Borrowing–developing–lending new ideas

While all firms bring in new ideas from outside, the central firms we studied have adopted an unusual and aggressive perspective in this sphere. They scan their horizons for all sorts of opportunities and utilize a formula we call *borrow–develop–lend*. 'Borrow' means that the strategic center deliberately buys or licenses some existing technological ideas from a third party; 'develop' means that it takes these outside ideas and adds value by developing them further in its own organization. This commercialization can then be exploited or 'lent' with great rapidity through its stellar system, creating new adjuncts to

leverage to the greatest advantage. Borrowing ideas, which are subsequently developed and exploited, stretches the organization and forces it to grow its capabilities and competencies. It demands a new way of thinking.

In the Italian packaging machinery sector, lead producers follow this strategy. They borrow designs of a new machine from specialist designers or customers. These designs are then prototyped. From these prototypes, small and medium-sized partners or specialists often improve the design in a unique way, such as improving the flows and linkages. The focal firm then re-purchases and exploits the modified design, licensing to producers for the final development and marketing phase. Thus we see a 'to-and-fro' pattern of development between the central firm and its many partners.

Sun also used the borrow–develop–lend approach in their project to build a new workstation delivering 'more power with less cost.' They borrowed existing technology from other parties, recombined and developed them further inside Sun, and then licensed them to third parties for development and sale under the Sun brand.

The borrow–develop–lend principle helps the central firm reduce the cost of development, make progress more quickly, and, most importantly, undertake projects which would normally lie outside its scope. This approach contrasts with the procedures used by other large firms. Although these firms may buy ideas from other sources, large firms usually have a slower pace of development and rarely match the speed of exploitation achieved through networking and re-lending the idea to third parties. The strategic center seems to avoid the *not-invented-here* syndrome, where innovations and ideas are rejected because they are not internally created and developed.

From the view of independent inventors, the strategic center is an attractive organization with which to do business. The central firms have a track record of rapid commercialization (usually offering large incentives to those with ideas). They emphasize moving quickly from ideas to market by a simultaneous learning process with partners, thereby offering a competitive advantage over other developers. Finally, the willingness to involve others means rapid diffusion with fast payback, thus lessening the risks.

Perceptions of the competitive process

Firms in the same industry experience varying degrees of competitive rivalry. The joint venture, formal agreements, or the use of cross shareholdings are mechanisms used to create common ties, encourage a common view, and unite firms against others in the industry. Strategic centers also create this sense of cooperation across competing enterprises.

Competitive success requires the integration of multiple capabilities (e.g. innovation, productivity, quality, responsiveness to customers) across internal and external organizational boundaries. Such integration is a big challenge to most organizations. Strategic centers rise to this challenge and create a sense of common purpose across multiple levels in the value chain and across different sectors. They achieve a combination of specialized capability and large-scale integration at the same time, despite the often destructive rivalry between buyers and customers. Strategic purchasing partnerships are commonly used to moderate this rivalry, but few firms are able to combine both horizontal and vertical linkages.

In building up their partner's capabilities and competencies, strategic centers convey an unusual perspective to their partners on the nature of the competitive process. This perspective permits the partners to take a holistic view of the network, seeing the collective as a unit that can achieve competitive advantage. In this respect, the whole network acts like a complex integrated firm spanning many markets.

Table 7.2.2 illustrates how the actions of the strategic center differ from other organizations. Chain stores are a good example of organizations that coordinate activities across many actors, yet at a single stage of the value chain. In contrast, the narrowly defined, vertically integrated firm coordinates across many stages but not across many markets or actors. Only the strategic center and the large multi-market, vertically integrated organization are able to coordinate across many markets and many stages of the value chain.

Beyond the hollow organization

Although the strategic center outsources more activities than most organizations, it is not hollow. Unlike the traditional broker that is merely a glorified arranger, the central firms we studied understand that they have to develop some critical core competencies. These competencies are, in general, quite different from those stressed by most

TABLE 7.2.2 Different kinds of competition across sectors and stages of the value chain

	Single units within the sector	Multiple units within the sector or across related sectors
Multiple stages of the value chain	▪ Vertical integration; or ▪ Value-added partnerships	▪ Strategic centers and their webs of partners; or ▪ Large integrated multi-market organizations
Single stages of the value chain	▪ Traditional adversarial firm	▪ Chain stores; or ▪ Simple networks

managers in traditional firms. The agenda for the central firm consists of:

- **The idea**. Creating a vision in which partners play a critical role.
- **The investment**. A strong brand image and effective systems and support.
- **The climate**. Creating an atmosphere of trust and reciprocity.
- **The partners**. Developing mechanisms for attracting and selecting partners.

Sharing a business idea

Most of the central firms we studied are small, lean, and focused operations. They employ comparatively few people and are very selective in what they do. Yet, they have an unusual ability to conceptualize a business idea that can be shared not only internally, but with other partners. In the case of Benetton, this idea has a few key elements such as: mass fashion for young people, and the notion of a strategic network to orchestrate and fulfill this vision. In food-machinery, the key idea of the central firms is to solve the client's problems, rather than selling existing competencies, while new partners are developed in response to customer needs – a novel notion in this sector. These simple ideas are not easy to create or sustain.

These ideas have been able to capture the imagination of the employees and their partners. They also encapsulate strategy and so contain, in the language of Prahalad and Hamel (1990, Reading 6.2 in this book), the features of a clear strategic intent. Common to all the business ideas we studied, there is a notion of partnership which includes the creation of a learning culture and the promotion of systems experiments so as to outpace rival competing organizations. The strategic centers view their role as one of leading and orchestrating their systems. Their distinctive characteristics lie in their ability to perceive the full business idea and understand the role of all the different parties in many different locations across the whole value chain. The managers in the strategic center have a dream and they orchestrate others to fulfill that dream.

This vision of the organization is not just an idea in the minds of a few managers, it is a feature that is shared throughout the organization. Many of the strategic centers we studied admit that their visions have emerged over time, they are not the work of a moment. Their vision is dynamic, for as their network grows and as the environment changes, the organizational vision also changes. This is not the case in the less successful alliances. They showed the typical characteristics of most organizations, multifaceted views of the world and a less-than-clear expression of their vision.

Clearly, vision is reinforced by success. The ability of central firms to deliver profits and growth for the partners helps cement a vision in their minds and makes their claims credible. It creates a cycle where success breeds clarity, which in turn helps breed more success.

Brand power and other support

To maintain the balance of power in the network, all central firms retain certain activities. The control of the brand names and the development of the systems that integrate the network are two activities that give the organization a pivotal role and allow it to exercise power over the system.

Some of the firms we observed were involved in consumer markets where branding is important. The brand name, owned by the central firm, was promoted by the activities of the partners, who saw the brand as a shared resource. They were encouraged to ensure its success, and quite often these efforts helped the brand become famous in a short period of time. While the brand and marketing are not so vital in producer goods markets, they are still important – and the strategic center neglects these at its peril. Its importance is highlighted by the experiences of one of the less successful organizations we studied. This aerospace firm had problems as a result of the inability of its members to relinquish many of the aspects of marketing to a single central firm.

To retain its power, the central firm must ensure that the information between partners flows freely and is not filtered. Communication is a costly activity, and developing effective communication systems is always the responsibility of the strategic center. These systems are not only electronically based, but include all other methods of communication. Often there is a style for meeting among the partners, which is set and monitored by the central firm. The quality of information is a key requirement if the central firm is to mandate effectively the stream of activities scattered among different firms.

Trust and reciprocity

Leveraging the skills of partners is easy to conceive but hard to implement. The difficulties occur because it takes many partners operating effectively to make the system work, but the negative behavior of only a few can bring the whole system to a halt. The strategic vision requires all its members to contribute all the time without fail. This is a considerable demand. The typical organizational response to such a need is to circumscribe the contracts with outsiders in a tight legalistic manner. But this is not always wise; contract making and policing can be difficult and expensive. Formal contracts are relatively inflexible and are suitable only where the behavior is easy to describe and is relatively inflexible. But the relationships are creative and flexible and so very difficult to capture and enforce contractually.

The approach of the central firms we studied is to develop a sense of trust and reciprocity in the system. This trust and reciprocity is a dynamic concept and it can be very tight. The tightness is apparent in each party agreeing to perform its known obligations. This aspect has similarities to contracts in the sense that obligations are precisely understood. But Anglo-Saxon contracts are typically limited in the sense that partners are not expected to go beyond the contract. In contrast, in a network perspective, the behavior is prescribed for the unknown, each promising to work in a particular manner to resolve future challenges and difficulties as they arise. This means that each partner will promise to deliver what is expected, and that future challenges will also be addressed positively. If there are uncertainties and difficulties in the relationships, these will be resolved after the work is done. If one party goes beyond (in the positive sense) the traditional contract, others will remember and reciprocate at a later date.

Trust and reciprocity are complements, not substitutes, to other obligations. If partners do not subscribe to the trust system, they can hold the whole system hostage whenever they are asked to do something out of the ordinary, or even in the normal course of events. Such behavior will cause damage to all, and the system will break up. Only with trust can the system work in unison.

The Benetton franchising system is perhaps an extreme version of this trust system. In the continent of Europe, Benetton does not use legal contracts, rather it relies on the unwritten agreement. This, it claims, focuses everyone's attention on making the expectations clear. It also saves a great deal of time and expense. Many other strategic centers also rely on trust, but utilize contracts and formal controls as a complement. Central firms develop rules for settling disputes (for there will be disputes even in a trust system). The central firm also ensures that rewards are distributed in a manner which encourages partners to reinforce the positive circle. Benetton has encountered limits to its approach in the US, where the cultural emphasis on law and contracts has come into conflict with Benetton's strategy.

In sharp contrast are the other less successful systems we studied. There, trust was used on a very limited scale, since most organizations had difficulty in getting partners to deliver even that which was promised. Broken promises and failed expectations were common in the defense systems. Very low anticipated expectations of partner reciprocity were a common feature of the Scottish network and appliance sectors. Most organizations believed that anything crucial had to be undertaken in-house.

Trust is delicate, and it needs fostering and underpinning. One of the ways in which positive behavior is encouraged is to ensure that the profit-sharing relationships give substantial rewards to the partners. None of the central firms we studied seeks to be the most profitable firm in the system; they are happy for others to take the bulk of the profit. In Benetton, a retailer may find his or her capital investment paid back in three years. In Corning, some partners have seen exceptional returns. This seemingly altruistic behavior, however, does not mean that the rewards to the central firm are small.

Partner selection

The central firms we studied recognize that creating success and a long-term perspective must begin with the partner selection process. In building a network, partners must be selected with great care. Initially, the central firms followed a pattern of trial and error, but following successful identification of the key points in the selection process, they became more deliberate. The many new styles of operation and new ways of doing things are not easy to grasp, and they are quite difficult to codify – especially at the early stages of the selection process. As time passes, a partner profile emerges together with a selection procedure aimed at creating the correct conditions for the relationships. These relationships require coordination among all the partners, a common long-term perspective, an acceptance of mutual adaptation, and incremental innovation.

When we looked at the details of the selection procedure, there was a difference between those central firms that had a few large partners and those that had many small-scale partners. In the case of the network composed of a few, large firm alliances, the selection criterion is typically based on careful strategic considerations. There is the question of matching capabilities and resources, as well as considerations of competition.

However, most important are the organizational features based on a compatibility of management systems, decision processes, and perspectives – in short, a cultural fit.

The selection process must also be tempered by availability. Typically, there are few potential partners to fit the ideal picture. Perhaps it is for this reason that some Japanese and European firms start the process early on by deliberately spinning off some of their internal units to create potential partners. Typically these units will contain some of their best talents. However, these units will have a cultural affinity and a mutual understanding, which makes the partnership easier.

In the case of the large network composed of many small partners, the center acts as a developer of the community. Its managers must assume a different role. Apple called some of its managers 'evangelists' because they managed the relationships with 3,000 third-party developers. So that they could keep constant contact with them, they used images of the 'Figurehead' and the 'Guiding Light.'

Simultaneous structuring and strategizing

Of all the battles firms face, the most difficult is not the battle for position, nor is it even the battle between strong firms and weak firms following the same strategic approaches. Rather, it is the battle between firms adopting different strategies and different approaches to the market. In these battles, the winners are usually those who use fewer and different resources in novel combinations. The central firms we studied fit this category, for they have typically dominated their sectors by stretching and leveraging modest resources to great effect. In trying to understand these battles of stretch and leverage, others have stressed the technical achievements of central firms such as lean production, technical innovation, or flexible manufacturing and service delivery. To be sure, these advances are important and provide partial explanations for the success of Sun, Nintendo, Benetton,

Apple, and others. Equally important, if not more important, are new ideas on the nature of strategizing and structuring. Strategizing is a shared process between the strategic center and its partners; structuring of the relationships between the partners goes hand in hand and is seen as a key part of the strategy.

Strategy conception and implementation of ideas is shared between central firms and their webs of partners. Here they differ from most conventional organizations, which neither share their conceptions of strategy with other organizations nor insist that their partners share their ideas with them in a constructive dialogue. While all firms form partnerships with some of their suppliers and customers, these linkages rarely involve sharing ideas systematically. Subcontracting relationships are usually deeper and more complex, and many firms share their notions of strategy with their subcontractors, but the sharing is nearly always limited. Alliances demand even greater levels of commitment and interchange, and it is common for firms involved in alliances to exchange ideas about strategy and to look for strategic fit and even reshaping of strategic directions. Networks can be thought of as a higher stage of alliances, for in the strategic center there is a conscious desire to influence and shape the strategies of the partners, and to obtain from partners ideas and influences in return.

This conscious desire to share strategy is reflected in the way in which central firms conceive of the boundaries of their operations. Most organizations view their joint ventures and subcontractors as beyond the boundaries of their firm, and even those involved in alliances do not think of partners as an integral part of the organization. Even firms that are part of a franchise system (and thus have a more holistic perspective) do not view their relationships as a pattern of multilateral contracts. Going beyond the franchise view, central firms and their participants communicate multilaterally across the whole of the value chain. In the words of Johanson and Mattsson (1992), they have a 'network theory,' a perception of governing a whole system.

Strategizing and structuring in the central firms we studied reverses Chandler's famous dictum about structure following strategy. When partner's competencies are so crucial to the developments of the business idea of the strategic center, the winners are building strategy and structure simultaneously whereas the losers are signing agreements without changing their organizational forms to match them. When each partner's resources and competencies are so essential to the success of the enterprise, new forms must be designed. To achieve this, structuring must come earlier, alongside strategizing, and both require an interaction among partners to create a platform of flexibility and capability. This behavior challenges much of what is received managerial practice and avoids some of the traps that webs of alliances face.

Like the large integrated cohesive organization, networked firms are able to believe as a single competitive entity which can draw on considerable resources. However, the network form avoids many of the problems of large integrated firms, who typically find themselves paralyzed in the struggle between freedom and control. By focusing attention on the matters where commonality is important (e.g. product design) and by allowing each unit to have freedom elsewhere, cooperation is fostered, time and energy spent in monitoring is reduced, and resources are optimized. In this way, the networked organization succeeds in bridging the gap between centralization and decentralization. But cooperation can dull the edge of progress, and the organizations in our study have avoided this trap by fostering a highly competitive spirit.

Marketing and information sharing

The way in which information is collected and shared in the system reveals how structure and strategy go hand in hand. The gathering of information is a central activity in any organization. A strategic feature of a network of alliances is that the firms in the system are closely linked for the sharing of information.

Members of the network exchange not only hard data about best practice, but also ideas, feelings, and thoughts about customers, other suppliers, and general market trends.

The central firm structures the information system so that knowledge is funneled to the areas that need it the most. Members specializing in a particular function have access to others in the system performing similar tasks, and share their knowledge. This creates a level playing field within the network system. It also provides the opportunity for the members to focus and encourage the development of competitive advantage over rivals.

One of the basic premises in our network view is that new information leading to new ways of doing things emerges in a process of interaction with people and real-life situations. It follows that the 'information ability' of the firm depends critically on a scheme of interactions. The difficulty is that the generation of new information cannot be planned, but has to emerge. Thus, the task of the manager is one of designing a structure which provides an environment favorable for interactions to form, and for new information to be generated. Such a structure is a network.

Our study found, as have others, that the availability of large amounts of high quality information on many aspects of the business facilitated more rapid responses to market opportunities. Information condensed through the network is 'thicker' than that condensed through the brokerage market, but is 'freer' than in the hierarchy.

The need for a sophisticated system was clear when we contrasted the central firms we studied with other firms. In these other firms, we often found that critical information was guarded, not shared. As is so common among organizations, individual players are either afraid of being exploited or they have a desire to exploit the power they have through knowledge. Even in traditional franchise systems, information is typically passed to the center for filtering before being shared. In the large integrated firm, centralization also causes unnecessary filtering. With centralization, the process of collecting and distributing information can be cumbersome and slow. Moreover, power to manipulate the information can be accidentally or intentionally misused by a small central group.

Some of the 'control group' of firms we studied did share their information, with adverse consequences. For example, defense contractors, unable to create an effective strategic network, found the partners sometimes used the shared information to their own advantage, and then did not reciprocate. The knowledge was exploited by partners to create superior bargaining positions. Opportunities to foster collective interest were missed, and in extreme cases, partners used the information to bolster a rival alliance to the detriment of the original information provider.

Learning races

Whereas identifying opportunities for growth is facilitated by information sharing, responding to the opportunity is more difficult. Here we see some of the clearest evidence that structure and strategy go hand in hand. First and foremost, the central firms we studied reject the idea of doing everything themselves. Instead, they seek help from others to respond to the opportunities they face. When the knowledge and capabilities exist within the network, the role of the center is to orchestrate the response so that the whole system capitalizes on the opportunity.

It frequently happens that opportunities require an innovative response, and it is common for strategic centers to set up 'learning races.' Here, partners are given a common goal (say a new product or process development) with a prize for the first to achieve the target. The prize may be monetary, but more commonly it is the opportunity to lead off the exploitation of the new development. There is a catch, the development must be shared with others in the network. Learning races create a sense of competition and rivalry, but within an overall common purpose.

Nintendo uses carefully nurtured learning races with its partners to create high quality rapid innovation. Partners are typically restricted in the number of contributions they can make. In the case of software design, the limit may be three ideas a year. These restrictions force a striving for excellence, and the consequence is a formidable pace of progress.

Learning races can be destructive rather than constructive if the partners do not have the skills and resources. The strategic centers we studied get around these difficulties by sharing knowledge and in effect allowing the whole network to 'borrow' skills and competencies from each other.

It is important to understand the role of new members in the process of creating innovations. Many central firms follow the twin strategies of internal and external development. Internal development involves offering existing partners a possibility of sharing in the growth markets. External development involves the finding of new partners to fill the gaps and accelerate the possibilities. New partners typically fit the pattern set by existing partners. These newly found 'look alike' firms allow the strategic center to truncate development of the necessary capabilities, leveraging off earlier experiences developed by the existing partners. By making growth a race between old and new partners, speed is assured and scale effects exploited. Our strategic centers fostered positive rivalry rather than hostility by ensuring that both old and new partners share in the final gains. When pursuing rapid growth, the twin tracks of internal and external development can lessen tensions. Because they are independent, existing members can respond to the new demands as they wish. But, if they do not respond positively, the central firm can sign up new partners to fill the gaps. The stresses and strains of growth can thus be reduced for each of the members of the network.

Conclusions

The strategically minded central firms in our study view the boundaries of the organization differently because their conception and implementation of strategy are shared with a web of partners. This attitude contrasts sharply with most organizations, which view their joint ventures and subcontractors as existing beyond the boundaries of their firm. Even those involved in alliances typically do not think of partners as an integral part of their organization; they rarely share their conceptions of strategy and even fewer insist that their partners share their strategy with them in a constructive dialogue. In contrast, strategic centers communicate strategic ideas and intent multilaterally across the whole of the value chain. They have a network view of governing a whole system.

Strategic centers reach out to resolve classic organizational paradoxes. Many subcontracting and alliance relationships seemed to be mired in the inability to reconcile the advantages of the market with those of the hierarchy. Strategic centers are able to create a system that has the flexibility and freedom of the market coupled with long-term holistic relationships, ensuring the requisite strategic capabilities across the whole system. Another paradox exists between creativity and discipline. Most organizations oscillate between having ample creativity and little discipline, or too much discipline and not enough creativity. Through their unusual attitude to structuring and strategizing, strategic centers attain leading-edge technological and market developments while retaining rapid decision-making processes.

All organizations have much to learn from studying strategic centers and their unusual conception of the managerial task. Strategic centers have taken modest resources and won leadership positions in a wide variety of sectors. They have brought a new way of thinking about business and organizing. Much of what they do is at the cutting edge, and they are shining examples of how firms can change the rules of the game by creative and imaginative thinking.

READINGS ON THE INDUSTRY CONTEXT

Actually, the first reading here is not entirely representative of the industry dynamics perspective. In selecting a reading, we were faced by the problem that almost all contributions to the strategic management literature by researchers taking an industry dynamics perspective have been written in academic journals and do not make for easy reading. There are many excellent works, but none that are accessible enough to act as an opening reading in this debate. Few strategists like to hear that they have little influence over their industry and that they should play by the rules: this message is hardly inspiring, if not outright frustrating, and it definitely does not sell books, which might partially explain why few proponents of the industry dynamics perspective have written for an audience of practicing managers.

As a compromise, therefore, the debate will be started off by an author who is strongly affiliated with the industry dynamics perspective, but who is not fully in their camp. This author is Michael Porter, and the article selected is appropriately entitled 'Industry Evolution'. In this reading, taken from his classic book *Competitive Strategy*, Porter expands on his basic premises, as discussed in Reading 5.1. In his view, a company's profitability is heavily influenced by the structure of the industry in which it competes. Some industries have a poor structure, making it difficult for even the best firms to make a profit. Other industries, however, have a more advantageous structure, making it much easier to show a good performance. In Porter's opinion, how the game of competition is played in each industry is largely determined by the underlying economics. The industry structure presents the strict rules to which companies must comply. As an industry's structure evolves, Porter sees two processes at work that determine which companies will survive and profit over the longer term. On the one hand, Porter recognizes 'natural selection' processes, whereby only the fittest survive and firms that are not suited to the new environment become extinct. For instance, Porter argues that the selection of fit companies is particularly strong as industries move into a mature phase of development: 'when growth levels off in an industry . . . there is a period of turmoil as intensified rivalry weeds out the weaker firms'. On the other hand, Porter also believes that companies can adapt themselves to changes in the industry's structure, although he emphasizes that they first must understand the drivers of change. So far, Porter's arguments fully coincide with the industry dynamics perspective. However, besides compliance to the industry context, Porter mentions the possibility of 'co-makership' as well. Or, in his own terms, he believes that firms can have some influence on the evolution of the industry's structure. Thus, each company does have a certain degree of strategic freedom to determine its own fate, but ultimately the autonomous development of the industry structure is crucially important to the survival and profitability of the company.

To open the debate on behalf of the industry leadership perspective, a reading by Charles Baden-Fuller and John Stopford has been selected, with the telling title 'The Firm Matters, Not the Industry'. In a direct reference to Porter, they state that their view 'contrasts sharply with the popular, but misguided, school of thought that believes that the fortune of a business is closely tied to its industry'. They point out that only a fraction of the differences in profitability between companies can be attributed to industry characteristics, while more than half of the profit variations are due to the choice of strategy. Their conclusion is that the given industry circumstances are largely unimportant – it's how a firm plays the game that matters. In their opinion, high profitability is not the consequence of complying with some preset rules, but the result of acting creatively and imaginatively. For instance, they challenge the widely held belief that high market share is important for profitability. Nor do they agree that the competitive game dictates generic strategies, as Porter suggests. They do not even believe that there is such a thing as a mature industry. In their view, the industry context does not present any fixed rules that cannot be avoided or changed by innovative companies. Their advice, therefore, is to remain imaginative and to adopt approaches that counter traditional solutions.

<table>
<tr><td>READING
8.1</td><td></td></tr>
</table>

Industry evolution

By Michael Porter[1]

Structural analysis gives us a framework for understanding the competitive forces operating in an industry that are crucial to developing competitive strategy. It is clear, however, that industries' structures change, often in fundamental ways. Entry barriers and concentration have gone up significantly in the US brewing industry, for example, and the threat of substitutes has risen to put a severe squeeze on acetylene producers.

Industry evolution takes on critical importance for formulation of strategy. It can increase or decrease the basic attractiveness of an industry as an investment opportunity, and it often requires the firm to make strategic adjustments. Understanding the process of industry evolution and being able to predict change are important because the cost of reacting strategically usually increases as the need for change becomes more obvious and the benefit from the best strategy is the highest for the first firm to select it. For example, in the early post-war farm equipment business, structural change elevated the importance of a strong exclusive dealer network backed by company support and credit. The firms that recognized this change first had their pick of dealers to choose from.

This article will present analytical tools for predicting the evolutionary process in an industry and understanding its significance for the formulation of competitive strategy.

Basic concepts in industry evolution

The starting point for analyzing industry evolution is the framework of structural analysis (see Chapter 5). Industry changes will carry strategic significance if they promise to affect the underlying sources of the five competitive forces; otherwise changes are important only in a tactical sense. The simplest approach to analyzing evolution is to ask the following question: Are there any changes occurring in the industry that will affect each element of structure? For example, do any of the industry trends imply an increase or decrease in mobility barriers? An increase or decrease in the relative power of buyers or suppliers? If this question is asked in a disciplined way for each competitive force and the economic causes underlying it, a profile of the significant issues in the evolution of an industry will result.

Although this industry-specific approach is the place to start, it may not be sufficient, because it is not always clear what industry changes are occurring currently, much less which changes might occur in the future. Given the importance of being able to predict evolution, it is desirable to have some analytical techniques that will aid in anticipating the pattern of industry changes we might expect to occur.

The product life cycle

The grandfather of concepts for predicting the probable course of industry evolution is the familiar product life cycle. The hypothesis is that an industry passes through a number of phases or stages – introduction, growth, maturity, and decline – illustrated in Figure 8.1.1. These stages are defined by inflection points in the rate of growth of industry sales. Industry growth follows an S-shaped curve because of the process of innovation and diffusion of a new product. The flat introductory phase of industry growth reflects the difficulty of overcoming buyer inertia and stimulating trials of the new product. Rapid growth occurs as many buyers rush into the market once the product has proven itself successful. Penetration of the product's potential buyers is eventually reached, causing the rapid growth to stop and to level off to the underlying rate of growth of the relevant buyer group. Finally, growth will eventually taper off as new substitute products appear.

As the industry goes through its life cycle, the nature of competition will shift. I have summarized in Table 8.1.1 the most common predictions about how an industry will change over the life cycle and how this should affect strategy.

The product life cycle has attracted some legitimate criticism:

- The duration of the stages varies widely from industry to industry, and it is often not clear what stage of the life cycle an industry is in. This problem diminishes the usefulness of the concept as a planning tool.

- Industry growth does not always go through the S-shaped pattern at all. Sometimes industries skip maturity, passing straight from growth to decline. Sometimes industry growth revitalizes after a period of decline, as has occurred in the motorcycle and bicycle industries and recently in the radio broadcasting industry. Some industries seem to skip the slow takeoff of the introductory phase altogether.

- Companies can *affect* the shape of the growth curve through product innovation and repositioning, extending it in a variety of ways. If a company takes the life cycle as given, it becomes an undesirable self-fulfilling prophesy.

- The nature of competition associated with each stage of the life cycle is *different* for different industries. For example, some industries start out highly concentrated

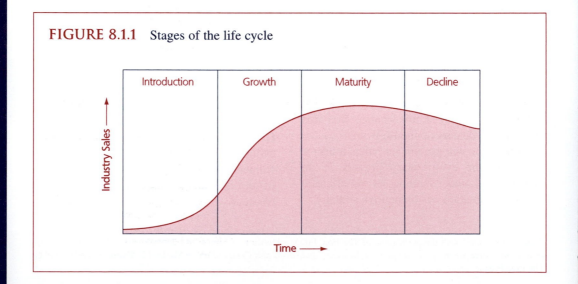

FIGURE 8.1.1   Stages of the life cycle

TABLE 8.1.1 Predictions of product life cycle theories about strategy, competition, and performance

	Introduction	Growth	Maturity	Decline
Buyers and buyer behavior	▪ High-income purchaser ▪ Buyer inertia ▪ Buyers must be convinced to try the product	▪ Widening buyer group ▪ Consumer will accept uneven quality	▪ Mass market ▪ Saturation ▪ Repeat buying ▪ Choosing among brands is the rule	▪ Customers are sophisticated buyers of the product
Products and product change	▪ Poor quality ▪ Product design and development key ▪ Many different product variations; no standards ▪ Frequent design changes ▪ Basic product designs	▪ Products have technical and performance differentiation ▪ Reliability key for complex products ▪ Competitive product improvements ▪ Good quality	▪ Superior quality ▪ Less product differentiation ▪ Standardization ▪ Less rapid product changes – more minor annual model changes ▪ Trade-ins become significant	▪ Little product differentiation ▪ Spotty product quality
Marketing	▪ Very high advertising/sales ▪ Creaming price strategy ▪ High marketing costs	▪ High advertising, but lower percent of sales than introductory ▪ Most promotion of ethical drugs ▪ Advertising and distribution key for nontechnical products	▪ Market segmentation ▪ Efforts to extend life cycle ▪ Broaden line ▪ Service and deals more prevalent ▪ Packaging important ▪ Advertising competition ▪ Lower advertising/sales	▪ Low advertising/sales and other marketing
Manufacturing and distribution	▪ Overcapacity ▪ Short production runs ▪ High skilled-labor content ▪ High production costs ▪ Specialized channels	▪ Undercapacity ▪ Shift toward mass production ▪ Scramble for distribution ▪ Mass channels	▪ Some overcapacity ▪ Optimum capacity ▪ Increasing stability of manufacturing process ▪ Lower labor skills ▪ Long production runs with stable techniques ▪ Distribution channels pare down their lines to improve their margins ▪ High physical distribution costs due to broad lines ▪ Mass channels	▪ Substantial overcapacity ▪ Mass production ▪ Specialty channels
R&D	▪ Changing production techniques			
Foreign trade	▪ Some exports	▪ Significant exports ▪ Few imports	▪ Falling exports ▪ Significant imports	▪ No exports ▪ Significant imports
Overall strategy	▪ Best period to increase market share ▪ R&D, engineering are key functions	▪ Practical to change price or quality image ▪ Marketing the key function	▪ Bad time to increase market share, particularly if low-share company ▪ Having competitive costs becomes key ▪ Bad time to change price image or quality image ▪ 'Marketing effectiveness' key	▪ Cost control key

TABLE 8.1.1   *continued*

	Introduction	Growth	Maturity	Decline
Competition	▪ Few companies	▪ Entry ▪ Many competitors ▪ Lots of mergers and casualties	▪ Price competition ▪ Shakeout ▪ Increase in private brands	▪ Exits ▪ Fewer competitors
Risk	▪ High risk	▪ Risks can be taken here because growth covers them up	▪ Cyclicality sets in	
Margins and profits	▪ High prices and margins ▪ Low profits ▪ Price elasticity to individual seller not as great as in maturity	▪ High profits ▪ Highest profits ▪ Fairly high prices ▪ Lower prices than introductory phase ▪ Recession resistant ▪ High P/Es ▪ Good acquisition climate	▪ Falling prices ▪ Lower profits ▪ Lower margins ▪ Lower dealer margins ▪ Increased stability of market shares and price structure ▪ Poor acquisition climate – tough to sell companies ▪ Lowest prices and margins	▪ Low prices and margins ▪ Falling prices ▪ Prices might rise in late decline

and stay that way. Others, like bank cash dispensers, are concentrated for a significant period and then become less so. Still others begin highly fragmented; of these some consolidate (automobiles) and some do not (electronic component distribution). The same divergent patterns apply to advertising, research and development (R&D) expenditures, degree of price competition, and most other industry characteristics. Divergent patterns such as these call into serious question the strategic implications ascribed to the life cycle.

The real problem with the product life cycle as a predictor of industry evolution is that it attempts to describe *one* pattern of evolution that will invariably occur. And except for the industry growth rate, there is little or no underlying rationale for why the competitive changes associated with the life cycle will happen. Since actual industry evolution takes so many different paths, the life cycle pattern does not always hold, even if it is a common or even the most common pattern of evolution. Nothing in the concept allows us to predict when it will hold and when it will not.

A framework for forecasting evolution

Instead of attempting to describe industry evolution, it will prove more fruitful to look underneath the process to see what really drives it. Like any evolution, industries evolve because some forces are in motion that create incentives or pressures for change. These can be called *evolutionary processes*.

Every industry begins with an *initial structure* – the entry barriers, buyer and supplier power, and so on that exist when the industry comes into existence. This structure is usually (though not always) a far cry from the configuration the industry will take later in its development. The initial structure results from a combination of underlying economic and technical characteristics of the industry, the initial constraints of small industry size, and the skills and resources of the companies that are early entrants. For example, even an industry like automobiles with enormous possibilities for economies of scale started out with labor-intensive, job-shop production operations because of the small volumes of cars produced during the early years.

The evolutionary processes work to push the industry toward its *potential structure*, which is rarely known completely as an industry evolves. Embedded in the underlying technology, product characteristics, and nature of present and potential buyers, however, there is a range of structures the industry might possibly achieve, depending on the direction and success of research and development, marketing innovations, and the like.

It is important to realize that instrumental in much industry evolution are the investment decisions by both existing firms in the industry and new entrants. In response to pressures or incentives created by the evolutionary process, firms invest to take advantage of possibilities for new marketing approaches, new manufacturing facilities, and the like, which shift entry barriers, alter relative power against suppliers and buyers, and so on. The luck, skills, resources, and orientation of firms in the industry can shape the evolutionary path the industry will actually take. Despite potential for structural change, an industry may not actually change because no firm happens to discover a feasible new marketing approach; or potential scale economies may go unrealized because no firm possesses the financial resources to construct a fully integrated facility or simply because no firm is inclined to think about costs. Because innovation, technological developments, and the identities (and resources) of the particular firms either in the industry or considering entry into it are so important to evolution, industry evolution will not only be hard to forecast with certainty but also an industry can potentially evolve in a variety of ways at a variety of different speeds, depending on the luck of the draw.

Evolutionary processes

Although initial structure, structural potential, and particular firms' investment decisions will be industry-specific, we can generalize about what the important evolutionary processes are. There are some predictable (and interacting) dynamic processes that occur in every industry in one form or another, though their speed and direction will differ from industry to industry:

- long-run changes in growth;
- changes in buyer segments served;
- buyer's learning;
- reduction of uncertainty;
- diffusion of proprietary knowledge;
- accumulation of experience;
- expansion (or contraction) in scale;
- changes in input and currency costs;
- product innovation;
- marketing innovation;
- process innovation;
- structural change in adjacent industries;
- government policy change;
- entries and exits.

Key relationships in industry evolution

In the context of this analysis, *how* do industries change? They do not change in a piecemeal fashion, because an industry is an *interrelated system*. Change in one element of an industry's structure tends to trigger changes in other areas. For example, an innovation in marketing might develop a new buyer segment, but serving this new segment may trigger changes in manufacturing methods, thereby increasing economies of scale. The firm reaping these economies first will also be in a position to start backward integration, which will affect power with suppliers – and so on. One industry change, therefore, often sets off a chain reaction leading to many other changes.

It should be clear from the discussion here that whereas industry evolution is always occurring in nearly every business and requires a strategic response, there is no one way in which industries evolve. Any single model for evolution such as the product life cycle should therefore be rejected. However, there are some particularly important relationships in the evolutionary process that I will examine here.

Will the industry consolidate?

It seems to be an accepted fact that industries tend to consolidate over time, but as a general statement, it simply is not true. In a broad sample of 151 four-digit US manufacturing industries in the 1963–72 time period, for example, 69 increased in four-firm concentration more than two percentage points, whereas 52 decreased more than two percentage points in the same period. The question of whether consolidation will occur in an industry exposes perhaps the most important interrelationships among elements of industry structure – those involving competitive rivalry, mobility barriers, and exit barriers.

Industry concentration and mobility barriers move together

If mobility barriers are high or especially if they increase, concentration almost always increases. For example, concentration has increased in the US wine industry. In the standard-quality segment of the market, which represents much of the volume, the strategic changes (high advertising, national distribution, rapid brand innovation, and so on) have greatly increased barriers to mobility. As a result, the larger firms have gotten further ahead of smaller ones, and few new firms have entered to challenge them.

No concentration takes place if mobility barriers are low or falling

Where barriers are low, unsuccessful firms that exit will be replaced by new firms. If a wave of exit has occurred because of an economic downturn or some other general adversity, there may be a temporary increase in industry concentration. But at the first signs that profits and sales in the industry are picking up, new entrants will appear. Thus a shake-out when an industry reaches maturity does not necessarily imply long-run consolidation.

Exit barriers deter consolidation

Exit barriers keep companies operating in an industry even though they are earning subnormal returns on investment. Even in an industry with relatively high mobility barriers, the leading firms cannot count on reaping the benefits of consolidation if high exit barriers hold unsuccessful firms in the market.

Long-run profit potential depends on future structure

In the period of very rapid growth early in the life of an industry (especially after initial product acceptance has been achieved), profit levels are usually high. For example, growth in sales of skiing equipment was in excess of 20 percent per year in the late 1960s, and nearly all firms in the industry enjoyed strong financial results. When growth levels off in an industry, however, there is a period of turmoil as intensified rivalry weeds out the weaker firms. All firms in the industry may suffer financially during this adjustment period. Whether or not the remaining firms will enjoy above-average profitability will depend on the level of mobility barriers, as well as the other structural features of the industry. If mobility barriers are high or have increased as the industry has matured, the remaining firms in the industry may enjoy healthy financial results even in the new era of slower growth. If mobility barriers are low, however, slower growth probably means the end of above-average profits for the industry. Thus mature industries may or may not be as profitable as they were in their developmental period.

Changes in industry boundaries

Structural change in an industry is often accompanied by changes in industry boundaries. Industry evolution has a strong tendency to shift these boundaries. Innovations in the industry or those involving substitutes may effectively enlarge the industry by placing more firms into direct competition. Reduction in transportation cost relative to timber cost, for example, has made timber supply a world market rather than one restricted to continents. Innovations increasing the reliability and lowering the cost of electronic surveillance devices have put them into effective competition with security guard services. Structural changes making it easier for suppliers to integrate forward into the industry may well mean that suppliers effectively become competitors. Or buyers purchasing private label goods in large quantities and dictating product design criteria may become effective competitors in the manufacturing industry. Part of the analysis of the strategic significance of industry evolution is clearly an analysis of how industry boundaries may be affected.

Firms can influence industry structure

Industry structural change can be influenced by firms' strategic behavior. If it understands the significance of structural change for its position, the firm can seek to influence industry change in ways favorable to it, either through the way it reacts to strategic changes of competitors or in the strategic changes it initiates.

Another way a company can influence structural change is to be very sensitive to external forces that can cause the industry to evolve. With a head start, it is often possible to direct such forces in ways appropriate to the firm's position. For example, the specific form of regulatory changes can be influenced; the diffusion of innovations coming from outside the industry can be altered by the form that licensing or other agreements with innovating firms take; positive action can be initiated to improve the cost or supply of complementary products through providing direct assistance and help in forming trade associations or in stating their case to the government; and so on for the other important forces causing structural change. Industry evolution should not be greeted as a fait accompli to be reacted to, but as an opportunity.

READING 8.2

The firm matters, not the industry

READING

8.2

By Charles Baden-Fuller and John Stopford[1]

Introduction

It is the firm that matters, not the industry. Successful businesses ride the waves of industry misfortunes; less successful businesses are sunk by them. This view contrasts sharply with the popular, but misguided, school of thought that believes that the fortune of a business is closely tied to its industry. Those who adhere to this view believe that

[1]Source: This article has been adapted from Chapter 2 of *Rejuvinating the Mature Business*, by Charles Baden-Fuller and John Stopford, published by Routledge in 1992. Used with permission.

some industries are intrinsically more attractive for investment than others. They (wrongly) believe that if a business is in a profitable industry, then its profits will be greater than if the business is in an unprofitable industry.

The role of the industry in determining profitability

Old views can be summarized as follows:

- Some industries are intrinsically more profitable than others.
- In mature environments it is difficult to sustain high profits.
- It is environmental factors that determine whether an industry is successful, not the firms in the industry.

New views can be summarized as follows:

- There is little difference in the profitability of one industry versus another.
- There is no such thing as a mature industry, only mature firms; industries inhabited by mature firms often present great opportunities for the innovative.
- Profitable industries are those populated by imaginative and profitable firms; unprofitable industries have unusually large numbers of uncreative firms.

This notion that there are 'good' and 'bad' industries is a theme that has permeated many strategy books. As one famous strategy writer (Porter, 1980) put it:

The state of competition in an industry depends on five basic competitive forces. . . . The collective strength of these forces determines the ultimate profit potential in the industry, where profit potential is measured in terms of long-run return on invested capital. . . . The forces range from intense in industries like tires, paper and steel – where no firm earns spectacular returns – to relatively mild like oil-field equipment and services, cosmetics and toiletries – where high returns are quite common.

Unfortunately, the writer overstates his case, for the evidence does not easily support his claim. Choosing good industries may be a foolish strategy; choosing good firms is far more sensible. As noted in Table 8.2.1, recent statistical evidence does not support the view that the choice of industry is important. At best only 10 per cent of the differences in profitability between one business unit and another can be related to their choice of industry. By implication, nearly 90 per cent of profitability variations are not explained by the choice of industry, and *at least half appear to be attributable to the choice of strategy.* Put simply, the correct choice of strategy appears to be at least five times more important than the correct choice of industry.

TABLE 8.2.1   The role of industry factors determining firm performance

Percentage of business units' profitability explained by	
Choice of industry	8.3 percent
Choice of strategy	46.4 percent
Parent company	0.8 percent
Not explained – random	44.5 percent

Adapted from Rumelt (1991).

Mature industries offer good prospects for success

It is often stated that market opportunities are created rather than found. Thus market research would never have predicted the large potential of xerography, laptop computers, or the pocket cassette recorder. Leaps of faith may be required. By analogy, low-growth mature markets or troubled industries are arguably ones that may offer greater chances of rewards than ones that appear to be glamorous and profitable. Our reasoning is simple. In general, profitable industries are more profitable because they are populated by more imaginative and more creative businesses. These businesses create an environment that attracts customers, grows the industry revenues, and makes the industry attractive. But creative and innovative businesses are also more fiercely competitive. To win in such environments may be difficult, as the pace of change may be rapid and the minimum standards high. In contrast, many less profitable industries are populated by sleepy, uncreative businesses that fail to innovate. In such environments, the potential for success by a creative newcomer is greater. The demands of competition may be less exacting and the potential for attracting customers is better.

We do not wish to overstate our case, but rather to force the reader to focus attention away from the mentality of labeling and pre-judging opportunities based only on industry profitability. For example, outsiders often point to low-growth industries and suggest that the opportunities are less than those in high-growth industries. Yet the difference in growth rates may be dependent on the ability of businesses in these industries to be creative and innovative. Until Honda came, the motorcycle market was in steady decline. By their innovations – of new bicycles with attractive features sold at reasonable prices – the market was once again revived. Thus we suggest that the growth rate of the industry is a reflection of the kinds of businesses in the industry, not the intrinsic nature of the environment.

Large market share is the reward, not the cause of success

We believe that many managers are mistaken in the value they ascribe to market share. A large share of the market is often the symptom of success, but it is not always its cause. Banc One and Cook achieved significant positions in their industries because they were successful. For these organizations the sequence of events was success followed by growth, which was then cemented into greater success. Banc One has been doing things differently from many of its competitors for many years. It emphasized operational efficiency and it quickly captured a significant position as a low cost, high quality data processor for other banks and financial service companies. It also emphasized service, in particular service to retail and commercial customers, which contrasted with the approach of many other banks that sought to compete solely on price or failed to appreciate what the customer really wanted. Mergers and growth have been an important part of Banc One's strategy, but in every case, the merged organizations have been changed to fit the philosophy of Banc One.

Market share and profitability

Old views can be summarized as follows:

- Large market share brings lower costs and higher prices and so yields greater profits.
- Small-share firms cannot challenge leaders.

New views can be summarized as follows:

- Large market share is the reward for efficiency and effectiveness.
- If they do things better, small-share firms can challenge the leaders.

For creative organizations we see an upward spiral (Figure 8.2.1), and for organizations that are not creative, we see the cycles shown in Figure 8.2.2.

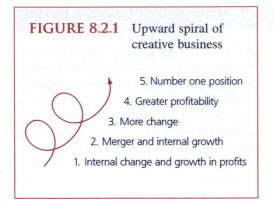

FIGURE 8.2.1   Upward spiral of creative business

5. Number one position

4. Greater profitability

3. More change

2. Merger and internal growth

1. Internal change and growth in profits

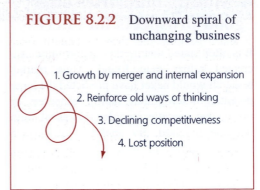

FIGURE 8.2.2   Downward spiral of unchanging business

1. Growth by merger and internal expansion

2. Reinforce old ways of thinking

3. Declining competitiveness

4. Lost position

Our assertions run counter to much of what has been written in conventional books on strategy, and what is believed in many corporate boardrooms (see Exhibit 8.1.1). There is a common but incorrect belief among managers that being number one or number two in an industry gives the business unique advantages and that these are greatest in industries characterized by slow growth. With a large market share, it is often argued, the business can achieve lower costs and charge higher prices than its rivals. In slow-growth markets, it is argued, this may prove to be a decisive factor. This thinking ignores the importance of innovation, and believes that it is the size of the business that confers the advantage, not the new ways of doing things.

These false beliefs are widespread. They appear in many guises. At one extreme there are chief executives who say, 'We are only interested in industries where we hold a number one or number two position.' Such statements, if unaccompanied by an empha-sis on innovation, will give out the wrong signal that high share will lead to success. At a more mundane level, managers are encouraged to write in their plans, 'We should dominate the industry and seek success by capturing a number one position.' Again, such statements are dangerous where the writer and reader believe that share by itself will bring success.

Growing market share is not the panacea for an organization's ills, not even in mature slow-growing markets. The belief that gaining market share will lead to greater profitability comes from confusing cause and effect. Many successful businesses do have a large market share, but the causality is usually from success to share, not the other way. Successful businesses often (but not always) grow because they have discovered an overwhelming source of competitive advantage, such as quality at low cost. Such advantages can be used to displace the market share of even the most entrenched incumbents.

EXHIBIT 8.1.1 MARKET SHARE AND PROFITABILITY

There is a lively debate on the importance of market share in *explaining* business unit profitability. By *explaining* we do not mean *causing*. High market share could be the consequence of profitability, or the cause of both.

Those who advocate that large market share *leads* to greater profits point to the importance of several causal factors. First, large market share gives rise to the need to deliver large volumes of the service or good. These increased volumes in turn give rise to opportunities for costs savings by exploiting scale economies in production, service delivery, logistics, and marketing. Second, large market

EXHIBIT 8.1.1 MARKET SHARE AND PROFITABILITY

share permits the firm to benefit from experience or learning effects that also lower costs. Third, larger market share may allow the firm to charge higher prices. A product or service with a large share may seem intrinsically less risky to consumers. Finally, with a large market share, new entrants may be discouraged because they perceive the incumbent to have a substantial commitment to the industry through perceived or actual sunk costs.

In contrast, there are several who argue that these supposed benefits of large share are overrated. It is innovation that matters, innovators that realize new ways of competing can achieve their advantages by new approaches that do not necessarily need large market shares. However, those with new approaches may win market share, in which case large share is a reward for success. This Darwinian view of the market suggests that the competitive process is one where success goes to the firm that successfully innovates.

The strongest proponents of the importance of market share as a cause of success are Buzzell and Gale. Using the PIMS database drawn from a very large sample of business units across a range of industries, they asserted the existence of a strong relationship between relative market share and profitability. The figures below

(Buzzell and Gale, 1987) suggest that a firm that has first rank in an industry will be more than twice as profitable as one of fourth rank.

Industry rank (by market share)	1	2	3	4	≤5
Pretax profits/ sales (per cent)	12.7	9.1	7.1	5.5	4.5

However, these figures are misleading, for in a very large proportion of the industries studied, the firm with largest rank was *not* the most profitable. Often the picture is quite different; indeed according to the statistics published in Buzzell and Gale (1987) only 4 percent of the differences in profitability of one business unit versus another could be explained by differences in market share. Schmalensee (1985), in his extensive study of more than 400 firms in US manufacturing, found that less than 2 percent of the variations in profitability between one business and another could be explained by differences in market share. Market share effects appear to be relatively unimportant across a wide sample of industries. Of course, market share may be important in specific instances, but this only goes to reinforce our basic point that the critical success is dependent on getting the right strategy.

Competing recipes

The crucial battles amongst firms in an industry are often centered around differing approaches to the market. Even in the so-called mature industries, where incumbent strategies have evolved and been honed over long time periods, it is new ideas that displace the existing leaders. Traditional wisdom has overstated the power of the generic approach

(see Exhibit 8.2.2) and underplayed the role of innovation. Banc One established its premier position by rejecting conventional orthodoxy and emphasizing aspects hitherto neglected by industry leaders. Cook won in the steel castings industry by emphasizing quality and service to the customer. Hotpoint emphasized variety and quality in its approach to both the retailers and the final consumers. No single approach works well in

EXHIBIT 8.2.2   THE FALLACY OF THE GENERIC STRATEGY

It has been fashionable to suggest that there are a few *stable generic strategies* that offer fundamental choices to the organization. Typically these are described as a choice between a *low cost strategy* or a *differentiated strategy*. The low cost strategy involves the sacrifice of something – speed, variety, fashion, or even quality – in order to keep costs low, the lowest in the industry. In contrast, the high cost, differentiated strategy involves the focus on the very factors ignored by the others. The advocates of generic strategy make an (implicit or explicit) assertion: that the opposites cannot be reconciled. According to the generic strategists, it is not possible to be both low cost and high quality, or low cost and fashionable, or low cost and speedy. Trying to reconcile the opposites means being *stuck in the middle*. This, it is suggested, is the worst of both worlds.

Generic strategies are a fallacy. The best firms are striving all the time to reconcile the opposites. Cook did find a way to be both high quality and low cost, so, too, many of the other creative firms we studied. At any point in time, there are some combinations that have not yet been resolved, but firms strive to resolve them. Until McDonald's, the idea of consistency and low price for fast food had not been achieved on a large scale. McDonald's solved that problem. Benetton was but one of many firms that resolved the dilemma of fashion at low cost. Given the enormous rewards that accrue to those who can resolve the dilemmas of the opposites, it is not surprising that there are no *lasting or enduring generic strategies*.

all industries, but rather a multiple set of approaches. Here we emphasize the more fundamental point: the real competitive battles are fought out between firms with a diversity of approaches to the market.

The dynamics of competition in traditional industries

The old view is:

- Competition is based on firms following well-defined traditional (or generic) approaches to the market.

The new view is:

- The real battles are fought among firms taking different approaches, especially those that counter yesterday's ideas.

Conclusions

Organizations that have become mature and suffer from poor performance typically view themselves as prisoners of their environment. Often their managers blame everyone but themselves for their poor performance. Labelling their environment as mature or hostile, they identify excess capacity, unfair competition, adverse exchange rates, absence of demand, and a host of other factors to explain why they are doing badly. Alas, too often these external factors are not really the causes of their demise but rather the symptoms of their failure. This conclusion is not so new; others have made the point before, yet their words appear to have been forgotten. Hall (1980) in an article in the *Harvard Business Review* noted:

Even a cursory analysis of the leading companies in the eight basic industries leads to an important observation: survival and prosperity are possible even when the business environment turns hostile and industry trends change from favourable to unfavourable. In this regard, the casual advice frequently offered to competitors in basic industries – that is diversify, dissolve or be prepared for below average returns – seems oversimplified and even erroneous.

Of course all industries experience the roller coaster of economic upswings and down-swings, but there are organizations that appear to ride the waves and others that appear to be submerged by them.

Those who are submerged all too often clutch at the wrong things in trying to escape their drowning. Seeking simple solutions such as industry recipes, the value of market share, or the need to amass large resources, they fail to appreciate the extent to which the rules of the game in an industry are always changing.

READINGS ON THE ORGANIZATIONAL CONTEXT

To open the debate on behalf of the organizational leadership perspective, a reading has been selected entitled 'Defining Leadership and Explicating the Process', which is by one of the 'god-fathers' of organizational theory, Richard Cyert. In this article, Cyert starts by summarizing the functions of a leader: determining the organizational structure, selecting managers, setting strategic objectives, controlling internal and external information flows, maintaining morale and making important decisions. But while some authors who take an organizational leadership perspective tend to conjure up an image of the leader as an octopus, with many long arms performing all of these tasks at the same time, Cyert has a more human, two-armed individual in mind. His view of the leader is not the control freak, who wants to run the organization single-handedly, but a person who can 'heavily influence the process of determining the goals of the organization', and then can 'have the participants in the organization behave in the ways that the leader believes are desirable'. This definition of leadership has two important ingredients. First, Cyert argues that leaders need to take the initiative in determining a vision and organizational goals, although they do this in interaction with other organizational members. Second, Cyert argues that leaders need to focus on modifying people's behaviors. To get people to move in the desired direction, he states that it is not so important what a leader decides or tells people to do. Rather, an effective leader 'controls the allocation of the attention focus of the participants in the organization . . . so that their attention is allocated to the areas that the leader considers important'. In this way, Cyert believes, organizational members will voluntarily align their behaviors with where the leader wants to go. He admits that 'this conception of leadership might strike some as making the leader a manipulative person', but feels that if leaders have a genuine belief in what they are doing and have an honest dedication to the people in the organization, exerting this type of leadership is justified. Although Cyert is well aware that organizations are complex systems of interacting human beings, his unquestioned supposition throughout the reading is that leadership is *possible* and *necessary*. As many writers taking an organizational leadership perspective, the demand for top management control is an implicit assumption – the main issue discussed is how to get power and how to exert control. Cyert's preference is for more indirect control, implicitly leaving some room for bottom-up self-organization.

As the reading to represent the organizational dynamics perspective, an article by Ralph Stacey has been selected, entitled 'Strategy as Order Emerging from Chaos'. Stacey argues that top managers cannot, and should not even try, to control the organization and its strategy. In his view, the organizational dynamics involved in strategy formation, learning and change are too complex to simply be controlled by managers. He states that 'sometimes the best thing a manager can do is to let go and allow things to happen'. The resulting chaos, he argues, does not mean that the organization will be a mess – a lack of control, he assures, does not mean that the organization will be adrift. His reasoning is that non-linear feedback systems, such as organizations, have a self-organizing ability, which 'can produce controlled behavior, even though no one is in control'. In his view, real strategic change requires the chaos of contention and conflict to destroy old recipes and to encourage the quest for new solutions. The 'self-organizing processes of political interaction and complex learning' ensure that chaos does not result in disintegration. Hence, in Stacey's opinion, it is management's task to help create a situation of bounded instability in which strategy can emerge. Managers do have a role in organizations, but it can hardly be called leadership – 'leaders' must direct their efforts at influencing the organizational context in such a way that the right conditions prevail for self-organization to take place. 'Leaders' are largely facilitators, making it possible for new and unexpected strategies to develop spontaneously.

READING

9.1

Defining leadership and explicating the process

Richard M. Cyert[1]

It is true that organizations, whether for-profit or not-for-profit, are in need of leadership. Most people in leadership positions in organizations tend to be managers rather than leaders. They administer, allocate resources, resolve conflicts, and go home at night convinced that they have done a good day's work. They may have, but they have not provided the organization with the critical ingredient that every organization needs – leadership (Zalesnik, 1977; Bavelas, 1964).

It is possible to generalize three broad functions that a leader performs. I specify these functions as organizational, interpersonal, and decisional. The organizational function involves the development of the organizational structure and the selection of people to manage the various segments of an organization. It involves the determination of the goal structure and the control of the internal and external information flows. This func-tion requires the leader to make certain that the participants in the organization and the relevant groups external to the organization are knowledgeable about the organization.

The interpersonal function involves the maintenance of morale in the organization. It reflects the degree of concern about the humanness of the organization. It requires the leader to pay attention to individual concerns.

The decision function involves the making of decisions that must be made in order for the organization to progress toward the achievement of its goals. This is the function that has traditionally been associated with leadership.

Nature of leadership

Although there is little agreement on the def-inition of leadership, most students of leader-

[1] Source: This article was adapted from 'Defining Leadership and Explicating the Process', R.M. Cyert in *Non-Profit Management & Leadership*, Vol. 1, No. 1: © 1990 Jossey-Bass Inc. Publishers. This material is used by permission of John Wiley & Sons, Inc.

ship would agree that the three functions just described are clearly a part of the definition. In a broad sense, the leader is attempting to have the participants in the organization behave in the ways that the leader believes are desirable. A major step in performing the organizational function is to define desirable behavior.

Desirability is determined by the goals of the organization. The leader should heavily influence the process of determining the goals of the organization. The determination of a goal structure for an organization is the result of a series of interactions among the participants and between the participants and the leader. The goal structure represents the vision of the leader and of the organization's other members. Projecting a vision for the organization is another characteristic that is commonly associated with leadership.

The vision embedded in the goal structure is essentially a map that is used as a guide for the direction of the organization. Clearly, the map is more detailed as one's view shifts to sub-units within the organization. At the top leadership position, a number of broad principles are specified to guide the overall construction of the vision.

These principles relate to the process by which the organization's vision can be constantly modified and reshaped. The specification of strategic principles and of the process by which the vision is modified is another characteristic of leadership. The leader is the helmsman, and the goal structure, together with the strategic principle, is the means by which the leader steers the organization. But, an organization is an interactive system of human beings, and its performance depends on the behavior of individuals. Regardless of the policies that are promulgated, the participants in the organization will determine the destiny of the organization by their productivity.

The goal structure is important in the leading of an organization. However, organizations can have conflicting goals (Cyert and March, 1963), primarily because they tend to goals sequentially. Also, each unit in an organization can focus on different goals. These goals may conflict, but they can all be embraced by the organization (Birnbaum, 1988).

A definition of leadership

The concept of attention focus is one of the most important variables in organization theory (March and Simon, 1958; Cyert and March, 1963). Participants in an organization allocate their attention to a variety of matters. The amount of attention allocated to each matter has been a subject of study. It can affect the organization in crucial ways. For example, if attention is not given to problems concerned with the future, the organization may flounder from myopia – too much attention to immediate problems. Clearly, the problems, concerns, ideas, concepts, and so on to which the participants pay attention will determine the long-run viability of the organization. The control of this allocation of attention is vital to the organization.

In discussing the formation of the organizational coalition, Cyert and March (1963, p. 39) argue that one of the five basic mechanisms for a theory of coalition formation is 'an attention-focus mechanism'; however, 'we know rather little about the actual mechanisms that control this attention factor.' In this paper, I argue that the leadership function is one of the mechanisms that controls the attention factor.

In fact, my definition of leadership is that the leader controls the allocation of the attention focus of the participants in the organization. The leader of any organization, no matter how small or large it is, affects the allocation of attention by participants. In a decentralized, structured organization, standard operating procedures determine the allocation of attention if the leader does not intervene. In general, in any organization where managers dominate, structured rules tend to influence the allocation of attention, but the leader will try to capture the attention focus of the participants so that their attention is allocated to the areas that the leader considers important.

The issues or problems on which the leader attempts to focus attention reflect, at least in part, the vision of the organization that exists in the leader's mind. This vision will generally have been developed from discussions with relevant participants, from the leader's experience and knowledge, and from his or her assessment of the organization's future in the light of existing information. This vision will change over time as the leader gets feedback from the organization's performance. As the vision changes, so does the priority of individual issues and problems to which the leader wishes to allocate the attention of participants. Organizations are dynamic, and attention allocation is an ongoing and always necessary process. Leadership, in the sense in which I have defined it here, must also be continuous.

Leadership, as I define it here, must also have substance. A leader cannot succeed in allocating attention without a strong intellectual position for a particular attention focus. This position can only come from a knowledge of the organization and of the area in which it functions. This need for specific knowledge is one of the reasons why it is difficult for executives to move from an organization in one industry to an organization in a different industry. The executive may be able to function as a manager, but he or she will have more difficulty functioning as a leader.

A second definition of leadership

Subgroups develop in every organization. Participants involved in the same department or in similar endeavors form a natural alliance (March and Simon, 1958). Important individuals in an organization can constitute subgroups in and of themselves. The point is that subgroups can develop a goal structure of their own, and this goal structure may conflict with that of the central organization.

The leader must bring about conformity between subgroup goals and the goals of the central organization. In other words, the leader must convince the members of the subgroup to give up or modify their goals and adopt the central organization's goals. In some cases, of course, the leader may decide that the central goals should be changed in the direction of the subgroup's goals. The point is that the leader cannot tolerate conflicting goals in the organization (Vroom and Jago, 1988). There must be a single goal structure, and everyone in the organization must accept it if the organization's goals are to be achieved. The concept of teamwork – of everyone working together – is a necessity for any organization.

Definitions of leadership and the three leadership functions

Having defined leadership, it is now logical for us to discuss the methods that one uses in the act of leadership. However, before we move to that topic, it will be useful to relate our two definitions of leadership – which really are essentially one – to the three functions of leadership discussed earlier.

In order to understand the leader's role, we need to go back to the distinction between managers and leaders. Every leader must perform some managerial functions, even though every manager cannot take a leadership role.

For example, in an effort to change organizational performance, many managers attempt to change the structure of their organizations. Currently, in an effort to reduce costs, many managers are attempting to reduce the number of hierarchical levels. Sometimes, the structure is changed by modifying the reporting relationship among units. The level at which decisions are made can also be changed. The organization can become more centralized or more decentralized with respect to decision making. Yet, changes in organizational structure alone are not likely to have any lasting impact on the organization's performance unless the structure affects the basic desire of participants to improve their performance.

The leader recognizes that it is necessary to focus the attention of participants on factors that will change performance. Thus, the leader makes changes in structure for their effect on attention focus, not because he or she believes that organizational structure alone can change the performance of participants. If the leader wishes to focus attention on costs, he or she looks at changes in the organization's structure that will encourage participants to allocate their attention to costs. Increased decentralization will often accomplish such a shift. The point is that leaders look at organizational tasks with a view to the impact that their actions will have on the attention focus of participants. Attention focus is central to the performance of the organizational function of leadership.

A similar statement can be made about the interpersonal function. The leader's role is to relate to the participants in ways that will affect their attention focus. The interpersonal function of leadership is sometimes viewed as one that holds the leader responsible for making everyone in the organization feel good. Friendliness and openness can be good for an organization if they help participants to focus their attention on the elements that the leader deems to be important. The interpersonal function is extremely important, but the leader must relate his or her actions in this area to the desired impact on attention focus. There is ample evidence that there is a low correlation between high morale and high productivity (Misumi, 1985).

The relation between the decisional function and attention focus is perhaps the most interesting of the three. Bavelas (1964, p. 206) defined leadership in terms of decision-making: 'leadership consists of the continuous choice-making process that permits the organization as a whole to proceed toward its objectives despite all sorts of internal and external perturbations.' More explicitly, he regards leadership as consisting of the reduction of uncertainty; this reduction is achieved by making choices.

This definition, which is close to the commonly accepted view of leadership, is quite different from those propounded here. My definitions focus on the leader's responsibility for modifying the behavior of participants in the organization. They assume that behavior is affected by the items to which individuals allocate their attention. The leader is able to capture the attention focus of participants. The leader gets participants to allocate attention to the items that he or she deems to be important. There is no question that the decisions that a leader makes are ways of making the priorities for attention clear. That is the aspect of decision making that in my view is part of leadership, not the fact that decision making reduces uncertainty. Nevertheless, it could be argued that influencing the allocation of attention tends to reduce uncertainty.

Studies of decision-making tend to show that decisions are rarely made by a single individual without regard to the views of the members of the organization. Leadership in an organization has to be less individualistic than it is in a combat situation where the leader may single-handedly eliminate a machine gun nest. Decision making in an organization must take into account the fact that members of the organization are interested in the direction that the organization takes. If the leader has captured the attention focus of the members, then it is possible to demonstrate 'the highest expressions of personal leadership' (Bavelas, 1964) and carry the organization along with those expressions.

Methods of leadership

If leadership is adequately encompassed by my definitions, we may ask how leadership is actually implemented in an organization. How does a person act in an organization when he or she plays a leadership role and wants to exert leadership?

There are at least three general approaches that are taken. They can be classified as communication, role modeling, and reward systems. I will discuss each of these approaches.

Communication

The first action that influences attention focus is oral interaction. These talks are ways of capturing the attention focus of participants. The ultimate aim is to change the behavior of people in the organization by influencing their focus. The underlying theory is that individuals' behavior is controlled by their attention focus. Put another way, the leader brings about the behavior that he or she desires by convincing participants to focus their attention on the ideas and actions that the leader considers important.

The interesting and difficult problem is that the methods of communication in organizations, are not well defined (March and Simon, 1958). In general, it is best to use a variety of communication channels. These channels can vary from one-on-one discussions to departmental meetings and meetings of the whole faculty and staff.

The leader also uses written communication. Again, different approaches must be found. Written communications can vary from personal letters to letters to the whole organization and formal reports. Even articles written for newspapers or other publications can be used to explicate the leader's desired priorities for the allocation of attention among participants.

Communication is perhaps the most important mechanism of leadership. The leader must have a clear understanding of the message that he or she is communicating, and he or she must be aware that the goal of communication is to influence the allocation of attention of the organization's members.

Role model

As a way of continuing to communicate with members of the organization, the leader must take into account the impact of his or her behavior on the attention focus of participants. The actions of the leader clearly represent the ideas that he or she considers to be important. If a university president is trying to emphasize research as an activity of impor-

tance, he or she should engage in research activity as well as emphasize research in the direct communications that he or she makes. Role modeling is a case in which actions speak as loudly as words.

The leader's activities are widely known among the members of any organization. Thus, the leader has ample opportunity to affect the attention focus of participants by demonstrating the factors that are important in his or her own behavior. In other words, role modeling is a form of communication. The leader's behavior exerts leadership whether the leader intends it or not.

Reward system

The reward system that the leader establishes is another way of reinforcing the attention focus of members. The relationship between particular rewards and performance is not well established. An organization cannot offer a specific monetary award and achieve a particular performance. However, a leader can use rewards to reinforce the priority system for attention allocation that he or she has established. The reward system can lead to both honor and money for recipients. The reward system is also a means of communicating the leader's priorities to participants. Obviously, a reward system cannot guarantee that performance in teaching will improve, but it can supplement the leader's effort to capture the attention focus of participants and allocate attention to areas that the leader considers important.

Conclusion

The theory of leadership just outlined is essentially a simple one. It assumes that participants in an organization behave in accordance with their focus attention. Behavior follows from the items on which they focus. From this perspective, leadership is the effort to capture the attention focus of the members of an organization. Three mechanisms help to perform the leadership function: communication between leader and participants, role modeling, and reward systems. The three mechanisms are alike in that all are ways of communicating the matters on which the leader wants members to focus their attention. There are other, related mechanisms. My list is not exhaustive. In all cases, the effort is to capture the attention focus of participants.

This conception of leadership might strike some as making the leader a manipulative person (Glassman, 1986). The key is that the leader must believe in what he or she is expressing. Mintzberg (1989) has put it exactly right: 'To my mind, key to the development of an organization ideology, in a new or existing organization, is a leadership with a genuine belief in mission and an honest dedication to the people who must carry it out.'

It is obvious, although I have not emphasized it, that a leader must have the ability and the knowledge needed to select the right items for the attention focus of participants (Mintzberg, 1982). That is, the items singled out for attention must enable the organization to attain its goals. The process of capturing the attention focus is also a dynamic one. The items on which the leader wishes participants to focus will change, and the leader must be perceptive enough to select the new items properly.

Although I have simplified the nature of leadership and the methods by which leadership can be exerted, I do not mean to imply that leadership is anything but complex. In any organization of significant size, the leader uses a system composed of many variables. To attend to the appropriate constituencies and focus their attention on the appropriate items requires thought, planning, energy, conviction, and an ability to persuade.

<table>
<tr><td>READING

9.2</td></tr>
</table>

Strategy as order emerging from chaos

By Ralph Stacey[1]

READING 9.2

There are four important points to make on the recent discoveries about the complex behaviour of dynamic systems, all of which have direct application to human organizations.

Chaos is a form of instability where the specific long-term future is unknowable

Chaos in its scientific sense is an irregular pattern of behavior generated by well-defined nonlinear feedback rules commonly found in nature and human society. When systems driven by such rules operate away from equilibrium, they are highly sensitive to selected tiny changes in their environments, amplifying them into self-reinforcing virtuous and vicious circles that completely alter the behavior of the system. In other words, the system's future unfolds in a manner dependent upon the precise detail of what it does, what the systems constituting its environments do, and upon chance. As a result of this fundamental property of the system itself, specific links between cause and effect are lost in the history of its development, and the

[1]Source: This article was reprinted from *Long Range Planning*, Vol. 26, No. 1, R. Stacey, 'Strategy as Order Emerging from Chaos', pp. 10–17, © 1993. With permission from Elsevier.

specific path of its long-term future development is completely unpredictable. Over the short term, however, it is possible to predict behavior because it takes time for the consequences of small changes to build up.

Is there evidence of chaos in business systems? We would conclude that there was if we could point to small changes escalating into large consequences; if we could point to self-reinforcing vicious and virtuous circles; if we could point to feedback that alternates between the amplifying and the damping. It is not difficult to find such evidence.

Creative managers seize on small differences in customer requirements and perceptions to build significant differentiators for their products. Customers may respond to this by switching from other product offerings, leading to a virtuous circle; or they may switch away, causing the kind of vicious circle that Coca-Cola found itself caught up in when it made that famous soft drink slightly sweeter.

Managers create, or at the very least shape, the requirements of their customers through the product offerings they make. Sony created a requirement for personal hi-fi systems through its Walkman offering, and manufacturers and operators have created requirements for portable telephones. Sony and Matsushita created the requirement for video recorders, and when companies supply information systems to their clients, they rarely do so according to a complete specification – instead, the supplier shapes the requirement. When managers intentionally shape customer demands through the offerings they make, this feeds back into customer responses, and managers may increase the impact by intentionally using the copying and spreading effects through which responses to product offerings feed back into other customers' responses. When managers do this, they are deliberately using positive feedback – along with negative feedback controls to meet cost and quality targets, for example – to create business success.

A successful business is also affected by many amplifying feedback processes that are outside the control of its managers and pro-duce effects that they did not intend. Successful businesses are quite clearly characterized by feedback processes that flip between the negative and the positive, the damping and the amplifying; that is, they are characterized by feedback patterns that produce chaos. The long-term future of a creative organization is absolutely unknowable, and no one can intend its future direction over the long term or be in control of it. In such a system long-term plans and visions of future states can be only illusions.

But in chaos there are boundaries around the instability

While chaos means disorder and randomness in the behavior of a system at the specific level, it also means that there is a qualitative pattern at a general, overall level. The future unfolds unpredictably, but it always does so according to recognizable family-like resemblances. This is what we mean when we say that history repeats itself, but never in the same way. We see this combination of unpredictable specific behavior within an overall pattern in snowflakes. As two nearby snowflakes fall to the earth, they experience tiny differences in temperature and air impurities. Each snowflake amplifies those differences as they form, and by the time they reach the earth they have different shapes – but they are still clearly snowflakes. We cannot predict the shape of each snowflake, but we can predict that they will be snowflakes. In business, we recognize patterns of boom and recession, but each time they are different in specific terms, defying all attempts to predict them.

Chaos is unpredictable variety within recognizable categories defined by irregular features, that is, an inseparable intertwining of order and disorder. It is this property of being bounded by recognizable qualitative patterns that makes it possible for humans to cope with chaos. Numerous tests have shown that our memories do not normally store information in units representing the precise characteristics of the individual shapes or events we perceive. Instead, we store information about the strength of connection between individual units perceived. We combine information together into categories or concepts using family resemblance-type features. Memory emphasizes general structure, irregular category features, rather than specific content. We remember the irregular patterns rather than the specific features and we design our next actions on the basis of these memorized patterns. And since we design our actions in this manner, chaotic behavior presents us with no real problem. Furthermore, we are adept at using analogical reasoning and intuition to reflect upon experience and adapt it to new situations, all of which is ideally suited to handling chaos.

Unpredictable new order can emerge from chaos through a process of spontaneous self-organization

When nonlinear feedback systems in nature are pushed far from equilibrium into chaos, they are capable of creating a complex new order. For example, at some low temperature the atoms of a particular gas are arranged in a particular pattern and the gas emits no light. Then, as heat is applied, it agitates the atoms causing them to move, and as this movement is amplified through the gas it emits a dull glow. Small changes in heat are thus amplified, causing instability, or chaos, that breaks the symmetry of the atoms' original behavior. Then at a critical point, the atoms in the gas suddenly all point in the same direction to produce a laser beam. Thus, the system uses chaos to shatter old patterns of behavior, creating the opportunity for the new. And as the system proceeds through chaos, it is confronted with critical points where it, so to speak, makes a choice between different options for further development. Some options represent yet further chaos and others lead to more complex forms of orderly behavior, but which will occur is inherently unpredictable. The choice itself is made by spontaneous self-organization amongst the components of the system in which they, in effect, communicate with each other, reach a consensus, and commit to a new form of behavior. If a more complex form of orderly behavior is reached, it has what scientists call a dissipative structure, because continual attention and energy must be applied if it is to be sustained – for example, heat has to be continually pumped into the gas if the laser beam is to continue. If the system is to develop further, then the dissipative structure must be short-lived; to reach an even more complex state, the system will have to pass through chaos once more.

It is striking how similar the process of dealing with strategic issues in an organization is to the self-organizing phenomenon just outlined. The key to the effectiveness with which organizations change and develop new strategic directions lies in the manner in which managers handle what might be called their strategic issue agenda. That agenda is a dynamic, unwritten list of issues, aspirations, and challenges that key groups of managers are attending to. Consider the steps managers can be observed to follow as they handle their strategic issue agenda:

- **Detecting and selecting small disturbances.** In open-ended strategic situations, change is typically the result of many small events and actions that are unclear, ambiguous, and confusing, with consequences that are unknowable. The key difficulty is to identify what the real issues, problems, or opportunities are, and the challenge is to find an appropriate and creative aspiration or objective. In these circumstances the organization has no alternative but to rely on the initiative of individuals to notice and pursue some issue, aspiration, or challenge. In order to do this, those individuals have to rely on their experience-based intuition and ability to detect analogies between one set of ambiguous circumstances and another.

- **Amplifying the issues and building political support.** Once some individual detects some potential issue, that individual begins to push for organizational attention to it. A complex political process of building special interest groups to support an issue is required before it gains organizational attention and can thus be said to be on the strategic issue agenda.

- **Breaking symmetries.** As they build and progress strategic issue agendas, managers are in effect altering old mental models, existing company and industry recipes, to come up with new ways of doing things. They are destroying existing perceptions and structures.

- **Critical points and unpredictable outcomes.** Some issues on the agenda may be dealt with quickly, while others may attract attention, continuous or periodic, for a very long time. How quickly an issue is dealt with depends upon the time required to reach enough consensus and commitment to proceed to action. At some critical point, an external or internal pressure in effect forces a choice. The outcome on whether and how to proceed to action over the issue is unpredictable because it depends upon the context of power, personality, and group dynamic within which it is being handled. The result may or may not be action, and action will usually be experimental at first.

- **Changing the frame of reference.** Managers in a business come to share memories of what worked and what did not work in the past – the organizational memory. In this way they build up a business philosophy, or culture, establishing a company recipe and in common with their rivals an industry recipe too. These recipes have a powerful effect on what issues will subsequently be detected and attended to; that is, they constitute a frame of reference within which managers interpret what to do next. The frame of reference has to be continually challenged and changed because it can easily become inappropriate to new circumstances. The dissipative structure of consensus and commitment is therefore necessarily short-lived if an organization is to be innovative.

These phases constitute a political and learning process through which managers deal with strategic issues, and the key point about these processes is that they are spontaneous and self-organizing: no central authority can direct anyone to detect and select an open-ended issue for attention, simply because no one knows what it is until someone has detected it; no one can centrally organize the factions that form around specific issues; nor can anyone intend the destruction of old recipes and the substitution of new ones since it is impossible to know what the appropriate new ones are until they are discovered. The development of new strategic direction requires the chaos of contention and conflict, and the self-organizing processes of political interaction and complex learning.

Chaos is a fundamental property of nonlinear feedback systems, a category that includes human organizations

Feedback simply means that one action or event feeds into another; that is, one action or event determines the next according to some relationship. For example, one firm repackages its product and its rival responds in some way, leading to a further action on the part of the first, provoking in turn yet another response from the second, and so on. The feedback relationship may be linear, or proportional, and when this is the case, the first firm will repackage its product and the second will respond by doing much the same. The feedback relationship could be nonlinear, or nonproportional, however, so that when the first firm repackages its product, the second introduces a new product at a lower price; this could lead the first to cut prices even further, so touching off a price war. In other words, nonlinear systems are those that use amplifying (positive) feedback in some way. To see the significance of positive feedback, compare it with negative feedback.

All effective businesses use negative or damping feedback systems to control and regulate their day-to-day activities. Managers fix short-term targets for profits and then prepare annual plans or budgets, setting out the time path to reach the target. As the business moves through time, outcomes are measured and compared with annual plan projections to yield variances. Frequent monitoring of those variances prompts corrective action to bring performance indicators back onto their planned paths; that is, variances feed back into corrective action and the feedback takes a negative form, so that when profit is below target, for example, offsetting action is taken to restore it. Scheduling, budgetary, and planning systems utilize negative feedback to keep an organization close to a predictable, stable equilibrium path in which it is adapted to its environment. While negative feedback controls a system according to prior intention, positive feedback produces explosively unstable equilibrium where changes are amplified, eventually putting intolerable pressure on the system until it runs out of control.

The key discovery about the operation of nonlinear feedback systems, however, is that there is a third choice. When a nonlinear feedback system is driven away from stable equilibrium toward explosive unstable equilibrium, it passes through a phase of bounded instability – there is a border between stability and instability where feedback flips autonomously between the amplifying and the damping to produce chaotic behavior; a paradoxical state that combines both stability and instability.

All human interactions take the form of feedback loops simply because the consequences of one action always feed back to affect a subsequent one. Furthermore, all human interactions constitute nonlinear feedback loops because people under- and overreact. Since organizations are simply a vast web of feedback loops between people, they must be capable of chaotic, as well as stable and explosively unstable, behavior. The key

question is which of these kinds of behaviors leads an organization to success. We can see the answer to this question if we reflect upon the fundamental forces operating on an organization.

All organizations are powerfully pulled in two fundamentally different directions:

- **Disintegration.** Organizations can become more efficient and effective if they divide tasks, segment markets, appeal to individual motivators, empower people, promote informal communication, and separate production processes in geographic and other terms. These steps lead to fragmenting cultures and dispersed power that pull an organization toward disintegration, a phenomenon that can be seen in practice as companies split into more and more business units and find it harder and harder to maintain control.

- **Ossification.** To avoid this pull to disintegration, and to reap the advantages of synergy and coordination, all organizations are also pulled to a state in which tasks are integrated, overlaps in market segments and production processes managed, group goals stressed above individual ones, power concentrated, communication and procedures formalized, and strongly shared cultures established. As an organization moves in this direction it develops more and more rigid structures, rules, procedures, and systems until it eventually ossifies, consequences that are easy to observe as organizations centralize.

Thus, one powerful set of forces pulls every organization toward a stable equilibrium (ossification) and another powerful set of forces pulls it toward an explosively unstable equilibrium (disintegration). Success lies at the border between these states, where managers continually alter systems and structures to avoid attraction either to disintegration or to ossification. For example, organizations typically swing to centralization in one period, to decentralization in another, and back again later on. Success clearly lies in a nonequilibrium state between stable and unstable equilibria; and for a nonlinear feedback system, that is chaos.

Eight steps to create order out of chaos

When managers believe that they must pull together harmoniously in pursuit of a shared organizational intention established before they act, they are inevitably confined to the predictable – existing strategic directions will simply be continued or innovations made by others will simply be imitated. When, instead of this, managers create the chaos that flows from challenging existing perceptions and promote the conditions in which spontaneous self-organization can occur, they make it possible for innovation and new strategic direction to emerge. Managers create such conditions when they undertake actions of the following kind.

Develop new perspectives on the meaning of control

The activity of learning in a group is a form of control that managers do not normally recognize as such. It is a self-organizing, self-policing form of control in which the group itself discovers intention and exercises control. Furthermore, we are all perfectly accustomed to the idea that the strategic direction of local communities, nation-states, and international communities is developed and controlled through the operation of political sytems, but we rarely apply this notion to organizations. When we do, we see that a sequence of choices and actions will continue in a particular direction only while those espousing that direction continue to enjoy sufficient support. This constitutes a form of control that is as applicable to an organization when it faces the conflicts around open-ended change, as it is to a nation. The lesson is that self-organizing processes can produce controlled behavior even though no one is in control – some-

times the best thing a manager can do is to let go and allow things to happen.

Design the use of power

The distribution of power and the way in which it is used provide very important boundaries around the group learning process from which new strategic directions emerge. The application of power in particular forms has fairly predictable consequences for group dynamics. Where power is applied as force and consented to out of fear, the group dynamic will be one of submission, or where such power is not consented to, the group dynamic will be one of rebellion, either covert or overt. Power may be applied as authority, and the predictable group dynamic here is one in which members of the group suspend their critical faculties and accept instructions from those above them. Groups in states of submission, rebellion, or conformity are incapable of complex learning, that is, the development of new perspectives and new mental models.

The kind of group dynamics that are conducive to complex learning occur when highly competitive win/lose polarization is removed, and open questioning and public testing of assertions encouraged. When this happens, people use argument and conflict to move toward periodic consensus and commitment to a particular issue. That consensus and commitment cannot, however, be the norm when people are searching for new perspectives – rather, they must alternate between conflict and consensus, between confusion and clarity. This kind of dynamic is likely to occur when they most powerfully alternate the form in which they use their power: sometimes withdrawing and allowing conflict; sometimes intervening with suggestions; sometimes exerting authority.

Encourage self-organizing groups

A group will be self-organizing only if it discovers its own challenges, goals, and objectives. Mostly, such groups need to form spontaneously – the role of top managers is simply to create the atmosphere in which this can happen. When top managers do set up a group to deal with strategic issues, however, they must avoid the temptation to write terms of reference, set objectives, or prod the group to reach some predetermined view. Instead top managers must present ambiguous challenges and take the chance that the group may produce proposals they do not approve of. For a group of managers to be self-organizing, it has to be free to operate as its members jointly choose, within the boundaries provided by their work together. This means that when they work together in this way, the normal hierarchy must be suspended for most of the time. Members are there because of the contributions they are able to make and the influence they can exert through those contributions and their own personalities. This suspension of the normal hierarchy can take place only if those on higher levels behave in a manner that indicates that they attach little importance to their position for the duration of the work of the group.

Provoke multiple cultures

One way of developing the conflicting countercultures required to provoke new perspectives is to rotate people between functions and business units. The motive here is to create cultural diversity as opposed to the current practice of using rotation to build a cadre of managers with the same management philosophy. Another effective way of promoting countercultures is that practiced by Canon and Honda, where significant numbers of managers are hired at the same time, midway through their careers in other organizations, to create sizeable pockets of different cultures that conflict with the predominant one.

Present ambiguous challenges instead of clear long-term objectives or visions

Agendas of strategic issues evolve out of the clash between different cultures in self-organizing groups. Top managers can provoke this activity by setting ambiguous challenges and presenting half-formed issues for others to develop, instead of trying to set clear long-term objectives. Problems without objectives should be intentionally posed to provoke the emotion and conflict that lead to active search for new ways of doing things. This activity of presenting challenges should also be a two-way one, where top executives hold themselves open to challenge from subordinates.

Expose the business to challenging situations

Managers who avoid taking chances face the certainty of stagnation and therefore the high probability of collapse in the long term, simply because innovation depends significantly on chance. Running for cover because the future is unknowable is in the long run the riskiest response of all. Instead, managers must intentionally expose themselves to the most challenging of situations. In his study of international companies, Michael Porter concludes that those who position themselves to serve the world's most sophisticated and demanding customers, who seek the challenge of competing with the most imaginative and competent competitors, are the ones who build sustainable competitive advantage on a global scale.

Devote explicit attention to improving group learning skills

New strategic directions emerge when groups of managers learn together in the sense of questioning deeply held beliefs and altering existing mental models rather than simply absorbing existing bodies of knowledge and sets of techniques. Such a learning process may well be personally threatening and so arouse anxiety that leads to bizarre group dynamics – this is perhaps the major obstacle to effective organizational learning. To overcome it, managers must spend time explicitly exploring how they interact and learn together – the route to superior learning is self-reflection in groups.

Create resource slack

New strategic directions emerge when the attitudes and behavior of managers create an atmosphere favourable to individual initiative and intuition, to political interaction, and to learning in groups. Learning and political interaction are hard work, and they cannot occur without investment in spare management resources. A vital precondition for emergent strategy is thus investment in management resources to allow it to happen.

Conclusion

Practicing managers and academics have been debating the merits of organizational learning as opposed to the planning conceptualization of strategic management. That debate has not, however, focused clearly on the critical unquestioned assumptions upon which the planning approach is based, namely, the nature of causality. Recent discoveries about the nature of dynamic feedback systems make it clear that cause and effect links disappear in innovative human organizations, making it impossible to envision or plan their long-term futures. Because of this lack of causal connection between specific actions and specific outcomes, new strategic directions can only emerge through a spontaneous, self-organizing political and learning process. The planning approach can be seen as a specific approach applicable to the short-term management of an organization's existing activities, a task as vital as the development of a new strategic direction.

READINGS ON THE INTERNATIONAL CONTEXT

As the opening reading, representing the global convergence perspective, 'The Globalization of Markets' by Theodore Levitt has been selected. This article, published in the early 1980s, has probably been the most influential at starting the debate about globalization in the business literature. Levitt's thesis is that the world is quickly moving towards a converging commonality. He believes that 'the world's needs and desires have been irrevocably homogenized'. The force driving this process is technology, which has facilitated communication, transport and travel, while allowing for the development of superior products at low prices. His conclusion is that 'the commonality of preference leads inescapably to the standardization of products, manufacturing, and the institutions of trade and commerce'. The old-fashioned multinational corporation, that adapted itself to local circumstances, is 'obsolete and the global corporation absolute'. While a clear proponent of the global convergence perspective, it should be noted that Levitt's bold prediction of global convergence is focused on the globalization of *markets*. In particular, he is intent on pointing out that converging consumer demand in international markets facilitates – even necessitates – the reaping of economies of scale through the standardization of products, marketing and production. With this emphasis on the demand side, Levitt pays far less attention to the supply side – the globalization of industries and the competition within industries – that other global convergence proponents tend to accentuate (see Porter, 1990a; Prahalad and Doz, 1987). And although he strongly advises companies to become 'global corporations', he does not further detail what a global company should look like (see Bartlett and Ghoshal, 1995). Overall, Levitt views globalization more as growing international similarity, while paying less attention to the possibility of growing international integration, as some other authors do.

As a direct response to 'the sweeping and somewhat polemic character' of Levitt's argumentation, Susan Douglas and Yoram Wind have written an article, 'The Myth of Globalization', that has been selected as representative of the international diversity perspective. Douglas and Wind believe that many of the assumptions underlying Levitt's global standardization philosophy are contradicted by the facts. They argue that the convergence of customer needs is not a one-way street; divergence trends are noticeable as well. Furthermore, they believe that Levitt is mistaken in arguing that economies of scale in production and marketing are an irreversible force driving globalization. According to Douglas and Wind, many new technologies have actually lowered the minimum efficient scale of operation, while there are also plenty of industries where economies of scale are not an important issue. The authors conclude by outlining the specific circumstances under which a strategy of global standardization might be effective. Under all other circumstances, Douglas and Wind reiterate, the international strategist will have to deal with the existence of international diversity and search for the right balance between global standardization and local adaptation.

The globalization of markets

By Theodore Levitt[1]

A powerful force drives the world toward a converging commonality, and that force is technology. It has proletarianized communication, transport, and travel. It has made isolated places and impoverished peoples eager for modernity's allurements. Almost everyone everywhere wants all the things they have heard about, seen, or experienced via the new technologies.

The result is a new commercial reality – the emergence of global markets for standardized consumer products on a previously unimagined scale of magnitude. Corporations geared to this new reality benefit from enormous economies of scale in production, distribution, marketing, and management. By translating these benefits into reduced world prices, they can decimate competitors that still live in the disabling grip of old assumptions about how the world works.

Gone are accustomed differences in national or regional preference. Gone are the days when a company could sell last year's models – or lesser versions of advanced products – in the less developed world. And gone are the days when prices, margins, and profits abroad were generally higher than at home.

The globalization of markets is at hand. With that, the multinational commercial world nears its end, and so does the multinational corporation.

The multinational and the global corporation are not the same thing. The multinational corporation operates in a number of countries, and adjusts its products and practices in each – at high relative costs. The global corporation operates with resolute constancy – at low relative cost – as if the entire world (or major regions of it) were a single entity; it sells the same things in the same way everywhere.

[1]Source: Reprinted by permission of *Harvard Business Review*. From 'The Globalization of Markets' by T. Levitt, May–June 1983, Vol. 61. © 1983 by Harvard Business School Publishing Corporation, all rights reserved.

Which strategy is better is not a matter of opinion but of necessity. World-wide communications carry everywhere the constant drumbeat of modern possibilities to lighten and enhance work, raise living standards, divert, and entertain. The same countries that ask the world to recognize and respect the individuality of their cultures insist on the wholesale transfer to them of modern goods, services, and technologies. Modernity is not just a wish but also a widespread practice among those who cling, with unyielding passion or religious fervor, to ancient attitudes and heritages.

Who can forget the televized scenes during the 1979 Iranian uprisings of young men in fashionable French-cut trousers and silky body shirts thirsting with raised modern weapons for blood in the name of Islamic fundamentalism?

In Brazil, thousands swarm daily from preindustrial Bahian darkness into exploding coastal cities, there quickly to install television sets in crowded corrugated huts and, next to battered Volkswagens, make sacrificial offerings of fruit and fresh-killed chickens to Macumban spirits by candlelight.

A thousand suggestive ways attest to the ubiquity of the desire for the most advanced things that the world makes and sells – goods of the best quality and reliability at the lowest price. The world's needs and desires have been irrevocably homogenized. This makes the multinational corporation obsolete and the global corporation absolute.

Living in the Republic of Technology

Daniel J. Boorstin, author of the monumental trilogy *The Americans*, characterized our age as driven by 'the Republic of Technology (whose) supreme law . . . is convergence, the tendency for everything to become more like everything else.'

In business, this trend has pushed markets toward global commonality. Corporations sell standardized products in the same way everywhere – autos, steel, chemicals, petroleum, cement, agricultural commodities and equipment, industrial and commercial construction, banking and insurance services, computers, semiconductors, transport, electronic instruments, pharmaceuticals, and telecommunications, to mention some of the obvious.

Nor is the sweeping gale of globalization confined to these raw material or high-tech products, where the universal language of customers and users facilitates standardization. The transforming winds whipped up by the proletarianization of communication and travel enter every crevice of life.

Commercially, nothing confirms this as much as the success of McDonald's from the Champs Elysées to the Ginza, of Coca-Cola in Bahrain and Pepsi-Cola in Moscow, and of rock music, Greek salad, Hollywood movies, Revlon cosmetics, Sony televisions, and Levi jeans everywhere. 'High-touch' products are as ubiquitous as high-tech.

Starting from opposing sides, the high-tech and the high-touch ends of the commercial spectrum gradually consume the undistributed middle in their cosmopolitan orbit. No one is exempt and nothing can stop the process. Everywhere everything gets more and more like everything else as the world's preference structure is relentlessly homogenized.

Consider the cases of Coca-Cola and Pepsi-Cola, which are globally standardized products sold everywhere and welcomed by everyone. Both successfully cross multitudes of national, regional, and ethnic taste buds trained to a variety of deeply ingrained local preferences of taste, flavor, consistency, effervescence, and aftertaste. Everywhere both sell well. Cigarettes, too, especially American-made, make year-to-year global inroads in territories previously held in the firm grip of other, mostly local, blends.

These are not exceptional examples. (Indeed their global reach would be even greater were it not for artificial trade barriers.) They exemplify a general drift toward the homogenization of the world and how companies distribute, finance, and price products.

Nothing is exempt. The products and methods of the industrialized world play a single tune for all the world, and all the world eagerly dances to it.

Ancient differences in national tastes or modes of doing business disappear. The commonality of preference leads inescapably to the standardization of products, manufacturing, and the institutions of trade and commerce. Small nation-based markets transmogrify and expand. Success in world competition turns on efficiency in production, distribution, marketing, and management, and inevitably becomes focused on price.

The most effective world competitors incorporate superior quality and reliability into their cost structures. They sell in all national markets the same kind of products sold at home or in their largest export market. They compete on the basis of appropriate value – the best combinations of price, quality, reliability, and delivery for products that are globally identical with respect to design, function, and even fashion.

That, and little else, explains the surging success of Japanese companies dealing world-wide in a vast variety of products – both tangible products like steel, cars, motorcycles, hi-fi equipment, farm machinery, robots, microprocessors, carbon fibers, and now even textiles, and intangibles like banking, shipping, general contracting, and soon computer software. Nor are high-quality and low-cost operations incompatible, as a host of consulting organizations and data engineers argue with vigorous vacuity. The reported data are incomplete, wrongly analyzed, and contradictory. The truth is that low-cost operations are the hallmark of corporate cultures that require and produce quality in all that they do. High quality and low costs are not opposing postures. They are compatible, twin identities of superior practice.

To say that Japan's companies are not global because they export cars with left-side drives to the United States and the European continent, while those in Japan have right-side drives, or because they sell office machines through distributors in the United States but directly at home, or speak Portuguese in Brazil is to mistake a difference for a distinction. The same is true of Safeway and Southland retail chains operating effectively in the Middle East, and to not only native but also imported populations from Korea, the Philippines, Pakistan, India, Thailand, Britain, and the United States. National rules of the road differ, and so do distribution channels and languages. Japan's distinction is its unrelenting push for economy and value enhancement. That translates into a drive for standardization at high quality levels.

Vindication of the Model T

If a company forces costs and prices down and pushes quality and reliability up – while maintaining reasonable concern for suitability – customers will prefer its world-standardized products. The theory holds at this stage in the evolution of globalization, no matter what conventional market research and even common sense may suggest about different national and regional tastes, preferences, needs, and institutions. The Japanese have repeatedly vindicated this theory, as did Henry Ford with the Model T. Most important, so have their imitators, including companies from South Korea (television sets and heavy construction), Malaysia (personal calculators and microcomputers), Brazil (auto parts and tools), Colombia (apparel), Singapore (optical equipment), and yes, even from the United States (office copiers, computers, bicycles, castings), Western Europe (automatic washing machines), Rumania (housewares), Hungary (apparel), Yugoslavia (furniture), and Israel (pagination equipment).

Of course, large companies operating in a single nation or even a single city don't standardize everything they make, sell, or do. They have product lines instead of a single product version, and multiple distribution channels. There are neighborhood, local, regional, ethnic, and institutional differences, even within metropolitan areas. But although companies customize products for particular market segments, they know that success in a world with homogenized demand requires a search for sales opportunities in similar segments across the globe in order to achieve the economies of scale necessary to compete.

Such a search works because a market segment in one country is seldom unique; it has close cousins everywhere precisely because technology has homogenized the globe. Even small local segments have their global equivalents everywhere and become subject to global competition, especially on price.

The global competitor will seek constantly to standardize his offering everywhere. He will digress from this standardization only after exhausting all possibilities to retain it, and he will push for reinstatement of standardization whenever digression and divergence have occurred. He will never assume that the customer is a king who knows his own wishes.

Trouble increasingly stalks companies that lack clarified global focus and remain inattentive to the economics of simplicity and standardization. The most endangered companies in the rapidly evolving world tend to be those that dominate rather small domestic markets with high value-added products for which there are smaller markets elsewhere. With transportation costs proportionately low, distant competitors will enter the now-sheltered markets of those companies with goods produced more cheaply under scale-efficient conditions. Global competition spells the end of domestic territoriality, no matter how diminutive the territory may be.

When the global producer offers his lower costs internationally, his patronage expands exponentially. He not only reaches into distant markets, but also attracts customers who previously held to local preferences and now capitulate to the attractions of lesser prices. The strategy of standardization not only responds to world-wide homogenized markets but also expands those markets with aggressive low pricing. The new technological juggernaut taps an ancient motivation – to make one's money go as far as possible. This

is universal – not simply a motivation but actually a need.

The hedgehog knows

The difference between the hedgehog and the fox, wrote Sir Isaiah Berlin in distinguishing between Dostoevski and Tolstoy, is that the fox knows a lot about a great many things, but the hedgehog knows everything about one great thing. The multinational corporation knows a lot about a great many countries and congenially adapts to supposed differences. It willingly accepts vestigial national differences, not questioning the possibility of their transformation, not recognizing how the world is ready and eager for the benefit of modernity, especially when the price is right. The multinational corporation's accommodating mode to visible national differences is medieval.

By contrast, the global corporation knows everything about one great thing. It knows about the absolute need to be competitive on a world-wide basis as well as nationally and seeks constantly to drive down prices by standardizing what it sells and how it operates. It treats the world as composed of few standardized markets rather than many customized markets. It actively seeks and vigorously works toward global convergence. Its mission is modernity and its mode, price competition, even when it sells top-of-the-line, high-end products. It knows about the one great thing all nations and people have in common: scarcity.

Nobody takes scarcity lying down; everyone wants more. This in part explains division of labor and specialization of production. They enable people and nations to optimize their conditions through trade. The median is usually money.

Experience teaches that money has three special qualities: scarcity, difficulty of acquisition, and transience. People understandably treat it with respect. Everyone in the increasingly homogenized world market wants products and features that everybody else wants. If the price is low enough, they will take highly standardized world products, even if these aren't exactly what mother said was suitable, what immemorial custom decreed was right, or what market-research fabulists asserted was preferred.

The implacable truth of all modern production – whether of tangible or intangible goods – is that large-scale production of standardized items is generally cheaper within a wide range of volume than small-scale production. Some argue that CAD/CAM (computer aided design/computer aided manufacturing) will allow companies to manufacture customized products on a small scale – but cheaply. But the argument misses the point. If a company treats the world as one or two distinctive product markets, it can serve the world more economically than if it treats it as three, four, or five product markets.

Different cultural preferences, national tastes and standards, and business institutions are vestiges of the past. Some inheritances die gradually; others prosper and expand into mainstream global preferences. So-called ethnic markets are a good example. Chinese food, pitta bread, country and western music, pizza, and jazz are everywhere. They are market segments that exist in world-wide proportions. They don't deny or contradict global homogenization but confirm it.

Many of today's differences among nations as to products and their features actually reflect the respectful accommodation of multinational corporations to what they believe are fixed local preferences. They believe preferences are fixed, not because they are but because of rigid habits of thinking about what actually is. Most executives in multinational corporations are thoughtlessly accommodating. They falsely presume that marketing means giving the customer what he says he wants rather than trying to understand exactly what he'd like. So they persist with high-cost, customized multinational products and practices instead of pressing hard and pressing properly for global standardization.

I do not advocate the systematic disregard of local or national differences. But a company's sensitivity to such differences does not require that it ignore the possibilities of doing things differently or better.

With persistence and appropriate means, barriers against superior technologies and economics have always fallen. There is no recorded exception where reasonable effort has been made to overcome them. It is very much a matter of time and effort.

A failure in global imagination

Many companies have tried to standardize world practice by exporting domestic products and processes without accommodation or change – and have failed miserably. Their deficiencies have been seized on as evidence of bovine stupidity in the face of abject impossibility. Advocates of global standardization see them as examples of failures in execution.

In fact, poor execution is often an important cause. More important, however, is failure of nerve – failure of imagination.

Consider the case for the introduction of fully automatic home laundry equipment in Western Europe at a time when few homes had even semiautomatic machines.

The growing success of small, low-powered, low-speed, low-capacity, low-priced Italian machines, even against the preferred but highly priced and highly promoted brand in West Germany, was significant. It contained a powerful message that was lost on managers confidently wedded to a distorted version of the marketing concept according to which you give the customer what he says he wants. In fact the customers said they wanted certain features, but their behavior demonstrated they'd take other features provided the price and the promotion were right.

In this case it was obvious that under prevailing conditions, people preferred a low-priced automatic over any kind of manual or semiautomatic machine and certainly over higher priced automatics, even though the low-priced automatics failed to fulfil all their expressed preferences. The supposedly meticulous and demanding German consumers violated all expectations by buying the simple, low-priced Italian machines.

This case illustrates how the perverse practice of the marketing concept and the absence of any kind of marketing imagination let multinational attitudes survive when customers actually want the benefits of global standardization. People were asked what features they wanted in a washing machine rather than what they wanted out of life. Selling a line of products individually tailored to each nation is thoughtless. Managers who took pride in practicing the marketing concept to the fullest did not, in fact, practice it at all. Data do not yield information except with the intervention of the mind. Information does not yield meaning except with the intervention of imagination.

Cracking the code of Western markets

Since the theory of the marketing concept emerged a quarter of a century ago, the more managerially advanced corporations have been eager to offer what customers clearly want rather than what is merely convenient. They have created marketing departments supported by professional market researchers of awesome and often costly proportions. And they have proliferated extraordinary numbers of operations and product lines – highly tailored products and delivery systems for many different markets, market segments, and nations.

Significantly, Japanese companies operate almost entirely without marketing departments or market research of the kind so prevalent in the West. Yet, in the colorful words of General Electric's chairman John F. Welch Jr., the Japanese, coming from a small cluster of resource-poor islands, with an entirely alien culture and an almost impenetrably complex language, have cracked the code of Western markets. They have done it not by looking with mechanistic thoroughness at the way markets are different but rather by searching for meaning with a deeper wisdom. They have discovered the one great thing all markets have in common – an overwhelming desire for dependable, world-standard modernity in all things, at aggressively low prices. In response, they deliver irresistible value everywhere, attracting people with products that market-research technocrats described with superficial certainty as being unsuitable and uncompetitive.

The wider a company's global reach, the greater the number of regional and national preferences it will encounter for certain product features, distribution systems, or promotional media. There will always need to be some accommodation to differences.

In its highly successful introduction of Contac 600 (the timed-release decongestant) into Japan, SmithKline Corporation used 35 wholesalers instead of the 1000-plus that established practice required. Daily contacts with the wholesalers and key retailers, also in violation of established practice, supplemented the plan, and it worked.

Denied access to established distribution institutions in the United States, Komatsu, the Japanese manufacturer of lightweight farm machinery, entered the market through over-the-road construction equipment dealers in rural areas of the Sunbelt, where farms are smaller, the soil sandier and easier to work. Here inexperienced distributors were able to attract customers on the basis of Komatsu's product and price appropriateness.

In cases of successful challenge to prevailing institutions and practices, a combination of product reliability and quality, strong and sustained support systems, aggressively low prices, and sales-compensation packages, as well as audacity and implacability, circumvented, shattered, and transformed very different distribution systems. Instead of resentment, there was admiration.

The differences that persist throughout the world despite its globalization affirm an ancient dictum of economics – that things are driven by what happens at the margin, not at the core. Thus, in ordinary competitive analysis, what's important is not the average price but the marginal price, what happens not in the usual case but at the interface of newly erupting conditions. What counts in commercial affairs is what happens at the cutting edge. What is most striking today is the underlying similarities of what is happening now to national preferences at the margin. These similarities at the cutting edge cumulatively form an overwhelming, predominant commonality everywhere.

To refer to the persistence of economic nationalism (protective and subsidized trade practices, special tax aids, or restrictions for home market producers) as a barrier to the globalization of markets is to make a valid point. Economic nationalism does have a powerful persistence. But, as with the present almost totally smooth internationalization of investment capital, the past alone does not shape or predict the future.

Reality is not a fixed paradigm, dominated by immemorial customs and derived attitudes, heedless of powerful and abundant new forces. The world is becoming increasingly informed about the liberating and enhancing possibilities of modernity. The persistence of the inherited varieties of national preferences rests uneasily on increasing evidence of, and restlessness regarding, their inefficiency, costliness, and confinement. The historic past, and the national differences respecting commerce and industry it spawned and fostered everywhere, is now subject to relatively easy transformation.

Cosmopolitanism is no longer the monopoly of the intellectual and leisure classes; it is becoming the established property and defining characteristic of all sectors everywhere in the world. Gradually and irresistibly it breaks down the walls of economic insularity, nationalism, and chauvinism. What we see today as escalating commercial nationalism is simply the last violent death rattle of an obsolete institution.

The successful global corporation does not abjure customization or differentiation for the requirements of markets that differ in product preferences, spending patterns, shopping preferences, and institutional or legal arrangements. But the global corporation accepts and adjusts to these differences only reluctantly, only after relentlessly testing their immutability, after trying in various ways to circumvent and reshape them.

READING

The myth of globalization

By Susan Douglas and Yoram Wind[1]

10.2

In recent years, globalization has become a key theme in every discussion of international strategy. Proponents of the philosophy of 'global' products and brands, such as Professor Theodore Levitt of Harvard, and the highly successful advertising agency, Saatchi & Saatchi, argue that in a world of growing internationalization, the key to success is the development of global products and brands, in other words, a focus on standardized products and brands worldwide. Others, however, point to the numerous

[1]Source: This article was reprinted from *Columbia Journal of World Business*, Winter 1987, S. Douglas and Y. Wind, 'The Myth of Globalization', pp. 19–29, © 1987. With permission of Elsevier.

barriers to standardization, and suggest that greater returns are to be obtained from adapting products and marketing strategies to the specific characteristics of individual markets.

The growing integration of international markets as well as the growth of competition on a world-wide scale implies that adoption of a global perspective has become increasingly imperative in planning strategy. However, to conclude that this mandates the adoption of a strategy of universal standardization appears naive and oversimplistic. In particular, it ignores the inherent complexity of operations in international markets, and the formulation of an effective strategy to penetrate these markets. While global products and brands may be appropriate for certain markets and in targeting certain segments, adopting such an approach as a universal strategy in relation to all markets may not be desirable, and may lead to major strategic blunders. Furthermore, it implies a product orientation, and a product-driven strategy, rather than a strategy grounded in a systematic analysis of customer behavior and response patterns and market characteristics.

The purpose of this article is thus to examine critically the notion that success in international markets necessitates adoption of a strategy of global products and brands. Given the restrictive characteristic of this philosophy, a somewhat broader perspective in developing global strategy is proposed which views standardization as merely one option in the range of possible strategies which may be effective in global markets.

The traditional perspective on international strategy

Traditionally, discussion of international business strategy has been polarized around the debate concerning the pursuit of a uniform strategy world-wide versus adaptation to specific local market conditions. On the one hand, it has been argued that adoption of a uniform strategy world-wide enables a company to take advantage of the potential synergies arising from multicountry operations, and constitutes the multinational company's key competitive advantage in international markets. Others however, have argued that adaptation of strategy to idiosyncratic national market characteristics is crucial to success in these markets.

Fayerweather, in his seminal work in international business strategy, described the central issue as one of conflict between forces toward unification and those resulting in fragmentation. He pointed out that within a multinational firm, internal forces created pressures toward the integration of strategy across national boundaries. On the other hand, differences in the sociocultural, political, and economic characteristics of countries as well as the need for effective relations with the host society, constitute fragmenting influences that favor adaptation to the local environment.

Recent discussion of global competitive strategy echoes the same theme of the dichotomy between the forces that have triggered the globalization of markets and those that constitute barriers to global competition. Factors such as economies of scale in production, purchasing, faster accumulation of learning from operating world-wide, decrease in transportation and distribution costs, reduced costs of product adaptation, and the emergence of global market segments have encouraged competition on a global scale. However, barriers such as governmental and institutional constraints, tariff barriers and duties, preferential treatment of local firms, transportation costs, differences in customer demand, and so on, call for nationalistic or 'protected niche' strategies.

Compromise solutions such as 'pattern standardization' have also been proposed. In this case, a global promotional theme or positioning is developed, but execution is adapted to the local market. Similarly, it has been pointed out that even where a standardized product is marketed in a number of countries, its positioning may be adapted in each market. Conversely, the positioning may be uniform across countries, but the product itself adapted or modified.

Although this debate first emerged in the 1960s, it has recently taken on a new vigor with the widely publicized pronouncements of proponents of 'global standardization' such as Professor Levitt and Saatchi & Saatchi.

The sweeping and somewhat polemic character of their argument has sparked a number of counterarguments as well as discussion of conditions under which such a strategy may be most appropriate. It has, for example, been pointed out that the potential for standardization may be greater for certain types of products such as industrial goods or luxury personal items targeted to upscale consumers, or products with similar penetration rates. Opportunities for standardization are also likely to occur more frequently among industrialized nations, and especially the Triad countries where customer interests as well as market conditions are likely to be more similar than among developing countries.

The role of corporate philosophy and organizational structure in influencing the practicality of implementing a strategy of global standardization has also been recognized. Here, it has been noted that few companies pursue the extreme position of complete standardization with regard to all elements of the marketing mix, and business functions such as R&D, manufacturing, and procurement in all countries throughout the world. Rather, some degree of adaptation is likely to occur relative to certain aspects of the firm's operations or in certain geographic areas. In addition, the feasibility of implementing a standardized strategy will depend on the autonomy accorded to local management. If local management has been accustomed to substantial autonomy, considerable opposition may be encountered in attempting to introduce globally standardized strategies.

An examination of such counterarguments suggests that there are a number of dangers in espousing a philosophy of global standardization for all products and services, and in relation to all markets world-wide. Furthermore, there are numerous difficulties and con-straints to implementing such a strategy in many markets, stemming from external market conditions (such as government and trade regulation, competition, the marketing infrastructure, and so on), as well as from the current structure and organization of the firm's operations.

The global standardization philosophy: The underlying assumptions

An examination of the arguments in favor of a strategy of global products and brands reveals three key underlying assumptions:

- Customer needs and interests are becoming increasingly homogeneous world-wide.
- People around the world are willing to sacrifice preferences in product features, functions, design, and the like for lower prices at high quality.
- Substantial economies of scale in production and marketing can be achieved through supplying global markets.

There are, however, a number of pitfalls associated with each of these assumptions. These are discussed here in more detail.

Homogenization of the world's wants

A key premise of the philosophy of global products is that customers' needs and interests are becoming increasingly homogeneous world-wide. But while global segments with similar interests and response patterns may be identified in some product markets, it is by no means clear that this is a universal trend. Furthermore, there is substantial evidence to suggest an increasing diversity of behavior within countries, and the emergence of idiosyncratic country-specific segments.

Lack of evidence of homogenization.
In a number of product markets ranging from watches, perfume, and handbags to soft drinks and fast foods, companies have successfully identified global customer segments, and developed global products and brands targeted to these segments. These include such stars as Rolex, Omega and Le Baume & Mercier watches, Dior, Patou or Yves St. Laurent perfume. But while these brands are highly visible and widely publicized, they are often, with a few notable exceptions such as Classic Coke or McDonald's, targeted to a relatively restricted upscale international customer segment.

Numerous other companies, however, adapt lines to idiosyncratic country preferences, and develop local brands or product variants targeted to local market segments. The Findus frozen food division of Nestlé, for example, markets fish cakes and fish fingers in the United Kingdom, but beef bourguignon and coq au vin in France, and vitello con funghi and braviola in Italy. Similarly, Coca-Cola in Japan markets Georgia, cold coffee in a can, and Aquarius, a tonic drink, as well as Classic Coke and Hi-C.

Growth of intracountry segmentation price sensitivity.   Furthermore, there is a growing body of evidence that suggests substantial heterogeneity within countries. In the United States, for example, the VALS (Value of American Lifestyles) study has identified nine value segments, while other studies have identified major differences in behavior between regions and subcultural segments. Many other countries are also characterized by substantial regional differences as well as different lifestyle and value segments.

Similarly, in industrial markets, while some global segments, often consisting of firms with international operations, can be identified, there also is considerable diversity within and between countries. Often local businesses constitute an important market segment and, especially in developing countries, may differ significantly in technological sophistication, business philosophy and strat-egy, emphasis on product quality, and service and price, from large multinationals.

The evidence thus suggests that the similarities in customer behavior are restricted to a relatively limited number of target segments, or product markets, while for the most part, there are substantial differences between countries. Proponents of standardization counter that the international strategist should focus on similarities among countries rather than differences. This may, however, imply ignoring a major part of a local market, and the potential profits that may be obtained from tapping other market segments.

Universal preference for low price at acceptable quality

Another critical component of the argument for global standardization is that people around the world are willing to sacrifice preferences in product features, functions, design, and the like for lower prices, assuming equivalent quality. Aggressive low pricing for quality products that meet the common needs of customers in markets around the world is believed to further expand the global markets facing the firm. Although an appealing argument, this has three major problems.

Lack of evidence of increased price sensitivity.   Evidence to suggest that customers are universally willing to trade off specific product features for a lower price is largely lacking. While in many product markets there is invariably a price-sensitive segment, there is no indication that this is on the increase. On the contrary, in many product and service markets, ranging from watches, personal computers, and household appliances to banking and insurance, an interest in multiple product features, product quality, and service appears to be growing.

Low price positioning is a highly vulnerable strategy.   Also, from a strategic point of view, emphasis on price positioning may be undesirable, especially in international markets, since it offers no long-term competitive advantage. A price-positioning strategy is always vulnerable to new technological developments that may lower costs, as well as to attack from competitors with lower overhead, and lower operating or labor costs. Government subsidies to local competitors may also undermine the effectiveness of a price-positioning strategy. In addition, price-sensitive customers typically are not brand or source loyal.

Standardized low price can be overpriced in some countries and underpriced in others.

Finally, a strategy based on a combination of a standardized product at a low price, when implemented in countries that vary in their competitive structure as well as the level of economic development, is likely to result in products that are overdesigned and overpriced for some markets and underdesigned and underpriced for others. Cost advantages may also be negated by transportation and distribution costs as well as tariff barriers and/or price regulation.

Economies of scale of production and marketing

The third assumption underlying the philosophy of global standardization is that a key force driving strategy is product technology, and that substantial economies of scale can be achieved by supplying global markets. This does, however, neglect three critical and interrelated points:

1   Technological developments in flexible factory automation enable economies of scale to be achieved at lower levels of output and do not require production of a single standardized product.

2   Cost of production is only one and often not the critical component in determining the total cost of the product.

3   Strategy should not be solely product driven but should take into account the other components of a marketing strategy, such as positioning, packaging, brand name, advertising, PR, consumer and trade promotion and distribution.

Developments in flexible factory automation.

Recent developments in flexible factory automation methods have lowered the minimum efficient scale of operation and have thus enabled companies to supply smaller local markets efficiently, without requiring operations on a global scale. However, diseconomies may result from such operations due to increased transportation and distribution costs, as well as higher administrative overhead, and additional communication and coordination costs.

Furthermore, decentralization of production and establishment of local manufacturing operations enables diversification of risk arising from political events, fluctuations in foreign exchange rates, or economic instability. Recent swings in foreign exchange rates, coupled with the growth of offshore sourcing have underscored the vulnerability of centralizing production in a single location. Government regulations relating to local component and/or offset requirements create additional pressures for local manufacturing. Flexible automation not only implies that decentralization of manufacturing and production may be cost efficient but also makes minor modifications in products or models in the latter stages of production feasible, so that a variety of model versions can be produced without major retooling. Adaptations to product design can thus be made to meet differences in preferences from one country to another without loss of economies of scale.

Production costs are often a minor component of total cost.

In many consumer and service industries, such as cosmetics, detergents, pharmaceuticals, or financial institutions, production costs are a small fraction of total cost. The key to success in these markets is an understanding of the tastes and purchase behavior of target customers' distribution channels, and tailoring products and strategies to these rather than production efficiency. In the detergent industry, for example, mastery of mass-merchandising techniques and an effective brand management system are typically considered the key elements in the success of the giants in this field, such as Procter & Gamble (P&G) or Colgate-Palmolive.

The standardization philosophy is primarily product driven. The focus on product- and brand-related aspects of strategy in discussions of global standardization is misleading since it ignores the other key strategy variables. Strategy in international markets should also take into consideration other aspects of the marketing mix, and the extent to which these are standardized across country markets rather than adapted to local idiosyncratic characteristics.

Requisite conditions for global standardization

The numerous pitfalls in the rationale underlying the global standardization philosophy suggests that such a strategy is far from universally appropriate for all products, brands, or companies. Only under certain conditions is it likely to prove a 'winning' strategy in international markets. These include:

- the existence of a global market segment;
- potential synergies from standardization;
- the availability of a communication and distribution infrastructure to deliver the firm's offering to target customers world-wide.

Existence of global market segments

As noted previously, global segments may be identified in a number of industrial and consumer markets. In consumer markets these segments are typically luxury- or premium-type products. Global segments are, however, not limited to such product markets, but also exist in other types of markets, such as motorcycle, record, stereo equipment, and computer, where a segment with similar needs and wants can be identified in many countries.

In industrial markets, companies with multinational operations are particularly likely to have similar needs and requirements world-wide. Where the operations are integrated or coordinated across national boundaries, as in the case of banks or other financial institutions, compatibility of operational systems and equipment may be essential. Consequently, they may seek vendors who can supply and service their operations world-wide, in some cases developing global contrasts for such purchases. Similarly, manufacturing companies with world-wide operations may source globally in order to ensure uniformity in quality, service and price of components, and other raw materials throughout their operations.

Marketing of global products and brands to such target segments and global customers enables development of a uniform global image throughout the world. In some markets such as perfume or fashions, association with a specific country of origin or a foreign image in general may carry a prestige connotation. In other cases, for example, Sony electronic equipment, McDonald's hamburgers, Hertz or Avis car rental, IBM computers, or Xerox office equipment, it may help to develop a world-wide reputation for quality and service. Just as multinational corporations may seek uniformity in supply world-wide, some consumers who travel extensively may be interested in finding the same brand of cigarettes and soft drinks, or hotels, in foreign countries. This may be particularly relevant in product markets used extensively by international travelers.

While the existence of a potential global segment is a key motivating factor for developing a global product and brand strategy, it is important to note that the desirability of such a strategy depends on the size and economic viability of the segment in question, the strength of the segment's preference for the global brand, as well as the ability to reach the segment effectively and profitably.

Synergies associated with global standardization

Global standardization may also have a number of synergistic effects. In addition to those associated with a global image noted above, opportunities may exist for the transfer of good ideas for products or promotional strategies from one country to another.

The standardization of strategy and operations across a number of countries may also enable the acquisition or exploitation of specific types of expertise that would not be feasible otherwise. Expertise in assessing country risk or foreign exchange risk, or in identifying and interpreting information relating to multiple country markets, for example, may be developed.

Such synergies are not, however, unique to a strategy of global standardization, but may also occur wherever operations and strategy are coordinated or integrated across country markets. In fact, only certain scale economies associated with product and advertising copy standardization, and the development of a global image as discussed earlier, are unique to global standardization.

Availability of an international communication and distribution infrastructure

The effectiveness of global standardization also depends to a large extent on the availability of an international infrastructure of communications and distribution. As many corporations have expanded overseas, service organizations have followed their customers abroad to supply their needs world-wide.

Advertising agencies such as Saatchi & Saatchi, McCann Erickson, and Young & Rubicam now have an international network of operations throughout the world, while many research agencies can also supply services in major markets world-wide. With the growing integration of financial markets, banks, investment firms, insurance and other financial institutions are also becoming increasingly international in orientation and are expanding the scope of their operations in world markets. The physical distribution network of shippers, freight forwarding, export and import agents, customs clearing, invoicing and insurance agents is also becoming increasingly integrated to meet demand for international shipment of goods and services.

Improvements in telecommunications and in logistical systems have considerably increased capacity to manage operations on a global scale and hence facilitate adoption of global standardization strategies. The spread of telex and fax systems, as well as satellite linkages and international computer linkages, all contribute to the shrinking of distances and facilitate globalization of operations. Similarly, improvements in transportation systems and physical logistics such as containerization and computerized inventory and handling systems have enabled significant cost savings as well as reducing time required to move goods across major distances.

Operational constraints to effective implementation of a standardization strategy

While adoption of a standardized strategy may be desirable under certain conditions, there are a number of constraints that severely restrict the firm's ability to develop and implement a standardized strategy.

External constraints to effective standardization

The numerous external constraints that impede global standardization are well recognized. Here, four major categories are highlighted, namely

1 government and trade restrictions;
2 differences in the marketing infrastructure, such as the availability and effectiveness of promotional media;
3 the character of resource markets, and differences in the availability and costs of resources;

4 differences in competition from one country to another.

Government and trade restrictions.

Government and trade restrictions, such as tariff and other trade barriers, product, pricing or promotional regulation, frequently hamper standardization of the product line, pricing, or promotional strategy. Tariffs or quotas on the import of key materials, components, or other resources may, for example, affect production costs and thus hamper uniform pricing or alternatively result in the substitution of other components and modifications in product design. Local content requirements or compensatory export requirements, which specify that products contain a certain proportion of components manufactured locally or that a certain volume of production is exported to offset imports of components or other services, may have a similar impact.

The existence of cartels such as the European steel cartel, or the Swiss chocolate cartel, may also impede or exclude standardized strategies in countries covered by these agreements. In particular, they may affect adoption of a uniform pricing strategy as the cartel sets prices for the industry. Cartel members may also control established distribution channels, thus preventing use of a standardized distribution strategy. Extensive grey markets in countries such as India, Hong Kong, and South America may also affect administered pricing systems, and require adjustment of pricing strategies.

The nature of the marketing infrastructure.

Differences in the marketing infrastructure from one country to another may hamper use of a standardized strategy. These may, for example, include differences in the availability and reach of various promotional media, in the availability of certain distribution channels or retail institutions, or in the existence and efficiency of the communication and transportation network. Such factors may, therefore, require considerable adaptation of strategy of local market conditions.

Interdependencies with resource markets.

Yet another constraint to the development of standardized strategies is the nature of resource markets, and their operation in different countries throughout the world as well as the interdependency of these markets with marketing decisions. Availability and cost of raw materials, as well as labor and other resources in different locations, will affect not only decisions regarding sourcing of and hence the location of manufacturing activities but also marketing strategy decisions such as product design. For example, in the paper industry, availability of cheap local materials such as jute and sugar cane may result in their substitution for wood fiber.

Cost differentials relative to raw materials, labor, management, and other inputs may also influence the trade-off relative to alternative strategies. For example, high packaging cost relative to physical distribution may result in use of cheaper packaging with a shorter shelf life and more frequent shipments. Similarly, low labor costs relative to media may encourage a shift from mass media advertising to labor-intensive promotion such as personal selling and product demonstration.

Availability of capital, technology, and manufacturing capabilities in different locations will also affect decisions about licensing, contract manufacturing, joint ventures, and other 'make-buy' types of decisions for different markets, as well as decisions about countertrade, reciprocity, and other long-term relations.

The nature of the competitive structure.

Differences in the nature of the competitive situation from one country to another may also suggest the desirability of adaptation strategy. Even in markets characterized by global competition, such as agricultural equipment and motorcycles, the existence of low-cost competition in certain countries may suggest the desirability of marketing stripped-down models or lowering prices to meet such competition. Even where competitors are predominantly other multinationals, preemption of established distribution networks may encourage adoption of innovative distribution methods or direct distribution to short-circuit an entrenched position. Thus, the existence of global competition does not necessarily imply a need for global standardization.

All such aspects thus impose major constraints on the feasibility and effectiveness of a standardized strategy, and suggest the desirability or need to adapt to specific market conditions.

Internal constraints to effective standardization

In addition to such external constraints on the feasibility of a global standardization strategy, there are also a number of internal constraints that may need to be considered. These include compatibility with the existing network of operations overseas, as well as opposition or lack of enthusiasm among local management toward a standardized strategy.

Existing international operations. Proponents of global standardization typically take the position of a novice company with no operations in international markets, and hence fail to take into consideration the fit of the proposed strategy with current international activities. In practice, however, many companies have a number of existing operations in various countries. In some cases, these are joint ventures, or licensing operations or involve some collaboration in purchasing, manufacturing or distribution with other companies. Even where foreign manufacturing and distribution operations are wholly owned, the establishment of a distribution network will typically entail relationships with other organizations, for example, exclusive distributor agreements.

Such commitments may be difficult if not impossible to change in the short run, and may constitute a major impediment to adoption of a standardized strategy. If, for example, a joint venture with a local company has been established to manufacture and market a product line in a specific country or region, resistance from the local partner (or government authorities) may be encountered if the parent company wishes to shift production or import components from another location. Similarly, a licensing contract will impede a firm from supplying the products covered by the agreement from an alternative location for the duration of the contract, even if it becomes more cost efficient to do so.

Conversely, the establishment of an effective dealer or distribution network in a country or region may constitute an important resource to a company. The addition of new products to the product line currently sold or distributed by this network may therefore provide a more efficient utilization of company resources than expanding to new countries or geographic regions with the existing line, as this would require substantial investment in the establishment of a new distribution network.

In addition, overseas subsidiaries may currently be marketing not only core products and brands from the company's domestic business, but may also have added or acquired local or regional products and brands in response to local market demand. In some cases, therefore, introduction of a global product or brand may be likely to cannibalize sales of local or regional brands.

Advocates of standardization thus need to take into consideration the evolutionary character of international involvement, which may render a universal strategy of global products and brands suboptimal. Somewhat ironically, the longer the history of a multinational corporation's involvement in foreign or international markets, and the more diversified and far-flung its operations, the more likely it is that standardization will not lead to optimal results.

Local management motivation and attitudes. Another internal constraint concerns the motivation and attitudes of local management with regard to standardization. Standardized strategies tend to facilitate or result in centralization in the planning and organization of international activities. Especially if input from local management is limited, this may result in a feeling that strategy is 'imposed' by corporate headquarters, and/or not adequately adapted or appropriate in view of specific local market characteristics and conditions. Local management is likely to take the view 'it won't work here – things are different,' which will reduce their motivation to implement a standardized strategy effectively.

A framework for classifying global strategy options

The adoption of a global perspective should not be viewed as synonymous with a strategy of global products and brands. Rather, for most companies such a perspective implies consideration of a broad range of strategic options of which standardization is merely one.

In essence, a global perspective implies planning strategy relative to markets worldwide rather than on a country-by-country basis. This may result in the identification of opportunities for global products and brands and/or integrating and coordinating strategy across national boundaries to exploit potential synergies of operating on an international scale. Such opportunities should, however, be weighed against the benefits of adaptation to idiosyncratic customer characteristics.

The development of an effective global strategy thus requires a careful examination of all international options in terms of standardization versus adaptation open to the firm.

A firm's international operations are likely to be characterized by a mix of strategies, including not only global products and brands, but also some regional products and brands and some national products and brands. Similarly, some target segments may be global, others regional, and others national. Hybrid strategies of this nature thus enable a company to take advantage of the benefits of standardization and potential synergies from operating on an international scale, while at the same time not losing those afforded by adaptation to specific country characteristics and customer preferences.

READINGS ON ORGANIZATIONAL PURPOSE

Selecting the first reading to represent the shareholder value perspective was a simple task. Alfred Rappaport's highly influential book *Creating Shareholder Value* is the classic reading in the field. Although the largest part of his book details how the shareholder value approach can be applied to planning and performance evaluation processes, the first chapter is a compelling exposition of his underlying views on the purpose of a business organization. This first chapter, entitled 'Shareholder Value and Corporate Purpose', has been reprinted here. Rappaport's argument is straightforward – the primary purpose of corporations should be to maximize shareholder value. Therefore, 'business strategies should be judged by the economic returns they generate for shareholders, as measured by dividends plus the increase in the company's share price'. Unlike some other proponents of the shareholder value perspective, Rappaport does not explicitly claim that shareholders have the moral right to demand the primacy of profitability. His argument is more pragmatic – failing to meet the objective of maximizing shareholder value will be punished by more expensive financing. A company's financial power is ultimately determined by the stock markets. Hence, management's ability to meet the demands of the various corporate constituencies depends on the continuing support of its shareholders. Creating shareholder value, therefore, precedes the satisfaction of all other claims on the corporation. It should be noted, however, that Rappaport's arrows are not directed at the demands of employees, customers, suppliers or debtholders, but at top management. He carefully states that senior executives may in some situations pursue objectives that are not to the benefit of shareholders. His preferred solution is not to change corporate governance structures, but to more tightly align the interests of both groups, for example by giving top managers a relatively large ownership position and by tying their compensation to shareholder return performance (in later writings he does favor more structural reforms; e.g. Rappaport, 1990).

The reading on behalf of the stakeholder values perspective is also a classic – 'Stockholders and Stakeholders: A New Perspective on Corporate Governance', by Edward Freeman and David Reed. This article in *California Management Review* and Freeman's subsequent book *Strategic Management: A Stakeholder Approach* were instrumental in popularizing the stakeholder concept. In their article, Freeman and Reed challenge 'the view that stockholders have a privileged place in the business enterprise'. They deplore the fact that 'it has long been gospel that corporations have obligations to stockholders . . . that are sacrosanct and inviolable'. They argue that there has been a long tradition of management thinkers who believe that corporations have a broader responsibility towards other stakeholders than only the suppliers of equity financing. It is their conviction that such a definition of the corporation, as a system serving the interests of multiple stakeholders, is superior to the shareholder perspective. Their strong preference for the stakeholder concept is largely based on the pragmatic argument that, in reality, stakeholders have the power to seriously affect the continuity of the corporation. Stakeholder analysis is needed to understand the actual claims placed by constituents on the firm and to evaluate each stakeholder's power position. Stakeholder management is a practical response to the fact that corporations cannot afford to ignore or downplay the interests of the claimants. Only here and there do Freeman and Reed hint that corporations have the moral responsibility to work on behalf of all stakeholders (which Freeman does more explicitly in some of his later works, e.g. Freeman and Gilbert, 1988; Freeman and Liedtka, 1991). In their opinion, the consequence of the stakeholder concept for corporate governance is that 'there are times when stakeholders must participate in the decision-making process'. However, they believe that if boards of directors adopt a stakeholder outlook and become more responsive to the demands placed on corporations, structural reforms to give stakeholders a stronger role in corporate governance will not be necessary.

READING 11.1

Shareholder value and corporate purpose

By Alfred Rappaport[1]

Corporate mission statements proclaiming that the primary responsibility of management is to maximize shareholders' total return via dividends and increases in the market price of the company's shares abound. While the principle that the fundamental objective of the business corporation is to increase the value of its shareholders' investment is widely accepted, there is substantially less agreement about how this is accomplished.

On the cover of its 1984 annual report Coca-Cola states that 'to increase shareholder

[1]Source: This article was adapted with the permission of The Free Press, a Division of Simon & Schuster Adult Publishing Group, from *Creating Shareholder Value: The New Standard for Business Performance* by Alfred Rappaport. © 1986 by Alfred Rappaport. All rights reserved.

value over time is the objective driving this enterprise.' On the very next page the company goes on to say that to accomplish its objective 'growth in annual earnings per share and increased return on equity are still the names of the game.' In contrast, Hillenbrand Industries, a producer of caskets and hospital equipment, also declares its intention to provide a superior return to its shareholders, but to accomplish that objective management is focusing not on earnings but rather on creating 'shareholder value,' which, it explains in the 1984 annual report, 'is created when a company generates free cash flow in excess of the shareholders' investment in the business.'

Both Coca-Cola and Hillenbrand Industries acknowledge their responsibility to maximize return to their respective shareholders. However, Coca-Cola emphasizes accounting indicators, earnings-per-share growth, and return on equity, while Hillenbrand Industries emphasizes the cash-flow based shareholder value approach to achieve shareholder returns. There are material differences between these two approaches to assessing a company's investment opportunities. Maximizing earnings-per-share growth or other accounting numbers may not necessarily lead to maximizing return for shareholders.

The growing interest

Numerous surveys indicate that a majority of the largest industrial companies have employed the shareholder value approach in capital budgeting for some time. Capital budgeting applications deal with investment projects such as capacity additions rather than total investment at the business level. Thus, we sometimes see a situation where capital projects regularly exceed the minimum acceptable rate of return, while the business unit itself is a 'problem' and creates little or no value for shareholders. This situation can arise because capital expenditures typically represent only a small percentage of total company outlays. For example, capital expenditures amount to about 10 percent of total outlays at General Motors, a particularly capital intensive company.

During the past 10 years, the shareholder value approach has been frequently applied not only to internal investments such as capacity additions, but also to opportunities for external growth such as mergers and acquisitions. Recently a number of major companies such as American Hospital Supply, Combustion Engineering, Hillenbrand Industries, Libbey-Owens-Ford, Marriott, and Westinghouse have found that the shareholder value approach can be productively extended from individual projects to the entire strategic plan. A strategic business unit (SBU) is commonly defined as the smallest organizational unit for which integrated strategic planning, related to a distinct product that serves a well-defined market, is feasible. A strategy for an SBU may then be seen as a collection of product-market related investments and the company itself may be characterized as a portfolio of these investment-requiring strategies. By estimating the future cash flows associated with each strategy, a company can assess the economic value to shareholders of alternative strategies at the business unit and corporate levels.

The interest in shareholder value is gaining momentum as a result of several recent developments.

- The threat of corporate take-overs by those seeking undervalued, undermanaged assets.
- Impressive endorsements by corporate leaders who have adopted the approach.
- The growing recognition that traditional accounting measures such as EPS and ROI are not reliably linked to increasing the value of the company's shares.
- Reporting of returns to shareholders along with other measures of performance in the business press such as *Fortune*'s annual ranking of the 500 leading industrial firms.
- A growing recognition that executives' long-term compensation needs to be more closely tied to returns to shareholders.

Endorsements of the shareholder value approach can be found in an increasing number of annual reports and other corporate publications. One of the more thoughtful statements appears in Libbey-Owens-Ford's 1983 annual report and is reproduced as Exhibit 11.1.1. Combustion Engineering's vice president for finance states that 'a primary financial objective for Combustion Engineering is to create shareholder value by earning superior returns on capital invested in the business. This serves as a clear guide for management action and is the conceptual framework on which CE's financial objectives and goals are based.'

EXHIBIT 11.1.1 LIBBEY-OWENS-FORD STATEMENT

A GREATER EMPHASIS ON SHAREHOLDER VALUE

Libbey-Owens-Ford's mission statement specifies that its primary responsibility is to its shareholders, and that the company has a continuing requirement to increase the value of our shareholders' investment in LOF. This is not just a contemporary business phrase, but the basis for a long-term company strategy. It evaluates business strategies and plans in terms of value to our shareholders, not just on the incremental income that the results will contribute to the bottom line. It requires a greater emphasis on developing strategies and plans that will increase shareholder value as measured by the market appreciation of our stock and dividends.

Traditional Accounting Measures May Not Tell the Entire Story

Traditionally, the most popular way to determine whether a company is performing well is through such accounting measurements as earnings per share (EPS) and return on investment. These measures do, of course, give an indication of a company's performance, but they can be misleading in that often they do not measure the increase or decrease in shareholder value. Sustained growth as measured by EPS does not necessarily reflect an increase in stock value.

This occurs because earnings do not reflect changes in risk and inflation, nor do they take into account the cost of added capital that may have been invested in the business to finance its growth. Yet these are critical considerations when you are striving to increase the value of the shareholders' investment.

Cash Flow Analysis is Emphasized

LOF stresses the importance of cash flow measurement and performance. Individual operating companies must analyze the cash flow effects of running their businesses. Where cash comes from and what cash is used for must be simply and clearly set forth. LOF's cash and short-term investments increased $46.3 million during 1983.

The Shareholder Value Approach

The shareholder value approach taken by LOF emphasized economic cash flow analysis in evaluating individual projects and in determining the economic value of the overall strategy of each business unit and the corporation as a whole. Management looks at the business units and the corporation and determines the minimum operating return necessary to create value. It then reviews the possible contribution of alternative strategies and evaluates the financial feasibility of the strategic plan, based on the company's cost of capital, return on assets, the cash flow stream and other important measurements.

This disciplined process allows LOF to objectively evaluate all its corporate investments, including internal projects and acquisitions, in light of our primary goal to increase shareholder value.

Source: Libbey-Owens-Ford Company 1983 Annual Report.

Whether or not executives agree with the well-publicized tactics of raiders such as Carl Icahn and T. Boone Pickens, they recognize that the raiders characterize themselves as champions of the shareholders. The raiders attack on two fronts. First, they are constantly searching for poorly managed companies, where aggressive changes in strategic directions could dramatically improve the value of the stock. Second, they identify undervalued assets that can be redeployed to boost the stock price. As a result, many executives recognize a new and compelling reason to be concerned with the performance of their company's stock.

Executives have also become increasingly aware that many accrual-based accounting measures do not provide a dependable picture of the current and future performance of an organization. Numerous companies have sustained double-digit EPS growth while providing minimal or even *negative* returns to shareholders. Hillenbrand Industries, for example, points out in its 1984 annual report (p. 4) that 'public companies that focus on achieving short-term earnings to meet external expectations sometimes jeopardize their ability to create long-term value.'

Considerable attention has focused recently on the problems associated with rewarding executives on the basis of short-term accounting-based indicators. As a reflection of the increasing scrutiny under which executive compensation has come, business publications such as *Fortune* and *Business Week* have begun to publish compensation surveys that examine the correlation between the executives' pay and how well their companies have performed based on several measures – including returns to shareholders. For example, *Business Week*'s executive compensation scoreboard now includes a 'pay-performance index' for 255 companies in 36 industries. The index shows how well the top two executives in each company were paid relative to how shareholders fared. The index is the ratio of the executive's three-year total pay as a percent of the industry average to the shareholders' total three-year return as a percent of the industry average. If an executive's pay and shareholders' return are both at the industry average, the index is 100. The lower the index, the better shareholders fared. The broad range in the pay-performance index, even within industries, has further fueled the interest in achieving shareholder value. For the 1982–1984 period, for example, *Business Week* reported a pay-performance index of 59 for Roger Smith, CEO of General Motors, and an index of 160 for Phillip Caldwell, CEO of Ford Motor.

When the shareholder value approach first gained attention toward the end of the 1970s, even the executives who found the concept an intriguing notion tended to think that the approach would be very difficult to implement. The task of educating managers seemed substantial, and they were also not eager to develop a new planning system if it might involve upheaval in the corporate information system. Recent advances in technology have put impressive analytical potential at management's disposal. Managers' decisions are now greatly facilitated by microcomputer software. New approaches thus can more readily be incorporated without displacing existing information systems.

Management versus shareholder objectives

It is important to recognize that the objectives of management may in some situations differ from those of the company's shareholders. Managers, like other people, act in their self-interest. The theory of a market economy is, after all, based on individuals promoting their self-interests via market transactions to bring about an efficient allocation of resources. In a world in which principals (e.g. stockholders) have imperfect control over their agents (e.g. managers), these agents may not always engage in transactions solely in the best interests of the principals. Agents have their own objectives and it may sometimes pay them to sacrifice the principals' interests. The problem is exacerbated in large corporations where it is difficult to identify the interests of a diverse set of stockholders ranging from institutional investors to individuals with small holdings.

Critics of large corporations often allege that corporate managers have too much power and that they act in ways to benefit themselves at the expense of shareholders and other corporate constituencies. The argument is generally developed along the following lines. Responsibility for administering companies or 'control' is vested in the hands of professional managers and thereby has been separated from 'ownership.' Since the ownership of shares in large corporations tends to be diffused, individual shareholders are said to have neither influence on nor interest in corporate governance issues such as the election of board members. Therefore, boards are largely responsive to management which, in turn, can ignore shareholders and run companies as they see fit.

The foregoing 'separation of ownership and control' argument advanced by Berle and Means in 1932 has been a persistent theme of corporate critics during the intervening years. There are, however, a number of factors that induce management to act in the best interests of shareholders. These factors derive from the fundamental premise that the greater the expected unfavorable consequences to the manager who decreases the wealth of shareholders, the less likely it is that the manager will, in fact, act against the interests of shareholders.

Consistent with the above premise, at least four major factors will induce management to adopt a shareholder orientation: (1) a relatively large ownership position, (2) compensation tied to shareholder return performance, (3) threat of take-over by another organization, and (4) competitive labor markets for corporate executives.

Economic rationality dictates that stock ownership by management motivates executives to identify more closely with the shareholders' economic interests. Indeed, we would expect that the greater the proportion of personal wealth invested in company stock or tied to stock options, the greater would be management's shareholder orientation. While the top executives in many companies often have relatively large percentages of their wealth invested in company stock, this is much less often the case for divisional and business unit managers. And it is at the divisional and business unit levels that most resource allocation decisions are made in decentralized organizations.

Even when corporate executives own shares in their company, their viewpoint on the acceptance of risk may differ from that of shareholders. It is reasonable to expect that many corporate executives have a lower tolerance for risk. If the company invests in a risky project, stockholders can always balance this risk against other risks in their presumably diversified portfolios. The manager, however, can balance a project failure only against the other activities of the division or the company. Thus, managers are hurt by the failure more than shareholders.

The second factor likely to influence management to adopt a shareholder orientation is compensation tied to shareholder return performance. The most direct means of linking top management's interests with those of shareholders is to base compensation, and particularly the incentive portion, on market returns realized by shareholders. Exclusive reliance on shareholder returns, however, has its own limitations. First, movements in a company's stock price may well be greatly influenced by factors beyond management control such as the overall state of the economy and stock market. Second, shareholder returns may be materially influenced by what management believes to be unduly optimistic or pessimistic market expectations at the beginning or end of the performance measurement period. And third, divisional and business unit performance cannot be directly linked to stock price.

Rather than linking incentive compensation directly to the market returns earned by shareholders, most *Fortune* 500 companies tie annual bonuses and long-term performance plans to internal financial goals such as earnings or accounting return on investment. These accounting criteria can often conflict with the way corporate shares are valued by the market. If incentives were largely based on earnings, for example, management might well be motivated to pursue economically unsound strategies when viewed from the perspective of shareholders. In such a situation what is economically irrational from the shareholder viewpoint may be a perfectly rational course of action for the decision-making executives.

The third factor affecting management behavior is the threat of take-over by another company. Tender offers have become a commonly employed means of transferring corporate control. Moreover the size of the targets continues to become larger. During the 1979–1985 period, 77 acquisitions each in excess of $1 billion were completed. The threat of take-over is an essential means of constraining corporate managers who might choose to pursue personal goals at the expense of shareholders. Any significant exploitation of shareholders should be reflected in a lower stock price. This lower price, relative to what it might be with more efficient management, offers an attractive take-over opportunity for another company which in many cases will replace incumbent management. An active market for corporate control places limits on the divergence of interests between management and shareholders and thereby serves as an important counterargument to the 'separation of ownership and control' criticisms.

The fourth and final factor influencing management's shareholder orientation is the labor market for corporate executives. Managerial labor markets are an essential mechanism for motivating management to function in the best interests of shareholders. Managers compete for positions both within and outside of the firm. The increasing number of executive recruiting firms and the length of the 'Who's News' column in the *Wall Street Journal* are evidence that the managerial labor market is very active. What is less obvious is how managers are evaluated in this market. Within the firm, performance evaluation and incentive schemes are the basic mechanisms for monitoring managerial performance. As seen earlier, the question here is whether these measures are reliably linked to the market price of the company's shares.

How managers communicate their value to the labor market outside of their individual firms is less apparent. While the performance of top-level corporate officers can be gleaned from annual reports and other publicly available corporate communications, this is not generally the case for divisional managers. For corporate level executives, the question is whether performance for shareholders is the dominant criterion in assessing their value in the executive labor market. The question in the case of division managers is, first, how does the labor market monitor and gain insights about their performance and second, what is the basis for valuing their services.

'Excellence' and restructuring

Two of the most visible business phenomena of the first half of the 1980s have been the publication of Peters and Waterman's *In Search of Excellence* and the unprecedented surge in the restructuring of companies. The 'excellence phenomenon' certainly provided no obvious encouragement for management to link its decisions more closely with the objective of maximizing returns to shareholders. In contrast, the more recent restructuring movement is clearly a manifestation of top management's growing concern with its company's share price and shareholder returns.

As US corporations began the 1980s, saddled with a decade of inflation and lagging productivity, nothing could have come as better news than the idea that not all excellent companies are Japanese. It was in this climate that *In Search of Excellence*, published in 1982, became an absolute sensation. Its longevity on the top of the best-seller list along with its wide coverage in the business press provided an extraordinary platform for the authors' ideas.

The basic purpose of *In Search of Excellence* was to identify key attributes of corporate excellence that are common among successful American corporations. To choose the 'excellent' companies, Peters and Waterman began by assembling a list of 62 US companies that were considered 'successful' by business leaders, consultants, members of the business press, and business school professors. From that list they selected 36 'excellent' companies based on superior performance for such financial measures as return on total capital, return on equity, return on sales, and asset growth. Eight attributes of corporate excellence were identified – a bias for action; staying close to the customer; autonomy and entrepreneurship; productivity through people; hands-on, value-driven management; sticking to the knitting; simple organization form and lean staff; and simultaneous loose-tight properties.

Even though the 'excellent' firms exhibited superior financial (accounting) performance over the 1960–1980 period, they did not provide consistently superior returns to shareholders via dividends plus share price appre-

ciation. The excellent companies did not perform significantly better than the market. Indeed, they did not consistently outperform their respective industry groups or closest competitors. These results once again raise questions about the use of accounting measures to gauge the economic performance of corporations. Since the eight attributes of corporate excellence are not associated with systematically superior returns to shareholders, efforts to emulate these attributes may be ill-advised.

While *In Search of Excellence* became 'must reading' in many organizations during 1982 and 1983, a certain degree of disenchantment set in during the following two years as a number of 'excellent' companies experienced strategic setbacks. Atari, Avon Products, Caterpillar Tractor, Digital Equipment, Hewlett-Packard, Levi Strauss, and Texas Instruments serve as examples.

But if emulating excellent companies has lost some of its luster, a new focal point of interest has captured the imagination of management during the past couple of years – restructuring. Hardly a day passes without some company announcing a major restructuring of its businesses or capital structure. Restructuring involves diverse activities such as divestiture of underperforming businesses or businesses that do not 'fit,' spinoffs directly to shareholders, acquisitions paid for with 'excess cash,' stock repurchases, debt swaps, and liquidation of overfunded pension funds. In many cases, these restructurings are motivated by a desire to foil a take-over bid by so-called 'raiders' who look for undermanaged companies where changes in strategic direction could dramatically increase the value of the stock, and for companies with high liquidation values relative to their current share price. There is, of course, no better means of avoiding a take-over than increasing the price of the stock. Thus, increasing share price has become the fundamental purpose of corporate restructuring.

In contrast to the earlier euphoria over emulating excellent companies, the current restructuring movement is solidly based on shareholder value creation principles. In 1985, the Standard & Poor's 500 appreciated 26 percent in price. Goldman Sachs estimates that corporate restructuring accounted for about 30 percent of that price change. However, the early stage of the restructuring movement, which I call 'Phase I restructuring,' is largely based on one-time transactions such as those listed above rather than changes in day-to-day management of the business.

The necessary agenda for the second half of the 1980s seems clear. Companies need to move from Phase I restructuring to Phase II restructuring. In Phase II, the shareholder value approach is employed not only when buying and selling businesses or changing the company's capital structure, but also in the planning and performance monitoring of all business strategies on an ongoing basis. Frequently, the most difficult issue in this area is how to go about estimating the impact of strategies on shareholder value. Fortunately, relatively straightforward approaches do exist for estimating the shareholder value created by a business strategy, and an increasing number of major companies have begun to use them.

Most companies already use the same discounted cash-flow techniques used in the shareholder value approach to assess the attractiveness of capital investment projects and to value prospective acquisition targets. This approach can be extended to estimate the value creation potential of individual business units and the strategic plan for the entire company.

In Phase II restructuring it will also become increasingly important that executive compensation be tied closely to the shareholder value driven plans so that management will be strongly motivated to make decisions consistent with creating maximum returns to shareholders. A successful implementation of Phase II restructuring not only ensures that management has met its fiduciary responsibility to develop corporate performance evaluation systems consistent with the parameters investors use to value the company, but also minimizes the Phase I concern that a take-over of an undermanaged company is imminent.

Rationale for shareholder value approach

Business strategies should be judged by the economic returns they generate for shareholders, as measured by dividends plus the increase in the company's share price. As management considers alternative strategies, those expected to develop the greatest sustainable competitive advantage will be those that will also create the greatest value for shareholders. The 'shareholder value approach' estimates the economic value of an investment (e.g. the shares of a company, strategies, mergers and acquisitions, capital expenditures) by discounting forecasted cash flows by the cost of capital. These cash flows, in turn, serve as the foundation for shareholder returns from dividends and share-price appreciation.

The case for why management should pursue this objective is comparatively straightforward. Management is often characterized as balancing the interests of various corporate constituencies such as employees, customers, suppliers, debtholders, and stockholders. As Treynor (1981) points out, the company's continued existence depends upon a financial relationship with each of these parties. Employees want competitive wages. Customers want high quality at a competitive price. Suppliers and debtholders each have financial claims that must be satisfied with cash when they fall due. Stockholders as residual claimants of the firm look for cash dividends and the prospect of future dividends which is reflected in the market price of the stock.

If the company does not satisfy the financial claims of its constituents, it will cease to be a viable organization. Employees, customers, and suppliers will simply withdraw their support. Thus, a going concern must strive to enhance its cash-generating ability. The ability of a company to distribute cash to its various constituencies depends on its ability to generate cash from operating its businesses and on its ability to obtain any additional funds needed from external sources.

Debt and equity financing are the two basic external sources. The company's ability to borrow today is based on projections of how much cash will be generated in the future. Borrowing power and the market value of the shares both depend on a company's cash-generating ability. The market value of the shares directly impacts the second source of financing, that is, equity financing. For a given level of funds required, the higher the share price, the less dilution will be borne by current shareholders. Therefore, management's finan-cial power to deal effectively with corporate claimants also comes from increasing the value of the shares. Treynor, a former editor of the *Financial Analysts Journal*, summarizes this line of thinking best:

> *Those who criticize the goal of share value maximization are forgetting that stockholders are not merely the beneficiaries of the corporation's financial success, but also the referees who determine management's financial power.*
>
> *Any management – no matter how powerful and independent – that flouts the financial objective of maximizing share value does so at its own peril.*

READING 11.2

Stockholders and stakeholders: A new perspective on corporate governance

By Edward Freeman and David Reed[1]

Management thought has changed dra-matically in recent years. There have been, and are now underway, both conceptual and practical revolutions in the ways that management theorists and managers think about organizational life. The purpose of this article is to understand the implications of one of these shifts in world view; namely, the shift from 'stockholder' to 'stakeholder.'

The stakeholder concept

It has long been gospel that corporations have obligations to stockholders, holders of the firm's equity, that are sacrosanct and invio-lable. Corporate action or inaction is to be driven by attention to the needs of its stock-holders, usually thought to be measured by stock price, earnings per share, or some other financial measure. It has been argued that the proper relationship of management to its stockholders is similar to that of the fiduciary to the *cestui que trustent*, whereby the interests of the stockholders should be dutifully cared for by management. Thus, any action taken by management must ulti-mately be justified by whether or not it fur-thers the interests of the corporation and its stockholders.

---

[1]Source: © 1983, by the Regents of the University of California. Reprinted from the *California Management Review*, Vol. 25, No. 3. By permission of the Regents.

There is also a long tradition of departure from the view that stockholders have a privileged place in the business enterprise. Berle and Means (1932) were worried about the 'degree of prominence entitling (the corporation) to be dealt with as a major social institution.' Chester Barnard argued that the purpose of the corporation was to serve society, and that the function of the executive was to instill this sense of moral purpose in the corporation's employees (Barnard, 1938). Public relations and corporate social action have a history too long to be catalogued here. However, a recent development calls for a more far-reaching change in the way that we look at corporate life, and that is the good currency of the idea of 'stakeholders.'

The stakeholder notion is indeed a deceptively simple one. It says that there are other groups to whom the corporation is responsible in addition to stockholders: those groups who have a stake in the actions of the corporation. The word *stakeholder*, coined in an internal memorandum at the Stanford Research Institute in 1963, refers to 'those groups without whose support the organization would cease to exist.' The list of stakeholders originally included shareowners, employees, customers, suppliers, lenders, and society. Stemming from the work of Igor Ansoff and Robert Stewart (in the planning department at Lockheed) and, later, Marion Doscher and Stewart (at SRI), stakeholder analysis served and continues to serve an important function in the SRI corporate planning process.

From the original work at SRI, the historical trail diverges in a number of directions. In his now classic *Corporate Strategy: An Analytic Approach to Business Policy for Growth and Expansion*, Igor Ansoff (1965) makes limited use of the theory:

> While as we shall see later, 'responsibilities' and 'objectives' are not synonymous, they have been made one in a 'stakeholder theory' of objectives. This theory maintains that the objectives of the firm should be derived by balancing the conflicting claims of the various 'stakeholders' in the firm: managers, workers, stockholders, suppliers, vendors.

Ansoff goes on to reject the stakeholder theory in favor of a view which separates objectives into 'economic' and 'social' with the latter being a 'secondary modifying and constraining influence' on the former.

In the mid-1970s, researchers in systems theory, led by Russell Ackoff (1974) 'rediscovered' stakeholder analysis, or at least took Ansoff's admonition more seriously. Propounding essentially an open systems view of organizations, Ackoff argues that many social problems can be solved by the redesign of fundamental institutions with the support and interaction of stakeholders in the system.

A second trail from Ansoff's original reference is the work of William Dill, who in concert with Ackoff, sought to move the stakeholder concept from the periphery of corporate planning to a central place. In 1975 Dill argued:

> For a long time, we have assumed that the views and the initiative of stakeholders could be dealt with as externalities to the strategic planning and management process: as data to help management shape decisions, or as legal and social constraints to limit them. We have been reluctant, though, to admit the idea that some of these outside stakeholders might seek and earn active roles with management to make decisions. The move today is from stakeholder influence towards stakeholder participation.

Dill went on to set out a role for strategic managers as communicators with stakeholders and considered the role of adversary groups such as Nader's Raiders in the strategic process. For the most part, until Dill's paper, stakeholders had been assumed to be nonadversarial, or adversarial only in the sense of labor-management relations. By broadening the notion of stakeholder to 'people outside . . . who have ideas about what the economic and social performance of the enterprise should include,' Dill set the stage for the use of the stakeholder concept as an umbrella for strategic management.

A related development is primarily responsible for giving the stakeholder concept a boost; namely, the increase in concern with the social involvement of business. The corporate social responsibility movement is too diverse and has spawned too many ideas, concepts, and techniques to explain here. Suffice it to say that the social movements of the sixties and seventies – civil rights, the antiwar movement, consumerism, environmentalism, and women's rights – served as a catalyst for rethinking the role of the business enterprise in society. From Milton Friedman to John Kenneth Galbraith, there is a diversity of arguments. However, one aspect of the corporate social responsibility debate is particularly relevant to understanding the good currency of the stakeholder concept.

In the early 1970s the Harvard Business School undertook a project on corporate social responsibility. The output of the project was voluminous, and of particular importance was the development of a pragmatic model of social responsibility called 'the corporate social responsiveness model' (Ackerman and Bauer, 1976). It essentially addressed Dill's question with respect to social issues: 'How can the corporation respond proactively to the increased pressure for positive social change?' By concentrating on responsiveness instead of responsibility, the Harvard researchers were able to link the analysis of social issues with the traditional areas of strategy and organization.

By the late 1970s the need for strategic management processes to take account of nontraditional business problems in terms of government, special interest groups, trade associations, foreign competitors, dissident shareholders, and complex issues such as employee rights, equal opportunity, environmental pollution, consumer rights, tariffs, government regulation, and reindustrializa-

tion had become obvious. To begin to develop these processes, The Wharton School began, in 1977 in its Applied Research Center, a 'stakeholder project.' The objectives of the project were to put together a number of strands of thought and to develop a theory of management which enabled executives to formulate and implement corporate strategy in turbulent environments. Thus, an action research model was used whereby stakeholder theory was generated by actual cases.

To date the project has explored the implications of the stakeholder concept on three levels: as a management theory; as a process for practitioners to use in strategic management; and as an analytical framework.

At the theoretical level the implications of substituting *stakeholder* for *stockholder* needs to be explicated. The first problem at this level is the actual definition of *stakeholder*. SRI's original definition is too general and too exclusive to serve as a means of identifying those external groups who are strategically important. The concentration on generic stakeholders, such as society and customers, rather than specific social interest groups and specific customer segments produces an analysis which can only be used as a background for the planning process. Strategically useful information about the actions, objectives, and motivations of specific groups, which is needed if management is to be responsive to stakeholder concerns, requires a more specific and inclusive definition.

We propose two definitions of *stakeholder*: a wide sense, which includes groups who are friendly or hostile, and a narrow sense, which captures the essence of the SRI definition. but is more specific.

- **The wide sense of stakeholder.** Any identifiable group or individual who can affect the achievement of an organization's objectives or who is affected by the achievement of an organization's objectives. (Public interest groups, protest groups, government agencies, trade associations, competitors, unions, as well as employees, customer segments, shareowners, and others are stakeholders, in this sense.)

- **The narrow sense of stakeholder.** Any identifiable group or individual on which the organization is dependent for its continued survival. (Employees, customer segments, certain suppliers, key government agencies, shareowners, certain financial institutions, as well as others are all stakeholders in the narrow sense of the term.)

While executives are willing to recognize that employees, suppliers, and customers have a stake in the corporation, many resist the inclusion of adversary groups. But from the standpoint of corporate strategy, *stakeholder* must be understood in the wide sense: strategies need to account for those groups who can affect the achievement of the firm's objectives. Some may feel happier with other words, such as *influencers*, *claimants*, *publics*, or *constituencies*. Semantics aside, if corporations are to formulate and implement strategies in turbulent environments, theories of strategy must have concepts, such as the wide sense of *stakeholder*, which allow the analysis of all external forces and pressures whether they are friendly or hostile. In what follows we will use *stakeholder* in the wide sense, as our primary objective is to elucidate the questions of corporate governance from the perspective of strategic management.

A second issue at the theoretical level is the generation of prescriptive propositions which explain actual cases and articulate regulative principles for future use. Thus, a *post hoc* analysis of the brewing industry and the problem of beverage container legislation, combined with a similar analysis of the regulatory environments of public utilities have led to some simple propositions which serve as a philosophical guideline for strategy formulation. For example:

- Generalize the marketing approach: understand the needs of each stakeholder, in a similar fashion to understanding customer needs, and design products, services, and programs to fulfill those needs.

- Establish negotiation processes: understand the political nature of a number of stakeholders, and the applicability of concepts and techniques of political science, such as coalition analysis, conflict management, and the use and abuse of unilateral action.

- Establish a decision philosophy that is oriented towards seizing the initiative rather than reacting to events as they occur.

- Allocate organizational resources based on the degree of importance of the environmental turbulence (the stakeholders' claims).

Other prescriptive propositions can be put forth, especially with respect to issues of corporate governance. One proposition that has been discussed is to 'involve stakeholder groups in strategic decisions,' or 'invite stakeholders to participate in governance decisions.' While propositions like this may have substantial merit, we have not examined enough cases nor marshalled enough evidence to support them in an unqualified manner. There are cases where participation is appropriate. Some public utilities have been quite successful in the use of stakeholder advisory groups in matters of rate setting. However, given the breadth of our concept of stakeholder we believe that co-optation through participation is not always the correct strategic decision.

The second level of analysis is the use of stakeholder concepts in strategy formulation processes. Two processes have been used so far: the *Stakeholder Strategy Process* and the *Stakeholder Audit Process*. The Stakeholder Strategy Process is a systematic method for analyzing the relative importance of stakeholders and their cooperative potential (how they can help the corporation achieve its objectives) and their competitive threat (how they can prevent the corporation from achieving its objectives). The process is one which relies on a behavioral analysis (both actual and potential) for input, and an explanatory model of stakeholder objectives and resultant strategic shifts for output. The Stakeholder

Audit Process is a systematic method for identifying stakeholders and assessing the effectiveness of current organizational strategies. By itself, each process has a use in the strategic management of an organization. Each analyzes the stakeholder environment from the standpoint of organizational mission and objectives and seeks to formulate strategies for meeting stakeholder needs and concerns.

The use of the stakeholder concept at the analytical level means thinking in terms which are broader than current strategic and operational problems. It implies looking at public policy questions in stakeholder terms and trying to understand how the relationships between an organization and its stakeholders would change given the implementation of certain policies.

One analytical device depicts an organization's stakeholders on a two-dimensional grid map. The first dimension is one of 'interest' or 'stake' and ranges from an equity interest to an economic interest or marketplace stake to an interest or stake as a 'kibitzer' or influencer. Shareowners have an equity stake; customers and suppliers have an economic stake; and single-issue groups have an influencer stake. The second dimension of a stakeholder is its power, which ranges from the formalistic or voting power of stockholders to the economic power of customers to the political power of special interest groups. By *economic power* we mean 'the ability to influence due to marketplace decisions' and by *political power* we mean 'the ability to influence due to use of the political process.'

Figure 11.2.1 represents this stakeholder grid graphically. It is of course possible that a stakeholder has more than one kind of both stake and power, especially in light of the fact that there are stakeholders who have multiple roles. An employee may be at once shareholder, customer, employee, and even kibitzer. Figure 11.2.1 represents the prevailing world view. That is, shareholders and directors have formal or voting power; customers, suppliers, and employees have economic power; and government and special interest groups have political power. Moreover, management concepts and principles have evolved to treat this 'diagonal case.' Managers learn how to handle stockholders and boards via their ability to vote on certain key decisions, and conflicts are resolved by the procedures and processes written into the corporate charter or by methods which involve formal legal parameters.

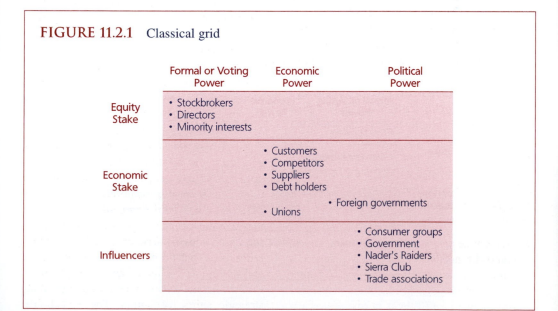

FIGURE 11.2.1 Classical grid

	Formal or Voting Power	Economic Power	Political Power
Equity Stake	• Stockbrokers • Directors • Minority interests		
Economic Stake		• Customers • Competitors • Suppliers • Debt holders • Unions	• Foreign governments
Influencers			• Consumer groups • Government • Nader's Raiders • Sierra Club • Trade associations

Strategic planners, marketers, financial analysts, and operations executives base their decisions on marketplace variables, and an entire tradition of management principles is based on the economic analysis of the marketplace. Finally, public relations and public affairs managers and lobbyists learn to deal in the political arena. As long as the real world approximately fits into the diagonal, management processes may be able to deal effectively with them. A more thoughtful examination, however, reveals that Figure 11.2.1 is either a straw man or that shifts of position have occurred. In the auto industry, for instance, one part of government has acquired economic power in terms of the imposition of import quotas or the trigger price mechanism. The Securities and Exchange Commission might be looked at as a kibitzer with formal power in terms of disclosure and accounting rules. Outside directors do not necessarily have an equity stake, especially those women, minorities, and academics who are becoming more and more normal for the boards of large corporations. Some kibitzer groups are buying stock and acquiring an equity stake, and while they also acquire formal power, their main source of power is still political. Witness the marshalling of the political process by church groups in bringing up, at annual meetings, issues such as selling infant formula in the Third World or investing in South Africa. Unions are using their political power as well as their formal clout as managers of large portions of pension funds to influence the company. Customers are being organized by consumer advocates to exercise the voice option and to politicize the marketplace. In short, the real world looks more like Figure 11.2.2. (Of course, each organization will have its own individual grid.) Thus, search for alternative applications of traditional management processes must begin, and new concepts and techniques are needed to understand the shifts that have occurred and to manage in the new environment.

There is a need to develop new and innovative management processes to deal with the current and future complexities of management issues. At the theoretical level, stakeholder analysis has been developed to enrich the economic approach to corporate strategy by arguing that kibitzers with political power must be included in the strategy process. At the strategic level, stakeholder analysis takes a number of groups into account and analyzes their strategic impact on the corporation.

FIGURE 11.2.2   'Real world' stakeholder grid

	Formal or Voting Power	Economic Power	Political Power
Equity Stake	• Stockbrokers • Directors • Minority interests		• Dissident stockholders
Economic Stake		• Suppliers • Debt holders • Customers • Unions	• Local governments • Foreign governments • Consumer groups • Unions
Influencers	• Government • SEC • Outside directors	• EPA/OSHA	• Nader's Raiders • Government • Trade associations

Stakeholder analysis and corporate democracy

The debate on corporate governance and, in particular, corporate democracy has recently intensified. Proposals have been put forth to make the corporation more democratic, to encourage shareholder participation and management responsiveness to shareholder needs, and to make corporations more responsive to other stakeholder needs and, hence, to encourage the participation of stakeholders in the governance process. Reforms from cumulative voting to audit committees have been suggested.

Corporate democracy has come to have at least three meanings over the years, which prescribe that corporations should be made more democratic: by increasing the role of government, either as a watchdog or by having public officials on boards of directors; by allowing citizen or public participation in the managing of its affairs via public interest directors and the like; or by encouraging or mandating the active participation of all or many of its shareholders. The analysis of the preceding section has implications for each of these levels of democratization.

The propositions of stakeholder analysis advocate a thorough understanding of a firm's stakeholders (in the wide sense) and recognize that there are times when stakeholders must participate in the decision-making process. The strategic tools and techniques of stakeholder analysis yield a method for determining the timing and degree of such participation. At the absolute minimum this implies that boards of directors must be aware of the impact of their decisions on key stakeholder groups. As stakeholders have begun to exercise more political power and as marketplace decisions become politicized, the need for awareness to grow into responsiveness has become apparent. Thus, the analytical model can be used by boards to map carefully the power and stake of each group. While it is not the proper role of the board to be involved in the implementation of tactical programs at the operational level of the corporation, it must set the tone for how the company deals with stakeholders, both traditional marketplace ones and those who have political power. The board must decide not only whether management is managing the affairs of the corporation, but indeed, what are to count as the affairs of the corporation. This involves assessing the stake and power of each stakeholder group.

Much has been written about the failure of senior management to think strategically, competitively, and globally. Some have argued that American businesspersons are 'managing [their] way to economic decline' (Hayes and Abernathy, 1980). Executives have countered the critics with complaints about the increase in the adversarial role of government and in the number of hostile external interest groups. Yet if the criteria for success for senior executives remains fixated on economic stakeholders with economic power and on short-term performance on Wall Street, the rise of such a turbulent political environment in a free and open society should come as no surprise. If the board sees itself as responsive only to the shareholder in the short term, senior management will continue to manage towards economic decline.[2] We have argued that the problem of governing the corporation in today's world must be viewed in terms of the entire grid of stakeholders and their power base. It is only by setting the direction for positive response and negotiation at the board level that the adversarial nature of the business-government relationship can be overcome.

---

[2] It is arguable whether responsiveness to nonmarket stakeholders is in the long-term interest of the corporation. We believe that there is no need to appeal to utilitarian notions of greatest social good or altruism or social responsibility. Rather the corporation fulfills its obligations to shareholders in the long term only through proper stakeholder management. In short we believe that enlightened self-interest gives both reasons why (personal motivation) and reasons for (social justification) taking stakeholder concerns into account. The development of this argument is, however, beyond our present scope.

If this task of stakeholder management is done properly, much of the air is let out of critics who argue that the corporation must be democratized in terms of increased direct citizen participation. Issues which involve both economic and political stakes and power bases must be addressed in an integrated fashion. No longer can public affairs, public relations, and corporate philanthropy serve as adequate management tools. The sophistication of interest groups who are beginning to use formal power mechanisms, such as proxy fights, annual meetings, the corporate charter, to focus the attention of management on the affairs of the corporation has increased. Responsive boards will seize these opportunities to learn more about those stakeholders who have chosen the option of voice over the Wall Street Rule. As boards direct management to respond to these concerns, to negotiate with critics, to trade off certain policies in return for positive support, the pressure for mandated citizen participation will subside.

REFERENCES

Abell, D. (1980) *Defining the Business: The Starting Point of Strategic Planning*, Prentice Hall, Englewood Cliffs, NJ.

Ackoff, R.L. (1974) *Redesigning the Future*, Wiley, New York.

Ackoff, R.L. (1980) *Creating the Corporate Future*, Wiley, Chichester.

Albert, M. (1991) *Capitalisme contre Capitalisme*, Seuil, Paris.

Aldrich, H.E. (1979) *Organizations and Environments*, Prentice Hall, Englewood Cliffs, NJ.

Aldrich, H.E. (1999) *Organizations Evolving*, Sage, London.

Aldrich, H.E., and Fiol, C.M. (1994) 'Fools Rush In? The Institutional Context of Industry Creation', *Academy of Management Review*, Vol. 19, No. 4, pp. 645–670.

Alkhafaji, A.F. (1989) *A Stakeholder Approach to Corporate Governance: Managing a Dynamic Environment*, Quorum Books, Westport, CT.

Allison, G.T. (1969) 'Conceptual Models and The Cuban Missile Crisis', *The American Political Science Review*, No. 3, September, pp. 689–718.

Allison, G.T. (1971) *Essence of Decision: Explaining the Cuban Missile Crisis*, Little Brown, Boston.

Amabile, T.M. (1998) 'How to Kill Creativity', *Harvard Business Review*, Vol. 76, No. 5, September–October, pp. 76–87.

Amit, R., and J. Livnat (1988) 'Diversification and the Risk–Return Trade-off', *Academy of Management Journal*, Vol. 31, No. 1, March, pp. 154–165.

Amit, R., and C. Zott (2001) 'Value Creation in E-business', *Strategic Management Journal*, Vol. 22, pp. 493–520.

Anderson, J.R. (1983) *The Architecture of Cognition*, Harvard University Press, Cambridge, MA.

Andrews, K. (1987) *The Concept of Corporate Strategy*, Irwin, Homewood. IL.

Anslinger, P.L., and T.E. Copeland (1996) 'Growth Through Acquisitions: A Fresh Look', *Harvard Business Review*, Vol. 74, No. 1, January–February, pp. 126–135.

Ansoff, H.I. (1965) *Corporate Strategy: An Analytic Approach to Business Policy for Growth and Expansion*, McGraw-Hill, New York, pp. 44.

Ansoff, H.I. (1991) 'Critique of Henry Mintzberg's The "Design School": Reconsidering the Basic Premises of Strategic Management', *Strategic Management Journal*, September, pp. 449–461.

Ansoff, H.I., and McDonnell. E. (1990) *Implanting Strategic Management, Second Edition*, Prentice Hall, New York.

Anthony, W.P., Bennett, R.H., Maddox, E.N., and Wheatley, W.J. (1993) 'Picturing the Future: Using Mental Imagery to Enrich Strategic Environmental Assessment', *Academy of Management Executive*, Vol. 7, No. 2, pp. 43–56.

Argyris, C. (1990) *Overcoming Organizational Defenses: Facilitating Organizational Learning*, Prentice Hall, Boston, MA.

Armstrong, J.S. (1982) 'The Value of Formal Planning for Strategic Decisions: Review of Empirical Research', *Strategic Management Journal*, Vol. 3, pp. 197–211.

Arthur, W.B. (1994) *Increasing Returns and Path Dependence in the Economy*, University of Michigan Press, Ann Arbor, MI.

Arthur, W.B. (1996) 'Increasing Returns and the New World of Business', *Harvard Business Review*, Vol. 74, No. 4, July–August, pp. 100–109.

Astley, W.G., and Van der Ven, A.H. (1983) 'Central Perspectives and Debates in Organization Theory', *Administrative Science Quarterly*, Vol. 28, No. 2, June, pp. 245–273.

Axelrod, R. (1976) *The Structure of Decision: The Cognitive Maps of Political Elites*, Princeton University Press, Princeton, New York.

Axelrod, R. (1984) *The Evolution of Cooperation*, Basic Books, New York.

Axelsson, B., and Easton, G. (1992) *Industrial Networks: A New View of Reality*, Wiley, New York.

Badaracco, J.L. (1991) *The Knowledge Link: How Firms Compete Through Strategic Alliances*, Harvard Business School Press, Boston, MA.

Baden-Fuller, C., and Pitt, M. (1996) *Strategic Innovation*, Routledge, London.

Baden-Fuller, C., and Stopford, J.M. (1992) *Rejuvenating the Mature Business*, Routledge, London.

Bailey, A., and Johnson, G. (1992) 'How Strategies Develop in Organizations', in D. Faulkner, and G. Johnson (eds.), *The Challenge of Strategic Management*, Kogan Page, London.

Bain, J.S. (1959) *Industrial Organization*, Wiley, New York.

Barney, J.B. (1991) 'Firm Resources and Sustained Competitive Advantage', *Journal of Management*, Vol. 17, No. 1, pp. 99–120.

Barney, J.B., Wright, M., and Ketchen, D.J. (2001) 'The Resource-Based View of the Firm: Ten Years After 1991', *Journal of Management*, Vol. 27, No. 6, pp. 625–641.

Bartlett, C.A., and Ghoshal, S. (1987) 'Managing Across Borders: New Organizational Responses', *Sloan Management Review*, Vol. 29, No. 1, Fall, pp. 43–53.

Bartlett, C.A., and Ghoshal, S. (1989) *Managing across Borders: The Transnational Solution*, Harvard Business School Press, New York.

Bartlett, C.A., and Ghoshal, S. (1994) 'Changing the Role of Top Management: Beyond Strategy to Purpose', *Harvard Business Review*, November–December, pp. 79–88.

Bartlett, C.A., and Ghoshal, S. (1995) *Transnational Management: Text, Cases, and Readings in Cross-Border Management*, Second Edition, R.D. Irwin Inc., Homewoood, IL.

Bass, B.M. (1990) *Bass and Stogdill's Handbook of Leadership*, Third Edition, The Free Press, New York.

Bate, P. (1994) *Strategies for Cultural Change*, Butterworth-Heinemann, Oxford.

Baum, J.A.C., and Singh, J.V. (eds.) (1994) *Evolutionary Dynamics of Organizations*, Oxford University Press, Oxford.

Baysinger, B.D., and Hoskisson, R.E. (1990) 'The Composition of Boards of Directors and Strategic Control: Effects of Corporate Strategy', *Academy of Management Review*, Vol. 15, No. 1, January, pp. 72–81.

Bazerman, M.H. (1990) *Judgment in Managerial Decision Making*, Second Edition, Wiley, New York.

Behling, O., and Eckel, N.L. (1991) 'Making Sense Out of Intuition', *Academy of Management Executive*, Vol. 5, No. 1, pp. 46–54.

Beinhocker, E.D. (1999) 'Robust Adaptive Strategies', *Sloan Management Review*, Vol. 40, No. 3, Spring, pp. 95–106.

Bennis, W. (1989) *On Becoming a Leader*, Addison-Wesley, Reading, MA.

Bennis, W., and Nanus, B. (1985) *Leaders: The Strategies for Taking Charge*, Harper & Row, New York.

Berle, A.A., and Means, G.C. (1932) *The Modern Corporation and Private Property*, Transaction Publishers, McMillan, New York.

Best, M.H. (1990) *The New Competition: Institutions of Industrial Restructuring*, Polity, Cambridge.

Bettis, R.A., Bradley, S.P., and Hamel, G. (1992) 'Outsourcing and Industrial Decline', *Academy of Management Executive*, pp. 7–22.

Bettis, R.A., and Donaldson, L. (1990) 'Market Discipline and The Discipline of Management', *Academy of Management Review*, Vol. 15, No. 3, July, pp. 367–368.

Birkenshaw, J., and Hood, N. (1998) *Multinational Corporate Evolution and Subsidiary Development*, Macmillan Press Ltd., London.

Blair, M. (1995) *Ownership and Control: Rethinking Corporate Governance for the Twenty-First Century*, Brookings Institution, Washington.

Bleeke, J., and Ernst, D. (1991) 'The Way to Win in Cross Border Alliances', *Harvard Business Review*, Vol. 69, No. 6, November–December, pp. 127–135.

Bourgeois, L.J., and Brodwin, D.R. (1983) 'Putting Your Strategy into Action', *Strategic Management Planning*, March–May.

Bower, J.L. (1970) *Managing the Resource Allocation Process*, Harvard Business School Press, Boston, MA.

Bower, J.L., and Christensen, C.M. (1995) 'Disruptive Technologies: Catching the Wave', *Harvard Business Review*, Vol. 73, No. 1, January–February, pp. 43–53.

Brandenburger, A.M., and Nalebuff, B.J. (1996) *Co-opetition*, Currency Doubleday, New York.

Brown, S.L., and K.M. Eisenhardt (1998) *Competing on the Edge: Strategy as Structured Chaos*, Harvard Business School Press, Boston, MA.

Bucholz, R.A. (1986) *Business Environment and Public Policy*, Prentice Hall, Englewood Cliffs, NJ.

Buckley, P.J., and Casson, M.C. (1976) *The Future of the Multinational Enterprise*, Macmillan, London.

Buckley, P.J., and Casson, M.C. (1985) *The Economic Theory of the Multinational Enterprise*, Macmillan, London.

Buono, A.F., and Nichols, L.T. (1985) *Corporate Policy, Values and Social Responsibility*, Praeger, New York.

Burgelman, R.A. (1983) 'Corporate Entrepreneurship and Strategic Management: Insights from a Process Study', *Management Science*, Vol. 29, No. 12, pp. 1349–1364.

Burgelman, R.A. (1991) 'Intraorganizational Ecology of Strategy Making and Organizational Adaptation: Theory and Field Research', *Organization Science*, Vol. 2, No. 3, pp. 239–262.

Burgelman, R.A., and Grove, A.S. (1996) 'Strategic Dissonance', *California Management Review*, Vol. 38, No. 2.

Buzzell, R.D., and Gale, B.T. (1987) *The PIMS Principles: Linking Strategy to Performance*, The Free Press, New York.

Calder, B. (1977) 'An Attribution Theory of Leadership', in B. Staw and B. Salanck (eds.), *New Directions in Organizational Behavior*, St. Clair, Chicago.

Calori, R. and CESMA (1988) 'How Successful Companies Manage Diverse Businesses', *Long Range Planning*, Vol. 21, No. 3, pp. 80–89.

Calori, R., and de Woot, P. (eds.) (1994) *A European Management Model: Beyond Diversity*, Prentice Hall, Hemel Hempstead.

Campbell, A., and Goold, M. (1998) *Synergy: Why Links Between Business Units Often Fail and How to Make Them Work*, Capstone Publishing, Oxford.

Campbell, A., Goold, M., and Alexander, M. (1995) 'The Value of the Parent Company', *California Management Review*, Vol. 38, No. 1, Fall, pp. 79–97.

Campbell, A., and Tawadey, K. (eds.) (1990) *Mission and Business Philosophy*, Butterworth-Heinemann, Oxford.

Campbell, A., and Yeung, S. (1991) 'Creating a Sense of Mission', *Long Range Planning*, Vol. 24, No. 4, August, pp.10–20.

Cannella, A.A., and Monroe, M.J. (1997) 'Contrasting Perspectives on Strategic Leaders: Toward a More Realistic View of Top Managers, *Journal of Management*, Vol. 23, No. 3, pp. 213–237.

Cannon, T. (1992) *Corporate Responsibility*, Pitman, London.

Carpenter, M.A., and Golden, B.R. (1997) 'Perceived Managerial Discretion: A Study of Cause and Effect', *Strategic Management Journal*, Vol. 18, No. 3, March, pp. 187–206.

Carroll, A.B. (1993) *Business and Society: Ethics and Stakeholder Management*, Second Edition, South-Western Publishing, Cincinnati.

Chaffee, E.E. (1985) 'Three Models of Strategy', *Academy of Management Review*, Vol. 10, No. 1, January, pp. 89–98.

Chakravarthy, B.S., and Lorange, P. (1991) *Managing the Strategy Process: A Framework for a Multibusiness Firm*, Prentice Hall, Englewood Cliffs, NJ.

Chakravarthy, B.S., and Perlmutter, H.W. (1985) 'Strategic Planning for a Global Business', *Columbia Journal of World Business*, Vol. 20, Summer, pp. 3–10.

Chandler, A.D. (1962) *Strategy and Structure: Chapters in the History of the American Industrial Enterprise*, MIT Press, Cambridge, MA.

Chandler, A.D. (1990) *Scale and Scope*, Belknop, Cambridge, MA.

Charkham, J. (1994) *Keeping Good Company: A Study of Corporate Governance in Five Countries*, Oxford University Press, Oxford.

Chatterjee, S. (1986) 'Types of Synergy and Economic Value: The Impact of Acquisitions on Merging and Rival Firms', *Strategic Management Journal*, Vol. 7, No. 2, March–April, pp. 119–139.

Chen, C.C., and Meindl, J.R. (1991) 'The Construction of Leadership Images in the Popular Press: The Case of Donald Burr and People Express', *Administrative Science Quarterly*, Vol. 36, No. 4, December, pp. 521–551.

Chesbrough, H.W., and Teece, D.J. (1996) 'Organizing for Innovation: When is Virtual Virtuous?', *Harvard Business Review*, Vol. 74, No. 1, January–February, pp. 65–73.

Child, J. (1972) 'Organizational Structure, Environment, and Performance: The Role of Strategic Choice', *Sociology*, January, pp. 2–22.

Child, J. and Faulkner, D. (1998) *Strategies of Cooperation: Managing Alliances, Networks, and Joint Ventures*, Oxford University Press, Oxford.

Christensen, C.M. (1997) *The Innovator's Dilemma*, HarperBusiness, New York.

Christensen, C.R., Andrews, K.R., Bower, J.L., Hamermesh, R.G., and Porter, M.E. (1987) *Business Policy: Text and Cases*, Sixth Edition, Irwin, Homewood, IL.

Clarke, T. (1998) 'The Stakeholder Corporation: A Business Philosophy for the Information Age', *Long Range Planning*, Vol. 31, No. 2, April, pp. 182–194.

Clarkson, M.B.E. (1995) 'A Stakeholder Framework For Analyzing and Evaluating Corporate Social Performance', *Academy of Management Review*, Vol. 20, No. 1, January, pp. 92–117.

Cochran, Ph.L., and Wartick, S.L. (1994) 'Corporate Governance: A Review of the Literature', in R.I. Tricker (ed.), *International Corporate Governance: Text, Readings and Cases*, Prentice Hall, Singapore.

Collins, J.C., and Porras, J.I. (1994) *Built to Last: Successful Habits of Visionary Companies*, HarperBusiness, New York.

Collins, J.C., and Porras, J. (1996) 'Building Your Company's Vision', *Harvard Business Review*, Vol. 75, No. 5, September–October, pp. 65–77.

Collis, D.J., and Montgomery, C.A. (1995) 'Competing on Resources: Strategy in the 1990s', *Harvard Business Review*, Vol. 73, No. 4, July–August, pp. 118–128.

Conger J.A. (1999) 'Charismatic and Transformational Leadership in Organizations', *The Leadership Quarterly*, Vol. 10, No. 2, Summer, pp. 145–179.

Contractor, F.J., and Lorange, P. (1988) *Cooperative Strategies in International Business*, Lexington Books, Lexington, MA.

Cummings, S., and Davies, J. (1994) 'Mission, Vision, Fusion', *Long Range Planning*, Vol. 27, No. 6, December, pp. 147–150.

Cusumano, M.A., and Gawer, A. (2002) 'The Elements of Platform Leadership', *Sloan Management Review*, Vol. 43, No. 3, Spring, pp. 51–58.

Cyert, R.M. (1990) 'Defining Leadership and Explicating the Process', *Non-Profit Management & Leadership*, Vol. 1, No. 1, Fall, pp. 29–38.

Daft, R., and Weick, K. (1984) 'Toward a Model of Organizations as Interpretation Systems', *Academy of Management Review*, Vol. 9, pp. 284–295.

D'Aveni, R.A. (1994) *Hypercompetition: Managing the Dynamics of Strategic Maneuvering*, The Free Press, New York.

D'Aveni, R.A. (1999) Strategic Supremacy through Disruption and Dominance, *Sloan Management Review*, Vol. 40, No. 3, pp. 127–135.

David, F.R. (1989) 'How Companies Define Their Mission', *Long Range Planning*, Vol. 22, No. 1, February, pp. 90–97.

Day, D.L. (1994) 'Raising Radicals: Different Processes for Championing Innovative Corporate Ventures', *Organization Science*, Vol. 5, No. 2, May, pp. 148–172.

Day, D.V. and Lord, R.G. (1992) 'Expertise and Problem Categorization: The Role of Expert Processing in Organizational Sense-Making', *Journal of Management Studies*, Vol. 29, pp. 35–47.

Day, G.S. (1990) *Market Driven Strategy, Processes for Creating Value*, The Free Press, New York.

Day, G.S. (1994) 'The Capabilities of Market-Driven Organizations', *Journal of Marketing*, Vol. 58, No. 4, October, pp. 37–52.

De Bono, E. (1970) *Lateral Thinking*, Harper & Row, New York.

Demb, A., and Neubauer, F.F. (1992) *The Corporate Board: Confronting the Paradoxes*, Oxford University Press, Oxford.

Dicken, P. (1992) *Global Shift: The Internationalisation of Economic Activity*, Chapman, London.

Dierickx, I., and Cool, K. (1989) 'Asset Stock Accumulation and Sustainability of Competitive Advantage', *Management Science*, Vol. 35, No. 12, December, pp. 1504–1511.

DiMaggio, P.J., and Powell, W.W. (1983) 'The Iron Cage Revisited: Institutional Isomorphism and Collective Rationality in Organizational Fields', *American Sociological Review*, Vol. 48, No. 2, April, pp. 147–160.

Dimsdale, N., and Prevezer, M. (eds.) (1994) *Capital Markets and Corporate Governance*, Oxford University Press, Oxford.

Dixit, A.K., and Nalebuff, B.J. (1991) *Thinking Strategically: The Competitive Edge in Business, Politics, and Everyday Life*, W.W. Norton, New York.

Donaldson, G., and Lorsch, J.W. (1983) *Decision Making at the Top: The Shaping of Strategic Direction*, Basic Books, New York.

Donaldson, L., and Davis, J.H. (1995) 'Boards and Company Performance: Research Challenges the Conventional Wisdom', *Corporate Governance*, Vol. 2, pp. 151–160.

Donaldson, T. (1989) *Ethics in International Business,* Oxford University Press, London.

Donaldson, T., and Preston, L.E. (1995) 'The Stakeholder Theory of the Corporation: Concepts, Evidence, and Implications', *Academy of Management Review*, Vol. 20, No. 1, January, pp. 65–91.

Dosi, G., and B. Kogut (1993) 'National Specificities and the Context of Change: The Co-evolution of Organization and Technology', in B. Kogut, (ed.) *Country Competitiveness: Technology and the Organizing of Work*, Oxford University Press, Oxford.

Douglas, S.P., and Wind, Y. (1987) 'The Myth of Globalization', *Columbia Journal of World Business*, Vol. 22, Winter, pp. 19–29.

Doz, Y., and Hamel, G. (1998) *The Alliance Advantage: The Art of Creating Vale Through Partnering*, Harvard Business School Press, Boston, MA.

Dretske, F. (1981) *Knowledge and the Flow of Information*, MIT Press, Cambridge, MA.

Drucker, P.F. (1984) 'The New Meaning of Corporate Social Responsibility', *California Management Review*, Vol. 26, No. 2, Winter, pp. 53–63.

Duncan, R.B. (1976) 'The Ambidextrous Organization: Designing Dual Structures for Innovation', in R.H. Kilmann, L.R. Pondy, and D.P. Slevin, (eds.), *The Management of Organizational Design*, Elsevier, New York, pp. 167–188.

Dunning, J. (1986) *Japanese Participation in British Industry: Trojan Horse or Catalyst for Growth?*, Croom Helm, Dover, NH.

Dunning, J. (1993) *The Globalization of Business*, Routledge, London.

Dunning, J.H. (1981) *International Production and the Multinational Enterprise*, Allen and Unwin, London.

Durand, T. (1996) *Revisiting Key Dimensions of Competence*, paper presented to the SMS Conference, Phoenix.

Dutton, J.E. (1988) 'Understanding Strategic Agenda Building and its Implications for Managing Change', in L.R. Pondy, R.J. Boland, Jr., and H. Thomas (eds.) (1988) *Managing Ambiguity and Change*, Wiley, Chichester.

Dyer, J.H. and Singh, H. (1998) 'The Relational View: Cooperative Strategy and Sources of Interorganizational Competitive Advantage', *Academy of Management Review*, Vol. 23, No. 4, pp. 660–679.

Dyer, J.H., Kale, P. and Singh, H. (2001) 'How to Make Strategic Alliances Work', *Sloan Management Review*, Vol. 42, No. 4, Summer, pp. 37–43.

Eden, C. (1989) 'Using Cognitive Mapping for Strategic Options Development and Analysis (SODA)', in J. Rosenhead (ed.), *Rational Analysis in a Problematic World*, Wiley, London.

Eisenhardt, K.M. (1989) 'Agency Theory: An Assessment and Review', *Academy of Management Review*, Vol. 14, No. 1, January, pp. 57–74.

Eisenhardt, K.M., and Brown, S.L. (1997) 'The Art of Continuous Change: Linking Complexity Theory and Time-Paced Evolution in Relentlessly Shifting Organizations', *Administrative Science Quarterly*, Vol. 42, No. 1, March, pp. 1–34.

Eisenhardt, K.M., and Galunic, D.C. (2000) 'Coevolving: At Last, a Way to Make Synergies Work', *Harvard Business Review*, Vol. 78, No. 1, January–February, pp. 91–101.

Elster, J. (1999) *Alchemies of the Mind: Rationality and the Emotions*, Cambridge University Press, Cambridge.

Epstein, E.M. (1987) 'The Corporate Social Policy Process: Beyond Business Ethics, Corporate Social Responsibility, and Corporate Social Responsiveness', *California Management Review*, Vol. 29, No. 3, Spring, pp. 99–114.

Etzioni, A. (1961) *A Comparative Analysis of Complex Organizations*, The Free Press, New York.

Evans, J.S. (1991) 'Strategic Flexibility for High Technology Maneuvers: A Conceptual Framework', *Journal of Management Studies*, Vol. 28, January, pp. 69–89.

Evans, P.B., and Wurster, T.S. (1997) 'Strategy and the New Economics of Information', *Harvard Business Review*, Vol. 76, No. 5, September–October, pp. 71–82.

Falsey, T.A. (1989) *Corporate Philosophies and Mission Statements*, Quorum Books, New York.

Finkelstein, S., and Hambrick, D.C. (1996) *Strategic Leadership: Top Executives and Their Effects on Organizations*, West, St. Paul.

Floyd, S.W., and Wooldridge, B. (2000) *Building Strategy from the Middle: Reconceptualizing Strategy Process*, Sage, Thousand Oaks.

Freeman, R.E. (1984) *Strategic Management: A Stakeholder Approach*, Pitman/Ballinger, Boston, MA.

Freeman, R.E., and Gilbert, D.R., Jr. (1988) *Corporate Strategy and the Search for Ethics*, Prentice Hall, Englewood Cliffs, NJ.

Freeman, R.E., and Liedtka, J. (1991) 'Corporate Social Responsibility: A Critical Approach', *Business Horizons*, July–August.

Freeman, R.E., and Reed, D.L. (1983) 'Stockholders and Stakeholders: A New Perspective on Corporate Governance', *California Management Review*, Vol.25, No.3, Spring, pp. 88–106.

French, J., and Raven, B.H. (1959) 'The Bases of Social Power', in D. Cartwright (ed.), *Studies of Social Power*, Institute for Social Research, Ann Arbor, MI.

Friedman, M. (1990) 'The Social Responsibility of Business is to Increase Its Profits', *The New York Times Magazine*, September 13 1970. Reprinted in W.M. Hoffman and J.M. Moore (eds.), *Business Ethics*, McGraw-Hill, New York.

Fuchs, P.H., Mifflin, K.E., Miller, D., and Whitney, J.O. (2000) 'Strategic Integration: Competing in the Age of Capabilities', *California Management Review*, Vol. 42, No. 3, Spring, pp. 118–147.

Gambetta, D. (ed.) (1988) *Trust: Making and Breaking Cooperative Relations*, Blackwell, New York.

Gerlach, M. (1992) *Alliance Capitalism: The Social Organization of Japanese Business*, University of California Press, Berkeley, CA.

Gersick, C.J.G. (1991) 'Revolutionary Change Theories: A Multilevel Exploration of the Punctuated Equilibrium Paradigm', *Academy of Management Review*, Vol. 17, No. 1, January, pp. 10–36.

Ghemawat, P. (1991) *Commitment: The Dynamic of Strategy*, The Free Press, New York.

Ghoshal, S., and Mintzberg, H. (1994) 'Diversifiction and Diversifact', *California Management Review*, Vol. 37, No. 1, Fall, pp. 8–27.

Gilbert, X., and Strebel, P. (1989) 'From Innovation to Outpacing', *Business Quarterly*, Summer, pp. 19–22.

Gioia, D.A., and Chittipeddi, K. (1991) 'Sensemaking and Sensegiving in Strategic Change Intuition', *Strategic Management Journal*, Vol. 12, pp. 433–448.

Gnyawali, D.R., and Madhavan, R. (2001) 'Cooperative Networks and Competitive Dynamics: A Structural Embeddedness Perspective', *Academy of Management Review*, Vol. 26, No. 3, pp. 431–445.

Gomes-Casseres, B. (1994) 'Group Versus Group: How Alliance Networks Compete', *Harvard Business Review*, Vol. 72, No. 4, July–August, pp. 62–74.

Goold, M., and Campbell, A. (1987) *Strategies and Styles: The Role of the Centre in Managing Diverse Corporations*, Basil Blackwell, Oxford.

Goold, M., Campbell, A., and Alexander, M. (1994) *Corporate-Level Strategy: Creating Value in the Multibusiness Company*, Wiley, New York.

Goold, M., and Lansdell, S. (1997) *Survey of Corporate Strategy Objectives, Concepts and Tools*, Ashridge Strategic Management Centre.

Goold, M., and Luchs, K. (1993) 'Why Diversify? Four Decades of Management Thinking', *Academy of Management Executive*, Vol. 7, No. 3, August, pp. 7–25.

Goold, M., and Quinn, J.J. (1990) *Strategic Control: Milestones for Long-Term Performance*, Hutchinson, London.

Govindarajan, V. (1988) 'A Contingency Approach to Strategy Implementation at the Business-Unit Level: Integrating Administrative Mechanisms with Strategy', *Academy of Management Journal*, Vol. 31, No. 4, December, pp. 828–853.

Govindarajan, V. and Gupta, A.K. (1999) 'Taking Wal-Mart Global: Lessons from Retailing's Giant', *Strategy & Business*, No. 4.

Grabher, G. (ed.) (1993) *The Embedded Firm: On the Socioeconomics of Industrial Networks*, Routledge, London.

Granovetter, M.S. (1985) 'Economic Action and Social Structure: The Problem Of Embeddedness', *American Journal of Sociology*, Vol. 91, pp. 481–501.

Grant, R.M. (1991) 'The Resource-Based Theory of Competitive Advantage: Implications for Strategy Formulation', *California Management Review*, Vol. 33, No. 3, Spring, pp. 114–135.

Greenwood, R. and Hinings, C.R. (1996) 'Understanding Radical Organizational Change: Bringing Together the Old and the New Institutionalism', *Academy of Management Review*, Vol. 21, No. 4, October, pp. 1022–1054.

Greiner, L.E. (1972) 'Evolution and Revolution as Organizations Grow', *Harvard Business Review*, Vol. 50, No. 4, July–August, pp. 37–46.

Grinyer, P.H., Al-Bazzaz, S. and Yasai-Ardekani, M. (1986) 'Towards a Contingency Theory of Corporate Planning: Findings in 48 U.K. Companies', *Strategic Management Journal*, Vol. 7, pp. 3–28.

Grinyer, P.H., Mayes, D., and McKiernan, P. (1987) *Sharpbenders: The Secrets of Unleashing Corporate Potential*, Blackwell, Oxford.

Gulati, R. (1998) 'Alliances and Networks', *Strategic Management Journal*, Vol. 19, No. 4, pp. 293–317.

Guthrie, J., and Turnbull, S. (1994) 'Audit Committees: Is There a Role for Corporate Senates and/or Stakeholder Councils?', *Corporate Governance*, Vol. 3, pp. 78–89.

Håkansson, H. and Johanson, J. (1993) 'The Network as a Governance Structure: Interfirm Cooperation beyond Markets and Hierarchies', in G. Grabner (ed.), *The Embedded Firm: On the Socioeconomics of Industrial Networks*, Routledge, London, pp. 35–51.

Hambrick, D.C. (ed.) (1989) 'Guest Editor's Introduction: Putting Top Managers Back in the Strategy Picture', *Strategic Management Journal,* Vol. 10, Special Issue, Summer, pp. 5–15.

Hambrick, D.C., and Abrahamson, E. (1995) 'Assessing the Amount of Managerial Discretion in Different Industries: A Multi-Method Approach', *Academy of Management Journal*, Vol. 38, No. 5, October, pp. 1427–1441.

Hambrick, D.C., and Finkelstein, S. (1987) 'Managerial Discretion: A Bridge between Polar Views of Organizational Outcomes', in B.M. Staw and L.L. Cummings (eds.), *Research in Organizational Behavior,* Vol. 9, pp. 369–406.

Hambrick, D.C., Geletkanycz, M.A., and Fredrickson, J.W. (1993) 'Top Executive Commitment to the Status Quo: Some Tests of Its Determinants', *Strategic Management Journal*, Vol. 14, No. 6, pp. 401–418.

Hambrick, D.C., and Mason, P. (1984) 'Upper Echelons: The Organization as a Reflection of Its Top Managers', *Academy of Management Review*, Vol. 9, No. 2, April, pp. 193–206.

Hamel, G. (1996) 'Strategy as Revolution', *Harvard Business Review*, July–August, Vol. 74, No. 4, pp. 69–82.

Hamel, G., Doz, Y.L., and Prahalad, C.K. (1989) 'Collaborate with Your Competitors – and Win', *Harvard Business Review*, Vol. 67, No. 1, January–February, pp. 133–139.

Hamel, G., and Prahalad, C.K. (1985) 'Do You Really Have a Global Strategy?', *Harvard Business Review*, Vol. 63, No. 4, July–August, pp. 139–148.

Hamel, G., and Prahalad, C.K. (1989) 'Strategic Intent', *Harvard Business Review*, May–June, pp. 63–77.

Hamel, G., and Prahalad, C.K. (1993) 'Strategy as Stretch and Leverage', *Harvard Business Review*, Vol. 71, No. 2, March–April, pp. 75–84.

Hamel, G., and Prahalad, C.K. (1994) *Competing for the Future*, Harvard Business School Press, Boston, MA.

Hamilton, G.G., and Woolsey Biggart, N. (1988) 'Market, Culture and Authority: A Comparative Analysis of Management and Organization in the Far East', *American Journal of Sociology*, Vol. 94, pp. 52.

Hammer, M. (1990) 'Reengineering Work: Don't Automate, Obliterate', *Harvard Business Review*, Vol. 68, No. 4, July–August, pp. 104–111.

Hammer, M., and Champy, J. (1993) *Reengineering the Corporation: A Manifesto for Business Revolution*, HarperCollins, New York.

Hampden-Turner, C. (1990) *Charting the Corporate Mind: From Dilemma to Strategy*, Basil Blackwell, Oxford.

Hampden-Turner, C., and Trompenaars, A. (1993) *The Seven Cultures of Capitalism: Value Systems for Creating Wealth in the United States, Japan, Germany, France, Britain, Sweden and the Netherlands*, Doubleday, New York.

Hampden-Turner, C., and Trompenaars, F. (2000) *Building Cross-Cultural Competence: How to Create Wealth from Conflicting Values*, Yale University Press, New Haven, CT.

Hannan, M.T., and Freeman, J. (1977) 'The Population Ecology of Organizations', *American Journal of Sociology*, Vol. 82, No. 5, March, pp. 929–964.

Hannan, M.T., and Freeman, J. (1989) *Organizational Ecology*, Harvard University Press, Cambridge, MA.

Haour, G. and Cho, H.J. (2000) *Samsung Electronics Co. Ltd in the 1990s: Sustaining Competitiveness*, IMD Business Case.

Harbison, J., and Pekar, P. (2000) *Smart Alliances: A Practical Guide to Repeatable Success*, Jossey-Bass, San Francisco.

Harrigan, K.R. (1985) 'Vertical Integration and Corporate Strategy', *Academy of Management Journal*, Vol. 28, No. 2, June, pp. 397–425.

Hart, O.D. (1995) *Firms, Contracts and Financial Structure*, Clarendon Press, Oxford.

Hart, S.L. (1992) 'An Integrative Framework for Strategy-Making Processes', *Academy of Management Review*, Vol. 17, No. 2, pp. 327–351.

Haspeslagh, P. (1982) 'Portfolio Planning: Uses and Limits', *Harvard Business Review*, Vol. 60, No. 1, January–February, pp. 58–73.

Haspeslagh, P., and Jemison, D. (1991) *Managing Acquisitions: Creating Value through Corporate Renewal*, The Free Press, New York.

Hax, A.C. (1990) 'Redefining the Concept of Strategy and the Strategy Formation Process', *Planning Review*, May–June, pp. 34–40.

Hax, A.C., and Maljuf, N.S. (1984) *Strategic Management: An Integrative Approach*, Prentice Hall, Englewood Cliffs, NJ.

Hayes, R.H. (1985) 'Strategic Planning: Forward in Reverse?', *Harvard Business Review*, Vol. 63, No. 6, November–December, pp. 111–119.

Hedley, B. (1977) 'Strategy and the "Business Portfolio"', *Long Range Planning*, Vol. 10, No. 1, February, pp. 9–15.

Hedlund, G. (1986) 'The Hypermodern MNC: A Heterarchy?', *Human Resource Management*, Vol. 25, pp. 9–35.

Henderson, B.D. (1979) *On Corporate Strategy*, ABT Books, Cambridge, MA.

Hendry, J. (1995) Culture, Community and Networks: The Hidden Cost of Outsourcing, *European Management Journal*, Vol. 13, No. 2, pp. 193–200.

Henry, J. (ed.) (1991) *Creative Management*, Sage in association with the Open University, London.

Hill, C.W.L. (1994) 'The Functions of the Headquarters Unit in Multibusiness Firms', in R. Rumelt, D. Teece and D. Schendel (eds.), *Fundamental Issues in Strategy Research*, Harvard University Press, Cambridge, MA.

Hill, C.W.L., and Hoskisson, R.E. (1987) 'Strategy and Structure in the Multiproduct Firm', *Academy of Management Review*, Vol. 12, No. 2, April, pp. 331–341.

Hitt, M., Harrison, J., and Ireland, R. (2001) *Mergers and Acquisitions: A Guide to Creating Value for Shareholders*, Oxford University Press, New York.

Hofer, C., and Schendel, D. (1978) *Strategy Formulation: Analytical Concepts*, West, St. Paul.

Hoffman, W.M. (1989) 'The Cost of a Corporate Conscience', *Business and Society Review*, Vol. 94, Spring, pp. 46–47.

Hogarth, R.M. (1980) *Judgement and Choice: The Psychology of Decision*, Wiley, Chichester.

Hoskisson, R.E. (1999) 'Theory and Research in Strategic Management: Swings of a Pendulum', *Journal of Management*, May–June, pp. 1–50.

Hosmer, L.T. (1994) 'Strategic Planning as if Ethics Mattered', *Strategic Management Journal*, Vol. 15, Summer, pp. 17–34.

House, R.J., and R.N. Aditya (1997) 'The Social Science Study of Leadership: Quo Vadis?', *Journal of Management*, Vol. 23, No. 3, May–June, pp. 409–474.

Hout, T.M., Porter, M.E., and Rudden, E. (1982) 'How Global Companies Win Out', *Harvard Business Review*, Vol. 60, No. 5, September–October, pp. 98–108.

Hrebiniak, L.G., and Joyce, W.F. (1985) 'Organizational Adaptation: Strategic Choice and Environmental Determinism', *Administrative Science Quarterly*, Vol. 30, No. 3, September, pp. 336–349.

Hurst, D. (1995) *Crisis and Renewal*, Harvard Business School Press, Boston, MA.

Hurst, D.K. (1986) 'Why Strategic Management is Bankrupt', *Organizational Dynamics*, Vol. 15, Autumn, pp. 4–27.

Hurst, D.K., Rush, J.C. and White, R.E. (1989) 'Top Management Teams and Organizational Renewal', *Strategic Management Journal*, Vol. 10, No. 1, pp. 87–105.

Imai, M. (1986) *Kaizen: The Key to Japan's Competitive Success*, McGraw-Hill, New York.

Ireland, R. D. and Hitt, M.A. (1999) 'Achieving and Maintaining Strategic Competitiveness in the 21st Century: The Role of Strategic Leadership', *Academy of Management Executive*, Vol. 13, No. 1, February, pp. 43–57.

Isenberg, D.J. (1984) 'How Senior Managers Think', *Harvard Business Review*, November–December, Vol. 63, No. 6, pp. 81–90.

Itami, H. (1987) *Mobilizing Invisible Assets*, Harvard University Press, Cambridge, MA.

James, B.G. (1985) *Business Wargames*, Penguin, Harmondsworth.

Janis, I.L. (1989) *Crucial Decisions: Leadership in Policymaking and Crisis Management*, The Free Press, New York.

Jarillo, J.C. (1988) 'On Strategic Networks', *Strategic Management Journal*, Vol. 9, No. 1, January–February, pp. 31–41.

Jaworski, B., and Kohli, A.K. (1993) 'Market Orientation: Antecedents and Consequences', *Journal of Marketing*, Vol. 57, No. 3, July, pp. 53–70.

Jelinek, M. (1979) *Institutionalizing Innovation*, Praeger, New York.

Jensen, M.C. (1991) 'Corporate Control and the Politics of Finance', *Journal of Applied Corporate Finance*, Vol. 4, pp. 13–33.

Jensen, M.C., and Meckling, W.H. (1976) 'Theory of the Firm, Managerial Behavior, Agency Costs, and Ownership Structure', *Journal of Financial Economics*, Vol. 3, No. 4, October, pp. 305–360.

Johnson, B. (1996) *Polarity Management*, HRD Press Inc, Amherst, MA.

Johnson, G. (1987) *Strategic Change and the Management Process*, Basil Blackwell, Oxford.

Johnson, G. (1988) 'Rethinking Incrementalism', *Strategic Management Journal*, Vol. 9, No. 1, January–February, pp. 75–91.

Jones, T.M. (1995) 'Instrumental Stakeholder Theory: A Synthesis of Ethics and Economics', *Academy of Management Review*, Vol. 20, No.2 , April, pp. 404–437.

Kagono, T., Nonaka, I., Sakakibara, K. and Okumura, A. (1985) *Strategic vs. Evolutionary Management: A US–Japan Comparison of Strategy and Organization*, North Holland, Amsterdam.

Kanter, R.M. (1983) *The Change Masters: Innovation for Productivity in the American Corporation*, Basic Books, New York.

Kanter, R.M. (1989) *When Giants Learn to Dance*, Simon & Schuster, New York.

Kanter, R.M. (1994) 'Collaborative Advantage: The Art of Alliances', *Harvard Business Review*, Vol. 72, No. 4, July–August, pp. 96–108.

Kanter, R.M. (2002) 'Strategy as Improvisational Theater', *Sloan Management Review*, Vol. 43, No. 2, pp. 76–81.

Kao, J. (1996) *Jamming: The Art and Discipline of Business Creativity*, HarperBusiness, New York.

Kaplan, R.S., and Norton, D.P. (2001) *The Strategy-Focused Organization: How Balanced Scorecard Thrive in the New Business Environment*, Harvard Business School Press, Boston, MA.

Kaplan, S. (1989) 'The Effects of Management Buyouts on Operating Performance and Value', *Journal of Financial Economics*, Vol. 24, No. 2, October, pp. 217–254.

Kay, J. (1989) 'Myths and Realities', in E. Davis (ed.) *1992: Myths and Realities*, Centre for Business Strategy, London.

Kay, J. (1993) *Foundations of Corporate Success: How Business Strategies Add Value*, Oxford University Press, Oxford.

Keasey, K., Thompson, S., and Wright, M. (eds.) (1997) *Corporate Governance: Economic, Management, and Financial Issues*, Oxford University Press, Oxford.

Kelley, R.E. (1988) 'In Praise of Followers', *Harvard Business Review*, Vol. 66, No. 6, November–December, pp. 142.

Kessler, E.H., and Chakrabarthi, A.K. (1996) 'Innovation Speed: A Conceptual Model of Context, Antecedents, and Outcomes', *Academy of Management Review*, Vol. 21, No. 4, October, pp. 1143–1191.

Ketchen, D.J., Thomas, J.B., and McDaniel, R.R. (1996) 'Process, Content and Context: Synergistic Effects on Organizational Performance', *Journal of Management*, Vol. 22, pp. 231–257.

Kets de Vries, M.F.R. (1994) 'The Leadership Mystique', *Academy of Management Executive*, Vol. 8, No. 3, August, pp. 73–92.

Kets de Vries, M.F.R., and Miller, D. (1984) *The Neurotic Organization*, Jossey-Bass, San Francisco.

Kets de Vries, M.F.R., and Miller, D. (1988) *Unstable at the Top: Inside the Troubled Organization*, New American Library, New York.

Kim, W.C. and Mauborgne, R. (1999) 'Strategy, Value Innovation, and the Knowledge Economy', *Sloan Management Review*, Vol. 40, No. 3, Spring, pp. 41–54.

Klein, K.J. and House, R.J. (1998) 'Further Thoughts on Fire: Charismatic Leadership and Levels of Analysis', in F. Dansereau and F.J. Yammarino (eds.), *Leadership: The Multi-Level Approaches*, Vol. 2, JAI Press, Stamford, CT, pp. 45–52.

Klein, N. (2000) *No Logo: Taking Aim at the Brand Bullies*, Flamingo, London.

Klemm, M., Sanderson, S. and Luffman, G. (1991) 'Mission Statements', *Long Range Planning*, Vol. 24, No. 3, June, pp. 73–78.

Klimoski, R. and Mohammed, S. (1994) 'Team Mental Model: Construct or Metaphor', *Journal of Management*, Vol. 20, pp. 403–437.

Knight, D., Pearce, C.L., Smith, K.G., Olian, J.D., Sims, H.P., Smith, K.A. and Flood, P. (1999) 'Top Management Team Diversity, Group Process, and Strategic Consensus', *Strategic Management Journal*, Vol. 20, pp. 445–465.

Kogut, B. (ed.) (1993) *Country Competitiveness: Technology and the Organizing of Work*, Oxford University Press, Oxford.

Kogut, B., and Zander, U. (1993) 'Knowledge of the Firm and the Evolutionary Theory of the Multinational Corporation', *Journal of International Business Studies*, Vol. 24, No. 4, pp. 625–646.

Kono, T. (1999) 'A Strong Head Office Makes a Strong Company', *Long Range Planning*, Vol. 32, No. 2, pp. 225–236.

Kotter, J.P. (1982) *The General Managers*, The Free Press, New York.

Kotter, J.P. (1990) 'What Leaders Really Do', *Harvard Business Review*, Vol. 68, No. 3, May–June, pp. 103.

Krüger, W. (1996) 'Implementation: The Core Task of Change Management', *CEMS Business Review*, Vol. 1, pp. 77–96.

Krugman, P.R. (1990) *Rethinking International Trade*, MIT Press, Cambridge, MA.

Kuhn, T.S. (1970) *The Structure of Scientific Revolutions*, University of Chicago Press, Chicago.

Kukalis, S. (1991) 'Determinants of Strategic Planning Systems in Large Organizations: A Contingency Approach', *Journal of Management Studies*, Vol. 28, pp. 143–160.

Lado, A.A., Boyd, N.G., and Hanlon, S.C. (1997) 'Competition, Cooperation and the Search for Economic Rents: A Syncretic Model', *Academy of Management Review*, Vol. 22, No. 1, January, pp. 110–141.

Langley, A. (1989) 'In Search of Rationality: The Purposes Behind the Use of Formal Analysis in Organizations', *Administrative Science Quarterly*, Vol. 34, No. 4, pp. 598–631.

Langley, A. (1995) 'Between "Paralysis by Analysis" and "Extinction by Instinct"', *Sloan Management Review*, Vol. 36, No. 3, Spring, pp. 63–76.

Langtry, B. (1994) 'Stakeholders and the Moral Responsibilities of Business', *Business Ethics Quarterly*, Vol. 4, pp. 431–443.

Lawrence, P.R., and Lorsch, J.W. (1967) *Organization and Environment*, Harvard University Press, Cambridge, MA.

Lenz, R.T., and Lyles, M. (1985) 'Paralysis by Analysis: Is Your Planning System Becoming Too Rational?', *Long Range Planning*, Vol. 18, No. 4, pp. 64–72.

Leonard-Barton, D. (1992) 'Core Capabilities and Core Rigidities: A Paradox in Managing New Product Development', *Strategic Management Journal*, Vol. 13, Special Issue, Summer, pp. 111–125.

Leonard-Barton, D. (1995) *Well-Springs of Knowledge: Building and Sustaining the Sources of Innovation*, Harvard Business School Press, Boston, MA.

Lessem, R., and Neubauer, F.F. (1994) *European Management Systems*, McGraw-Hill, London.

Levenhagen, M., Porac, J.F. and Thomas, H. (1993) 'Emergent Industry Leadership and the Selling of Technological Visions: A Social Constructionist View', in J. Hendry, G. Johnson and J. Newton (eds.), *Strategic Thinking: Leadership and the Management of Change*, Wiley, Chichester.

Levitt, T. (1960) 'Marketing Myopia', *Harvard Business Review*, Vol. 38, July–August, pp. 45–56.

Levitt, T. (1983) 'The Globalization of Markets', *Harvard Business Review*, Vol. 61, No. 3, May–June, pp. 92–102.

Levy, D. (1994) 'Chaos Theory and Strategy: Theory, Application, and Managerial Implications, *Strategic Management Journal*, Vol. 15, pp. 167–178.

Lewin, K. (1947) 'Frontiers in Group Dynamics: Social Equilbria and Social Change', *Human Relations*, Vol. 1, pp. 5–41.

Lewis, M. (2000) 'Exploring Paradox, Toward a More Comprehensive Guide', *Academy of Management Review*, Vol. 25, No. 4, pp. 760–776.

Lieberman, M.B., and Montgomery, D.B. (1988) 'First Mover Advantages', *Strategic Management Journal*, Vol. 9, No. 1, January–February, pp. 41–58.

Lieberman, M.B. and Montgomery, D.B. (1998) 'First-Mover (Dis)Advantages: Retrospective and Link with the Resource-Based View', *Strategic Management Journal*, Vol. 19, No. 12, December, pp. 1111–1126.

Liebeskind, J. (1996) 'Knowledge, Strategy and the Theory of the Firm', *Strategic Management Journal*, Vol. 17, Special Issue, Winter, pp. 93–107.

Liedtka, J. (2000) 'In Defense of Strategy as Design', *California Management Review*, Vol. 42, No. 3, pp. 8–30.

Long, W.F., and Ravenscraft, D.J. (1993) 'Decade of Debt: Lessons from LBOs in the 1980s', in M.M. Blair (ed.), *The Deal Decade: What Takeovers and Leveraged Buyouts Mean for Corporate Governance*, Brookings Institution, Washington.

Lorange, P. (1980) *Corporate Planning: An Executive Viewpoint*, Prentice Hall, Englewood Cliffs, NJ.

Lorange, P., and Roos, J. (1992) *Strategic Alliances: Formation, Implementation, and Evolution*, Blackwell, Cambridge, MA.

Lorange, P., and Vancil, R.F. (1977) *Strategic Planning Systems*, Prentice Hall, Englewood Cliffs, NJ.

Lorenzoni, G., and Baden-Fuller, C. (1995) 'Creating a Strategic Center to Manage a Web of Partners', *California Management Review*, Vol. 37, No. 3, Spring, pp. 146–163.

Lowendahl, B.R. (1997) *Strategic Management of Professional Business Service Firms*, Copenhagen Business School Press, Copenhagen.

Lubatkin, M., and Chatterjee, S. (1994) 'Extending Modern Portfolio Theory into the Domain of Corporate Diversification: Does It Apply?', *Academy of Management Journal*, Vol. 37, No. 1, pp. 109–136.

Lyles, M.A. and Schwenk, C.R. (1992) 'Top Management, Strategy and Organizational Knowledge Structures', *Journal of Management Studies*, Vol. 29, pp. 155–174.

Lyon, D.W., Lumpkin, G.T., and Dess, G.G. (2000) 'Enhancing Entrepreneurial Orientation Research: Operationalizing and Measuring a Key Strategic Decision Making Process', *Journal of Management*, Vol. 26, pp. 1055–1085.

MacDonald, S. (1995) 'Too Close for Comfort?: The Strategic Implications of Getting Close to the Customer', *California Management Review*, Vol. 37, Summer, pp. 8–27.

Mahoney, J.T. (1992) 'The Choice of Organizational Form: Vertical Financial Ownership Versus Other Methods of Vertical Integration', *Strategic Management Journal*, Vol. 13, No. 8, pp. 559–584.

Maidique, M.A. (1980) 'Entrepreneurs, Champions, and Technological Innovation', *Sloan Management Review*, Vol. 21, pp. 18–31.

Makridakis, S. (1990) *Forecasting, Planning, and Strategy for the 21st Century*, The Free Press, New York.

March, J.G., and Simon, H.A. (1958) *Organizations*, Wiley, New York.

March, J.G., and Simon, H.A. (1993) *Organizations*, Second Edition, Blackwell, Cambridge, MA.

Markides, C. (1998) 'Strategic Innovation in Established Companies', *Sloan Management Review*, Vol. 39, No. 3, Spring, pp. 31–42.

Marx, T.G. (1991) 'Removing the Obstacles to Effective Strategic Planning', *Long Range Planning*, Vol. 24, No. 4, August, pp. 21–28.

Mason, R.O., and Mitroff, I.I. (1981) *Challenging Strategic Planning Assumptions*, Wiley, New York.

McCaskey, M.B. (1982) *The Executive Challenge: Managing Change and Ambiguity*, Pitman, Boston, MA.

McCoy, C.S. (1985) *Management of Values*, Ballinger, Cambridge, MA.

McGrew, A.G. and Lewis, P.G. (eds.) (1992) *Global Politics: Globalisation and the Nation-State*, Polity Press, Cambridge.

Meindl, J.R., Ehrlich, S.B., and Dukerich, J.M. (1985) The Romance of Leadership, *Administrative Science Quarterly*, Vol. 30, No. 1, March, pp. 78–102.

Meyer, A.D. (1982) 'Adapting to Environmental Jolts', *Administrative Science Quarterly*, Vol. 27, No. 4, December, pp. 515–537.

Meyer, A.D., Brooks, G., and Goes, J. (1990) 'Environmental Jolts and Industry Revolutions: Organizational Responses to Discontinuous Change', *Strategic Management Journal*, Vol. 11, No. 2, February, pp. 93–110.

Miller, C.C., and Cardinal, L.B. (1994) 'Strategic Planning and Firm Performance: A Synthesis of More Than Two Decades of Research', *Academy of Management Journal*, Vol. 37, No. 6, pp. 1649–1665.

Miller, D. (1990) *The Icarus Paradox: How Excellent Companies Can Bring About Their Own Downfall*, Harper Business, New York.

Miller, D., Eisenstat, R., and Foote, N. (2002) 'Strategy from the Inside-Out: Building Capability-Creating Organizations', *California Management Review*, Vol. 44, No. 3, Spring, pp. 37–54.

Miller, D., and Friesen, P.H. (1980) 'Momentum and Revolution in Organizational Adaptation', *Academy of Management Journal*, Vol. 23, No. 4, December, pp. 591–614.

Miller, D., and Friesen, P.H. (1984) *Organizations: A Quantum View*, Prentice Hall, Englewood Cliffs, NJ.

Mintzberg, H. (1984) 'Who Should Control the Corporation?', *California Management Review*, Vol. 27, No. 1, Fall, pp. 90–115.

Mintzberg, H. (1990) 'The Design School: Reconsidering the Basic Premises of Strategic Management', *Strategic Management Journal*, Vol. 11, No. 3, pp. 171–195.

Mintzberg, H. (1991) 'The Effective Organization: Forces and Forms', *Sloan Management Review*, Vol. 32, No. 2, Winter, pp. 54–67.

Mintzberg, H. (1993) 'The Pitfalls of Strategic Planning', *California Management Review*, Vol. 36, No. 1, Fall, pp. 32–45.

Mintzberg, H. (1994a) 'The Fall and Rise of Strategic Planning', *Harvard Business Review*, Vol. 73, No. 1, January–February.

Mintzberg, H. (1994b) *The Rise and Fall of Strategic Planning*, Prentice Hall, Englewood Cliffs, NJ.

Mintzberg, H., Ahlstrand, B., and Lampel, J. (1998) *Strategy Safari: A Guided Tour Through the Wilds of Strategic Management*, The Free Press, New York.

Mintzberg, H., and Waters, J.A. (1985) 'Of Strategies: Deliberate and Emergent', *Strategic Management Journal*, Vol. 6, No. 3, July–September, pp. 257–272.

Mitchell, R.K., Agle, B.R., and Wood, D.J. (1997) 'Toward a Theory of Stakeholder Identification and Salience: Defining the Principle of Who and What Really Counts', *Academy of Management Review*, Vol. 22, No. 4, October, pp. 853–886.

Moore, G.A. (2000) *'Living on the Fault Line: Managing for Shareholder Value in the Age of the Internet'*, HarperBusiness, New York.

Moore, J.F. (1996) *The Death of Competition: Leadership and Strategy in the Age of Business Ecosystems*, HarperBusiness, New York.

Morgan, G. (1986) *Images of Organization*, Sage, London.

Morgan, G. (1993) *Imaginization: The Art of Creative Management*, Sage, Newbury Park, CA.

Nanus, B. (1992) *Visionary Leadership: Creating a Compelling Sense of Direction for Your Organization*, Jossey-Bass, San Francisco.

Nelson, R., and Winter, S. (1982) *An Evolutionary Theory of Economic Change*, Harvard University Press, Cambridge, MA.

Nishiguchi, T. (1994) *Strategic Industrial Sourcing: The Japanese Advantage*, Oxford University Press, New York.

Nonaka, I. (1988a) 'Toward Middle-Up-Down Management: Accelerating Information Creation', *Sloan Management Review*, Vol. 29, No.3, Spring, pp. 9–18.

Nonaka, I. (1988b) 'Creating Organizational Order Out of Chaos: Self-Renewal in Japanese Firms', *California Management Review*, Vol. 30, No. 3, Spring, pp. 9–18.

Nonaka, I. (1991) 'The Knowledge-Creating Company', *Harvard Business Review*, Vol. 69, No. 6, November–December, pp. 96–104.

Nonaka, I., and Konno, N. (1998) 'The Concept of "Ba": Building a Foundation for Knowledge Creation', *California Management Review*, Vol. 40, No. 3, Spring, pp. 40–54.

Noorderhaven, N.G. (1995) *Strategic Decision Making*, Addison-Wesley, Wokingham.

Norman, R., and Ramirez, R. (1993) 'From Value Chain to Value Constellation: Designing Interactive Strategy', *Harvard Business Review*, July–August, pp. 65–77.

Ocasio, W. (1997) Towards an Attention-Based View of the Firm', *Strategic Management Journal*, Vol. 18, Special Issue, July, pp. 187–206.

Ohmae, K. (1982) *The Mind of the Strategist: The Art of Japanese Business*, McGraw-Hill, New York.

Ohmae, K. (1990) *The Borderless World: Power and Strategy in the Interlinked Economy*, Fontana, London.

Oliver, C. (1991) 'Strategic Responses to Institutional Processes', *Academy of Management Review*, Vol. 16, No. 1, January, pp. 145–179.

Oliver, C. (1997) 'Sustainable Competitive Advantage: Combining Institutional and Resource-based Views', *Strategic Management Journal*, Vol. 18, No. 9, October, pp. 697–713.

Oliver, N. and Wilkinson, B. (1988) *The Japanization of British Industry*, Basil Blackwell, London.

Ouchi, W.G. (1980) 'Markets, Bureaucracies, and Clans', *Administrative Science Quarterly*, Vol. 25, No. 1, pp. 129–142.

Parkinson, J.E. (1993) *Corporate Power and Responsibility*, Oxford University Press, Oxford.

Parolini, C. (1999) *The Value Net*, Wiley, Chichester.

Pascale, R.T. (1984) 'Perspectives on Strategy: The Real Story Behind Honda's Success', *California Management Review*, Vol. 26, No. 3, pp. 47–72.

Pascale, R.T. (1990) *Managing on the Edge: How Successful Companies Use Conflict to Stay Ahead*, Viking Penguin, London.

Patel, P., and Pavitt, K. (1991) 'Large Firms in the Production of the World's Technology: An Important Case of "Non-Globalisation"', *Journal of International Business Studies*, Vol. 22, No. 1, pp. 1–21.

Pearce, J.A. (1982) 'The Company Mission as a Strategic Tool', *Sloan Management Review*, Spring, pp. 15–24.

Penrose, E.T. (1959) *The Theory of the Growth of the Firm*, Wiley, New York.

Peteraf, M.A. (1993) 'The Cornerstones of Competitive Advantage: A Resource-Based View', *Strategic Management Journal*, Vol. 14, pp. 179–191.

Peters, T.J., and Waterman, R.H. (1982) *In Search of Excellence*, Harper & Row, New York.

Pettigrew, A. (1977) 'Strategy Formulation as a Political Process', *International Studies of Management and Organization*, Vol. 7, Summer, pp. 47–72.

Pettigrew, A. (1992) 'The Character and Significance of Strategy Process Research', *Strategic Management Journal*, Vol. 13, pp. 5–16.

Pettigrew, A., and Whipp, R. (1991) *Managing Change for Competitive Success*, Basil Blackwell, Oxford.

Pfeffer, J. (1977) 'The Ambiguity of Leadership', *Academy of Management Review*, Vol. 2, No. 1, January, pp. 104–112.

Pfeffer, J. (1981) *Power in Organizations*, Pitman, Marshfield, MA.

Pfeffer, J. (1992) *Managing with Power: Politics and Influence in Organizations*, Harvard Business School Press, Boston, MA.

Pfeffer, J., and Salancik, G. (1978) *The External Control of Organizations: A Resource Dependency Perspective*, Harper & Row, New York.

Pfeffer, J. and Sutton, R.I. (1999a) 'Knowing "What" to Do is Not Enough: Turning Knowledge Into Action', *California Management Review*, Vol. 42, No. 1, Fall, pp. 83–108.

Pfeffer, J., and Sutton, R.I. (1999b) *The Knowing-Doing Gap*, Harvard Business School Press, Boston, MA.

Piercy, N.F., and Morgan, N.A. (1994) 'Mission Analysis: An Operational Approach', *Journal of General Management*, Vol. 19, No. 3, pp. 1–16.

Pinchot, G., III. (1985) *Intrapreneuring: Why You Don't Have to Leave the Company to Become an Entrepreneur*, Harper & Row, New York.

Piore, M., and Sabel, C.F. (1984) *The Second Industrial Divide*, Basic Books, New York.

Polanyi, M. (1958) *Personal Knowledge*, University of Chicago Press, Chicago.

Polanyi, M. (1966) *The Tacit Dimension*, Routledge & Kegan Paul, London.

Pondy, L.R. (1983) 'Union of Rationality and Intuition in Management Action', in S. Srivastava (ed.), *The Executive Mind*, Jossey-Bass, San Francisco.

Pondy, L.R., Boland, J.R. and Thomas, H. (eds.) (1988) *Managing Ambiguity and Change*, Wiley, New York.

Poole, M.S., and Van de Ven, A.H. (1989) 'Using Paradox to Build Management and Organization Theories', *Academy of Management Review*, Vol. 14, No. 4, pp. 562–578.

Porac, J.F., Thomas, H., and Baden-Fuller, C. (1989) 'Competitive Groups as Cognitive Communities: The Case of Scottish Knitwear Manufacturers', *Journal of Management Studies*, Vol. 26, pp. 397–416.

Porter, M.E. (1980) *Competitive Strategy: Techniques for Analyzing Industries and Competitors,* The Free Press, New York.

Porter, M.E. (1985) *Competitive Advantage: Creating and Sustaining Superior Performance*, The Free Press, New York.

Porter, M.E. (1986) *Competition in Global Industries*, The Free Press, New York.

Porter, M.E. (1987) 'From Competitive Advantage to Corporate Strategy', *Harvard Business Review*, Vol. 65, No. 3, May–June, pp. 43–59.

Porter, M.E. (1990a) *The Competitive Advantage of Nations*, Macmillan, London.

Porter, M.E. (1990b) 'New Global Strategies for Competitive Advantage', *Planning Review*, Vol. 18, No. 3, May–June, pp. 4–14.

Porter, M.E. (1991) 'Towards a Dynamic Theory of Strategy', *Strategic Management Journal*, Vol. 12, pp. 95–117.

Porter, M.E. (1996) 'What is Strategy?', *Harvard Business Review*, Vol. 74, No. 6, November–December, pp. 61–78.

Porter, M.E. (2001) 'Strategy and the Internet', *Harvard Business Review*, Vol. 80, No. 3, March, pp. 62–78.

Powell, T.C. (1992) 'Strategic Planning as Competitive Advantage', *Strategic Management Journal*, Vol. 13, pp. 551–558.

Powell, W. (1990) Neither Market nor Hierarchy: Network Forms of Organization, *Research in Organizational Behavior*, Vol. 12, pp. 295–336.

Powell, W.W. (1991) 'Expanding the Scope of Institutional Analysis', in W.W. Powell and P.J. DiMaggio (eds.), *The New Institutionalism in Organizational Analysis*, University of Chicago Press, Chicago, pp. 183–203.

Prahalad, C.K., and Bettis, R.A. (1986) 'The Dominant Logic: A New Linkage between Diversity and Performance', *Strategic Management Journal*, Vol. 7, No. 6, November–December, pp. 485–601.

Prahalad, C.K., and Doz, Y. (1987) *The Multinational Mission: Balancing Local Demands and Global Vision*, The Free Press, New York.

Prahalad, C.K., and Hamel, G. (1990) 'The Core Competence of the Corporation', *Harvard Business Review*, Vol. 68, No. 3, May–June, pp. 79–91.

Quinn, J.B. (1978) 'Strategic Change: "Logical Incrementalism"', *Sloan Management Review*, Fall, pp. 7–21.

Quinn, J.B. (1980a) *Strategies for Change*, Irwin, Homewood, IL.

Quinn, J.B. (1980b) 'Managing Strategic Change', *Sloan Management Review*, Summer, pp. 3–20.

Quinn, J.B. (1985) 'Managing Innovation: Controlled Chaos', *Harvard Business Review*, Vol. 63, No. 3, May–June, pp. 73–84.

Quinn, J.B. (1992) *The Intelligent Enterprise: A Knowledge and Service Based Paradigm for Industry*, The Free Press, New York.

Quinn, J.B. (2002) 'Strategy, Science and Management', *Sloan Management Review*, Vol. 43, No. 4.

Quinn, R.E. (1988) *Beyond Rational Management: Mastering the Paradoxes and Competing Demands of High Performance*, Jossey-Bass, San Francisco.

Quinn, R.E., and Cameron, K.S. (1988) *Paradox and Transformation: Toward a Theory of Change in Organization and Management*, Ballinger Publishing, Cambridge, MA.

Ramanujam, V., and Varadarajan, P. (1989) 'Research on Corporate Diversification: A Synthesis', *Strategic Management Journal*, Vol. 10, No.6, November–December, pp. 523–551.

Rappaport, A. (1986) *Creating Shareholder Value: The New Standard for Business Performance*, The Free Press, New York.

Rappaport, A. (1990) 'The Staying Power of the Public Corporation', *Harvard Business Review*, January–February, Vol. 68, No. 1, p. 96.

Raynor, M.E., and Bower, J.L. (2001) 'Lead From the Center: How to Manage Diverse Businesses', *Harvard Business Review*, Vol. 80, No. 5, May, pp. 93–100.

Redding, S.G. (1990) *The Spirit of Chinese Capitalism*, Walter de Gruyter, Berlin.

Reid, S. (2002) *How to Think: Building Your Mental Muscle*, Prentice Hall, London.

Reve, T. (1990) 'The Firm as a Nexus of Internal and External Contracts', in M. Aoki, B. Gustafsson, and O.E. Williamson (eds.), *The Firm as a Nexus of Treaties*, Sage, London.

Richardson, G. (1972) 'The Organization of Industry', *Economic Journal*, Vol. 82, pp. 833–896.

Rittel, H. (1972), 'On the Planning Crisis: Systems Analysis of the First and Second Generations', *Bedriftsokonomen*, No. 8, pp. 390–396.

Rittel, H., and Webber, M. (1973) 'Dilemmas in a General Theory of Planning', *Policy Sciences*, Vol. 4, pp. 155–169.

Robinson, R.B. (1982) 'The Importance of Outsiders in Small Firm Strategic Planning', *Academy of Management Journal*, Vol. 25, pp. 80–93.

Rowe, W.G. (2001) 'Creating Wealth in Organizations: The Role of Strategic Leadership', *Academy of Management Executive*, Vol. 15, No. 1, February, pp. 81–94.

Ruigrok, W., and Van Tulder, R. (1995) *The Logic of International Restructuring*, Routledge, London.

Rumelt, R.P. (1974) *Strategy, Structure, and Economic Performance*, Harvard University Press, Cambridge, MA.

Rumelt, R.P. (1980) 'The Evaluation of Business Strategy', in W.F. Glueck (ed.), *Business Policy and Strategic Management*, Third Edition, McGraw-Hill, New York.

Rumelt, R.P. (1982) 'Diversification Strategy and Profitability', *Strategic Management Journal*, Vol. 3, No. 4, October–December, pp. 359–369.

Rumelt, R.P. (1996) 'Inertia and Transformation', in C.A. Montgomery (ed.), *Resource-based and Evolutionary Theories of the Firm: Towards a Synthesis*, Kluwer Academic Publishers, Boston, pp. 101–132.

Sanchez, R., Heene, A. and Thomas, H. (eds.) (1996) *Dynamics of Competence-Based Competition*, Elsevier, London.

Schein, E.H. (1985) *Organizational Culture and Leadership*, Jossey-Bass, San Francisco.

Schein, E.H. (1993) 'On Dialogue, Culture, and Organizational Learning', *Organizational Dynamics*, Vol. 22, No. 2, pp. 40–51.

Schelling, T. (1960) *The Strategy of Conflict*, Harvard University Press, Cambridge.

Schneider, S.S. (ed.) (1991) 'Interpreting Organizational Leadership', *Organization Studies*, Special Issue, Vol. 12.

Schoemaker, P.J.H. and Russo, J.E. (1993) 'A Pyramid of Decision Approaches', *California Management Review*, Vol. 36, No. 1, Fall, pp. 9–32.

Schumpeter, J.A. (1950) *Capitalism, Socialism and Democracy*, Third Edition, Harper & Row, New York.

Schwenk, C.R. (1984) 'Cognitive Simplification Processes in Strategic Decision-Making', *Strategic Management Journal*, Vol. 5, No. 2, April–June, pp. 111–128.

Schwenk, C.R. (1988) *The Essence of Strategic Decision Making*, Lexington Books, Lexington, MA.

Scott, W.R. (1995) *Institutions and Organizations*, Sage, Thousand Oaks, CA.

Selznick, P. (1957) *Leadership in Administration: A Sociological Interpretation*, Harper & Row, New York.

Senge, P.M. (1990a) 'The Leader's New Work: Building Learning Organizations', *Sloan Management Review*, Vol. 32, No. 1, Fall, pp. 7–23.

Senge, P. (1990b) *The Fifth Discipline: The Art and Practice of the Learning Organization*, Doubleday, New York.

Seth, A. (1990) 'Value Creation in Acquisitions: A Re-Examination of Performance Issues', *Strategic Management Journal*, Vol. 11, No. 2, February, pp. 99–115.

Shapiro, C., and Varian, H. (1998) *Information Rules: A Strategic Guide to the Network Economy*, Harvard Business School Press, Cambridge, MA.

Simon, H.A. (1957) *Models of Man*, Wiley, New York.

Simon, H.A. (1972) 'Theories of Bounded Rationality', in C. McGuire and R. Radner (eds.), *Decision and Organization*, North-Holland, Amsterdam, pp. 161–176.

Simon, H.A. (1987) 'Making Management Decisions: The Role of Intuition and Emotion', *Academy of Management Executive*, Vol. 1, No. 1, pp. 57–64.

Simonin, B. (1997) 'The Importance of Collaborative Know-How', *Academy of Management Journal*, Vol. 40, No. 5, pp. 1150–1174.

Simons, R. (1994) 'How New Top Managers Use Control Systems as Levers of Strategic Renewal', *Strategic Management Journal*, Vol. 15, No. 3, March, pp. 169–189.

Simons, R. (1995) *Levers of Control: How Managers Use Innovative Control Systems to Drive Strategic Renewal*, HBS Press, Boston, MA.

Sims, H.P., and Lorenzi, P. (1992) *The New Leadership Paradigm: Social Learning and Cognition in Organizations*, Sage, London.

Sirower, M.L. (1997) *The Synergy Trap: How Companies Lose the Acquisition Game*, The Free Press, New York.

Slywotski, A.J. (1996) *Value Migration*, Harvard Business School Press, Boston, MA.

Smircich, L., and Stubbart, C. (1985) 'Strategic Management in an Enacted World', *Academy of Management Review*, Vol. 10, No. 4, pp. 724–736.

Solomon, R.C. (1992) *Ethics and Excellence: Cooperation and Integrity in Business*, Oxford University Press, New York.

Spencer, A. (1983) *On the Edge of the Organization: The Role of the Outside Director*, Wiley, New York.

Spender, J.C. (1989) *Industry Recipe: An Enquiry into the Nature and Sources of Managerial Judgment*, Basil Blackwell, New York.

Stacey, R.D. (1992) *Managing Chaos: Dynamic Business Strategies in an Unpredictable World*, Kogan Page, London.

Stacey, R.D. (1993a) 'Strategy as Order Emerging from Chaos', *Long Range Planning*, Vol. 26, No. 1, pp. 10–17.

Stacey, R.D. (1993b) *Strategic Management and Organizational Dynamics*, Pitman, London.

Stacey, R.D. (1996) *Strategic Management and Organizational Dynamics*, Second Edition, Pitman, London.

Stacey, R.D. (2001) *Complex Responsive Processes in Organizations: Learning and Knowledge Creation*, Routledge, London.

Stalk, G., Evans, P., and Shulman, L.E. (1992) 'Competing on Capabilities: The New Rules of Corporate Strategy', *Harvard Business Review,* Vol. 70, No. 2, March–April, pp. 57–69.

Starbuck, W., and Milliken, F. (1988) 'Challenger: Fine-Tuning the Odds Until Something Breaks', *Journal of Management Studies*, Vol. 25, No. 4, July.

Steiner, G.A. (1979) *Strategic Planning: What Every Manager Must Know*, The Free Press, New York.

Sternberg, E. (1997) 'The Defects of Stakeholder Theory', *Corporate Governance: an International Review*, Vol. 5, No. 1, January, pp. 3–10.

Stinchcombe, A.L. (1965) 'Social Structure and Organizations', in J.G. March (ed.), *Handbook of Organizations*, Rand McNally, Chicago, pp. 142–193.

Stone, C.D. (1975) *Where the Law Ends*, Harper & Row, New York.

Stopford, J.M., and Wells, L.T. (1972) *Strategy and Structure of Multinational Enterprise*, Basic Books, New York.

Strebel, P. (1992) *Breakpoints: How Managers Exploit Radical Business Change*, Harvard Business School Press, Boston, MA.

Strebel, P. (1994) 'Choosing the Right Change Path', *California Management Review*, Vol. 36, No. 2, Winter, pp. 29–51.

Sutcliffe, K.M., and Huber, G.P. (1998) 'Firm and Industry Determinants of Executive Perceptions of the Environment', *Strategic Management Journal*, Vol. 19, pp. 793–807.

Sykes, A., (1994) 'Proposals for Internationally Competitive Corporate Governance in Britain and America', *Corporate Governance*, Vol. 2, No. 4, pp. 187–195.

Tannenbaum, R., and Schmidt, W.H. (1958) How to Choose a Leadership Pattern, *Harvard Business Review*, Vol. 36, No. 2, March–April, pp. 95–101.

Teece, D.J., Pisano, G., and Shuen, A. (1997) 'Dynamic Capabilities and Strategic Management', *Strategic Management Journal*, Vol. 18, No. 7, August, pp. 509–533.

Thompson, A.A., and Strickland, A.J., III (1995) *Strategic Management: Concepts and Cases*, Eighth Edition, Irwin, Chicago.

Thompson, J.D. (1967) *Organizations in Action*, McGraw-Hill, New York.

Thorelli, H.B. (1986) 'Networks: Between Markets and Hierarchies', *Strategic Management Journal*, Vol. 7, No. 1, January–February, pp. 37–51.

Tichy, N., and E. Cohen (1997) *The Leadership Engine: How Winning Companies Build Leaders at Every Level*, HarperCollins, New York.

Tirole, J. (1988) *The Theory of Industrial Organization*, MIT Press, Cambridge, MA.

Trautwein, F. (1990) 'Merger Motives and Merger Prescriptions', *Strategic Management Journal*, Vol. 11, No. 4, May–June, pp. 283–295.

Treacy, M., and F. Wiersema (1995) *The Discipline of Market Leaders*, Addison-Wesley, Reading, MA.

Trice, H.M., and Beyer, J.M. (1993) *The Cultures of Work Organizations*, Prentice Hall, Englewood Cliffs, NJ.

Tricker, R.I. (1994) *International Corporate Governance: Text, Readings and Cases*, Prentice Hall, Singapore.

Tucker, R.C. (1968) 'The Theory of Charismatic Leadership', *Daedalus*, Vol. 97, No. 3, pp. 731–756.

Tushman, M.L., Newman, W.H. and Romanelli, E. (1986) 'Convergence and Upheaval: Managing the Unsteady Pace of Organizational Evolution', *California Management Review*, Vol. 29, No. 1, Fall, pp. 29–44.

Tushman, M.L., and O'Reilly, C.A., III (1996) 'Ambidextrous Organizations: Managing Evolutionary and Revolutionary Change', *California Management Review*, Vol. 38, No. 4, Summer, pp. 8–30.

Tushman, M.L., and O'Reilly, C.A., III (1997) *Winning Through Innovation: A Practical Guide to Leading Organizational Change and Renewal*, Harvard Business School Press, Boston, MA.

Tversky, A., and Kahneman, D. (1986) 'Rational Choice and the Framing of Decisions', *Journal of Business*, Vol. 59, No. 4, pp. 251–278.

Van der Heyden, K. (1996) *Scenarios: The Art of Strategic Conversation*, Wiley, New York.

Van Tulder, R., and Junne, G. (1988) *European Multinationals and Core Technologies*, Wiley, London.

Vernon, R. (1966) 'International Investment and International Trade in the Product Life Cycle', *Quarterly Journal of Economics*, Vol. 80, No. 2, May, pp. 190–207.

Von Winterfeldt, D., and Edwards, W. (1986) *Decision Analysis and Behavioral Research*, Cambridge University Press, Cambridge.

Vroom, V.H., and Jago, A.G. (1988) *The New Leadership: Managing Participation in Organizations*, Prentice Hall, Englewood Cliffs, NJ.

Waldman, D.A., and Yammarino, F.H. (1999) 'CEO Charismatic Leadership: Levels-of-Management and Levels-of-Analysis Effects', *Academy of Management Review*, Vol. 24, No. 2, pp. 266–285.

Walsh, J. (1995) 'Managerial and Organizational Cognition: Notes From a Trip Down Memory Lane', *Organization Science*, Vol. 6, pp. 280–321.

Wartick, S.L., and Wood, D.J. (1998) *International Business and Society*, Blackwell, Oxford.

Waterman, R.H., Peters, T.J., and Philips, J.R. (1980) 'Structure is Not Organization', *Business Horizons*, Vol. 23, June, pp. 14–26.

Webster, F. (1994) *Market Driven Management: Using the New Marketing Concept to Create a Customer-oriented Company*, Wiley, New York.

Weick, K.E. (1979) *The Social Psychology of Organizing*, Random House, New York.

Weick, K.E., and Bourgnon, M.G. (1986) 'Organizations as Cognitive Maps', in H.P. Sims Jr. and D.A. Gioia (eds.) *The Thinking Organization*, Jossey-Bass, San Francisco, pp. 102–135.

Weidenbaum, M., and Hughes, S. (1996) *The Bamboo Network: How Expatriate Chinese Entrepreneurs Are Creating a New Economic Superpower in Asia*, The Free Press, New York.

Wernerfelt, B. (1984) 'A Resource-Based View of the Firm', *Strategic Management Journal*, Vol. 5, No. 2, April–June, pp. 171–180.

Weston, J.F., Chung, K.S. and Hoag, S.E. (1990) *Mergers, Restructuring, and Corporate Control*, Prentice Hall, Englewood Cliffs, NJ.

Wheatley, M.J., and Kellner-Rogers, M. (1996) 'Self-Organization: The Irresistible Future of Organizing, Strategy, and Leadership', Vol. 24, No. 4, pp. 18–25.

Wheelen, T.L., and Hunger, J.D. (1992) *Strategic Management and Business Policy*, Fourth Edition, Addison-Wesley, Reading, MA.

Whitley, R.D. (1999) *Divergent Capitalisms: The Social Structuring and Change of Business Systems*, Oxford University Press, Oxford.

Wildavsky, A. (1979) *Speaking Truth to Power: The Art and Craft of Policy Analysis*, Little, Brown & Co., Toronto.

Williamson, O.E. (1975) *Markets and Hierarchies: Analysis and Antitrust Implications*, The Free Press, New York.

Williamson, O.E. (1979) 'Transaction Cost Economics: The Governance of Contractual Relations', *Journal of Law and Economics*, Vol. 22, pp. 223–261.

Williamson, O.E. (1985) *The Economic Institutions of Capitalism*, The Free Press, New York.

Williamson, O.E. (1991) 'Strategizing, Economizing, and Economic Organization', *Strategic Management Journal*, Vol. 12, Special Issue, Winter, pp. 75–94.

Wilson, D.C. (1992) *A Strategy of Change*, London, Routledge.

Wilson, I. (2000) 'From Scenario Thinking to Strategic Action', *Technological Forecasting and Social Change*, Vol. 65, No. 1, September, pp. 23–29.

Yip, G.S. (1993) *Total Global Strategy: Managing for Worldwide Competitive Advantage,* Prentice Hall, London.

Yoshimori, M. (1995) 'Whose Company Is It? The Concept of the Corporation in Japan and the West', *Long Range Planning*, Vol. 28, pp. 33–45.

Yukl, G. (1994) *Leadership in Organizations*, Third Edition, Prentice Hall, Englewood Cliffs, NJ.

Zahra, S.A., and Pearce, J.A. (1989) 'Boards of Directors and Corporate Financial Performance: A Review and Integrative Model', *Journal of Management*, Vol. 15, pp. 291–334.

INDEX